Second Edition

Management Accounting

Wayne J. Morse
Clarkson University

James R. Davis
Clemson University

Al L. Hartgraves
Emory University

Addison-Wesley Publishing Company
Reading, Massachusetts • Menlo Park, California • New York
Don Mills, Ontario • Wokingham, England • Amsterdam • Bonn
Sydney • Singapore • Tokyo • Madrid • Bogotá • Santiago • San Juan

Sponsoring Editor: Herbert E. Smith
Production Supervisor: Kazia Navas
Production Coordination: Sherry Berg
Text Designer: Marie E. McAdam
Cover Designer: Marshall Henrichs
Art Consultant: Loretta M. Bailey
Illustrator: George Nichols
Copyeditor: Margaret E. Hill
Permissions Editor: Mary Dyer
Manufacturing Supervisor: Roy E. Logan

Library of Congress Cataloging-in-Publication Data

Morse, Wayne J.
    Management accounting.
    Includes bibliographical references and index.
    1. Managerial accounting.   I. Davis, James Richard, 1947–   II. Hartgraves, Al L.
III. Title.
HF5635.M864   1988   658.1'511   87-11570
ISBN 0-201-15760-8

Preface

This book is concerned with the development and use of accounting information within specific organizations for the purposes of planning, control, and the analysis of special decisions. The topics discussed are important to all students of business and management regardless of their career objectives. *Management Accounting, Second Edition*, is intended for use by students who have had previous exposure to financial accounting. However, the amount of financial accounting background required varies, depending on what managerial accounting coverage the instructor chooses to stress for this course. In the typical situation, where students have completed a course in financial accounting, any or all material may be used. Even if students in a professional development program or in an accelerated survey course have not been exposed to journal entries, all but Chapters 11 and 12 on product costing and cost allocation may be used. The flow of product costs is introduced and illustrated in Chapter 2 with the aid of diagrams rather than journal entries.

GOALS OF THE TEXT

We have attempted to make this book **relevant, flexible, clear,** and **accurate.** The text is relevant to the educational objectives of students of business and management. The book is flexible so that it may be compatible with the backgrounds of different students, the curricula of different institutions, and the course objectives of different instructors. Extensive efforts have been made to produce a text that is clear and accurate. This should maximize the student's knowledge and understanding of management accounting while minimizing the time required of the instructor to explain material contained in the text. The instructor is thereby freed to provide additional enrichment or assistance, depending on the needs of individual students. Actions taken to meet these four goals are outlined below.

Relevant

- Emphasis is on accounting information as a management tool rather than as an end. Topics in management accounting are related to the functions of management.
- Illustrations of the use of management accounting in merchandising, service, manufacturing, not-for-profit, and government organizations are presented.
- Considerable attention is given to how standards are developed and to the interpretation of standard cost variances.
- The text includes a major (optional) appendix on budgeting in not-for-profit organizations.
- The use of quantitative models as decision aids is clearly illustrated, in a nontechnical manner, in an optional chapter.
- The impact of taxes on a wide variety of management decisions is clearly illustrated and discussed in an optional chapter. This chapter may be of particular value to students not planning to enroll in a tax course.
- Financial statement analysis and the statement of resource flows are presented in a manner that emphasizes their relevance to internal planning and control.
- The impact of changing prices on the use of managerial accounting data for internal planning and control, including capital budgeting, is discussed.

Flexible

- Once the first three chapters are covered, the remaining material can be sequenced in a variety of ways. (See Organization and Course Outlines.)
- The material can be packaged into a concise short course or a full semester.
- A wide variety of assignment material allows the instructor to adapt the text to a variety of teaching styles, program emphases, and time constraints.
- The text contains over 700 questions, exercises, and problems for class use or homework assignment.
- Numerous representative problems have been adapted from professional examinations.
- Redundant assignment material makes it possible for the instructor to vary similar assignments between sections and subsequent course offerings.
- Numerous appendixes lend flexibility to coverage of material.

- The mechanics of product costing is placed in optional chapters, which may be emphasized, surveyed, or omitted.
- Alternative sequencing of material can provide a product-costing emphasis, a planning-and-control emphasis, or a broad survey.
- Case-type problem material can be used to promote a discussion of issues raised in other chapters, or even other courses.

Clear

- Learning Objectives presented at the start of each chapter provide an orientation to the chapter material and its structure.
- The purpose or primary learning objective of each chapter is clearly stated and highlighted in the introduction to each chapter.
- The writing style is direct, and important relationships are always expressed in words.
- Wide margins allow for notes.
- The generous use of topical headings and subheadings promote readability and learning.
- Color illustrations emphasize key points.
- Key terms are highlighted when first introduced, listed at the end of each chapter, and defined in a glossary at the back of the book.
- A summary at the end of each chapter reiterates key points contained in the chapter.
- Review questions at the end of each chapter ask the student to recall basic concepts presented in the chapter. The questions are sequenced in the order in which topics are introduced in the chapter.
- Review problems at the end of all but Chapter 1 allow students to test and receive immediate feedback on their mastery of technical material contained in the accompanying chapter. The solutions to all review problems are contained at the end of the exercises and problems in the accompanying chapter. The end-of-chapter problems also provide detailed assignments related to the material presented in the chapter.
- The end-of-chapter exercises reinforce the student's knowledge of technical material contained in the accompanying chapter. Exercises are generally short and sequenced in the order in which topics are introduced in the accompanying chapter.
- The topical coverage of each exercise and problem is clearly identified in a boldfaced heading.
- Assignment materials based on chapter appendixes are clearly identified with boldfaced headings.

Accurate
- All materials have been prepared, reviewed, revised, and proofread by the authors.
- Developmental and marketing reviews by instructors at other institutions guided the authors in the preparation and revision of the text, and helped fine tune the finished product.
- Text and assignment materials have been classroom-tested.

CHANGES IN THE SECOND EDITION

The primary focus of the revision has been on improving the clarity of presentation. Special emphasis was placed on Chapter 6, Operating Budgets; Chapter 8, Performance Evaluation of Standard Cost Centers; Chapter 11, Product Costing; and Chapter 14, Capital Budgeting. In addition to these changes, the Tax Reform Act of 1986 necessitated a comprehensive revision of Chapter 15, and pronouncements of the Financial Accounting Standards Board necessitated changes in the portion of Chapter 16 dealing with the statement of resource flows.

In addition to the major changes mentioned above, learning objectives were added to the beginning of each chapter, and significant attention was given to the development of additional assignment material and the revision of old assignment material. Review problems have been added to Chapters 2 through 17. The review problems are placed after the review questions accompanying the chapter and the complete solution to each review problem is placed at the end of the exercises and problems accompanying the chapter. While many books place review problem solutions immediately after each problem, we believe separating the solution from the problem helps encourage students to work the problem before examining the solution. The number of problems and exercises accompanying all chapters after Chapter 1 has been increased to a minimum of 30. With each chapter having at least 12 review questions, a minimum of 42 assignment items accompanies each chapter. When the new exercises and problems are combined with revisions made to old exercises and problems, more than 50 percent of the exercises and problems accompanying each chapter are new or revised. A checklist of key figures for solutions is located in the back of the textbook.

In addition to the changes already mentioned in Chapters 6, 8, 11, 14, 15, and 16, the following topics in other chapters received significant attention in the preparation of the second edition:

- Professional accountants (Chapter 1)
- Cost-volume-profit graphs (Chapter 4)
- Operating leverage (Chapter 4, Appendix A)
- Sales mix analysis (Chapter 4, Appendix B)
- Flexible budgets emphasize efficiency (Chapter 7)

- Reconciling budgeted and actual income (Chapter 7)
- Management considerations in transfer pricing (Chapter 9)
- Applying transfer pricing (Chapter 9)
- Suboptimization (Chapter 9)
- Introduction to the assignment of common costs (Chapter 12)
- Economic lot size (Chapter 13)

SUPPLEMENTS

A variety of supplementary materials accompany the text:

- A solutions manual contains:

  Alternative course outlines.

  An evaluation of all assignment materials as to level of difficulty and estimated completion time.

  Solutions to all review questions, exercises, and problems. These completed solutions are designed to serve as transparency masters.

- Transparency acetates for solutions to all problems.

- An instructor's resource guide, prepared by Professors Donald Keller, Paul Krause, and Samir Nissan of California State University, Chico, contains:

  Alternative course outlines.

  A detailed lecture outline of each chapter.

  Identification of key concepts presented in each chapter plus additional ideas and explanation of how these concepts can be presented.

  Lecture aids for each chapter, such as transparency masters.

  Additional examples with solutions of materials presented in each chapter, illustrating important concepts.

- A test bank, prepared by Professors Donald Keller, Paul Krause, and Samir Nissan of California State University, Chico, is available in hardcopy or disk for use on the IBM personal computer or compatibles.

- A student study guide, prepared by Al Hartgraves, reemphasizes and reinforces basic concepts and techniques. For each chapter it contains:

  A list of learning objectives.

  A chapter review outline.

  A self test, including multiple-choice questions, completion questions, and up to four exercises.

  Solutions to the self test.

- Computer spreadsheet exercises, for use with Lotus 1-2-3 on the IBM personal computer or compatibles, which include a student manual and diskette.

ORGANIZATION AND COURSE OUTLINES

The text is divided into four parts. It is likely that most instructors will cover most or all of the material in Part I, Essential Elements of Management Accounting, and Part II, Planning and Control. Part III, Product Costing and Cost Allocation, focuses on a set of topics some instructors may wish to emphasize while others may prefer to omit or defer to a cost accounting course. Part IV, Selected Topics for Further Study, contains a variety of topics which may be assigned by the instructor to achieve particular course objectives.

The following outlines are intended to illustrate two of the alternative ways of sequencing text material. The first alternative, which emphasizes product costing, is most appropriate for students who will not take a cost accounting course. The second alternative, which emphasizes planning and control, is most appropriate for students who will take a cost accounting course. The second alternative might also be used in an introductory management accounting course taught at the graduate level, especially if the optional topics are included. Additional outlines are contained in the *Instructor's Resource Guide*.

Alternative Assignment Schedules: Product Costing Emphasis

Chapter	Title
1	Accounting and Management
2	Basic Cost Concepts
3	Cost Behavior Analysis
11	Product Costing
*11	Appendix A: Normal Factory Overhead Accounting
12	The Assignment of Common Costs
*12	Appendix: Joint Products and By-Products
4	Cost-Volume-Profit Analysis
*5	Relevant Costs for Management Decisions
6	Operating Budgets
7	Responsibility Accounting and Flexible Budgets
8	Performance Evaluation of Standard Cost Centers
8	Appendix A: A Closer Look at Fixed Overhead Variances
*11	Appendix B: Product Costing Using Standard Costs
*9	Control of Decentralized Operations
*10	Inventory Valuation Approaches and Segment Reporting**
*Appendix	Time Value of Money
*14	Capital Budgeting

* May be deleted on the basis of time constraints.

** Coverage of Chapter 10 may be limited to absorption and variable costing.

Alternative Assignment Schedules: Planning and Control Emphasis

Chapter	Title
1	Accounting and Management
2	Basic Cost Concepts
3	Cost Behavior Analysis
4	Cost-Volume-Profit Analysis
5	Relevant Costs for Management Decisions
*13	Relevant Costs for Quantitative Models
6	Operating Budgets
*6	Appendix: Not-for-Profit Budgeting
7	Responsibility Accounting and Flexible Budgets
8	Performance Evaluation of Standard Cost Centers
9	Control of Decentralized Operations
10	Inventory Valuation Approaches and Segment Reporting
*Appendix	Time Value of Money
*14	Capital Budgeting
*15	Impact of Taxes on Capital Budgeting and Other Management Decisions**
*16	Financial Statement Analysis and the Statement of Resource Flows†
*17	The Impact of Changing Prices

ACKNOWLEDGMENTS

Management Accounting could not have been completed without the generous cooperation, assistance, and support of numerous individuals and organizations. We are indebted to the following professors who offered helpful comments on the first edition of this textbook or reviewed the manuscript for the second:

Garth Blanchard (University of Puget Sound)

Charles Caldwell (University of South Carolina)

James B. Edwards (University of South Carolina)

Jeff Gillespie (University of Delaware)

Larzette Hale (Utah State University)

Douglas A. Johnson (Arizona State University)

---

* May be deleted on the basis of time constraints.

** Coverage of Chapter 15 may be limited to the impact of taxes on capital budgeting.

† Coverage of Chapter 16 may be limited to Financial Statement Analysis.

William Lawler (Babson College)

John Marquart (University of Michigan, Flint)

Susan Milstein (Western Maryland College)

Daniel J. O'Mara (Villanova University)

Ron Pawliczek (Boston College)

Ray Powell (University of Notre Dame)

Edward B. Schwan (Susquehanna University)

G. A. Swanson (Tennessee Technological University)

William C. Tuthill (Emory University)

Richard Veazey (Grand Valley State College)

Ara Volkan (University of South Alabama)

A special note of thanks goes to our students at Clarkson University, Clemson University, and Emory University. We are indebted to them both for their comments on the first edition and for their feedback on material new to the second. We also wish to express our appreciation to Professor Richard Veazey of Grand Valley State College and the following sixteen students in his summer course who class-tested the second edition: Jean Block, Robert Boogaard, Susan Burkheimer, Darrell Claeys, David Dornbos, David Emaus, Terrance Feravich, Cheryl Fifield, James Fox, Thomas Garrison, Robert Huizenga, Connie Mahon, David McLary, Patrick Pokorny, Stephen Price, Kathryn VanderWeele.

Appreciation is extended to the Institute of Management Accounting of the National Association of Accountants for permission to use adaptations of problem materials from past Certificate in Management Accounting examinations; these materials are identified as "CMA Adapted." We are also indebted to the American Institute of Certified Public Accountants and the Institute for Internal Auditors for permission to use adaptations of materials from their professional examinations; these materials are identified as "CPA Adapted" or "IIA Adapted."

Comments or suggestions from users are most welcome.

Potsdam, NY	W.J.M.
Clemson, SC	J.R.D.
Atlanta, GA	A.L.H.

Brief Contents

Contents

Essential Elements of Management Accounting

CHAPTER 1

Accounting and Management

LEARNING
OBJECTIVES

Upon completion of this chapter you should:

- Be familiar with the primary functions of managers.
- Understand the role of management accounting information in managing profit and not-for-profit organizations.
- Be able to identify the duties of the controller and the treasurer.
- Understand the relationship of the various accounting functions to the controller's department.
- Know the differences and similarities between management accounting and financial accounting.

An **organization** is a group of people united to achieve a common goal. As students, instructors, employees, citizens, relatives, sports players, and, perhaps, volunteers, we are members of a variety of organizations. The members who direct the affairs of an organization are identified as **managers.** In the process of performing their duties, managers use many kinds of information, including that provided by management accounting.

The purpose of this chapter is to provide an overview of **management accounting,** which is concerned with providing information to managers and other persons inside specific organizations. Because management accounting is concerned with providing information to managers, we begin by discussing some important characteristics of organizations and the functions of management. We then describe how managers use accounting terms, relationships, and information in performing their duties. We also consider the duties of accountants and the relationships that exist among managers, accountants, and other information specialists.

Accounting is broadly classified into financial accounting and management accounting. This classification is based on differences in the relationship between the organization and the person or persons to whom information is supplied. To provide an orientation to the study of management accounting, we carefully distinguish between these two types of accounting. We conclude this chapter by summarizing why managers and management accountants must thoroughly understand management accounting.

ORGANIZATIONS AND THEIR GOALS

Organizations vary widely in their goals. Whereas the goal of a college or university is to provide educational services, the goal of a department store or a steel company is to earn a profit by providing customers with goods, and the goal of the Red Cross is to provide humanitarian service. An organization is likely to have several goals. The local department store, for example, which has profit and providing customers with consumer goods as goals, may also support cultural activities and local charities with the goal of being regarded as a good community citizen.

We frequently distinguish between organizations on the basis of profit motive. **For-profit organizations** have profit as a primary goal, and **not-for-profit organizations** do not have profit as a goal. Clearly, the General Electric Company is a for-profit organization, whereas the City of New York and the Red Cross are not-for-profit organizations.[1] Regardless of the presence or absence of a profit motive, an organization should use resources efficiently in accomplishing its goals. Every dollar the Salvation Army spends for fuel is a dollar that cannot be used to feed the indigent. Private not-for-profit organizations (such as colleges) and government units (such as cities) can go bankrupt if they are unable to meet their financial obligations. The common need to use resources efficiently indicates the existence of a common need for a good accounting system that will help management plan, organize, and control the use of the organization's limited resources.

FUNCTIONS OF MANAGEMENT

Smooth functioning organizations do not just happen. They are a result of the actions of the managers who are responsible for their operation. Management entails planning, organizing, and controlling. In all but the smallest organizations, the manager's job is to get things done through people. The manager of the local department store does not order goods, stock shelves, place advertising, operate the cash register, drive the delivery truck, or record accounting transactions. The manager has to decide what tasks are needed and how they should be accomplished (planning). The manager then assigns these tasks to other people (organizing) and ensures that they are properly completed (controlling).

Planning

Planning, which is the formulation of a scheme or program for the accomplishment of a specific purpose or goal, consists of two basic activities: (1) setting goals and (2) selecting a way to accomplish these goals. A distinction is often made between long-range planning and short-range planning. Long-range planning emphasizes the selection of goals that the organization hopes to achieve over several years and the selection of programs that will enable the organization to achieve these goals. Short-range planning is based on the organization's long-range plan as well as its current situation and focuses on specific activities to be taken in the near term to move the organization from its current situation

---

[1] The term *nonprofit* is frequently used to refer to what we have identified as *not-for-profit* organizations. We avoid this term because it can be confused with a *non-profit* (i.e., zero or negative profit) situation.

toward its long-range goals. Short-range planning involves both the interpretation of long-range goals into performance objectives for the coming year and the selection of specific actions to achieve these objectives. The following example illustrates the difference between long-range and short-range plans.

Good Department Stores currently operates three stores in the suburbs of a large metropolitan area. Professional people such as engineers, scientists, doctors, lawyers, and managers live in this market area. Good's long-range plans are to achieve the highest annual dollar sales volume of all suburban department stores in the market area and to provide their investors with an acceptable level of earnings. Important elements of this plan include: the opening of one new store during each of the next five years, a reorientation of merchandise lines toward goods likely to be purchased by professional people, and increased support of cultural activities. Good's short-range plans for the coming year call for the hiring of personnel and the acquisition of merchandise for one new store currently under construction. Discontinuing the sale of hardware, expanding the offerings of furniture and women's business apparel, adding an art department, and starting a Good Summer Concert Series are also among management's plans. Management believes these activities will produce a 40 percent increase in sales revenue and a 35 percent increase in after-tax profits during the coming year.

Good's short-range plans are made in the light of its long-range plans. Care is taken to ensure that the short-range plans support the long-range goals. Short-range goals are more specific than long-range goals; they have to be because they are statements of what management hopes to accomplish next year.

Organizing

Through **organizing,** the process of making the organization into a well-ordered whole, management attempts to structure and divide the tasks that need to be done. Specific people are assigned specific tasks. Within a formal structure established to show the relationships between organization members, authority is delegated to managers and other employees who are subsequently held accountable for the activities they control.

An **organization chart** illustrates the formal set of relationships that exist among the elements of an organization. An organization chart for Good Department Stores is shown in Exhibit 1–1. The blocks represent organizational units, and the lines represent the relationships between organizational units. Top management delegates authority, which flows down the organization, to use resources for limited purposes to subordinate managers who, in turn, delegate more limited authority to accomplish more structured tasks to their subordinates. Responsibility increases as one moves up the organization. People at the bottom of the chart are responsible for specific tasks, but the president (chairman, agency head) is responsible for the operation of the entire organization.

Following the formal sequence of authority and responsibility (sometimes referred to as the chain of command), a problem in the Appliance Department

EXHIBIT 1-1   Good Department Stores Organization Chart

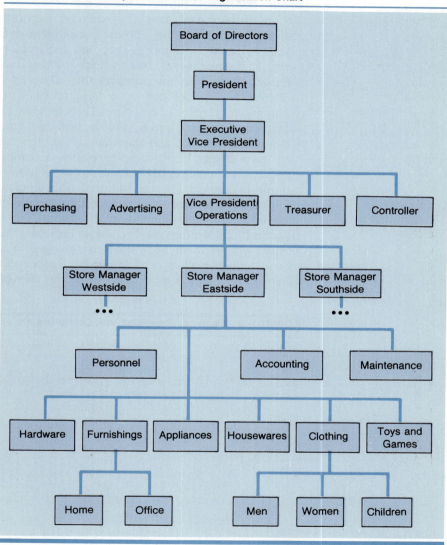

of the Eastside Store is first brought to the attention of the Store Manager and then to the Vice President of Operations by the Store Manager. Normally, the head of the Appliance Department does not take the problem directly to the attention of a manager two or more levels above him or her because this action violates the chain of command.

A distinction is made between line and staff managers. Line managers are directly responsible for the activities that create and distribute the goods and services of the organization. They exercise authority over all other managers and employees below them on the organization chart. Staff managers, on the other hand, exercise authority over only the employees in their own departments. Staff departments exist to help facilitate line activities. Although staff members often advise line managers, they do not exercise authority over them. In Exhibit 1–1 we see that Good Department Stores has two levels of staff organizations, corporate and store. The corporate staff units are Purchasing, Advertising, Treasurer, and Controller. Staff departments at the store level are Personnel, Accounting, and Maintenance. All other units are line departments. Note that a change in plans can necessitate a change in the organization. For example, Good's plan to discontinue the sale of hardware and add an art department during the coming year will necessitate an organizational change.

In addition to the formal relationships specified in the organization chart, many informal relationships develop between individuals and organizational units. Such relationships can become so important that the organization cannot function without them. Many times knowledgeable and persuasive individuals exert an influence on the organization far in excess of what their formal position would suggest; this is especially true in the case of staff members who are

EXHIBIT 1–2   Planning, Organizing, and Controlling Are a Continuous Cycle

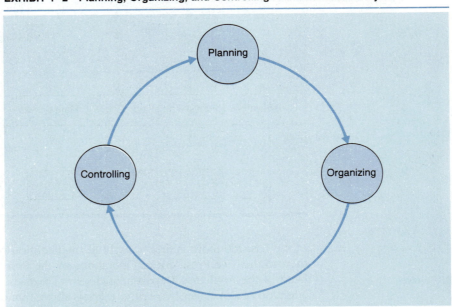

experts in a specialized area and offer advice concerning that area to line managers.

Controlling

Controlling is the process of ensuring that results agree with plans. In the process of controlling operations, management compares actual performance with plans. If actual results deviate significantly from plans, management either attempts to bring operations into line with the original plan or adjusts the plan. The original plan is adjusted if management determines that it is no longer appropriate because of changed circumstances. Hence, the process of controlling feeds back into the process of planning to form a continuous cycle. This cycle is illustrated in Exhibit 1–2.

ACCOUNTING AS A MANAGEMENT TOOL

Managers make extensive use of accounting in the performance of their functions. This is true regardless of the nature of their business. Accounting information is important in managing a volunteer fire department, a religious organization, the city of Chicago, and General Motors. There are two basic reasons for this: (1) accounting terms are the language of business, and (2) accounting relationships serve as a model of the organization.

Accounting Terms Are the Language of Business

Accounting terms are an important part of every manager's vocabulary. Because financial data provide a common denominator for measuring and summarizing widely diverse activities, accounting terms are a basic means of communication within and between organizations. The need to summarize widely diverse activities becomes increasingly important as we move up the organization chart. Good's President would be overwhelmed by detailed information on the unit sales of specific items in individual stores, but could easily understand a summary of sales in terms of dollars of sales revenue. Note, however, that the manager of the Home Furnishing Department in a particular store would want detailed unit sales information. Dollars also provide a convenient measure of effectiveness in for-profit organizations. By looking at the bottom line of the income statement, a manager can immediately determine if the organization met its profit goal for the period.

Accounting Relationships Model the Organization

A **model** is a simplified representation of some real-world phenomenon. Managers study models to obtain an understanding of the related real-world phenomenon, and they use models to predict the impact of a proposed action. A proper understanding and use of models leads to better decisions. Because the accounting system used to classify and summarize data reported in general purpose financial statements touches every area of activity within an organization, accounting relationships serve as a model of the organization.

An understanding of the organization's accounting system helps the manager understand the organization and the interrelationships that exist within it. The statement of financial position (balance sheet) serves as an economic picture of the organization at a particular moment. The income statement and the statement of resource flows (cash or working capital) summarize the economic activity of the organization during a period of time. An understanding of these and other accounting reports also helps the manager understand the organization. These statements are particularly valuable in planning; for example, a manager who is familiar with the income statement can use it to quickly predict the probable impact of a proposed action on net income.

Accounting Information Assists in Planning, Organizing, and Controlling

Accounting relationships are used extensively in planning, organizing, and controlling activities. These relationships provide the framework used to develop the budget for the coming year. A **budget** is a formal plan of action expressed in monetary terms. An organization's budget for the coming year includes projected financial statements and detailed schedules indicating the financial consequences of all expected activities. In budgeting, the same accounting relationships that are used to report the financial implications of transactions after they have occurred are also used to predict the financial consequences of transactions before they occur. By analyzing the financial consequences of alternative actions, management is better able to select those transactions that lead to the most desirable outcome(s).

The budgeting process also assists management in its organizing function. Detailed supporting schedules for revenues, expenditures, costs, and activities are drawn up for all units of the organization. Because all these pieces must fit together in the overall budget, flaws in organizational design become apparent as the budgeting process is nearing completion.

Accounting information also assists management in controlling operations subsequent to the adoption of a budget. During and after the budget period, management is provided with **performance reports** that compare actual results with plans. Performance reports may be prepared for the organization as a whole or for any area of responsibility within the organization. They may report on revenues, or costs, or both. A report measuring the effectiveness of the Maintenance Department of the Eastside Good Department Store in controlling costs is presented in Exhibit 1–3. The differences between actual and allowed costs are identified as **variances.** Expenditures of less than the allowed amounts are **favorable variances** (F), and expenditures of more than the allowed amounts are **unfavorable variances** (U).

Copies of this performance report are provided to the Maintenance Department supervisor and to the store manager. The maintenance supervisor, who uses the report as a *scorecard*, can determine from it how well he or she is doing. The store manager, who uses the report as an *attention director,* can determine from it whether or not he or she should inquire further or take some

EXHIBIT 1–3   Typical Performance Report

**Good Departmental Stores: Eastside
Maintenance Department Performance Report
For the month of September, 19×2**

	Actual Costs	Allowed Costs	Variance*
Salaries and wages	$14,000	$12,000	$2,000 U
Utilities	800	850	50 F
Supplies	300	210	90 U
Equipment rentals	1,000	1,000	—
Totals	$16,100	$14,060	$2,040 U

* F = Favorable
   U = Unfavorable

action regarding the performance of the Maintenance Department. This is consistent with the concept of **management by exception,** whereby managers focus their attention on those aspects of operations that are not operating as planned, rather than constantly inquiring about all aspects of performance. If the store manager deemed any of the variances in Exhibit 1–3 to be significant, the manager would inquire further about their cause. If the unfavorable variance for salaries and wages was caused by an increase in wage rates, management might revise the budget (change its plans) for this item. If the variance was caused by excessive labor hours due to poor supervision, management would attempt to bring operations into conformity with the original plans.

Performance reports are developed for all units and subunits in the organization, and all revenues and costs incurred by the organization during a period should appear in at least one of these performance reports. Furthermore, some manager, or group of managers, should be held responsible for the generation of revenues or incurrence of each cost. The process of developing a system to assign revenues and costs to responsible managers assists management in its organizing and controlling functions. If problems are encountered in assigning responsibility for revenues and costs, the most likely cause is either a weakness in organization structure or a failure to communicate areas of authority and responsibility to organization members. The resolution of responsibility problems is accompanied by the development of a clearer organizational structure and a better understanding of the delegation of authority and responsibility within the organization.

Though we are particularly concerned with the role of monetary data, non-monetary data are an important part of planning and control systems. Non-monetary data increase in importance as we move down the organization chart.

Performance reports stated in terms of units of production, pounds of materials, and hours of labor are more useful to clerks, factory workers, and first level production supervisors who work with physical units rather than with monetary symbols. First level managers must be able to speak to their subordinates in terms of units of activity and to their supervisors in accounting terms.

Nonmonetary measures of performance are also important in organizations where units of output cannot be related to revenue generation and profit. This is likely to be the case in the research and development department of a for-profit organization as well as for many activities of not-for-profit organizations, especially government agencies. It is difficult, for example, to determine the bottom-line impact of a good fire department. A budgeting and performance evaluation technique known as management by objectives is widely used in organizations where activities cannot be related to profit.

Under a program of **management by objectives** the head of an agency or department and the head's immediate superior agree to a set of short-run nonmonetary objectives. Care is taken to ensure that the short-run objectives are in agreement with the overall objectives of the organization. The short-run objectives are subsequently used as a performance measure for the agency or department head. One possible objective for a fire department might be to reduce the average response time to a fire alarm from five to four minutes.

Accounting Information Assists in Problem Solving

Accounting information is useful in evaluating unusual problems or opportunities. For example, a supplier might offer to provide a major component that goes into a manufactured product. The manufacturer must determine whether it is better to continue to manufacture the component or to purchase it from the supplier. A detailed analysis of cost data helps determine the costs to manufacture the component, which are then compared to the costs to buy the component. Another example might involve a government agency contracting with a university to provide educational services on the basis of the costs of those services. In this case it must be clearly understood by both the government agency and the university how costs are to be determined. As a final example, consider the case of a bank that is trying to determine whether to continue or discontinue operating a particular branch. Before deciding, the bank should carefully analyze how the bank's total revenues and expenses will change if the branch is closed. In these and many other examples discussed in later chapters, the proper accounting information focuses on how revenues or costs, or both, differ under each alternative.

External Forces Increase the Importance of Accounting

A number of forces outside business organizations have increased the importance of accounting information as a basis for management decisions. Large insurance companies often require hospitals to justify their rates by using prescribed accounting procedures for cost assignments. Several government agencies award contracts on the basis of cost plus a specified allowance for profit.

The U.S. Government has occasionally imposed controls limiting price increases to amounts that can be justified by documented increases in costs. Numerous lawsuits are initiated in an attempt to recover damages caused by the alleged failure of persons or organizations to complete their contractual obligations. The damage claims are based on cost data, and the success of the suit, or the defense, often centers on how well the parties demonstrate an understanding of cost concepts and develop and explain cost data supporting their position. In this type of environment, all managers should have a basic understanding of cost concepts.

ACCOUNTANTS IN THE ORGANIZATION

Accounting activities within an organization are usually under the overall supervision of the **controller,** who is the organization's chief accountant.[2] Many people erroneously equate "controller" with "control" and assume that the controller regulates, directs, or dominates the organization. In fact, as shown in the organization chart illustrated in Exhibit 1–1, the controller is a top management staff member. As a staff member, the controller does not have any formal authority to direct the activities of anyone outside the controller's department but does, however, exert a strong influence on other members of the organization. This influence comes about because of the controller's role in coordinating the development of the budget and because the position provides the controller with an in-depth understanding and detailed knowledge of the organization, making him or her a valuable advisor.

Duties of the Controller

As the organization's chief accountant, the controller is responsible for a widely diverse set of activities. Although they vary from organization to organization, the duties most frequently assigned to the controller's office include:

- Designing, installing, and maintaining the accounting system.
- Preparing financial statements for external users.
- Coordinating the development of the budget.
- Accumulating and analyzing cost data.
- Preparing and analyzing performance reports.
- Providing information for problem solving and special decisions.
- Consulting with management about the meaning of accounting information.
- Planning and administrating taxes.
- Designing, installing, and maintaining computer-based information systems.

[2] The word controller is occasionally spelled "comptroller." The pronunciation remains the same as the first spelling, and both refer to the same position.

Somewhat related to the controller's function is that of the treasurer. The **treasurer** is the officer responsible for money management and serves chiefly as the custodian of the organization's funds. Typical duties of the treasurer include:

- Receiving, maintaining custody of, and disbursing monies and securities.
- Investing the organization's funds.
- Directing the granting of credit.
- Maintaining sources of short-term borrowing.
- Establishing and maintaining a market for the organization's debt and equity securities.

The positions of the controller and the treasurer are sometimes combined into the single position of **chief financial executive.** Other titles of this combined position include chief financial officer and vice president of finance.

Organization of the Controller's Department

As a member of top management, the controller personally performs few of the above duties. Rather, the actual execution of these tasks is delegated to members of the controller's department. The organization chart for a typical controller's department is illustrated in Exhibit 1–4. By studying this exhibit from left to right, you should be able to determine where each of the duties listed above would be performed in the controller's department. The first two duties (designing, installing, and maintaining the accounting system; preparing financial statements for external users) are part of General Accounting, and the next three are part of Cost Planning and Analysis.

The actual structure of a controller's department varies between organizations. The duties assigned Special Studies, Electronic Data Processing, and Internal Auditing in Exhibit 1–4 are likely to be performed elsewhere. The Special Studies section is assigned the task of providing information for problem solving and special decisions. This unit also spends considerable time consulting with management about the meaning of accounting information.[3] Establishing a separate accounting unit for special studies was one of the major recommendations of a research effort conducted by Herbert A. Simon and others more than thirty years ago. They believed that the unstructured, analytic tasks of providing information for problem solving and special studies could not be performed effectively by the persons who were responsible for record keeping.[4] The required, day-to-day record keeping activities that have near-term due dates would always be done first, and frequently to the exclusion of unstructured tasks. Although our experiences support this conclusion, many organizations request account-

---

[3] Many other persons within the controller's department would also provide such consultations in conjunction with their other duties.

[4] Herbert A. Simon et al., *Centralization vs. Decentralization in Organizing the Controller's Department* (New York: Controllership Foundation, 1954).

EXHIBIT 1–4   Organization Chart of a Controller's Department

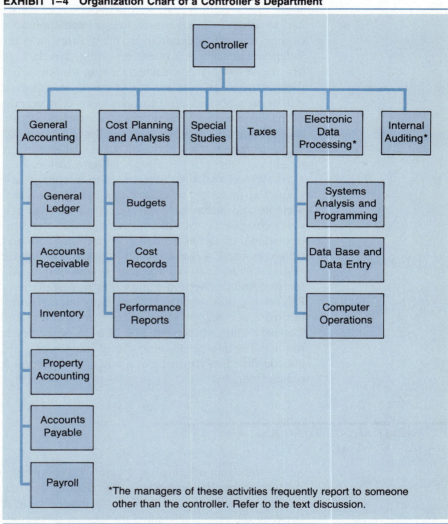

*The managers of these activities frequently report to someone other than the controller. Refer to the text discussion.

ants, who are performing more structured tasks, to complete special studies as staff time is available.

Electronic data processing (EDP) involves the storage, manipulation, retrieval, and communication of data by electronic means. Electronic data processing systems almost always involve the use of computers. Because the first large-scale applications of EDP systems were in accounting (payroll, receivables, payables), the responsibility for EDP operations has traditionally been placed under the overall direction of the controller. Today, however, an ever-increasing amount of computer time in large organizations is devoted to nonaccounting applications: engineering, scientific, personnel management, word processing, and so forth. To recognize and encourage applications of electronic data processing across functional areas, many firms have now established EDP as an independent staff department reporting directly to top management. In many organizations electronic data processing activities are placed within a department that has the more inclusive title of management information systems (MIS). The title of management information systems is broad enough to include all aspects of management accounting, but MIS activities are usually related to electronic data storage and processing. Regardless of where EDP activities are placed in the organization, the controller has a vital interest in the availability, accuracy, timeliness, and security of financial information.

Internal auditing is intended to safeguard an organization's assets from fraud and theft, and to ensure that the organization's accounting records are accurate and adequate. Many organizations also rely on internal auditing to verify compliance with management's policies and procedures and to promote operational efficiency. Since 1977, when the Foreign Corrupt Practices Act was passed by the U.S. Congress, all publicly held American companies have been *required* to maintain an adequate system of internal control. Even though the Internal Auditing section is presented as part of the Controller's Department in Exhibit 1–4, the internal auditors most often report to the president or board of directors. Many persons believe that reporting to the board strengthens the internal auditor's independence. The U.S. Securities and Exchange Commission requires the internal auditing staff of many public corporations to report to the outside directors[5] regardless of where the internal audit staff is placed in the organization chart.

FINANCIAL ACCOUNTING AND MANAGEMENT ACCOUNTING

Accounting is an information system.[6] We previously indicated that accounting is broadly classified into financial accounting and management accounting and that this classification is based on the difference in the relationship that exists between the organization and the person or persons to whom information is supplied. **Financial accounting** is concerned with providing financial information to persons outside the firm, especially investors, creditors, labor unions,

---

[5] Outside directors are members of the organization's board of directors who are independent of management. That is, they are neither officers nor employees of the organization.

[6] *Information* is something that contributes to knowledge. Data taken alone do not contribute to knowledge. The number 500 is a datum, but, taken by itself, it is not knowledge. An advertisement stating that a local discount store is selling color television sets for $500 is information. It contributes to our knowledge.

and the general public. **Management accounting** is concerned with providing financial information to persons inside the organization, especially managers. This difference in orientation results in significant differences between these two types of accounting.

Financial Accounting Has an External Orientation

Financial accounting is concerned with the development of *general purpose* financial statements (such as the statement of financial position and the income statement) that are intended for the primary use of persons *external* to the organization. These statements, which are *highly aggregated* and, therefore, provide little detail, are summaries of the financial affairs of all the organization's subunits and activities and are typically issued quarterly and annually. Compared to the frequency with which management accounting reports are issued (daily, weekly, monthly), financial accounting reports cover *relatively long time periods*.

Financial accounting statements report on management's handling of the affairs of the organization in the *past*. The U.S. Securities and Exchange Commission *requires* publicly held corporations to issue financial statements. To ensure conformity, understandability, and fairness, general purpose financial statements are prepared in accordance with *external standards* imposed by the public accounting profession (in the form of generally accepted accounting principles) and by regulatory agencies (such as the U.S. Securities and Exchange Commission). A significant feature of these external standards is their emphasis on *objectivity*. General purpose financial statements should not be influenced by emotion, surmise, or personal prejudice. They should be based on observable phenomena, such as the historical cost actually paid for a product or service.

You should not interpret the preceding comments on external reporting as implying that management has little interest in financial accounting. Managers can benefit greatly from financial accounting information. Management often uses financial statements as a starting point in evaluating and planning the overall affairs of the firm. Because financial accounting data are widely available, managers can learn a great deal about their firm's operations by a comparative financial analysis of their own and competing firms. Financial accounting numbers, such as net income, or ratios, such as earnings per share of common stock, are often used as goals. Furthermore, financial accounting statements are a major means of communication with persons outside the firm. Obviously, management is most interested in the content of this message. Finally, employees, who have a personal interest in the economic health of the organization for which they work, can gain an understanding of this economic health by studying their firm's financial statements.

Management Accounting Has an Internal Orientation

Management accounting is concerned with providing information to managers and other persons *inside* the organization. Management accounting reports are *special purpose*. Designed to fit the specific needs of individual or group decision makers, they emphasize factors under the decision makers' control. In this regard management accounting might be called a decision support system. At lower levels of management, planning and control decisions must be made quite frequently. To serve the needs of these desicion makers, management accounting provides information for *relatively short periods of time*—a month, a week, a day, or even some portion of a day. Because managers are primarily concerned with the impact of their decisions on the future performance of the organization, management accounting reports are *future oriented.* Past and current activities are reported to the extent that this information helps management plan for the future or ensure future conformance with current plans. Management accounting reports exist to serve the needs of management. Because they are *not required* by law, the development and use of these reports are subject to a cost-benefit analysis. Management accounting reports should only be provided if the perceived benefits of their development and use exceed the related costs.

No external standards are imposed on information provided to internal users. Consequently, management accounting reports may be quite *subjective.* In developing a budget, management is more interested in a subjective estimate of next year's sales volume than in an objective report on last year's sales. The significant differences between management accounting and financial accounting are summarized in Exhibit 1–5.

Professional Accountants

Public corporations are required by law to have outside auditors independently evaluate their general purpose financial statements. This audit is performed to determine whether or not the statements are prepared in accordance with generally accepted accounting principles. In the United States the persons who perform these independent evaluations are designated as **Certified Public Accountants (CPAs).** In Canada and several other countries they are designated as **Chartered Accountants (CAs).** All CPAs have passed an examination and met the education and experience requirements of the state in which they are certified. The CPA is widely recognized as a professional designation. Indeed,

EXHIBIT 1–5   Differences Between Financial and Management Accounting

Financial Accounting	Management Accounting
Provides information to external users	Provides information to internal users
Generates general purpose financial statements	Generates special purpose financial statements and reports
Statements highly aggregated; provide little detail	Statements and reports may be disaggregated; provide much detail
Relatively long time period	May be relatively short time period
Reports on past	Reports on past or outlines future plans
Required by law	Not required by law
Must conform to externally imposed standards	Has no externally imposed standards
Emphasizes objective data	Allows subjective data

until recent years, U.S. business executives often cited the CPA as the only available guide to the professional competence of American accountants. This situation has changed since the National Association of Accountants (NAA) established the Institute of Certified Management Accountants and a program to recognize professional competence and educational attainment in the field of management accounting. The program leads to designation as a **Certified Management Accountant (CMA).** According to a booklet distributed by the Institute:

> *A Certified Management Accountant is well prepared to be an active participant in management. The CMA program is founded upon the dynamic role the management accountant plays in the management process. The program recognizes all aspects of business, with the focus on the development and analysis of information used in decision making. A CMA has demonstrated the knowledge and professional skills to become an influential member of the management team.*[7]

The CMA examination is a comprehensive five-part examination that covers all aspects of accounting as well as related disciplines. Its interdisciplinary nature is reflected in the names given the five parts of the exam:

1. Economics and business finance.
2. Organization and behavior, including ethical considerations.
3. Periodic reporting standards, auditing, and taxes.
4. Internal reporting and analysis.
5. Decision analysis, including modeling, and information systems.[8]

The interdisciplinary nature of the CMA examination is intended to reflect the dual role of the management accountant as both an accountant and a member of the management team. Robert Shultis, former Executive Director of the National Association of Accountants, has even expressed the view that "the management accountant needs to be a businessman *first* and an accountant *second.*"[9]

Statements on Management Accounting

The National Association of Accountants established a Management Accounting Practices (MAP) Committee in 1969 to express the official position of the NAA on accounting and financial reporting issues raised by standard setting groups and to develop guidelines on management accounting concepts, policies, and practices. The MAP Committee has promulgated these guidelines in a continuing series of Statements on Management Accounting. These statements have dealt with a wide variety of topics, ranging from the definition of important terms

---

[7] *Certified Management Accountant,* Institute of Certified Management Accountants, 1986–1987 announcement, p. 1.

[8] Additional information about the CMA program is available from the Institute of Certified Management Accountants, 10 Paragon Drive, Montvale, NJ 07645-1759.

[9] Robert Shultis, "Management and Management Accountants," *Survey of Business,* Fall, 1981, p. 6.

and issues in cost and performance measurement to standards of ethical conduct for management accountants. References are made to several of these statements in this text.

The MAP Committee takes a very broad view of management accounting and the functions performed by management accountants. According to Statement on Management Accounting Number 1B, persons involved in such functions as controllership, treasury, financial analysis, planning and budgeting, cost accounting, internal audit, systems, and general accounting are management accountants. Based on this list of functions, all professional personnel in the controller's department, and many within the treasury department would be management accountants.

The MAP Committee also defines management accounting very broadly. In Statement on Management Accounting Number 1A, management accounting is defined as

> *the process of identification, measurement, accumulation, analysis, preparation, interpretation, and communication of financial information used by management to plan, evaluate, and control within an organization and to assure appropriate use of and accountability for its resources. Management accounting also comprises the preparation of financial reports for nonmanagement groups such as shareholders, creditors, regulatory agencies, and tax authorities.*

This broad definition of management accounting is somewhat troublesome when attempting to delineate the scope of this text or the content of management accounting courses. Accordingly, for the purpose of defining the subject matter included in this text, a more traditional view is taken. Thus, this text restricts management accounting to that segment of accounting concerned with providing financial information to managers and other persons within specific organizations.

SUMMARY

Accounting is an information system that is classified into financial accounting and management accounting. Financial accounting is concerned primarily with providing information to persons outside the organization. Management accounting is concerned primarily with providing information to persons inside the organization.

A manager is someone who directs the affairs of an organization. In planning, organizing, and controlling the activities of an organization, managers use many types of information, including that provided by management accounting. To perform their jobs, managers need to have a thorough understanding of accounting in general and management accounting in particular. Managers use accounting terms to communicate with employees, other managers, and persons in other organizations. They use accounting information as a basis for decision making and are very much involved in budgeting. Accounting reports are used to evaluate their performance and the performance of others. Accountants must also have a thorough understanding of management accounting concepts to ensure that the accounting information system supplies the information management needs for planning and controlling ongoing operations and for solving special problems.

KEY TERMS

Budget
Certified Management Accountant
  (CMA)
Certified Public Accountant (CPA)
Chartered Accountant (CA)
Chief financial executive
Controller
Controlling
Electronic data processing
Favorable variance
Financial accounting
For-profit organization
Internal auditing
Management accounting

Management by exception
Management by objectives
Managers
Model
Not-for-profit organization
Organization
Organization chart
Organizing
Performance report
Planning
Treasurer
Unfavorable variance
Variance

REVIEW QUESTIONS

The review questions at the end of each chapter are intended to assist in reviewing conceptual material. These questions are arranged in the same order that material is covered in the chapter.

1–1 Why do not-for-profit organizations need a good accounting system?

1–2 Identify and briefly describe the three functions of management.

1–3 What is the proper relationship between short-range and long-range planning?

1–4 Distinguish between the authority of staff and line managers. Why do staff departments exist?

1–5 What characteristic of accounting data is largely responsible for top management's wide use of accounting?

1–6 Why is a model useful to management?

1–7 How does the accounting model of the firm assist in planning?

1–8 How does accounting assist in controlling?

1–9 How does budgeting and the development of a system of responsibility accounting assist in organizing?

1–10 The controller frequently exerts a stronger influence on the affairs of line managers than one would expect from a staff officer. Why?

1–11 Identify several duties frequently assigned the controller.

1–12 Identify several duties frequently assigned the treasurer.

1–13 Why should the responsibility for special studies be assigned to a separate unit within the controller's department?

1–14 Why is electronic data processing frequently under the overall direction of the controller? Why are many large organizations establishing separate departments for electronic data processing?

1–15 Distinguish between financial and management accounting on the basis of the following: specificity of reports, users who receive reports, level of aggregation in reports, relative time period between reports, time orientation of reports (past, future), legal requirements for reporting, external pressures specifying content and form of reports, and emphasis on objective data.

CHAPTER 2

Basic Cost Concepts

Upon completion of this chapter you should:

- Be familiar with the basic components of cost measurement systems.
- Be able to identify the various types of inventories in service, merchandising, and manufacturing organizations.
- Know the difference between product costs and period costs.
- Be familiar with the three elements of product costs for manufactured inventories.
- Be able to prepare a statement of cost of goods manufactured and sold.
- Understand generally how predetermined rates are established for applying factory overhead costs to manufactured inventory.
- Be familiar with several basic cost concepts for management decision making, including sunk costs, relevant costs, and opportunity costs.

Cost is generally defined as a monetary measure of the economic sacrifice made to obtain some product or service. The economic sacrifice can be a cash expenditure, the giving up of another valuable asset, the forgoing of an economically desirable opportunity, or the incurrence of an obligation to pay cash in the future. Cost measurement is a significant aspect of financial and management accounting. However, although the general definition of cost is adequate for most external purposes, a variety of cost concepts and related measurements are needed for internal planning and control.

The purpose of this chapter is to introduce cost concepts and measurements that are widely used in management accounting. In the course of our study, we will determine how costs are best measured for different purposes. Much of the material presented here is an overview with in-depth coverage contained in subsequent chapters.

Managers, in order to communicate with one another and with accountants, must be familiar with cost concepts. Accountants must be equally familiar with cost concepts to ensure that the accounting information system provides management with the information it needs. Both managers and accountants should understand the basic cost measurements that comprise a significant part of the accounting model of the organization, which is used to plan and control organizational activities.

DIFFERENT COSTS FOR DIFFERENT PURPOSES

Accountants and managers employ many different cost concepts, such as historical costs, budgeted costs, future costs, allowed costs, relevant costs, opportunity costs, and sunk costs, to name just a few. These cost concepts are not used randomly; instead, *different costs are used for different purposes*. Consider, for example, some of the alternative inventory costs that might be used in a department store. For the purpose of external reporting, the cost of goods sold is based on the historical cost actually paid for inventory. In developing a budget for next year, the store's management predicts the future cost of inventory purchases. The performance of the store's purchasing agent is evaluated by comparing the actual cost of purchases to the planned or allowed cost of purchases.

Cost Measurement Systems

Though purpose is the primary consideration in selecting a cost concept, a system of cost measurement also needs one or more cost objectives, a determination of the cost elements assignable to each objective, and one or more techniques for assigning cost elements to cost objectives. The **costing purpose** is the basic reason a cost concept is used and a cost measurement is made, the **cost objectives** are the objects or activities to which costs are assigned, the **cost elements** are the detailed categories of costs assignable to a cost objective, and the **costing techniques** are the procedures used to assign cost elements to cost objectives.

One purpose of a public corporation's accounting system is to provide general purpose financial statements to persons outside the organization. For this purpose each major type of asset, such as buildings, is a cost objective. The cost elements assignable to buildings include the amount paid to purchase them and the cost of major improvements. Alternative costing techniques for measuring the adjusted cost of buildings include straight-line, sum-of-the-years'-digits, and double-declining-balance depreciation.

Costs and Benefits of Cost Measurement

Cost measurement is intended to provide useful information. In general, information should not be developed unless the benefits derived from its use exceed its acquisition cost. Exceptions to this generalization occur when forces outside the organization (such as government agencies) require the disclosure of certain information.

Many corporations are legally required to maintain an accounting system capable of providing cost data for inclusion in general purpose financial statements. It is possible to estimate the cost of installing and operating this system, but the related benefits are difficult to quantify. To a large extent the benefits accrue to shareholders, creditors, and other persons outside the organization.

Even with a system primarily designed for external reporting, many cost reducing measures are taken that do not significantly reduce the accuracy of cost measurement. One example is the treatment of transportation-in on goods purchased for resale. Theoretically, these costs should be assigned to inventory items at the time of purchase and included in the valuation of ending inventory and cost of sales. In practice, however, the less costly and slightly less accurate treatment of immediately assigning transportation-in to a separate expense account is widely used.

Because management accounting information is not required by law, it should be provided only if the benefits obtained from the information exceed the costs of its measurement and processing. To reduce costs, wherever the information needs of management can be satisfied with data accumulated for external reporting, the data used for external reporting may be rearranged in a format suitable for management. Consider, for example, the cost of merchandise in a department store. For external reporting purposes, the financial accounting system must account for the actual cost of merchandise purchased either as merchandise inventory or as cost of goods sold. For the purpose of evaluating the performance of the purchasing department, the management accounting system compares the actual cost of purchases to the allowed cost of purchases. Although actual cost data are contained in both the external financial statements and the internal reports, they are configured differently.

Because much management accounting information is derived from the financial accounting information system, much of this chapter is devoted to costing objectives, elements, and techniques developed for external reporting. Study of this chapter will provide an understanding of the accounting data base used in both financial and management accounting.

INVENTORY COSTS IN DIFFERENT ORGANIZATIONS

The importance and complexity of inventory cost measurement varies widely among organizations. The importance of inventory costing is a function of the dollar size of inventories, whereas the complexity of inventory costing is a function of the number of major inventory categories and the number of cost elements assigned to each category. Using inventory as a basis, we can distinguish between service, merchandising, and manufacturing organizations. **Service organizations** perform work for others. Included in this category are banks, barbershops, hospitals, restaurants, movie theaters, electric utilities, schools, most government agencies, railroads, bus companies, and accounting firms. **Merchandising organizations** buy and sell goods. Included in this category are department stores, grocery stores, wholesale distributors, shoe stores, and discount stores. **Manufacturing organizations** process raw materials into finished products. Included in this category are automobile manufacturers, steel mills, computer manufacturers, and furniture makers.

In general, service organizations have a low percentage of their total assets invested in inventory, which usually consists only of the supplies needed to facilitate their operations. Merchandising organizations usually have a high percentage of their total assets invested in inventory. Their most significant inventory is merchandise purchased for resale, but they also have supplies inventories.

Manufacturing organizations convert raw materials into finished products that are sold to other organizations and, like merchandisers, usually have a high percentage of their total assets invested in inventories. However, rather than just one inventory category, manufacturing organizations have three major categories: raw materials, work-in-process, and finished goods. **Raw materials inventories** contain the physically existing items that are to be converted into a finished product. **Work-in-process inventories** contain materials that are in the process of being converted into a finished product. **Finished goods inventories** contain the manufactured products that are intended for sale to others.

Manufacturing organizations also have investments in supplies inventories. Some of these supplies are used to facilitate production. Others are used in selling and administrative activities. The cost of supplies that are used in production, such as lubricating oils and small tools, are a cost element of the finished product.

Exhibit 2–1 illustrates the flow of inventory costs in service, merchandising, and manufacturing organizations. Note that in all three types of organizations all inventories are eventually consumed or sold and become expenses.[1]

PRODUCT COSTING AND SERVICE COSTING

The process of assigning costs to inventories as they are converted from raw materials to finished goods is called **product costing.** Product costs must be determined for the purposes of inventory valuation and expense measurement in required general purpose financial statements. Product cost information is also used by management to plan and control firm activities.

The process of assigning costs to services is called **service costing.** Examples of service costing include measuring the cost of check processing (for a bank), instructional hours (for a college), operating room minutes (for a hospital), and passenger miles (for an airline). Though costs are seldom accumulated by service categories in external financial statements, service cost information is used internally to plan and control firm activities. The management of a bank, for example, might like to know the cost of processing a check drawn on a customer's account or the cost of processing an application for a personal loan. This information would assist in budgeting, pricing, and performance evaluation.

This chapter is presented in the context of product costing, rather than service costing, because product costing concepts are more fully developed and easier to generalize and understand. Note, however, that most product costing concepts are applicable to service costing.

---

[1] For the purposes of this classification, agriculture might be included in the category of manufacturing organizations. A cattle ranch, for example, has a high percentage of its total assets invested in cattle (work-in-process). The cattle are raised from calves (raw material) and sold to slaughterhouses or feed lots when they obtain sufficient size (finished goods).

EXHIBIT 2–1   Inventory Costs in Various Organizations

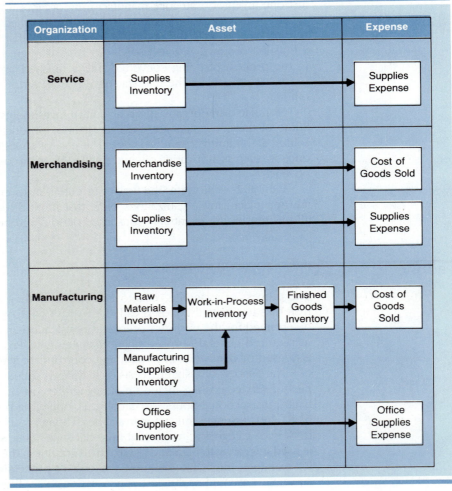

PRODUCT COSTS FOR EXTERNAL REPORTING

In financial accounting it is important to differentiate between unexpired costs and expired costs. **Unexpired costs** are recorded as assets on the statement of financial position, and **expired costs** are deducted from revenues on the income statement. A cost is classified as an asset, or an unexpired cost, to the extent that the cost objective it is related to has a potential to generate future revenues from the sale or use of the asset or to avoid future costs. For instance, the cost of merchandise inventory is an asset to a retail store because future revenues can be generated from the sale of merchandise; the cost of an apartment building is an asset to its owners because future revenues can be generated from apartment rentals; and the cost of prepaid insurance is an asset because the purchaser can avoid the cost of buying additional insurance for the coverage period.

As a cost objective loses its revenue producing or cost avoidance potential, the costs assigned to that objective are reclassified as expired costs. The loss may be sudden or gradual. Thus, the cost of merchandise inventory is reclassified as the costs of goods sold when the merchandise is sold, the cost of an apartment building is depreciated over the building's life, and the cost of prepaid insurance is reclassified as insurance expense with the passage of the coverage period.

The difference between expired and unexpired costs is often difficult to discern. Consider the case of a newly constructed office building. Because the building presumably has a future service potential, the cost of the building is initially recorded as an asset. As this service potential is realized, the cost of the building is systematically reclassified as an expense. The accounting problem is how and when to properly record the expiration of the cost of the building. To resolve this problem several alternative depreciation procedures are used. Even though these procedures may not accurately depict the decline in the value of the building, they do assign its costs, in an understandable manner, to the periods that benefit from the use of the building.

Depreciation procedures are complex, but they are not so complex as the techniques used to differentiate expired from unexpired product costs. Because manufactured products can be sold, they have a future service potential. Consequently, *the cost of raw materials and other costs incurred to transform raw materials into finished goods become part of the cost of the finished goods.* These costs are recorded as assets, since they are unexpired costs, until the finished goods are sold, when they become an expense, that is, the cost of goods sold.

Product Costs and Period Costs

In manufacturing organizations, an important distinction is made between costs assigned to products and nonproduct costs that expire during the period. **Product costs** are costs assigned to products. They are expensed when the products are sold. **Period costs** are expired nonproduct costs. They are always recorded as an expense.

For external reporting purposes, product costs include the costs of raw materials and all other factors necessary to transform raw materials into finished products. Because all manufacturing costs "attach to" or are "absorbed by" the units produced, external reports are often said to state manufacturing inventories on an *absorption cost* basis. *According to the* **absorption cost basis of external reporting,** *all manufacturing costs are product costs, and all selling and administrative costs are period costs.*

The proper treatment of several product and period costs is illustrated in Exhibit 2–2. Note in particular that depreciation, expired insurance, the cost of utilities, and so forth, are not automatically classified as period costs. When these costs are incurred in connection with manufacturing activities, they are product costs; when they are incurred in connection with other activities, they are period costs. The future service potential of factory buildings and equipment is transformed into the future service potential of manufactured products. Depreciation on manufacturing buildings and equipment is absorbed by the product; hence, this depreciation is a product cost. The future service potential of office buildings and equipment expires with the passage of time. Depreciation on office buildings and equipment is not absorbed by products; hence, this depreciation is a period cost.

EXHIBIT 2–2   Product Costs and Period Costs

Product Costs Are Related to Manufacturing Activities

Raw materials used
Manufacturing supplies used
Production employees' wages
Depreciation on plant
Expired insurance on plant
Production supervisors' salaries
Plant maintenance
Plant utilities
Production equipment rent
Plant office supplies used

They Are Assigned to the Asset Inventory

Work-in-Process Inventory

Finished Goods Inventory

They Are Expensed When Inventory Is Sold

Cost of Goods Sold

Period Costs Are Not Related to Manufacturing Activities

Nonfactory office supplies used
General and administrative salaries
Depreciation on showroom
Expired insurance on showroom
President's salary
Showroom maintenance
Nonfactory office utilities
Nonfactory office rent

They Are Expensed As Incurred

Various Selling and Administrative Expenses

EXHIBIT 2–3   Three Product Costs

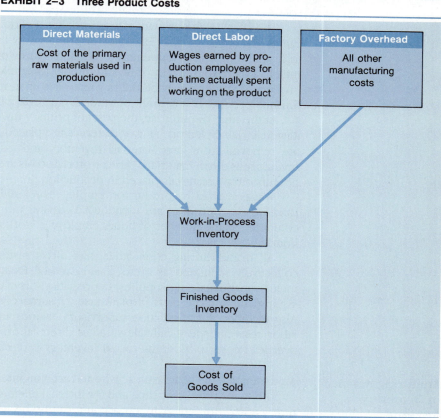

Three Product Costs

The manufacture of even a simple product, such as a wooden rowboat, requires three basic ingredients: materials (such as wood), labor (such as that of a boat craftsman), and production facilities (such as a building to work in, a saw, and a hammer). Corresponding to these three basic ingredients, product costs are classified into three categories: direct materials, direct labor, and factory overhead. Just as materials, labor, and production facilities are combined to produce a finished product, the costs of direct materials, direct labor, and factory overhead are accumulated to obtain the cost of finished goods. Exhibit 2–3 illustrates that these costs are accumulated in Work-in-Process[2] as production takes place and transferred to Finished Goods Inventory when production is completed. Product

---

[2] Account titles are capitalized to make it easier to determine when reference is being made to a physically existing item, such as work-in-process inventory, and the account Work-in-Process, which discloses the costs assigned to work-in-process inventory.

costs are finally assigned to Cost of Goods Sold when the finished goods are sold.

The costs of the primary raw materials converted into finished goods are called **direct materials.** Examples of primary raw materials include iron ore to a steel mill, coiled aluminum to a manufacturer of aluminum siding, cow's milk to a dairy, logs to a sawmill, and lumber to a builder. Note that the finished product of one firm may be the raw materials of another. Two-by-fours are the finished product of a sawmill but the raw material of a carpenter.

At the time of purchase, the costs of primary raw materials are assigned to Raw Materials Inventory. As raw materials are placed in production, their costs are removed from Raw Materials Inventory and assigned to Work-in-Process Inventory as direct materials. Direct materials costs are computed as the number of units of raw materials placed in production times their related cost per unit.

Wages earned by production employees *for the time they actually spend working on a product* are identified as **direct labor.** Direct labor costs are computed as the number of hours employees work on production times their hourly wage rate.

All manufacturing costs other than direct materials and direct labor are collectively identified as **factory overhead.**[3] Examples of factory overhead include manufacturing supplies; depreciation on manufacturing buildings and equipment; and the costs of plant taxes, insurance, maintenance, and utilities. Also included are production supervisors' salaries and all other manufacturing labor costs not specifically classified as direct labor. The assignment of factory overhead costs to Work-in-Process Inventory is discussed later in this chapter.

Analyzing Activity in Inventory Accounts

An understanding of account activity and account interrelationships is extremely important for product costing and for internal planning and control. During any time period, the activity in any account can be broken down into four parts:

Beginning balance + Increases − Decreases = Ending balance.

Knowing any three of these items, we can always find the fourth. Typical accounts and their activity include:

Cash	Merchandise Inventory	Accounts Payable
Beginning balance	Beginning balance	Beginning balance
+ Cash receipts	+ Purchases	+ Purchases on account
= Total cash available	= Total available	= Total payable
− Cash disbursements	− Cost of goods sold	− Payments on account
= Ending balance	= Ending balance	= Ending balance

---

[3] Factory overhead is also called "manufacturing overhead," "burden," "manufacturing burden," and "overhead." All but the last of these terms are acceptable. The word "overhead" by itself does not indicate the type of overhead. Merchandising organizations occasionally refer to administrative costs as overhead.

The totals are inserted for computational ease. Assume that the management of a department store is trying to budget purchases for the coming year. The beginning merchandise inventory costs $50,000, and management desires to have an inventory of $45,000 at the end of the year. If the cost of goods sold is budgeted to be $350,000, knowledge of account activity can be used to budget purchases:

Activity	Given Information	Solution
Beginning balance	$ 50,000	$ 50,000
+ Purchases	+ ?	+345,000
= Total available	$?	$395,000
− Cost of goods sold	−350,000	−350,000
= Ending balance	$ 45,000	$ 45,000

Purchases should be budgeted at $345,000.

Activity in one account always affects at least one other account. Inventory purchased on account in a merchandising organization increases Merchandise Inventory and Accounts Payable. Payments on account reduce Cash and Accounts Payable. Inventory issued to the factory in a manufacturing organization decreases Raw Materials Inventory and increases Work-in-Process Inventory. A complete analysis of a manufacturing organization's inventory account relationships is presented in Exhibit 2–4.

In Exhibit 2–4 the cost of raw materials placed in production reduces Raw Materials Inventory and increases Work-in-Process Inventory. The total additions

EXHIBIT 2–4   Analysis of Activity in Manufacturing Inventory Accounts

to Work-in-Process Inventory are collectively identified as **current manufacturing costs,** and the total costs assigned to products completed are collectively identified as the **cost of goods manufactured.** The cost of goods manufactured is deducted from Work-in-Process Inventory and added to Finished Goods Inventory. Once the relationships between inventory accounts are known, items of interest (such as the cost of materials placed in production, the cost of goods manufactured, or the cost of goods sold) are readily determined. Consider the following example.

On September 1, 19x4, the beginning inventory balances of the Harmon Manufacturing Company were

Raw Materials Inventory	$ 5,000
Work-in-Process Inventory	8,000
Finished Goods Inventory	11,000

During the month of September, raw materials costing $12,000 were purchased. Direct labor and factory overhead costs were $20,000 and $15,000, respectively.

The September 30 inventory account balances were

Raw Materials Inventory	$ 7,000
Work-in-Process Inventory	14,000
Finished Goods Inventory	6,000

An analysis of activity in inventory accounts is presented in Exhibit 2–5. For computational ease the ending balance in each account is subtracted from the total to determine the items of interest:

Cost of materials placed in production	$10,000
Cost of goods manufactured	39,000
Cost of goods sold	44,000

This example focused on inventory account activity. Cost of goods sold is, of course, just one item on the income statement. Harmon's September income statement would also include revenues and other expenses. Harmon's September 30 statement of financial position would include inventory and many other assets, as well as liability and shareholders' equity accounts.

Because activity in one account always affects at least one other account, the analysis here is incomplete. The acquisition of raw materials and direct labor

EXHIBIT 2–5   Analysis of Harmon's Inventory Accounts

Raw Materials Inventory

Beginning balance		$ 5,000
Purchases		12,000
Total available		$17,000
Ending balance		− 7,000
Cost of materials placed in production (direct materials)		$10,000

Work-in-Process Inventory

Beginning balance		$ 8,000
Current manufacturing costs:		
Direct materials	$10,000	
Direct labor	20,000	
Factory overhead	15,000	45,000
Total costs in process		$53,000
Ending balance		−14,000
Cost of goods manufactured		$39,000

Finished Goods Inventory

Beginning balance		$11,000
Cost of goods manufactured		39,000
Total goods available for sale		$50,000
Ending balance		− 6,000
Cost of goods sold		$44,000

and the incurrence of factory overhead costs affect many other accounts. We have ignored these accounts for the moment in order to emphasize the essential inventory relationships found in product costing.

Statement of Cost of Goods Manufactured

The activity in Raw Materials and Work-in-Process is formally summarized in a **statement of cost of goods manufactured.** Harmon Manufacturing Company's September 19x4 Statement of Cost of Goods Manufactured is presented in Exhibit 2–6. To show the relationship between this statement and the income statement, Harmon's September 19x4 Income Statement is also presented in the exhibit. For this example assume September sales of $90,000 and selling and administrative expenses of $30,000.

The activity in all major inventory accounts can be summarized in a single **statement of cost of goods manufactured and sold,** such as the one presented in Exhibit 2–7, along with an accompanying income statement. These statements, like all formal accounting statements, begin with a heading that indicates the name of the organization, the name of the statement, and the statement date or time period. Statement formats and details vary. Factory overhead may, for example, be itemized rather than be presented as a single amount.

Combined Product Costs

A clear association exists between the physical product and the direct materials and direct labor costs. Direct materials and direct labor costs are easily traced to finished goods. The number of units of raw materials that enter into each finished unit can be counted, and the time production employees work to produce a finished unit can be measured. Because of this direct association with the finished product, direct materials and direct labor costs are jointly identified as **direct product costs** or **prime product costs.**

EXHIBIT 2–6   Statement of Cost of Goods Manufactured

Harmon Manufacturing Company
Statement of Cost of Goods Manufactured
For the month ending September 30, 19x4

Current manufacturing costs:			
Cost of materials placed in production:			
Raw materials, 9/1/x4	$ 5,000		
Purchases	12,000		
Total available	$17,000		
Raw materials, 9/30/x4	− 7,000	$10,000	
Direct labor		20,000	
Factory overhead		15,000	$45,000
Work-in-process, 9/1/x4			8,000
Total costs in process			$53,000
Work-in-process, 9/30/x4			−14,000
Cost of goods manufactured			$39,000

Harmon Manufacturing Company
Income Statement
For the month ending September 30, 19x4

Sales		$90,000
Cost of goods sold:		
Finished goods inventory, 9/1/x4	$11,000	
Cost of goods manufactured	39,000	
Total goods available for sale	$50,000	
Finished goods inventory, 9/30/x4	− 6,000	−44,000
Gross profit		$46,000
Selling and administrative expenses		−30,000
Net income		$16,000

EXHIBIT 2–7   Statement of Cost of Goods Manufactured and Sold

Harmon Manufacturing Company
Statement of Cost of Goods Manufactured and Sold
For the month ending September 30, 19x4

Current manufacturing costs:			
Cost of materials placed in production:			
Raw materials, 9/1/x4	$ 5,000		
Purchases	12,000		
Total available	$17,000		
Raw materials, 9/30/x4	– 7,000	$10,000	
Direct labor		20,000	
Factory overhead		15,000	$45,000
Work-in-process, 9/1/x4			8,000
Total costs in process			$53,000
Work-in-process, 9/30/x4			–14,000
Cost of goods manufactured			$39,000
Finished goods inventory, 9/1/x4			11,000
Total goods available for sale			$50,000
Finished goods inventory, 9/30/x4			– 6,000
Cost of goods sold			$44,000

Harmon Manufacturing Company
Income Statement
For the month ending September 30, 19x4

Sales	$90,000
Cost of goods sold	–44,000
Gross profit	$46,000
Selling and administrative expenses	–30,000
Net income	$16,000

All product costs other than direct materials and direct labor are classified as factory overhead. It is difficult to associate factory overhead costs with specific units of product. Factory overhead costs (such as depreciation on plant, insurance on plant, production supervisors' salaries, plant maintenance, and plant utilities) are incurred to facilitate the production of all products. Because it is difficult to establish an explicit (direct) association between these costs and individual units of product, factory overhead costs are often identified as **indirect product costs.**

Direct labor and factory overhead costs, which are incurred to convert raw materials into finished goods, are jointly identified as **conversion costs.** The relationships between these new cost terms are illustrated in Exhibit 2–8. The

EXHIBIT 2–8   Product Costing Terminology

September 19x4 amounts for the Harmon Manufacturing Company are as follows:

Direct product costs:		
Direct materials	$10,000	
Direct labor	20,000	$30,000
Prime product costs:		
Direct materials	$10,000	
Direct labor	20,000	$30,000
Indirect product costs		
(factory overhead)		$15,000
Conversion costs:		
Direct labor	$20,000	
Factory overhead	15,000	$35,000

Note that direct materials refers to the cost of materials placed in production rather than the cost of materials purchased.

A Closer Look at Factory Overhead

As production occurs, direct materials, direct labor, and factory overhead are assigned to Work-in-Process. Direct materials costs are transferred from Raw Materials Inventory. The number of units of raw materials transferred to the factory multiplied by the related cost per unit equals the direct materials cost. Direct labor costs are the number of direct labor hours worked times the appropriate rate per direct labor hour. But what about overhead?

Factory overhead is the most broadly defined and difficult to measure product cost. It includes all production costs other than those specifically identified as direct materials and direct labor. If there is a company-subsidized cafeteria in the plant, factory overhead will even include depreciation on the kitchen sink.

Selecting a Basis for Overhead Application. The costs and benefits of alternative measurement techniques are important considerations in the accumulation and assignment of factory overhead. As a cost reducing measure, all factory overhead costs may be grouped together into a single collection of related costs, called a **cost pool.** These costs are then assigned (applied) to Work-in-Process Inventory on the basis of some factor that has a high correlation with the incurrence of overhead, is common to all products, and is easy to measure. Frequently used bases of overhead application include direct labor dollars, direct labor hours, and machine hours.

The variety and different natures of factory overhead costs make it difficult to accurately apply them using a single application basis. Some factory overhead costs are related to people, others are related to the existence of buildings and equipment, and still others are related to the use of buildings and equipment. Accuracy could be improved by grouping overhead costs into two or more cost pools that have common characteristics and applying each on a separate basis. For example, labor related costs might be pooled and applied on the basis of labor hours, whereas equipment related costs might be placed in another cost pool and applied on the basis of machine hours. This should be done only if the management accountant believes the increased accuracy is worth the added cost of operating the more complex cost measurement system.[4]

Using Predetermined Overhead Rates. The timely assignment of actual factory overhead costs is difficult because the amount of many overhead costs cannot be determined until after the period. September's electric utility and water bills, for example, may not be received until mid-October. Waiting until September's actual overhead costs are known would necessitate an undesirable delay in product costing. September's statement of cost of goods manufactured could not be prepared until mid to late October.

To overcome this timing problem, and other problems such as smoothing the work load of the bookkeepers, most firms use a predetermined rate to assign factory overhead costs. A **predetermined factory overhead rate** is determined at the start of the year by dividing the predicted overhead costs for the year by the predicted activity for the year. A predetermined overhead rate per direct labor hour is computed as

$$\text{Predetermined overhead rate per direct labor hour} = \frac{\text{Predicted total overhead for the year}}{\text{Predicted total direct labor hours for the year}}.$$

---

[4] Cost systems that use two or more factory overhead cost pools are discussed in Chapter 12.

Using a predetermined overhead rate based on direct labor hours, we compute the assignment of overhead to Work-in-Process Inventory as

$$\begin{array}{l}\text{Factory overhead}\\\text{assigned to}\\\text{Work-in-Process Inventory}\end{array} = \begin{array}{l}\text{Actual}\\\text{direct}\\\text{labor}\\\text{hours}\end{array} \times \begin{array}{l}\text{Predetermined}\\\text{overhead rate per}\\\text{direct labor hour.}\end{array}$$

Late in 19x3 Harmon Manufacturing Company predicted a 19x4 activity level of 25,000 direct labor hours with factory overhead totaling $187,500. Using this information, their 19x4 predetermined overhead rate per direct labor hour was computed as

$$\begin{array}{l}\text{Predetermined}\\\text{overhead rate}\end{array} = \frac{\$187,500}{25,000}$$

$$= \$7.50 \text{ per direct labor hour.}$$

If 2,000 direct labor hours were used in September 19x4, the applied overhead would equal $15,000:

$$2,000 \times \$7.50 = \$15,000.$$

When a predetermined overhead rate is used, monthly variations between actual and applied factory overhead are expected. In some months actual overhead is less than applied overhead; in some months it can be more. If the difference between cumulative actual and cumulative applied overhead builds up in a single direction over a period of time, it will be necessary to change the predetermined overhead rate. Underapplied and overapplied overhead costs are considered further in Chapter 11.

Materials and Labor Costs in Factory Overhead. As discussed earlier, direct materials costs include only the costs of primary raw materials clearly identified with the finished product, and direct labor costs include only the wages earned by production employees for time spent working on products. All other materials and labor costs are elements of factory overhead. Materials and labor costs normally in factory overhead include: indirect materials, indirect labor, idle time, overtime premiums, and employee fringe benefits.

Indirect materials are relatively low cost materials that are difficult to associate with specific units of final product. Wood is a primary raw material in the manufacture of wooden bookcases; its cost is a direct materials cost. Nails, screws, glue, and varnish are indirect materials whose costs are assigned to Manufacturing Supplies Inventory at the time of purchase and transferred to the factory overhead cost pool as they are used.

Indirect labor includes the salaries and wages earned by production employees for the time they spend performing all production related tasks, except physically working on the product. Production related tasks include receiving instructions, oiling machinery, and cleaning the work area. Salaries earned by production supervisors and wages earned by maintenance personnel may also be classified as indirect labor.

Idle time is time employees are not working on the product or performing other production related tasks. Included in this category are the time employees wait for instructions, materials, or repairs. Unless idle time becomes excessive, the salaries and wages paid employees for idle time are regarded as a normal operating cost and included in the factory overhead cost pool. In most organizations it is difficult to structure activities so that employees have no unassigned time. Some employers also pay idle time wages to employees who report for work when no work is available.

Overtime premiums are bonus wages in excess of the regular hourly rate that are paid to production employees for working more than the regular number of hours. Employees who regularly work 40 hours per week receive an overtime premium for working more than 40 hours. Assume an employee whose regular wage rate is $12 per hour is entitled to a 50 percent overtime premium. If the employee works 45 hours in a given week, the employee's total wages will be $570.

Regular hourly wages (45 × $12)	$540
Overtime premium (5 × $6)	30
Total wages	$570

Overtime premiums are usually treated as factory overhead even if the overtime hours are identified with particular units of product. Overtime is the result of the overall level of activity. If there were less activity, products worked on during overtime hours would be worked on during regular hours. Accordingly, overtime premiums are spread over all production as part of factory overhead. In the above example, $540 is classified as direct labor, and $30 is classified as factory overhead.

Employee fringe benefits are additional labor costs paid by the employer on behalf of the employees. Employee fringe benefits are not included in the computation of employees' salary or wage rates, nor are they disclosed on employees' pay stubs as part of gross earnings or as a deduction in arriving at net earnings. Typical employee fringe benefits include: the employer's share of social security (FICA) taxes, federal and state unemployment taxes, workmen's compensation insurance, medical insurance premiums, employer paid pension plans, and vacation pay.

In the past, employee fringe benefits were a small percentage of total labor costs. Because of their relatively small size, management accountants believed that the increased accuracy that would result from separately accounting for them was not worth the additional bookkeeping cost. Consequently, the cost of employee fringe benefits has traditionally been assigned to the factory overhead cost pool.

However, a recent U.S. Chamber of Commerce survey reported that, in many organizations, employee fringe benefits now exceed 35 percent of the total labor bill. This has led some management accountants to question the propriety of the traditional method of accounting for them. There is a concern that employee fringe benefits will dominate the factory overhead cost pool and cause an inaccurate allocation of either the employee fringe benefits or the other overhead costs. Rather than mixing the cost of fringe benefits with other overhead costs, many firms now place employee fringe benefits in a separate cost pool and assign them to products on the basis of direct labor costs.

COST CONCEPTS FOR MANAGEMENT ACTION

The product costing concepts and techniques introduced above are used to develop the historical cost information presented in general purpose financial statements. Management is interested in historical cost information primarily because it is useful in controlling current operations and planning future operations.

Historical Costs for Prediction and Control

To plan a trip you need to know your current location, your destination, and alternative ways of traveling between them. Likewise, to plan for the future a manager must understand the organization's current situation, its goals, and alternative ways of traveling between them. A manager can obtain an understanding of where the organization is (its current economic situation) by studying historical cost data and reports. A detailed analysis of historical cost data also assists in determining whether the organization has the capabilities needed to achieve its goals. If, for example, an organization's plant is old and its production costs exceed competitor's selling prices, the organization cannot currently compete in the market for its final product.

Management is often interested in how costs respond to changes in the volume of activity. Some costs increase in direct proportion to increases in activity, whereas others do not change at all. An analysis of historical cost data provides an excellent starting point in determining cost behavior. Furthermore, predictions of future costs are often based on historical cost relationships, adjusted for changes in prices and technology. Cost behavior is studied in Chapter 3, and predicted cost relationships are used for profit planning in Chapters 4 through 6.

Subsequent to planning, actual (historical) costs are accumulated and analyzed for the purpose of controlling operations. In Chapters 7 through 10, performance reports are developed that compare allowed and actual costs. Special attention is given to the problem of determining who is responsible for each cost.

Sunk Costs and Relevant Costs

Although an analysis of historical cost information is a useful starting point in predicting future costs, it is the predicted future costs, rather than the historical costs, that are of interest to decision makers. In and of themselves, historical costs are irrelevant to decisions about the future. In the context of decision making, historical costs are called sunk costs.

Sunk costs result from past decisions that management no longer has control over. Because sunk costs cannot be changed, they are irrelevant to decisions about the future and should be omitted from any analysis prepared to assist in decision making. Including sunk costs makes it difficult for management to focus on important decision variables; furthermore, management may be misled into making bad decisions on the basis of sunk costs that cannot be changed.

Relevant costs are future costs that differ among competing alternatives. Because relevant costs can be changed by management decisions (selecting one alternative rather than another), they should be included in any analysis prepared to assist in decision making. Assume management is evaluating the desirability of replacing a four-function calculator with a new ten-function calculator that has several memory units. The old calculator was purchased yesterday for $25 and has a used sales value of $15. The new calculator costs $90. Using the new calculator rather than the old one will save three labor hours per week at a cost of $15 per hour. For simplicity assume a planning period is 10 weeks, at the end of which both calculators will cease to operate and have a zero salvage value.

The cost of the calculator purchased yesterday is irrelevant to a decision to keep it or replace it with a new calculator. The relevant factors for this decision are the cost of the new calculator, the disposal value of the old calculator, and the cost savings derived from using the new, rather than the old, calculator. The net benefit of acquiring the new calculator is $375.

Labor cost reduction (10 wk. × 3 hr. per wk. × $15 per hr.)		$450
Additional investment:		
Cost of new calculator	$90	
Less disposal value of old calculator	−15	−75
Net benefit		$375

The $25 cost of the old calculator was not included in the analysis because it is a sunk cost.

Sunk costs are not relevant to an economic analysis of decisions about the future, but they do have behavioral implications. Even though it is economically advantageous to acquire the new calculator, a manager might be reluctant to do so, because of a concern that this new decision should reflect poorly on the decision to acquire the old calculator. Sometimes accounting procedures increase this fear when, for example, it is necessary to compute and disclose a "loss" on the disposal of an old asset. This is a situation where good decisions will be made only if managers and management accountants clearly understand the proper uses and limits of accounting data.

Opportunity Cost

An **opportunity cost** is the net cash inflow that could be obtained if the resources committed to one action were used in the most desirable other alternative. An opportunity cost results from a forgone opportunity. By selecting one opportunity, management forgoes an alternative. Other things equal, management desires to select the alternative with the smallest total cost, including any opportunity cost. Consequently, opportunity costs are relevant costs and, as such, should always be considered in decision making. Note, however, that because there are no cash receipts or cash expenditures incurred in connection with a forgone opportunity, opportunity costs are not recorded in the accounting records.

Opportunity costs are a significant part of the cost of your education. How much more could you earn this year, at your current education and skill level, if you were not enrolled in college? $10,000? If so, $10,000 is the opportunity cost of your college education this year. This opportunity cost should be added to tuition, room, board, books, and so forth in computing your total educational investment.[5]

What, then, is the opportunity cost of acquiring the new calculator? The answer depends on the best other alternative use of the $75 additional investment. If the money were to remain in a noninterest bearing checking account or earn $6 interest in a short-term savings certificate, the best other alternative action would be to invest in the savings certificate, so the opportunity cost would be $6. In this case, the $6 opportunity cost should be compared to the net benefits of the new calculator to determine the net advantage or disadvantage of purchasing the calculator. The net economic advantage of purchasing the calculator would, therefore, be $369 ($375 net benefit − $6 opportunity cost).

It is important to understand that the opportunity cost of an action is a function of the *other* alternative actions. Investing in the savings certificate has an opportunity cost of $375 because this is the net cash inflow from the most desirable other action, namely, buying the calculator. Likewise, the opportunity cost of leaving the $75 in a noninterest bearing checking account is $375.

SUMMARY

Though cost is generally defined as a monetary measure of the economic sacrifice made to obtain some product or service, different cost concepts and measurements are required for different purposes. A system for cost measurement includes a costing purpose, cost objectives, cost elements, and costing

---

[5] The benefits of this investment will accrue in the future. Ways to equate monetary future benefits with current investments are considered in Chapter 14. There are, of course, many nonmonetary benefits associated with a college education.

techniques. For the purpose of external reporting, products are important cost objectives in manufacturing organizations. The cost of a product contains three major cost elements: direct materials, direct labor, and factory overhead. The pooling of all product costs other than direct materials and direct labor into a single factory overhead cost pool and the application of factory overhead to products using a predetermined overhead rate are important product costing techniques.

In manufacturing organizations a distinction is made between product costs and period costs. Product costs are assigned to products and accounted for as assets until the product is sold. At that time they become an expense, that is, the cost of goods sold. Period costs are nonproduct costs that are accounted for as expenses in the period their service potential expires.

Product costing is emphasized in this chapter because product costing is well developed, easily generalized and understood, and required for external reporting. Many of the concepts discussed here are also applicable to service costing. The accounting system used for product costing also provides the data used for many management accounting purposes.

In and of themselves, historical costs are not relevant to an economic analysis of the future. They are sunk costs that management can no longer control. An economic analysis prepared to assist management in making decisions should focus on relevant costs, that is, on future costs that differ among competing alternatives.

KEY TERMS

Absorption cost basis of external
   reporting
Conversion costs
Cost
Cost element
Cost objective
Cost of goods manufactured
Cost pool
Costing purpose
Costing technique
Current manufacturing costs
Direct labor
Direct materials
Direct product costs
Employee fringe benefits
Expired cost
Factory overhead
Finished goods inventory
Idle time
Indirect labor
Indirect materials
Indirect product costs

Manufacturing organization
Merchandising organization
Opportunity cost
Overtime premium
Period cost
Predetermined factory overhead
   rate
Prime product costs
Product cost
Product costing
Raw materials inventory
Relevant cost
Service costing
Service organization
Statement of cost of goods
   manufactured
Statement of cost of goods
   manufactured and sold
Sunk cost
Unexpired cost
Work-in-process inventory

REVIEW QUESTIONS

2–1 What relationships exist among costing purpose, cost objectives, cost elements, and costing techniques?

2–2 Why is management accounting information subject to more stringent cost-benefit analysis than financial accounting information?

2–3 Distinguish among service, merchandising, and manufacturing organizations on the basis of the importance and complexity of inventory cost measurement.

2–4 Distinguish among raw materials, work-in-process, and finished goods inventories.

2–5 Distinguish between product costing and service costing. Why do we emphasize product costing rather than service costing in this chapter?

2–6 In general, how do we determine whether a cost is an expired cost or an unexpired cost?

2–7 When is depreciation a product cost? When is depreciation a period cost?

2–8 What are the three major product cost elements?

2–9 How can you determine when a manufacturing cost should be classified as factory overhead?

2–10 Which product cost element is both a prime cost and a conversion cost?

2–11 What are the characteristics of a good basis of overhead application?

2–12 How are predetermined overhead rates developed? Why are they widely used?

2–13 What labor costs are often elements of factory overhead?

2–14 Of what use are historical costs in planning for the future?

2–15 Are opportunity costs relevant costs? Why or why not?

REVIEW PROBLEM

Cost Statements and Terminology

On January 1, 19x7, the beginning inventory balances of the Poston Manufacturing Company were as follows:

Raw Materials Inventory	$ 3,000
Work-in-Process	8,200
Finished Goods Inventory	15,000

During January, raw materials costing $6,000 were purchased. Direct labor and factory overhead costs were $8,000 and $20,000, respectively.

The January 31 inventory account balances were as follows:

Raw Materials Inventory	$ 2,500
Work-in-Process	6,000
Finished Goods Inventory	13,000

January sales of finished goods amounted to $75,000 and selling and administrative expenses totaled $25,050.

Requirements

a) Prepare a statement of cost of goods manufactured and an income statement for January 19x7.

b) Prepare a statement of cost of goods manufactured and sold and an income statement for January 19x7.

c) Determine each of the following for January:

1. Direct product costs.
2. Prime product costs.
3. Indirect product costs.
4. Conversion costs.

The solution to this problem is found at the end of the Chapter 2 exercises and problems.

EXERCISES

2–1 Cost Terms: Matching

For each of the numbered phrases or statements, select the *most appropriate* term. Each term is used only once.

1. Has three inventory categories
2. Objects or activities costs are assigned to
3. Sold to other organizations
4. Benefit forgone
5. Performs work for others
6. Cannot be changed
7. Manufacturing costs except direct materials and labor
8. Future costs that differ
9. Total additions to Work-in-Process
10. These costs are assigned to inventories

a. Product costs
b. Service organization
c. Sunk cost
d. Relevant costs
e. Opportunity cost
f. Cost objectives
g. Manufacturing organization
h. Current manufacturing costs
i. Finished goods
j. Factory overhead

2–2 Cost Terms: Matching

For each of the numbered phrases or statements, select the *most appropriate* term. Each term is used only once.

1. Direct labor and factory overhead
2. Direct materials and direct labor
3. Used to assign cost elements to cost objectives
4. Selling and administrative expenses
5. Buys and sells goods
6. Being converted to a finished product
7. All manufacturing costs are product costs
8. A collection of related costs
9. A measure of economic sacrifice
10. Transferred to Finished Goods Inventory

a. Costing technique
b. Merchandising organization
c. Work-in-process
d. Absorption cost basis of external reporting
e. Cost of goods manufactured
f. Cost pool
g. Cost
h. Direct product costs
i. Period costs
j. Conversion costs

2–3 Classification of Product and Period Costs

Classify the following costs incurred by a furniture manufacturer as product costs or period costs. Further classify the product costs as direct or indirect product costs.

1. Rent on cars used by salespersons
2. Depreciation on factory
3. Power and water consumed in the factory
4. Advertising in national magazines
5. Broken saw blades
6. Vacation pay of production workers
7. Carpenters' wages
8. Depreciation on table saws
9. Glue used in furniture assembly
10. Supervisors' salaries
11. Materials used in packing finished goods prior to shipment
12. Participation in regional trade shows
13. Management training seminar
14. Depreciation on corporate headquarters
15. Prime lumber

2–4 Classification of Product and Period Costs

Classify the following costs incurred by an automobile manufacturer as product costs or period costs. Further classify the product costs as direct materials or conversion.

1. Salaries of legal staff
2. Automobile window glass
3. Depreciation on word processor in president's office
4. Plant fire department
5. Automobile tires
6. Automobile bumpers
7. Wages paid assembly line maintenance workers
8. Salary of corporate controller
9. Automobile engines
10. Subsidy of plant cafeteria
11. Wages paid assembly line production workers
12. National sales meeting in Detroit
13. Overtime premium paid assembly line workers
14. Advertising on national television
15. Depreciation on assembly line

2–5 Account Activity and Interrelationships

For each of the following independent cases find the required information.

1. *Cash*

Beginning balance	$ 30,000
Ending balance	25,000
Cash receipts	130,000

Find: Cash disbursements

2. *Merchandise Inventory*

Purchases	$104,000
Cost of goods sold	80,000
Ending balance	70,000

Find: Beginning balance

3. *Accounts Payable* (to suppliers)

Ending balance	$ 65,000
Payments on account	302,000
Beginning balance	88,000

Find: Purchases on account

4. *Accounts Receivable*

Sales on account	$260,000
Collections on account	291,000
Beginning balance	57,000

Find: Ending balance

5. *Merchandise Inventory*

Beginning balance	$15,000
Ending balance	45,000
Cost of goods sold	95,000

Accounts Payable (to suppliers)

Beginning balance	$ 5,000
Ending balance	6,000

Find: Payments on account when all purchases are on account

6. *Merchandise Inventory*

Beginning balance	$ 39,000
Ending balance	29,000
Purchases	110,000

Accounts Receivable

Beginning balance	$ 23,000
Ending balance	120,000

Find: Collections on account when all sales are on account and the selling price is 150 percent of cost

2–6 Account Activity and Interrelationships

For each of the following independent cases find the required information.

1. *Raw Materials*

Beginning balance	$ 7,000
Ending balance	14,000
Purchases	48,000

Find: Direct materials

2. *Work-in-Process*

Ending balance	$22,000
Cost of goods manufactured	21,000
Beginning balance	8,000

Find: Current manufacturing costs

3. *Finished Goods Inventory*

Cost of goods manufactured	$62,000
Ending balance	20,000
Cost of goods sold	61,000

Find: Beginning balance

4. *Merchandise Inventory*

Purchases	$210,000
Cost of goods sold	223,000
Beginning balance	41,000

Find: Ending balance

5. *Raw Materials*

Beginning balance	$ 8,500
Ending balance	12,000
Direct materials	42,000

Accounts Payable (to suppliers)

Ending balance	$11,000
Beginning balance	6,000

Find: Payments on account when all purchases are on account

6. *Finished Goods Inventory*

Beginning balance	$ 22,000
Cost of goods manufactured	100,000
Ending balance	30,000

Accounts Receivable

Beginning balance	$ 16,000
Ending balance	50,000

Find: Collections on account when all sales are on account and the selling price is 200 percent of cost

2–7 Analyzing Activity in Inventory Accounts

Selected data concerning the past fiscal year's operations of the Hull Manufacturing Company are presented below.

Raw materials used	$290,000
Total manufacturing costs charged to production during the year (includes raw materials, direct labor, and factory overhead applied at a rate of 60 percent of direct labor cost)	686,000
Cost of goods available for sale	826,000
Selling and general expenses	25,000

	Inventories	
	Beginning	*Ending*
Raw materials	$70,000	$ 80,000
Work-in-process	80,000	30,000
Finished goods	90,000	110,000

Required: Determine each of the following:

1. The cost of raw materials purchased.
2. The direct labor costs charged to production.
3. The cost of goods manufactured.
4. The cost of goods sold.

2–8 Statements: Cost of Goods Manufactured, Income

Information from the records of the Alexandria Manufacturing Company is given below for August 19x4.

Sales	$205,000
Selling and administrative expenses	83,000
Purchases of raw materials	20,000
Direct labor	15,000
Factory overhead	32,000

	Inventories	
	August 1	*August 31*
Raw materials	$ 7,000	$ 5,000
Work-in-process	14,000	11,000
Finished goods	15,000	19,000

Requirements

a) Prepare a statement of cost of goods manufactured and an income statement for August.

b) Determine each of the following:

Direct product costs.
Prime product costs.
Indirect product costs.
Conversion costs.

2–9 Statements: Cost of Goods Manufactured and Sold, Income

Information from the records of Grand Rapids Products is given below for January 19x7.

Sales	$350,000
Selling and administrative expenses	55,000
Purchases of raw materials	90,000
Direct labor	120,000
Overhead is applied using a predetermined overhead rate of 130 percent of direct labor.	

	Inventories	
	January 1	January 31
Raw materials	$12,000	$ 8,000
Work-in-process	50,000	25,000
Finished goods	30,000	40,000

Requirements

a) Prepare a statement of cost of goods manufactured and sold and an income statement for January.

b) Determine each of the following:

  Direct product costs.
  Prime product costs.
  Indirect product costs.
  Conversion costs.

2–10 Developing and Using a Predetermined Overhead Rate

The following predictions were made for 19x9:

Total factory overhead for the year	$1,375,000
Total direct labor hours for the year	125,000

Actual results for January 19x9 were as follows:

Factory overhead	$82,000
Direct labor hours	8,000

Requirements

a) Determine the 19x9 predetermined overhead rate per direct labor hour.

b) Using the 19x9 predetermined overhead rate, determine the factory overhead applied to Work-in-Process during January.

c) Determine the amount of any overapplied or underapplied overhead at the end of January.

2–11 Developing and Using a Predetermined Overhead Rate

The following predictions were made for 19x2:

Total factory overhead for the year	$380,000
Total machine hours for the year	20,000

Actual results for February 19x2 were as follows:

Factory overhead	$55,200
Machine hours	3,100

Requirements

a) Determine the 19x2 predetermined overhead rate per machine hour.

b) Using the 19x2 predetermined overhead rate per machine hour, determine the factory overhead applied to Work-in-Process during February.

c) As of February 1, actual overhead was underapplied by $4,000. Determine the cumulative amount of any overapplied or underapplied overhead at the end of February.

2–12 Assignment of Overtime Premium

Susan Dove is a telephone installer in a college-oriented community. During the last week of August she spent 25 hours installing telephones in Riverview Apartments, 23 hours installing telephones in Sam's Luxury Apartments, and 3 hours on general tasks. Mrs. Dove has a regular 40-hour workweek, with scheduled daily hours from 8 A.M. to 12 P.M. and from 1 P.M. to 5 P.M., Monday through Friday. Of the 23 hours at Sam's Luxury Apartments, 11 were after 5 P.M. Mrs. Dove's wage rate is $9 per hour with time-and-a-half for overtime.

Required: Determine the amount of Mrs. Dove's labor cost that should be assigned to each apartment complex. Explain why some of Mrs. Dove's labor costs should be assigned to overhead.

2–13 Determining and Classifying Labor Related Costs

Joan Keller works on the assembly line of the National Computer Company. She installs cathode ray picture tubes in personal computers. Because of the high demand for the company's products, Joan often works overtime hours. During a recent week her total reported time was 48 hours, with 42 hours spent working on the assembly line.

The base wage rate for assembly line workers is $12 per hour. Employee fringe benefits amount to 40 percent of the base wage rate. Employees are paid time-and-a-half for overtime. The regular workweek is 40 hours.

Requirements

a) Determine the total wages and benefits earned by Joan Keller.

b) If all earnings other than the base wages paid for working on products are classified as factory overhead, classify Keller's total earnings as direct labor and factory overhead.

c) If base wages paid for working on products and related fringe benefits are classified as direct labor, with all other earnings classified as factory overhead, classify Keller's total earnings as direct labor and factory overhead.

2–14 Determining and Classifying Labor Related Costs

Gary Dicer is a teller at the Big Bucks National Bank. During a recent week he worked a total of 52 hours, with 38 hours spent at a drive-up banking window and 14 hours spent on breaks and miscellaneous tasks.

The base wage rate for tellers is $6 per hour. Employee fringe benefits amount to 30 percent of the base wage rate. Employees are paid time-and-a-half for overtime. The regular workweek is 40 hours.

Requirements

a) Determine the total wages and benefits earned by Gary Dicer.

b) To determine the cost of bank activities, Big Bucks classifies the earnings of tellers as direct labor and operating overhead. If all earnings other than the base wages paid for working at the teller's window are classified as operating overhead, classify Dicer's total earnings as direct labor and operating overhead.

c) If base wages paid for working at the teller's window and related fringe benefits are classified as direct labor, with all other earnings classified as operating overhead, classify Dicer's total earnings as direct labor and operating overhead.

2–15 Establishing Overhead Cost Pools

A cost pool is a collection of related costs. Presented are a number of factory overhead costs. Classify these costs by number into one of three cost pools:

Pool 1: The existence of buildings and equipment.

Pool 2: The use of buildings and equipment.

Pool 3: The availability and use of direct labor.

Factory overhead costs:

1. Depreciation on buildings and machinery.
2. Power.
3. Water.
4. Fringe benefits.
5. Idle time wages.
6. Property taxes.
7. Supervisors' salaries.
8. Property insurance on buildings and equipment.
9. Overtime premiums.
10. Lubricants for machines.
11. Safety hats and shoes.
12. Night and weekend security.
13. Subsidy of employee cafeteria.

2–16 Relevant Costs

Sally Byte is a computer science major just starting her senior year. To complete her extensive programming assignments, Sally goes to the computer lab every Saturday and Sunday. Because she lives off campus and does not have a car, she takes the bus to and from campus at a round trip cost of $1.20.

A local Computer Shack store has offered to rent Sally a computer terminal and modem (a telephone connection) so that she can complete her programming assignments at home by dialing the college computer. The rental fee is $300 for the academic year, payable in advance. The academic year is 30 weeks long.

If Sally rents the modem, she will be able to work four additional hours each week at a part-time job that pays $4 per hour.

Required: Determine the net benefit of renting the computer terminal and modem for the 30-week academic year.

2–17 Relevant Costs

John Bright recently spent $5 to purchase a regular flashlight that operates on two size D batteries. While walking through a discount store, John came upon a rechargeable flashlight that was on sale for $20. The promotional literature indicated that the rechargeable flashlight could be plugged into an electric outlet and recharged for only $0.25.

Additional information:

- Size D batteries cost $0.50 each.
- John will replace batteries or recharge the flashlight an average of four times a year.
- The expected life of both flashlights is 5 years.
- A friend has offered to pay John $2.00 for the regular flashlight.

Required: Determine the net benefit (or cost) of replacing the regular flashlight with a rechargeable flashlight.

2–18 Sunk Costs Versus Relevant Costs

A medium-sized consulting firm has a number of portable computers for the use of its professional staff. The firm's bookkeeper, Mr. Eyeshade, is responsible for issuing the computers to authorized persons and seeing that they are returned in good condition.

A recently hired employee checked out a computer and was crossing the street on her way to her first assignment when she slipped and fell on the ice, breaking a leg. The computer crashed to the ground and slid under the wheels of a speeding taxicab. Bystanders called an ambulance and the sound of the ambulance siren brought Mr. Eyeshade to the window. After surveying the scene, the employee with a broken leg, the damaged computer, and the angry taxi driver, Mr. Eyeshade observed, "I'm glad the computer was fully depreciated."

Required: Comment. Be sure to distinguish between relevant and irrelevant costs. What would Mr. Eyeshade's reaction have been if the computer were not fully depreciated?

2–19 Opportunity Costs

Matrix Products paid $10,000 for a specialized machine and then discovered that the market for the product the machine was intended to produce had completely disappeared. Matrix Products has two offers for the machine:

1. A machine shop has offered to buy the machine for $4,000 with the intention of disassembling it and reselling the machine's parts.

2. A promotional firm has offered to rent the machine for one year. They would pay a rental fee of $5,000; however, Matrix Products would have to spend $1,500 modifying the machine. At the end of the year the machine would be worthless.

Required: Determine the opportunity cost associated with each alternative. Which offer should Matrix Products accept?

2–20 Opportunity Costs

Mr. Fury purchased an antique Plymouth for $4,000 and spent another $16,000 reconditioning it. Mr. Fury is currently considering three alternative uses for the car:

1. DeSoto's Auto Museum has offered Mr. Fury a lease-purchase agreement that involves leasing the car to the museum for one year with the museum purchasing the car at the end of the year. The lease payment of $3,000 and the purchase price of $20,000 are both payable at the end of the year.

2. A local car buff has offered Mr. Fury $20,000 in cash for the car. If Mr. Fury accepts this offer, he will invest the money in a one year bank certificate that pays 10 percent interest.

3. He can keep the car in a local warehouse for one year, and then sell it for $25,000. The storage costs of $1,000 are payable at the end of the year.

Required: Determine the opportunity cost of each action.

PROBLEMS

2–21 Statements: Cost of Goods Manufactured, Income

Presented is information from the records of the Rocking Chair Craft Shop for June 19x2.

Purchases:	
Lumber	$ 4,500
Glue, paint, sandpaper, and small tools	100
Office supplies	210
Sales	18,000
Salaries: Selling and administrative (including	
fringe benefits of $250)	2,000
Wages: Production (including fringe benefits of $400)	3,000
Rent	2,000*
Utilities	600*
Advertising	350

	Inventories	
	June 1	June 30
Lumber	$ 2,200	$ 800
Glue, paint, etc.	250	300
Office supplies	75	90
Finished goods	12,000	8,000

* Of these costs 60 percent are assigned to manufacturing and 40 percent to selling and administration.

Production employee fringe benefits are classified as factory overhead. There is no beginning or ending inventory of work-in-process.

Requirements

a) Prepare a statement of cost of goods manufactured and an income statement. Actual overhead costs are assigned to products.

b) Determine each of the following:

Direct product costs.
Prime product costs.
Indirect product costs.
Conversion costs.

2–22 Statements: Cost of Goods Manufactured, Income

Presented below is information from the records of the Saskatchewan River Production Company for July 19x3.

Purchases:	
Raw materials	$ 70,000
Manufacturing supplies	3,500
Office supplies	1,200
Sales	425,700
Administrative salaries	12,000
Direct labor	117,500
Production employees' fringe benefits	4,000*
Sales commissions	50,000
Production supervisors' salaries	7,200
Depreciation on plant	14,000
Depreciation on office	20,000
Plant maintenance	10,000
Plant utilities	35,000
Office utilities	8,000
Office maintenance	2,000
Production equipment rent	6,000
Office equipment rent	1,300

	Inventories	
	July 1	July 31
Raw materials	$17,000	$15,000
Manufacturing supplies	1,500	3,000
Office supplies	600	1,000
Work-in-process	51,000	40,000
Finished goods	35,000	27,100

* Classified as factory overhead.

Requirements

a) Prepare a statement of cost of goods manufactured and an income statement. Actual overhead costs are assigned to products.

b) Determine each of the following:

Direct product costs.
Prime product costs.
Indirect product costs.
Conversion costs.

2–23 Correcting Erroneous Statements: Cost of Goods Manufactured, Income

Presented are two reports prepared by the former accountant of Misclassification Manufacturing Corporation:

Misclassification Manufacturing Corporation
Statement of Cost of Goods Manufactured and Income
For the month ended December 31, 19x5

Sales		$200,000
Less direct materials		− 40,000
Gross profit		$160,000
Less other expenses:		
Cost of goods sold (computed below)	$89,000	
Office supplies	500	
Manufacturing utilities	2,000	
Office utilities	500	− 92,000
Net income		$ 68,000

Misclassification Manufacturing Corporation
Statement of Cost of Goods Sold
For the month ending December 31, 19x5

Finished goods inventory 12/1/x5			$30,000
Work-in-process 12/1/x5			6,000
Total			$36,000
Current manufacturing costs:			
Salaries and wages:			
Direct labor	$10,000		
Other manufacturing	4,000		
Sales	8,000		
Administrative	6,000	$28,000	
Other:			
Manufacturing supplies	$ 3,000		
Manufacturing depreciation	7,000		
Insurance on showroom	2,000		
Miscellaneous factory overhead	13,000	25,000	−53,000
Total work-in-process			$89,000
Work-in-process 12/31/x5			− 0
Cost of goods sold			$89,000

Additional information:

■ The 12/31/x5 finished goods inventory was $4,000.

■ Dividends of $10,000 were declared and paid during December.

■ All amounts, except those specifically computed in the presented statements, are correct.

Requirements

a) Prepare a statement of cost of goods manufactured and an income statement in good form.

b) Determine each of the following:

Direct product costs.
Prime product costs.
Indirect product costs.
Conversion costs.

2–24 Correcting Erroneous Statements: Cost of Goods Manufactured, Income

Presented is a financial statement prepared by the former accountant of the Southern Snowshoe Company:

Southern Snowshoe Company
Statement of Inventories, Revenues, and Expenses
For the year ending December 31, 19x3

Sales		$80,000
Net of finished goods inventory change:		
Finished goods inventory, 1/1/x3	$20,000	
Finished goods inventory, 12/31/x3	−30,000	10,000
Net sales		$90,000
Materials expenses:		
Direct materials	$14,000	
Factory supplies	2,800	
Office supplies	450	
Work-in-process, 1/1/x3	2,000	−19,250
Gross profit		$70,750
Labor expenses:		
Sales salaries and wages	$ 3,000	
Administrative salaries and wages	4,000	
Indirect labor	4,000	
Office utilities	300	
Direct labor	35,000	−46,300
Labor profit		$24,450
Miscellaneous costs:		
Factory utilities	$ 3,000	
Telephone and direct mail advertising	8,000	
Packing and transportation-out	12,000	
Factory depreciation	4,000	
Miscellaneous factory overhead	6,000	−33,000
Miscellaneous profit		$ (8,550)
Dividends declared and paid expense		15,000
Dividend profit		$ 6,450

Additional information:

- The 12/31/x3 work-in-process is $1,800.

- All amounts, except those specifically computed in the presented statement, are correct.

Requirements

a) Prepare a statement of cost of goods manufactured and an income statement in good form.

b) Determine each of the following:

Direct product costs.
Prime product costs.
Indirect product costs.
Conversion costs.

2–25 Account Interrelationships: Missing Production Data

Supply the missing data in each independent case in the following table.

	Case 1	Case 2	Case 3	Case 4
Raw materials, beginning	$ 5,000	$ 3,000	$?	$ 3,000
Purchases	10,000	?	20,000	7,000
Raw materials, ending	8,000	5,000	6,000	2,000
Direct materials	?	20,000	30,000	?
Direct labor	12,000	?	40,000	?
Factory overhead	20,000	20,000	?	30,000
Current manufacturing costs	?	65,000	?	90,000
Work-in-process, beginning	15,000	?	10,000	5,000
Work-in-process, ending	16,000	35,000	20,000	?
Cost of goods manufactured	?	105,000	90,000	80,000
Finished goods, beginning	25,000	?	20,000	10,000
Finished goods, ending	10,000	10,000	50,000	?
Cost of goods sold	?	98,000	?	70,000

2–26 Account Interrelationships: Missing Data

Supply the missing data in each independent case.

	Case 1	Case 2	Case 3	Case 4
Sales	$50,000	$?	$?	$?
Raw materials, beginning	10,000	13,000	?	5,300
Purchases	?	13,000	2,500	31,400
Raw materials, ending	8,000	?	500	6,200
Direct materials	?	20,000	2,000	?
Direct labor	20,000	25,000	6,000	?
Factory overhead	10,000	8,000	?	29,200
Current manufacturing costs	55,000	?	12,000	?
Work-in-process, beginning	?	8,000	8,000	5,300
Work-in-process, ending	5,000	7,000	?	4,000
Cost of goods manufactured	55,000	?	19,000	82,000
Finished goods, beginning	?	6,000	1,500	8,000
Finished goods, ending	25,000	?	500	10,000
Cost of goods sold	?	55,000	?	?
Gross profit	10,000	9,000	?	10,500
Other expenses	8,000	?	5,000	3,500
Net income (loss)	?	(4,000)	1,000	?

2–27 Statement of Cost of Goods Manufactured and Sold from Percent Relationships

Information about the Portion Company for the year ending December 31, 19x1, is given below.

- Sales $400,000
- Direct materials   64,000
- Factory overhead is 150 percent of direct labor.
- The beginning inventory of finished goods is 20 percent of the cost of goods sold.
- The ending inventory of finished goods is twice the beginning inventory.
- The gross profit is 20 percent of sales.
- There is no beginning or ending work-in-process.

Required: Prepare a statement of cost of goods manufactured and sold for 19x1. *Hint:* Set up the statement format and start the solution from known information.

2–28 Income Statement and Statement of Cost of Goods Manufactured from Percent Relationships

Information about the Lots-O-Luck Company for the year ending December 31, 19x1, is as follows:

- Sales $350,000
- Net income   5,000
- Ending inventories:

  Raw materials   18,000
  Work-in-process   8,000
  Finished goods   67,000

- Inventory changes:

  Ending raw materials are twice beginning raw materials.
  Ending work-in-process is one-third larger than beginning work-in-process.
  Finished goods inventory increased by $15,000 during the year.

- Selling and administrative expenses are five times net income.
- Prime costs are 60 percent of manufacturing costs.
- Conversion costs are 80 percent of manufacturing costs.

Required: Prepare an income statement and a statement of cost of goods manufactured for 19x1. *Hint:* Set up the statement formats and start the solution from known information.

2–29 Statement of Cost of Goods Manufactured with Predetermined Overhead and Labor Cost Classification

Presented is information pertaining to Little Bear Productions for December 19x4.

Purchases of raw materials	$ 41,000
Sales	310,000
Supervisors' salaries (production), including fringe benefits	20,000
Depreciation on office	17,500
Depreciation on plant	35,000
Plant utilities	51,000
Plant insurance	6,000
Purchases of office supplies	350
Plant property taxes	40,000

	Inventories	
	December 1	December 31
Raw materials	$ 3,000	$ 5,000
Office supplies	250	150
Work-in-process	25,000	15,000
Finished goods	12,000	18,000

Additional information:

- Factory overhead is applied to products at the rate of 200 percent of direct labor dollars.

- Employee base wages are $10 per hour.

- Employee fringe benefits amount to 50 percent of the base wage rate. They are classified as factory overhead.

- During December, production employees worked 9,000 hours, including 8,500 spent working on products.

Requirements

a) Prepare a statement of cost of goods manufactured.

b) Determine underapplied or overapplied overhead for December.

2–30 Statements: Cost of Goods Manufactured, Income with Predetermined Overhead and Labor Cost Classification

Presented is information pertaining to Big Bear, Incorporated, for April 19x9.

Sales	$200,000
Purchases:	
Raw materials	35,000
Manufacturing supplies	800
Office supplies	500
Salaries (including fringe benefits):	
Administrative	6,000
Production supervisors	3,600
Sales	15,000
Depreciation:	
Plant and machinery	8,000
Office and office equipment	4,000
Utilities:	
Plant	5,250
Office	890

	Inventories	
	April 1	April 30
Raw materials	$5,000	$3,500
Manufacturing supplies	1,000	1,100
Office supplies	900	800
Work-in-process	2,000	2,300
Finished goods	8,000	9,000

Additional information:

- Factory overhead is applied to products at 80 percent of direct labor dollars.
- Employee base wages are $12 per hour.
- Employee fringe benefits amount to 40 percent of the base wage rate. They are classified as factory overhead.
- During April, production employees worked 5,600 hours, including 4,800 regular hours and 200 overtime hours spent working on products.
- Employees are paid a 50 percent overtime premium.

Requirements

a) Prepare a statement of cost of goods manufactured and an income statement.

b) Determine underapplied or overapplied overhead for April.

c) Recompute direct labor and actual factory overhead assuming employee fringe benefits for direct labor hours are classified as direct labor.

REVIEW PROBLEM SOLUTION

a) **Poston Manufacturing Company**
Statement of Cost of Goods Manufactured
For the month ending January 31, 19x7

Current manufacturing costs:			
Cost of materials placed in production:			
Raw materials, 1/1/x7	$3,000		
Purchases	6,000		
Total available	$9,000		
Raw materials, 1/31/x7	−2,500	$ 6,500	
Direct labor		8,000	
Factory overhead		20,000	$34,500
Work-in-process, 1/1/x7			8,200
Total costs in process			$42,700
Work-in-process, 1/31/x7			− 6,000
Cost of goods manufactured			$36,700

Poston Manufacturing Company
Income Statement
For the month ending January 31, 19x7

Sales		$75,000
Cost of goods sold:		
Finished goods inventory, 1/1/x7	$15,000	
Cost of goods manufactured	36,700	
Total goods available for sale	$51,700	
Finished goods inventory, 1/31/x7	−13,000	−38,700
Gross profit		$36,300
Selling and administrative expenses		−25,050
Net income		$11,250

b) **Poston Manufacturing Company**
Statement of Cost of Goods Manufactured and Sold
For the month ending January 31, 19x7

Current manufacturing costs:			
Cost of materials placed in production:			
Raw materials, 1/1/x7	$3,000		
Purchases	6,000		
Total available	$9,000		
Raw materials, 1/31/x7	−2,500	$ 6,500	
Direct labor		8,000	
Factory overhead		20,000	$34,500
Work-in-process, 1/1/x7			8,200
Total costs in process			$42,700
Work-in-process, 1/31/x7			− 6,000
Cost of goods manufactured			$36,700
Finished goods inventory, 1/1/x7			15,000
Total goods available for sale			$51,700
Finished goods inventory, 1/31/x7			−13,000
Cost of goods sold			$38,700

Poston Manufacturing Company
Income Statement
For the month ending January 31, 19x7

Sales	$75,000
Cost of goods sold	−38,700
Gross profit	$36,300
Selling and administrative expenses	−25,050
Net income	$11,250

c) **1.** Direct product costs:

Direct materials	$ 6,500	
Direct labor	8,000	$14,500

2. Prime product costs:

Direct materials	$ 6,500	
Direct labor	8,000	$14,500

3. Indirect product costs
(factory overhead):

	$20,000

4. Conversion costs:

Direct labor	$ 8,000	
Factory overhead	20,000	$28,000

CHAPTER 3

Cost Behavior Analysis

Upon completion of this chapter you should:

- Be able to prepare a graph showing the relationship between the amount of cost and the volume of activity for any given cost element, and determine the slope of the line representing the relationship.

- Understand the following important cost behavior patterns: variable, fixed, mixed, and step.

- Be thoroughly familiar with the total cost equation: Total costs = Fixed costs + (Variable costs per unit × Unit volume).

- Have a general awareness of the differences and similarities between the accounting and economic models of cost behavior.

- Be able to separate mixed costs into their variable and fixed components using the high-low, scatter diagram, and least-squares methods.

- Understand the importance of selecting an appropriate independent variable.

- Understand the effect of changing prices and technology on cost estimation and cost prediction.

Activities undertaken to achieve an organization's short-range and long-range objectives result in the incurrence of various costs. Because economic resources are limited, managers must carefully control both costs and the activities that cause them. To plan and control costs, managers must know how costs respond to changes in activity. Some costs increase in direct proportion to changes in activity, whereas others do not change at all. Still others, which do not change throughout a range of activity, will then increase suddenly to a different amount. Managers need to know which costs will change, the circumstances that cause them to change, and the amount they will change.

The purpose of this chapter is to introduce **cost behavior analysis,** which is the study of how costs respond to changes in the volume of activity. We will study the major cost behavior patterns used in accounting models, mention several representative costs that display each pattern, and survey methods used to estimate cost behavior.

PLOTTING COST BEHAVIOR

The relationship between the volume and the total cost of an activity is often illustrated with a graph, such as the one in Exhibit 3–1(a). Volume of activity, the independent variable that causes the incurrence of costs, is measured on the horizontal axis. Total cost, the dependent variable that responds to changes in volume, is measured on the vertical axis. Combinations of observed activity and cost are represented by dots. Total cost and total volume increase up and to the right from the origin (where the horizontal and vertical axes intersect). Each unit of activity, in Exhibit 3–1(a), results in the incurrence of an additional $1 in total costs.

By compressing the measurement scale, it is possible to move the individual dots so close together that the relationship between volume and total cost appears to be a solid line. In Exhibit 3–1(b) the unit cost is still $1, but the range of activity is now 0 to 500 units rather than 0 to 5 units. For ease of

EXHIBIT 3–1   Plotting Cost Behavior

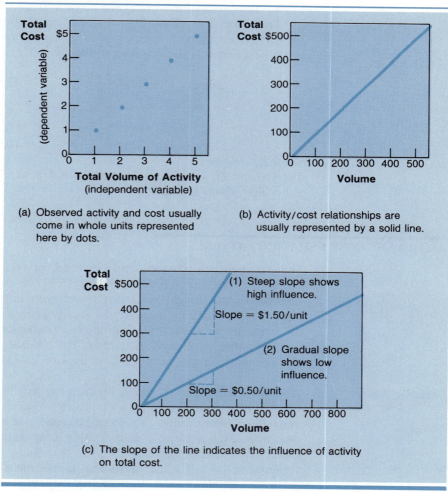

(a) Observed activity and cost usually come in whole units represented here by dots.

(b) Activity/cost relationships are usually represented by a solid line.

(c) The slope of the line indicates the influence of activity on total cost.

presentation, lines are often used to represent cost behavior even when the scale of activity is such that dots might be better. In cost behavior analysis, the horizontal axis is, by convention, labeled "volume" rather than "total volume of activity," "total activity," or "total volume." Because there are a variety of cost concepts, care should be taken to label the vertical axis "total cost," "average cost," "unit cost," or whatever other term is appropriate.

The slope of a line measures the change in the dependent variable for each unit of change in the independent variable. In cost behavior analysis, the slope indicates the responsiveness of costs to changes in volume. The slope of the total cost line is the incremental cost of one unit. In Exhibit 3–1(c) the slope of line (1) illustrates a situation where volume has a relatively large influence on total cost, whereas the slope of line (2) illustrates a situation where volume has a relatively small influence on total cost.

The slope of a straight line is computed as the change in the total cost between two selected volumes divided by the difference between the two volumes. The slopes of the two lines in Exhibit 3–1(c) are

$$\text{Slope of line (1)} = \frac{\$450 - \$300}{300 - 200} = \$1.50 \text{ per unit,}$$

and

$$\text{Slope of line (2)} = \frac{\$150 - \$100}{300 - 200} = \$0.50 \text{ per unit.}$$

The 300 and 200 unit volumes were randomly selected. Any pair of volumes on either line would give identical results.

IMPORTANT COST BEHAVIOR PATTERNS

Four cost behavior patterns—variable, fixed, mixed (or semivariable), and step costs—are widely used in accounting models. Although the behavior of each is illustrated with a straight line drawn between zero units and an arbitrarily chosen high volume of activity, management is only interested in cost behavior within the range of *probable* activity. Illustrated cost behavior patterns are seldom valid over the entire range of *possible* activity. This limitation will be examined further immediately after the introduction of important total cost behavior patterns.

Variable Costs

A **variable cost** is a cost that is uniform for each incremental unit of volume. Total variable costs change in direct proportion to changes in volume, equaling zero dollars when activity is zero and increasing at a constant amount per unit of activity. Typical variable costs include sales commissions, direct materials, direct labor, cost of goods sold in merchandising, postage in magazine publishing, gasoline in trucking, and asphalt in road maintenance. A behavior pattern for total variable costs is illustrated in Exhibit 3–2(a) by an upward sloping straight line that starts at the origin. The slope of this line represents the variable cost per unit. The equation for total variable costs is

$$\text{Total variable costs} = \text{Variable cost per unit} \times \text{Unit volume.}$$

A 50 percent increase in volume results in a 50 percent increase in total variable costs. If hamburger patties cost Big Burger Restaurant $0.50 each, and Big Burger serves 10,000 hamburgers during February, the cost of hamburger patties consumed is $5,000 (10,000 × $0.50). If volume increases 50 percent in March, the cost of hamburger patties consumed increases proportionally, to $7,500 (15,000 × $0.50).

EXHIBIT 3–2   Important Total Cost Behavior Patterns

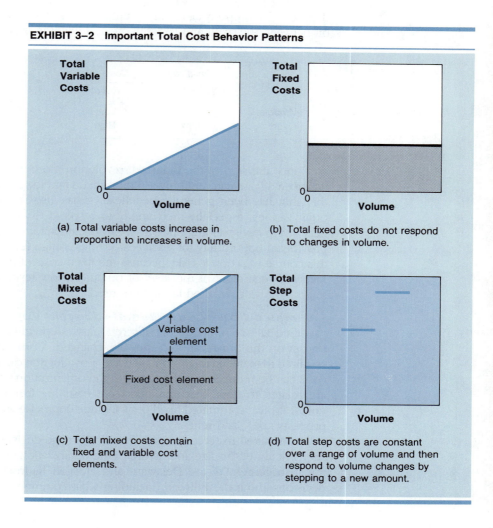

(a) Total variable costs increase in proportion to increases in volume.

(b) Total fixed costs do not respond to changes in volume.

(c) Total mixed costs contain fixed and variable cost elements.

(d) Total step costs are constant over a range of volume and then respond to volume changes by stepping to a new amount.

Fixed Costs

A **fixed cost** is a cost that does not respond to changes in the volume of activity within a given period. Total fixed costs are a constant amount per period regardless of the level of activity. Typical fixed costs include depreciation, supervisors' salaries, property taxes, rent, advertising, research and development, and charitable contributions. Total fixed costs are illustrated in Exhibit 3–2(b) by a straight line drawn parallel to the horizontal axis. Because fixed costs do not respond to changes in activity, the slope of the line is zero.

Organizations can control the relative portions of their variable and fixed costs by making long-run decisions about their methods of operation. For example, the frame of an automobile can be welded by skilled laborers or by robots. If the welding is performed by skilled labor, the direct labor cost per unit will be relatively high. If the welding is performed by a robot, fixed costs, such as depreciation, property taxes, and maintenance, will be relatively high. The trade-off between the fixed and variable costs of welding is summarized as follows:

	Relative Welding Costs	
	Skilled Labor	Robot
Variable	High	Low
Fixed	Low	High

Since the start of the industrial revolution more than 200 years ago, there has been a systematic shift toward more fixed and fewer variable costs. Though this shift has been generally beneficial, it has also reduced the flexibility of organizations, especially their ability to respond to decreases in activity. The decision to have welding operations performed automatically by a machine can provide an opportunity for great cost savings at high levels of output. However, this course of action is risky because the fixed costs of machine ownership are incurred regardless of the level of output. At low levels of output total costs might be lower if skilled labor were used.

Committed Fixed Costs Maintain Current Capacity. Fixed costs are classified as "committed" or "discretionary," depending on their immediate impact on the organization if they are changed. **Committed fixed costs** are required to maintain the current service or production capacity. Ordinarily, these costs can be reduced only by reducing the organization's capacity. Because they are related to capacity, committed fixed costs are frequently called **capacity costs.** Typical committed fixed costs include depreciation, supervisors' salaries, property taxes, and rent.

Committed fixed costs result from long-range decisions made by top management about the size and nature of the organization. For example, years ago the management of the Delaware and Hudson Railroad made a number of decisions about the railroad, including what communities the railroad would serve. Track was laid on the basis of these decisions, and the Delaware and Hudson now pays property taxes each year on the railroad's miles of track. These property taxes can be reduced by disposing of track. However, reducing the track will also reduce the railroad's capacity to serve.

Capacity is usually thought of in terms of a maximum *volume* of activity, such as the number of automobiles that can be produced in a month, the number of beds in a hospital, the number of seats in a church, and the monthly passenger seat miles in an airplane. There is also a *quality* dimension to current capacity. For example, a restaurant can retain its seating capacity while reducing its committed fixed costs by selling nonessential depreciable assets and reducing expenditures on entertainment, maintenance, heating, cooling, and so forth. The physical capacity remains, but the quality is lower; the restaurant is not what it was before the cost reductions.

Discretionary Fixed Costs Do Not Affect Current Capacity. **Discretionary fixed costs,** sometimes called **managed fixed costs,** are set at a fixed amount each year at the discretion of management. It is possible to change these costs and not change production or service capacity in the near-term. Typical discretionary fixed costs include advertising, charitable contributions, employee training programs, and research and development.

Expenditures on discretionary fixed costs are frequently regarded as investments in the future. Research and development, for example, is undertaken to produce new or improved products that can be profitably produced and sold in future periods. During periods of financial well-being, organizations may make large expenditures on discretionary cost items. Conversely, during periods of financial stress, organizations will likely reduce discretionary expenditures before reducing capacity costs. Managers should, of course, exercise care before making drastic changes in the level of funding of discretionary cost items. Fluctuations in funding reduce the effectiveness of long-range programs. A high-quality research staff may be difficult to reassemble if key personnel are laid off; even the contemplation of such layoffs may reduce the staff's effectiveness. In all periods discretionary costs are subject to debate and are likely to be changed in the give and take of the budgeting process. The alternative designation, managed fixed costs, is intended to reflect the importance of management's judgment in setting their amount.

Mixed Costs

Mixed costs, sometimes called **semivariable costs,** contain a fixed and a variable cost element. Total mixed costs are positive (like fixed costs) when volume is zero, and they increase in a linear fashion (like total variable costs) as volume increases. Typical mixed costs include power, maintenance, and automobile rental charges. Some power is required to light buildings and to provide the heat necessary to keep water pipes from freezing in the winter, and additional power is required to operate machinery. Some maintenance is required to prevent the deterioration of buildings and equipment, and additional maintenance is required as the use of these assets increases. Finally, automobiles are frequently rented on the basis of a fixed charge per day plus an additional charge per mile driven. Total mixed costs are illustrated in Exhibit 3–2(c) by an upward sloping straight line that starts above the origin. The equation for total mixed costs is

$$\begin{array}{c}\text{Total mixed} \\ \text{costs}\end{array} = \begin{array}{c}\text{Fixed} \\ \text{costs}\end{array} + \left(\begin{array}{c}\text{Variable cost} \\ \text{per unit}\end{array} \times \begin{array}{c}\text{Unit} \\ \text{volume}\end{array}\right).$$

Because of the presence of fixed costs, total mixed costs do not increase in proportion to volume. Assume Big Burger Restaurant pays a franchise fee of $1,000 per month plus 2 percent of sales. The franchise fee for a month when sales revenue totals $50,000 is $2,000 [$1,000 + ($50,000 × 0.02)]. If sales revenue increases by 50 percent, only the variable cost element of the franchise fee will increase, whereas the fixed element will remain $1,000.

Step Costs

Step costs are constant within a range of activity but different between ranges of activity. Total step costs increase in a steplike fashion as volume increases. The steps are caused by input indivisibilities. Typical step costs include the salaries of quality inspectors and production supervisors. In some states the maximum legal first grade student-to-teacher ratio is 25 to 1. These laws cause first grade instructional costs to follow a step pattern. The first step is fixed over the range of 1 to 25 students. The 26th student requires the addition of a second full-time teacher. The third step starts with the 51st student, and so forth.

Step costs are illustrated in Exhibit 3–2(d) by a series of lines drawn parallel to the horizontal axis. Moving to the right, each line steps up to a level higher than the preceding line. The discontinuity that occurs at each increment makes step costs difficult to analyze, to represent by an equation, or to graphically illustrate in a chart depicting the total effect of several different costs. To overcome these problems, step costs are frequently approximated by mixed or fixed costs. The selection of a proxy depends on the range of activity included in each step and the cost difference between steps.

Step costs are approximated by mixed costs when there are many steps and the cost difference between steps is small. The illustration in Exhibit 3–3(a) shows that the mixed cost approximation passes through the midpoint of each step and intersects the vertical axis at one half the height of the first step. The mixed cost approximation is subject to a maximum error of one half the cost difference between steps. The mixed cost approximation may be used if this error is acceptable.

Step costs are approximated by fixed costs when one step includes all the organization's probable range of volume. The illustration in Exhibit 3–3(b) shows that the fixed cost approximation is drawn through the step in the expected range of volume and extended parallel to the horizontal axis. The fixed cost approximation is only valid in the activity range of a single step. Large

EXHIBIT 3–3   Step Costs Approximated by Mixed and Fixed Costs

(a) Step costs are approximated by mixed costs when there are many steps and the difference between steps is small.

(b) Step costs are approximated by fixed costs when one step includes all the normal range of volume.

errors can occur if this approximation is used to predict step costs outside this range. If the difference between steps is large, and one step does not include the expected range of activity, step costs must be analyzed as step costs.

Total Costs for the Organization

An organization's total costs consist of the sum of its variable, fixed, mixed, and step costs. With mixed costs approximating step costs, a behavior pattern for total costs is developed by combining variable, fixed, and mixed costs, as in Exhibit 3–4.

The equation for total costs is

$$\text{Total costs} = \text{Fixed costs} + \left(\text{Variable costs per unit} \times \text{Unit volume}\right).$$

EXHIBIT 3–4   Total Cost Behavior

Variable costs are layered on top of fixed costs.

In the equation for total costs, fixed costs and the fixed element of mixed costs are both included in the "fixed costs." Likewise, variable costs and the variable cost element of mixed costs are both included in the "variable costs." The equation for total costs corresponds to the general equation for a straight line:

$$Y = a + bX,$$

where Y = the value of the dependent variable,
a = a constant term,
b = the slope of the line, and
X = the value of the independent variable.

To save space we will occasionally use the general equation.

ECONOMIC COST PATTERNS AND THE RELEVANT RANGE

The use of straight lines in accounting models of cost behavior assumes a linear relationship between cost and volume, with each unit of additional volume being accompanied by a uniform increment in total costs. Accountants identify this uniform increment as the variable cost of one unit. The relationship between volume and the variable cost per unit is illustrated in Exhibit 3–5(a). Note that the vertical axis is labeled unit cost rather than total cost. Because the variable cost of each unit is identical, the slope of the unit cost line in Exhibit 3–5(a) is zero.

Economic models show a curvilinear relationship between cost and volume, with each unit of additional volume being accompanied by a varying increment in total cost. Economists identify the varying increment in total cost as the **marginal cost** of one unit. The relationship between volume and marginal cost is illustrated in Exhibit 3–5(b). At low volumes marginal costs are relatively high. They decline and level off as production becomes more efficient and then start to rise because of the existence of capacity constraints and increases in operating costs.

The economists' short-run total cost pattern is illustrated in Exhibit 3–6(a). The vertical axis intercept represents capacity costs. Note the influence of mar-

EXHIBIT 3–5   Incremental Costs in Accounting and Economic Cost Behavior Models

(a) In accounting models the variable cost of each unit is uniform.

(b) In economic models the marginal cost of each unit changes.

ginal costs. The initial slope of the total cost line is quite steep in the range where marginal costs are high. The slope becomes less steep for a while as marginal costs decline and then increases again as marginal costs increase.

The economists' cost behavior patterns certainly sound plausible. The initially high marginal costs might represent a production situation where there is much excess capacity and idle time. Employees complete their assignments at a leisurely pace; indeed, they may try to make work. Marginal costs logically decline and then level off in the optimal range of production for which the plant was designed to operate. Again, we expect marginal costs to rise as capacity limits are reached. Near capacity, older equipment is brought out of retirement, new employees with little or no experience are hired, and experienced employees are paid overtime premiums to work additional hours.

EXHIBIT 3–6   Economic Cost Patterns and the Relevant Range

Total Costs

Expected range of
← operations for which →
plant is designed

0
0   Volume

(a) Economist's curvilinear total cost pattern

Total Costs

Relevant range
← for which linear →
patterns are valid

0
0   Volume

(b) Linear approximation of economist's pattern

If the economists' total cost pattern is valid, how can we reasonably approximate it with a straight line? The answer to this question is in the notion of a relevant range. A linear pattern may be a poor approximation of the economists' curvilinear pattern over the entire range of possible activity, but a linear pattern is often sufficiently accurate within the range of probable operations. The range of operations within which a linear cost function is a good approximation of the economists' curvilinear cost function is called the **relevant range.** Linear estimates of cost behavior are only valid within the relevant range. Managers and accountants must exercise extreme care when making statements about cost behavior outside the relevant range, which is illustrated in Exhibit 3–6(b).

AVERAGE COSTS

According to the absorption cost basis of external reporting, all manufacturing costs are product costs that are assigned to the units produced each period. For a single product company, the absorption cost of each unit is an average cost, computed as the cost of goods manufactured divided by the number of units produced. In the absence of beginning or ending inventories of work-in-process, the cost of goods manufactured is the same as the current manufacturing costs, and the average cost per unit is computed as the current manufacturing costs divided by the number of units produced. The following example illustrates the computation of average costs and the effect of volume on this amount.

The Springfield Bean Company manufactures bean bag chairs. The unit variable and monthly fixed production costs are as follows:

	Variable Costs	Fixed Costs
Direct materials	$2.75	
Direct labor	1.50	
Factory overhead	0.75	$3,000
Total	$5.00	$3,000

In the absence of beginning or ending inventories of work-in-process, the equations for the total manufacturing costs per month and the average cost per unit produced during a given month are

$$\text{Total manufacturing costs} = \$3,000 + \$5X,$$

$$\begin{aligned}\text{Average cost per unit} &= (\$3,000 + \$5X)/X \\ &= \$3,000/X + \$5,\end{aligned}$$

where X represents the unit volume.

The total and average production costs at several unit volumes are computed here and illustrated in Exhibit 3–7.

Volume	Total Fixed Costs	Total Variable Costs (Volume × $5)	Total Manufacturing Costs	Average Cost per Unit
100	$3,000	$ 500	$3,500	$35.00
200	3,000	1,000	4,000	20.00
300	3,000	1,500	4,500	15.00
400	3,000	2,000	5,000	12.50
500	3,000	2,500	5,500	11.00

The average cost declines as volume increases because fixed costs are spread over a larger number of units.

If the Springfield Bean Company regularly produced 300 bags per month, the average cost per unit would be $15. Although this cost would be used to value inventory and compute the cost of goods sold in external financial statements, it should not be used for internal planning and control. A manager may be tempted to conclude that the unit cost reported in external financial statements represents the incremental cost of producing one unit. If this cost is $15, the manager might budget production costs for 250 units as $3,750 ($15 × 250) and conclude that production was inefficient if the actual costs of producing 250 units were $4,250. A proper analysis of cost behavior reveals that $4,250 is, in fact, the expected production costs of 250 units:

$$\text{Total costs} = \$3,000 + (\$5 \times 250) = \$4,250.$$

EXHIBIT 3–7   Total and Average Costs

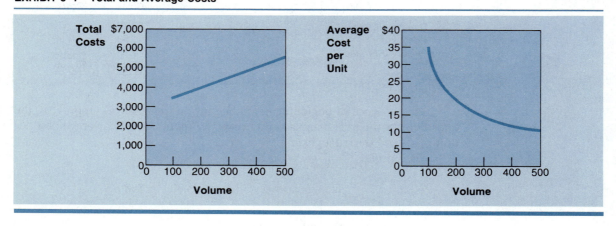

Here we see the significance of different costs for different purposes. Though average costs are widely used for external reporting, total costs should be used for internal planning and control. *Bad decisions can occur if cost information developed for one purpose is incorrectly used for another purpose.*

DETERMINING COST BEHAVIOR

Cost behavior is often determined through an analysis of historical cost data. To properly estimate the relationship between activity and cost, it is necessary (1) to be familiar with basic cost behavior patterns, (2) to understand the characteristics of the accounting data base, and (3) to be knowledgeable of cost estimating techniques. The first part of this chapter introduced important cost behavior patterns. A significant feature of the accounting data base, discussed in Chapter 2, is its orientation to information needed for external reporting. Managers must be very cautious in using these data for internal purposes. As illustrated in the preceding section, average costs presented in financial statements are of limited use in planning and control. To obtain appropriate data, it may be necessary to analyze individual cost elements rather than final cost figures.

Estimating Mixed Costs

Costs known to display a variable or a fixed cost pattern are readily estimated by studying the costs of a representative period. Unit variable costs are estimated by dividing total variable costs by unit volume, and fixed costs are estimated by totaling the known fixed costs of the period. It is the mixed costs that cause most cost estimation problems.

Assume the Springfield Bean Company incurred the following production costs in April 19x3 when 4,000 bean bag chairs were produced:

Direct materials		$11,000
Direct labor		6,000
Factory overhead:		
Supervisors' salaries	$1,800	
Depreciation	800	
Utilities and maintenance	3,400	6,000
Total		$23,000

Direct materials and direct labor are known to display variable cost patterns. Assuming April 19x3 is a representative month, the variable costs of direct materials and direct labor are $2.75 and $1.50, respectively:

$$\text{Variable costs per unit} = \frac{\text{Total variable costs}}{\text{Unit volume}},$$

$$\text{Variable cost of direct materials} = \frac{\$11,000}{4,000}$$

$$= \$2.75,$$

$$\text{Variable cost of direct labor} = \frac{\$6,000}{4,000}$$

$$= \$1.50.$$

Assuming supervisors' salaries and depreciation are fixed costs, total fixed costs amount to $2,600:

Supervisors' salaries	$1,800
Depreciation	800
Total	$2,600

Utilities and maintenance are neither wholly variable nor wholly fixed; they are mixed costs that contain fixed and variable cost elements. According to a basic rule of algebra, two equations are needed to determine two unknowns. Following this rule at least two observations are needed to determine the variable and the fixed cost elements of a mixed cost.

High-Low Cost Estimation. The most straightforward approach to determining the variable and fixed elements of mixed costs is to use the **high-low method of cost estimation.** This method utilizes data from two time periods, a representative high volume period and a representative low volume period, to estimate fixed and variable costs. Assuming identical fixed costs in both periods, the difference in total costs between these two periods is due entirely to the difference in total variable costs, and the variable costs per unit are found by dividing the difference in total costs by the difference in activity. The general formula to find variable costs using the high-low method is

$$\text{Variable costs per unit} = \frac{\text{Difference in total costs}}{\text{Difference in activity}}.$$

Once the variable costs per unit are determined, the fixed costs, which are identical in both periods, are computed by estimating the total variable costs of either the high or the low volume period and subtracting them from the corresponding total costs:

$$\text{Fixed costs} = \text{Total costs} - \text{Variable costs.}$$

Assume April and May 19x2 are representative high and low volume periods. The mixed costs and production volumes in these months are shown below.

	Utilities and Maintenance	Unit Production
April	$3,400	4,000
May	2,650	3,000

Equations for total mixed costs are

$$\text{April:} \quad \$3,400 = a + b(4,000),$$

$$\text{May:} \quad \$2,650 = a + b(3,000),$$

where a = fixed costs per month, and
b = variable costs per unit (the slope of the mixed cost line).

$$b = \frac{\$3,400 - \$2,650}{4,000 - 3,000}$$

$$= \frac{\$750}{1,000}$$

$$= \$0.75$$

The variable cost element is $0.75 per unit.

The fixed element of Springfield's monthly utilities and maintenance costs is found by substituting the $0.75 for b in *either* the April or May total cost equation:

$$\text{April:} \quad \$3,400 = a + \$0.75(4,000)$$
$$a = \$3,400 - \$0.75(4,000)$$
$$= \$3,400 - \$3,000$$
$$= \$400,$$

or

$$\text{May:} \quad \$2,650 = a + \$0.75(3,000)$$
$$a = \$2,650 - \$0.75(3,000)$$
$$= \$2,650 - \$2,250$$
$$= \$400.$$

The fixed cost is $400 per month. The use of the high-low method to estimate the variable and fixed elements of this mixed cost is illustrated in Exhibit 3–8.

Springfield Bean Company's cost estimating equation for total monthly production costs is determined by adding together the total cost equations for variable and fixed costs.

EXHIBIT 3–8   High-Low Cost Estimation

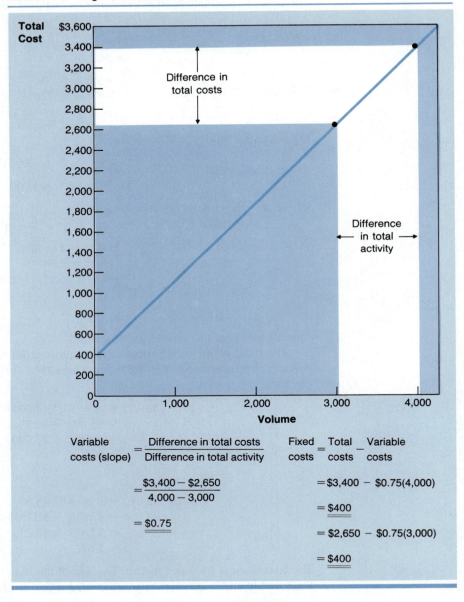

$$\text{Variable costs (slope)} = \frac{\text{Difference in total costs}}{\text{Difference in total activity}}$$

$$= \frac{\$3,400 - \$2,650}{4,000 - 3,000}$$

$$= \underline{\underline{\$0.75}}$$

$$\text{Fixed costs} = \text{Total costs} - \text{Variable costs}$$

$$= \$3,400 - \$0.75(4,000)$$

$$= \underline{\underline{\$400}}$$

$$= \$2,650 - \$0.75(3,000)$$

$$= \underline{\underline{\$400}}$$

	Fixed Costs	Variable Costs
Direct materials		$2.75X
Direct labor		1.50X
Factory overhead:		
Supervisors' salaries	$1,800	
Depreciation	800	
Utilities and maintenance	400	0.75X
Total costs =	$3,000 +	$5.00X

This cost estimating equation can be used to predict total production costs in a subsequent period. If July 19x2 production is budgeted at 3,800 units, the budgeted production costs are $22,000:

$$\$3,000 + \$5.00(3,800) = \$22,000.$$

If detailed cost information is not available, the high-low method can be applied to total cost data. Similar results are obtained because the total costs consist of fixed and variable cost elements.

In using the high-low method, *it is very important to select high and low volumes representative of normal operating conditions.* As illustrated in Exhibit 3–9, the periods of highest and lowest activity may not be representative of normal operating conditions. Even within the usual range of activity, the results of a particular period might not be representative if there was a strike, a materials shortage, a severe storm, or some other abnormal event. Because management is interested in predicting cost behavior under normal operating conditions, cost estimating equations should be developed from data reflecting normal operating conditions. Professional judgment is required to select the appropriate data.

EXHIBIT 3–9   Selecting Representative High and Low Volumes

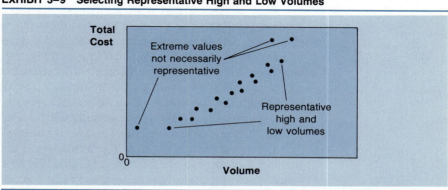

Scatter Diagrams. A **scatter diagram** is a graph of past volume and cost data, with individual observations represented by dots. Plotting historical volume and cost data on a scatter diagram is a useful approach to cost estimation, especially when used in conjunction with other cost estimating techniques such as the high-low method. The scatter diagram in Exhibit 3–9 would help identify representative high and low volumes. A scatter diagram is also useful in determining if costs can be reasonably approximated by a straight line.

Scatter diagrams are sometimes used alone as a basis of cost estimation. This requires the use of professional judgment to draw a representative straight line through the plot of historical data. Typically, the analyst tries to ensure that an equal number of observations are on either side of the line. Once a line is drawn, cost estimates at any representative volume are made by studying the line. Alternatively, an equation for the line may be developed by applying the high-low method to any two points on the line.

Exhibit 3–10(b) illustrates the use of the scatter diagram method to estimate the Springfield Bean Company's total production costs. The specific values of each observation are presented in Exhibit 3–10(a). Studying this line, the estimated production costs at 3,000 units are approximately $18,000.

Least-Squares Method. The **least-squares method** of developing a cost estimating equation is conceptually similar to the scatter diagram method. However, the least-squares method uses a mathematical criterion, rather than professional judgment, to develop a cost estimating equation. The mathematical criterion is to fit a straight line to the observed data in a manner that minimizes the sum of the squared vertical differences between the observations and the line. The least-squares criterion is illustrated in Exhibit 3–11.

The observations plotted in Exhibit 3–11 are the same as in Exhibit 3–10. The line drawn through the data is based on an equation developed using the least-squares method. The deviations are measured as the differences between the estimated cost and the actual cost at each observation.

Many managers and management accountants believe the least-squares method is superior to the high-low and the scatter diagram methods of cost estimation. The least-squares method can use all available data, rather than just two observations, as does the high-low method. Its use of a mathematical criterion provides an objective approach to cost estimation, rather than the subjective approach involved in visually fitting a line through a scatter diagram. Most significant, the least-squares method can provide information on how good the cost estimating equation fits the historical cost data and information needed to construct probability intervals for cost estimates.

The computations required to estimate fixed and variable costs using the least-squares method are illustrated in Appendix A of this chapter. Until recent years these computations were regarded as too complex for practical application. Today there is little need to perform them manually. Computers of all sizes and

EXHIBIT 3–10   Use of Scatter Diagram in Cost Estimation

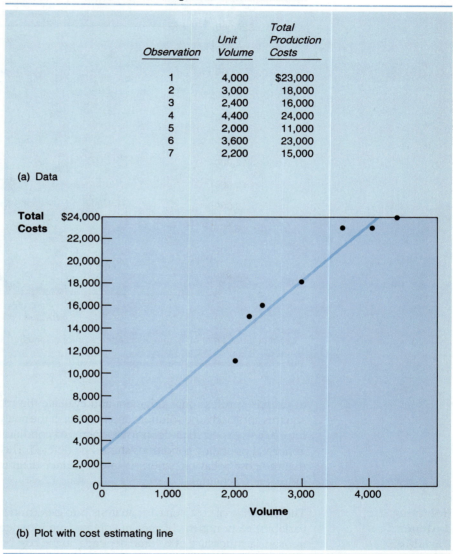

Observation	Unit Volume	Total Production Costs
1	4,000	$23,000
2	3,000	18,000
3	2,400	16,000
4	4,400	24,000
5	2,000	11,000
6	3,600	23,000
7	2,200	15,000

(a) Data

(b) Plot with cost estimating line

many hand calculators have programs available to perform least-squares calculations. Users need only provide paired observations of volume and cost.

With computational ease has come widespread application and an increased danger of inappropriate use. The analyst should not merely feed raw data into a computer and accept the output as truth. He or she must always be prepared

EXHIBIT 3–11   Least-Squares Criterion

Least-squares criterion is to minimize the sum of all squared vertical differences.

to exercise professional judgment and evaluate the reasonableness of the least-squares approach, the solution, and the data. If the analyst's objective is to predict future costs expected under normal operating conditions, observations reflecting abnormal operating conditions should be deleted. The analyst should also verify that the cost behavior pattern is linear. Scatter diagrams assist in both of these judgmental activities.

Selecting the Independent Variable

The objective of cost behavior analysis is to determine how cost (the dependent variable) responds to changes in volume (the independent variable). The most appropriate measure of volume depends on the cost being studied. The measure of volume should have a logical relationship to the cost being studied, and it should be easy to measure. The sales volume of a department store in Miami, Florida, is logically related to the number of persons who enter the store; the store's sales are not logically related to the number of fish in a New England pond. Although the factory overhead of a furniture manufacturer may be mathematically related to the amount of sawdust swept from the factory floor, sawdust is a bad basis for estimating overhead because of measurement difficulties and because residual items do not have a causal influence on the incurrence of overhead.

Care must also be taken to ensure that the independent and dependent variables are properly matched within each observation. In merchandising organizations, goods are purchased before they are sold. Though the cost of goods sold is matched with sales within each observation, the cost of purchases is matched with sales only when goods are purchased and sold in the same period. In manufacturing organizations, raw materials are purchased before they are used in production, and finished goods are produced before they are sold. Though the cost of goods sold is matched with sales within each observation, the current manufacturing costs are matched with sales only when goods are produced and sold in the same period. If production and sales differ, production volume rather than sales volume should be used as the independent variable in an analysis of manufacturing costs. In an analogous manner, if the purchases and use of raw materials differ, the volume of purchases rather than the volume of production should be used as the independent variable in an analysis of purchasing costs.

In selecting an independent variable for cost behavior analysis, it is important to determine the activity that causes the incurrence of the cost being analyzed. Professional judgment is very important in selecting an activity measure for a particular cost. Statistical measures, such as the correlation coefficient, are often used to assist in this effort. However, an activity measure should not be selected solely on the basis of a high past correlation with cost. A high correlation between two variables does not prove that one causes the other. Changes in both variables may be caused by a third variable, or the correlation between the two variables may be a chance event that will not recur. Factory overhead and sawdust may be correlated in a furniture plant, but unless sawdust is a major product of the plant it should not be treated as an independent variable. Both factory overhead and sawdust are caused by a third variable, the production of furniture. The correlation coefficient is discussed further in Appendix B of this chapter.

THE IMPACT OF CHANGING PRICES AND TECHNOLOGY

Cost estimation is the determination of previous or current relationships between cost and activity. Historical data from the accounting data base are used in cost estimation. **Cost prediction** is the forecasting of future relationships between cost and activity and is a frequent purpose of cost estimation. As a starting point in the prediction of future costs, managers study cost behavior by analyzing historical cost data.

Cost estimation and cost prediction are made difficult by changes in technology and prices. If an automobile manufacturer changes from skilled labor to computer controlled assembly procedures, the past data are of little or no value in predicting future costs. Only data accumulated subsequent to the initiation of the new assembly technique are useful in predicting the cost of robot assembly.

If prices have remained stable in the past but then uniformly increase by 20 percent, cost estimating equations developed for previous periods will underpredict future costs. In this example all that is required is a 20 percent increase in the prediction.

Unfortunately, adjustments for price changes are seldom this simple. The prices of various cost elements are likely to change at different rates and at different times. Furthermore, there are apt to be several different price levels included in the past data used to develop cost estimating equations. During periods of changing prices only data reflecting a single price level should be used in cost estimation and cost prediction. The analyst should always be suspicious of old data. If data from different price levels are used, an attempt should be made to restate the data to a single price level. Procedures used to do this are discussed in Chapter 17.

One response to the cost prediction problems resulting from changing prices is to use something other than cost as the dependent variable. It is, for example, possible to substitute direct labor hours for direct labor dollars and kilowatt hours for the cost of electricity. In terms of kilowatt hours, the monthly use of electricity might be stated as

$$\text{Total kilowatt hours} = 20{,}000 + 50X,$$

where $X =$ unit volume.

If X is budgeted at 5,000 units, the total use of electricity is predicted to be 270,000 [20,000 + (50 × 5,000)] kilowatt hours. If the current cost of electricity is 12 cents per kilowatt hour, this translates into an electric bill of $32,400 ($0.12 × 270,000).

A disadvantage of this approach is that it must be implemented on a very disaggregated basis. Data for labor costs and electric costs can be added together and analyzed in total. Because labor hours and kilowatt hours cannot be added, they must be analyzed separately before totaling the final cost predictions for each cost element.

SUMMARY

Activities undertaken to achieve an organization's objectives result in the incurrence of costs. Because economic resources are limited, the costs that result from activity also limit activity. Consequently, managers must plan and control both costs and activities. To plan and control costs, managers must know how costs respond to changes in activity.

Managers must be familiar with variable, fixed, mixed, and step costs. A variable cost is the uniform incremental cost of each additional unit. Total variable costs change in direct proportion to changes in volume. A fixed cost does not respond to changes in the volume of activity within a given period. Total fixed costs are a constant amount regardless of the level of activity. Mixed costs contain a fixed and a variable cost element, they are positive when volume is zero, and they increase in a linear fashion as volume increases. Step costs are constant within a range of activity but different between ranges of activity. Total step costs increase in a steplike fashion as volume increases.

The cost behavior of a particular activity is often determined through an analysis of historical cost data. Three techniques used to develop an equation for total cost behavior are the high-low method, the scatter diagram method, and the least-squares method. The high-low method uses data from a representative high volume period and a representative low volume period. The scatter diagram method requires the use of professional judgment to draw a representative straight line through a plot of historical data. The least-squares method fits a straight line to the observed data in a manner that minimizes the sum of the squared deviations between individual observations and the line.

Regardless of the cost estimating technique used, the development of a cost estimating equation should be guided by professional judgment. The analyst must be familiar with the characteristics of the accounting data base, the data must display a linear trend within the relevant range, and observations reflecting abnormal operating conditions should be deleted from the analysis. Particular care should be taken to ensure that the data base reflects constant technology and a single price level. Even when proper precautions are taken, cost predictions are only valid within the relevant range and for the current technology and price level.

APPENDIX A
LEAST-SQUARES COST ESTIMATION

The equation for a straight line is

$$Y = a + bX,$$

where Y = the value of the dependent variable,
a = a constant term,
b = the slope of the line, and
X = the value of the independent variable.

The objective of least-squares cost estimation is to fit this equation to observations of X and Y in a manner that minimizes the sum of the squared differences between the actual and estimated values of Y. Mathematicians have proved that the appropriate values of a and b can be found by the simultaneous solution of the following equations:

$$\sum XY = a \sum X + b \sum X^2, \tag{3-1}$$

$$\sum Y = an + b \sum X, \tag{3-2}$$

where Σ is a capital sigma, meaning "the sum of" (i.e., ΣXY means the sum of the products of X and Y) and

n = the number of observations.

The above equations, called the **normal equations,** are used to compute the constant term and the slope that best meets the least-squares criterion.

The computations required to apply the normal equations to the data in Exhibit 3–10(a) are shown below.

Observation	Unit Volume X	Total Costs Y	XY	X²
1	4,000	$ 23,000	92,000,000	16,000,000
2	3,000	18,000	54,000,000	9,000,000
3	2,400	16,000	38,400,000	5,760,000
4	4,400	24,000	105,600,000	19,360,000
5	2,000	11,000	22,000,000	4,000,000
6	3,600	23,000	82,800,000	12,960,000
7	2,200	15,000	33,000,000	4,840,000
	21,600	$130,000	427,800,000	71,920,000

Substituting these values into the normal equations we obtain

$$427,800,000 = a21,600 + b71,920,000, \tag{3-3}$$

$$130,000 = a7 + b21,600. \tag{3-4}$$

We can solve for b by eliminating a from an equation for the difference between Eqs. (3–3) and (3–4). To do this, we must have the same coefficient for a in each equation. This can be accomplished in a number of ways. We will multiply Eq. (3–3) by 7 and Eq. (3–4) by 21,600. Doing this we obtain

$$2,994,600,000 = 151,200a + 503,440,000b \tag{3-5}$$

$$2,808,000,000 = 151,200a + 466,560,000b \tag{3-6}$$

$$186,600,000 = \qquad\qquad 36,880,000b \tag{3-7}$$

Equation (3–7) is the difference between Eqs. (3–5) and (3–6). Solving Eq. (3–7) for b, we obtain

$$b = \frac{186,600,000}{36,880,000} = 5.06 \quad \text{(rounded)}.$$

We can solve for a by substituting the value of b in any equation containing a. Doing this in Eq. (3–4), we obtain

$$7a = 130,000 - (5.06)(21,600)$$
$$7a = 20,704$$
$$a = 20,704/7 = 2,958 \quad \text{(rounded)}.$$

The resulting cost estimating equation is

$$\text{Total costs} = \$2,958 + \$5.06X.$$

Computations involving large numbers are often simplified by expressing the numbers in thousands. In thousands, the unit volume and total cost of observation 1 are 4 and \$23, respectively. The value of XY then becomes 92, and the value of X^2 becomes 16. Restating all seven observations into thousands and solving for a and b, we obtain \$2.958 and \$5.06. The slope of the line (value of b) is not affected when all data are expressed in thousands. However, the vertical axis intercept (value of a) is \$2.958 thousand, that is, \$2,958, not \$2.958.

In addition to the constant term and the slope, the correlation coefficient, the coefficient of determination, and the standard error of the estimate are often computed when the least-squares method is used. The **correlation coefficient,** a standardized measure of the degree to which two variables move together, is discussed in Appendix B of this chapter. The **coefficient of determination** is a measure of the percent of variation in the dependent variable that is explained by the cost estimating equation; it indicates how good the equation fits the historical data. The **standard error of the estimate** is a measure of the variability of actual costs around the cost estimating equation; it is used to construct probability intervals for cost estimates. Readers interested in studying this further should consult a basic statistics or cost accounting book.

APPENDIX B
THE CORRELATION COEFFICIENT

The **correlation coefficient** is a standardized measure of the degree to which two variables move together and can take on values between -1 and $+1$. Negative correlation implies that the two variables move in opposite directions;

as one increases the other decreases. Positive correlation implies that the two variables move in the same direction; as one increases the other also increases. A correlation coefficient of zero implies that the movement of the two variables is unrelated.

When two variables that are logically related have a high correlation, knowledge of a change in one variable is useful in predicting a change in the other. Management accountants use the correlation coefficient to assist in selecting the best basis for overhead application and for cost estimation. In the selection process the management accountant is usually looking for the basis of activity measurement that has the highest correlation with total costs.

Assume we are trying to determine the best basis for applying overhead to products. We selected four possible bases and calculated their past correlation with total overhead.

Basis	Correlation with Total Overhead
Direct labor hours	0.752
Direct labor dollars	0.885
Machine hours	0.630
Number of employee coffee breaks	−0.100

We would select direct labor dollars as the basis of overhead application; it has the highest correlation with total overhead. Note that the number of employee coffee breaks had a small negative correlation with total overhead. This indicates a slight tendency for total overhead to decrease as the number of employee coffee breaks increases. This may be due to such factors as reduced power consumption by machines while employees are away on breaks.

The basis selected to apply overhead must also be logical and easy to implement. Direct labor dollars has a logical relationship to overhead and, in most organizations, it is easy to relate direct labor dollars to individual products. Even if the number of employee coffee breaks had the highest positive correlation with total overhead, we would not use it as a basis for overhead application. A large positive relationship between these variables does not seem logical. And it would be difficult to relate employee coffee breaks to individual products.

Mathematicians have developed the following equation to compute the correlation coefficient:

$$ r = \frac{\Sigma(X - \bar{X})(Y - \bar{Y})}{\sqrt{\Sigma(X - \bar{X})^2 \ \Sigma(Y - \bar{Y})^2}} , $$

where

r = the correlation coefficient

$\overline{X}$ = the average value of the independent variable, computed as ΣX divided by n

$\overline{Y}$ = the average value of the dependent variable, computed as ΣY divided by n

$\Sigma(X - \overline{X})(Y - \overline{Y})$ = the sum of each difference between individual values of X and $\overline{X}$ multiplied by the corresponding difference between individual values of Y and $\overline{Y}$

$\Sigma(X - \overline{X})^2$ = the sum of the squared differences between X and $\overline{X}$ and

$\Sigma(Y - \overline{Y})^2$ = the sum of the squared differences between Y and $\overline{Y}$.

The average unit volume, $\overline{X}$, and the average total production cost, $\overline{Y}$, for the data in Exhibit 3–10(a) are 3,086 and $18,571, respectively.

$$\overline{X} = (4,000 + 3,000 + 2,400 + 4,400 + 2,000 + 3,600 + 2,200)/7$$
$$= 3,086 \quad \text{(rounded)}$$

$$\overline{Y} = (\$23,000 + \$18,000 + \$16,000 + \$24,000 + \$11,000 + \$23,000 + \$15,000)/7$$
$$= \$18,571 \quad \text{(rounded)}$$

The computation of the correlation coefficient between unit volume and total production costs is presented in Exhibit 3–12. The correlation coefficient of 0.962 indicates a high positive relationship between these two variables. An increase in unit volume has a high statistical correlation with an increase in total production costs. It appears that unit volume is a good basis for estimating total production costs.

EXHIBIT 3–12   Computation of the Correlation Coefficient

Observation	X	$(X - \overline{X})$	$(X - \overline{X})^2$	Y	$(Y - \overline{Y})$	$(Y - \overline{Y})^2$	$(X - \overline{X})(Y - \overline{Y})$
1	4,000	914	835,396	$23,000	4,429	19,616,041	4,048,106
2	3,000	−86	7,396	18,000	−571	326,041	49,106
3	2,400	−686	470,596	16,000	−2,571	6,610,041	1,763,706
4	4,400	1,314	1,726,596	24,000	5,429	29,474,041	7,133,706
5	2,000	−1,086	1,179,396	11,000	−7,571	57,320,041	8,222,106
6	3,600	514	264,196	23,000	4,429	19,616,041	2,276,506
7	2,200	−886	784,996	15,000	−3,571	12,752,041	3,163,906
			5,268,572			145,714,287	26,657,142

$$r = \frac{26,657,142}{\sqrt{(5,268,572)(145,714,287)}} = 0.962$$

KEY TERMS

Capacity cost
Committed fixed cost
Cost behavior analysis
Cost estimation
Cost prediction
Discretionary fixed cost
Fixed cost
High-low method of cost estimation
Least-squares method of cost
  estimation

Managed fixed cost
Marginal cost
Mixed cost
Relevant range
Scatter diagram
Semivariable cost
Step cost
Variable cost

APPENDIX KEY TERMS

Coefficient of determination
Correlation coefficient

Normal equations
Standard error of the estimate

REVIEW QUESTIONS

3–1   In cost behavior analysis, what is the relationship between the cost and the volume of an activity?

3–2   How do you compute the slope of a straight line?

3–3   Briefly describe four widely used total cost behavior patterns.

3–4   What long-run trade-offs are there between fixed and variable costs?

3–5   Under what circumstances are step costs approximated by mixed costs? By fixed costs?

3–6   In what range of activity is a straight line often a reasonable approximation of the economist's short-run total cost pattern?

3–7   Why do average unit costs decline as volume increases?

3–8   Average inventory costs are widely used for what purpose? Give an example of a purpose they should not be used for.

3–9   What minimum number of observations of past data are necessary to estimate the fixed and variable elements of mixed costs?

3–10   Why should we use data reflecting normal operating conditions as a basis for developing cost estimating equations?

3–11   Name two reasons why scatter diagrams are used in conjunction with the high-low and least-squares methods of cost estimation.

3–12   What is the least-squares criterion?

3–13   Why might current unit sales not be a good activity measure for the cost of current purchases in a manufacturing organization?

3–14   Distinguish between cost estimation and cost prediction on the basis of their time orientation.

3–15   Name two dynamic factors which limit the usefulness of historical cost data in cost prediction.

REVIEW PROBLEM

Estimating Cost Behavior and Predicting Future Costs

Dan's Submarine Sandwich Shop reported the following results for April and May 19x2.

	April	May
Unit sales	2,100	2,700
Cost of food sold	$1,575	$2,025
Wages and salaries	1,525	1,675
Rent on building	1,500	1,500
Depreciation on equipment	200	200
Utilities	710	770
Supplies	225	255
Miscellaneous	113	131
Total	$5,848	$6,556

Requirements

a) Identify each cost as being variable, fixed, or mixed.

b) Develop a schedule identifying the amount of each cost that is fixed per month or variable per unit. Total the amounts in each category to develop a cost estimating equation for total monthly costs.

c) Predict total and average costs for monthly volumes of 1,000 units and 2,000 units.

d) Explain why the average costs differ at these two volumes.

The solution to this problem is found at the end of the Chapter 3 exercises and problems.

EXERCISES

3–1 Classifying Cost Behavior

Classify the total costs of each of the following as variable, fixed, mixed, or step.

a) Pulpwood in a paper mill.

b) Salaries of two supervisors.

c) Real estate taxes.

d) Direct labor.

e) Salaries of quality inspectors.

f) Electric power in a factory.

g) Raw materials used in production.

h) Automobiles rented on the basis of a fixed charge per day plus an additional charge per mile driven.

i) Sales commissions.

j) Depreciation on office equipment.

3–2 Classifying Cost Behavior

Classify the total costs of each of the following as variable, fixed, mixed, or step.

a) Maintenance costs at a college.

b) Property taxes on a building.

c) Rent on a photocopy machine charged as a fixed amount per month plus an additional charge per copy.

d) Cost of goods sold in a bookstore.

e) Salaries paid temporary instructors in a college as the number of sections offered of a course varies.

f) Lumber used by a house construction company.

g) The costs of operating a research department.

h) The cost of hiring a dance band for three hours.

i) Typing paper used in a steno pool.

j) Electric power in a restaurant.

3–3 Classifying Cost Behavior

For each situation, select the most appropriate cost behavior pattern. Lines represent the cost behavior pattern. The vertical axis represents total costs. The horizontal axis represents total volume. Dots represent actual costs. Each pattern may be used more than once.

Pattern

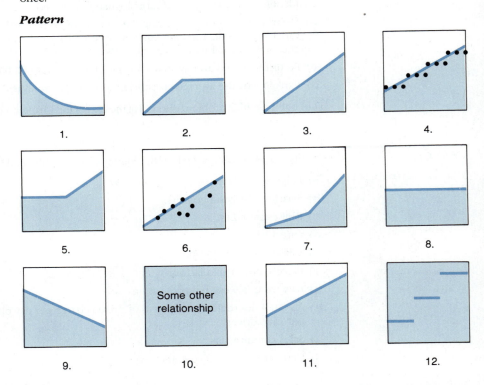

1.   2.   3.   4.

5.   6.   7.   8.

9.   10.   11.   12.

Some other relationship

Situation

a) Variable costs per unit.

b) Total mixed costs.

c) Total fixed costs.

d) Average fixed costs per unit.

e) Total current manufacturing costs.

f) High-low cost estimation influenced by unusual observations.

g) Employees are paid $10 per hour for the first forty hours worked each week and $15 per each additional hour.

h) Employees are paid $10 per hour and guaranteed a minimum weekly wage of $200.

i) A consultant is paid $50 per hour with a maximum fee of $1,000.

j) Total variable costs.

k) Salaries of social workers where each social worker can handle a maximum of 20 cases.

l) A water bill where a flat fee of $800 is charged for the first 100,000 gallons and additional water costs $0.005 per gallon.

m) Variable costs properly used to estimate step costs.

n) Total direct materials costs.

o) Rent on exhibit space at a convention.

3–4 Classifying Cost Behavior

For each situation, select the most appropriate cost behavior pattern. Lines represent the cost behavior pattern. The vertical axis represents total costs. The horizontal axis represents total volume. Dots represent actual costs. Each pattern may be used more than once.

Pattern

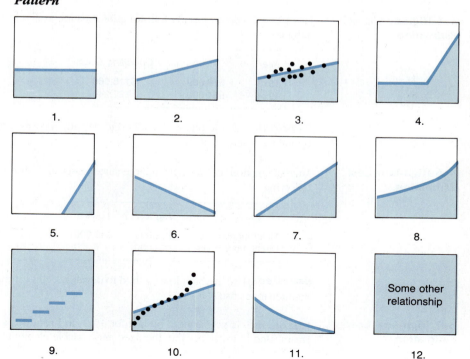

1.	2.	3.	4.
5.	6.	7.	8.
9.	10.	11.	12. Some other relationship

Situation

a) A telephone bill where a flat fee is charged for the first twenty calls per month and additional calls cost $0.25 each.

b) Total selling and administrative costs.

c) Total direct labor costs.

d) Total overtime premium paid production employees.

e) Average total cost per unit.

f) Salaries of supervisors when each can supervise a maximum of ten employees.

g) Total idle time costs when employees are paid for a minimum forty-hour week.

h) Direct materials costs per unit.

i) High-low method properly used to estimate cost behavior.

j) Electric power consumption in a restaurant.

k) Total costs when high volumes of production require the use of overtime and obsolete equipment.

l) Total sales commissions.

m) A linear cost estimation valid only within the relevant range.

n) Average variable costs per unit.

o) Once the capacity of a plant that has only fixed costs is reached, additional parts are purchased from outside vendors.

3–5 High-Low Cost Estimation

Jack's Taxi Company has the following information available about fleet miles and operating costs.

Year	Miles	Operating Costs
19x3	556,000	$115,060
19x4	684,000	132,340

Required: Use the high-low method to develop a cost estimating equation for annual operating costs.

3–6 High-Low Cost Estimation

An examination of monthly maintenance costs and direct labor hours reveals the following:

	Highest	Lowest
Maintenance	$64,000	$40,800
Direct labor hours	13,000	7,200

Required: Use the high-low method to develop a cost estimating equation for monthly maintenance costs.

3–7 High-Low Cost Estimation

Jackson, Inc., is preparing a budget for 19x1 and requires a breakdown of the cost of steam used in its factory into the fixed and variable elements. The following data on the cost of steam used and direct labor hours worked are available for the last six months of 19x0:

Month	Cost of Steam	Direct Labor Hours
July	$ 15,850	3,000
August	13,400	2,050
September	16,370	2,900
October	19,800	3,650
November	17,600	2,670
December	18,500	2,650
Total	$101,520	16,920

Required: Use the high-low method to develop an equation for the monthly cost of steam.

(CPA Adapted)

3–8 High-Low Cost Estimation and Predetermined Overhead Rates

Presented is information on 19x7 and 19x8 factory overhead and direct labor hours:

	19x7	19x8
Factory overhead	$156,000	$187,400
Direct labor hours	55,500	71,200

Management predicts that 60,000 direct labor hours will be used in 19x9.

Required: Determine the 19x9 predetermined overhead rate per direct labor hour.

3–9 High-Low Cost Estimation and Predetermined Overhead Rates

Tastee-Treat Company prepares, packages, and distributes six frozen vegetables. The different vegetables are prepared in large batches. Manufacturing overhead is assigned to batches by a predetermined rate on the basis of direct labor hours. The manufacturing overhead costs incurred by the company during two recent years are presented below.

	19x2	19x3
Direct labor hours worked	2,760,000	2,160,000
Manufacturing overhead costs incurred (adjusted for changes in current prices and wage rates)		
Indirect labor	$11,040,000	$ 8,640,000
Employee benefits	4,140,000	3,240,000
Supplies	2,760,000	2,160,000
Power	2,208,000	1,728,000
Heat and light	552,000	552,000
Supervision	2,865,000	2,625,000
Depreciation	7,930,000	7,930,000
Property taxes and insurance	3,005,000	3,005,000
Total overhead costs	$34,500,000	$29,880,000

Required: Tastee-Treat Company expects to operate at a 2,300,000 direct labor hour level of activity in 19x4. Using the data from two recent years, calculate the rate Tastee-Treat should employ to assign manufacturing overhead to its products during 19x4.

(CMA Adapted)

3–10 Scatter Diagrams and High-Low Cost Estimation

Presented are monthly production and cost data.

Month	Volume	Total Cost
1	3,000	$40,000
2	1,500	28,000
3	4,000	65,000
4	2,800	39,000
5	2,300	32,000
6	1,000	20,000
7	2,000	30,000

Requirements

a) Using information from the high and low volume months, develop a cost estimating equation for monthly production costs.

b) Plot the data on a scatter diagram. Using information from *representative* high and low volume months, develop a cost estimating equation for monthly production costs.

c) What factors might cause the difference in the equations developed in requirements (a) and (b)?

3–11 Scatter Diagrams and High-Low Cost Estimation

From April 1 through October 31 the Central County Highway Department hires temporary employees to mow and clean the right-of-way along county roads. A county road commissioner has asked you to assist her in determining the variable labor cost of mowing and cleaning a mile of road. The following information is available regarding 19x5 operations.

Month	Miles Mowed and Cleaned	Labor Cost
April	350	$7,500
May	300	7,000
June	400	8,500
July	250	5,000
August	375	8,000
September	200	4,500
October	100	4,300

Requirements

a) Using information from the high and low volume months, develop a cost estimating equation for monthly labor costs.

b) Plot the information on a scatter diagram. Using information from *representative* high and low volume months, develop a cost estimating equation for monthly labor costs.

c) What factors might cause the difference in the equations developed in requirements (a) and (b)?

d) Adjust the equation developed in requirement (b) to incorporate the effect of a 7 percent increase in wages.

3–12 Computing Average Unit Costs

The total monthly operating costs of Del Rio Chili To Go are

$$\$10{,}000 + \$0.30X,$$

where X = servings of chili.

Requirements

a) Determine the average cost per serving at each of the following monthly volumes: 10, 100, 200, 400, 800.

b) Determine the monthly volume at which the average cost per serving is $0.50.

3–13 Computing Average Unit Costs: Review of Relevant Costs

The local chapter of a professional organization is organizing a one-day continuing education program. Program costs are as follows:

Advertising	$1,000 per program
Instructor's fee	600 per program
Room rental and set-up	200 per program
Instructional materials	20 per participant
Lunch and coffee breaks	15 per participant

Requirements

a) Develop an equation for total program costs.

b) Determine the average cost per participant at each of the following volumes: 10, 20, 30, 50.

c) Determine the volume at which the average cost per participant is $50.

d) The program is scheduled for October 1, 19x4. The budgeted advertising expenditures are made on September 1, and a $100 nonrefundable deposit for the room rental and set-up is made on September 15. All other costs, except the instructor's fee, are payable at the start of the program. The instructor's fee is payable at the end of the program.

   One week before the scheduled date of the program, the chapter's director of continuing education becomes concerned about a lack of preregistered participants and considers whether or not to cancel the program. Identify the sunk and relevant costs for this decision, and develop a cost estimating equation that contains only relevant costs.

3–14 Developing an Equation from Average Costs

The average unit cost at a volume of 4,000 units is $2.00, and the average unit cost at a volume of 10,000 units is $1.25.

Required: Develop an estimating equation for total cost.

3–15 Developing an Equation from Average Costs

The Dog House is a pet hotel located on the outskirts of town. In March, when dog (occupancy) days were at an annual low of 500, the average cost per dog day was $18.50. In July, when dog days were at a capacity level of 3,100, the average cost per dog day was $5.50.

Requirements

a) Develop an equation for *monthly* operating costs.

b) Determine the average cost per dog day at an *annual* volume of 24,000 dog days.

3–16 Mixed Cost Approximation of Step Costs

The Civic Center has asked you to develop a cost estimating equation for ticket takers. Ticket takers are on duty for a one-hour period starting 45 minutes before a performance is scheduled to begin. Ticket takers are paid $8 per hour, and each ticket taker can collect a maximum of 1,000 tickets per hour.

Requirements

a) The labor cost of ticket takers is a step function with each step being 1,000 tickets collected. Develop a mixed cost approximation of the cost of taking tickets.

b) Use the equation developed in requirement (a) to estimate the labor cost of collecting 10,000 and 10,001 tickets. What is the dollar amount of the error with this approximation?

3–17 Mixed Cost Approximation of Step Costs

Quality Aviation manufactures guidance systems for single-engine aircraft. To ensure a high level of conformance between the performance of each unit and product specifications, Quality Aviation recently instituted a program management called "Total Quality Assurance." As part of this program, all purchased parts are inspected when they are received, and additional inspections are performed at various points during manufacturing, as well as before finished goods are approved for shipment.

Given the intensive and extensive nature of the inspection program, management has determined that one inspector is needed for each 100 guidance systems produced per week. Inspectors are paid at the rate of $15 per hour for a forty-hour week. The union contract specified they will be paid for forty hours even if they work fewer than forty hours.

Requirements

a) Develop a mixed cost approximation of the weekly cost of inspecting aircraft guidance systems.

b) Use the equation developed in requirement (a) to estimate the cost of inspecting 500 and 501 guidance systems per week. What is the dollar amount of the error with this approximation?

c) Assuming inspectors are paid a 50 percent overtime premium, how should management respond when production temporarily increases from 480 to 510 units per week?

3–18 Automatic Versus Manual Processing

The Fast Photo Company operates a 60-minute film development and print service. The current service, which relies extensively on manual operations, has monthly operating costs of $5,000 plus $2 per roll of film developed and printed. Management is evaluating the desirability of acquiring a machine that will automatically develop film and make prints. If the machine is acquired, the monthly fixed costs of the service will increase to $23,000, and the variable costs of developing and printing a roll of film will decline to $1.40.

Requirements

a) Determine the total costs of developing and printing 20,000 and 50,000 rolls per month:

With the current process.
With the automatic process.

b) Determine the monthly volume at which the total operating costs of both processes are identical.

3–19 Automatic Versus Manual Processing

The Kopy Tat Photocopy Service processes 1,000,000 photocopies per month at its midtown service center. Approximately 60 percent of the photocopies, 600,000 per month, require collating. Collating is currently performed by high school and college students who are paid $4.00 per hour. Each student collates an average of 5,000 copies per hour.

Management is contemplating the lease of an automatic collating machine that has a monthly capacity of 5,000,000 photocopies with operating costs of $795 plus $0.05 per 1,000 units collated.

Requirements

a) Determine the total costs of collating 500,000 and 1,500,000 copies per month:

With the student help.
With the collating machine.

b) Determine the monthly volume of collating at which the total operating costs of both processes are equal.

c) Should Kopy Tat acquire the automatic collating machine at this time?

PROBLEMS

3–20 Cost Behavior Analysis with Changing Prices

The Wildcat Auto Insurance Company has asked you to develop an equation that will be useful in predicting the labor cost of processing insurance claims. The following information regarding the operation of their claims office is available.

Year	Claims Processed	Labor Hours	Labor Dollars
19x2	3,300	3,700	$18,500
19x3	4,200	4,300	21,500
19x4	3,200	3,500	21,000
19x5	5,000	5,300	31,800
19x6	4,000	4,400	44,000
19x7	3,600	4,000	40,000

Wage rates have increased substantially over the six-year period from 19x2 through 19x7. However, no additional increases are expected until 19x9.

Required: Develop an equation to predict the 19x8 labor cost of processing claims. Use the high-low method.

3–21 Cost Behavior Analysis with Changing Prices

Julie Schultz is trying to develop an equation to predict the cost of electricity consumed at an apartment she rents each summer. Julie believes that the primary factor affecting monthly power consumption is the amount by which the average daily high temperature exceeds 75 degrees Fahrenheit. Presented is information Julie has accumulated from her electric bill and the local newspaper:

Period	Average Daily High Temperature	Kilowatt Hours Used	Electric Bill
June 19x3	82.1	1,780	$133.50
July 19x3	93.6	3,490	261.75
August 19x3	89.4	2,800	210.00
June 19x4	81.0	1,690	160.55
July 19x4	90.1	3,100	294.50
August 19x4	86.3	2,250	213.75
June 19x5	80.4	1,510	173.65
July 19x5	90.1	2,950	339.25
August 19x5	87.6	2,550	258.75

The cost of electricity per kilowatt hour (KWH) has increased during each of the past three years and is anticipated to be 13.5 cents per KWH during 19x6.

Required: Develop an equation to predict the 19x6 monthly cost of electricity for the apartment.

3–22 Cost Behavior Analysis in a Restaurant: High-Low Method

The Pizza House Restaurant has the following information available regarding costs at various levels of monthly sales.

	5,000	8,000	10,000
Monthly sales in units	5,000	8,000	10,000
Cost of food sold	$ 5,250	$ 8,400	$10,500
Wage and fringe benefits of restaurant employees	4,250	4,400	4,500
Fees paid delivery help	1,250	2,000	2,500
Rent on building	1,200	1,200	1,200
Depreciation on equipment	300	300	300
Utilities	500	560	600
Supplies (soap, floor wax, etc.)	150	180	200
Administrative costs	1,300	1,300	1,300
Total	$14,200	$18,340	$21,100

Requirements

a) Identify each cost as being variable, fixed, or mixed.

b) Develop a schedule identifying the amount of each cost that is fixed per month or variable per unit. Total the amounts under each category to develop an equation for total monthly costs.

c) Predict total costs for a monthly sales volume of 9,500 units.

3–23 Cost Behavior Analysis in a Store: High-Low Method

The Eleventh Avenue Convenience Store has the following information available regarding costs and revenues for two recent months.

	April	May
Sales revenue	$60,000	$100,000
Cost of goods sold	−36,000	− 60,000
Gross profit	$24,000	$ 40,000
Less other expenses:		
Advertising	$ 600	$ 600
Utilities	4,200	5,600
Salaries and commissions	3,200	4,000
Supplies (bags, cleaning		
supplies, etc.)	320	400
Depreciation	2,300	2,300
Administrative costs	1,900	1,900
Total	−12,520	− 14,800
Net income	$11,480	$ 25,200

Requirements

a) Identify each cost as being fixed, variable, or mixed.

b) Develop a schedule identifying the amount of each cost that is fixed per month or variable per sales dollar. Express fixed costs as an amount per month and variable costs as a portion of sales revenue. Develop a cost estimating equation for total monthly costs.

c) Predict total costs for a monthly sales volume of $70,000.

3–24 Average Costs and Internal Decisions

The production supervisor of Confusion Reigns bursts into your office declaring that accounting information is of little or no use to him:

"Back in early August I asked the accounting department for production cost information. They told me that the July production costs were $13 per unit. Well, I knew that July was a typical month in which we had good cost control, so I used the $13 amount in my production cost budgets for August and September.

In August I was scheduled to produce 12,000 units, so I budgeted my costs at $156,000 (12,000 × $13). I figured that something was wrong when actual costs turned out to be $150,000. However, when the vice president congratulated me for saving $6,000, I decided to keep my mouth shut. But last month was a disaster! In September I produced 5,000 units at a budgeted cost of $65,000 (5,000 × $13), and the V.P. is now demanding an explanation of the $15,000 difference between the budgeted costs and the actual costs of $80,000. I am totally confused because I believe I did an equally good job of controlling costs in all three months. You've got to help me!"

The first thing you did was obtain the following statements for the months in question.

Confusion Reigns
Statements of Cost of Goods Manufactured
For the months of July, August, and September, 19x2

	July	August	September
Current manufacturing costs:			
Raw materials	$ 30,000	$ 36,000	$15,000
Direct labor	50,000	60,000	25,000
Factory overhead	50,000	54,000	40,000
Total	$130,000	$150,000	$80,000
Work-in-process, beginning	0	0	0
Total costs-in-process	$130,000	$150,000	$80,000
Work-in-process, ending	— 0	— 0	— 0
Cost of goods manufactured	$130,000	$150,000	$80,000
Units manufactured	10,000	12,000	5,000

Required: Prepare a report explaining what happened. Based on your analysis, did the production supervisor do an equally good job of controlling costs in all three months?

3–25 Selecting an Independent Variable: Scatter Diagrams

Valley Production Company produces backpacks that are sold to sporting goods stores throughout the Rocky Mountains. Presented is information on production costs and inventory changes for five recent months.

	January	February	March	April	May
Finished goods inventory in units:					
Beginning	30,000	40,000	50,000	30,000	60,000
Manufactured	60,000	90,000	80,000	90,000	100,000
Available	90,000	130,000	130,000	120,000	160,000
Sold	− 50,000	− 80,000	−100,000	− 60,000	−120,000
Ending	40,000	50,000	30,000	60,000	40,000
Manufacturing costs	$300,000	$500,000	$450,000	$450,000	$550,000

Requirements

a) With the aid of scatter diagrams, determine whether units sold or units manufactured is a better predictor of manufacturing costs.

b) Prepare an explanation for your answer to requirement (a).

c) Which independent variable, units sold or units manufactured, should be a better predictor of selling costs? Why?

3–26 Selecting a Basis of Overhead Allocation: Scatter Diagrams

The Roth Company manufactures two products, A and B. In the past, factory overhead costs have been allocated equally to all products on the basis of the number of units produced. However, Mr. Roth is concerned that this method does not provide a proper cost basis for product pricing. Mr. Roth has noted that most of the company's factory overhead costs are related to the use of machinery, and that each unit of product A requires twice as many machine hours as a unit of product B. Consequently, he believes the allocation should be made on the basis of machine hours.

You have been asked to study this matter and determine the more accurate basis of allocating factory overhead costs. The following information is available.

Month	Units Produced A	Units Produced B	Units Produced Total	Machine Hours	Factory Overhead
1	50	100	150	300	$30,000
2	200	100	300	500	40,000
3	100	50	150	250	25,000
4	150	50	200	350	30,000
5	50	350	400	450	32,000
6	100	300	400	500	35,000

Requirements

a) With the aid of scatter diagrams, determine whether units produced or machine hours is the better basis of overhead application.

b) Which product is assigned too few overhead costs, and which product is assigned too many overhead costs, when the allocation is made on the basis of units produced? Explain your answer. If prices are based on cost, what may happen to the prices Roth charges for its products compared to the prices of competitors' products?

3–27 Selecting a Basis for Predicting Shipping Expenses

The Tyson Company assembles and sells computer boards in western Pennsylvania. In an effort to improve the planning and control of shipping expenses, management is trying to determine which of three variables—units shipped, weight shipped, or sales value of units shipped—has the closest relationship with shipping expenses. The following information is available.

Month	Units Shipped	Weight Shipped (lbs.)	Sales Value of Units Shipped	Shipping Expenses
May	3,000	6,200	$50,000	$2,500
June	5,000	8,000	55,000	3,500
July	4,000	8,100	40,000	3,000
August	7,000	10,000	57,000	5,000
September	6,000	7,000	70,000	4,000
October	4,500	8,000	80,000	3,800

Requirements

a) With the aid of scatter diagrams, determine whether units shipped, weight shipped, or sales value of units shipped has the closest relationship with shipping expenses.

b) Using the independent variable that appears to have the closest relationship to shipping expense, develop a high-low cost estimating equation for total monthly shipping expenses.

c) Use the equation developed in requirement (b) to predict total shipping expenses in a month when 5,000 units, weighing 7,000 lbs., with a total sales value of $57,000 are shipped.

3–28 Least-Squares Cost Estimation (Appendix A)

The Quartz Watch Repair Center is trying to determine the cost of repairing a quartz watch. The following information is available regarding the number of units repaired and labor hours.

Week	Watches Repaired	Labor Hours
1	150	45
2	50	20
3	75	25
4	200	60
5	175	40
6	250	50

Requirements

a) Determine the average and the incremental time to repair a quartz watch. Use the least-squares method to compute the incremental time. Round your answer to three decimal places.

b) Predict the total labor hours required for a week when 200 quartz watches are repaired. If the labor cost is $12 per hour, what is the predicted total labor cost for this week?

3–29 Least-Squares Cost Estimation (Appendix A)

The following information is available about shipping costs.

Month	Pounds Shipped	Total Shipping Cost
January	5,000	$12,000
February	7,000	16,000
March	6,000	15,000
April	9,000	17,000

Required: Use the least-squares method to develop an equation for total monthly shipping costs. Round answers to three decimal places. *Hint:* Perform calculations in thousands, and then adjust the constant term in your answer.

3–30 Predicting Selling Expenses (Appendix B)

The Grackly Company is trying to determine the best independent variable to use in predicting selling expenses. In the past this prediction has been made on the basis of expected unit sales. However, the increasing diversity of the company's products has led the sales manager to suggest that expected sales revenue might be a better predictor. You have gathered the following information:

Month	Units Sold	Sales Revenue	Selling Expense
1	5,000	$25,000	$2,200
2	7,000	35,000	2,400
3	6,000	20,000	1,800
4	9,000	40,000	3,200
5	8,000	30,000	2,400

Requirements

a) Use the correlation coefficient to determine the best predictor of selling expenses.

b) Use the least-squares method to develop an equation for predicting monthly selling expenses. Select the basis of prediction that has the highest correlation with actual selling expenses. If you select sales revenue as the independent variable, variable costs should be expressed as a portion of sales revenue.

3–31 Selecting a Basis of Overhead Application (Appendix B)

Presented is information on manufacturing activity and total overhead costs for five recent months.

Month	Direct Labor Hours	Machine Hours	Total Factory Overhead
April	20,000	6,000	$ 90,000
May	40,000	10,000	150,000
June	30,000	8,000	140,000
July	60,000	10,000	260,000
August	50,000	6,000	160,000

Requirements

a) Use the correlation coefficient to determine the best basis of overhead application.

b) Use the least-squares method to develop an equation to predict monthly overhead. Select the basis of prediction that has the highest correlation with actual overhead.

c) Modify the equation developed above to predict annual overhead, and then compute the predetermined overhead rate for a year when management predicts the use of 480,000 direct labor hours and 120,000 machine hours.

REVIEW PROBLEM SOLUTION

a) Fixed costs are easily identified. They are the same at each activity level. Variable and mixed costs are determined by dividing the total cost for an item by unit sales at two activity levels. The quotients of variable cost items will be the same at both activity levels. The quotients of mixed costs will differ, being lower at the higher activity level because the fixed costs are spread over a larger number of units.

Cost	Behavior
Cost of food sold	Variable
Wages and salaries	Mixed
Rent on building	Fixed
Depreciation on equipment	Fixed
Utilities	Mixed
Supplies	Mixed
Miscellaneous	Mixed

b)

	Fixed Costs	Variable Costs
Cost of food sold ($1,575/2,100)		$0.75X
Wages and salaries		
($1,675 − $1,525)/(2,700 − 2,100)		0.25X
$1,525 − $0.25(2,100)	$1,000	
Rent on building	1,500	
Depreciation on equipment	200	
Utilities ($710 − $770)/(2,700 − 2,100)		0.10X
$710 − $0.10(2,100)	500	
Supplies ($255 − $225)/(2,700 − 2,100)		0.05X
$225 − $0.05(2,100)	120	
Miscellaneous		
($131 − $113)/(2,700 − 2,100)		0.03X
$113 − $0.03(2,100)	50	
Total	$3,370	$1.18X

Total costs $= \$3,370 + \$1.18X$

where $X =$ unit sales.

c)

Volume	Total Cost	Average Cost
1,000	$4,550	$4.550
2,000	$5,730	$2.865

d) The average costs differ at 1,000 and 2,000 units because the fixed costs are being spread over differing numbers of units. The larger the number of units, the smaller the average fixed cost per unit.

CHAPTER 4

Cost-Volume-Profit Analysis

Upon completion of this chapter you should:

- Be able to prepare an income statement under the functional approach and the contribution approach.
- Understand the concept of contribution margin and be able to compute the contribution margin ratio.
- Be able to prepare a cost-volume-profit graph showing total revenues, total costs, profit or loss, and break-even point.
- Be able to compute the break-even point by three methods: graph, formula, and contribution.
- Be able to determine the sales volume required to achieve a desired before-tax or after-tax profit.
- Be able to prepare a profit-volume graph.
- Be familiar with the limiting assumptions of the cost-volume-profit model.

Cost-volume-profit analysis is a technique used to examine the relationships between volume, total costs, total revenues, and profit. Cost-volume-profit analysis is particularly useful in the early stages of planning because it provides a framework for discussing planning issues and for organizing relevant data.

Cost-volume-profit analysis is widely used in for-profit and not-for-profit organizations, and it is equally applicable to service, merchandising, and manufacturing activities. In for-profit organizations cost-volume-profit analysis is used to answer such questions as: How many photocopies must the College Avenue Copy Service produce to earn a profit of $20,000? At what sales volume will Burger King's total costs and total revenues be equal? What profit will General Electric earn at an annual sales volume of 3 billion dollars? What will happen to the profits of Duff's Smorgasbord if there is a 20 percent increase in the cost of food and a 10 percent increase in the selling price of meals?

In not-for-profit organizations cost-volume-profit analysis is used to plan service levels, plan fund-raising activities, and determine funding requirements: How many meals can the Downtown Salvation Army serve with an annual budget of $200,000? How many tickets must be sold for the benefit concert to raise $10,000? Given current tuition rates and projected enrollments, how much money must City University obtain from other sources?

The purpose of this chapter is to introduce cost-volume-profit analysis. We begin by developing a profit formula and presenting a new type of income statement based on that formula. Next we examine cost-volume-profit relationships and illustrate their use in planning. Then we summarize the assumptions that are an inherent part of cost-volume-profit analysis. Appendices A and B consider operating leverage, which is a measure of the responsiveness of income to changes in sales, and methods of analyzing the effect on profits of changes in the portion of sales derived from different products.

A BASIC ASSUMPTION

In Chapter 2 *cost* was defined as a monetary measure of the economic sacrifice made to obtain some product or service. The cost of a product or service that has a future service or revenue generating potential is recorded as an asset, whereas the cost of a product or service that has been consumed or no longer has a revenue generating potential is recorded as an expense. An important distinction was made between product costs and period costs. *Product costs*—which include the cost of raw materials and other factors necessary to transform raw materials into finished goods—are recorded as assets until the finished goods are sold; at that time they become the expense cost of goods sold. *Period costs*—which are expired nonproduct costs, such as selling or administrative expenses—are recorded as expenses in the period they are incurred.

To simplify the discussion of cost-volume-profit relationships, inventories are assumed to be constant or at zero. All merchandise is sold and all supplies are consumed in the period they are purchased. In manufacturing organizations raw materials are converted into finished goods in the period they are purchased, and finished goods are sold in the period they are produced. With this assumption, product costs and period costs are both expenses of the period in which they are incurred. By limiting the discussion to these two types of costs, the words "cost" and "expense" have equivalent meaning and may be used interchangeably. In cost-volume-profit analysis, the word "cost(s)" refers to product costs and period costs that are expenses of the period in which they are incurred. Additional assumptions of cost-volume-profit analysis are discussed at the end of this chapter.

THE PROFIT FORMULA

An organization's profit is equal to the difference between its total revenues and its total costs:

$$\text{Profit} = \text{Total revenues} - \text{Total costs.}$$

Total revenues are a function of the unit sales volume and the unit selling price:

$$\frac{\text{Total}}{\text{revenues}} = \frac{\text{Selling}}{\text{price}} \times \frac{\text{Unit}}{\text{volume.}}$$

The computation of profit can be expanded to include the detailed elements of revenues and costs:

$$\text{Profit} = \left(\frac{\text{Selling}}{\text{price}} \times \frac{\text{Unit}}{\text{volume}} \right) - \left[\frac{\text{Fixed}}{\text{costs}} + \left(\frac{\text{Variable costs}}{\text{per unit}} \times \frac{\text{Unit}}{\text{volume}} \right) \right].$$

$$P = S \cdot V_u - [FC + (VC_u \times V_u)]$$

Given information on the selling price, the fixed costs per period, and the variable costs per unit, this formula is used to determine profit at any specified volume. Consider the following example.

The Benchmark Card Company manufactures high-quality seasonal greeting cards that are sold at $8 per box of 100 cards. Variable and fixed costs are shown below.

Variable Costs per Box			Fixed Costs per Month	
Manufacturing:			Factory overhead	$ 5,000
Direct materials	$1.00		Selling and	
Direct labor	0.50		administrative	10,000
Factory overhead	0.50	$2.00	Total	$15,000
Selling and				
administrative		1.00		
Total		$3.00		

If Benchmark produces and sells 4,000 boxes of cards in October 19x7, their profit would be $5,000.

$$\text{Profit} = (\$8 \times 4{,}000) - [\$15{,}000 + (\$3 \times 4{,}000)]$$
$$= \$5{,}000.$$

ALTERNATIVE INCOME STATEMENTS

Assuming Benchmark does not maintain beginning or ending inventories, and that monthly production equals monthly sales, the cost of goods manufactured is the cost of goods sold, and a detailed list of current manufacturing costs can be disclosed in the income statement as the cost of goods sold. There are two alternative formats for disclosing manufacturing and other costs in an income statement. Each is discussed and illustrated below.

Functional Income Statements Classify Expenses by Function

Benchmark Card Company's income statement is presented at the top of Exhibit 4–1 in the form most frequently used for external reporting. This statement is called a **functional income statement** because costs are classified according to function, such as manufacturing or selling and administrative. Variable and fixed costs are included within each functional category. The cost of goods sold includes variable and fixed manufacturing costs; likewise, the selling and administrative expenses include variable and fixed costs. For the purpose of exposition, detailed computations of cost of goods sold and selling and administrative expenses are shown in Exhibit 4–1. In reality, it is unlikely that each functional cost would be further classified by cost behavior.

One immediate problem with a functional income statement is the difficulty of relating it to the profit formula where costs are classified according to behavior rather than function. The cost and profit consequences of changes in sales volume are not readily apparent in a functional income statement, especially when cost information is presented at an aggregated level. *For planning and control purposes, costs should be classified by behavior.* This classification assists in determining how costs and, hence, profits respond to changes in volume.

Contribution Income Statements Classify Expenses by Cost Behavior

A contribution income statement is presented at the bottom of Exhibit 4–1. Such statements are used for internal planning and control. In a contribution income statement costs are classified according to behavior. The variable manufacturing costs and the variable selling and administrative expenses are grouped together and subtracted from revenues. The difference between rev-

---

EXHIBIT 4–1   Functional and Contribution Income Statements

Benchmark Card Company
Functional Income Statement
For the month of October, 19x7

Sales (4,000 × $8)		$32,000
Cost of goods sold:		
Direct materials (4,000 × $1)	$ 4,000	
Direct labor (4,000 × $0.50)	2,000	
Variable factory overhead (4,000 × $0.50)	2,000	
Fixed factory overhead	5,000	−13,000
Gross profit		$19,000
Selling and administrative expenses:		
Variable (4,000 × $1)	$ 4,000	
Fixed	10,000	−14,000
Net income		$ 5,000

Benchmark Card Company
Contribution Income Statement
For the month of October, 19x7

Sales (4,000 × $8)			$32,000
Less variable costs:			
Cost of goods sold:			
Direct materials (4,000 × $1)	$4,000		
Direct labor (4,000 × $0.50)	2,000		
Factory overhead (4,000 × $0.50)	2,000	$ 8,000	
Selling and administrative			
(4,000 × $1)		4,000	−12,000
Contribution margin			$20,000
Less fixed costs:			
Factory overhead		$ 5,000	
Selling and administrative		10,000	−15,000
Net income			$ 5,000

enues and variable costs, called the **contribution margin,** is the amount of money contributed to cover fixed costs and to provide a profit. The fixed manufacturing costs and the fixed selling and administrative expenses are also grouped together and subtracted from the contribution margin to obtain net income.

When production and sales are equal (no beginning or ending inventories), the same net income will be obtained with either type of income statement. However, the gross profit (or gross margin) in a functional income statement will seldom be the same as the contribution margin in a contribution income statement. This is because the computation of gross profit includes a deduction for fixed manufacturing costs while excluding a deduction for variable selling and administrative expenses. The mixing of fixed and variable costs in the computation of a *manufacturing* firm's gross profit makes it difficult to determine how gross profit responds to changes in sales volume. Note, however, that a *merchandising* firm's cost of goods sold includes only the variable cost of goods purchased and sold; hence, the gross profit of a merchandising firm represents a contribution or margin that is available to cover selling and administrative costs and to provide for a profit. It should change in direct proportion to changes in sales volume.

Unit Contribution Margin. For planning purposes it is useful to express sales, variable costs, and contribution margin by dollars per unit, as a percentage of the total dollar amount of sales, or both. Condensing Benchmark's October 19x7 contribution income statement, we obtain the following:

	Total	Per Unit	Percent of Sales
Sales (4,000 units)	$32,000	$8	100.0
Variable costs	−12,000	−3	−37.5
Contribution margin	$20,000	$5	62.5
Fixed costs	−15,000		
Net income	$ 5,000		

The **unit contribution margin** is the difference between the unit selling price and the unit variable costs, including the variable cost of goods sold and the variable selling and administrative costs. The unit contribution margin is also described as the dollar amount that each unit sold contributes to cover fixed costs and to provide for a profit. This relationship is often used to determine the effect on profit of changes in the unit sales volume.

The change in profit is calculated as follows:

$$\frac{\text{Change}}{\text{in profit}} = \frac{\text{Unit contribution}}{\text{margin}} \times \frac{\text{Change in}}{\text{unit volume.}}$$

$$\Delta P = C_m \times \Delta V_u$$

Management may want to know what will happen to Benchmark's profit if sales increase by 500 units. With a unit contribution margin of $5, the impact on profit of a 500 unit increase in sales volume is quickly computed as $5 multiplied by 500:

$$\$5 \times 500 = \$2,500 \qquad \text{increase in profit.}$$

If the current profit is $5,000 at a monthly volume of 4,000 units, the new profit will be $7,500 at a monthly volume 500 units higher.

Current profit	$5,000
Increase (500 × $5)	2,500
New profit	$7,500

We could use the profit formula to compute the new profit and then subtract the current profit from this amount to determine the increase; however, this approach is more time consuming. Alternatively, we could start with the current contribution income statement and show the impact of the possible sales increase on revenues and variable costs:

	Current 4,000 Units	Increase 500 Units	New 4,500 Units
Sales ($8 per unit)	$32,000	$4,000	$36,000
Variable costs ($3 per unit)	−12,000	−1,500	−13,500
Contribution margin	$20,000	$2,500	$22,500
Fixed costs	−15,000	—	−15,000
Net income	$ 5,000	$2,500	$ 7,500

In addition to being a useful way of presenting information to management, this also illustrates one of the advantages of contribution income statements for internal planning. The effect of a volume change is much easier to illustrate with a contribution income statement than with a functional income statement.

Contribution Margin Ratio. The **contribution margin ratio,** which is the ratio of contribution margin to sales revenue, indicates the portion of each sales dollar that is available to cover fixed costs and provide for a profit. It is computed as the contribution margin divided by sales revenue:

$$\frac{\text{Contribution}}{\text{margin ratio}} = \frac{\text{Contribution}}{\text{margin}} \div \frac{\text{Sales}}{\text{revenue.}}$$

$$CM_r = \frac{CM}{SR}$$

The calculation may be made on total dollars ($20,000 ÷ $32,000 = 0.625) or on dollars per unit ($5 ÷ $8 = 0.625).

Using the contribution margin ratio, the profit impact of a change in sales revenue is easily determined as the change in sales revenue multiplied by the contribution margin ratio:

$$\Delta P = \Delta R_T \cdot CM_r$$

$$\frac{\text{Change}}{\text{in profit}} = \frac{\text{Change in}}{\text{total revenues}} \times \frac{\text{Contribution}}{\text{margin ratio.}}$$

Benchmark has a contribution margin ratio of 0.625. If Benchmark's monthly sales increase by $4,000, their monthly profit will increase by $2,500:

$$\text{Change in profit} = \$4,000 \times 0.625$$
$$= \$2,500 \text{ increase.}$$

The unit contribution margin and the contribution margin ratio are equally useful in determining the effect on profit of volume changes in single product firms. However, because sales dollars provide a common denominator that can be meaningfully added across products, *the contribution margin ratio is easier to use in firms that sell several products in a constant sales mix.* A furniture company may sell several different styles of desks, tables, and bookcases. Given the different selling prices, costs, and contribution margins of each product, calculating the change in profit for total revenues using the contribution margin ratio is much simpler than aggregating the information from each product's unit contribution margin and unit selling price.

Variable Cost Ratio. The **variable cost ratio** indicates the portion of each sales dollar that is used to cover variable costs. It provides useful information regarding an organization's cost structure. The variable cost ratio is computed as variable costs divided by sales revenue:

$$VC_r = \frac{VC}{SR}$$

$$\frac{\text{Variable}}{\text{cost ratio}} = \frac{\text{Variable}}{\text{costs}} \div \frac{\text{Sales}}{\text{revenue.}}$$

This calculation may be made on total dollars ($12,000 ÷ $32,000 = 0.375) or on dollars per unit ($3 ÷ $8 = 0.375). Note that the contribution margin ratio can be computed as 1.000 minus the variable cost ratio (1.000 − 0.375 = 0.625). Of each sales dollar received by Benchmark, 37.5 percent goes to cover variable costs and 62.5 percent goes to cover fixed costs and provide for a profit.

COST-VOLUME-PROFIT RELATIONSHIPS

A **cost-volume-profit graph** illustrates the relationships between volume, total revenues, total costs, and profit. Its usefulness comes from its depicting revenue and cost relationships over a range of activity, rather than only at selected volumes. Although less precise than quantitative schedules, this representation of an organization's revenues and costs allows management to view the relative amount of important variables at any graphed volume without making computations. A comparison of graphs illlustrating the costs, revenues, and profits of alternative products or production procedures assists management in selecting the most desirable product or method of operation.

The Benchmark Card Company's cost-volume-profit graph is presented in Exhibit 4–2. Total revenues and total costs are measured on the vertical axis, and volume of activity is measured in units on the horizontal axis. Separate lines are drawn for total costs and total revenues. When total costs exceed total revenues, losses occur, and when total revenues exceed total costs, profits occur. The amount of profit or loss at a given volume is depicted by the vertical distance between the total revenue and the total cost lines. The **break-even point** occurs at the unit or dollar sales volume where total revenues equal total costs. Graphically, this happens when the total revenue and total cost lines intersect.

Before developing a cost-volume-profit graph, it is necessary to obtain information on the behavior of costs and revenues. The three lines graphed in Exhibit 4–2 are developed as follows:

1. A line representing monthly fixed costs of $15,000 is drawn parallel to the horizontal axis. The distance between the horizontal axis and this line depicts Benchmark's monthly fixed costs.

2. Variable costs are layered on top of fixed costs to obtain total costs. To draw this line, it is necessary to determine total costs at some selected volume.

EXHIBIT 4–2   Typical Cost-Volume-Profit Graph

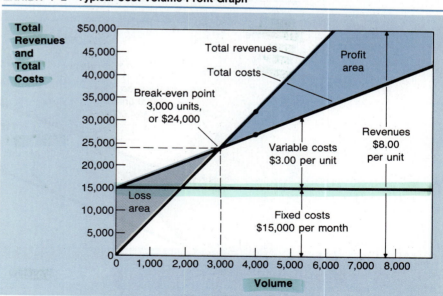

At 4,000 units Benchmark's total costs are $27,000 [$15,000 + ($3 × 4,000)]. This point is plotted on the graph, and a straight line is drawn through it and the point where the fixed cost line intersects the vertical axis. The distance between the total cost line and the fixed cost line represents Benchmark's variable costs at each level of production.

3. A straight line depicting total revenues is drawn through the origin and a point representing total revenues at some selected volume. At 4,000 units Benchmark's total revenues are $32,000 ($8 × 4,000). The distance between the total revenue line and the horizontal axis represents Benchmark's total revenues at each level of sales.

A widely used variation of the cost-volume-profit graph is presented in Exhibit 4–3. Here a line is drawn first for variable costs with fixed costs layered on top of variable costs to obtain total costs. By layering fixed costs on top of variable costs, this graph emphasizes the contribution margin available to cover fixed costs and to provide for a profit. The contribution margin is represented by the vertical distance between the total revenue and the total variable cost lines. Up to the break-even point, the entire contribution margin goes to cover fixed costs; at the break-even point, the contribution margin equals the fixed costs; and beyond the break-even point, the contribution margin is large enough to cover fixed costs and provide for a profit.

EXHIBIT 4–3   Cost-Volume-Profit Graph Emphasizing the Contribution Margin

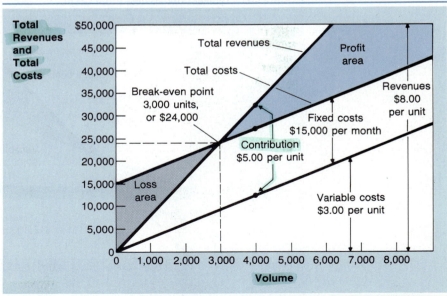

The lines in Exhibit 4–3 are developed in a manner similar to those in Exhibit 4–2. Straight lines are drawn through plotted values at a selected volume and at the appropriate vertical axis intercepts. A useful feature of this second graph is its relationship to the contribution income statement. Compare the contribution income statement in Exhibit 4–1 with the graph in Exhibit 4–3. The income statement is merely a formal presentation of the relationships graphed at 4,000 units. With the graph it is easy to determine income statement amounts at other volumes.

Another variation of the cost-volume-profit graph is shown in Exhibit 4–4. Here total revenues are shown on the horizontal axis as well as on the vertical axis. The objective is to show total costs and the profit or loss at each dollar sales volume. The graph in Exhibit 4–4 is most appropriate for multiple-product firms, where the concept of unit sales volume has less meaning. For single-product firms, or for the purpose of analyzing the cost-volume-profit relationships of an individual product, the graphs in Exhibit 4–2 or 4–3 are preferred because they contain more information (that is, information regarding the unit sales volume) than the graph in Exhibit 4–4.

Determining the Break-even Point

Three approaches are widely used to determine the break-even point: (1) the graphic approach, (2) the formula approach, and (3) the contribution approach. Each is used to determine the break-even point in units or sales dollars.

EXHIBIT 4–4 Cost-Volume-Profit Graph Emphasizing Total Revenues

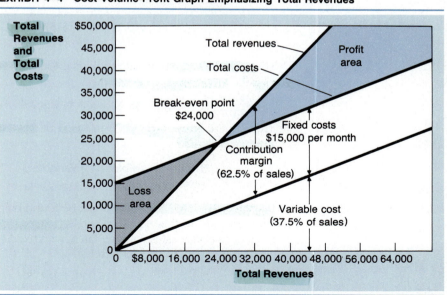

Graphic Approach. The graphic approach involves the graphing of cost-volume-profit relationships. The break-even point in units or sales dollars is then determined by studying the graph. In Exhibits 4–2, 4–3, and 4–4 the break-even point is 3,000 units, or 24,000 sales dollars. The break-even point always occurs where the total revenue and total cost lines intersect.

Formula Approach. The formula approach to determining the break-even point involves the use of the profit formula with profits set equal to zero.

$$\text{Profit} = \left(\begin{matrix}\text{Selling}\\\text{price}\end{matrix} \times \begin{matrix}\text{Unit}\\\text{volume}\end{matrix}\right) - \left[\begin{matrix}\text{Fixed}\\\text{costs}\end{matrix} + \left(\begin{matrix}\text{Variable costs}\\\text{per unit}\end{matrix} \times \begin{matrix}\text{Unit}\\\text{volume}\end{matrix}\right)\right] = 0.$$

With zero profits, total revenues equal total costs.

Total Revenues	Total Costs

$$\begin{matrix}\text{Selling}\\\text{price}\end{matrix} \times \begin{matrix}\text{Unit}\\\text{volume}\end{matrix} = \begin{matrix}\text{Fixed}\\\text{costs}\end{matrix} + \left(\begin{matrix}\text{Variable costs}\\\text{per unit}\end{matrix} \times \begin{matrix}\text{Unit}\\\text{volume}\end{matrix}\right).$$

The break-even unit volume is now computed by placing prices and costs in this equation and solving for unit volume. Let X equal the break-even *unit* volume. Then, with a selling price of $8 per box, variable costs of $3 per box, and fixed costs of $15,000 per month:

$$\$8X = \$15,000 + \$3X.$$

Solving for X:

$$\$8X - \$3X = \$15,000$$
$$\$5X = \$15,000$$
$$X = \$15,000/\$5$$
$$= 3,000 \text{ units.}$$

The break-even point in sales dollars is found by multiplying the unit selling price by the break-even unit volume:

$$\$8 \times 3,000 = \$24,000.$$

Alternatively, the break-even point in terms of sales dollars can be found using the variable cost ratio:

$$\begin{matrix}\text{Total}\\\text{revenues}\end{matrix} = \begin{matrix}\text{Fixed}\\\text{costs}\end{matrix} + \left(\begin{matrix}\text{Variable}\\\text{cost ratio}\end{matrix} \times \begin{matrix}\text{Total}\\\text{revenue}\end{matrix}\right).$$

The break-even dollar sales volume can be found by placing fixed costs and the variable cost ratio in this equation and solving for total revenues. Let X equal the break-even *dollar* sales volume. Then, with fixed costs of $15,000 per month and a variable cost ratio of 37.5 percent,

$$X = \$15,000 + 0.375X.$$

Solving for X:

$$X - 0.375X = \$15,000$$
$$0.625X = \$15,000$$
$$X = \$15,000/0.625$$
$$= \$24,000.$$

Contribution Approach. Focusing on the final computation in the formula approach provides a third approach to determining the break-even unit or dollar sales volume. With fixed costs of \$15,000 and a unit contribution margin of \$5, the unit break-even point was computed as

$$\frac{\$15,000}{\$5} = 3,000 \text{ units.}$$

The unit break-even volume indicates the number of unit contribution margins needed to cover the fixed costs. With fixed costs of \$15,000 and a \$5 unit contribution margin, 3,000 unit contribution margins are required to break even. In general,

$$BE_u = \frac{FC}{uC_M}$$

$$\frac{\text{Break-even point}}{\text{in units}} = \frac{\text{Fixed costs}}{\text{Unit contribution margin}}.$$

In sales dollars, the break-even point was found as follows:

$$\frac{\$15,000}{0.625} = \$24,000,$$

$$CM_r = 1 - VC_r$$

where 0.625 is the contribution margin ratio. Recall that the contribution margin ratio is one minus the variable cost ratio.

To contribute \$15,000 to cover fixed costs, a total revenue of \$24,000 is required. This is verified as follows:

$$\$24,000 \times 0.625 = \$15,000.$$

In general,

$$BE_\$ = \frac{FC}{CM_r}$$

$$\frac{\text{Break-even point}}{\text{in sales dollars}} = \frac{\text{Fixed costs}}{\text{Contribution margin ratio}}.$$

Profit Planning

Cost-volume-profit relationships are used to determine profit or loss at any specified level of activity. The Benchmark Card Company, for example, anticipates a profit of \$5,000 at a sales volume of 4,000 units, or 32,000 sales dollars. Using the graphs in Exhibits 4–2, 4–3, and 4–4, observe that a volume of 1,000 units, or 8,000 sales dollars, should result in a loss of \$10,000.

Margin of Safety. The **margin of safety** is the excess of actual or budgeted sales over break-even sales. Expressed in units or sales dollars, the margin of safety indicates the amount that sales could decline before losses occur. The

Benchmark Card Company's margin of safety for October 19x7 is 1,000 units, or $8,000.

	Units	Sales Dollars
Anticipated sales	4,000	$32,000
Break-even sales	−3,000	−24,000
Margin of safety	1,000	$ 8,000

Activity Planning. Establishing profit objectives is an important part of planning in for-profit organizations. Profit objectives are determined in many ways. They can be set at a percentage of last year's profits, at a percentage of total assets at the start of the current year, or at a percentage of average owner's equity over some past period. They might be based on a profit trend, or they might be expressed as a percent of sales. The economic outlook for the firm's products and anticipated changes in products, costs, and technology are also considered in establishing profit objectives.

Before incorporating profit plans into a detailed budget, it is useful to obtain some preliminary information on the feasibility of profit plans. Cost-volume-profit analysis is one way of doing this. By manipulating cost-volume-profit relationships, management can determine the sales volume required to obtain a desired profit. Management would then evaluate the feasibility of this sales volume. If the profit plans are feasible, a complete budget might be developed for this activity level. The required sales volume may be infeasible because of market conditions or because the required volume exceeds production capacity, in which case management might lower its profit objective or consider other ways of achieving it. Alternatively, the required sales volume might be less than management believes the firm is capable of producing and selling, in which case management would raise its profit objective.

Assume Benchmark's management desires to know the unit sales volume required to achieve a monthly profit of $12,000. Using the formula approach, the required unit sales volume is determined by setting profits equal to $12,000 and solving for X, the *unit* sales volume:

$$
\begin{aligned}
\text{Profit} &= \text{Revenues} - \text{Costs} \\
\$12{,}000 &= \$8X - (\$15{,}000 + \$3X) \\
\$8X - \$3X &= \$15{,}000 + \$12{,}000 \\
X &= (\$15{,}000 + \$12{,}000)/\$5 \\
&= 5{,}400 \text{ units.}
\end{aligned}
$$

The required dollar sales volume is found by multiplying 5,400 units times the unit selling price:

$$
\$8 \times 5{,}400 = \$43{,}200.
$$

Alternatively, the dollar sales volume required to achieve a monthly profit of $12,000 can be found using the profit formula with the variable cost ratio:

$$\$12,000 = X - (\$15,000 + 0.375X)$$
$$X - 0.375X = \$15,000 + \$12,000$$
$$X = (\$15,000 + \$12,000)/0.625$$
$$= \$43,200,$$

where X equals the dollar sales volume.

Once again, the final computation in the formula approach provides a contribution approach to determining the required unit or dollar sales volume. The alternative computations using the contribution approach are shown below.

	Volume required to achieve a desired profit	
	X = Units	**X = Sales dollars**
In general:		
$X =$	$\dfrac{\text{Fixed costs} + \text{Desired profit}}{\text{Unit contribution margin}}$	$\dfrac{\text{Fixed costs} + \text{Desired profit}}{\text{Contribution margin ratio}}$
For Benchmark:		
$X =$	$\dfrac{\$15,000 + \$12,000}{\$5}$	$\dfrac{\$15,000 + \$12,000}{0.625}$
$=$	5,400 units	$43,200

In units the contribution approach indicated the number of physical units of production and sales needed to cover the fixed costs and provide the desired profit. In sales dollars the contribution approach indicated the total sales revenue required to provide a total contribution equal to the fixed costs and the desired profit.

The Impact of Income Taxes. Income taxes are imposed on individuals and for-profit organizations by units of government. The amount of an individual's or an organization's income tax is determined by laws that specify the calculation of taxable income (the income subject to tax) and the calculation of the amount of tax on taxable income. Income taxes are computed as a percentage of taxable income with increases in taxable income usually subject to progressively higher tax rates. The laws governing the computation of taxable income differ in many ways from the accounting principles and standards that guide the computation of accounting income. Consequently, taxable income and accounting income are seldom the same.

In the *early stages* of profit planning, income taxes are sometimes incorporated into an organization's cost-volume-profit model by assuming that taxable income and accounting income are equal and that the tax rate is constant. Although these assumptions are seldom true, they are useful because they assist management in developing an early prediction of the sales volume required to earn a desired after-tax profit. Once management has developed a general plan, this early prediction should be refined with the advice of tax experts.

Assuming income taxes are imposed at a constant rate per dollar of before-tax profit, income taxes are computed as before-tax profit multiplied by the tax rate. An organization's after-tax profit is equal to its before-tax profit minus income taxes:

$$\frac{\text{After-tax}}{\text{profit}} = \frac{\text{Before-tax}}{\text{profit}} - \left(\frac{\text{Before-tax}}{\text{profit}} \times \frac{\text{Tax}}{\text{rate}}\right).$$

After-tax profit can also be expressed as before-tax profit times 1 minus the tax rate.

$$\frac{\text{After-tax}}{\text{profit}} = \frac{\text{Before-tax}}{\text{profit}} \times \left(1 - \frac{\text{Tax}}{\text{rate}}\right).$$

This formula can be rearranged to isolate before-tax profit as follows:

$$\frac{\text{Before-tax}}{\text{profit}} = \frac{\text{After-tax profit}}{(1 - \text{Tax rate})}.$$

Since all costs and revenues in the profit formula are expressed on a before-tax basis, the most straightforward way of determining the volume required to earn a desired after-tax profit is to

1. Determine the required before-tax profit,
2. Substitute the required before-tax profit into the profit formula,
3. Solve for the required volume using the formula or the contribution approach.

Assume that the Benchmark Card Company is subject to a 40 percent tax rate, and that management desires to earn a November 19x7 after-tax profit of $12,000. The required before-tax profit is readily determined to be $20,000:

$$\frac{\text{Required before-}}{\text{tax profit}} = \frac{\$12,000}{1 - 0.40}$$

$$= \$20,000.$$

Using the contribution approach, a sales volume of 7,000 units or $56,000 is required to earn a before-tax profit of $20,000, shown as follows.

	Volume required to achieve a before-tax profit	
	X = Units	**X = Sales dollars**
In general:		
$X = $	$\dfrac{\text{Fixed costs} + \text{Before-tax profit}}{\text{Unit contribution margin}}$	$\dfrac{\text{Fixed costs} + \text{Before-tax profit}}{\text{Contribution margin ratio}}$
For Benchmark:		
$X = $	$\dfrac{\$15{,}000 + \$20{,}000}{\$5}$	$\dfrac{\$15{,}000 + \$20{,}000}{0.625}$
=	7,000 units	$56,000

It is apparent that *income taxes increase the sales volume required to earn a desired after-tax profit.* A 40 percent tax rate increased the sales volume required for Benchmark to earn a profit of $12,000 from 5,400 to 7,000 units, or from $43,200 to $56,000. These amounts are verified in Exhibit 4–5.

Sensitivity Analysis   **Sensitivity analysis** is the study of the responsiveness of a model's dependent variable(s) to changes in one or more of the model's independent variables. It is often applied to an organization's cost-volume-profit model to determine how profits or some other variable will respond to some proposed change. Managers are particularly interested in performing sensitivity analysis on those variables

EXHIBIT 4–5   Contribution Income Statement with Income Taxes

Benchmark Card Company
Contribution Income Statement
Planned for the month of November, 19x7

Sales (7,000 × $8)		$56,000
Less variable costs:		
Cost of goods sold (7,000 × $2.00)	$14,000	
Selling and administrative (7,000 × $1.00)	7,000	−21,000
Contribution margin		$35,000
Less fixed costs:		
Factory overhead	$ 5,000	
Selling and administrative	10,000	−15,000
Income before taxes		$20,000
Income taxes ($20,000 × 0.40)		− 8,000
Net income		$12,000

that are most likely to change. Knowing what will happen to profits if cost or revenue or volume changes assists management in developing contingency plans that can be implemented as soon as an event occurs.

The management of the Benchmark Card Company might, for example, anticipate a decline in sales if the U.S. Post Office announces a December 15 increase in the cost of first class postage. To determine the possible profit impact of this change and to evaluate alternative responses, management would use sensitivity analysis. Possible responses might include doing nothing, instituting an offsetting reduction in selling prices, increasing advertising to encourage potential customers to mail early, lobbying to delay the postage increase, or introducing a new holiday postcard that can be mailed at a lower rate. By analyzing each alternative in advance, management will know what action to initiate if an increase in first class postage is announced.

To offset this increase in postage, management is considering a reduction in selling price from $8 to $7 per box of cards. Management needs to know the number of boxes Benchmark will have to sell at the new, lower price to earn a monthly before-tax profit of $20,000.

The $1 reduction in selling price would reduce the unit contribution margin from $5 to $4 ($7 − $3). With fixed costs of $15,000 the unit sales volume required to earn a before-tax profit of $20,000 is now 8,750:

$$X = \frac{\$15,000 + \$20,000}{\$4}$$

$$= 8,750 \text{ units.}$$

This is an increase of 1,750 units:

Required sales volume at $7 selling price	8,750
Required sales volume at $8 selling price	−7,000
Increase in required sales volume	1,750

PROFIT-VOLUME GRAPHS

In cost-volume-profit graphs, profits are represented by the difference between total revenues and total costs. When management is primarily interested in the impact on profits of changes in sales volume, and less interested in the related revenues and costs, a profit-volume graph is sometimes used instead of a cost-volume-profit graph. A **profit-volume graph** illustrates the relationship between volume and profits; it does not illustrate revenues and costs. A manager primarily interested in profit-volume relationships prefers a profit-volume graph because it clearly illustrates profits. Profits are read directly from a profit-volume graph rather than being computed as the difference between total revenues and total costs.

The Benchmark Card Company's monthly profit-volume graph is presented in Exhibit 4–6. Profit or loss is measured on the vertical axis, and volume is measured in units on the horizontal axis, which intersects the vertical axis at zero profit. A single line, representing total profit, is drawn intersecting the vertical axis at a zero unit sales volume loss equal to the fixed costs. The profit line crosses the horizontal axis at the break-even unit sales volume. The profit or loss at any volume is depicted by the vertical distance between the profit line and the horizontal axis.

The profit line is drawn by determining and plotting profit or loss at two different volumes and then drawing a straight line through the plotted values. Perhaps the easiest values to select are the loss at a volume of zero (this amount is the fixed costs) and the volume at which the profit line crosses the horizontal axis (this is the break-even unit sales volume). It is also possible, using the profit formula, to determine profit or loss at any other volumes. Note that the slope of the profit line is equal to the unit contribution margin, the amount by which profits increase, or losses decrease, as one additional unit is sold.

EXHIBIT 4–6   Typical Profit-Volume Graph

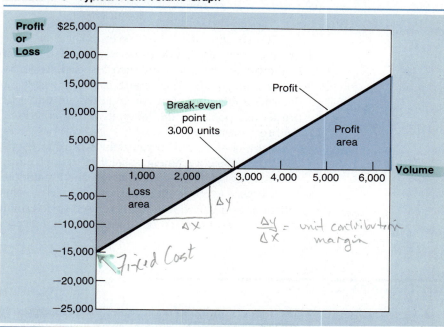

NOT-FOR-PROFIT APPLICATIONS

Cost-volume-profit relationships and related break-even concepts are widely used in not-for-profit organizations. To make these concepts more acceptable in such organizations, they might be renamed "cost-volume-contribution" or "cost-volume-subsidy" relationships. Although managers of not-for-profit organizations are not specifically interested in earning a profit for the organization as a whole, they often desire that some activities provide a positive contribution that can be used to subsidize other activities. Consider the following example.

Martha Montgomery is a candidate for the U.S. House of Representatives. To obtain money to finance her campaign, a fund-raising dinner with a required donation of $100 per plate is scheduled in a rented hall. The costs of renting and decorating the hall are $3,000. The variable cost of each meal served is $30. The total contribution to Martha Montgomery's campaign can be expressed as a function of the number of persons who attend the dinner. Substituting desired contribution for desired profits, campaign organizers can determine the number of tickets they must sell to net $25,000 from the dinner:

$$\frac{\text{Required number}}{\text{of tickets}} = \frac{\text{Fixed costs} + \text{Desired contribution}}{\text{Donation per unit} - \text{Variable costs per unit}}$$

$$= \frac{\$3,000 + \$25,000}{\$100 - \$30}$$

$$= 400 \text{ tickets.}$$

The concept of the break-even point is also widely used in not-for-profit organizations. The Student Association of City University may be interested in the break-even point for such association-sponsored activities as concerts, festivals, and plays. They could also use cost-volume-profit relationships to determine the amount of any required subsidy if ticket sales fall short of the break-even point, or the amount of any contribution if ticket sales exceed the break-even point.

Many not-for-profit organizations provide goods or services for less than cost: The U.S. government subsidizes school lunches, civic orchestras stage children's concerts for a nominal fee, and the tuition charged by most colleges is inadequate to cover operating costs. Here cost-volume-profit relationships (or variations of the profit formula) are used to determine the required subsidy, or the activity level that can be supported with a given subsidy.

LIMITING ASSUMPTIONS

The models and graphs presented in this chapter are subject to a number of limiting assumptions. Although these assumptions do not negate the usefulness of these models in the early stages of planning, they do suggest the need for further analysis before plans are completed. This additional analysis is normally reflected in an organization's budget for a coming period. Among the more important assumptions are:

1. *All costs are classified as fixed or variable.* Step costs must be approximated by fixed or mixed costs, and mixed costs must be broken down into their fixed and variable cost elements.

2. *The total cost function is linear.* This assumption may be valid only within a relevant range. Over the entire range of possible volumes, changes in productivity and efficiency are likely to result in a curvilinear cost function.

3. *The total revenue function is linear.* Unit selling prices are assumed to be constant over the entire range of possible volumes. This implies a purely competitive market for final products. In some economic models (monopolistic and oligopolistic), where the demand for a product responds to price changes, the revenue function is curvilinear. In these situations the linear approximation is accurate only within a limited range of activity.

4. *The analysis is for a single product or the sales mix of multiple products is constant.* The sales mix refers to the relative portion of unit or dollar sales that is derived from each product or service. If multiple products have different unit costs or revenues, changes in the sales mix will cause changes in the slopes of total revenue or cost lines, or both. Changes in the sales mix are examined in Appendix B to this chapter.

5. *Inventories are constant.* This assumption means that all current expenditures for acquiring or producing inventories are reported as expenses on the current income statement. In the absence of this assumption, current manufacturing or inventory acquisition costs can be greater or less than the expenses reported on the income statement. This assumption, which was discussed at the beginning of this chapter, is examined further in Chapter 10.

SUMMARY

Cost-volume-profit analysis is used to examine the relationships among volume, total costs, total revenues, and profit. Because cost-volume-profit analysis provides a framework for discussing planning issues and organizing relevant data, it is widely used in the early stages of planning.

We illustrated the usefulness of this technique in determining the break-even point, the margin of safety, and the volume required to earn a desired profit with and without income taxes. In all these applications we used either the unit contribution margin or the contribution margin ratio. The unit contribution margin is the difference between the unit selling price and the unit variable costs. The contribution margin ratio is the ratio of contribution margin to sales dollars. In making short-run decisions managers should think in terms of these concepts. We will use them frequently in subsequent chapters.

APPENDIX A
OPERATING LEVERAGE

Operating leverage is a measure of the responsiveness of income to changes in sales. An organization's operating leverage at a *given sales volume* is computed as contribution margin divided by net income.

$$\text{Operating leverage} = \frac{\text{Contribution margin}}{\text{Net income}}$$

$$OL = \frac{CM\text{\#}}{NI}$$

Information regarding a firm's operating leverage can be used to assist in profit planning. Multiplying a proposed percentage change in sales by a firm's operating leverage indicates the percentage effect the proposed change will have on income.

$$\frac{\text{Percentage change}}{\text{in income}} = \frac{\text{Percentage change}}{\text{in sales}} \times \frac{\text{Operating}}{\text{leverage}}$$

Recall that the Benchmark Card Company manufactures a product that has a unit selling price of $8, variable costs of $3, and monthly fixed costs of $15,000. At a monthly volume of 4,000 units, Benchmark has a contribution margin of $20,000 [($8 − $3) × 4,000] and realizes an income of $5,000 ($20,000 − $15,000). At this sales volume, Benchmark's operating leverage is 4 ($20,000 contribution margin/$5,000 income).

With an operating leverage of 4, a 37.5 percent increase in sales, from 4,000 to 5,500 units, should result in a 150 percent increase in income:

$$\frac{\text{Percentage change}}{\text{in income}} = 37.5\% \times 4$$

$$= \underline{150\%}$$

With an increase in income of $7,500 ($5,000 × 1.50) Benchmark's monthly profits would be $12,500 ($5,000 current + $7,500 increase), as verified below.

	Current 4,000 Units	Increase 1,500 Units	New 5,500 Units
Sales ($8 per unit)	$32,000	$12,000	$44,000
Variable costs ($3 per unit)	−12,000	− 4,500	−16,500
Contribution margin	$20,000	$ 7,500	$27,500
Fixed costs	−15,000	− 0	−15,000
Net income	$ 5,000	$ 7,500	$12,500

The difference between contribution margin and net income, fixed costs, is a constant. Because of this mathematical relationship, net income constitutes a larger portion of contribution margin as sales volume increases. This dispro-portionate increase in net income, as sales volume increases, produces a decrease in operating leverage, computed as the ratio of contribution margin to net income. The numerator, contribution margin, changes at a slower rate than the denominator, net income.

Because operating leverage varies with sales volume, it is important to specify both operating leverage and a corresponding sales volume. If, for exam-ple, the current sales volume was 5,000 units and management was contem-plating the effect of a 10 percent increase in sales to 5,500 units, it would be inappropriate to use an operating leverage of 4 to predict the effect of the increased sales on profits. At 5,000 units the operating leverage is 2.5 ($25,000 contribution margin/$10,000 net income). If sales increase by 10 percent, profits will increase by 25 percent (10 percent increase in sales × 2.5 operating leverage), or $2,500 ($10,000 × 0.25), not by 40 percent (10 percent increase in sales × 4 operating leverage).

At the break-even point, where profits are zero, operating leverage is unde-fined because division by zero is undefined. Operating leverage is highest *near* the break-even point, where a percentage change in sales has the greatest per-centage effect on profits. As demonstrated above for the Benchmark Card Com-pany, the absolute value of operating leverage is lower at sales volumes farther from the break-even volume.

In addition to its use in profit planning, operating leverage is also used as an indication of an organization's cost structure. The higher the portion of an organization's fixed costs (in comparison with variable costs), the higher its operating leverage. In evaluating different firms and alternative ways of pro-ducing goods or providing services, information of operating leverage is useful in determining the sensitivity of income to changes in sales. The higher a firm's operating leverage, the more sensitive are its profits to changes in sales volume. Consider the following example.

The High Fixed Card Company manufactures a product that has a unit selling price of $8, variable costs of $1.50, and monthly fixed costs of $21,000. At a monthly volume of 4,000 units, High Fixed has a contribution of $26,000 [($8.00 − $1.50) × 4,000] and a before-tax profit of $5,000 ($26,000 − $21,000). Although High Fixed and Benchmark have identical profits at a monthly sales volume of 4,000 units, High Fixed's profits are more sensitive to changes in sales. This higher sensitivity can be determined by comparing Benchmark's and High Fixed's operating leverages:

	High Fixed	Benchmark
Contribution margin	$26,000	$20,000
Net income	÷5,000	÷5,000
Operating leverage	5.2	4.0

High Fixed's higher operating leverage results from its greater use of resources that have fixed costs (its fixed costs are $21,000, whereas Benchmark's are only $15,000).

If monthly sales increase by 12.5 percent to 4,500 units, High Fixed's profits will increase more than Benchmark's:

	High Fixed	Benchmark
Percentage change in sales	12.5%	12.5%
Operating leverage	×5.2	×4.0
Percentage change in profits	65.0%	50.0%

Conversely, if monthly sales decrease, High Fixed's profits will decrease more than Benchmark's.

In addition to helping management plan for the future, investors use information on operating leverage to predict how businesses will perform in different economic conditions. Given their cost structures, High Fixed will perform better during periods of economic growth, whereas Benchmark will perform better during periods of economic contraction. With information on operating leverage and predictions of future economic activity, investors are better able to make sound investment decisions.

APPENDIX B
SALES MIX ANALYSIS

Sales mix refers to the relative portion of unit or dollar sales that are derived from each product. One of the limiting assumptions of the basic cost-volume-profit model is that the analysis is for a single product or the sales mix is constant. When the sales mix is constant, managers of multiple-product organizations can use the average unit contribution margin, or the average contribution margin ratio, to determine the break-even point or the sales volume required to earn a desired profit. Often, however, management is interested in the effect of a change in the sales mix, rather than in the effect of a change in the sales volume at a constant mix. In this situation it is necessary to determine either the average unit contribution margin or the average contribution margin ratio for each alternative mix.

Unit Sales Analysis   Assume the Benchmark Card Company sells two kinds of greeting cards, Deluxe and Regular. At a 1:1 (one-to-one) unit sales mix, where Benchmark sells one box of Regular cards for every box of Deluxe cards, the following revenue and cost information is available:

	Deluxe Box	Regular Box	Average Box
Unit selling price	$12.00	$4.00	$8.00
Unit variable costs	− 3.00	−3.00	−3.00
Unit contribution margin	$ 9.00	$1.00	$5.00*
Fixed costs per month			$15,000

* At a 1:1 unit sales mix, 50 percent of the units are Deluxe and 50 percent of the units are Regular; hence, the average unit contribution margin is $5.00 [($9.00 × 0.50) + ($1.00 × 0.50)].

Benchmark's current monthly break-even sales volume is 3,000 units ($15,000/$5), consisting of 1,500 boxes of Deluxe cards and 1,500 boxes of Regular cards.

Product	Total Sales (Units)		Sales Mix (Units)		Product Sales (Units)
Deluxe cards	3,000	×	0.50	=	1,500
Regular cards	3,000	×	0.50	=	1,500

The current unit sales mix is represented by the top line in Exhibit 4–7.

EXHIBIT 4–7   Sales Mix Analysis: Unit Sales Approach

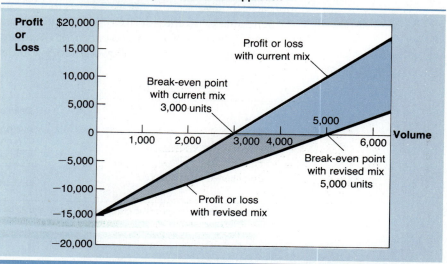

Benchmark's management wants to know what the break-even unit sales volume would be if the unit sales mix became $1:3$, that is, 25 percent Deluxe and 75 percent Regular. There are no changes in prices or costs.

At the revised mix the average unit contribution margin would be $3 per box [($9 × 0.25) + ($1 × 0.75)], and the break-even unit sales volume would be 5,000 units ($15,000/$3), consisting of 1,250 boxes of Deluxe cards and 3,750 boxes of Regular cards.

Product	Total Sales (Units)		Sales Mix (Units)		Product Sales (Units)
Deluxe cards	5,000	×	0.25	=	1,250
Regular cards	5,000	×	0.75	=	3,750

The revised mix is represented by the bottom line in Exhibit 4–7. The effect of the shift in the mix would be to increase the break-even unit sales volume. This occurs because a greater portion of the unit sales in the revised mix comes from Regular cards, which have a lower unit contribution margin.

Sales Dollar Analysis

The preceding analysis focused on unit sales and the unit contribution margin. The sales mix was expressed in terms of units. An alternative approach is to focus on dollar sales and the unit contribution margin ratio. Following this approach, the sales mix is expressed in terms of sales dollars.

Benchmark currently derives 75 percent of its sales revenue from Deluxe cards and 25 percent of its sales revenue from Regular cards. At a current monthly sales volume of $32,000, the following information is available:

	Deluxe	Regular	Total
Sales	$24,000	$8,000	$32,000
Less variable costs	− 6,000	−6,000	−12,000
Contribution margin	$18,000	$2,000	$20,000
Contribution margin ratio	0.75	0.25	0.625*

* At a sales dollar mix consisting of 75 percent Deluxe and 25 percent Regular, the overall contribution margin ratio is 0.625 [(0.75 Deluxe contribution margin ratio × 0.75 Deluxe sales dollars) + (0.25 Regular contribution margin ratio × 0.25 Regular sales dollars)].

With fixed costs of $15,000 per month, Benchmark's current monthly break-even dollar sales volume is $24,000 ($15,000/0.625), consisting of $18,000 from Deluxe card sales and $6,000 from Regular card sales.

Product	Break-even Sales (Dollars)		Sales Mix (Dollars)		Product Sales (Dollars)
Deluxe cards	$24,000	×	0.75	=	$18,000
Regular cards	$24,000	×	0.25	=	$ 6,000

The current unit sales mix is represented by the top line in Exhibit 4–8.

Benchmark's management wants to know what the break-even dollar sales volume would be if the dollar sales mix became 30 percent Deluxe and 70 percent Regular. There are no changes in prices or costs.

At the revised mix, the average contribution margin ratio would be 0.40 [(0.75 Deluxe contribution margin ratio × 0.30 Deluxe sales dollars) + (0.25 Regular contribution margin ratio × 0.70 Regular sales dollars)], and the break-even dollar sales volume would be $37,500 ($15,000/0.40), consisting of $11,250 from Deluxe cards and $26,250 from Regular cards.

EXHIBIT 4–8   Sales Mix Analysis: Sales Dollar Approach

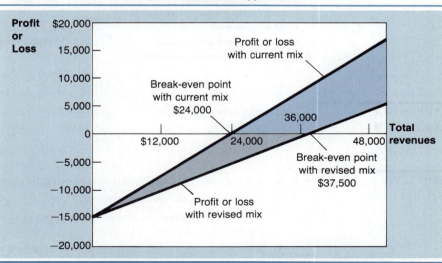

Product	Total Sales (Dollars)		Sales Mix (Dollars)		Product Sales (Dollars)
Deluxe cards	$37,500	×	0.30	=	$11,250
Regular cards	$37,500	×	0.70	=	$26,250

The revised mix is represented by the bottom line in Exhibit 4–8. The effect of the shift in the mix would be to increase the break-even dollar sales volume. This occurs because a greater portion of the sales revenue in the revised mix comes from Regular cards, which have a lower contribution margin ratio.

Sales mix analysis is an interesting and important topic in multiple-product firms. Management must be just as concerned with the mix of product sales as they are with the total unit or dollar volume of sales. A shift in the sales mix can lead to unexpected results. Profits may decline with an increase in unit or dollar sales if the sales mix shifts to products with smaller contribution margins. Conversely, profits may increase even though unit or dollar sales decrease, if the sales mix shifts to products with larger contribution margins. Other things being equal, management should strive to increase sales of products that have higher contribution margins.

KEY TERMS

Break-even point
Contribution income statement
Contribution margin
Contribution margin ratio
Cost-volume-profit analysis
Cost-volume-profit graph
Functional income statement

Margin of safety
Profit-volume graph
Sales mix
Sensitivity analysis
Unit contribution margin
Variable cost ratio

APPENDIX KEY TERM

Operating leverage

REVIEW QUESTIONS

4–1   At what stage of planning is cost-volume-profit analysis particularly useful? Why?

4–2   Present the profit equation in detail.

4–3   Why is a contribution income statement superior to a functional income statement for planning and control purposes?

4–4   What is the unit contribution margin? What does it tell us?

4–5   Distinguish between the contribution margin ratio and the variable cost ratio.

4–6 Using the contribution approach, how is the unit break-even point computed? In words, what does it tell us?

4–7 Using the contribution approach, how is the break-even dollar sales volume computed?

4–8 Using the contribution approach, how do we determine the unit sales volume required to earn a desired profit?

4–9 Using the contribution approach, how do we determine the dollar sales volume required to earn a desired profit?

4–10 What assumptions are made when income taxes are incorporated into cost-volume-profit models?

4–11 Given a desired after-tax profit and a tax rate, how do we determine the desired before-tax profit?

4–12 Why is sensitivity analysis often applied to an organization's cost-volume-profit model?

4–13 Why do some managers prefer profit-volume graphs to cost-volume-profit graphs?

4–14 Name three uses of cost-volume-profit models in not-for-profit organizations.

4–15 Name five assumptions that limit the usefulness of cost-volume-profit models.

REVIEW PROBLEM

Income Statements and Cost-Volume-Profit Analysis

The Memorabilia Cup Company produces keepsake beverage containers for educational institutions that are sold for $40 per box of 50 containers. Variable and fixed costs are shown below:

Variable Costs per Box		Fixed Costs per Month	
Manufacturing:			
Direct materials	$15	Factory overhead	$15,000
Direct labor	3	Selling and	
Factory overhead	10	administrative	10,000
Total manufacturing	$28	Total fixed	$25,000
Selling and			
administrative	2		
Total variable	$30		

In September 19x3, Memorabilia produced and sold 3,000 boxes.

Requirements

a) Prepare a functional income statement for September.

b) Prepare a contribution income statement for September.

c) Determine Memorabilia's unit contribution margin and contribution margin ratio.

d) Determine Memorabilia's monthly break-even point in units.

e) Determine the dollar sales volume required to produce a monthly profit of $5,000. Ignore taxes.

f) Assuming Memorabilia is subject to a 40 percent income tax, determine the monthly unit sales volume required to produce a monthly after-tax profit of $4,500.

The solution to this problem is found at the end of the Chapter 4 exercises and problems.

EXERCISES

4–1 Functional and Contribution Income Statements

The Central Ohio Company produces a product that is sold for $15 per unit. Variable and fixed costs are shown below.

Variable Costs per Unit			Fixed Costs per Month	
Manufacturing:			Factory overhead	$20,000
Direct materials	$5		Selling and	
Direct labor	2		administrative	10,000
Factory overhead	2	$ 9	Total	$30,000
Selling and				
administrative		3		
Total		$12		

The company produced and sold 12,000 units during July of 19x1. There were no beginning or ending inventories.

Requirements

a) Prepare functional and contribution income statements for July.

b) Which of these income statements is more useful to management? Why?

c) Compute the unit contribution margin, and use it to determine the impact on profit of a 600 unit decrease in sales.

d) Compute the contribution margin ratio, and use it to determine the impact on profit of a $12,000 increase in sales revenue.

4–2 Functional and Contribution Income Statements

The Alberta Company produces a product that is sold for $50 per unit. Variable and fixed costs are shown below.

Variable Costs per Unit			Fixed Costs per Month	
Manufacturing:			Factory overhead	$40,000
Direct materials	$ 8		Selling and	
Direct labor	12		administrative	20,000
Factory overhead	10	$30	Total	$60,000
Selling and				
administrative		5		
Total		$35		

The company produced and sold 6,000 units during May 19x3. There were no beginning or ending inventories.

Requirements

a) Prepare functional and contribution income statements for May.

b) Explain why gross profit in the functional income statement differs from contribution margin in the contribution income statement.

c) Compute the unit contribution margin, and use it to determine the impact on profit of a 200 unit increase in sales.

d) Compute the contribution margin ratio, and use it to determine the impact on profit of a $10,000 increase in sales revenue.

4–3 Contribution Margin Concepts

At a price of $12 the estimated monthly sales of a product is 10,000 units. Variable costs include manufacturing, $6, and distribution, $1. Fixed costs are $24,000 per month.

Requirements

Determine each of the following:

a) Unit contribution margin.

b) Monthly break-even unit sales volume.

c) Monthly profit. (Ignore taxes.)

d) Monthly margin of safety in units.

4–4 Contribution Margin Concepts

At a monthly volume of $20,000 a company incurs variable costs of $8,000 and fixed costs of $9,000.

Requirements

Determine each of the following:

a) Variable cost ratio.

b) Contribution margin ratio.

c) Monthly break-even dollar sales volume.

d) Monthly margin of safety in dollars.

4–5 Contribution Margin Concepts

In 19x5 the Duke Art Shop had the following experience:

	Fixed	Variable	
Sales			$800,000
Costs:			
Goods sold		$300,000	
Labor	$160,000	60,000	
Supplies	2,000	5,000	
Utilities	12,000	3,000	
Rent	24,000	—	
Advertising	6,000	2,000	
Miscellaneous	6,000	10,000	
Total costs	$210,000	$380,000	−590,000
Net income			$210,000

Requirements

a) Determine the annual break-even dollar sales volume.

b) Determine the current margin of safety in dollars.

c) What is the annual break-even dollar sales volume if management makes a decision that increases fixed costs by $52,500?

4–6 Cost-Volume-Profit Graphs with Sensitivity Analysis

Presented is a typical cost-volume-profit graph.

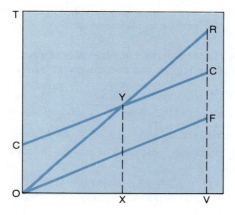

Requirements

a) Identify each of the following:

    1. Line OF.

    2. Line OR.

    3. Line CC.

    4. The difference between lines OF and OV.

    5. The difference between lines CC and OF.

    6. The difference between lines CC and OV.

    7. The difference between lines OR and OF.

    8. Point X.

    9. Area CYO.

    10. Area RCY.

b) Indicate the effect of each of the following independent events on lines CC, OR, and the break-even point:

    1. A decrease in fixed costs.

    2. An increase in the unit selling price.

3. An increase in unit variable costs.

4. An increase in fixed costs and a decrease in the unit selling price.

5. A decrease in fixed costs and a decrease in the unit variable costs.

4–7 Preparing Cost-Volume-Profit Graphs

Little Nero's Pizza Shop has the following monthly revenue and cost functions.

$$\text{Total revenues} = \$6.00X,$$

$$\text{Total costs} = \$9,000 + \$1.50X.$$

Requirements

a) Prepare a graph, similar to that in Exhibit 4–2, illustrating Little Nero's cost-volume-profit relationships. The vertical axis should vary between $0 and $18,000, with increments of $3,000. The horizontal axis should vary between 0 units and 3,000 units, with increments of 500 units.

b) Prepare a graph, similar to that in Exhibit 4–3, illustrating Little Nero's cost-volume-profit relationships. Use the same scale for the graph as in requirement (a).

c) What does the graph prepared for requirement (b) emphasize?

d) Prepare a graph, similar to that in Exhibit 4–4, illustrating Little Nero's cost-volume-profit relationships. Use the same scale for the graph as in requirement (a). Be sure to label the horizontal axis in dollars.

e) What is the objective of the graph in requirement (d)? When is it most appropriate to use this type of graph?

4–8 Preparing Cost-Volume-Profit Graphs

The Mountain View Custard Shop has the following monthly revenue and cost functions:

$$\text{Total revenues} = \$1.25X,$$

$$\text{Total costs} = \$3,000 + \$0.75X.$$

Requirements

a) Prepare a graph, similar to that in Exhibit 4–2, illustrating Mountain View's cost-volume-profit relationships. The vertical axis should vary between $0 and $12,500 in increments of $2,500. The horizontal axis should vary between 0 and 10,000 units in increments of 2,000 units.

b) Prepare a graph, similar to that in Exhibit 4–3, illustrating Mountain View's cost-volume-profit relationships. Use the same scale for the graph as in requirement (a).

c) What does the graph prepared for requirement (b) emphasize?

d) Prepare a graph, similar to that in Exhibit 4–4, illustrating Mountain View's cost-volume-profit relationships. Be sure to label the horizontal axis in dollars.

e) What is the objective of the graph in requirement (d)? When is it most appropriate to use this type of graph?

4–9 Profit Planning with Taxes

In 19x5 the Fenwick Processing Company had the following income statement:

Sales		$950,000
Variable costs:		
Variable cost of goods sold	$420,000	
Variable selling and administrative expenses	150,000	−570,000
Contribution margin		$380,000
Fixed costs:		
Fixed factory overhead	$110,000	
Fixed selling and administrative expenses	80,000	−190,000
Net income before taxes		$190,000
Income taxes @ 0.36		− 68,400
Net income		$121,600

Requirements

a) Determine the 19x5 break-even point in sales dollars.

b) Determine the 19x5 margin of safety in sales dollars.

c) What is the break-even point in sales dollars if management makes a decision that increases fixed costs by $50,000?

d) What dollar sales volume is required to provide an after-tax net income of $200,000? Assume fixed costs are $190,000.

e) Prepare an abbreviated contribution income statement to verify that the solution to requirement (d) will provide the desired after-tax income.

4–10 Profit Planning with Taxes

The Brown Manufacturing Company produces a product that is sold for $35 per unit. Variable and fixed costs are shown below.

Variable Costs per Unit		Fixed Costs per Year	
Manufacturing	$18	Manufacturing	$ 80,000
Selling and administrative	7	Selling and administrative	30,000
Total	$25	Total	$110,000

Last year Brown manufactured and sold 20,000 units to obtain a net income after taxes of $49,500.

Requirements

a) Determine the tax rate Brown paid last year.

b) What unit sales volume is required to provide an after-tax net income of $88,000?

c) If Brown reduces the unit variable cost by $2.50 and increases fixed manufacturing costs by $20,000, what unit sales volume is required to provide an after-tax income of $88,000?

d) What assumptions are made about taxable income and tax rates in requirements (a) through (c)?

4–11 Profit Planning with Taxes

Pawnee Company operated at normal capacity during the current year producing 40,000 units of its single product. Sales totaled 40,000 units at an average price of $20 per unit. Variable manufacturing costs were $8 per unit, and variable marketing costs were $4 per unit sold. Fixed costs were incurred uniformly throughout the year and amounted to $188,000 for manufacturing and $64,000 for marketing. There was no year-end work-in-process inventory.

Requirements

a) Determine Pawnee's break-even point in sales dollars for the current year.

b) Pawnee is subject to an income tax rate of 30 percent. Determine the number of units required to be sold in the current year to earn an after-tax income of $126,000.

c) Pawnee's variable manufacturing costs are expected to increase 10 percent in the coming year. Determine Pawnee's break-even point in sales dollars for the coming year.

d) Assuming Pawnee's variable manufacturing costs do increase by 10 percent in the coming year, determine the selling price that will yield the current contribution margin ratio in the coming year.

(CMA Adapted)

4–12 Profit-Volume Graph: Identification and Analysis

Presented is a typical profit-volume graph.

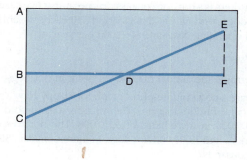

Requirements

a) Identify each of the following:

1. Area BDC.
2. Area DEF.
3. Point D.

4. Line AC.
5. Line BC.
6. Line EF.

b) Indicate the effect of each of the following on line CE and the break-even point.

1. An increase in the unit selling price.
2. An increase in the variable costs per unit.

3. A decrease in fixed costs.

4. An increase in fixed costs and a decrease in the unit selling price.

5. A decrease in fixed costs and an increase in the variable costs per unit.

4–13 Preparing Cost-Volume-Profit and Profit-Volume Graphs

Maritime Petro operates several self-service gas stations in the Maritime Provinces of Canada. Maritime Petro has a selling price of $0.90 per liter. Variable operating costs are $0.70 per liter, and fixed operating costs are $80,000 per month.

Requirements

a) Determine the monthly break-even point in liters.

b) Prepare a cost-volume-profit graph for Maritime Petro. Use a format that emphasizes the contribution margin. The vertical axis should vary between 0 dollars and $540,000 in increments of $90,000. The horizontal axis should vary between 0 liters and 600,000 liters in increments of 100,000 liters. Label the graph in thousands.

c) Prepare a profit-volume graph for Maritime Petro. The vertical axis should vary between $(100,000) and $60,000 in increments of $20,000. The horizontal axis should vary between 0 liters and 600,000 liters in increments of 100,000 liters. Label the graph in thousands.

d) Evaluate the profit-volume graph. In what ways is it superior and in what ways is it inferior to the traditional cost-volume-profit graph?

4–14 Preparing Cost-Volume-Profit and Profit-Volume Graphs

Happy Hawkers is a hot dog concession operator at five baseball stadiums. Happy Hawkers sells hot dogs, with all the fixings, for $1.50 each. Variable costs are $1.20 per hot dog, and fixed operating costs are $150,000 per year.

Requirements

a) Determine the annual break-even point in hot dogs.

b) Prepare a cost-volume-profit graph for Happy Hawkers. Use a form that emphasizes the contribution margin. The vertical axis should vary between 0 dollars and $1,500,000 in increments of $250,000. The horizontal axis should vary between 0 hot dogs and 1,000,000 hot dogs, in increments of 250,000 hot dogs. Label the graph in thousands.

c) Prepare a profit-volume graph for Happy Hawkers. The vertical axis should vary between $(200,000) and $200,000 in increments of $100,000. The horizontal axis should vary as described in requirement (b). Label the graph in thousands.

d) Evaluate the profit-volume graph. In what ways is it superior and in what ways is it inferior to the traditional cost-volume-profit graph?

4–15 Not-for-Profit Applications

Determine the solution to each of the following independent cases.

1. Lakeside College has annual fixed operating costs of $5,000,000 and variable operating costs of $1,000 per student. Tuition is $4,000 per student for the academic year. The projected enrollment for the coming year is 1,500 students. Expected revenues from endowments and federal and state grants are $250,000. Determine the amount Lakeside must obtain from other sources.

2. The Lakeside College Student Association is planning a fall concert. Expected costs of renting a hall, hiring a band, and so forth, are $30,000. Assuming 5,000 persons attend the concert, determine the break-even price per ticket. How much will the association lose if this price is charged and only 4,250 tickets are sold?

3. City Hospital has a contract with the city to provide indigent health care on an out-patient basis for $25 per visit. The patient will pay $5 of this amount, and the city will pay the balance of $20. Determine the amount the city will have to pay if the hospital has 10,000 patient visits.

4. A civic organization is engaged in a fund-raising program. On Civic Sunday they will sell newspapers at $1.25 each. The organization will pay $0.75 for each newspaper. Costs of the necessary permits, signs, and so forth, are $500. Determine the amount they will raise if 5,000 newspapers are sold.

5. Christmas for the Needy is a civic organization that provides Christmas presents to disadvantaged children. The annual costs of this activity are $5,000 plus $10 per present. Determine the number of presents the organization can provide with $20,000.

4–16 High-Low Cost Estimation and Profit Planning

Presented are comparative 19x8 and 19x9 income statements for Montana Products, Inc.

Montana Products, Inc.
Comparative Income Statements
For the years ending December 31, 19x8 and 19x9

	19x8	19x9
Unit sales	5,000	8,000
Sales revenue	$ 65,000	$104,000
Expenses	− 75,000	− 90,000
Net income (loss)	$(10,000)	$ 14,000

Requirements

a) Determine the break-even point in units.

b) Determine the unit sales volume required to earn a profit of $10,000.

4–17 High-Low Cost Estimation and Profit Planning

Presented are comparative 19y3 and 19y4 income statements for Nevada Products, Inc.

Nevada Products, Inc.
Comparative Income Statements
For the years ending 19y3 and 19y4

	19y3	19y4
Sales revenue	$500,000	$300,000
Expenses	−440,000	−360,000
Net income (loss)	$ 60,000	$ (60,000)

Requirements

a) Determine the break-even point in sales dollars.

b) Determine the dollar sales volume required to earn a profit of $180,000.

PROBLEMS

4–18 Cost-Volume-Profit Relationships: Missing Data

Supply the missing data in each independent case.

	Case 1	Case 2	Case 3	Case 4
Unit sales	1,000	800	? *4300*	? *3000*
Sales revenue	$20,000	? *1600*	? *137,600*	$60,000
Variable cost per unit	$ 10	$ 1	$ 12	? *5*
Contribution margin	?	$800	? *80,000*	? *45,000*
Fixed costs	$ 8,000	? *400*	$80,000	? *30,000*
Net income	?	$400	? *6000*	? *15,000*
Unit contribution margin	?	? *1*	? *20*	$ 15
Break-even point (units)	?	? *400*	4,000	2,000
Margin of safety (units)	?	? *400*	300	1,000

4–19 Cost-Volume-Profit Relationships: Missing Data

Supply the missing data in each independent case.

	Case 1	Case 2	Case 3	Case 4
Sales revenue	$100,000	$80,000	?	?
Contribution margin	$ 60,000	?	$20,000	?
Fixed costs	$ 30,000	?	?	?
Net income	?	$15,000	$10,000	?
Variable cost ratio	?	0.25	?	0.20
Contribution margin ratio	?	?	0.40	?
Break-even point (dollars)	?	?	?	$25,000
Margin of safety (dollars)	?	?	?	$15,000

4–20 Cost Analysis

In 1979 Winnebago Industries Inc. reported a loss of $4.2 million on sales of $214.6 million. In an effort to save the company, John K. Hanson reduced the firm's employees to 1,400 from 4,000 and sold two assembly plants. This reduced Winnebago's break-even point to 100 million sales dollars. In 1981 Winnebago reported a profit of $10.1 million on sales of $146.6 million.

Required: Determine Winnebago's margin of safety, contribution margin ratio, variable cost ratio, and fixed costs during 1981. Round calculations to four decimal places.

4–21 Potpourri of Profit Planning without Taxes

1. Lindsay Company reported the following results from sales of 5,000 units of product A for June 19x1.

Sales	$200,000
Variable costs	120,000
Fixed costs	60,000
Operating income	20,000

Assume that Lindsay increases the selling price of product A by 10 percent on July 1, 19x1. How many units of product A would have to be sold in July 19x1 in order to generate an operating income of $20,000?

2. Singer, Inc., sells product R for $5 per unit. The fixed costs are $210,000, and the variable costs are 60 percent of the selling price. Determine the dollar sales volume required for Singer to realize a profit of 10 percent of sales.

3. Birney Company is planning its advertising campaign for 19x1 and has prepared the following budget data based on a zero advertising expenditure.

Normal plant capacity	200,000 units
Sales	150,000 units
Selling price	$25.00 per unit
Variable manufacturing costs	$15.00 per unit
Fixed costs:	
Manufacturing	$800,000
Selling and administrative	$700,000

An advertising agency claims that an aggressive advertising campaign would enable Birney to increase its unit sales by 20 percent. What is the maximum amount that Birney can pay for advertising and obtain an operating profit of $200,000?

4. Pitt Company is considering a proposal to replace existing machinery used for the manufacture of product A. The new machines are expected to cause increased annual fixed costs of $120,000; however, variable costs should decrease by 20 percent because of a reduction in direct labor hours and more efficient usage of direct materials. Before this change was under consideration, Pitt had budgeted product A sales and costs for 19x1 as follows:

Sales	$2,000,000
Variable costs	70 percent of sales
Fixed costs	$400,000

Assuming that Pitt implemented the above proposal by January 1, 19x1, what would be the increase in budgeted operating profit for product A for 19x1?

(CPA Adapted)

4–22 Break-even Analysis in a Not-for-Profit Organization

Melford Hospital operates a general hospital, but rents space to separately owned entities rendering specialized services, such as pediatrics and psychiatric. Melford charges each separate entity for patients' services such as meals and laundry and for administrative services such as billings and collections. Space and bed rentals are fixed charges for the year, based on bed capacity rented to each entity.

Melford charged the following costs to Pediatrics for the year ended June 30, 19x2:

	Patient Days (Variable)	Bed Capacity (Fixed)
Dietary	$ 600,000	
Janitorial		$ 70,000
Laundry	300,000	
Laboratory	450,000	
Pharmacy	350,000	
Repairs and maintenance		30,000
General and administrative		1,300,000
Rent		1,500,000
Billings and collections	300,000	
Total	$2,000,000	$2,900,000

In addition to the above charges from Melford Hospital, Pediatrics incurred the following personnel costs:

	Annual Salaries
Supervising nurses	$100,000
Nurses	200,000
Aids	180,000
Total	$480,000

These salaries are fixed within the ranges of annual patient-days considered in this problem.

During the year ended June 30, 19x2, Pediatrics charged each patient $300 per day, had a capacity of 60 beds, and had revenues of $6,000,000 for 365 days. Pediatrics operated at 100 percent of capacity on 90 days during the year ended June 30, 19x2. It is estimated that during these 90 days the demand exceeded 80 beds (Pediatrics' capacity is 60 beds). Melford has an additional 20 beds available for rent during the year ending June 30, 19x3. Such additional rental would proportionately increase Pediatrics' annual fixed charges based on bed capacity.

Requirements

a) Calculate the minimum number of patient-days required for Pediatrics to break even for the year ending June 30, 19x3, if additional beds are not rented. Patient demand is unknown, but assume that revenue per patient-day, cost per patient-day, cost per bed, and salary rates for the year ending June 30, 19x3, remain the same as for the year ended June 30, 19x2.

b) Assume that patient demand, revenue per patient-day, cost per patient-day, cost per bed, and salary rates for the year ending June 30, 19x3, remain the same as for the year ended June 30, 19x2. Prepare a schedule of increases in revenue and increases in costs for the year ending June 30, 19x3, in order to determine the net increase or decrease in earnings from an additional 20 beds if Pediatrics rents this extra capacity from Melford.

(CPA Adapted)

4–23 Cost-Volume-Profit Analysis of Alternative Products

Siberian Ski Company recently expanded its manufacturing capacity to allow production of up to 15,000 pairs of cross-country skis of the mountaineering model or the touring model. The sales department assures management that it can sell between 9,000 and 13,000 of either product this year. Because the models are very similar, Siberian Ski will produce only one of the two models.

The following information was compiled by the accounting department.

	Model	
	Mountaineering	Touring
Selling price per unit	$88.00	$80.00
Variable costs per unit	$52.80	$52.80

Fixed costs will total $369,600 if the mountaineering model is produced, but only $316,800 if the touring model is produced. Siberian Ski Company is subject to a 40 percent income tax rate.

Requirements

a) Determine the contribution margin ratio of the touring model.

b) If Siberian Ski Company desires an after-tax net income of $24,000, how many pairs of touring model skis will the company have to sell? Round answer to nearest unit.

c) Determine the *unit* sales volume at which Siberian Ski Company would make the same before-tax profit or loss regardless of the ski model it decides to produce. Also determine the resulting before-tax profit or loss.

d) Determine the *dollar* sales volume at which Siberian Ski Company would make the same before-tax profit or loss regardless of the ski model it decides to produce. Also determine the resulting before-tax profit or loss. *Hint:* Work with contribution margin ratios.

e) What action should Siberian Ski Company take if the annual sales of either model were guaranteed to be at least 12,000 pairs? Why?

f) Determine how much the unit variable costs of the touring model would have to change before both models have the same break-even point in units. Round calculations to the nearest cent.

g) Determine the new unit break-even point of the touring skis if their variable costs per unit decrease by 10 percent and their fixed costs increase by 10 percent. Round answer to nearest unit.

(CMA Adapted)

4–24 Alternative Production Procedures and Operating Leverage (Appendix)

Candice Corporation has decided to introduce a new product. The new product can be manufactured by either a capital intensive method or a labor intensive method. The manufacturing method will not affect the quality of the product. The predicted manufacturing costs for each method are as follows:

	Capital Intensive	Labor Intensive
Direct materials	$5.00	$5.60
Direct labor		
(0.5 hours × $12)	6.00	
(0.8 hours × $9)		7.20
Variable overhead		
(0.5 labor hours × $6)	$3.00	
(0.8 labor hours × $6)		4.80
Fixed overhead per year	$2,440,000	$1,320,000

Candice's market research department has recommended an introductory unit sales price of $30. The incremental selling costs are predicted to be $500,000 per year plus $2 per unit sold.

Requirements

a) Calculate the annual break-even point in units of the new product if Candice uses the:

   1. Capital intensive manufacturing method.

   2. Labor intensive manufacturing method.

b) Determine the annual unit volume at which Candice would be indifferent between the two manufacturing methods. Indicate when Candice should use each of the two methods.

c) Management must decide which manufacturing method to employ. One factor it must consider is operating leverage.

   1. Explain operating leverage and the relationship between operating leverage and the volatility of earnings.

   2. Determine the operating leverage of each manufacturing method at an annual volume of 250,000 units. Round your answer to two decimal places.

   3. Explain the difference in operating leverage.

(CMA Adapted)

4–25 Contribution Income Statements and Operating Leverage (Appendix)

The Woodchopper Company cuts and sells firewood in Vermont and New Hampshire. The wood is sold by the face cord, which is a stack 4 feet high, by 2 feet deep, by 8 feet long. The Woodchopper Company pays high school and college students to saw, split, and transport the wood using company-owned equipment. Woodchopper uses newspaper advertising extensively in the fall and maintains a toll-free "hot line" to accept customer orders. The selling price is $45 per cord, variable costs are $25 per cord, and fixed costs are $20,000 per year. In 19x6 Woodchopper sold 1,400 cords.

Requirements

a) Prepare a contribution income statement for the year ended December 31, 19x6.

b) Determine Woodchopper's operating leverage.

c) Using Woodchopper's current operating leverage, calculate the percentage change in profits if sales increase 50 percent, to 2,100 cords per year.

d) Could the operating leverage determined for requirement (b) be used to calculate the percentage change in profits if sales increased 5 percent, from 2,000 cords to 2,100 cords? Explain your answer.

e) Woodchopper's management is considering the desirability of purchasing several log-splitting machines. This will increase their annual fixed costs while reducing their variable costs. What effect will this acquisition have on Woodchopper's operating leverage? Explain your answer.

4–26 Contribution Income Statements and Operating Leverage (Appendix)

The Alabama Berry Basket harvests early season strawberries for shipment throughout the eastern United States in late March. The strawberry farm is maintained by a permanent staff of ten employees and a large number of seasonal workers who pick and pack strawberries. The strawberries are sold in crates containing 100 individually packaged one-quart containers. Affixed to each one-quart container is the distinctive Alabama Berry Basket logo inviting buyers to enjoy "the berry best strawberries in the world" and an invitation to visit the Alabama Berry Basket, located near Interstate Highway 65. The selling price is $90 per crate, variable costs are $80 per crate, and fixed costs are $275,000 per year. In 19x8 Alabama Berry Basket sold 40,000 crates.

Requirements

a) Prepare a contribution income statement for the year ended December 31, 19x8.

b) Determine Alabama Berry Basket's operating leverage. 3.2

c) Using Alabama Berry Basket's current operating leverage, calculate the percentage change in profits if sales decreased 10 percent, to 36,000 containers per year. 32%

d) Could the operating leverage determined for requirement (b) be used to calculate the percentage change in profits if sales increased 20 percent, from 30,000 crates to 36,000 crates? Explain your answer.

e) Management is considering the desirability of purchasing several berry-picking machines. This will increase their annual fixed costs to $375,000 while reducing their variable costs to $77.50 per crate. Calculate the effect this acquisition will have on operating leverage. Explain the change in operating leverage. 4.0

4–27 Unit Sales Analysis of Break-even Point for Multiple Products (Appendix)

Presented is information regarding the Triangle Company's three products.

	A	B	C
Unit selling price	$5.00	$7.00	$6.00
Unit variable costs	−4.00	−5.00	−3.00
Unit contribution margin	$1.00	$2.00	$3.00

Triangle sells two units of A for each unit of B and three units of B for each unit of C. Fixed costs are $90,000 per month.

Required: Determine the unit sales of product A at the monthly break-even point.

4–28 Sales Dollars Analysis of Break-even Point for Multiple Products (Appendix)

Bob's Tax Service prepares tax returns for low to middle income taxpayers. Bob's service operates January 2 through April 15 at a counter in a local department store. All jobs are classified into one of three categories: standard, multiform, and complex. Presented is information on each category.

	Standard	Multiform	Complex
Billing rate	$50	$125	$250
Average variable cost	−30	− 75	−150
Average contribution margin	$20	$ 50	$100
Returns prepared last year	1,750	500	250

All employees are paid on a per-return basis. The fixed costs of rent, utilities, and so forth, were $30,000 last year.

Requirements

a) Determine Bob's break-even dollar sales volume.

b) Determine Bob's margin of safety in sales dollars.

c) Prepare a profit-volume graph.

4–29 Unit Sales Analysis of Break-even Point for Multiple Products (Appendix)

Tennessee Instruments manufactures and sells two types of hand calculators: student and professional. Information about selling prices and costs follows:

	Student	Professional
Unit selling price	$20.00	$50.00
Unit variable costs:		
Manufacturing	$ 7.00	$15.00
Selling	3.00	5.00
Total	−10.00	−20.00
Unit contribution margin	$10.00	$30.00
Fixed costs are $60,000 per month.		

Monthly calculator sales total 5,000 units. The current sales mix is 50 percent student calculators and 50 percent professional calculators. Management believes that a $10 reduction in the price of professional calculators will change the mix to 40 percent student calculators and 60 percent professional calculators while increasing the monthly calculator sales to 6,000 units.

Requirements

a) Determine the current unit break-even point and monthly profit.

b) Determine the revised unit break-even point and monthly profit with the reduced price for professional calculators.

c) Prepare a profit-volume graph that contains profit lines for the current mix and prices as well as for the revised mix and prices.

d) Based on your analysis, what action do you recommend?

4–30 Sales Dollars Analysis of Break-even Point for Multiple Products (Appendix)

Currently, the Corner Lunch Counter only sells Super Burgers. During a typical month, the Counter reports a profit of $9,000, with sales of $50,000 and fixed costs of $21,000. Management desires to introduce a new Super Chicken Sandwich. The new sandwich will sell for $3 and have variable costs of $1.80. The addition of Super Chickens will require the counter to hire additional personnel and purchase new equipment. These actions will increase monthly fixed costs by $7,760.

In the short run, management believes that 10,000 Super Chickens will be sold each month. However, almost all the sales will come from regular customers who will switch from Super Burgers to Super Chickens. Consequently, monthly sales of Super Burgers will decline to $20,000.

In the long run, management believes that Super Chicken sales will increase to 15,000 units per month and that Super Burger sales will increase to $75,000 per month.

Requirements

a) Determine each of the following:

1. The current monthly break-even point in sales dollars. — 24,000

2. The short-run monthly profit and break-even point in sales dollars subsequent to the introduction of Super Chickens. <32403>

3. The long-run monthly profit and break-even point in sales dollars subsequent to the introduction of Super Chickens. Round your answer to the nearest dollar.

34,740 →

b) Prepare a profit-volume graph with profit lines for the current, short-run, and long-run mixes. Label the horizontal axis in sales dollars.

REVIEW PROBLEM SOLUTION

a)

Memorabilia Cup Company
Functional Income Statement
For the month of September, 19x3

Sales (3,000 × $40)		$120,000
Cost of goods sold:		
Direct materials (3,000 × $15)	$45,000	
Direct labor (3,000 × $3)	9,000	
Variable factory overhead (3,000 × $10)	30,000	
Fixed factory overhead	15,000	− 99,000
Gross profit		$ 21,000
Selling and administrative expenses:		
Variable (3,000 × $2)	$ 6,000	
Fixed	10,000	− 16,000
Net income		$ 5,000

b) **Memorabilia Cup Company**
Contribution Income Statement
For the month of September, 19x3

Sales (3,000 × $40)			$120,000
Less variable costs:			
Cost of goods sold:			
Direct materials (3,000 × $15)	$45,000		
Direct labor (3,000 × $3)	9,000		
Factory overhead			
(3,000 × $10)	30,000	$84,000	
Selling and administrative			
(3,000 × $2)		6,000	− 90,000
Contribution margin			$ 30,000
Less fixed costs:			
Factory overhead	$15,000		
Selling and administrative	10,000		− 25,000
Net income			$ 5,000

c)

	Per Unit
Selling price	$40
Variable costs	−30
Contribution margin	$10

$$\frac{\text{Contribution}}{\text{margin ratio}} = \frac{\text{Unit contribution margin}}{\text{Selling price}}$$

$$= \$10/\$40$$

$$= \underline{\underline{0.25}}$$

d) Contribution approach:

$$\frac{\text{Break-even point}}{\text{in units}} = \frac{\text{Fixed costs}}{\text{Unit contribution margin}}$$

$$= \frac{\$25,000}{\$10}$$

$$= \underline{\underline{2,500}} \text{ units}$$

Formula approach:

$$\text{Profit} = \left(\begin{array}{c}\text{Selling} \\ \text{price}\end{array} \times \begin{array}{c}\text{Unit} \\ \text{volume}\end{array}\right) - \left[\begin{array}{c}\text{Fixed} \\ \text{costs}\end{array} + \left(\begin{array}{c}\text{Variable costs} \\ \text{per unit}\end{array} \times \begin{array}{c}\text{Unit} \\ \text{volume}\end{array}\right)\right]$$

$$\$0 = \$40X - [\$25,000 + \$30X]$$

$$X = \underline{\underline{2,500}} \text{ units}$$

e) Dollar sales for a monthly profit of $5,000 $= \dfrac{\text{Fixed costs + Required before-tax profit}}{\text{Contribution margin ratio}}$

$$= \frac{\$25,000 + \$5,000}{0.25}$$

$$= \underline{\underline{\$120,000}}$$

f) Required before-tax profit $= \dfrac{\text{Desired after-tax profit}}{1.0 - \text{Tax rate}}$

$$= \frac{\$4,500}{1 - 0.40}$$

$$= \underline{\underline{\$7,500}}$$

Unit sales for a monthly after-tax profit of $4,500 $= \dfrac{\text{Fixed costs + Required before-tax profit}}{\text{Unit contribution margin}}$

$$= \frac{\$25,000 + \$7,500}{\$10}$$

$$= \underline{\underline{3,250}} \text{ units}$$

CHAPTER 5

Relevant Costs for
Management Decisions

Upon completion of this chapter you should:

- Understand how the concept of relevant costs is used in decision making.
- Be able to distinguish between relevant and nonrelevant costs for special decisions.
- Be able to organize relevant costs in a manner that clearly indicates how they differ under each decision alternative.
- Be familiar with the differential analysis approach to cost analysis.
- Understand the application of differential analysis to important decisions, including: evaluating multiple changes in profit plans, accepting or rejecting special orders, deciding to make or buy a part or service, determining how best to use limited resources, and deciding to sell a product at some stage of completion or to process it further.
- Understand the basic alternative approaches to pricing products and services, including economic and cost-based approaches.

Cost-volume-profit analysis was presented in Chapter 4 as a useful framework for discussing planning issues and organizing relevant data. Cost-volume-profit analysis is especially useful in the early stages of planning. The overview it provides helps managers avoid getting lost in the details of individual decisions. Yet, despite the immense value of cost-volume-profit analysis, a sharper focus is often needed to make specific decisions. This need is particularly evident in multiple-product or multiple-service organizations. Here managers are frequently faced with the problem of too much rather than too little information.

When evaluating alternative actions, management should not place all information within the framework of their organization's overall cost-volume-profit model or profit formula. Instead, they should focus their attention on those costs and revenues that differ under alternative actions.

The purpose of this chapter is to examine concepts used to identify and analyze cost information for specific management decisions. While examining these concepts, a number of decision situations are discussed: whether to accept or reject a special order, whether to make or buy a part or service, how best to use limited capacity, whether to sell a product or process it further, and what price to charge for a product or service.

The decision situations presented here are not exhaustive; they are only intended to illustrate relevant cost concepts. Once these concepts are understood, they can be applied to a variety of management decisions. Because income taxes would unnecessarily complicate the discussion of relevant cost concepts, they are omitted from the examples presented in this chapter.

Although the emphasis in this chapter is on identifying and analyzing cost information, it is important to keep in mind that decisions should not be based solely on the criterion of short-run cost minimization or profit maximization. A proper analysis of cost information *assists* management in making decisions; however, management must also consider legal, ethical, social, and other non-quantitative factors. These factors may lead management to select a course of action other than that suggested by cost information alone.

RELEVANT COSTS AND DIFFERENTIAL ANALYSIS

Cost concepts for management action were introduced in Chapter 2. *Relevant costs* were defined as future costs that differ among competing alternatives, and *sunk costs* were defined as costs that result from past decisions management no longer has control over. Management must avoid being influenced by sunk costs that cannot be changed or by future costs that are not affected by the decision at hand. *The key to effective cost analysis is to (1) identify the relevant costs (and revenues), and (2) organize them in a manner that clearly indicates how they differ under each alternative.* Consider the following equipment replacement decision.

The Ace Stamping Company uses a Model I stamping machine to produce 10,000 widgets per year. Widgets sell for $15 each. Ace's variable and fixed costs are as follows:

Variable:	
Direct materials	$3 per unit
Direct labor	4 per unit
Factory overhead	1 per unit
Selling and administrative	1 per unit
Fixed:	
Factory overhead other than depreciation	$19,000 per year
Depreciation of Model I stamping machine	15,000 per year
Selling and administrative	12,000 per year

The Model I stamping machine is two years old and has a remaining useful life of four years. It cost $90,000 and has an estimated salvage value of zero dollars at the end of its useful life. Its current book value (original cost less accumulated depreciation) is $60,000, but its current disposal value is only $35,000.

Management is evaluating the desirability of replacing the Model I stamping machine with a new Model II stamping machine. The new machine costs $80,000, has a useful life of four years, and a predicted salvage value of zero dollars at the end of its useful life. Though the new machine has the same productive capacity as the old machine, its operating costs would be lower because it would require only one operator rather than the two needed by the old machine. Furthermore, it has fewer moving parts, so it would require less maintenance and use less power. The new labor and overhead costs are predicted to be as follows:

Direct labor	$2.00 per unit
Variable factory overhead	0.80 per unit
Fixed factory overhead other than depreciation	$16,000 per year

All other costs would be the same as for the old machine.

Identifying Relevant Costs

The decision at hand is either to keep the old Model I stamping machine or to replace it with a new Model II stamping machine. To assist management in making this decision, the accountant should prepare an analysis of those costs and revenues that differ under each alternative. Although the clearest presentation is one that contains only those costs and revenues that differ, the first objective of this chapter is to study the distinction between relevant and irrelevant items. To help accomplish this objective, a complete analysis of all costs and revenues under each alternative is presented in Exhibit 5–1. After evaluating the relevance of each item, a more focused differential analysis of relevant costs will be prepared.

The first thing to notice in Exhibit 5–1 is that many costs and revenues are the same under each alternative. These items are not relevant to the replacement decision. The only relevant items are those that have an entry in the difference column.

Future Revenues May Be Relevant. Revenues, which are inflows of resources from operations, are relevant if they differ between alternatives. Revenues in this example are not relevant because they are identical under each alternative. They would be relevant if the new machine had greater capacity that would be used, or if management intended to change the unit selling price should they acquire the new machine.

The keep or replace decision facing Ace's management might be called a **cost reduction proposal** because it is based on the assumption that the organization is committed to an activity and that management desires to minimize the cost of the activity. Here the alternatives are (1) continue operating with the old machine or (2) replace with a new machine.

Although this approach is appropriate for many activities, managers of for-profit organizations should always remember that they have another alternative; namely, discontinue operations. To simplify the analysis, managers normally do not consider the alternative to discontinue when operations appear to be profitable. However, if there is any doubt about an operation's profitability, this

EXHIBIT 5-1   **Complete Analysis of All Costs and Revenues**

	Complete Analysis of Four-Year Totals		
	(1) Keep Old Model I Machine	(2) Replace with New Model II Machine	(1) − (2) Difference (Effect of Replacement on Income)
Sales (10,000 units × $15 × 4 years)	$600,000	$600,000	
Costs:			
Direct materials			
(10,000 units × $3 × 4 years)	$120,000	$120,000	
Direct labor:			
Old (10,000 units × $4 × 4 years)	160,000		
New (10,000 units × $2 × 4 years)		80,000	$80,000
Variable overhead:			
Old (10,000 units × $1 × 4 years)	40,000		
New (10,000 units × $0.80 × 4 years)		32,000	8,000
Variable selling and administrative			
(10,000 units × $1 × 4 years)	40,000	40,000	
Fixed overhead except depreciation:			
Old ($19,000 × 4 years)	76,000		
New ($16,000 × 4 years)		64,000	12,000
Depreciation or write-off of old machine	60,000	60,000*	
Disposal value of old machine		(35,000)*	35,000
Cost of new machine		80,000	(80,000)
Fixed selling and administrative ($12,000 × 4 years)	48,000	48,000	
Total costs	−544,000	−489,000	
Net income	$ 56,000	$111,000	$55,000
Advantage of replacement		$55,000	

* A single loss on disposal of $25,000 ($60,000 − $35,000) would be shown on an income statement prepared for external users.

alternative should be considered. Because revenues will change if an operation is discontinued, revenues are relevant whenever this alternative is considered.

Outlay Costs May Be Relevant. Outlay costs are future costs that require future expenditures of cash or other resources. Outlay costs that differ under the decision alternatives at hand are relevant; those that do not differ are irrelevant. It is a mistake to assume that variable costs are always relevant and fixed costs always irrelevant. The relevant and the irrelevant outlay costs for Ace Stamping Company's equipment replacement decision are as follows:

Relevant Outlay Costs	*Irrelevant Outlay Costs*
Direct labor	Direct materials
Variable factory overhead	Variable selling and administrative
Fixed factory overhead	Fixed selling and administrative
except depreciation	
Cost of new machine	

Variable and fixed costs are included in both categories.

Because variable costs respond to changes in the volume of activity, they are relevant when decision alternatives have different activity levels. *Variable costs may not be relevant when decision alternatives have the same activity level.* In this case, variable costs will differ only if there is a difference in the variable cost per unit of activity.

The Model II stamping machine requires fewer operators, less maintenance, and less power. Hence, direct labor and variable overhead are relevant to the replacement decision. Because there is no change in the production and sales volume, nor any other change in selling or administrative procedures, the variable selling and administrative costs are not relevant.

Fixed costs may be relevant. A decision to increase activity may necessitate an increase in capacity and an accompanying increase in fixed costs. Conversely, a decision to reduce activity may provide an opportunity to reduce fixed costs. Alternative production or service procedures may have different fixed costs at the same activity level. This is the situation faced by the Ace Stamping Company. The Model II machine's fixed factory overhead is lower than the Model I's.

Because the fixed administrative costs are the same with both machines, they are irrelevant to the replacement decision. Indeed, fixed administrative costs, such as those incurred to pay the president's salary, have little or nothing to do with the operation of the stamping machine. These costs are not associated with the decision at hand.[1] The acquisition cost of the new machine is obviously relevant. This cost will be incurred only if the replacement alternative is selected.

Sunk Costs Are Never Relevant. *Though the relevance of outlay costs is determined by the decision at hand, sunk costs (aside from possible tax consequences) are never relevant.* Sunk costs result from past expenditures that cannot be changed. The cost of the Model I machine is a historical cost, not a future cost. This historical cost, and the related depreciation, result from the past decision to acquire the old machine. Even though all the outlay costs discussed above would be relevant to a decision to continue or discontinue operations, the sunk cost of the Model I machine is not relevant even to this decision.

---

[1] In textbook examples and problems, and in professional examinations, it is assumed, in the absence of specific information, that fixed costs do not differ between decision alternatives. This is a simplifying assumption. In practice the manager or the management accountant would have to ask many questions to determine whether or not fixed outlay costs are relevant to a decision situation.

If management elects to keep the old machine, its book value will be depreciated over its remaining useful life of four years, whereas if management elects to replace the old machine, its book value will be written off when it is replaced. Even if management elects to discontinue operations, the book value of the old machine must be disposed of.

Although the book value of the old machine has no economic significance, the accounting treatment of past costs can make it difficult for managers to regard them as irrelevant. If management replaces the old machine, a loss from disposal of $25,000 will be recorded in the year of replacement:

Book value	$60,000
Disposal value	−35,000
Loss on disposal	$25,000

Managers are often reluctant to have such a loss recorded out of fear that it will lead superiors to question the wisdom of past decisions. The loss acts as an attention-getting flag. A manager might prefer using the old machine, with lower total profits over the four-year period, to replacing it and being forced to record a loss on disposal.

From an economic viewpoint, a mistake made in acquiring the old machine cannot be corrected by continuing to use the old machine. When a preferred alternative is available, continued commitment to the original decision compounds the first mistake with a second. Though there is no easy solution to this behavioral problem, managers and management accountants should be aware of its potential impact.

Disposal and Salvage Values. Revenues are inflows of resources from operations. The Ace Stamping Company's revenues, which are from the sale of widgets, were discussed above. The sale of fixed assets is also a source of resources. Because the sale of fixed assets is a nonoperating item, cash inflows obtained from these sales are discussed separately.

The disposal value of the Model I machine is a relevant cash inflow. It is obtained only if the replacement alternative is selected. Any salvage value available at the end of the useful life of either machine would also be relevant. A loss on disposal may have a favorable tax impact if the loss can be offset against taxable gains or taxable income. In this case, though the book value of the old asset remains irrelevant, the expected tax reduction would be relevant.

Differential Analysis of Relevant Costs

Differential cost analysis is an approach to the analysis of relevant costs that focuses on the costs that differ under alternative actions. A differential analysis of relevant costs for the Ace Stamping Company's equipment replacement deci-

EXHIBIT 5–2   Differential Analysis of Relevant Costs

	Differential Analysis of Four-Year Totals		
	(1) Keep Old Model I Machine	(2) Replace with New Model II Machine	(1) − (2) Difference (Effect of Replacement on Income)
Costs:			
Direct labor:			
Old (10,000 units × $4 × 4 years)	$160,000		
New (10,000 units × $2 × 4 years)		$ 80,000	$80,000
Variable overhead:			
Old (10,000 units × $1 × 4 years)	40,000		
New (10,000 units × $0.80 × 4 years)		32,000	8,000
Fixed overhead except depreciation:			
Old ($19,000 × 4 years)	76,000		
New ($16,000 × 4 years)		64,000	12,000
Disposal value of old machine		(35,000)	35,000
Cost of new machine		80,000	(80,000)
Total	$276,000	$221,000	$55,000
Advantage of replacement		$55,000	

sion is presented in Exhibit 5–2. Replacement provides a net advantage of $55,000 over the life of both machines.[2]

A differential analysis of relevant costs and revenues (such as the one in Exhibit 5–2) is preferred to a complete analysis of all costs and revenues (such as the one in Exhibit 5–1) for a number of reasons:

- Focusing only on those items that differ provides a clearer picture of the impact of the decision at hand. Management is less apt to be confused by a differential analysis than by an analysis that intermingles relevant and irrelevant items.

- Because a differential analysis contains fewer items, it is easier and quicker to prepare.

- In complex situations, such as those encountered by multiple-product or multiple-plant firms, it is difficult, if not impossible, to develop complete firmwide statements to analyze all decision alternatives.

---

[2] Our current objectives are (1) to distinguish between relevant and irrelevant costs and (2) to demonstrate the advantages of analyzing only relevant costs. An analysis of long-lived projects should also consider the time value of money. The time value of money is discussed in Chapter 14 and in the appendix to this book.

Predicting Relevant Costs

Information on relevant costs is almost always given in textbook examples and problems. Here the task is to (1) distinguish between relevant and irrelevant costs and (2) properly classify the relevant costs. In practice the analyst would also have the difficult job of obtaining the relevant cost information, which is a very time-consuming process that requires questioning, observing, and analyzing. Obviously, an understanding of relevant cost concepts is a prerequisite to obtaining relevant cost information. Simply stated, the analyst must know what to look for. The knowledge of this helps guide the search for the few pieces of relevant information contained in voluminous sets of data.

Predicting relevant costs may involve an examination of past cost trends. If one of the alternatives under consideration is to continue operations as in the past, the techniques discussed in Chapter 3 can be used to estimate past costs and to develop predictions of future costs. The predicted operating costs of the Model I stamping machine would be developed in this manner.

It is more difficult to predict costs when technology changes. The substitution of the Model II for the Model I stamping machine is an example of a technological change. Because the Model II is new, the Ace Stamping Company's historical information is of little or no value in predicting its future operating costs. Cost predictions for the Model II machine must be deduced from information obtained from the manufacturer, other users, trade associations and publications, and engineers employed by Ace. Management should carefully evaluate the credibility of this information.

A **cost prediction error** is the difference between a predicted future cost and the actual amount of the cost when, or if, it is incurred. Because cost predictions may be inaccurate, management should determine how sensitive a decision is to prediction errors. This would include, for example, determining how much a prediction could change before affecting the decision.

The Ace Stamping Company's new machine has a net advantage of $55,000 over its four-year life; hence, cost predictions could increase by $55,000 before affecting the decision.[3] Given the size of the operating costs, a $55,000 prediction error seems unlikely. If the net advantage of the new machine were smaller, say $10,000, management might want to consider the likelihood of a $10,000 prediction error.

APPLICATIONS OF DIFFERENTIAL ANALYSIS

Differential analysis is used to provide information for a variety of planning and decision situations. Illustrated in this section are some of the more frequently encountered applications of differential analysis, including multiple changes in profit plans, whether to accept or reject a special order, whether to make or

[3] See footnote 2.

buy a product or service, how best to use limited resources, and whether to sell a product or process it further.

Multiple Changes in Profit Plans

Mind Trek, Ltd. manufactures an electronic game that is sold to distributors for $22 per unit. Manufacturing and other costs are as follows:

Variable Costs per Unit			Fixed Costs per Month	
Manufacturing:			Factory overhead	$30,000
Direct materials	$5.00		Selling and administrative	15,000
Direct labor	3.00		Total	$45,000
Factory overhead	2.00	$10.00		
Selling and administrative		2.00		
Total		$12.00		

The unit contribution margin is $10 ($22 selling price − $12 variable costs). Mind Trek's April 19x6 Contribution Income Statement is presented in Exhibit 5–3. The April 19x6 operations are typical. Monthly production and sales average 5,000 units, and monthly profits average $5,000.

Management wants to know the effect on monthly profits of the following three alternative actions.

1. Increasing the monthly advertising budget by $4,000, which should result in a 1,000 unit increase in monthly sales.

2. Increasing the unit selling price by $3, which should result in a 2,000 unit decrease in monthly sales.

EXHIBIT 5–3   Contribution Income Statement

Mind Trek, Ltd.
Contribution Income Statement
For the month of April 19x6

Sales (5,000 units × $22)			$110,000
Less variable costs:			
Cost of goods sold:			
Direct materials (5,000 units × $5)	$25,000		
Direct labor (5,000 units × $3)	15,000		
Factory overhead (5,000 units × $2)	10,000	$50,000	
Selling and administrative (5,000 units × $2)		10,000	− 60,000
Contribution margin			$ 50,000
Less fixed costs:			
Factory overhead		$30,000	
Selling and administrative		15,000	− 45,000
Net income			$ 5,000

3. Decreasing the unit selling price by $2, which should result in a 2,000 unit increase in monthly sales. However, because of capacity constraints, the last 1,000 units would be produced during overtime, when the direct labor costs increase by $1 per unit.

It is possible to develop contribution income statements for each alternative and then determine the profit impact of the proposed change by comparing the new net income with the current net income. A more direct approach is to use differential analysis and focus only on those items that differ under each alternative.

Alternative 1:

Profit increase from increased sales (1,000 units × $10)	$ 10,000
Profit decrease from increased advertising	(4,000)
Increase in monthly profit	$ 6,000

Alternative 2:

Profit decrease from reduced sales if there were no changes in prices or costs (2,000 units × $10)	$(20,000)
Profit increase from increased selling price [(5,000 units − 2,000 units) × $3]	9,000
Decrease in monthly profit	$(11,000)

Alternative 3:

Profit increase from increased sales if there were no changes in prices or costs (2,000 units × $10)	$ 20,000
Profit decrease from reduced selling price of all units [(5,000 units + 2,000 units) × $2]	(14,000)
Profit decrease from increased direct labor costs of the last 1,000 units (1,000 units × $1)	(1,000)
Increase in monthly profit	$ 5,000

Alternative 2 is undesirable because it would result in a decrease in monthly profit. Because Alternative 1 results in a larger increase in monthly profit, it is preferred to Alternative 3.

Special Orders

Assume a Brazilian distributor has proposed to place a special, one-time order for 1,000 units next month, at a reduced price of $12 per unit. The distributor will pay all packing and transportation costs, and there will be no incremental selling or administrative expenses associated with the order. Mind Trek has sufficient production capacity to produce the additional units without reducing sales to other customers. Management desires to know the profit impact of accepting the order. The following analysis focuses on those costs and revenues that will differ if the order is accepted.

Increase in revenues (1,000 units × $12)		$12,000
Increase in costs:		
Direct materials (1,000 units × $5)	$5,000	
Direct labor (1,000 units × $3)	3,000	
Variable factory overhead (1,000 units × $2)	2,000	−10,000
Increase in profits		$ 2,000

Accepting the order will result in a profit increase of $2,000.

If management were unaware of management accounting concepts, they might be tempted to compare the special order price to the average unit cost of goods sold used for financial accounting purposes. If management made their decision by comparing the special order price to the unit cost of goods sold found in Mind Trek's April 19x6 financial statements, they might reject the order. With all manufacturing costs assigned to the units produced, the April cost of goods sold averaged $16 per unit:

Cost of goods sold:		
Direct materials (5,000 units × $5)		$25,000
Direct labor (5,000 units × $3)		15,000
Factory overhead:		
Variable (5,000 units × $2)	$10,000	
Fixed	30,000	40,000
Total		$80,000
Unit production and sales		÷ 5,000
Average unit cost of goods sold		$ 16

Comparing the special order price of $12 per unit to the average unit cost of goods sold of $16, management might conclude the order would result in a loss of $4 per unit.

It is apparent that the $16 figure is composed of variable manufacturing costs of $10 per unit and fixed manufacturing costs of $30,000 spread over 5,000 units. But remember that management may not have detailed cost information. To obtain appropriate information for decision-making purposes, management must ask their accounting staff for the specific information needed. Different configurations of cost information are provided for different purposes. In the absence of special instructions the accounting staff will probably supply the most readily available data, namely, that used for financial reporting.

Importance of Time Span. The special order is a one-time order for 1,000 units that will use current excess capacity. Because no special setups or equipment are required to produce the order, it is appropriate to consider only variable costs in computing the order's profitability.

But what if the Brazilian distributor wanted Mind Trek to sign a multiyear contract to provide 1,000 units per month at $12 each? Under these circumstances management would be well advised to reject the order because there is a high probability that cost increases would make the order unprofitable in later years. At the very least, management should insist that a cost escalation clause be added to the purchase agreement, specifying that the selling price be increased to cover any cost increases and detailing how cost is computed.

Of more concern is the variable nature of all long-run costs. *In the long run all costs, including costs classified as fixed in a given period, are relevant.* To remain in business in the long run, Mind Trek must replace equipment, pay property taxes, pay administrative salaries, and so forth. Consequently, management should consider all costs (fixed and variable, manufacturing and non-manufacturing) in evaluating a long-term contract.

Full costs include all (fixed and variable) product and period costs. The average full cost per unit is sometimes used to approximate long-run variable costs. If accepting a long-term contract increases the monthly production and sales volume to 11,000 units, the average full cost per unit will be $16.09:

Direct materials	$ 5.00
Direct labor	3.00
Variable factory overhead	2.00
Fixed factory overhead ($30,000 ÷ 11,000 units)	2.73
Variable selling and administrative costs	2.00
Fixed selling and administrative costs ($15,000 ÷ 11,000 units)	1.36
Average full cost per unit	$16.09

If the Brazilian distributor agrees to pay separately all variable selling and administrative expenses associated with the contract, the estimated long-run variable costs are $14.09 per unit ($16.09 − $2.00). Many managers would say this is the minimum acceptable unit selling price for the order, especially if the order extends over a long period of time.

Opportunity Costs May Also Be Relevant. Recall from Chapter 2 that an *opportunity cost* is the net cash inflow that could be obtained if the resources committed to one action were used in the most desirable other alternative. Because Mind Trek has excess productive capacity, no opportunity cost is associated with accepting the Brazilian distributor's one-time order. There is no alternative use of the productive capacity in the short run, so there is no opportunity cost.

But what if Mind Trek were operating with no excess capacity? In this case accepting the special order would require either reducing regular sales or using overtime. To simplify the illustration, assume overtime production is not possible. Because Mind Trek is operating at capacity, there is an alternative use of the productive capacity and, hence, an opportunity cost associated with its use to fill the special order. Each unit sold to the Brazilian distributor could generate a $10 contribution from regular customers. Accepting the special order would cause Mind Trek to incur an opportunity cost of $10,000, the net benefit of the most desirable other action, selling to regular customers:

Lost sales to regular customers	1,000 units
Regular unit contribution margin	×$10
Opportunity cost of accepting special order	$10,000

Because this opportunity cost exceeds the $2,000 contribution derived from the special order, management should reject the special order. Accepting the order will reduce profits by $8,000 ($2,000 − $10,000).

Nonquantitative Considerations. Although an analysis of cost and revenue information may indicate that a special order would be profitable in the near term, management might still reject the order because of nonquantitative, short-run or long-run considerations. Because of a concern for the order's impact on regular customers, management might reject an order even if they had excess capacity. If the order involves a special low price, regular customers might demand a similar price reduction and threaten to take their business elsewhere. Alternatively, management might accept the special order even though they were operating at capacity if they believed there were long-term benefits associated with penetrating a new market. Legal factors must also be considered if the special order is from a buyer who competes with regular customers. These legal factors are discussed later in this chapter.

Make or Buy Decisions

Now suppose a foreign manufacturer has offered a one-year contract to supply Mind Trek with an electronic component at a cost of $2.20 per unit. If Mind Trek accepts the offer, they will be able to reduce materials costs by 10 percent and direct labor and variable factory overhead costs by 20 percent. Fixed factory overhead can be reduced by $20,000 per year. A differential analysis of Mind Trek's make or buy decision is presented in Exhibit 5–4. Making the component has a net advantage of $22,000.

But what if the space currently used to manufacture the electronic component can be rented to a third party for $40,000 per year? In this case the productive capacity has an alternative use, and the net cash flow from this alternative use is an opportunity cost of making the component. In analyzing the make or buy decision, this opportunity cost should be treated as a cost of making. Buying now has a net advantage of $18,000:

	Cost to Make	Cost to Buy	Difference (Effect of Buying on Income)
Cost to buy		$132,000	$(132,000)
Cost to make:			
Outlay*	$110,000		110,000
Opportunity	40,000		40,000
Total	$150,000	$132,000	$ 18,000
Advantage of buying		$18,000	

* See Exhibit 5–4.

Even if buying appears financially advantageous in the short run, management should not decide to buy before considering a variety of nonquantitative factors. Is the outside supplier attempting to use some temporarily idle capacity? If so, what will happen at the end of the contract period? Will the supplier extend the contract at all, or at a higher price? What impact would a decision to buy have on the morale of Mind Trek's employees? Will Mind Trek have to rehire laid-off employees after the contract expires? Will the outside supplier meet delivery schedules? Does the supplied part meet Mind Trek's quality standards, and will it continue to meet them? Organizations often manufacture

EXHIBIT 5–4   Differential Analysis for Make or Buy Decision

	(1) Cost to Make	(2) Cost to Buy	(1) – (2) Difference (Effect of Buying on Income)
Cost to buy ($2.20 × 60,000 units*)		$132,000	$(132,000)
Cost to make:			
Direct materials			
($5 × 0.10 × 60,000 units*)	$ 30,000		30,000
Direct labor			
($3 × 0.20 × 60,000 units*)	36,000		36,000
Variable factory overhead			
($2 × 0.20 × 60,000 units*)	24,000		24,000
Fixed factory overhead	20,000		20,000
Total	$110,000	$132,000	$ (22,000)
Advantage of making		$22,000	

* 5,000 units per month × 12 months = 60,000 units.

products or provide services they can obtain elsewhere in order to control quality and have an assured source of supply with on-time delivery.

How Best to Use Limited Resources

No doubt you have experienced time as a limiting resource. With two exams the day after tomorrow and a paper due next week, your problem was how to allocate limited study time. The solution depended on your objectives, your current status (grades, knowledge, skill levels, and so forth), and the available time. Given this information, you devised a work plan to most nearly meet your objectives.

Managers must also decide how best to use limited resources to accomplish organizational goals. A supermarket may lose sales because limited shelf space prevents stocking all available brands of cereal. A manufacturer may lose sales because limited machine or labor hours prevents filling all orders. Managers of for-profit organizations will likely find the problems of capacity constraints less troublesome than the problems of excess capacity; nonetheless, these problems are real.

The long-run solution to these problems may be to expand capacity. However, this is usually not feasible in the short run. Economic models suggest that another solution is to reduce demand by increasing the price. Again, this may not be desirable. The supermarket, for example, may want to maintain competitive prices, and the manufacturer might want to maintain a long-run price or to avoid accusations of "price-gouging."

The allocation of limited resources should be made only after a careful consideration of many nonquantitative factors. The following rule provides a useful starting point in making short-run decisions of how best to use limited resources: *To achieve short-run profit maximization, a for-profit organization should allocate limited resources in a manner that maximizes the contribution per unit of constraining factor.* The application of this rule is illustrated in the following example.

The Delta Manufacturing Company produces three products: A, B, and C. A limitation of 100 machine-hours per week prevents Delta from meeting the sales demand for these products. Product information is as follows:

	A	B	C
Unit selling price	$100	$80	$50
Unit variable costs	− 90	−50	−25
Unit contribution margin	$ 10	$30	$25
Machine-hours per unit	2	2	1

Product A has the highest selling price, product B has the highest unit contribution margin, and product C is shown below to have the highest contribution per machine-hour.

	A	B	C
Unit contribution margin	$10	$30	$25
Machine-hours per unit	÷ 2	÷ 2	÷ 1
Contribution per machine-hour	$ 5	$15	$25

Following the rule of maximizing the contribution per unit of constraining factor, Delta should use its limited machine-hours to produce product C. As shown in the following analysis, any other plan would result in lower profits.

	A	B	C
	Highest Selling Price	*Highest Contribution per Unit*	*Highest Contribution per Unit of Constraining Factor*
Machine hours available	100	100	100
Machine hours per unit	÷ 2	÷ 2	÷ 1
Weekly production	50	50	100
Unit contribution margin	×$10	× $30	× $25
Total contribution	$500	$1,500	$2,500

Despite this analysis, management may decide to produce some units of A, or B, or both to satisfy the requests of some "good" customers, or to offer a full product line. However, such decisions sacrifice short-run profits. Each machine-hour used to produce A or B has an opportunity cost of $25, the net cash flow from using that hour to produce a unit of C, the most desirable other alternative. Producing all A, for example, results in an opportunity cost of $2,500 (100 units of C × $25). The net disadvantage of producing all A is $2,000:

Contribution from A	$ 500
Opportunity cost of not producing C	− 2,500
Net disadvantage of producing A	$(2,000)

The opportunity cost of producing all C is $1,500. This is the net cash flow from the most desirable other alternative, producing B. However, when compared to producing B, producing C has a net advantage of $1,000:

Contribution from C	$2,500
Opportunity cost of not producing B	−1,500
Net advantage of producing C	$1,000

When an organization has alternative uses for several (rather than one) limiting resources, the optimal use of those resources cannot be determined using the rule for short-run profit maximization. In these situations techniques such as linear programming (discussed in Chapter 13) may be used to assist in determining the optimal mix of products or services.

Sell or Process Further

Single Product Decisions. When a product is saleable at various stages of completion, management must determine the product's most advantageous selling point. As each stage is completed, management must determine whether to sell it then or to process it further. Assume the Boston Rocking Company manufactures rocking chairs from precut and shaped wood. The chairs are saleable once they are assembled; however, Boston Rocking sands and paints all chairs before they are sold. Management wishes to know if this is the optimal selling point.

A complete listing of unit costs and revenues for the alternative selling points is as follows:

	Per Chair		
	Sell After Assembly	Sell After Painting	Difference (Effect of Painting on Income)
Selling price	$40	$75	$35
Assembly costs	(25)	(25)	
Sanding and painting costs		(12)	(12)
Contribution margin	$15	$38	$23
Advantage of painting		$23	

The chairs should be sold after they are painted. The sanding and painting operation has an additional contribution of $23 per unit.

Note that the assembly costs are the same under both alternatives. This illustrates that *all costs incurred prior to the decision point are irrelevant*. Given the existence of an assembled chair, the decision alternatives are to sell it now or process it further. A differential analysis for the decision to sell or process further should include only revenues and the incremental costs of further processing:

Increase in revenues:		
Sell after painting	$75	
Sell after assembly	−40	$35
Additional costs of sanding		
and painting		−12
Advantage of sanding and painting		$23

The identical solution is obtained if the selling price without further processing is treated as an opportunity cost:

Revenues after painting		$75
Additional costs of sanding		
and painting	$12	
Opportunity cost of not selling		
after assembly	40	−52
Advantage of sanding and painting		$23

By processing the chairs further, Boston Rocking has forgone the opportunity to receive $40 from its sale. Since the chair is already made, this $40 is the net cash inflow from the most desirable alternative; hence, it is the opportunity cost of painting.

Joint Product Decisions. Two or more products simultaneously produced from a common set of inputs by a single process are called **joint products.** Joint products are often found in basic industries that process natural raw materials, such as dairy products, chemicals, meat products, petroleum, and wood products. In the petroleum industry, crude oil is refined into fuel oil, gasoline, kerosene, lubricating oil, and other products.

The point in the process where the joint products become separately identifiable is called the **split-off point,** and product costs incurred prior to the split-off point are called **joint costs.** For external reporting purposes a number of techniques are used to allocate joint costs among joint products. (Some of these techniques are considered in the appendix to Chapter 12.) We are not interested in these techniques here, except to note that none of them provides information that is useful in determining what to do with a joint product once it is produced. Because joint costs are incurred prior to the decision point, they are sunk costs. Consequently, *joint costs are irrelevant to a decision to sell a joint product or process it further.*

THE PRICING DECISION

Product pricing is one of the most important and complex decisions facing management. The saleability of individual products or services is directly affected by pricing decisions, as is the profitability and even the survival of the organization. This section introduces some basic pricing concepts and indicates the important role of costs in pricing decisions.

Economic Approaches to Product Pricing

In economic models, the firm has a profit maximizing goal and known cost and revenue functions. The firm continues to produce as long as the marginal revenue derived from the sale of each additional unit exceeds the marginal cost of producing that unit. **Marginal revenue** is the varying increment in total revenue derived from the sale of an additional unit. **Marginal cost** is the varying increment in total cost required to produce and sell an additional unit. Profits are maximized by producing until marginal revenue equals marginal cost.

Economic models provide a useful framework for thinking about pricing decisions, but they are seldom used for day-to-day pricing decisions. Their primary weaknesses stem from the assumptions of profit maximization and known cost and revenue functions. Most for-profit organizations attempt to achieve a target profit rather than a maximum profit. One reason for this is an inability to determine the single set of actions out of all possible actions that will lead to profit maximization. Furthermore, managers are more apt to strive to satisfy a number of goals (such as profits for owners, job security for themselves and their employees, and being a "good" corporate citizen) than to strive for the maximization of a single profit goal. In any case, to maximize profits a company's management would have to know the cost and revenue functions of every product their firm sells. For most products this information either cannot be developed or cannot be developed at a reasonable cost.

Cost-Based Approaches to Product Pricing

Though cost is not the only consideration in product pricing, it is important. There are several reasons for this.

- *Cost data are available*. When hundreds of different prices must be set in a short time, cost may be the only feasible basis for product pricing.

- *Cost based prices are defensible*. Managers threatened by legal action or public scrutiny may feel secure using cost based pricing. They can argue that prices are set in a manner that provides a "fair" profit.

- *Revenues must exceed costs in the long run if the firm is to remain in business*. In the long run the unit selling price must exceed the full cost of each unit, including the product cost of the unit and a portion of all other costs.

In a typical pricing decision, management uses cost information to arrive at an initial selling price. Other available information about the market, competitors, and so forth, is then evaluated in arriving at a final selling price.

Price Setting in Single Product Companies. Determining the initial cost based price in a single product company is straightforward if everything is known but the selling price. In this case all known information can be substituted into the profit formula, which is then solved for the variable price.

Assume that Bright Rug Cleaning Company has annual fixed costs of $200,000 and variable costs of $10 per rug cleaned. Management desires to achieve a target profit of $30,000. The estimated annual volume is 10,000 units. As a matter of policy, management charges the same price regardless of the type, size, or shape of the rug. Using the profit formula, the unit price required to achieve the target profit is determined to be $33:

| Total revenue | Total costs | | Profit |
	Fixed	Variable	
(Price × 10,000) −	[$200,000 +	($10 × 10,000)] =	$30,000.

Solving for the price:

$$(\text{Price} \times 10{,}000) - \$300{,}000 = \$30{,}000$$
$$\text{Price} = \$330{,}000/10{,}000$$
$$= \$33.$$

To achieve its target profit, Bright would charge $33 to clean a rug.

Price Setting in Multiple-Product Companies. In multiple-product companies, desired profits are determined for the company as a whole, and standard procedures are established for determining the initial selling price of each product. These procedures typically specify the initial selling price as cost, plus a markup stated as a percentage of cost, which is determined by the cost base used in the computations. The larger the cost base for a given product the smaller the markup. Two possible cost bases that we consider are variable costs and manufacturing costs.

When the markup is based on variable costs, it must be large enough to cover all fixed costs and the target profit:

$$\frac{\text{Variable}}{\text{cost markup}} = \frac{\text{Predicted fixed costs} + \text{Target profit}}{\text{Predicted variable costs}}$$

Once the variable cost markup is determined, it is then used to determine the initial selling price of each product:

$$\frac{\text{Initial}}{\text{selling price}} = \frac{\text{Variable costs}}{\text{per unit}} + \left(\frac{\text{Variable costs}}{\text{per unit}} \times \frac{\text{Variable}}{\text{cost markup}} \right).$$

Assume the predicted 19x9 variable and fixed costs for Magnum Enterprises are as follows:

	Variable Costs		Fixed Costs
Manufacturing	$600,000	Manufacturing	$400,000
Selling and		Selling and	
administrative	200,000	administrative	200,000
Total	$800,000	Total	$600,000

To achieve a target profit of $200,000, Magnum Enterprises needs a 100 percent markup on variable costs:

$$\frac{\text{Variable}}{\text{cost markup}} = \frac{\$600,000 + \$200,000}{\$800,000} = 1.00.$$

Assume the following information is available about product A:

	Unit
Direct material	$ 4
Direct labor	4
Factory overhead:	
Variable	$2
Fixed	5 7
Total manufacturing costs	$15
Variable selling and administrative costs	$ 2

Variable costs for product A are $12 per unit:

	Unit
Direct material	$ 4
Direct labor	4
Variable factory overhead	2
Variable selling and administrative	2
Total variable costs	$12

Using the variable cost markup, the initial selling price of A is $24:

$$\text{Initial selling price} = \$12 + (\$12 \times 1.00)$$
$$= \$24.$$

To make appropriate pricing decisions, management must be aware of the variable costs of a product or service and the markup required to cover fixed costs and to provide for a target profit. One way of doing this is to break the markup on variable costs into two parts: one part to cover fixed costs and another part to provide for a profit. For Magnum Enterprises this might be done as follows:

	Product A
Variable costs	$12
Markup to cover fixed costs [($600,000/$800,000 = 0.75) × $12]	9
Markup to achieve target profit [($200,000/$800,000 = 0.25) × $12]	3
Initial price	$24

With this information management can readily see that any price in excess of $12 increases short-run profits or reduces short-term losses. However, all products must have an average markup of 75 percent on variable costs if the firm is to be profitable in the long run. Using this guideline, the suggested markup for product A is at least $9. To achieve target profits, all products must have an additional average markup of 25 percent on variable costs. The suggested additional markup for product A is $3 using this guideline. Management would modify this initial price to reflect current market conditions and other factors.

When the markup percentage is based on manufacturing costs, it must be large enough both to cover selling and administrative costs and to provide for the desired profit:

$$\text{Manufacturing cost markup} = \frac{\text{Predicted selling and administrative costs} + \text{Desired profit}}{\text{Predicted manufacturing costs}}.$$

To compute the manufacturing cost markup, it is necessary to determine the desired profit and to predict all costs for the pricing period. The initial prices of individual products are then computed as their unit manufacturing costs plus the markup.

$$\text{Initial selling price} = \text{Manufacturing costs per unit} + \left(\text{Manufacturing costs per unit} \times \text{Manufacturing cost markup} \right).$$

Magnum Enterprises has the following cost predictions for 19x9:

Manufacturing Costs		Selling and Administrative Costs	
Variable	$ 600,000	Variable	$200,000
Fixed	400,000	Fixed	200,000
Total	$1,000,000	Total	$400,000

To achieve a target profit of $200,000, Magnum Enterprises needs a 60 percent markup on manufacturing costs:

$$\frac{\text{Manufacturing}}{\text{cost markup}} = \frac{\$400,000 + \$200,000}{\$1,000,000}$$
$$= 0.60.$$

Using the manufacturing cost markup, with total manufacturing costs of $15, the initial selling price of product A is $24:

$$\text{Initial selling price} = \$15 + (\$15 \times 0.60)$$
$$= \$24.$$

Because of the availability of manufacturing cost data, this approach to product pricing is widely used. However, it has several weaknesses. The manufacturing cost markup indiscriminately mixes fixed and variable costs in the base and in the markup. If the variable selling and administrative expenses can be identified with individual products, they should be included in the base rather than in the markup. Conversely, the nonvarying nature of fixed manufacturing costs and the difficulty of accurately associating them with individual products suggest that they should be included in the markup rather than in the base.

Legal Forces Increase the Role of Costs

Cost has always been an important determinant of price in regulated industries such as utilities, communications, and transportation. In recent years a number of legal forces have greatly increased the role of costs in many other industries. Large government defense contracts, for example, are often awarded on the basis of cost, which is determined in a manner specified by government regulations, plus an allowance for profit. Medicare and Medicaid reimbursements to hospitals are often based on cost as well, which again is determined in a specified manner.

The **Robinson–Patman Act** prohibits charging purchasers different prices when these purchasers compete with one another in the sale of their products or services. There are three exceptions to the act:

1. The discriminatory lower price is in response to changing conditions in the market for, or the marketability of, the commodities involved (such as the sale of discontinued products);

2. The discriminatory lower price is made to meet an equally low price of a competitor; and

3. The discriminatory lower price makes only due allowance for specific cost differences, such as those resulting from long production runs and bulk shipments.

Management must always take care to ensure that accepting a special order does not violate the provisions of the Robinson–Patman Act.

SUMMARY

A number of decision situations were presented in this chapter, including whether to accept or reject a special order, whether to make or buy a product or service, how best to use limited resources, and whether to sell a product or process it further. When evaluating alternative actions such as these, managers should focus their attention on the decision at hand. They should evaluate only those costs and revenues that differ under each alternative.

Relevant costs include all future costs that differ among competing alternatives, namely, outlay costs that differ under each alternative, and sometimes an opportunity cost. An outlay cost is a future cost that requires a future expenditure. An opportunity cost is the net cash flow from the most desirable other alternative. When resources are limited, the initiation of one action requires management to forgo competing alternative actions. The net cash flow from the most desirable other alternative is the opportunity cost of the action selected.

Irrelevant costs, which include sunk costs and certain outlay costs, do not differ among competing alternatives. Sunk costs are historical costs resulting from past decisions. There is absolutely nothing management can do to change the total amount of these costs. All outlay costs are relevant to some decisions, such as the decision to continue or discontinue operations, but not all outlay costs are relevant to all decisions. Outlay costs that do not differ under decision alternatives are not relevant to that decision. A summary classification of relevant and irrelevant costs is presented in Exhibit 5–5.

Although this chapter has focused on short-run decisions, decisions should not be based solely on short-run cost minimization or profit maximization. This is especially true in price setting and determining whether to accept or reject a special order. Any price in excess of variable cost increases current profits. In the long run, all costs are variable. Accordingly, average prices must exceed the full cost of products or services if the firm is to remain in business in the long run.

EXHIBIT 5–5   Summary Classification of Relevant and Irrelevant Costs

Relevant Costs			Irrelevant Costs
Future costs that differ among competing alternatives			Costs that do not differ among competing alternatives
Opportunity Cost	**Outlay Costs**		**Sunk Cost**
Net cash flow from the best alternative	Future costs requiring future expenditures that differ	Future costs requiring future expenditures that do not differ	A historical cost resulting from a past decision

KEY TERMS

Cost prediction error
Cost reduction proposal
Differential cost analysis
Full cost
Joint cost
Joint products
Manufacturing cost markup

Marginal cost
Marginal revenue
Outlay costs
Robinson–Patman Act
Split-off point
Variable cost markup

REVIEW QUESTIONS

5–1   Distinguish between relevant and irrelevant revenues.

5–2   In evaluating a cost reduction proposal, what three alternatives are available to the management of a for-profit organization?

5–3   When are outlay costs relevant? When are outlay costs irrelevant?

5–4   Are variable costs always relevant? Why or why not?

5–5   Are fixed costs always irrelevant? Why or why not?

5–6   Are sunk costs ever relevant? Why or why not?

5–7   Why is a differential analysis of relevant items preferred to a detailed listing of all costs and revenues associated with each alternative?

5–8   In evaluating a special order management might erroneously compare the special price to the average unit cost of goods sold. Mention two ways that management can avoid this error.

5–9   What costs should be considered in evaluating a special order that will extend over several years?

5–10   When are opportunity costs relevant to the evaluation of a special order?

5–11   How should limited resources be used to achieve short-run profit maximization?

5–12   In the decision to sell or process further, of what relevance are costs incurred prior to the decision point? Explain your answer.

5–13   How is the optimal production and sales volume determined in economic models?

5–14   Why are cost data widely used as a starting point in pricing decisions?

5–15   In cost-based pricing, what is the most useful way of presenting the variable cost markup to management?

REVIEW PROBLEM

Applications of Differential Analysis

The Carbon Copy produces cartridge ribbons for electronic typewriters. The ribbons are sold to mail-order distributors for $4.80. Manufacturing and other costs are as follows:

Variable Costs per Unit		Fixed Costs per Month	
Direct materials	$2.00	Factory overhead	$15,000
Direct labor	0.20	Selling and administration	5,000
Factory overhead	0.25	Total	$20,000
Distribution	0.05		
Total	$2.50		

The variable distribution costs are for transportation to mail-order distributors. The current monthly production and sales volume is 15,000. Monthly capacity is 20,000 units.

Requirements

Determine the effect of the following on monthly profits. Each situation is to be evaluated independent of all others.

a) A $1.50 increase in the unit selling price should result in a 1,800 unit decrease in monthly sales.

b) A $1.80 decrease in the unit selling price should result in a 6,000 unit increase in monthly sales. However, because of capacity constraints, the last 1,000 units would be produced during overtime, when the direct labor costs increase by 50 percent.

c) A New Zealand distributor has proposed to place a special one-time order for 4,000 units next month at a reduced price of $4 per unit. The distributor would pay all transportation costs. There would be additional fixed selling and administrative costs of $500.

d) An Australian distributor has proposed to place a special one-time order for 8,000 units at a special price of $4 per unit. The distributor would pay all transportation costs. There would be additional fixed selling and administrative of $500. Assume overtime production is not possible.

e) A Mexican manufacturer has offered a one-year contract to supply cartridges for the ribbons at a cost of $1.00 per unit. If Carbon Copy accepts the offer, they will be able to reduce variable manufacturing costs by 40 percent and rent some space currently used to manufacture cartridges for $1,000 per month.

f) The cartridge ribbons are currently unpackaged; that is, they are sold in bulk. Packaging them individually would increase costs by $0.10 per unit. However, the units could now be sold for $5.05.

g) Carbon Copy produces a variety of carbon ribbons. The given information is for an average unit. Determine the variable cost markup required to earn an annual profit of $120,000.

The solution to this problem is found at the end of the Chapter 5 exercises and problems.

EXERCISES

5–1 Relevant Cost Terms: Matching

A company that produces three products, M, N, and O, is evaluating a proposal that will result in doubling the production of N and discontinuing the production of O. The facilities that are currently used to produce O will be devoted to the production of N. Furthermore, additional machinery will be acquired to produce N. The production of M will not be affected. All products have a positive contribution margin.

Presented are a number of phrases or statements related to the proposal. For each phrase or statement, select the most appropriate cost term. Each term is used only once.

1. Increased revenues from the sale of N
2. Increased variable costs of N
3. Property taxes on the new machinery
4. Revenues from the sale of M
5. Cost of the equipment used to produce O
6. Contribution margin of O
7. Variable costs of M
8. The salary of the company president

a. Opportunity cost
b. Sunk cost
c. Irrelevant variable outlay cost
d. Irrelevant fixed outlay cost
e. Relevant variable outlay cost
f. Relevant fixed outlay cost
g. Relevant revenues
h. Irrelevant revenues

5–2 Relevant Cost Terms: Matching

A company that produces and sells 4,000 units per month, but has the capacity to produce 5,000 units per month, is evaluating a one-time special order for 2,000 units from a large chain store. Accepting the order will result in an increase in variable manufacturing costs and certain fixed selling and administrative costs. It will also require the company to forgo the sale of 1,000 units to regular customers.

Presented are a number of statements related to the proposal. For each statement, select the most appropriate cost term. Each term is used only once.

1. Cost of equipment used to produce special order
2. Lost contribution margin from forgone sales to regular customers
3. Increased revenues from special order
4. Variable cost of 4,000 units sold to regular customers
5. Increase in fixed selling and administrative expenses
6. Revenues from 4,000 units sold to regular customers
7. Salary paid to supervisor who oversees manufacture of special order
8. Increased variable costs of special order

a. Irrelevant variable outlay cost
b. Irrelevant fixed outlay cost
c. Sunk cost
d. Relevant variable outlay cost
e. Relevant fixed outlay costs
f. Opportunity cost
g. Relevant revenues
h. Irrelevant revenues

5–3 Identifying Relevant Costs and Revenues

The Ames Company manufactures two components (A and B) and assembles them into a final product. Ames is evaluating two alternative proposals.

Proposal 1 calls for buying component B. This action would free up facilities to manufacture more units of component A and assemble more units of final product. Management believes the additional production can be sold at the current market price. No new assembly equipment would be needed.

Proposal 2 calls for replacing the equipment currently used to manufacture component B. The new equipment would operate with fewer workers and less power. The salvage value of the old equipment is equal to its removal costs.

Presented are a number of cost and revenue items related to the operations of the Ames Company. Under the columns for proposals 1 and 2 indicate whether each item is relevant or irrelevant to that proposal.

	Proposal 1	Proposal 2
1. Sales revenue		
2. Variable costs of assembling final product		
3. Direct materials—component A		
4. Direct materials—component B		
5. Direct labor—component A		
6. Direct labor—component B		
7. Variable overhead—component A		
8. Variable overhead—component B		
9. Cost of final assembly equipment		
10. Cost of A manufacturing equipment		
11. Cost of old B manufacturing equipment		
12. Cost of new B manufacturing equipment		
13. Variable selling and administrative costs		
14. Fixed selling and administrative costs		

5–4 Identifying Relevant Costs and Revenues

The village of Twin Falls operates a hydro plant on the west side of a river that flows through town. The village uses some of the electricity generated by the plant to operate a water treatment plant and sells the excess electricity to a local utility. The village council is evaluating two alternative proposals.

Proposal 1 calls for replacing the generators used in the plant with more efficient generators that will produce more electricity and have lower operating costs. The salvage value of the old generators is greater than their removal cost.

Proposal 2 calls for raising the level of the dam to retain more water for power generation and increasing the force of water flowing through the dam. This will significantly increase the amount of electricity generated by the plant. Operating costs will not be affected.

Presented are a number of cost and revenue items. Under the columns for proposals 1 and 2 indicate whether each item is relevant or irrelevant to that proposal.

	Proposal 1	Proposal 2
1. Cost of new fire engine		
2. Cost of old generators		
3. Cost of new generators		
4. Operating cost of old generators		
5. Operating cost of new generators		
6. Mayor's salary		
7. Depreciation on old generators		

8. Salvage value of old generators

9. Removal cost of old generators

10. Cost of raising dam

11. Maintenance costs of water plant

12. Revenues from sale of electricity

5–5 Classifying Relevant and Irrelevant Items

Taylor, Taylor, and Tower, Attorneys at Law, have been asked to represent a local client in proceedings to be held in Washington, D.C. Classify each of the following items on the basis of their relationship to this engagement. Items may have multiple classifications.

	Relevant Costs		Irrelevant Costs	
	Opportunity	Outlay	Outlay	Sunk

1. The case will require three attorneys to stay four nights in a Washington hotel. The predicted hotel bill is $1,200.

2. Taylor, Taylor, and Tower's professional staff is paid $800 per day for out-of-town assignments.

3. Last year, depreciation on Taylor, Taylor, and Tower's office was $12,000.

4. Round-trip transportation to Washington is expected to cost $250 per person for the engagement.

5. The firm has recently accepted an engagement that will require them to spend two weeks in Atlanta. The predicted out-of-pocket costs of this engagement are $8,500.

6. The firm has a maintenance contract on its word processing equipment that will cost $2,200 next year.

7. If the firm accepts the engagement in Washington, it will have to decline a conflicting engagement in Hilton Head that would have provided a net cash inflow of $7,200.

8. The firm's variable overhead is $8 per client hour.

9. The firm pays $50 per year for Mr. Tower's subscription to a law journal.

10. Last year the firm paid $3,500 to increase the insulation in its building.

5–6 Classifying Relevant and Irrelevant Items

Baltimore Computer Services maintains records and prepares reports for area businesses. Fantastic Clipper Hair Shoppes has asked Baltimore to maintain their payroll records for an annual fee of $800. Classify each of the following items on the basis of its relationship to the decision to accept or reject Fantastic Clipper's order. Items may have multiple classifications.

	Relevant Costs		Irrelevant Costs	
	Opportunity	Outlay	Outlay	Sunk

1. Baltimore Computer's President earned $60,000 last year.

2. Baltimore Computer intends to spend $10,000 on advertising next year.

3. Baltimore Computer owns 5 printers that cost $6,000 each.

4. The Fantastic Clipper job would require 2 labor-hours per month for data entry at $15 per hour.

5. The sales manager is paid a 2 percent commission on gross revenues.

6. Baltimore Computer's utility bills were $15,000 last year.

7. The Fantastic Clipper job would use supplies costing $75 per year.

8. Sam's Head House, a major competitor of Fantastic Clipper, currently uses Baltimore Computer Services. Sam indicated he will take his business

elsewhere if Baltimore accepts Fantastic's order. Sam's business provides an annual net cash inflow of $150.

9. Depreciation on Baltimore's computer will be $5,200 next year.

10. Variable overhead is $8.50 per labor-hour.

5-7 Special Order

The Produce Patch is a new health food restaurant situated on a busy highway in Pomona, California. The Produce Patch specializes in a chef's salad dinner selling for $6. Daily fixed costs are $1,500, and variable costs are $3 per meal. An average of 750 meals are served each day even though the capacity is 800 meals per day.

Requirements

a) Determine the current average cost per meal.

b) A bus load of 40 Girl Scouts, on their way home from the San Bernadino National Forest, stops by and the scoutmaster offers to bring them in if the scouts can all be served a meal for a total of $150. The owner refuses, saying he would lose $1.25 per meal if he accepted this offer. Comment.

c) A local businessman on a tomato juice break overhears the conversation with the scoutmaster and offers the owner a one-year contract to feed 300 of his employees at the special price of $3.75 per meal. Should the restaurant owner accept? Why or why not?

5-8 Special Order: High-Low Cost Estimation

The Quality Belt Company produces seat belts that are sold to North American automobile manufacturers. Although the company has a capacity of 300,000 belts per year, it is currently producing at an annual rate of 180,000 belts.

Quality Belt has received an order from a German manufacturer to purchase 60,000 belts at $9.50 each. Budgeted costs for 180,000 and 240,000 units are as follows:

Units	180,000	240,000
Manufacturing costs:		
Direct materials	$ 450,000	$ 600,000
Direct labor	315,000	420,000
Factory overhead	1,215,000	1,260,000
Total	$1,980,000	$2,280,000
Selling and administrative	765,000	780,000
Total	$2,745,000	$3,060,000
Costs per unit:		
Manufacturing	$11.00	$ 9.50
Selling and administrative	4.25	3.25
Total	$15.25	$12.75

Sales to North American manufacturers are priced at $20 per unit, but the sales manager believes Quality Belt should aggressively seek the German business even if it results in a loss of $3.25 per unit. She believes obtaining this order would open up several new markets for the company's product. The general manager is concerned about the ethical and legal problems associated with accepting the order. He also commented that Quality Belt cannot tighten its belt enough to absorb the $195,000 loss ($3.25 × 60,000) they would incur if the order is accepted.

Requirements

a) Determine the financial implications of accepting the order.

b) How would your analysis differ if Quality Belt were operating at capacity? Determine the net advantage or disadvantage of accepting the order under these circumstances.

c) Comment on the legal implications of accepting the order.

5–9 Make or Buy

Fresh Air Limited manufactures a line of room air fresheners. Management is currently evaluating the possible production of an air freshener for the passenger compartment of automobiles. Based on an annual volume of 10,000 units, the predicted cost of an auto air freshener is as shown below.

Direct materials	$ 8.00 per unit
Direct labor	1.50 per unit
Factory overhead	7.00 per unit
Total	$16.50 per unit

These cost predictions include an allocation of $50,000 in fixed factory overhead.

One of the component parts of the auto air freshener is a battery operated electric motor. Fresh Air does not currently manufacture battery operated electric motors. However, the above cost predictions are based on the assumption that Fresh Air will assemble such a motor.

The Mini Motor Company has offered to supply an assembled battery operated motor at a cost of $4.00 per unit, with a minimum annual order of 5,000 units. If Fresh Air accepts this offer, it will be able to reduce the variable labor and variable overhead costs of the auto air freshener by 50 percent. The electric motor's components will cost $2.00 if Fresh Air assembles the motors.

Requirements

a) Determine whether Fresh Air should make or buy the electric motor.

b) If Fresh Air could rent the space the motors would be assembled in for $8,000 per year, should they make or buy this component?

c) What additional factors should Fresh Air consider in deciding whether they should make or buy the electric motors?

5–10 Make or Buy   John Rahavy III, MD, is a general practitioner whose offices are located in the South Falls Professional Building. In the past Dr. Rahavy has operated his practice with a nurse, a receptionist/secretary, and a part-time bookkeeper. Dr. Rahavy, like many small town physicians, has billed his patients and their insurance companies from his own office. The part-time bookkeeper, who works 10 hours per week, is employed exclusively for this purpose.

The North Falls Physician's Service Center has offered to take over all of Dr. Rahavy's billings and collections for an annual fee of $7,500. If Dr. Rahavy accepts this offer, he will no longer need the bookkeeper. The bookkeeper's wages and fringe benefits amount to $8 per hour, and the bookkeeper works 50 weeks per year. With all the billings and collections done elsewhere, Dr. Rahavy will have 2 additional hours available per week to see patients. Dr. Rahavy sees an average of 3 patients per hour at an average fee of $30 per visit. His practice is expanding, and new patients often have to wait several weeks for an appointment. Dr. Rahavy has resisted expanding his office hours or working more than 50 weeks per year. Finally, if Dr. Rahavy subscribes to the computer service, he will no longer need to rent a records storage locker in the basement of the Professional Building. The locker rents for $100 per month.

Required: Determine whether or not Dr. Rahavy should subscribe to the service.

5–11 Limited Resources   The Cape Town Manufacturing Company, Ltd. produces three products: X, Y, and Z. A limitation of 200 labor-hours per week prevents Cape Town Manufacturing from meeting the sales demand for these products. Product information is as follows:

	X	Y	Z
Unit selling price	$160	$100	$200
Unit variable costs	−100	− 50	−180
Unit contribution margin	$ 60	$ 50	$ 20
Labor-hours per unit	4	2	4

Requirements

a) Determine the weekly contribution from each product when total labor-hours are allocated to the product with the highest:

   1. Unit selling price.

   2. Unit contribution margin.

   3. Contribution per labor-hour.

   Hint: Each situation is independent of the others.

b) What generalization can be made regarding the allocation of limited resources to achieve short-run profit maximization?

c) Determine the opportunity cost Cape Town Manufacturing will incur if management requires the weekly production of 10 units of X.

5–12 Limited Resources

John Drive, a regional sales representative for the Byte Computer Supply Company, has been working more than 80 hours per week calling on a total of 140 regular customers each month. Because of considerations of family and health, he has decided to spend no more than 40 hours per week, or 160 per month, with customers. Unfortunately, this cutback will require John to turn away some of his regular customers, or at least serve them less frequently than once a month. John has developed the following information to assist him in determining how to best allocate his time.

	Customer Classification		
	Large Business	Small Business	Individual
Number of customers	10	50	80
Average monthly sales per customer	$2,000	$1,000	$500
Commission percentage	5%	7%	10%
Hours per customer per monthly visit	4.0	2.0	2.5

Required: Develop a monthly plan indicating the number of customers he should call on in each classification to maximize his monthly sales commissions. Determine the monthly commissions he will earn if he implements this plan.

5–13 Sell or Process Further

The Finger Lakes Boat Company manufactures sailboat hulls at a cost of $4,200 per unit. The hulls are sold to boat yards for $5,000. Finger Lakes Boat Company is evaluating the desirability of adding masts, sails, and rigging to the hulls prior to sale. The additional parts would cost $1,500. However, the completed sailboats could then be sold for $5,800 each.

Required: Determine whether Finger Lakes should sell sailboat hulls or process them further into complete sailboats. Assume sales volume will not be affected.

5–14 Sell or Process Further

The Morristown Chemical Company processes raw material D into joint products E and F. Each 100 liters of D yields 60 liters of E and 40 liters of F. Raw material D costs $5 per liter, and it costs $100 to convert 100 liters of D into E and F. Product F can be sold immediately for $5 per liter or processed further into product G at an additional cost of $4 per liter. Product G can then be sold for $15 per liter.

Required: Determine whether product F should be sold or processed further into product G.

5–15 Single Product Price Setting

Presented is the 19y2 contribution income statement of Simplex Products.

Simplex Products
Contribution Income Statement
For the year ending December 31, 19y2

Sales (12,000 units)		$1,440,000
Less variable costs:		
Cost of goods sold	$480,000	
Selling and administrative	132,000	−612,000
Contribution margin		$ 828,000
Less fixed costs:		
Factory overhead	$520,000	
Selling and administrative	210,000	−730,000
Net income		$ 98,000

During the coming year it is expected that variable manufacturing costs will increase by $6 per unit and fixed manufacturing costs will increase by $48,000.

Requirements

a) If sales remain at 12,000 units, what price should Simplex charge to produce the same profit as last year?

b) Management believes that sales can be increased to 16,000 units if the selling price is lowered to $107. Is this action desirable?

c) After taking into consideration the expected increases in costs, what sales volume is needed to earn a profit of $98,000 with a unit selling price of $107?

5–16 Single Product Price Setting

Mary Morgan is planning to open a soft ice cream franchise. The franchise will operate in a resort community during June, July, and August. Fixed operating costs for the three-month period are projected to be $5,250. Variable costs per serving include the cost of the ice cream and cone, $0.25, and a franchise fee payable to Snowdrift Cooler, $0.05. A market analysis prepared by Snowdrift Cooler indicates that summer sales in the resort community should total 22,500 units.

Required: Determine the price Mary Morgan should charge for each ice cream cone to achieve a profit of $6,000 for the three-month period.

5–17 Relevant Cost Concepts

Benjamin Franklin observed that:

Time is money. He that can earn ten shillings a day by his labor and goes abroad or sits idle one-half of that day, though he spends but sixpense during his diversion or idleness, ought not to recon that the only expense; he has really spent, or rather thrown away, five shillings besides.

Required: Identify the relevant cost concepts referred to in this quote.

PROBLEMS

5–18 Multiple Changes in Profit Plans

Presented is the Mountainside Company's April 19x6 contribution income statement.

Mountainside Company
Contribution Income Statement
For the month of April, 19x6

Sales (10,000 units × $40)			$400,000
Less variable costs:			
Cost of goods sold:			
Direct materials (10,000 units × $5)	$ 50,000		
Direct labor (10,000 units × $14)	140,000		
Variable factory overhead			
(10,000 units × $6)	60,000	$250,000	
Selling and administrative			
(10,000 units × $5)		50,000	−300,000
Contribution margin (10,000 units × $10)			$100,000
Less fixed costs:			
Factory overhead		$ 50,000	
Selling and administrative		60,000	−110,000
Net income (loss)			$ (10,000)

In an attempt to improve the company's profit performance, management is considering a number of alternative actions. They have asked your help in evaluating the consequences of each.

Requirements

Determine the effect of each of the following on monthly profit. Each situation is to be evaluated independent of all others.

a) Purchasing automated assembly equipment. This action should reduce direct labor costs by $6 per unit. It will also increase variable overhead costs by $2 per unit and fixed factory overhead by $20,000 per month.

b) Reducing the unit selling price by $5 per unit. This should increase the monthly sales by 5,000 units. At this higher volume additional equipment and salaried personnel would be required. This will increase fixed factory overhead by $3,000 per month and fixed selling and administrative costs by $2,500 per month.

c) Buying rather than manufacturing a component of Mountainside's final product. This will increase direct materials costs by $15 per unit. However, direct labor will decline $4 per unit, variable factory overhead will decline $1 per unit, and fixed factory overhead will decline $10,000 per month.

d) Increasing the unit selling price by $3 per unit. This action should result in a 1,000 unit decrease in monthly sales.

e) Combining requirements (a) and (d).

5–19 Multiple Changes in Profit Plans: Multiple Products

Information on Flamingo Bay's three products follow.

	A	B	C
Unit sales per month	800	1,400	900
Selling price per unit	$ 5.00	$7.50	$4.00
Variable costs per unit	− 5.20	−6.00	−2.00
Unit contribution margin	$(0.20)	$1.50	$2.00

Requirements

Determine the effect of each of the following on monthly profits. Each situation is to be evaluated independent of all others.

a) Product A is discontinued.

b) Product A is discontinued, and the subsequent loss of customers causes sales of B to decline by 100 units.

c) The selling price of A is increased to $5.50 with a sales decrease of 200 units.

d) The price of B is increased to $8.00 with a sales decrease of 200 units. However, some of these customers shift to product A, and sales of product A increase by 100 units.

e) Product A is discontinued, and the plant in which A was produced is used to produce D, a new product. Product D has a unit contribution margin of $0.30. Monthly sales of product D are predicted to be 700 units.

f) The selling price of product C is increased to $5, and the selling price of product B is decreased to $7. Sales of C decline by 200 units, and sales of B increase by 300 units.

5–20 Multiple Product Price Setting

The Sussex Company's predicted 19x0 variable and fixed costs are as follows:

Variable Costs		Fixed Costs	
Manufacturing	$400,000	Manufacturing	$200,000
Selling and administrative	100,000	Selling and administrative	50,000
Total	$500,000	Total	$250,000

Sussex produces a wide variety of small tools. Information about one of these products, the type A clamp, is as follows:

	Unit
Direct materials	$ 5
Direct labor	7
Factory overhead:	
Variable	6
Fixed	6
Total manufacturing costs	$24
Variable selling and administrative costs	$ 3

Management has set a $150,000 profit goal for 19x1.

Requirements

a) Determine the markup percentage on variable costs required to earn the desired profit.

b) Use variable cost markup to determine a suggested selling price for the type A clamp.

c) For the type A clamp, break the markup on variable costs into separate parts for fixed costs and profit. Explain the significance of each part.

d) Determine the markup percentage on manufacturing costs required to earn the desired profit.

e) Use the manufacturing cost markup to determine a suggested selling price for the type A clamp.

f) Evaluate the variable and the manufacturing cost approaches to determining the markup percentage.

5–21 Multiple Product Price Setting

The Chesapeake Tackle Company produces a wide variety of commercial fishing equipment. In the past the prices of individual products have been set by product managers on the basis of professional judgment. John Marlin, the new Controller, believes this practice has led to the significant underpricing of some products (and lost profits) and the significant overpricing of other products (and lost sales volume). You have been asked to assist Mr. Marlin in developing a corporate approach to pricing. The output of your work should be a cost-based formula that can be used to develop initial selling prices for each product. Though product managers are allowed to adjust these prices to meet competition and take advantage of market opportunities, they must explain such deviations in writing.

You have obtained the following 19x4 cost information from the accounting records:

Manufacturing Costs		Selling and Administrative Costs	
Variable	$350,000	Variable	$ 50,000
Fixed	150,000	Fixed	200,000
Total	$500,000	Total	$250,000

In 19x4 Chesapeake reported earnings of $80,000. However, the Controller believes that proper pricing should produce earnings of at least $120,000 on the same sales mix and unit volume. Accordingly, you are to use the above cost information and a target profit of $120,000 in developing a pricing formula.

Selling and administrative expenses are not currently associated with individual products. However, you have obtained the following unit production cost information for the Tigershark Reel.

Variable manufacturing costs	$120 per unit
Fixed factory overhead	60 per unit
Total	$180 per unit

Requirements

a) Determine the standard markup percentage for each of the following cost bases. Round answers to three decimal places.

1. Full cost, including fixed and variable manufacturing costs, and fixed and variable selling and administrative costs.

2. Manufacturing costs plus variable selling and administrative costs.

3. Manufacturing costs.

4. Variable costs.

5. Variable manufacturing costs.

b) Explain why the markup percentages became progressively larger between parts 1 and 5 of requirement (a).

c) Determine the initial price of a Tigershark Reel using the manufacturing cost markup and the variable manufacturing cost markup.

d) Do you believe the Controller's approach to product pricing is reasonable? Why or why not?

5–22 Relevant Costs and Differential Analysis

The Third National Bank of Outback paid $50,000 for a check-sorting machine in January 19x1. The machine had an estimated life of 10 years and annual operating costs of $40,000, excluding depreciation. Although management is pleased with the machine, recent technological advances have made it obsolete. Consequently, as of January 19x5, the machine has a book value of $30,000, a remaining operating life of 6 years, and a salvage value of $0.

The manager of operations is evaluating a proposal to acquire a new Perfect Reader II—Optical Scanning and Sorting Machine. The new machine would cost $60,000 and reduce annual operating costs to $25,000, excluding depreciation. Because of expected technological improvements, the manager believes the new machine will have an economic life of only 6 years and no salvage value at the end of that life.

Prior to signing the papers authorizing the acquisition of the new machine, the president of The Third National Bank prepared the following analysis:

Six-year savings [($40,000 − $25,000) × 6 years]	$ 90,000
Cost of new machine	(60,000)
Loss on disposal of old machine	(30,000)
Advantage (disadvantage) of replacement	$ 0

After looking at these numbers he rejected the proposal and commented that he was ". . . tired of looking at marginal projects. This bank is in business to make a profit, not to break even. If you want to break even, go work for the government."

Requirements

a) Evaluate the president's analysis.

b) Prepare a differential analysis of six-year totals for the old and the new machine.

5-23 Cost Plus Pricing and a Special Order

Thousand Islands Propulsion Company produces a variety of electric trolling motors. Management follows a pricing policy of manufacturing cost plus 60 percent. In response to a request from Northern Sporting Goods, the following price has been developed for an order of 300 Minnow Motors (this is the smallest motor Thousand Island produces):

Manufacturing costs:	
Direct materials	$10,000
Direct labor	12,000
Factory overhead	18,000
Total	$40,000
Markup (60 percent)	24,000
Selling price	$64,000

Mr. Bass, the president of Northern Sporting Goods, rejected this price as too high and offered to purchase the 300 Minnow Motors at a price of $44,000.

Additional information:

- Thousand Islands has sufficient excess capacity to produce the motors.
- Factory overhead is applied on the basis of direct labor dollars.
- Budgeted factory overhead is $400,000 for the current year. Of this amount, $100,000 is fixed.
- Selling and administrative expenses are budgeted as follows:

Fixed	$90,000 per year
Variable	$20 per unit manufactured and sold

Requirements

a) The president of Thousand Islands Propulsion wants to know if he should allow Mr. Bass to have the Minnows for $44,000. Determine the effect on profits of accepting Mr. Bass' offer.

b) Briefly explain why you omitted certain costs from your analysis in requirement (a).

c) Assume Thousand Islands is operating at capacity and that they could sell the 300 Minnows at their regular markup.

  1. Determine the opportunity cost of accepting Mr. Bass' offer.

  2. Determine the effect on profits of accepting Mr. Bass' offer.

5-24 Special Order

Every Halloween the Glacier Ice Cream Shop offers a Trick-or-Treat package of 20 coupons for $3. The coupons are redeemable, by children of 12 or under, for a single-scoop cone of Glacier ice cream, with a limit of one coupon per child per visit. Coupon sales average 500 books per year. The printing costs are $60.

A single-scoop cone of Glacier Ice Cream normally sells for $0.60. The variable costs of a single-scoop cone are $0.40.

Requirements

a) Determine the loss if all coupons are redeemed without any other effect on sales.

b) Not all coupons will be redeemed. Assuming regular sales are not affected, determine the coupon redemption rate at which Glacier will break even on the offer.

c) Assuming regular sales are not affected and that each time a coupon is redeemed one additional single-scoop cone is sold at the regular price, determine the coupon redemption rate at which Glacier will break even on the offer.

d) Determine the profit or loss incurred on the offer if the coupon redemption rate is 60 percent and:

- One fourth of the redeemed coupons have no effect on sales.
- One fourth of the redeemed coupons result in additional sales of 2 single-scoop cones.
- One fourth of the redeemed coupons result in additional sales of 3 single-scoop cones.
- One fourth of the redeemed coupons come out of regular sales of single-scoop cones.

5–25 Applications of Differential Analysis

The Bird Box produces squirrel-proof bird feeders. The bird feeders are sold to mail-order distributors for $25.00. Manufacturing and other costs are as follows:

Variable Costs per Unit		Fixed Costs per Month	
Direct materials	$ 8.00	Factory overhead	$10,000
Direct labor	7.00	Selling and administrative	5,000
Factory overhead	2.00	Total	$15,000
Distribution	3.00		
Total	$20.00		

The variable distribution costs are for transportation to mail-order distributors. The current monthly production and sales volume is 5,000 units. Monthly capacity is 6,000 units.

Requirements

Determine the effect of each of the following on monthly profits. Each situation is to be evaluated independent of all others.

a) A $2.50 increase in the unit selling price should result in a 1,000 unit decrease in monthly sales.

b) A $2.00 decrease in the unit selling price should result in a 2,000 unit increase in monthly sales. However, because of capacity constraints, the last 1,000 units would be produced during overtime, when the direct labor costs increase by 60 percent.

c) A British distributor has proposed to place a special one-time order for 1,000 units next month at a reduced price of $20 per unit. The distributor would pay all transportation costs. There would be additional fixed selling and administrative costs of $100.

d) A Dutch distributor has proposed to place a special one-time order for 2,500 units at a special price of $20 per unit. The distributor would pay all transportation costs. There would be additional fixed selling and administrative costs of $200. Assume overtime production is not possible.

e) A Canadian manufacturer has offered a one-year contract to supply a squirrel guard that attaches to the bottom of the feeder at a cost of $4 per unit. If the Bird Box accepts the offer, they will be able to reduce variable manufacturing costs by 10 percent, reduce fixed costs by $500 per month, and rent some space currently used to manufacture bird feeders for $900 per month.

f) The bird feeders are currently sold assembled and ready for mounting. Selling the feeders unassembled would reduce costs by $5.00 per unit. However, the units could now be sold for only $21.00.

g) The Bird Box produces a variety of bird feeders. The given information is for an average unit. Determine the variable cost markup required to earn a monthly profit of $20,000.

5-26 Applications of Differential Analysis

Bush-Wack Expeditions offers guided back-country hiking/camping trips in British Columbia. Bush-Wack provides a guide and all necessary food and equipment at a fee of $50 per person per day. Bush-Wack currently provides an average of 600 guide-days per month in June, July, August, and September. Based on available equipment and staff, maximum capacity is 800 guide-days per month. Monthly variable and fixed operating costs are as follows:

Variable Costs per Guide-Day		Fixed Costs per Month	
Food	$ 5.00	Equipment rental	$ 5,000
Guide salary	25.00	Administration	5,000
Supplies	2.00	Advertising	2,000
Insurance	8.00	Total	$12,000
Total	$40.00		

Requirements

Determine the effect of each of the following on monthly profits. Each situation is to be evaluated independent of all others.

a) A $12 increase in the daily fee should result in a 200 unit decrease in monthly sales.

b) A $5 decrease in the daily fee should result in a 300 unit increase in monthly sales. However, because of capacity constraints, the last 100 guide-days would be provided by subcontracting to another firm at a cost of $46 per guide-day.

c) A French tour agency has proposed to place a special one-time order for 80 guide-days next month at a reduced fee of $45 per guide-day. The agency would pay all insurance costs. There would be additional fixed administrative costs of $200.

d) An Italian tour agency has proposed to place a special one-time order for 300 guide-days next month at a special fee of $45 per guide-day. The agency would pay all insurance costs. There would be additional fixed administrative costs of $200. Assume additional capacity beyond 800 guide-days is not available.

e) An Alberta outdoor supply company has offered to supply all necessary food and camping equipment at $7.50 per guide-day. This eliminates the current food costs and reduces the monthly equipment rental costs to $1,500.

f) Clients must currently carry a backpack and assist in camp activities such as cooking. Bush-Wack is considering the addition of mules to carry all food and equipment and the hiring of college students to perform camp activities such as cooking. This will increase variable costs by $10 per guide-day and fixed costs by $1,200 per month. However, 600 full-service guide-days per month could now be sold at $75.00 each.

g) Bush-Wack provides a number of different types of wilderness experiences. The given information is for an average tour. Determine the variable cost markup required to earn a monthly profit of $6,000.

5–27 Differential Analysis of Alternative Facilities

Williams Company owns and operates a nationwide chain of movie theaters. The 500 properties in the Williams chain vary from low volume, small town, single-screen theaters to high volume, big city, multiscreen theaters.

Management is considering installing machines that will make popcorn on the premises. These machines would allow the theaters to sell freshly popped popcorn daily rather than the prepopped popcorn that is currently purchased in large bags. This proposed feature would be properly advertised and is intended to increase patronage at the company's theaters.

The machines are available from a leasing company in several different sizes. The annual rental and operating costs vary with the size of the machine. The machine capacities and costs are shown below.

	Popper Model		
	Economy	Regular	Super
Annual capacity (boxes)	50,000	120,000	300,000
Costs:			
Annual machine rental	$8,000	$11,000	$20,000
Popcorn cost per box	0.13	0.13	0.13
Other costs per box	0.22	0.14	0.05
Cost of each box	0.08	0.08	0.08

Requirements

a) Calculate the sales volume in boxes at which the Economy Popper and the Regular Popper would earn the same profit.

b) Management can estimate the number of boxes to be sold at each theater. Present a decision rule, based on sales volume in boxes, that would enable Williams' management to select the most profitable machine without having to make a separate cost calculation for each theater.

c) Could management use the average number of boxes sold per seat for the entire chain and the capacity of each theater to develop the decision rule? Explain your answer.

(CMA Adapted)

5–28 Relevant Costs for Various Decisions

The income statement for Davann Co. presented below represents the operating results for the fiscal year just ended. Davann had sales of 1,800 tons of product during the current year. The manufacturing capacity of Davann's facilities is 3,000 tons of product.

Davann Co.
Income Statement
For the year ended December 31, 19y0

Sales	$900,000
Variable costs:	
Manufacturing	$315,000
Selling	180,000
Total variable costs	−495,000
Contribution margin	$405,000
Fixed costs:	
Manufacturing	$ 90,000
Selling	112,500
Administrative	45,000
Total fixed costs	−247,500
Net income before taxes	$157,500
Income taxes (40%)	− 63,000
Net income	$ 94,500

Requirements

a) Determine the 19y0 break-even volume in tons of product.

b) Determine the expected 19y1 after-tax net income, assuming a sales volume of 2,100 tons and no changes in selling prices or cost behavior.

c) Assume demand from regular customers equals 1,800 tons in 19y1 and there are no changes in regular selling prices or cost behavior. Davann has a potential foreign customer that has offered to buy 1,500 tons at $450 per ton. What net income after taxes would Davann make in 19y1 if it took this order and rejected some business from regular customers so as not to exceed capacity?

d) Assume Davann will have additional capacity in 19y1 and there are no changes in sales to regular customers, selling prices, or cost behavior. Davann plans to market its product at the regular price in a new territory. This will require an additional promotion program costing $61,500 annually. Additionally, an extra $25 per ton sales commission, over and above the current sales commission, would be required in the new territory. How many tons would have to be sold in the new territory to maintain Davann's current after-tax income of $94,500?

e) Davann is considering replacing a highly labor intensive process with an automatic machine. This would result in an increase of $58,500 in annual fixed manufacturing costs. The variable manufacturing costs would decrease by $25 per ton. Determine the new break-even volume in tons.

f) Davann estimates the per ton selling price will decline by 10 percent next year. If variable costs increase $40 per ton and fixed costs remain unchanged, what sales volume *in dollars* would be required to earn an after-tax net income of $94,500?

(CMA Adapted)

5–29 Potpourri of Relevant Costs

1. Plainfield Company manufactures Part G for use in its production cycle. The costs per unit for 10,000 units of Part G are as follows:

Direct materials	$ 3
Direct labor	15
Variable overhead	6
Fixed overhead	8
	$32

Verona Company has offered to sell Plainfield 10,000 units of Part G for $30 per unit. If Plainfield accepts Verona's offer, the released facilities could be used to save $45,000 in relevant costs in the manufacture of Part H. In addition $5 per unit of the fixed overhead applied to Part G would be totally eliminated. What alternative is more desirable and by what amount is it more desirable?

	Alternative	**Amount**
a)	Manufacture	$10,000
b)	Manufacture	$15,000
c)	Buy	$35,000
d)	Buy	$65,000

2. Boyer Company manufactures basketballs. The forecasted income statement for the year before any special orders is as follows:

	Amount	Per Unit
Sales	$4,000,000	$10.00
Manufacturing cost of goods sold	−3,200,000	− 8.00
Gross profit	$ 800,000	$ 2.00
Selling expenses	− 300,000	− 0.75
Operating income	$ 500,000	$ 1.25

Fixed costs included in the forecasted income statement are $1,200,000 in manufacturing cost of goods sold and $100,000 in selling expenses.

A special order offering to buy 50,000 basketballs for $7.50 each was made to Boyer. There will be no additional selling expenses if the special order is accepted. Assuming Boyer has sufficient capacity to manufacture 50,000 more basketballs, by what amount would operating income be increased or decreased as a result of accepting the special order?

a) $25,000 decrease

b) $62,500 decrease

c) $100,000 increase

d) $125,000 increase

3. Gandy Company has 5,000 obsolete desk lamps that are carried in inventory at a manufacturing cost of $50,000. If the lamps are reworked for $20,000, they could be sold for $35,000. Alternatively, the lamps could be sold for $8,000 to a jobber located in a distant city. In a decision model analyzing these alternatives, the sunk cost would be?

a) $8,000

b) $15,000

c) $20,000

d) $50,000

4. Kingston Company needs 10,000 units of a certain part to be used in its production cycle. The following information is available.

Cost to Kingston Company to make the part:	
Direct materials	$ 6
Direct labor	24
Variable overhead	12
Fixed overhead applied	15
Total	$57
Cost to buy the part from Utica Company	$53

If Kingston buys the part from Utica instead of making it, Kingston could not use the released facilities in another manufacturing activity. Sixty percent of the fixed overhead applied will continue regardless of what decision is made.

In deciding whether to make or buy the part, which of the following is the total relevant cost to make the part?

a) $342,000

b) $480,000

c) $530,000

d) $570,000

5. Yardley Corporation uses a joint process to produce products A, B, and C. Each product may be sold at its split-off point or processed further. Additional processing costs are entirely variable and are traceable to the respective products produced. Joint production costs for 19x5 were $50,000. Relevant data follow.

Product	Units Produced	Sales Value at Split-Off	Sales Value	Additional Costs
			Sales Values and Additional Costs If Processed Further	
A	20,000	$ 45,000	$60,000	$20,000
B	15,000	75,000	98,000	20,000
C	15,000	30,000	62,000	18,000
		$150,000		

To maximize profits, which products should Yardley subject to further processing?

a) A only

b) C only

c) B and C only

d) None, because of joint costs

6. Brike Company, which manufactures robes, has enough idle capacity available to accept a special order of 10,000 robes at $8 a robe. A predicted income statement for the year without this special order is as follows:

	Per Unit	Total
Sales	$12.50	$1,250,000
Manufacturing costs (variable)	$ 6.25	$ 625,000
Manufacturing costs (fixed)	1.75	175,000
Manufacturing costs (total)	− 8.00	− 800,000
Gross profit	$ 4.50	$ 450,000
Selling expenses (variable)	$ 1.80	$ 180,000
Selling expenses (fixed)	1.45	145,000
Selling expenses (total)	− 3.25	− 325,000
Operating income	$ 1.25	$ 125,000

Assuming no additional selling expenses, what would be the effect on operating income if the special order were accepted?

a) $8,000 increase

b) $17,500 increase

c) $32,500 decrease

d) $40,000 increase

(CPA Adapted)

5–30 Analysis of Relevant Costs for Decision Alternatives

Auer Company had received an order for a piece of special machinery from Jay Company. Just as Auer Company completed the machine, Jay Company declared bankruptcy, defaulted on the order, and forfeited the 10 percent deposit paid on the selling price of $72,500.

Auer's manufacturing manager identified the costs already incurred in the production of the special machinery for Jay as follows:

Direct materials used		$16,600
Direct labor incurred		21,400
Overhead applied:		
Manufacturing:		
Variable	$10,700	
Fixed	5,350	16,050
Fixed selling and		
administrative		5,405
Total cost		$59,455

Another company, Kaytell Corp., would be interested in buying the special machinery if it were reworked to Kaytell's specifications. Auer offered to sell the reworked special machinery to Kaytell as a special order for a net price of $68,400. Kaytell has agreed to pay the net price when it takes delivery in two months. The additional identifiable costs to rework the machinery to the specifications of Kaytell are as follows:

Direct materials	$ 6,200
Direct labor	4,200
Total	$10,400

A second alternative available to Auer is to convert the special machinery to the standard model. The standard model lists for $62,500. The additional identifiable costs to convert the special machinery to the standard model are:

Direct materials	$2,850
Direct labor	3,300
Total	$6,150

A third alternative for the Auer Company is to sell, as a special order, the machine as is (e.g., without modification) for a net price of $52,000. However, the potential buyer of the unmodified machine does not want it for 60 days. The buyer offers a $7,000 down payment with final payment upon delivery.

The following additional information is available regarding Auer's operations:

■ The sales commission rate on sales of standard models is 2 percent, whereas the sales commission rate on special orders is 3 percent. All sales commissions are calculated on net sales price (i.e., list price less cash discount, if any).

■ Normal credit terms for sales of standard models are 2/10, net/30, that is, customers who pay within 10 days receive a 2 percent cash discount; otherwise, the full sales price is due within 30 days. Ordinarily, customers take the discounts. Credit terms for special orders are negotiated with the customer.

■ The application rates for manufacturing overhead and the fixed selling and administrative costs are as follows:

Manufacturing:	
Variable	50 percent of direct labor costs
Fixed	25 percent of direct labor costs
Selling and administrative:	
Fixed	10 percent of the total of direct material, direct labor, and manufacturing overhead costs

■ Normal time required for rework is 1 month.

■ A surcharge of 5 percent of the sales price is placed on all customer requests for minor modifications of standard models.

■ Auer normally sells a sufficient number of standard models for the company to operate at a volume in excess of the break-even point.

Auer does not consider the time value of money in analyses of special orders and projects whenever the time period is less than one year because the effect is not significant.

Requirements

a) Determine the dollar contribution each of the three alternatives will make to the Auer Company's before-tax profits.

b) If Kaytell makes Auer a counteroffer, what is the lowest price Auer should accept for the reworked machinery from Kaytell? Explain your answer.

c) Discuss the influence fixed factory overhead cost should have on the sales prices quoted by Auer Company for special orders when

1. A firm is operating at or below the break-even point.

2. A firm's special orders constitute efficient utilization of unused capacity above the break-even volume.

(CMA Adapted)

5–31 Differential Analysis with Joint Costs

Helene's, a high fashion women's dress manufacturer, is planning to market a new cocktail dress for the coming season. Helene's supplies retailers in the east and mid-Atlantic states.

Four yards of material are required to lay out the dress pattern. Some material remains after cutting that can be sold as remnants.

The leftover material could also be used to manufacture a matching cape and handbag. However, if the leftover material is to be used for the cape and handbag, more care will be required in the cutting, which will increase the cutting costs.

The company expected to sell 1,250 dresses if no matching capes or handbags were available. Helene's market research reveals that dress sales will be 20 percent higher if a matching cape and handbag are available. The market research indicates that the cape or handbag will only sell well as optional accessories with the dress. The various combinations of dresses, capes, and handbags that are expected to be manufactured by Helene's and sold by retailers are as follows:

	Percent of Total
Complete sets of dress, cape, and handbag	70
Dress and cape	6
Dress and handbag	15
Dress only	9
Total	100

The material used in the dress costs $12.50 a yard or $50.00 for each dress. The cost of cutting the dress if the cape and handbag are not manufactured is estimated at $20.00 a dress, and the resulting remnants can be sold for $5.00 for each dress cut out. If the cape and handbag are to be manufactured, the cutting costs will be increased by $9.00 per dress. There will be no saleable remnants if the capes and handbags are manufactured in the quantities estimated.

The selling prices and the costs to complete the three items once they are cut are presented below.

	Selling Price Per Unit	Unit Cost to Complete (Excludes Cost of Material and Cutting Operation)
Dress	$200.00	$80.00
Cape	27.50	19.50
Handbag	9.50	6.50

Requirements

a) Calculate Helene's incremental profit or loss from manufacturing the capes and handbags in conjunction with the dresses.

b) Identify any nonquantitative factors that could influence Helene's management in its decision to manufacture the matching capes and handbags.

(CMA Adapted)

**REVIEW PROBLEM
SOLUTION**

Unit selling price	$4.80
Unit variable costs	−2.50
Unit contribution margin	$2.30

a)

Profit decrease from reduced sales if there were no changes in prices or costs (1,800 units × $2.30)		$ (4,140)
Profit increase from increase in selling price [(15,000 units − 1,800 units) × $1.50]		19,800
Increase in monthly profit		$15,660

b)

Profit increase from increased sales if there were no changes in prices or costs (6,000 units × $2.30)		$ 13,800
Profit decrease from reduced selling price of all units [(15,000 units + 6,000 units) × $1.80]		(37,800)
Profit decrease from increased direct labor costs of the last 1,000 units [1,000 units × ($0.20 × 0.50)]		(100)
Decrease in monthly profit		$(24,100)

c)

Increase in revenues (4,000 units × $4)		$16,000
Increase in costs:		
Direct materials (4,000 units × $2.00)	$8,000	
Direct labor (4,000 units × $0.20)	800	
Factory overhead (4,000 units × $0.25)	1,000	
Selling and administrative	500	−10,300
Increase in profits		$ 5,700

d)

Increase in revenues (8,000 units × $4)		$32,000
Increase in costs:		
Direct materials (8,000 units × $2.00)	$16,000	
Direct labor (8,000 units × $0.20)	1,600	
Factory overhead (8,000 units × $0.25)	2,000	
Selling and administrative	500	
Opportunity cost of lost regular sales [(15,000 units + 8,000 units − 20,000 unit capacity) × $2.30]	6,900	−27,000
Increase in profits		$ 5,000

e)

	Cost to Make	Cost to Buy	Difference (Effect of Buying on Income)
Cost to buy (15,000 units × $1)		$15,000	$(15,000)
Cost to make:			
Direct materials			
(15,000 units × $2.00 × 0.40)	$12,000		12,000
Direct labor			
(15,000 units × $0.20 × 0.40)	1,200		1,200
Factory overhead			
(15,000 units × $0.25 × 0.40)	1,500		1,500
Opportunity cost	1,000		1,000
Totals	$15,700	$15,000	$ 700
Advantage of buying	$700		

f) Increase in revenues:

Package individually (15,000 units × $5.05)	$75,750	
Sell in bulk (15,000 units × $4.80)	−72,000	$3,750
Additional packaging costs (15,000 units × $0.10)		−1,500
Advantage of individual packaging		$2,250

g)

Predicted annual fixed costs ($20,000 × 12 months)	$240,000
Predicted annual variable costs (15,000 units × $2.50 × 12)	450,000

$$\frac{\text{Variable}}{\text{cost markup}} = \frac{\$240,000 + \$120,000}{\$450,000}$$

$$= 0.80$$

PART II

Planning and Control

CHAPTER 6

Operating Budgets

Upon completion of this chapter you should:

- Understand the importance of budgeting.
- Understand the input/output, incremental, and minimum level approaches to budgeting, and when each approach is most likely to be used.
- Be aware of the alternative procedures used to collect budget information.
- Be familiar with the parts of a complete operating budget and how they are assembled within an organization.
- Be able to compile the following operating budgets for a small manufacturing firm: sales, production, purchases, manufacturing disbursements, selling expense, general and administrative expense, and cash.
- Be able to prepare a pro forma income statement and a pro forma balance sheet.
- Be aware of common problems encountered in budgeting.

The planning and control cycle involves anticipating future activities before they happen and undertaking measures to ensure they occur in a way that is in the best interest of the organization. More than simply forecasting what will take place and reporting what actually did take place, this cycle is an ongoing process of guiding, monitoring, and governing the organization. In this and the next four chapters, a structure for planning and controlling is developed, along with alternative procedures for reporting activities within this structure. *One purpose of this chapter is to develop a basic framework for financial planning.*

The process of projecting the operations of the organization and their financial impact into the future is called operations budgeting. An **operating budget** is a set of formal financial documents that reports expected revenues and expenses as well as all other expected operating and financing transactions for a future period of time (usually one year). *Another purpose of this chapter is to discuss the basic concepts and benefits of operating budgets and alternative approaches to budget preparation.* An example of a complete operations budget is developed, starting with the forecasting of sales and concluding with the preparation of pro forma financial statements. Throughout the chapter consideration is given to the behavioral implications of budgeting and the difficulties and problems often encountered in operations budgeting.

JUSTIFICATIONS OF BUDGETING

Preparing budgets is an important activity in all organizations. It requires making estimates about future needs and developments that may be difficult to predict and even more difficult to control. Many future events almost defy accurate prediction (e.g., a company trying to anticipate the cost of complying with union demands or federal regulations). Despite the difficulty and the inherent uncertainty involved in budgeting, numerous benefits normally accrue to firms whose managers engage in operations budgeting. These benefits include: systematic planning, improved communications and coordination among organizational elements, and an improved basis of performance evaluation.

Systematic Planning

Budgeting is planning for a future period and, as applied to the accounting aspects of an organization, requires management to systematically examine what is anticipated in its financial environment. This look into the future invariably compels management to establish goals and objectives for the future and, maybe more important, it helps management identify major problems that may develop later if corrective action is not taken. Budgeting moves the organization from an informal reaction method of management to a formal proactive method of management. As a result, less time is spent solving unanticipated problems, and more time is spent on positive measures and preventive actions.

Improved Communication

The operating budget encompasses the entire organization; hence, its preparation requires the participation of all levels of management. The process of compiling, reviewing, and revising budget data requires managers to communicate with each other and with subordinates and superiors.

Improved Coordination

Once completed, the operating budget becomes the plan of action for the entire organization and must therefore reflect the coordinated efforts of all components of the organization. The production and sales managers cannot make their plans independent of each other. The personnel department must know the needs of all other departments before it can budget its needs for new employees and training costs. The final version of the operating budget emerges after an extensive, and often lengthy, process of communication and coordination. It represents a synthesis of the experience and knowledge of management at every level of the organization.

Performance Evaluation

Effective control requires a basis for evaluating performance. The traditional bases for measuring performance are historical, industry, and budgeted data. The first two bases have some disadvantages. If *historical data* regarding the firm's performance are used for measuring current performance, past inefficiencies may be allowed to continue as long as the organization operates at the same level. Also, changes in the organization's operating environment will not be reflected in the basis on which performance is evaluated—for example, a change in the sales volume and mix of products demanded by customers.

Using *industry data* to measure performance has the disadvantage of comparing one organization to other companies that may be substantially different from it, thus leading to erroneous conclusions. Comparisons of one organization with others in an industry may be interesting, and they may provide a general perspective of how well one firm is doing compared to similar ones, but this is usually a poor basis for evaluating management's performance for a particular operating period.

Budgeted data prepared for the period under review is a more realistic basis for evaluating performance because the benchmarks are relevant and current. Comparing actual and budgeted data produces variances that are meaningful measures of performance.

MOTIVATION ASPECTS AND HUMAN BEHAVIOR

All organizations are composed of individuals who perform a wide variety of activities in pursuit of the organization's common goals. To accomplish these goals, it is important for management to recognize the effects that budgeting and performance evaluation methods and techniques may have on the behavior of the people in the organization.

Budgeting often produces strong reactions from employees. Some managers use budgets in such a way that employees perceive the budgets as a means of squeezing the last unit of productivity out of them, or merely as a means of identifying the poor performers. Because people inherently dislike restrictions on their behavior, we often see only the negative aspects of budgeting. Budgeting can and should be used as a means of bringing out the best in people without threatening their security and self-esteem.

Properly used, the operating budget can be an effective mechanism for motivating workers to higher levels of performance and productivity. Improperly developed and administered, it can foster feelings of animosity toward both management and the budget process. Research has shown that when workers participate in the preparation of budgets and feel that the budgets represent fair standards for evaluating their performance, they receive personal satisfaction from accomplishing the goals set forth in the budgets.

Another important motivational aspect of operating budgets is related to management's recognition that the budget is not infallible. Mistakes in prediction and judgment are sometimes made, and unforeseen circumstances often develop, necessitating modification of the budget. Unless top management is willing to recognize when changes in the budget are needed, support for the budget at lower levels will quickly erode. If the organization is to receive maximum benefit from the budget process, support for the budget at the top management level, as well as at lower levels, must be maintained. Achieving this support may be the most difficult challenge facing an organization that is undertaking budgeting for the first time.

Lower level managers will not respect the budget and the related performance reports if they perceive a lack of commitment by top management. Violations of the budget by top management can quickly destroy the effectiveness of the budget throughout the organization.

In summary, managers who follow the suggestions below are more likely to be successful in using budgets as a positive tool for accomplishing organizational goals through people.

1. Emphasize the importance of budgeting as a planning device.

2. Encourage wide participation in budget preparation at all levels of management.

3. Demonstrate through appropriate communications that the budget has the complete support of top management.

4. Recognize that the budget is not unalterable, that it may require modification if conditions change.

5. Use budget performance reports not just to identify the poor performer, but also to recognize good performance.

6. Conduct programs in budget education to provide new managers with information about the purposes of budgets and to dispel erroneous misconceptions that may exist.

FORMAL PLANNING CONCEPTS

Before an organization can develop operating budgets, management must decide which approaches to budgeting will be used for various activities. Widely used planning approaches to budgeting include (1) the input/output approach, (2) the incremental approach, and (3) the minimum level approach. Exhibit 6–1 contains a summary of the typical cost characteristics found when each approach to budgeting is used.

EXHIBIT 6–1   Planning Concepts

Approach to Budgeting	Typical Cost Characteristics
Input/output	Variable and mixed costs
Incremental	Discretionary fixed costs
Minimum level	Committed fixed costs

Input/Output Approach

The **input/output approach** budgets physical inputs and costs as a function of planned activity. This approach is often used for manufacturing and distribution activities where there are clearly defined relationships between effort and accomplishment. For example, if each unit produced requires two pounds of raw materials that cost $5 each, and the planned production volume is 25 units, then the budgeted inputs and costs for raw materials are 50 (25 × 2) pounds and $250 (50 × $5). Note that the budgeted inputs are a function of the planned outputs. The input/output approach starts with the planned outputs and works backward to budget the inputs. In evaluating the proposed budget, management would focus its attention on the physical and cost relationships between the inputs and the outputs. For variable costs, the input/output approach is most appropriate. This approach is seldom used for activities that do not have clearly defined input/output relationships, such as advertising, research and development, and executive training.

Incremental Approach

The **incremental approach** budgets costs for a coming period as a dollar or percentage change from the amount budgeted for (or spent during) some previous period. This approach is often used where the relationships between inputs and outputs are weak or nonexistent, particularly where fixed costs dominate. For example, it is difficult to establish a clear relationship between sales volume and advertising expenditures. Consequently, the budgeted amount of advertising for some coming period is often based on the budgeted or actual advertising expenditures in a previous period. If budgeted advertising expenditures for 19x1 were $200,000, the budgeted expenditures for 19x2 would be some increment based on $200,000. In evaluating the proposed 19x2 budget, management would accept the $200,000 base and focus its attention on a justification for the increment.

This approach to budgeting has been more widely used in government than in business organizations (see the appendix to this chapter). In seeking an annual budget appropriation, a department operating under the incremental approach would be required to justify only proposed expenditures in excess of its previous budget appropriation.

The primary advantage of the incremental approach is that it simplifies the budget process by considering only the increments in the various budget items, which in most cases would be smaller and easier to handle than the total budgeted amount. On the other hand, a major disadvantage is that existing waste and inefficiencies may escalate year after year without ever being discovered.

Minimum Level Approach

Using the **minimum level approach,** an organization establishes a base amount for all budget items and requires explanation or justification for any budgeted amount above the minimum. Under this method an absolute minimum amount of expenditures is presumed necessary to support ongoing activity in the organization. This method is very useful where many committed costs continue from period to period. Proponents of this approach maintain that requiring extensive justifications of budget items up to the minimum amount is an ineffective use of managerial time. Like the incremental approach, the minimum level approach is often used for activities that do not have clearly defined input/output relationships. For example, the corporate director of product development would need some minimum provision in the budget to support a minimum level of activity for ongoing projects. Additional increments might also be included first to support the current level of product development and second to undertake desirable new projects.

All three approaches are often used in the same organization. A manufacturing firm might, for example, use the input/output approach to budget manufacturing and distribution expenditures; the incremental approach to budget administrative salaries, advertising, and contributions; and the minimum level approach to budget research and development, employee training, and computer operations.

BUDGET PREPARATION

There are probably no two organizations that use the same budget development procedures, but there are two approaches to budgeting that seem to characterize budget preparation in most organizations: the *imposed budget* and the *participation budget*. These are sometimes referred to as, respectively, the *top-down* approach and the *bottom-up* approach.

Under the imposed budget, or top-down, approach to budget preparation, top management decides on the goals and objectives for the whole organization and communicates these to lower management levels. This *nonparticipative approach* to budgeting can have serious motivational consequences. Personnel who do not participate in budget preparation are likely to lack a commitment in achieving their part of the budget.

The participation budget uses the benefits of improved communication, coordination, and motivation. The participation budget requires managers at all levels, and in some cases even nonmanagers, to become involved in budget preparation. This approach is sometimes referred to as the bottom-up approach. Budget proposals are made first at the lowest level of management and then are integrated into the proposals for the next level, and so on, until the proposals reach the top level of management where the budget is completed. Although the imposed budget approach was used quite frequently in the past, today most companies encourage greater participation in budget preparation.

In the participative approach to budgeting, managers who are directly responsible for a given area have the initial input into the budgeting process for that area. This builds confidence into the budgeting process at the operating levels of the organization and is likely to promote a better budgeting system. Budget predictions are likely to be more accurate and the person responsible for the budget is more likely to strive to accomplish its objectives. These *self-*

imposed budgets reinforce the concept of participative management and should strengthen the overall budgeting process.

Also important to budget preparation are the types of forecasts used. Though the sales forecast is primary to most organizations, other types of forecasts vary in importance. Other forecasts or predictions often used include: estimates of uncollectibles, production output as a ratio of resources input, production days available, employee turnover and subsequent training of new employees, and cash balance needs per month. Because of the diverse sources of these predictions, the preparation process requires coordination of most of the functions in an organization. Unfortunately, with the forecasts come new and additional demands by those providing input; for example, marketing wants to change the product unit, production wants to operate only four days a week, and the treasurer wants a smaller daily cash balance.

Obviously, all requests cannot be included in the budget. Someone must be responsible for deciding which requests are most important to the organization. Most organizations have a **budget committee** that is responsible for supervising budget preparation and serves as a review board for evaluating requests for discretionary cost items and new projects. The final responsibility for decisions rests with the budget committee, which is usually composed of top-level managers. In addition, larger companies frequently will have a *budget office*, responsible to the controller, that performs a staff function of assisting the budget committee. The budget office is responsible for the preparation, distribution, and processing of forms used in gathering budget data and handles most of the work of actually formulating the budget schedules and reports. The budget office staff may also assist the budget committee by preparing various analyses and special reports.

Large organizations frequently have a full-time budgeting staff that works year-round on the budget. This does not mean that it takes twelve months to prepare the budget, or that once the annual budget is completed the budgeting staff has nothing else to do until the next year. Preparing a budget may take most of the year in some companies; also, the final budget is really never final—it may have to be revised several times during the course of the budget period. Furthermore, the multiyear, long-range plans of many companies are updated constantly to reflect changing conditions. Revisions and updating are part of the responsibility of the budget office.

BUDGETING PERIODS

Up to this point the normal budget period has been assumed to be one year. Although the annual budget period is certainly the most common, many organizations budget for shorter periods (such as a month or a quarter of a year) and for longer periods (such as two years, five years, or more). In addition to fixed length budget periods, two other types of budget periods are commonly used, *cycle budgeting* and *continuous budgeting*.

For some businesses, a fixed time period is not particularly relevant to the planning of operations. A company engaged in large construction projects might find it more advantageous to prepare a budget for the entire project life, which may be more than a year in some cases and less than a year in others. In these cases the firm may use cycle budgeting, which is appropriate when the entire life of the cycle or project represents a more useful planning horizon than an artificial period of one year. Such cycles could be reduced to shorter planning periods by breaking the overall project into several components, such as construction phases.

Another type of budgeting that is gaining in popularity is *continuous,* or *perpetual,* budgeting. Under continuous budgeting, the budget is based on a moving time-frame that extends over a fixed period. For example, an organization on a continuous four-quarter budget system adds a quarter to the budget at the end of each quarter of operations, thereby always maintaining a budget four quarters into the future. Under this system, plans for a full year into the future are always available; whereas under a fixed annual budget, operating plans for a full year ahead are available only at the beginning of the budget year. Because management is constantly involved in this type of budgeting, the budget process becomes an active and integral part of the management process. Management is forced to be future-oriented throughout the year, rather than just once each year. Continuous budgeting, which is now feasible with the aid of computers, helps to elevate the level of visibility and recognition of the planning function.

TYPES OF BUDGETS

The types of budgets that must be prepared vary, depending on the nature of the business and its activities. The operating cycle of most businesses, as shown in Exhibit 6–2, involves the conversion of cash into other assets, which are intended to produce revenues in excess of their costs. The cycle generally follows a path from cash, to inventory, to receivables, and back to cash. There are, of course, intermediate phases in the cycle such as the purchase or manufacture of inventories, payment of accounts payable, and the collection of receivables. The operating budget is merely a detailed model of the firm's operating cycle.

In most organizations the budgeting process begins with the development of the sales budget and concludes with the development of pro forma financial statements. Exhibit 6–3 depicts the annual budget assembly process in a manufacturing firm. Note how all the critical activities converge from sales toward cash and then toward the pro forma financial statements.

To illustrate the procedures involved in budget assembly, an operating budget will be developed for the All American Wagon Company (AAW) (a manufacturer of wooden wagons for children) for the year 19x5. The assembly sequence follows the overview illustrated in Exhibit 6–3. Each element of the budget process in Exhibit 6–3 is illustrated in a separate exhibit as given. Because

EXHIBIT 6–2   Operating Cycle

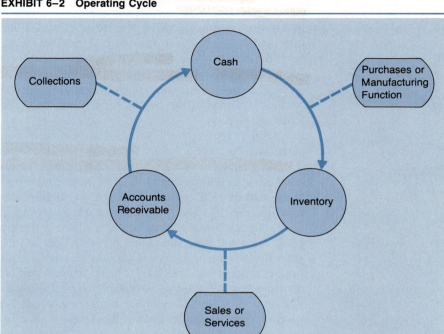

of the numerous elements in the budget process illustrated for AAW, you will find it useful to refer back to Exhibit 6–3 often.

The activities of a business can be summarized under three broad categories: operating activities, financing activities, and investing activities. For our purposes, and to simplify our discussion, assume that All American Wagon Company engaged in no investing activities during the budget period and that the only financing activity is short-term borrowing. Normal profit-related activities performed in conducting the daily affairs of an organization are called **operating activities.** These, of course, are the major concern of management in preparing operating budgets. The operating activities of the All American Wagon Company include:

1. Sales of goods or services.

2. Purchase of materials, labor, and overhead for the manufacture of saleable goods.

3. Purchase and use of goods and services classified as selling expenses.

4. Purchase and use of goods and services classified as general and administrative expenses.

In addition to preparing the budget for each operating activity, a cash budget is prepared that summarizes the projected cash receipts and disbursement for the budget period. The importance of cash planning makes the cash budget a vital part of the total budget process. Management must, for example, be aware of the need to borrow and have some idea when borrowed funds can be repaid.

The budgets for AAW provide information for each of the four quarters in 19x5 and totals for the year. The balance sheet at the end of 19x4, presented

EXHIBIT 6–3   Overview of Budget Assembly in a Manufacturing Firm

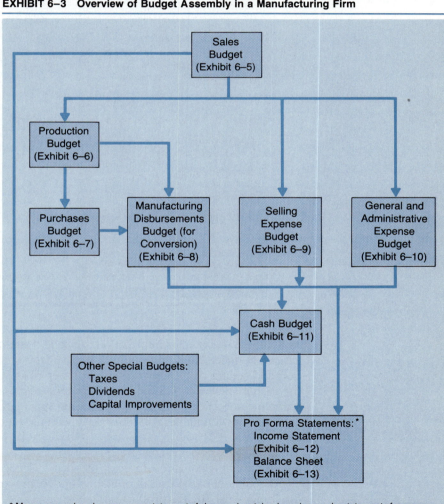

* Many companies also prepare a statement of changes in retained earnings and a statement of resource flows.

EXHIBIT 6–4   Initial Balance Sheet

All American Wagon Company
Balance Sheet
December 31, 19x4

Assets

Current Assets:

Cash	$ 15,000	
Accounts receivable (net)	19,200	
Inventory, raw materials*	5,720	
Inventory, finished goods (1,000 units)†	21,000	$ 60,920

Plant, property, and equipment:

Land		$ 60,000	
Buildings and equipment	$260,000		
Less accumulated depreciation	−124,800	135,200	195,200
Total assets			$256,120

Liabilities and stockholder's equity

Current liabilities:

Accounts payable		$ 17,200

Stockholder's equity:

Capital stock	$150,000	
Retained earnings	88,920	238,920
Total liabilities and stockholder's equity		$256,120

---

* Direct materials included $3,120 of lumber (1,560 sq. ft. of lumber at $2 per sq. ft.) and $2,600 of hardware sets (520 sets at $5 per set).

† Unit costs for 19x4 averaged $21 composed of direct materials, $11; direct labor, $6; variable overhead, $2; and fixed overhead, $2.

in Exhibit 6–4, contains information to use as a starting point in preparing the various budgets. The input/output approach is used to budget variable production and selling costs. The budgets for other costs are developed using either the incremental approach or the minimum level approach. Budgets to be prepared include sales, production, purchasing, manufacturing disbursements, selling expense, general and administrative expense, and cash.

Sales Budget

The **sales budget** contains a forecast of unit sales volume and sales dollars, and it may also contain a forecast of sales collections. The sales budget is a critical element in the overall operating budget process because so many of the other elements, such as production, purchases, labor needs, and other resource requirements, are based on projected sales. Management uses the best available information to forecast future market conditions accurately. These forecasts, when considered along with product development plans, promotion and advertising plans, and expected pricing policies, should lead to the most dependable sales predictions. The sales budget for 19x5 is presented in Exhibit 6–5.

Once the sales predictions are made, information on credit terms, collections policy, and past collection experience are used to develop a sales collections budget. Collections on sales normally include receipts from the current period's sales and the collections from sales of prior periods. An allowance for bad debts, which reduces each period's collections, is also predicted. Other items often included are sales discounts, allowances for volume discounts, and seasonal changes of sales prices and collections. For AAW 75 percent of the cash is collected in the quarter of sales and 24 percent in the quarter after the sales take place. Bad debts are budgeted at 1 percent of sales.

Production Budget

The **production budget** is based on sales predictions with adjustments for beginning inventory and desired ending inventory. It establishes the production quotas for each period necessary to cover sales and provide desired ending inventory levels. Assume AAW's experience indicates ending inventories should amount to 20 percent of the next quarter's expected sales. First we determine the total needs for sales and desired ending inventories and then subtract the expected beginning inventories from this amount. The difference is what the company needs to produce. The production budget for 19x5 is presented in Exhibit 6–6.

EXHIBIT 6–5   Sales Budget

All American Wagon Company
Sales Budget
For the year ended December 31, 19x5

	First Quarter	Second Quarter	Third Quarter	Fourth Quarter	Year Total
Sales (units)	5,000	6,000	8,500	5,500	25,000
Sales ($38 each)	$190,000	$228,000	$323,000	$209,000	$950,000
Collections on sales					
For current quarter (75% of sales)	$142,500	$171,000	$242,250	$156,750	$712,500
For previous quarter (24% of sales)	19,200*	45,600	54,720	77,520	197,040
Total	$161,700	$216,600	$296,970	$234,270	$909,540
Budgeted bad debts (1% of current quarter sales)	$ 1,900	$ 2,280	$ 3,230	$ 2,090	$ 9,500

* This is the January 1, 19x5, Accounts Receivable balance.

Note: The Accounts Receivable balance on December 31, 19x5, is $50,160 ($209,000 − $156,750 − $2,090).

EXHIBIT 6–6   Production Budget

All American Wagon Company
Production Budget
For the year ended December 31, 19x5
(In units)

	First Quarter	Second Quarter	Third Quarter	Fourth Quarter	Year Total
Wagons					
Budgeted sales (Exhibit 6–5)	5,000	6,000	8,500	5,500	25,000
Plus required ending inventory*	1,200	1,700	1,100	1,200†	1,200
Total inventory requirements	6,200	7,700	9,600	6,700	26,200
Less beginning inventory	−1,000	−1,200	−1,700	−1,100	−1,000
Budgeted production	5,200	6,500	7,900	5,600	25,200

* Equals 20 percent of the next quarter's sales.
† Sales for 19x6 are projected to be 6,000 units each quarter.

Purchases Budget

The **purchases budget** indicates the raw materials that must be acquired to meet production needs and ending inventory requirements. It may be referred to as a direct materials purchases budget if it contains only purchases of raw materials. However, it often contains factory supplies and may even contain office and selling supplies. For simplicity, the purchases budget developed in this chapter includes only purchases of raw materials.

This budget is critical to the overall budget process because it may contain the largest commitment of cash outflows from the organization. From this budget, cash disbursements for purchases are predicted based on the expected timing of payments on account. A firm often delays cash disbursements as long as possible within any available discount period. For AAW, payments for purchases are assumed to be made 50 percent in the quarter purchased and 50 percent in the next quarter.

AAW's purchases budget is shown in Exhibit 6–7. Supplies are assumed to be immaterial and therefore are assumed to be included in variable factory overhead and office expenses. For each wagon, the materials requirements consist of 3 square feet of lumber and one set of hardware, which includes such items as wheels, bolts and nuts, a tongue, and other assembly items. These sets come to the workstations prepackaged.

All purchases are made by a centralized purchasing department and the quarterly purchases budget is very helpful in controlling the activities of this department. By using appropriate procedures for getting bids and placing orders, the department helps the organization to minimize the cost of carrying inventory.

EXHIBIT 6–7   Purchases Budget

All American Wagon Company
Purchases Budget
For the year ended December 31, 19x5

	First Quarter	Second Quarter	Third Quarter	Fourth Quarter	Year Total
Production units (from Exhibit 6–6)	5,200	6,500	7,900	5,600	25,200
Lumber (sq. ft.)					
Target ending inventory*	1,950	2,370	1,680	1,800	1,800
Production needs**	15,600	19,500	23,700	16,800	75,600
Total requirements	17,550	21,870	25,380	18,600	77,400
Less beginning inventory	− 1,560	− 1,950	− 2,370	− 1,680	− 1,560
Purchases needed	15,990	19,920	23,010	16,920	75,840
Cost ($2 per sq. ft.)	× $2	× $2	× $2	× $2	× $2
Total lumber purchases	$31,980	$39,840	$46,020	$33,840	$151,680
Hardware sets (each)					
Target ending inventory*	650	790	560	600	600
Production needs	5,200	6,500	7,900	5,600	25,200
Total requirements	5,850	7,290	8,460	6,200	25,800
Less beginning inventory	− 520	− 650	− 790	− 560	− 520
Purchases needed	5,330	6,640	7,670	5,640	25,280
Cost ($5 per set)	× $5	× $5	× $5	× $5	× $5
Total hardware set purchases	$26,650	$33,200	$38,350	$28,200	$126,400
Total Purchases					
Lumber	$31,980	$39,840	$46,020	$33,840	$151,680
Hardware sets	26,650	33,200	38,350	28,200	126,400
Total	$58,630	$73,040	$84,370	$62,040	$278,080
Disbursements for purchases					
Payments of material purchases:					
For current quarter (50 percent)	$29,315	$36,520	$42,185	$31,020	$139,040
For previous quarter (50 percent)	17,200†	29,315	36,520	42,185	125,220
Total	$46,515	$65,835	$78,705	$73,205	$264,260

* Target ending inventory equal to 10 percent of next quarter's production.

** Each wagon requires three square feet of lumber.

† Unpaid balance at December 31, 19x4, reflects prior year payment terms.

Manufacturing Disbursements Budget

The **manufacturing disbursements budget,** which is based on an analysis of the production budget, is used to plan the conversion cost (labor and factory overhead) requirements for the budgeted volume of production. These requirements are then used to budget the actual disbursement dollars for labor and overhead. Recall that required disbursements for purchases of direct materials are included in the purchases budget.

Direct labor and overhead costs for each wagon produced by AAW have been estimated by management to be as follows:

Direct materials (lumber and hardware sets)	$11
Direct labor, $\frac{1}{2}$ hour at $20 per hour	10
Variable factory overhead, $\frac{1}{2}$ hour of direct labor at $8 per hour	4
Fixed factory overhead, $75,600/25,200 units	3
Total cost per unit	$28

Fixed manufacturing costs are as follows:

Fixed factory overhead requiring cash expenditures	$15,000 per quarter
Fixed factory overhead not requiring cash expenditures (depreciation)	$3,900 per quarter

Direct labor and factory overhead, except for depreciation, are acquired and paid for in the quarter they are used. Information on budgeted labor hours is presented in the upper portion of Exhibit 6–8. The budgeted manufacturing disbursements for conversion costs are presented in the lower portion of Exhibit 6–8. Depreciation is not included because cash flow is not associated with depreciation but is incurred in connection with the acquisition of fixed assets.

Selling Expense Budget

The **selling expense budget** presents the costs and disbursements the organization plans to incur in connection with sales and distribution. Budgeted selling expenses include variable selling expenses and fixed selling expenses other than depreciation of $4,000 per quarter. Note in the Selling Expense Budget, Exhibit 6–9, that the budgeted variable selling expenses are based on budgeted sales as a percentage of budgeted sales dollars. The budgeted fixed selling expenses are based on amounts obtained from the manager of the sales department. Budgeted selling costs for AAW are paid in the quarter they are incurred.

General and Administrative Expense Budget

The **general and administrative expense budget** presents the expected costs and disbursements for the overall administration of the organization, such as the accounting department, the computer center, and the president's office.

EXHIBIT 6–8   Manufacturing Disbursements Budget

All American Wagon Company
Manufacturing Disbursements Budget
For the year ended December 31, 19x5

	First Quarter	Second Quarter	Third Quarter	Fourth Quarter	Year Total
Budgeted production					
Wagons	5,200	6,500	7,900	5,600	25,200
Direct labor hours ($\frac{1}{2}$ hour per unit)	2,600	3,250	3,950	2,800	12,600
Manufacturing disbursements (for conversion)					
Direct labor					
$20 per hour	$52,000	$ 65,000	$ 79,000	$56,000	$252,000
Variable overhead					
$8 per direct labor hour	20,800	26,000	31,600	22,400	100,800
Fixed overhead	15,000	15,000	15,000	15,000	60,000
Total	$87,800	$106,000	$125,600	$93,400	$412,800

EXHIBIT 6–9   Selling Expense Budget

All American Wagon Company
Selling Expense Budget
For the year ended December 31, 19x5

	First Quarter	Second Quarter	Third Quarter	Fourth Quarter	Year Total
Budgeted sales (from Exhibit 6–5)	$190,000	$228,000	$323,000	$209,000	$950,000
Selling costs and disbursements					
Variable costs:					
Delivery (1% sales)	$ 1,900	$ 2,280	$ 3,230	$ 2,090	$ 9,500
Commissions (2% sales)	3,800	4,560	6,460	4,180	19,000
Miscellaneous (1% sales)	1,900	2,280	3,230	2,090	9,500
Total	$ 7,600	$ 9,120	$12,920	$ 8,360	$38,000
Fixed costs:					
Advertising	$ 2,250	$ 2,250	$ 2,250	$ 2,250	$ 9,000
Office expenses	1,250	1,250	1,250	1,250	5,000
Miscellaneous	1,000	1,000	1,000	1,000	4,000
Total	4,500	4,500	4,500	4,500	18,000
Total selling costs and disbursements	$12,100	$13,620	$17,420	$12,860	$56,000

Depreciation of $2,000 per quarter is omitted since it requires no cash disbursement. Note in Exhibit 6–10 that there are no variable general and administrative costs. This is because most expenditures categorized as general and administrative are related to top management operations that do not vary with current sales or production. For AAW all general and administrative costs except depreciation are assumed to be paid in the quarter they are incurred.

Cash Budget

The **cash budget** summarizes all cash receipts and disbursements expected to occur during the budget period. Almost all activities affect cash sooner or later. AAW's cash budget, presented in Exhibit 6–11, is affected by credit policies, sales discounts taken by customers, collection experiences, payment policies, purchase and volume discounts taken, and myriad other factors. The tax information is furnished by AAW's tax department, and the information for dividends by the Board of Directors. The cash budget shows the cash operating deficiencies and surpluses expected to occur at the end of each quarter. This information is used to predict cash borrowing, loan payment, and cash investment needs.

The cash maintenance policy for All American Wagon requires that a minimum balance of $15,000 be maintained at the end of each quarter. AAW has a line of credit with a major bank, with any interest on borrowed funds computed at the simple interest rate of 12 percent per year, or 1.0 percent per month. All necessary borrowing is assumed to occur at the start of each quarter in incre-

EXHIBIT 6–10   General and Administrative Expense Budget

All American Wagon Company
General and Administrative Expense Budget
For the year ended December 31, 19x5

	First Quarter	Second Quarter	Third Quarter	Fourth Quarter	Year Total
General and administrative costs and disbursements					
Compensation	$20,000	$20,000	$20,000	$20,000	$ 80,000
Research and development	5,000	5,000	5,000	5,000	20,000
Insurance	2,000	2,000	2,000	2,000	8,000
Property taxes	3,000	3,000	3,000	3,000	12,000
Miscellaneous	1,000	1,000	1,000	1,000	4,000
Total budgeted general and administrative costs and disbursements	$31,000	$31,000	$31,000	$31,000	$124,000

ments of one thousand dollars. The cash budget presented in Exhibit 6–11 indicates that AAW will need to borrow $18,000 at the beginning of the first quarter and $2,000 at the beginning of the second. At the end of the third quarter, AAW will be able to repay the loan.

EXHIBIT 6–11   Cash Budget

All American Wagon Company
Cash Budget
For the year ended December 31, 19x5

	First Quarter	Second Quarter	Third Quarter	Fourth Quarter	Year Total
Cash balance beginning	$ 15,000	$ 15,285	$ 15,430	$ 35,935	$ 15,000
Plus cash collections on sales (Exhibit 6–5)	161,700	216,600	296,970	234,270	909,540
Total available from operations	$176,700	$231,885	$312,400	$270,205	$924,540
Less budgeted disbursements:					
Purchasing (from Exhibit 6–7)	$ 46,515	$ 65,835	$ 78,705	$ 73,205	$264,260
Manufacturing (from Exhibit 6–8)	87,800	106,000	125,600	93,400	412,800
Selling (from Exhibit 6–9)	12,100	13,620	17,420	12,860	56,000
General and administrative (from Exhibit 6–10)	31,000	31,000	31,000	31,000	124,000
Other:					
Income taxes	2,000	2,000	2,000	1,200	7,200
Dividends	—	—	—	30,000	30,000
Total	−179,415	−218,455	−254,725	−241,665	−894,260
Excess (deficiency) cash available over disbursements	$ (2,715)	$ 13,430	$ 57,675	$ 28,540	$ 30,280
Short-term financing*					
New loans	$ 18,000	$ 2,000	—	—	$ 20,000
Repayments	—	—	$ (20,000)	—	(20,000)
Interest†	—	—	(1,740)	—	(1,740)
Net cash flow from financing	18,000	2,000	(21,740)	—	(1,740)
Cash balance, ending	$ 15,285	$ 15,430	$ 35,935	$ 28,540	$ 28,540

* Short-term loans are obtained in increments of $1,000 to maintain cash at a minimum balance of $15,000 at all times. Accordingly, new loans required are budgeted for the beginning of the quarter and repayments are budgeted for the end of the quarter. Loan repayments are made on a first-borrowed, first-repaid basis and interest is paid only at the time of repayment.

† Interest computation for repayment of $20,000 is ($18,000 × 9 months × 0.01 = $1,620) + ($2,000 × 6 months × 0.01 = $120) = $1,740.

PRO FORMA STATEMENTS

The preparation of operating budgets culminates in the preparation of *pro forma financial statements*. **Pro forma financial statements** are hypothetical statements that reflect the "as if" effects of the budgeted activities on the actual financial position of the organization. That is, the statements reflect what the results of operations will be if all the predictions in the budget are correct. The preparation of pro forma financial statements has been simplified greatly by computer programs, especially financial spreadsheets that permit the user to immediately determine the impact of any assumed changes. These statements may use either the functional or contribution format for the income statement with the balance sheet accounts reflecting the corresponding entries.

Exhibit 6–12 presents the pro forma income statement for the year ended December 31, 19x5, using the functional format. If all the predictions made in the operating budget are correct, All American will produce a net income for the year of $34,560. Note that just about every item on the pro forma income statement comes from one of the budget schedules. The only exceptions are depreciation expense and taxes. Depreciation expense is predicted by the company's chief accountant; it is based on historical asset costs. Income taxes are determined on the basis of predicted taxable income following rules established by the Internal Revenue Service.

The pro forma balance sheet, presented in Exhibit 6–13, shows the financial position of AAW at the end of 19x5, assuming all the budget predictions are correct. Sources of the pro forma balance sheet data are included as part of the exhibit.

POTENTIAL PROBLEMS OF BUDGETING

Like many other tools available to managers, budgeting offers the potential for vast benefits but also has potential pitfalls and problems. This section briefly mentions some of the more important problems that may be encountered in budgeting.

Preparation Time

Preparing a budget for a large company can be a massive task, requiring hundreds, and perhaps thousands, of hours of valuable management time. Careful coordination and planning are required to keep budget preparation from becoming too onerous for managers or from interfering with their other responsibilities. To minimize the time required by each manager, the budget preparation calendar should be carefully planned, and easy-to-use forms should be provided.

Accuracy

In some cases the prediction ability of management is very weak. The more limited management's ability to make the accurate forecasts and predictions that

EXHIBIT 6–12   Pro Forma Income Statement

All American Wagon Company
Pro Forma Income Statement (functional format)
For the year ended December 31, 19x5

Sales (Exhibit 6–5)			$950,000
Cost of goods sold:			
Finished goods inventory, 1/1/x5 (Exhibit 6–4)		$ 21,000	
Cost of materials placed in production:			
Raw materials, 1/1/x5 (Exhibit 6–4)	$ 5,720		
Purchases (Exhibit 6–7)	278,080		
Total available	$283,800		
Raw materials, 12/31/x5*	− 6,600	$277,200	
Direct labor (Exhibit 6–8)		252,000	
Variable factory overhead (Exhibit 6–8)		100,800	
Fixed factory overhead ($60,000 + $15,600**)		75,600	705,600
Total goods available for sale			$726,600
Finished goods inventory, 12/31/x5 (1,200 units × $28)†			− 33,600	−693,000
Gross profit			$257,000
Other operating expenses:			
Selling expenses (Exhibit 6–9)		$ 56,000	
Selling expenses, depreciation ($4,000 per quarter)		16,000	
General and administrative (Exhibit 6–10)		124,000	
General and administrative, depreciation			
($2,000 per quarter)		8,000	
Bad debt expense (Exhibit 6–5)		9,500	−213,500
Income from operations			$ 43,500
Interest expense (Exhibit 6–11)			− 1,740
Net income before taxes			$ 41,760
Allowance for income taxes			− 7,200
Net income			$ 34,560

* Lumber	1,800 sq. ft. × $2	$3,600
Hardware sets	600 sets × $5	3,000
Total		$6,600

** Depreciation = 4 × $3,900 = $15,600.

† AAW uses a FIFO cost flow assumption. Hence, the ending inventory includes goods manufactured during the current period at a unit cost of $28 ($705,600/25,200 units).

are necessary for the budget, the more limited the usefulness of a single budget becomes. This is particularly true for newer businesses. Rapidly changing economic conditions also make budgeting difficult. Even then, however, managers who study the budgetary impact of possible changes can learn what factors to monitor most closely and to develop contingency plans that can be implemented

EXHIBIT 6–13   Pro Forma Balance Sheet

All American Wagon Company
Pro Forma Balance Sheet
December 31, 19x5

Assets

Current assets:
Cash (Exhibit 6–11)	$ 28,540	
Accounts receivable (net) (Exhibit 6–5)	50,160	
Inventory, raw materials (Exhibit 6–12)	6,600	
Inventory, finished goods (Exhibit 6–12)	33,600	$118,900

Plant, property, and equipment:
Land		$ 60,000	
Buildings and equipment	$260,000		
Less accumulated depreciation	−164,400	95,600	155,600

Total assets			$274,500

Liabilities and stockholder's equity

Current liabilities:
Accounts payable (Exhibit 6–7)	$ 31,020

Stockholder's equity:
Capital stock	$150,000	
Retained earnings	93,480	243,480

Total liabilities and stockholder's equity		$274,500

Sources of data:

1. Cash balance was obtained from the cash budget.

2. Accounts receivable represents 24 percent of the fourth quarter sales that are expected to be collected in 19x6.

3. Raw material inventory represents the purchases of direct materials in the fourth quarter that will be used in manufacturing in 19x6.

4. The finished goods inventory values are at the 19x5 average unit costs of $28.

5. Land and buildings and equipment are the same as at the end of 19x4.

6. Accumulated depreciation is equal to the balance at the end of 19x4 increased by the 19x5 depreciation [$124,800 + $15,600 (building and equipment) + 16,000 (selling) + $8,000 (general and administrative)].

7. The balance in accounts payable is 50 percent of the fourth quarter purchases of direct materials ($62,040 × 0.50).

8. Capital stock is the same as at the end of 19x4.

9. Retained earnings is equal to the balance at the end of 19x4 plus pro forma net income less dividends of $30,000 reported in the cash budget.

if needed. Many statistical and mathematical techniques, such as those discussed in the appendix to Chapter 3, are available to improve the reliability of the budget data.

Budgetary Slack

Budgetary slack, sometimes referred to as "padding the budget," occurs when managers intentionally request more funds in the budget for their departments than they need to support the anticipated level of operations. If a department consistently produces large favorable variances—or even small favorable variances with little apparent effort—this may be a symptom of slack built into the budget. The desire by managers to pad their budgets may indicate poor relations between upper and lower management, or poor administration of the budget.

Economy and Industry Relations

Although each organization is a unique entity whose peculiar characteristics are reflected in its operations budget, most organizations are also affected by general economic or industry conditions. Any inability to obtain accurate and reliable information about these conditions can pose serious problems for managers trying to make predictions about their own companies. For example, many organizations that depend on external sources of funds have found it very difficult to predict the cost and availability of acquiring funds.

SUMMARY

Operating budgets are an integral part of the overall planning and control system. They represent management's expectations about the events and activities scheduled to occur during a specified future period. Budgets provide the basis for evaluating actual performance and modifying subsequent plans. Budgeting offers many potential benefits for organizations, including forcing managers to look at the future of the company, improving communication, improving coordination between various departments and functions in the organization, and motivating managers to achieve organizational objectives.

The input/output approach to budget planning is based on clearly defined relationships between effort and accomplishment. The incremental approach requires budget review of proposals in excess of the budgeted (or actual) expenditures for the previous period. The minimum level approach requires review of any budgeted amounts in excess of some minimum amount. The budgeting process is usually implemented on an annual schedule, although companies in certain industries find the cyclical approach more appropriate. Continuous budgeting consists of adding a new time unit to the end of the budget period upon completing a unit of time.

Most manufacturing organizations prepare budgets for sales, production, purchases, manufacturing disbursements, selling expenses, general and administrative expenses, and cash. Budget preparation culminates with the presentation of pro forma financial statements reflecting the "as if" effects on the company of carrying out the budget.

Feedback is an essential part of budgeting. Without interpretation of actual performance much of the benefit, including that of motivating people, would be lost. To receive maximum benefits from budgeting requires participation by all management levels, commitments by top management, and both positive and negative feedback.

Pitfalls of operations budgeting include placing excessive time demands on managers, expecting accurate and reliable predictions of all general economic and industry conditions, failure of top management to support the budget, poorly established organizational lines of authority and responsibility, and possible budgetary slack.

APPENDIX
NOT-FOR-PROFIT BUDGETING

In not-for-profit organizations, budgeting plays a vital role in planning and monitoring the effective and efficient use of scarce resources. In most not-for-profit organizations, the key element is budgeted revenue. It is often the primary determinant of all the expenditures in other parts of the budget. The budget is essentially a legal document for governmental units and a restraining document for nongovernmental units. Not-for-profit organizational agencies or units cannot exceed budgeted amounts until the proper authorities have approved budget amendments.

For most not-for-profit organizations the budget is the primary control element. It is through the budget process that the projected revenues and expenditures for each of the accounts are established. Two types of budgets, revenue budgets and appropriation budgets, are used by many organizations. **Revenue budgets** establish the amount expected to be collected from each revenue source during the upcoming period. **Appropriation budgets** provide the authorization for expenditures during the specified period.[1] Very seldom do agencies or units have equal revenues and expenditures. For example, many units of a municipality generate revenue, but others receive no revenue. A city-supported college receives revenue through student fees and contributions, whereas a city prison system receives no revenues. To make up for the deficits, a municipality will usually impose income taxes, sales taxes, or property taxes, which are allocated to the different agencies that do not raise enough revenue to be self-supporting.

---

[1] An appropriation is an authorization to make expenditures and incur obligations with limitations on amount, purpose, and time period.

Once the budget is approved, it is considered the authority for expenditures of funds to carry out the goals and objectives of each organizational unit. The budgetary control accounts are then created for the coming period (see Exhibit 6–14). The parent group (a state, a religious organization, a private college) establishes the general control accounts that break the budget into its major elements. For the Ohio Valley Children's Foundation the control accounts are Contributions, Service Fees, Interest Income, Children's Home, Summer Camp, and Emergency Care.

The revenue accounts represent an accounting of revenues from all sources and are used to maintain control of all revenues, much as the master budget does for a corporation. The estimated revenues are a function of the various revenue-generating activities of an organizational unit. The appropriations accounts represent an accounting of budgeted appropriations. The detailed appropriations accounts specify the funds allocated to the different areas of the organization.

Organizations use two types of budgeting to control the different operational units. In a **lump-sum budget** only general areas are allocated revenues and expenditures. Appropriations for a lump-sum budget appear in Exhibit 6–14. In this budget the Children's Home was allocated $1,500,000 for the period. In the other type of budget, a **line-item budget,** revenues and expenditures are assigned to specific categories and items of responsibility. Using this method, the $1,500,000 to the Children's Home is allocated by major categories. A line-item budget for the Children's Home might appear as in Exhibit 6–15. Using this budget, the management of the Children's Home would be required to adhere to the appropriation limits set for each category. Most organizations resist shifting funds from one line item to another without approval of the governing body. This type of budgeting places tight control over the expenditures, but it does not attempt to measure the efficiency or effectiveness of the expenditures.

EXHIBIT 6–14   Control Budget

Ohio Valley Children's Foundation
Budget for 19x6

Estimated revenues:		
Contributions	$1,000,000	
Service fees	600,000	
Interest income	400,000	$2,000,000
Appropriations:		
Children's Home	$1,500,000	
Summer Camp	200,000	
Emergency Care	275,000	−1,975,000
Balance to general fund		$ 25,000

EXHIBIT 6–15   Line-Item Budget

Children's Home
Ohio Valley Children's Foundation
Budget for 19x6

Estimated revenues:		
Contributions		$ 700,000
Appropriations:		
Building maintenance	$200,000	
Staff salaries and benefits	300,000	
Food and clothing	600,000	
Utilities	100,000	
Equipment	150,000	
Schooling	150,000	−1,500,000
Excess appropriations over revenues		$ (800,000)
Balance from general fund		800,000
Fund balance		$ 0

Revenue and Appropriation Budgets

Because revenues in most not-for-profit organizations come from many sources, each major source of revenue should be itemized, as in Exhibit 6–16 for the City of Dothan. For comparison purposes, Exhibit 6–16 also shows the actual revenues of the prior period.

The itemization of the revenue budget allows the city to evaluate each revenue source separately. Some revenue sources are more susceptible to prediction errors than others. For example, it is much easier to predict the revenue received from property taxes than it is to predict the fees collected from exhibitors in the city park.

Appropriation budgets show how each organizational unit is authorized to spend its resources or allocations during the budget period. The format of a given budget depends on the type of organizational unit and budget being used. The overall appropriation budget for the City of Dothan and a line-item budget for the fire department are shown in Exhibit 6–17. In this case there are only five line items.

Appropriation budgets are the primary basis for the evaluation and control of not-for-profit organizations. Nonprofit organizations generally emphasize accountability of funds rather than efficiency of operation; therefore, each operating period is measured by the funds expended (cash payments) rather than by the matching of revenues and expenses. To ensure adherence to the budgets, the manager of each operating unit is responsible for accepting the budget as the operating plan for the next period. Performance reports that compare actual results with the budgets are prepared to determine how well the plans were carried out. The City of Dothan fire department performance report for fiscal year 19x5–x6 is illustrated in Exhibit 6–18.

For most not-for-profit organizations, the performance report is the key means of evaluating a unit. Each item should be evaluated separately and both unfavorable and favorable variances should receive detailed analysis. For example, a department could have a favorable variance for salaries simply because not enough people were employed to carry out its services. In such a situation management would be able to evaluate whether or not the services were weakened because of the lack of personnel or if, in fact, the category was overbudgeted at the beginning of the period.

Approaches to Budget Preparation

The budgets of governmental units are authorized by law. The collection of revenues and the appropriation of expenses must conform with constitutional law and must be specifically authorized through an approved budgetary process. Once the budgets of governmental units are approved, they have binding legal authority. Rather than just being a guide to action, the budget of a governmental unit is a mandate to act. Frequently used approaches to preparing budgets in governments and other not-for-profit organizations include incremental budgeting, programming budgeting, and zero base budgeting.

EXHIBIT 6–16   Revenue Budgets

City of Dothan
Budgeted Revenue
Fiscal year 19x6–x7

	Actual 19x5–x6	Budget 19x6–x7
Taxes:		
Property	$2,000,000	$2,300,000
Sales	600,000	750,000
Total taxes	$2,600,000	$3,050,000
Fees and licenses:		
Business	$ 20,000	$ 25,000
Water sales	310,000	315,000
Police	32,000	40,000
Total fees and licenses	362,000	380,000
Other revenues:		
Federal and state grants	$ 150,000	$ 150,000
Investment income	25,000	30,000
Sales of equipment	10,000	25,000
Total other revenues	185,000	205,000
Total revenues budgeted	$3,147,000	$3,635,000

EXHIBIT 6–17   Budget Relationships

City of Dothan
Appropriation Budget
Fiscal year 19x6–x7

	Actual 19x5–x6	Budget 19x6–x7
Schools	$1,300,000	$1,350,000
Police	800,000	900,000
Fire	200,000	220,000
Water	47,000	50,000
Street maintenance	500,000	600,000
Administration and courts	200,000	275,000
Parks and recreation	100,000	240,000
Totals	$3,147,000	$3,635,000

City of Dothan
Fire Protection Budget
Fiscal year 19x6–x7

	Actual 19x5–x6	Budget 19x6–x7
Salaries	$160,000	$175,000
Maintenance (equipment)	20,000	10,000
Supplies	11,000	22,000
Operating expenses	5,000	8,000
Gas and oil	4,000	5,000
Total	$200,000	$220,000

EXHIBIT 6–18   Performance Report

City of Dothan
Fire Protection
Performance Report
Fiscal year 19x5–x6

	Actual	Budget	Variances*
Salaries	$160,000	$162,000	$2,000 F
Maintenance (equipment)	20,000	19,000	1,000 U
Supplies	11,000	18,000	7,000 F
Operating expenses	5,000	5,500	500 F
Gas and oil	4,000	4,000	—
Total	$200,000	$208,500	$8,500 F

* F = Favorable
  U = Unfavorable

Incremental budgeting, discussed earlier in the chapter, is often used where the relationships between inputs and outputs are weak or nonexistent. The input/output approach, also discussed earlier, is often difficult to use in not-for-profit organizations, thereby resulting in the popularity of incremental budgeting. As an example, the cost of police protection is not necessarily a function of the measurable output of the agency (arrests) but of the inputs (size of city, previous crime rate, and level of trained personnel).

In seeking an annual appropriation, an agency is required to justify only proposed expenditures in excess of its previous budget. Because input/output relationships are difficult to determine, this method considers only the increments from an established base. The biggest advantages of incremental budgeting are simplicity and ease of preparation. However, a major disadvantage is that current inefficiencies may continue undetected for years.

Planning, programming, and budgeting systems (PPBS) emphasize outputs of an organization in programmed areas rather than inputs. A program is a specific activity or set of activities established to achieve a desired objective, such as fire protection. PPBS is based on three control ideas: (1) It is a formal planning system, (2) it uses a program budget, and (3) it emphasizes cost-benefit analysis. PPBS requires a careful specification and analysis of program objectives for each area or agency as a first step. Next, the process analyzes, insofar as possible, the output of a program in terms of its objectives. The third step is to measure the total costs of the program for several periods into the future. The fourth step is to analyze alternatives and seek those that have the greatest benefits as related to the stated objectives. The fifth and last step is the systematic implementation of the selected alternatives.

PPBS emphasizes control through responsibility accounting. The key to successful PPBS is forcing agencies to back away from their current operations and to evaluate their overall objectives. Through such evaluations each agency head accepts the responsibility of current and planned activities and must account for the results. Unfortunately, PPBS has not been well received in recent years because of implementation difficulties. All managers involved in the process must be familiar with it, and its implementation is very time consuming.

Zero-base budgeting begins with the premise that every dollar of a budgeted expenditure must be justified, including current expenditures that are to be continued. Incremental budgeting starts with the current level of expenditures and requires justification only for any proposed increases. Unlike incremental budgeting, which usually allows account increase differentiation but often requires spending cuts across the board, zero-base budgeting permits each program, subject to available resources, to receive any allocations that can be justified and supported.

Zero-base budgeting, as a planning tool, forces management to identify the activities that each agency or department engages in, to evaluate these activities, and to rank them in order of priority. The availability of funds will determine how many of the activities will be implemented.

The zero-base budgeting approach often assumes that decision makers have the capacity to eliminate programs. However, the political forces in any jurisdiction are such that few programs, if any, can be eliminated in any given year. For this reason zero-base budgeting may be better applied to selected programs than to entire organizations. Proposals for zero-base budgeting for the federal government would have program review occur only once every four or five years, with all programs of a given agency or department reviewed in the same year.[2]

The basic steps in zero-base budgeting are (1) development of decision packages consisting of departmental or agency activities, (2) evaluation of each decision package, (3) ranking of decision packages, (4) compilation of acceptable decision packages into the budget up to the limit of available resources, and (5) monitoring, control, and follow-up.

A **decision package** identifies each activity or department or agency. Decision packages may relate to goods, services, geographic areas, capital projects, or any other activity that relates to the organization's goals and objectives. Each decision package must be complete and able to stand alone, and it must include all direct costs and the cost of support activities. The budget of a city library could be defined as a decision package.

Decision packages should include an evaluation of what the organization is getting for each proposed expenditure and an identification of the cost and benefit relationships. The effects of different spending levels on costs and benefits should also be determined. Because cost and benefit relationships are not always linear, significant increases in total benefits may be accomplished by small increases in total costs. By comparing the incremental effect of additional expenditures on different programs, decision makers are better able to determine the optimal funding level. For the city library the cost of adding video packages would have to be evaluated against the increased service to the public and the public's acceptance of the new service.

Starting at the lowest decision level in the organization, decision packages are ranked and reranked until some upper level of management establishes a final order of priority. For example, the library director ranked the new video packages as the top priority for the coming year, the city budget review committee ranked it in the top 20 percent of the new requests, and the city council placed it in the middle of all new budgetary needs. Starting with the highest ranked package, the organization approves decision packages as long as uncommitted funds exist. The rankings are made on a variety of economic, social, bureaucratic, and political criteria. The funds available determines the number of decision packages accepted; generally, they are accepted in descending order. Therefore, any reduction in funds should result in dropping only the marginal decision packages.

---

[2] Joel Havemann, "Congress Tries to Break Ground Zero in Evaluating Federal Programs," *National Journal*, Volume 8, 1976, p. 708.

Budgeting Problems

Like for-profit organizations, not-for-profit organizations have used budgeting for many years. The emphasis on formalized budgeting programs in government began long before that of most businesses. Although the benefit of experience has been a positive influence, there have also been some negative effects. Because many not-for-profit organizations have used budgeting for compliance rather than for coordinating and planning, many negative attitudes toward budgeting have developed.

For governments a budget is an authorization to spend that is founded in law. If an unusual occurrence causes activities to increase, the funding may be inadequate, but if the activities fall below planned levels, there will likely be an abundance of funds. For a given period the not-for-profit budget usually does not change. Another detrimental effect of the static (nonflexible) budget of not-for-profit organizations is that when a program does not spend all its budgeted funds, it may receive a smaller appropriation the following year. The fear of this occasionally sends managers into a spending frenzy at the end of the fiscal year, which usually results in wasted resources.

The inability of managers to obtain additional resources as their activities increase also has a negative effect. Because their agencies are funded for a definite period, usually one year, additional resources are usually unavailable. Managers often build slack into their budget, preparing their requests for all possible situations. These budget manipulations destroy confidence in the process and create situations where managers falsify inputs to ensure proper operations of their departments.

From these negative experiences two improvements can be suggested. First, organizations can strive to maintain flexible budgets where resources are related directly to activities. Second, organizations should commit their objectives to writing. Planning and control can be facilitated by the establishment of specific objectives, with funds appropriated on the basis of these objectives.

In not-for-profit organizations the revenue budget strongly influences the quantity and quality of services and programs. However, it should be remembered that revenue is not a goal in itself; it merely provides the means of operating the various programs and services that are desired. The appropriations budget is the organization's plan for using the resources that it has available. Revenue and appropriations budgets should be prepared in sufficient detail to provide control over the activities of not-for-profit organizations.

The budget plays a critical role in not-for-profit organizations because it represents approval for expenditures at each operating level. It is also a critical tool for management accounting. Traditional budgeting has focused on input and accountability, but recent advances in management accounting in not-for-profit organizations include the program budget and zero-base budgeting. Management is provided with a structure that establishes priorities and allows allocation of resources based on priorities. Zero-base budgeting has application in most areas of the not-for-profit sector. If possible, unit evaluations should also consider both efficiency and effective measures.

KEY TERMS

Bottom-up approach
Budget committee
Budgetary slack
Cash budget
Continuous budgeting
Cycle budgeting
General and administrative expense
    budget
Imposed budget
Incremental budgeting
Input/output approach
Manufacturing disbursements
    budget

Minimum level approach
Operating activities
Operating budget
Participation budget
Pro forma financial statements
Production budget
Purchases budget
Sales budget
Selling expense budget
Top-down approach

**APPENDIX
KEY TERMS**

Appropriations budget
Decision package
Line-item budget
Lump-sum budget

Planning, programming, and
    budgeting systems
Revenue budget
Zero-base budgeting

**REVIEW
QUESTIONS**

6–1   What is the relationship between budgeting and planning and control?

6–2   Does budgeting require formal planning? Identify and briefly describe three budget planning concepts.

6–3   Identify the types of organizations or situations the incremental approach to budgeting is best suited for.

6–4   Identify the advantages and disadvantages of the incremental approach to budgeting.

6–5   Discuss the three bases used for performance evaluation.

6–6   Why should motivational considerations be a part of budget planning and utilization?

6–7   Contrast the top-down and bottom-up approaches to budget preparation.

6–8   What is the role of the budget committee? Who should be on the budget committee?

6–9   Why are annual budgets not always desirable? What are some alternative budget periods?

6–10   Explain how continuous budgeting works.

6–11   Which budget brings together all other budgets? How is this accomplished?

6–12   What are pro forma statements?

6–13   Why is prediction ability important to budgeting?

6–14   Is budgetary slack a desirable feature? Can it be prevented?

REVIEW PROBLEM

Handy Company manufactures and sells two industrial products in a single plant. The new manager wants to have quarterly budgets and has prepared the following information for the first quarter of 19x1.

Estimated sales:

Drills	60,000 at $100 each
Saws	40,000 at $125 each

Predicted inventories:

	Beginning	Ending
Drills, finished	20,000	25,000
Saws, finished	8,000	10,000
Metal, raw materials	32,000 lbs.	36,000 lbs.
Plastic, raw materials	29,000 lbs.	32,000 lbs.
Handles, raw materials	6,000	7,000

Manufacturing requirements:

	Raw Materials	Direct Labor
Drills	Metal 5 lbs. at $8 per lb. Plastic 3 lbs. at $5 per lb. Handles 1 each at $3	2 hours at $12 per hour
Saws	Metal 4 lbs. at $8 per lb. Plastic 3 lbs. at $5 per lb.	3 hours at $16 per hour

Variable factory overhead is applied at the rate of $1.50 per direct labor hour for each product. Fixed factory overhead is $214,000 per quarter, including noncash expenditures of $156,000, and is allocated on total units completed.

Financial information:

- Beginning cash balance is $1,800,000.
- Purchases of raw materials and labor costs are paid for in quarter acquired.
- Overhead expenses are paid in the next quarter. The accounts payable for these expenses from the last quarter of 19x0 is $380,000.
- Sales are on credit and are collected 50 percent in current period and the remainder the next period. Last quarter's sales were $8,400,000. There are no bad debts.
- Selling and administrative expenses are paid quarterly and total $340,000 including $90,000 of depreciation.
- All unit costs for the first quarter of 19x1 are the same as for the last quarter of 19x0.

Requirements

For the first quarter of 19x1 prepare a:

a) Sales budget in dollars.

b) Production budget in units.

c) Purchases budget.

d) Manufacturing disbursements budget.

e) Cash budget.

f) Budgeted income statement using the functional format. *Hint:* First determine the total costs per unit.

The solution to this problem is found at the end of the Chapter 6 exercises and problems.

EXERCISES

6–1 Cash Budget

Wilson's Retail Company is planning a cash budget for the next three months. Estimated sales revenue is as follows:

Month	Sales Revenue	Month	Sales Revenue
January	$300,000	March	$200,000
February	225,000	April	175,000

All sales are on credit. Forty percent of the sales are collected during the month of sale, and 60 percent are collected during the next month.

Cost of goods sold is 70 percent of sales. Payments for merchandise sold are made in the month following the month of sale. Operating expenses to be paid amount to $41,000 each month and are paid during the month incurred.

The cash balance on February 1 is estimated to be $20,000.

Required: Prepare monthly cash budgets for February, March, and April.

6–2 Cash Budget

Boston Tea Company began July with a cash balance of $142,000. A cash receipts and payment budget for each six-month period is prepared in advance. Sales have been estimated as follows:

Month	Sales Revenue	Month	Sales Revenue
May	$120,000	September	$ 80,000
June	140,000	October	100,000
July	80,000	November	100,000
August	60,000	December	120,000

All sales are on credit with 75 percent collected during the month of sale, 20 percent collected during the next month, and 5 percent collected during the second month following the month of sale.

Cost of goods sold averages 70 percent of sales revenue. Ending inventory is one half of the next month's predicted cost of sales. The other half of the merchandise is acquired during the month of sale. All purchases are paid for in the <u>month after purchase.</u>

Operating costs are estimated at $18,000 each month and are paid for during the month incurred.

Required: Prepare monthly cash budgets for six months from July to December.

6–3 Cash Receipts

The sales budget for Cards, Inc., is forecasted as follows:

Month	Sales Revenue	Month	Sales Revenue
May	$60,000	July	$90,000
June	80,000	August	60,000

To prepare a cash budget, the company must determine the budgeted cash collections from sales. Historically, the following trend has been established regarding cash collection of sales:

60 percent in month of sale,

20 percent in month following sale,

15 percent in second month following sale,

5 percent uncollectible.

The company gives a 2 percent cash discount for payments made by customers during the month of sale. The accounts receivable balance on April 30 is $24,000, of which $7,000 represents uncollected March sales, and $17,000 represents uncollected April sales.

Required: Prepare a schedule of budgeted cash collections from sales for May, June, and July. Include a three-month summary of estimated cash collections.

6–4 Cash Receipts

Chicago Metal Company is currently estimating cash receipts for the next six months. The accounts receivable balance is to be estimated at the end of each month also. Cash sales are estimated at 10 percent of sales for the month. The balance of sales should be collected as follows:

50 percent during the month of sale,

40 percent during the following month,

10 percent during the second month following month of sale.

The accounts receivable balance at April 1 was $93,600. Budgeted and actual sales are as follows:

Month	Sales Revenue	Month	Sales Revenue
January	$200,000	April	$150,000
February	190,000	May	180,000
March	170,000	June	200,000

Required: Prepare a schedule of budgeted cash collections for each month of the second quarter. Determine the estimated balance of accounts receivable at the end of each month.

6–5 Cash Disbursements

Oregon Timber Company is in the process of preparing its budget for next year. Cost of goods sold has been estimated at 70 percent of sales. Lumber purchases and payments are to be made during the month preceding the month of sale. Wages are estimated at 15 percent of sales and are paid during the month of sale. Other operating costs amounting to 10 percent of sales are to be paid in the month following the month of sales. Additionally, a monthly lease payment of $10,000 is paid to BMI for computer services. Sales revenue is forecast as follows:

Month	Sales Revenue	Month	Sales Revenue
February	$100,000	May	$210,000
March	160,000	June	180,000
April	180,000	July	230,000

Required: Prepare a schedule of cash disbursements for April, May, and June.

6–6 Purchases Budget in Units and Dollars

Budgeted sales of The Record Shop for the first six months of 19x3 are as follows:

Month	Unit Sales	Month	Unit Sales
January	120,000	April	210,000
February	160,000	May	180,000
March	200,000	June	240,000

Beginning inventory for 19x3 is 40,000 units. The budgeted inventory at the end of a month is 40 percent of units to be sold the following month. Purchase price per unit is $3.

Required: Prepare a purchases budget in units and dollars for each month, January through May.

6–7 Purchases Budget in Units and Dollars

Unit sales estimates for Snow King Plow Company for next year are as follows:

Month	Unit Sales	Month	Unit Sales
January	45,000	March	90,000
February	60,000	April	93,000

There were 10,000 units of finished goods in inventory at the beginning of January. Plans are to have an inventory of finished product equal to one third of the sales for the next month.

Four hundred pounds of materials are required for each unit produced. Each pound of material costs $10. Inventory levels for materials are to be equal to one fourth of the needs for the next month. Materials inventory on January 1 was 5.5 million pounds.

Requirements

a) Prepare production budgets for January, February, and March.

b) Prepare a purchases budget in pounds and dollars for January and February.

6-8 Pro Forma Income Statement

Pendleton Company, a merchandising company, is developing its master budget for 19x2. The income statement for 19x1 is as follows:

Pendleton Company
Income Statement
For the year ending December 31, 19x1

Gross sales	$750,000
Less estimated uncollectible accounts	− 7,500
Net sales	$742,500
Cost of goods sold	−430,000
Gross profit	$312,500
Operating expenses (including $25,000 depreciation)	−200,500
Net income	$112,000

The following are management's goals and forecasts for 19x2.

1. Selling prices will increase by 8 percent, and sales volume will increase by 5 percent.

2. The cost of merchandise will increase by 4 percent.

3. All operating expenses are fixed and are paid in the month incurred. Price increases for operating expenses will be 10 percent.

4. The estimated uncollectibles are 1 percent of budgeted sales.

Required: Prepare a budgeted functional income statement for 19x2.

6-9 Pro Forma Income Statement

Big Burger Drive-in is planning a budget for the next fiscal year. Sales revenue has been estimated at $1,000,000. The cost of goods sold has been estimated at 70 percent of sales revenue. Depreciation on the office building and fixtures is budgeted at $50,000. Salaries and wages should amount to 15 percent of sales revenue. Advertising has been budgeted at $75,000, and utilities should amount to $20,000. Income tax is estimated at 40 percent of operating income.

Required: Prepare a pro forma functional income statement for the next fiscal year.

6–10 Sales Budget

Jennifer's T-shirt Shop has very seasonal sales. For 19x7 she is trying to decide whether to establish a sales budget based on average sales or sales estimated by quarter. The unit sales for 19x7 are expected to be 10 percent higher than 19x6 sales. Unit sales by quarter for 19x6 were as follows:

	Children's Shirts	Women's Shirts	Men's Shirts	Total Shirts
Winter quarter	200	200	100	500
Spring quarter	200	250	200	650
Summer quarter	400	300	200	900
Fall quarter	200	250	100	550
Total sales	1,000	1,000	600	2,600

Children's T-shirts sell for $4.00 each, women's sell for $8.00, and men's sell for $7.00.

Requirements

Assuming a 10 percent increase in sales, prepare a sales budget for each quarter of 19x7 using:

a) Average quarterly sales. *Hint:* Winter quarter children's shirts are 275 [(1,000 × 1.10)/4].

b) Actual quarterly sales. *Hint:* Winter quarter children's shirts are 220 [200 × 1.10].

c) Suggest advantages of each method.

6–11 Sales Budget

Quick Mix Company sells three products. The seasonal sales pattern for 19x6 is as follows:

		Products	
Quarter	Gravel	Limestone	Sand
1	10%	25%	20%
2	20	25	30
3	30	25	40
4	40	25	10
	100%	100%	100%

The annual sales budget shows forecasts of: Gravel, 150,000 tons; Limestone, 120,000 tons; and Sand, 180,000 tons. Next year's selling prices per ton will be: Gravel, $10; Limestone, $5; and Sand, $4.

Required: Prepare a sales budget in units and dollars by quarters for the company for the coming year.

6–12 General Budget (Appendix)

The City of Taylorsville has budgeted the following general fund revenues and appropriations for the 19x3 fiscal year.

Revenue forecasts:	
Property taxes	$400,000
Sales taxes	100,000
Income taxes	220,000
Sales revenue sharing	70,000
Appropriations:	
Police protection	$300,000
Fire protection	180,000
Public works	90,000
Administration	125,000
Health and welfare	100,000

Requirements

a) Set up a revenue and appropriation budget for 19x3.

b) Is this a lump-sum or line-item budget? Explain.

6–13 General Budget (Appendix) The Zuker Foundation has established the following revenue and appropriation budgets for 19x1.

Revenues:	
Donations	$800,000
Interest and dividends	250,000
Federal grants	620,000
Appropriations:	
Administration	$115,000
Research and development	980,000
Lab equipment	470,000

Requirements

a) Set up a revenue and appropriation budget for 19x1.

b) What happens if projected revenues do not equal appropriations?

6–14 General Budget (Appendix) The following accounts are from the general fund of the St. Louis General Hospital for October 19x4.

Cash	$100,000	Investments	$500,000
Taxes receivable	80,000	Accounts payable	86,000
Food preparation	44,000	Maintenance	41,000
Nursing services	781,000	Cafeteria revenue	15,000
Security costs	6,000	Patient charges	837,000
Supplies	41,000	Notes payable	400,000

Required: Prepare a revenue and appropriation budget for October 19x4.

6–15 Cash Budget (Appendix)

Tulsa Water Service had the following sales of water for selected months of 19x8.

Month	Sales Revenue	Month	Sales Revenue
February	$120,000	May	$150,000
March	130,000	June	170,000
April	140,000	July	190,000

All sales are on credit. Historically, 60 percent is collected in the month of sale, 30 percent during the first month following sale, and 10 percent in the second month following sale.

Cost of water averages 70 percent of sales revenue. Desired ending inventories are sufficient for 5 percent of the next month's sales. All purchases are paid during the month following purchase.

Operating costs of $20,000 are paid each month.

The April 1 cash balance is expected to be $20,000.

Required: Prepare a cash budget for April, May, and June.

PROBLEMS

6–16 Inventory and Purchases Budgets

The Midwest Belt Company sells men's and boys' belts that are cut to order. Each foot or fraction thereof sells for $2.00. Small belts average two feet, and large belts average three feet in length. The leather is purchased from a local tannery for 90 cents per foot. The buckles are purchased at $2.00 for the small size and $2.50 for the large size. No changes are expected in any of the purchasing and selling prices.

Sales should increase 20 percent this year over last year. Last year the company sold 300 small belts and 140 large belts during January and February. The inventories are as follows:

December 31 Actual		February 28 Target	
Leather (feet)	900	Leather (feet)	800
Small buckles	200	Small buckles	200
Large buckles	300	Large buckles	250

Purchases are made to provide sufficient stock for each two-month period.

Requirements

a) Prepare a purchases budget in units for total January and February purchases of buckles and leather.

b) Compute the budgeted cost of the raw materials to be used in manufacturing small and large belts during January and February.

6–17 Purchases Budget

Crown Candy Company manufactures various products to sell to retail stores. A sales budget for pecan turtles for the next several months is as follows:

Month	Budgeted Units in Boxes
June	20,000
July	24,000
August	30,000
September	36,000
October	40,000

There is no inventory of turtles on hand at June 1. During the summer the company desires an ending finished goods inventory of 10 percent of the following month's sales. The raw materials must be purchased one month before they are needed in production. The June 1 raw materials inventory meets these requirements.

Pecan turtles require direct materials as follows:

	Pounds of Materials per Box of Product
Caramel	3
Pecans	2
Chocolate	5

Required: Prepare a purchases budget in pounds of each ingredient for June and July. *Hint:* A production budget will be helpful.

6–18 Cash Budget

Cash budgeting of Carolina Apple is done on a quarterly basis. The company is planning its cash needs for the third quarter of 19x1 and the following information is available to assist in preparing a cash budget.

Budgeted income statements for July through October 19x1 are as follows:

	July	August	September	October
Sales	$18,000	$24,000	$28,000	$36,000
Cost of goods sold	−10,000	−14,000	−16,000	−20,000
Gross profit	$ 8,000	$10,000	$12,000	$16,000
Less other expenses:				
Selling	$ 2,300	$ 3,000	$ 3,400	$ 4,200
Administrative	2,600	3,000	3,200	3,600
Total	− 4,900	− 6,000	− 6,600	− 7,800
Net income	$ 3,100	$ 4,000	$ 5,400	$ 8,200

Additional information:

1. Other expenses, which are paid monthly, include $1,000 a month of depreciation.

2. Sales are 30 percent for cash and 70 percent on credit.

3. Credit sales are collected 20 percent in the month of sale, 70 percent one month after sale, and 10 percent two months after sale.

4. May sales were $15,000, and June sales were $16,000. Merchandise is paid for 50 percent in the month of purchase. The remaining 50 percent is paid in the following month. Accounts payable for merchandise at June 30 totaled $6,000.

5. The company maintains its ending inventory levels at 25 percent of the cost of goods to be sold in the following month. The inventory at June 30 is $2,500.

6. An equipment note of $5,000 per month is being paid through August.

7. The company must maintain a cash balance of at least $5,000 at the end of each month. The cash balance on June 30 is $5,100.

8. The company can borrow from its bank as needed. Borrowings must be in multiples of $100. All borrowings take place at the beginning of a month, and all repayments are made at the end of a month. At the time the principal is repaid, interest is also paid on the portion of the principal repaid. The interest rate is 12 percent per annum.

Requirements

a) Prepare a monthly schedule of budgeted operating cash receipts for July, August, and September.

b) Prepare a monthly purchases budget and a schedule of budgeted cash payments for purchases for July, August, and September.

c) Prepare a monthly cash budget for July, August, and September. Show borrowings from the company's bank and repayments to the bank as needed to maintain the minimum cash balance.

 6–19 Cash Budget

The Mobile Supply Company sells one product that is purchased for $20 and sold for $30. Budgeted sales in total dollars for next year are $720,000. The sales information needed for preparing the July budget is as follows:

Month	Sales Revenue	Month	Sales Revenue
May	$30,000	July	$48,000
June	42,000	August	60,000

Account balances at July 1 include:

Cash	$15,000
Merchandise inventory	16,000
Accounts receivable (sales)	23,000
Accounts payable (purchases)	15,000

The company pays for one half of its purchases in the month of purchase, and the remainder in the following month. End-of-month inventory must be 50 percent of the budgeted sales in units for the next month.

A 2 percent cash discount on sales is allowed if payment is made during the month of sale. Experience indicates that 50 percent of the billings will be collected during the month of sale, 40 percent in the following month, 8 percent in the next following month, and 2 percent will be uncollectible.

Total budgeted selling and administrative expenses (excluding bad debts) for the fiscal year are estimated at $186,000, of which half is fixed expense (inclusive of a $20,000 annual depreciation charge). Fixed expenses are incurred evenly during the year. The other selling and administrative expenses vary with sales. Expenses are paid during the month incurred.

Requirements

a) Prepare a schedule of estimated cash collections for July.

b) Prepare a schedule of estimated July cash payments for purchases. (Round calculations to the nearest dollar.)

c) Prepare schedules of all July selling and administrative expenses and of those requiring cash payments.

d) Prepare a cash budget in summary form for July.

6–20 Purchases Budget

Topper Toys makes plastic riding tractors that require 3 pounds of material. The company wants raw materials on hand at the beginning of each month equal to one half of the month's production needs. This requirement was met on April 1, the start of the second quarter. There are no work-in-process inventories. A sales budget in units for the next four months is given below.

Month	Unit Sales	Month	Unit Sales
April	15,000	June	24,000
May	18,000	July	26,000

Finished goods inventory at the end of each month must be equal to 40 percent of the next month's sales. On March 31 the finished goods inventory totaled 7,500 units.

Requirements

a) Prepare a production budget for April, May, and June.

b) Prepare a purchases budget for April and May.

6-21 Pro Forma Statements

Madison Butter Sales Company is preparing a budget for January and February of next year. The balance sheet as of December 31, 19x1 is given below.

Madison Butter Sales Company
Balance Sheet
December 31, 19x1

Assets		Equities	
Cash	$100,000	Accounts payable	$125,000
Accounts receivable	60,000	Operating expenses payable	10,000
Inventory	30,000	Miscellaneous payable	20,000
Equipment leasehold	60,000	Capital stock	25,000
		Retained earnings	70,000
Total assets	$250,000	Total equities	$250,000

Monthly sales data for the current year and the budgeted data for next year are as follows:

November 19x1	$180,000	February 19x2	$250,000
December 19x1	100,000	March 19x2	260,000
January 19x2	240,000	April 19x2	280,000

For 19x2 the following conditions are expected to be present:

- Forty percent of the sales revenue is collected during the month of sale, with the balance collected during the following month.

- Cost of goods sold is 60 percent of sales. Merchandise inventory sufficient for 20 percent of next month's sales is to be maintained at the end of each month. All butter purchased for resale is paid for in the month following the month of purchase.

- Operating expenses for each month are estimated at 10 percent of sales revenue. All operating expenses are paid during the following month.

- Income taxes are estimated at 40 percent of income before taxes. Income taxes are paid fifteen days after the end of the quarter. There were no taxes payable on December 31. The miscellaneous payables at December 31, 19x1 are to be paid during January 19x2.

Requirements

a) Prepare a budgeted income statement for the quarter ending March 31, 19x2 using a functional format. Do not prepare monthly statements.

b) Prepare a pro forma balance sheet as of March 31, 19x2. *Hint:* Prepare purchases and cash budgets.

6–22 Budgets and Pro Forma Statements

The Peyton Department Store prepares budgets quarterly. The following information is available for use in planning the second quarter budgets for 19x1.

**Peyton Department Stores
Balance Sheet
March 31, 19x1**

Assets		Equities	
Cash	$ 3,000	Accounts payable	$26,000
Accounts receivable	25,000	Dividends payable	17,000
Inventory	30,000	Rent payable	2,000
Prepaid insurance	2,000	Stockholders' equity	40,000
Fixtures	25,000		
Total assets	$85,000	Total equities	$85,000

Actual and forecasted monthly sales for selected months in 19x1 are as follows:

Month	Sales Revenue	Month	Sales Revenue
January	$60,000	May	$60,000
February	50,000	June	70,000
March	40,000	July	90,000
April	50,000	August	80,000

Monthly operating expenses are as follows:

Wages and salaries	$25,000
Depreciation	100
Utilities	1,000
Rent	2,000

Cash dividends of $17,000 are paid during the first month of each quarter and declared during the third month of each quarter for the next quarter. Operating expenses are paid as incurred, except insurance, rent, and depreciation. Rent is paid during the following month. The prepaid insurance is for five more months. Cost of goods sold is equal to one half of sales.

Beginning inventories are sufficient for 120 percent of the next month's sales. Purchases during any given month are paid in full during the following month. All sales are on account, with 50 percent collected during the month of sale, 40 percent during the next month, and 10 percent during the month thereafter.

Money can be borrowed and repaid in multiples of $1,000 at an interest rate of 12 percent per annum. The company desires a minimum cash balance of $3,000 at the first of each month. At the time the principal is repaid, interest is paid on the portion of principal that is repaid. All borrowing is at the start of the month, and all repayment is at the end of the month. Money is never repaid at the end of the month it is borrowed.

Requirements

a) Prepare a purchases budget for each month of the quarter ending June 30, 19x1.

b) Prepare a cash receipts schedule for each month of the quarter ending June 30, 19x1. Do not include borrowings.

c) Prepare a cash disbursements schedule for each month of the second quarter ending June 30, 19x1. Do not include repayments of borrowings.

d) Prepare a cash budget for each month of the quarter ending June 30, 19x1.

e) Prepare an income statement for each month of the quarter ending June 30, 19x1.

f) Prepare a pro forma balance sheet as of June 30, 19x1.

6–23 Behavioral Implications of Budgeting

Andrea Rawls, controller of Data Scientific, believes that effective budgeting greatly assists in meeting the goals and objectives of the organization. She argues that the budget serves as a blueprint for the operating activities during each reporting period and as such is an important control device. She believes that sound management evaluations can be based on the comparisons of performance and budgetary schedules and that employees respond more favorably when they participate in the budgetary process.

Jeff Cooke, treasurer of Data Scientific, agrees that budgeting is essential for overall organizational success, but argues that human resources are too valuable to spend much time planning and preparing the budgetary process. He thinks that the roles people play in budgetary preparation are not important in the final analysis of a budget's effectiveness.

Required: Contrast the participative versus imposed budgeting concepts and indicate how the ideas of Ms. Rawls and Mr. Cooke fit the two categories.

6–24 Behavioral Considerations and Budgeting

Scott Weidner, the Controller in the Division of Social Services for the state, recognizes the importance of the budgetary process for planning, control, and motivation purposes. He believes that a properly implemented participative budgeting process for planning purposes and a management by exception reporting procedure based on the participative budget will motivate his subordinates to improve productivity within their particular departments. Based on this philosophy, Weidner has implemented the following budget procedures.

- An appropriation target figure is given to each Department Manager. This amount is the maximum funding that each department can expect to receive in the next fiscal year.

- Department Managers develop their individual budgets within the following spending constraints as directed by the controller's staff.

    1. Expenditure requests cannot exceed the appropriation target.

    2. All fixed expenditures should be included in the budget. Fixed expenditures would include such items as contracts and salaries at current levels.

    3. All government projects directed by higher authority should be included in the budget in their entirety.

- The controller's staff consolidates the departmental budget requests from the various departments into one budget that is to be submitted for the entire division.

- Upon final budget approval by the legislature, the controller's staff allocates the appropriation to the various departments on instructions from the Division Manager. However, a specified percentage of each department's appropriation is held back in anticipation of potential budget cuts and special funding needs. The amount and use of this contingency fund is left to the discretion of the Division Manager.

- Each department is allowed to adjust its budget when necessary to operate within the reduced appropriation level. However, as stated in the original directive, specific projects authorized by higher authority must remain intact.

- The final budget is used as the basis of control for a management by exception form of reporting. Excessive expenditures by account for each department are highlighted on a monthly basis. Department Managers are expected to account for all expenditures over budget. Fiscal responsibility is an important factor in the overall performance evaluation of Department Managers.

Weidner believes his policy of allowing the Department Managers to participate in the budget process and then holding them accountable for their performance is essential, especially during these times of limited resources. He further believes the Department Managers will be motivated positively to increase the efficiency and effectiveness of their departments because they have provided input into the initial budgetary process and are required to justify any unfavorable performances.

Requirements

a) Explain the operational and behavioral benefits that generally are attributed to a participative budgeting process.

b) Identify deficiencies in Scott Weidner's participative budgetary policy for planning and performance evaluation purposes. For each deficiency identified, recommend how the deficiency can be corrected.

(CMA Adapted)

6–25 Comprehensive Budgets

Overton Products assembles and sells computer terminals in a single plant. The controller has decided to begin a new evaluation system, which includes quarterly budgets. She has prepared the following information for the first quarter of 19x1.

Estimated sales:
20,000 units at $100 each

Predicted inventories:

	Beginning	Ending
Finished units	5,000	6,000
Frames, raw materials	2,000	3,000
Tubes, raw materials	1,000	1,200

Manufacturing requirements per unit:

Raw Materials	Direct Labor
1 frame at $16	2 hours at $15 per hour
1 tube at $20	

Variable factory overhead is applied at the rate of $5 per direct labor hour. Fixed factory overhead is $147,000 per quarter, including noncash expenditures of $30,000, and is allocated to total units completed.

Financial information:

- Beginning cash balance is $300,000.
- Purchases of raw materials and labor costs are paid for in the quarter acquired.
- Overhead expenses are paid in the next quarter. The accounts payable for these expenses from the last quarter of 19x0 is $320,000.
- Sales are on credit and are collected 40 percent in current period and the remainder the next period. Last quarter's sales were $1,800,000. There are no bad debts.
- Selling and administrative expenses are paid quarterly and total $240,000 including $70,000 of depreciation.
- All unit costs for the first quarter of 19x1 are the same as for the last quarter of 19x0.

Requirements

For the first quarter of 19x1 prepare a:

a) Sales budget in dollars.

b) Production budget in units.

c) Purchases budget.

d) Manufacturing disbursements budget.

e) Cash budget.

f) Budgeted functional income statement. *Hint:* First determine the total costs per unit.

6–26 Comprehensive Budgets

Tuscaloosa Tire Company manufactures plastic tires for automated cleaning machines. It is completing its financial plans for 19x8 and is in need of assistance in the budgeting phase. You are provided the following information that may be useful in preparing the necessary budgets and schedules for 19x8.

Tuscaloosa Tire Company
Balance Sheet
December 31, 19x7

Assets

Current Assets:		
Cash	$200,000	
Accounts receivable (net)	294,000	$494,000
Plant, property, and equipment:		
Land	$100,500	
Buildings and equipment	$350,000	
Less accumulated depreciation	−118,000	232,000	332,500
Total assets		$826,500

Liabilities and stockholder's equity

Current liabilities:		
Accounts payable		$132,000
Stockholder's equity:		
Capital stock	$400,000	
Retained earnings	294,500	694,500
Total liabilities and stockholder's equity		$826,500

Estimated sales:

	First Quarter	Second Quarter	Third Quarter
Sales (units)	15,000	16,000	18,000
Sales ($30 each)	$450,000	$480,000	$540,000

All sales are on credit and are collected 30 percent in month of sale and 70 percent in month following sale. The company has a history of no bad debts. The sales from the last quarter of 19x7 were $420,000.

The company will have no inventories at the beginning of the year. Management desires 5,000 pounds of unmolded plastic at the end of the first quarter and 6,000 pounds at the end of the second quarter. Each wheel takes 2 pounds of plastic, including waste trimmings. There should be 2,000 wheel rims at the end of the first quarter and 2,500 at the end of the second quarter. Finished inventory should total 1,000 wheels at the end of the first quarter and 1,500 at the end of the second quarter.

Manufacturing requirements:

	Raw Materials	Direct Labor
Plastic	2 lbs. at $3 per lb.	One-half hour
Rims	1 each at $2	

Variable factory overhead is applied at the rate of $3 per direct labor hour for each finished unit. Fixed factory overhead is $170,000 per quarter, including noncash expenditures of $54,000, and is allocated on total units completed. Direct labor averages $20 per hour.

Additional information:

- Purchases of raw materials and labor costs are paid for in the quarter acquired.
- Overhead expenses are paid in the next quarter.
- The accounts payable on the balance sheet is for these expenses from the last quarter of 19x7.
- Selling and administrative expenses are paid quarterly and total $40,000, including $10,000 of depreciation.

Requirements

For the first and second quarters of 19x8 prepare a:

a) Sales budget in dollars.

b) Production budget in units.

c) Purchases budget.

d) Manufacturing disbursements budget.

e) Cash budget.

6–27 Reporting (Appendix)

Washington County makes the following report public on July 31 for its educational program.

Washington County
Annual Report
Education Program
July 31, 19x4

	Budget	Actual
Revenues (all sources)	$4,500,000	$4,400,000
Expenditures:		
Salaries	2,250,000	2,270,000
Maintenance	600,000	700,000
Other	1,650,000	1,580,000

Notes to report:

1. Revenues were lower than expected.

2. Teachers did not get a pay raise.

3. Twelve new buses were purchased.

Requirements

a) As a commissioner of Washington County, what additional information would you want in the body of the financial report?

b) What management accounting information could be furnished?

c) How could the notes section be improved?

6–28 Financial Statement (Appendix)

The City of Naples conducts all its activities through a general fund account. At the beginning of the 19x1 fiscal year the town's assets consisted of cash, $12,000; city hall, $132,000; city park, $19,500; and equipment, $68,000.

At the beginning of the year the town council approved the following line-item budget.

Budgeted revenues:	Taxes, $75,000; other revenues, $28,600
Appropriations:	Salaries, $56,000; supplies, $2,000; equipment, $3,000; contractual services, $14,000; miscellaneous, $2,000

Actual transactions for the year were as follows:

Revenues:	Taxes, $80,000; other revenues, $25,000
Expenditures:	Salaries, $55,500; supplies, $1,400; equipment, $3,000; contractual services, $14,000; miscellaneous, $1,500

Requirements

a) Prepare a budget statement of revenues and expenditures for the fiscal year ending October 31, 19x1, for the general fund of Naples.

b) Prepare a performance report for the year ended October 31, 19x1.

c) One citizen group complained that the cut in expenditures hurt the town park; another group complained that not enough was spent on streets. In preparing the next budget, what could you do to be more responsive to citizen groups?

6–29 Budget by Function (Appendix)

The city of Flowershine prepares functional budgets based on the estimated needs of its managers. These are limited by the general budget, which is approved by the city council. For 19x5 the council approved the following line-item general budget.

Salaries and wages	$ 800,000
Supplies	100,000
Repairs and parts	212,000
Capital expenditures (buildings)	400,000
Equipment purchases	170,000
General and miscellaneous	62,000
Total	$1,744,000

This budget is then allocated to the service functions based on a program evaluation of services. For 19x5 the needs are as follows:

	Utilities	Fire Protection	Police Protection	Welfare	Administration
Salaries and wages	10%	20%	30%	15%	25%
Supplies	40	15	20	10	15
Repairs and parts	20	30	40	5	5
Capital expenditures	50	5	10	5	30
Equipment purchases	30	35	20	5	10
General and miscellaneous	15	20	20	25	20

Required: Prepare a budget for each fund.

6–30 Budget Preparation (Appendix)

The Board of Education of the Victoria School District is developing a budget for the school year ending June 30, 19x1. The budgeted expenditures follow.

Victoria School District
Budgeted Expenditures
For the year ending June 30, 19x1

Current operating expenditures:		
Instruction:		
General	$1,401,600	
Vocational training	112,000	$1,513,600
Pupil service:		
Bus transportation	$ 36,300	
School lunches	51,700	88,000
Attendance and health service		14,000
Administration		46,000
Operation and maintenance of plant		208,000
Pensions, insurance, etc.		154,000
Total current operating expenditures		$2,023,600
Other expenditures:		
Capital outlays from revenues		$ 75,000
Debt service (annual installment		
and interest on long-term debt)		150,000
Total other expenditures		225,000
Total budgeted expenditures		$2,248,600

The following data are available.

1. The estimated average daily school enrollment of the school district is 5,000 pupils, including 200 pupils enrolled in a vocational training program.

2. Estimated revenues include equalizing grants-in-aid from the state of $150 per pupil. The grants were established by state law under a plan intended to encourage raising the level of education.

3. The federal government matches 60 percent of state grants-in-aid for pupils enrolled in a vocational training program. In addition, the federal government contributes toward the cost of bus transportation and school lunches a maximum of $12 per pupil based on total enrollment within the school district but not to exceed $6\frac{2}{3}$ percent of the state per-pupil equalization grants-in-aid.

4. Interest on temporary investment of school tax receipts and rents of school facilities are expected to be $75,000 and are earmarked for special equipment acquisitions listed as "Capital outlays from revenues" in the budgeted expenditures. Cost of the special equipment acquisitions will be limited to the amount derived from these miscellaneous receipts.

5. The remaining funds needed to finance the budgeted expenditures of the school district are to be raised from local taxation. An allowance of 9 percent of the local tax levy is necessary for possible tax abatements and losses. The assessed valuation of the property located within the school district is $80,000,000.

Requirements

a) Prepare a schedule computing the estimated total funds to be obtained from local taxation for the ensuing school year ending June 30, 19x1, for the Victoria School District.

b) Prepare a schedule computing the estimated current operating cost per regular pupil and per vocational pupil to be met by local tax funds. Assume that costs other than instructional costs are assignable on a per capita basis to regular and vocational students.

c) Without prejudice to your solution to requirement (a), assume that the estimated total tax levy for the ensuing school year ending June 30, 19x1, is $1,092,000. Prepare a schedule computing the estimated tax rate per $100 of assessed valuation of the property within the Victoria School District required to meet the tax levy.

(CPA Adapted)

REVIEW PROBLEM SOLUTION

a) **Handy Company**
Sales Budget
First Quarter, 19x1

Sales Product	Units	Price	Sales
Drills	60,000	$100	$ 6,000,000
Saws	40,000	125	5,000,000
Total			$11,000,000

Collections on sales

Current quarter's sales (50%)	$5,500,000
Previous quarter's sales (50%)	4,200,000
Total cash collections	$9,700,000

---

b) **Handy Company**
Production Budget
First Quarter, 19x1

	Drills	Saws
Budget sales	60,000	40,000
Plus required ending inventory	25,000	10,000
Total inventory requirements	85,000	50,000
Less beginning inventory	−20,000	−8,000
Budgeted production	65,000	42,000

c)   **Handy Company**
     Purchases Budget
     First Quarter, 19x1

Metal purchases

	Drills	Saws	Total
Production units (from part b)	65,000	42,000	
Metal	× 5 lbs.	× 4 lbs.	
Production needs	325,000 lbs.	168,000 lbs.	493,000 lbs.
Target ending inventory			36,000
Total metal needs			529,000
Less beginning inventory			− 32,000
Purchases needed			497,000 lbs.
Cost per lb.			× $8
Total purchases			$3,976,000

Plastic purchases

	Drills	Saws	Total
Production units (from part b)	65,000	42,000	107,000
Plastic			× 3 lbs.
Production needs			321,000 lbs.
Target ending inventory			32,000
Total plastic needs			353,000
Less beginning inventory			− 29,000
Purchases needed			324,000 lbs.
Cost per lb.			× $5
Total purchases			$1,620,000

Handle purchases

	Drills	Total
Production units (from part b)	65,000	65,000
Handles		× 1
Production needs		65,000
Target ending inventory		7,000
Total handle needs		72,000
Less beginning inventory		− 6,000
Purchases needed		66,000
Cost per handle		× $3
Total purchases		$ 198,000

Total purchases

Metal	$3,976,000
Plastic	1,620,000
Handles	198,000
Total	$5,794,000

d)   Handy Company
Manufacturing Disbursements Budget
First Quarter, 19x1

	Drills	Saws	Total
Budgeted production	65,000	42,000	
Direct labor hours per unit	× 2	× 3	
Total direct labor hours	130,000	126,000	
Labor rate	× $12	× $16	
Labor expenditures	$1,560,000	$2,016,000	$3,576,000
Direct labor hours	130,000	126,000	
Variable factory overhead rate	× $1.50	× $1.50	
Total variable overhead	$195,000	$189,000	$384,000
Fixed factory overhead			214,000
Total overhead			$598,000
Less noncash items			−156,000
Overhead expenditures to be paid next quarter			$442,000

e)   Handy Company
Cash Budget
First Quarter, 19x1

Cash balance, beginning	$1,800,000	
Plus cash collections (sales budget)	9,700,000	
Cash available from operations		$11,500,000
Less budgeted disbursements:		
Materials (Purchases budget)	$5,794,000	
Labor (Manufacturing disbursements budget)	3,576,000	
Overhead (last quarter)	380,000	
Selling and administrative ($340,000 − $90,000 depreciation)	250,000	−10,000,000
Cash balance, ending		$ 1,500,000

f) Schedule of Total Unit Costs

		Drills	Saws
Metal:	5 lbs. at $8	$40.00	
	4 lbs. at $8		$32.00
Plastic:	3 lbs. at $5	15.00	15.00
Handles:	1 each at $3	3.00	
Direct labor:	2 hrs. at $12	24.00	
	3 hrs. at $16		48.00
Variable factory overhead:	2 hrs. at $1.50	3.00	
	3 hrs. at $1.50		4.50
Fixed factory overhead:	$214,000/107,000*	2.00	2.00
Total unit costs		$87.00	$101.50

* From production budget.

Handy Company
Income Statement
First Quarter, 19x1

Sales (Sales budget)			$11,000,000
Less costs of goods sold:			
Finished goods inventory, beginning			
Drills (20,000 × $87)	$1,740,000		
Saws (8,000 × $101.50)	812,000	$ 2,552,000	
Cost of materials placed in production (Purchases budget):			
Metal (493,000 × $8)	$3,944,000		
Plastic (321,000 × $5)	1,605,000		
Handles (65,000 × $3)	195,000		
Total	$5,744,000		
Labor (Manufacturing disbursements budget)	3,576,000		
Variable overhead (Manufacturing disbursements budget)	384,000		
Fixed overhead	214,000	9,918,000	
Total goods available for sale		$12,470,000	
Finished goods inventory, ending			
Drills (25,000 × $87)	$2,175,000		
Saws (10,000 × $101.50)	1,015,000	− 3,190,000	− 9,280,000
Gross profit			$ 1,720,000
Selling and administrative expenses			− 340,000
Net income			$ 1,380,000

CHAPTER 7

Responsibility Accounting and Flexible Budgets

Upon completion of this chapter you should:

- Understand the importance of feedback reports in budgeting and in performance evaluation.
- Understand how the concept of responsibility accounting is used to structure a performance reporting system for organizations with more than one management level.
- Be familiar with the four primary types of responsibility centers (investment centers, profit centers, revenue centers, and cost centers).
- Know the difference between a standard cost center and a discretionary cost center.
- Be able to compute flexible budget cost variances and prepare a flexible budget performance report for a responsibility center.
- Be able to analyze revenue center performance and prepare variances for sales price and sales volume. Also be able to prepare, for revenue centers that incur costs, variances for selling expenses and net sales volume.
- Be able to reconcile budgeted and actual income using sales variances and flexible budget cost variances.

Feedback in the form of performance reports is essential if the benefits of budgeting are to be fully realized. Managers need to know how actual results compare with the current budget in order to control current operations and improve budgets for future periods. Consider a relatively simple situation where the unit cost of raw materials exceeds the cost allowed in the budget. A performance report addressed to the appropriate manager indicates the existence of the disparity, and the manager initiates an investigation to determine its cause. The manager may find that a new employee in the Purchasing Department is buying from unauthorized vendors or in small lots. In this case the manager will take action to bring performance into line with plans, perhaps by having the new employee work closely with a more experienced colleague. Alternatively, the investigation may reveal unanticipated price increases. In this case the budget should be revised to reflect the price increases, and the new prices should also be used in future budgets.

The importance of feedback to budgeting is illustrated in Exhibit 7–1. Here budgeting and performance evaluation are presented as a continuous cycle. Assume the cycle starts with the current budget. As the year passes, actual operating data are accumulated and compared with the current budget in the form of performance reports. The appropriate managers receive these reports and then obtain additional information to explain significant deviations from

EXHIBIT 7–1   The Budgeting–Performance Evaluation Cycle

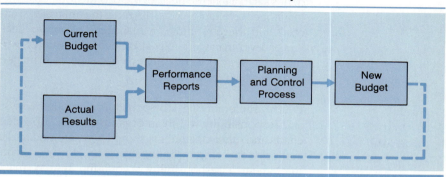

the budget. Based on this information, management attempts to improve current operations and plans for the future, which are summarized in the new budget. The new budget becomes the current budget and the cycle continues.

The purpose of this chapter is to examine the nature of financial performance reports and the concepts that underlie their development and use. The relationship between performance reports and organization structure, as well as the types of financial performance reports that are best suited to various activities, are discussed. Much of the material presented here is examined in greater detail in later chapters.

RESPONSIBILITY ACCOUNTING

By serving as a scorecard and an attention director, performance reports, which contain comparisons of actual results and plans, help managers determine and control the organization's activities. In accordance with the concept of management by exception, the absence of significant differences indicates that activities are proceeding as planned, whereas the presence of significant differences indicates a need either to take corrective action or to revise plans.

Performance reports should be prepared in accordance with the concept of **responsibility accounting,** which is the structuring of performance reports addressed to individual or group members of an organization in a manner that emphasizes the factors controllable by them. In responsibility accounting the focus is on specific units within the organization that are responsible for the accomplishment of specific activities or objectives. Performance reports are customized to emphasize the activities of each specific organizational unit. For example, a financial performance report addressed to the head of a production department contains manufacturing costs controllable by the department head;

it does not contain costs (such as advertising, sales commissions, or the president's salary) that the head of the production department cannot control. Including noncontrollable costs distracts the manager's attention from controllable costs and thereby dilutes a manager's efforts to deal with controllable items. Lower level managers may also become frustrated with the entire performance reporting system if they believe upper level managers expect them to control costs they cannot influence.

Financial Performance Reports and Corporate Structure

Before implementing a responsibility accounting system all areas of authority and responsibility within an organization must be clearly defined. Organization charts and other documents should be examined to determine an organization's authority and responsibility structure. However, when an attempt is made to implement a responsibility accounting system, management may find many instances of overlapping duties, of authority not commensurate with responsibility, and of expenditures for which no one appears responsible. These circumstances make the development of a responsibility accounting system difficult, but their resolution is a benefit of successful installation.

Though performance reports can be developed for areas of responsibility as narrow as a single worker, the basic responsibility unit in most organizations is the department. In manufacturing plants, separate responsibility centers are set up for individual production and service departments. In large universities, separate responsibility centers are set up for individual academic departments (such as accounting, psychology, and sociology) and service departments (such as admissions, cafeteria, and maintenance). When a large department performs a number of diverse and significant activities, responsibility accounting may be further refined so that a single department contains several responsibility centers with performance reports prepared for each.

An abbreviated organization chart for a manufacturing firm is presented in Exhibit 7–2. The short-run objective of the firm is to earn a profit by the production and sale of finished goods. The president and the executive vice president are responsible for overall operations and profitability. The authority to set selling prices and to incur costs in connection with the sale of goods is delegated to the vice president of sales, who in turn delegates a portion of this authority to each of two district sales managers. The authority to incur costs in connection with the manufacture of goods is delegated to the vice president of production, who in turn delegates a portion of this authority to each of two plant managers. Finally, each plant manager delegates the authority to incur costs, in connection with specific manufacturing activities, to department heads.

Commensurate with their authority, the responsibility of individual department heads is quite narrow. And, commensurate with greater authority, responsibility is broader at higher levels in the organization. A series of financial performance reports, illustrating expanding authority for manufacturing costs, is presented in Exhibit 7–3. A plant manager is responsible for more costs than

EXHIBIT 7–2   Partial Organization Chart of a Manufacturing Firm

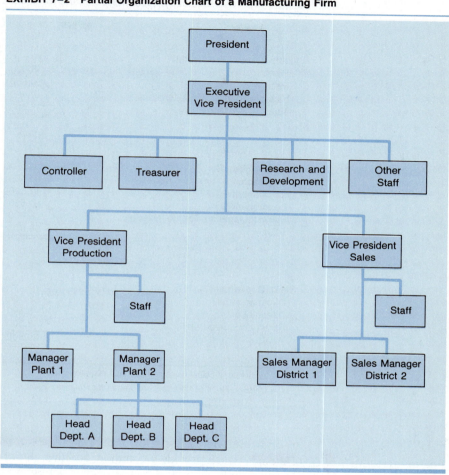

is a department head, and the vice president of production is responsible for more costs than is a single plant manager. Note how the performance reports tie together. The totals for the head of Department C are included as one line in the plant manager's report, and the totals for the manager of Plant 2 are included as one line in the report for the vice president of production. This aggregation takes place because the managers closest to actual activities need detailed information to control day-to-day activities, whereas upper level managers spend less time controlling activities and more time planning them.

EXHIBIT 7–3   Responsibility Accounting Reports for Manufacturing

	Actual Cost	Allowed Cost	Variance*
Vice president: Production			
Plant 1	$ 55,000	$ 54,800	$ 200 U
Plant 2	69,600	68,400	1,200 U
Vice president's office (itemized)	10,900	12,000	1,100 F
Total	$135,500	$135,200	$ 300 U

	Actual Cost	Allowed Cost	Variance*
Manager: Plant 2			
Department A	$ 25,400	$ 24,700	$ 700 U
Department B	17,500	18,000	500 F
Department C	20,500	19,900	600 U
Plant manager's office (itemized)	6,200	5,800	400 U
Total	$ 69,600	$ 68,400	$1,200 U

	Actual Cost	Allowed Cost	Variance*
Head: Department C			
Direct materials	$ 6,000	$ 5,000	$1,000 U
Direct labor	6,500	7,000	500 F
Factory overhead (itemized)	8,000	7,900	100 U
Total	$ 20,500	$ 19,900	$ 600 U

* F = Favorable, if actual costs are less than allowed costs.
  U = Unfavorable, if actual costs are greater than allowed costs.

Nonmonetary Performance Measures

An organization's basic performance reports are almost always stated in terms of dollars, which provide a common, additive unit of measure for all activities. Once the dollar impact of each activity is determined, the dollar measures can be summarized and reported up the corporate ladder. Furthermore, both the immediate supervisor of an activity and other managers far removed from the activity can understand the impact of dollars on cash flow and income. Dollars should not, however, be used to the exclusion of nondollar performance measures. A favorable variance that resulted from an unethical or illegal action should not be rewarded. Short-sighted managers may also take actions that appear favorable in the short run but are detrimental to the organization in the long run. Excessive pressures for employee productivity may result in strikes and employee turnover, and bargain purchases of raw materials may result in excess waste. These examples illustrate the need for upper level management to inquire about the causes of favorable as well as unfavorable variances. What is more, there should be some legitimate way for concerned employees to communicate with upper management without violating the chain of command. For example, an employee in a waste treatment department should be able to legitimately express a concern to upper management about a supervisor's illegal cost cutting measures. A corporate ombudsman might be useful in this regard.

The persons responsible for the accomplishment of specific activities, especially first line supervisors, should be routinely provided with dollar and nondollar performance measures. The nondollar measures should be stated in terms of the activities or resources for which first line supervisors are responsible. The head of a production department, for example, should receive information on materials use, labor hours, machine hours, units produced, defective units, scrap, and so forth. A district sales manager would like information on market share, number of orders, number of salespersons' visits, and customer complaints.

Frequency of Performance Reports

Performance reports must be provided with sufficient frequency for managers to take timely corrective action. Although performance reports for an entire year may assist in developing plans and evaluating managers' performance, they are of no use in adjusting operations during the year. On the other hand, daily or hourly performance reports may be of great value to some managers but a distraction to others. The solution to this dilemma is to recognize that different levels of management, and different personnel at each level, have differing needs for performance information. The head of a production department may require daily, hourly, or even continuous information about operations under his or her control, whereas a plant manager may need only weekly reports from each department head. Similarly, the vice president of production may require only monthly performance reports from each plant. The further a manager is from actual operations, the less the manager's need for frequent feedback. Higher level managers spend more time planning operations and motivating personnel to execute these plans, and lower level managers spend more time executing plans. Hence, lower level managers have greater need for frequent and fast feedback.

Types of Responsibility Centers

Under responsibility accounting, performance reports are prepared for departments, segments of departments, or groupings of departments that operate under the control and authority of a responsible manager. Each organizational unit for which performance reports are prepared is identified as a responsibility center. For the purpose of evaluating their financial performance, responsibility centers may be classified as investment centers, profit centers, revenue centers, or costs centers.

An investment center is responsible for the relationship between its profits and the total assets invested in the center. In general, the management of an investment center is expected to earn a target profit per dollar invested. Investment center managers are evaluated on the basis of how well they use the total resources entrusted to their care to earn a profit.

An investment center is the broadest and most inclusive type of responsibility center. The entire organization depicted in Exhibit 7–2 would be regarded as an investment center, with the president and the executive vice president being the investment center's management. These officials have more authority and responsibility than other managers and are primarily responsible for planning, organizing, and controlling firm activities. Their decisions regarding the size of the company determine the total assets for which they are responsible. Because of their authority regarding the size of corporate assets, they are held responsible for the relationship between profits and assets. Investment centers are discussed further in Chapter 9.

A **profit center** is responsible for the difference between revenues and costs. A profit center may refer to an entire organization but is more frequently a segment of an organization, such as a product line, marketing territory, or store. In the context of performance evaluation the word "profit" may not refer to the bottom line of an income statement; instead, it is likely to refer to the profit center's contribution to common corporate costs and profit. Profit is computed as the center's revenues less all costs identified with operating the center.

A large retail organization might evaluate each of its stores as a profit center, with the store manager being the administrative officer. The store manager, who has responsibility for the overall operation of the store, accepts the store's physical structure and the organization's investment in the store as givens. Though the store manager may request that additional investments be made for a variety of purposes, the manager seldom has the authority to make investment or financing decisions. Having limited authority regarding the size of the store's total assets, the store manager is not held responsible for the relationship between profits and assets. For making special analyses, management may, of course, evaluate the store as an investment center.

A **revenue center** is responsible for the generation of sales revenues. In Exhibit 7–2 there are three revenue centers: District 1, District 2, and the Vice President of Sales. A performance report is prepared for each district and the Vice President of Sales. Even though the basic performance report of a revenue center emphasizes sales, revenue centers are likely to be assigned responsibility for the controllable costs they incur in generating revenues. If revenues and costs are evaluated separately, the center has dual responsibility as a revenue center and as a cost center. If controllable costs are deducted from revenues to obtain some bottom-line contribution, the center is, in fact, being treated as a quasi-profit center.

A **cost center** is financially responsible only for the incurrence of costs; it does not have a revenue responsibility. A cost center may be as small as a segment of a department or large enough to include a major aspect of the organization, such as all manufacturing activities. The financial performance reports in Exhibit 7–3 illustrate an increasing responsibility for manufacturing costs. The head of a production department is responsible only for costs incurred in his or her department, but the vice president of manufacturing is responsible for all manufacturing costs. Cost centers are established for nonmanufacturing as well as for manufacturing activities. In Exhibit 7–2 each of the staff departments, such as the Controller's Department, is evaluated as a cost center. Cost centers are also established in merchandising, service, and not-for-profit organizations. Typical examples of these cost centers include the following:

Organization	Cost Center
Retail store	Advertising department
	Maintenance department
TV station	Audio/video engineering
	Buildings and grounds
College	History department
	Power plant
City government	Public safety (police and fire)
	Welfare

In the remainder of this chapter we introduce concepts that are important to the development of financial performance reports for cost and revenue centers. We conclude by illustrating how the performance reports of cost centers and revenue centers can be combined to reconcile the difference between an organization's budgeted and actual income. We will look closer at cost center performance reports in Chapter 8, investment centers are considered in Chapter 9, and performance reports for important segments of a business (profit centers) are examined in Chapter 10.

PERFORMANCE REPORTS FOR COST CENTERS

Financial performance reports for cost centers should always include a comparison of actual and allowed costs, with the difference identified as a variance. The variance is favorable if actual costs are less than allowed costs and unfavorable if actual costs are greater than allowed costs. These comparisons are made in total and for each type of controllable cost assigned to the cost center. The allowed costs used in performance reports are based on a flexible budget for the actual level of activity.

Development of Flexible Budgets

A budget that is based on a prior prediction of expected sales and production is called a **static budget.** The operating budget explained in Chapter 6 is a static budget. Budgets may also be drawn up for a series of possible production and sales volumes or adjusted to a particular level of production after the fact. These budgets, based on cost-volume-profit or cost-volume relationships, are called flexible budgets; they are used to determine what costs should have been for an attained volume of activity. Before a flexible budget can be developed, management must understand how costs respond to changes in activity.

Assume the Meridian Clock Company contains three departments, Production, Sales, and Administration. In this chapter we will develop financial performance reports for each of them, starting with the Production Department. The flexible budget cost estimating equation for total monthly production costs is as follows:

		Fixed Costs		Variable Costs
Direct materials				$10X
Direct labor				6X
Factory overhead		$50,000		4X
Total cost	=	$50,000	+	$20X

where X equals the number of units produced.

If management planned to produce 10,000 units in July 19x7, the budgeted manufacturing costs for July would amount to $250,000:

Meridian Clock Company
Manufacturing Budget
For the month of July, 19x7

Manufacturing costs:	
Direct materials (10,000 × $10)	$100,000
Direct labor (10,000 × $6)	60,000
Variable overhead (10,000 × $4)	40,000
Fixed overhead	50,000
Total	$250,000

Flexible Budgets Emphasize Efficiency

If actual production happened to equal 10,000 units, the performance of the Production Department in controlling costs could be based on a comparison of actual and budgeted manufacturing costs. But, if production were at some volume other than that specified in the original manufacturing budget, it would be inappropriate to compare actual manufacturing costs with the costs predicted in the original static budget. Doing so would intermix two separate Production Department responsibilities; namely, the manufacturing responsibility for production volume and the financial responsibility for cost control.

The original budget for production volume was set on the basis of predicted needs for sales and inventory requirements, taking into consideration materials, labor, and facilities constraints. In the absence of any changes in these needs, the Production Department's manufacturing responsibility for production volume is evaluated by comparing the actual and budgeted production volumes. If, however, production needs change, perhaps due to an unexpected increase or decrease in sales volume, the Production Department should attempt to make appropriate changes in its production volume. And, when the actual production volume is anything other than the originally budgeted amount, the Production Department's financial responsibility for cost control should be based on the actual level of production.

For the purpose of evaluating the financial performance of cost centers, a flexible budget is tailored, after the fact, to the actual level of activity. A **flexible budget variance** is computed for each cost as the difference between the actual cost and the flexible budget cost of producing a given quantity of product or service. Examples of performance reports for July manufacturing costs, based on static and flexible budgets, are presented in Exhibit 7–4. When the Production Department's financial performance is evaluated using the static budget, the actual cost of producing 11,000 units is compared to the budgeted cost of producing 10,000 units. The result is a series of large, unfavorable static budget variances, totaling $23,000. When the Production Department's financial performance is evaluated by comparing actual costs with costs allowed in a flexible budget that was drawn up for the actual production volume, the results are mixed. Direct materials have a $2,000 favorable flexible budget variance. Direct labor has a $4,000 unfavorable flexible budget variance. There is no variable overhead flexible budget variance. And fixed overhead has a $1,000 unfavorable variance. The net unfavorable flexible budget variance is $3,000.

Standard Costs

A **standard cost,** a budget for one unit of product, indicates what it should cost to produce one unit of product under efficient operating conditions. Standard costs can be developed from an engineering analysis or from an analysis of historical data adjusted for expected changes in the product, production technology, or costs. When standards are developed using historical data, management must be careful to ensure that past inefficiencies are excluded from current standards. The standard variable product costs for the Meridian Clock Company are $20 per unit, including direct materials, direct labor, and factory overhead costs of $10, $6, and $4, respectively. These standard costs were used in developing the flexible budget in Exhibit 7–4.

Standard costs are used for budgeting, performance evaluation, and product costing. In Chapter 6 standard costs for materials, labor, and overhead were used in developing the operating budget for the All American Wagon Company. In this chapter and in Chapter 8, standard costs are used for performance

EXHIBIT 7–4   Flexible Budgets and Performance Evaluation

Meridian Clock Company
Production Department Performance Report
For the month of July, 19x7

	Based on Static Budget			Based on Flexible Budget			
	Actual	Original Budget	Static Budget Variance*	Flexible Budget Formula	Actual	Flexible Budget	Flexible Budget Variance*
Volume	11,000	10,000			11,000	11,000	
Manufacturing costs:							
Direct materials	$108,000	$100,000	$ 8,000 U	$10/unit	$108,000	$110,000	$2,000 F
Direct labor	70,000	60,000	10,000 U	6/unit	70,000	66,000	4,000 U
Variable overhead	44,000	40,000	4,000 U	4/unit	44,000	44,000	0
Fixed overhead	51,000	50,000	1,000 U	$50,000/month	51,000	50,000	1,000 U
	$273,000	$250,000	$23,000 U		$273,000	$270,000	$3,000 U

* F = Favorable
   U = Unfavorable

evaluation. In Appendix B of Chapter 11, standard costs are used for product costing. When standard costs are used to value product inventories in external financial statements, the unit standard cost must also include an element for fixed overhead.[1] For purposes of internal planning and control, it is better to classify costs by their behavior. Accordingly, since fixed costs are constant in the short run without regard to the level of operations, they are treated as a lump sum in this chapter. In the Meridian Clock Company's flexible budget for manufacturing costs (see Exhibit 7–4), the budgeted fixed overhead does not vary with production volume.

To obtain the full benefit of standard costs, the standards must be based on realistic expectations. Some organizations intentionally set "tight" standards to motivate employees toward higher levels of production. The management of the Meridian Clock Company might set their standard for direct labor at $4 per unit, rather than at the expected $6 per unit, hoping that employees will strive toward the lower cost. The use of tight standards often causes planning and

---

[1] External reporting requires that inventories be stated on an absorption cost basis in which all manufacturing costs, including fixed costs, are product costs.

behavioral problems. Management expects them to result in unfavorable variances. Accordingly, tight standards should not be used to budget input requirements and cash flows—management expects to incur more labor costs than the standards allow. The use of tight standards can have undesirable behavioral effects if lower level managers and employees find that a second set of standards are used in the "real" budget or if they are constantly subject to unfavorable performance reports. They may come to distrust the entire budgeting and performance evaluation system, or they may quit trying to achieve any of the organization's standards.

Tight standards are more likely to occur in an imposed budget and less likely to occur in a participation budget where employees are actively involved in budget preparation. In a participation budget the problems may be to avoid loose standards that are easily attained and to avoid overstating the costs required to produce a product. Loose standards may fail to properly motivate employees; what is more, they may lead the company into an uncompetitive market position with costs and prices that are higher than those of competitors.

Standard and Discretionary Cost Centers

A distinction is often made between standard and discretionary cost centers. A standard cost center is a cost center that has clearly defined relationships between effort and accomplishment. A discretionary cost center is a cost center that does not have clearly defined relationships between effort and accomplishment.

The financial performance of standard cost centers is evaluated with the aid of flexible budgets drawn up for the actual level of activity. A production department is the most obvious example of a standard cost center. However, the growth of services and service industries, and the resultant need to control service costs, has led to an expanding use of standard cost centers. Standard cost centers can be established for any segment of a business for which it is possible to develop standard costs per unit of activity. Possible applications include the costs of packaging, transportation, commissions, utilities, room cleaning, residential fire inspection, laundry, automobile repair, and processing loan applications.

Recall that discretionary costs are set at a fixed amount at the discretion of management. Changing these costs does not affect production or service capacity in the near term. Because of the absence of a relationship between effort and accomplishment, the financial performance of a discretionary cost center cannot be evaluated with the aid of a flexible budget. Indeed, it is difficult to evaluate the performance of a discretionary cost center by any means. The best monetary evaluation is based on a comparison of the actual and budgeted costs for a given period, with the results identified as over budget or under budget.

If a research and development budget for 19x9 contained authorized expenditures of $1.5 million, but the actual 19x9 expenditures amounted to $1.2

million, the $300,000 difference is not necessarily favorable. Research and development was $300,000 under budget. Whether or not this is good or bad depends on what was accomplished during the year. If the money was saved by canceling a program critical to the organization's future, the net result is hardly favorable. Again, all the variance does is inform management that actual results were not in line with plans. Management must investigate further to determine the significance of the variance.

Though it is difficult to evaluate the under-budget performance of a discretionary cost center, an over-budget performance has an undesirable implication regardless of the results achieved. If, after the budget is approved, the manager of a discretionary cost center realizes the center's budget is inadequate, the manager should immediately request additional funds, or notify his or her supervisor of the need to reduce activity. Going over budget implies that the manager is unable to operate with the budgeted resources. Obviously, a manager should not be allowed unlimited use of the organization's resources. To control such use, the organization's treasurer is often prohibited from providing financial resources in excess of an authorized limit (like the limit on a bank credit card). If this limit is exceeded, the matter should be brought immediately to the attention of the next level of management.

In for-profit organizations, an increase in demand for a product or service is usually accompanied by an increase in financial resources that more than covers the increase in variable costs. This is often not the case in not-for-profit organizations. Here the funds provided for an activity may be fixed regardless of the level of the activity. A city in upstate New York might budget $1,000,000 per year for snow removal with the money collected from property taxes. If this budget is based on an average of five snowfalls per year at an average removal cost of $200,000 per snowfall, the city department responsible for snow removal may have to operate with this amount even if there are seven snowfalls. The problem is that the department, a natural standard cost center, receives resources as if it were a discretionary cost center. Consequently, the department may not have enough resources to do its job in periods of high activity, and it may have excess resources (which it might be tempted to waste) in periods of low activity. The unique problems of planning and control in not-for-profit organizations are considered further in the appendix to Chapter 6.

As management's ability to define the relationships between effort and accomplishment becomes more refined, there is a tendency for managers to replace discretionary cost centers with standard cost centers. A computer center that was initially established as a discretionary cost center may be changed to a standard cost center, once management determines the relationships between the computer's operating costs and some measure of its activity. A management that desires to better plan and control costs will encourage the evolution from discretionary to standard cost centers wherever practicable.

PERFORMANCE REPORTS FOR REVENUE CENTERS

The financial performance reports for revenue centers include a comparison of actual and budgeted revenues, with the difference identified as a variance. Revenue centers are sometimes assigned responsibility for controllable costs they incur in generating revenues. In this case they have a dual responsibility as a revenue center and as a cost center. Controllable costs may be deducted from revenues to obtain some bottom-line contribution. If the center is then evaluated on the basis of this contribution, it is being treated as a profit center.

Revenue Center Reports Reconcile with the Original Budget

If the organization is to meet its budgeted profit goal for a period, with its budgeted fixed and variable costs, the organization's revenue centers must meet their original revenue budgets. Consequently, the original budget (a static budget), rather than a flexible budget, is used to evaluate the financial performance of revenue centers.

Assume the Meridian Clock Company's sales budget for July 19x7 called for the sale of 10,000 units at $40 each. If Meridian actually sold 11,000 units at $39 each, the total revenue variance would be $29,000:

Actual revenues (11,000 × $39)	$429,000
Budgeted revenues (10,000 × $40)	−400,000
Revenue variance	$ 29,000 F

Because actual revenues exceeded budgeted revenues, the revenue variance is favorable. Note that two distinct events occurred to create the $29,000 favorable variance: the selling price declined from $40 to $39, and the sales volume increased from 10,000 to 11,000 units. These two causes of the total revenue variance are identified as the sales price variance and the sales volume variance.

The **sales price variance** indicates the impact on revenues of a change in selling price, given the actual sales volume. It is computed as the change in selling price times the actual sales volume:

$$V_{SP} = (SP_A - SP_B) \, Vol_S$$

$$\begin{pmatrix} \text{Sales} \\ \text{price} \\ \text{variance} \end{pmatrix} = \begin{pmatrix} \text{Actual} & & \text{Budgeted} \\ \text{selling} & - & \text{selling} \\ \text{price} & & \text{price} \end{pmatrix} \times \begin{pmatrix} \text{Actual} \\ \text{sales} \\ \text{volume.} \end{pmatrix}$$

The **sales volume variance** indicates the impact on revenues of the change in sales volume, assuming there was no change in selling price. It is computed as the difference between the actual and the budgeted sales volume times the budgeted selling price:

$$Var_{VOL} = (VOL_A - VOL_B) SP_{BUG}$$

| Sales volume variance | = | (Actual sales volume | − | Budgeted sales volume) | × | Budgeted selling price. |

The July sales price and volume variances for the Meridian Clock Company are $11,000 U and $40,000 F, respectively:

Sales price variance	= ($39 − $40) × 11,000	= $11,000 U
Sales volume variance	= (11,000 − 10,000) × $40 =	40,000 F
Total revenue variance		$29,000 F

The interpretation of variances is subjective. In this case we might say that if the increase in sales volume had not been accompanied by a decline in selling price, revenues would have increased $40,000. The $1 per unit decline in selling price cost the company $11,000 in revenues. Alternatively, we might note that a $1 reduction in the unit selling price was more than offset by an increase in sales volume.

In any case, variances are merely signals that actual results are not proceeding according to plan. They help managers identify potential problems and opportunities. An investigation into their cause(s) may even indicate that a manager who received a favorable variance was doing a poor job, whereas a manager who received an unfavorable variance was doing an outstanding job. Consider Meridian's favorable sales volume variance. This occurred because actual sales exceeded budgeted sales by 1,000 units or 10 percent, which on the surface indicates good performance. But what if the total market for the company's products exceeded the company's forecast by 20 percent? In this case Meridian's sales volume fell below its expected percentage share of the market, and the favorable variance may have occurred, despite a poor marketing effort, because of strong customer demand that competitors could not fill.

Revenue Center Reports Sometimes Include Costs

Controllable costs should also be considered when evaluating the overall performance of revenue centers. A failure to consider costs might encourage uneconomic selling practices, such as excessive advertising and entertaining, and spending too much time on small accounts. The controllable costs of revenue centers include variable and fixed selling costs. These costs are sometimes further classified into order getting and order filling costs. **Order getting costs** are costs incurred to obtain a customer's order, for example, advertising, salespersons' salaries and commissions, travel, telephone, and entertainment. **Order filling costs** are costs incurred to place finished goods in the hands of purchasers, for example, storing, packaging, and transportation. Many of these costs are fixed (committed and discretionary); others are variable.

The performance of a revenue center in controlling costs can be evaluated with the aid of a flexible budget drawn up for the actual level of activity. Assume the Meridian Clock Company's July 19x7 budget for the Sales Department calls for fixed costs of $10,000 and variable costs of $5 per unit sold. If the actual fixed and variable selling expenses for July are $9,500 and $65,000, respectively, the total cost variances assigned to the Sales Department are $9,500 unfavorable:

Meridian Clock Company
Sales Department Performance Report for Costs
For the month of July, 19x7

	Flexible Budget Formula	Actual	Flexible Budget	Flexible Budget Variance*
Volume		11,000	11,000	
Selling expenses:				
Variable	$5/unit	$65,000	$55,000	$10,000 U
Fixed	$10,000/month	9,500	10,000	500 F
Total		$74,500	$65,000	$ 9,500 U

*F = Favorable
U = Unfavorable

In evaluating the performance of the Sales Department as both a cost center and a revenue center, management would consider these cost variances as well as the revenue variances.

Revenue Centers Are Sometimes Evaluated as Profit Centers

Even though we have computed revenue and cost variances for Meridian's Sales Department, we are still left with an incomplete picture of the performance of this revenue center. Is the Sales Department's performance best represented by the $29,000 favorable revenue variance, by the $9,500 unfavorable cost variance, or by the net favorable variance of $19,500 ($29,000 F + $9,500 U)? Actually, it is inappropriate to attempt to obtain an overall measure of the Sales Department's performance by combining these separate revenue and cost variances. The combination of revenue and cost variances is only appropriate for a profit center and, so far, we have left out one important cost that must be assigned to the Sales Department before it can be treated as a profit center. That cost is the standard variable cost of goods sold.

As a profit center, the Sales Department acquires units from the Production Department and sells them outside the firm. Its total responsibilities include revenues, the standard variable cost of goods sold, and actual selling expenses. Note that the Sales Department is assigned the standard, rather than the actual, variable cost of goods sold. Because the Sales Department does not control production activities, it should not be assigned actual production costs. Doing so would result in the Production Department's variances being passed on to the Sales Department. Fixed manufacturing costs are not assigned to the Sales Department because short-run variations in sales volume do not normally affect the total amount of these costs.

To evaluate the Sales Department as a profit center, the computation of the sales volume variance must be adjusted for the corresponding variations in allowed costs. In its current form the sales volume variance does not consider that costs as well as revenues respond to changes in sales volume. Consequently, to evaluate the performance of a profit center, this variance must be stated net of its impact on the flexible budgets for manufacturing and selling costs. The standard variable costs that respond to changes in sales volume are as follows:

Direct materials	$10
Direct labor	6
Factory overhead	4
Selling	5
Total	$25

When standard variable costs are considered, the net impact of the sales volume variance is $15,000 favorable:

Sales volume variance [(11,000 − 10,000) × $40]	$40,000 F
Less increase in standard variable costs	
[(11,000 − 10,000) × $25]	−25,000
Net sales volume variance	$15,000 F

In general, the **net sales volume variance** indicates the impact of a change in sales volume on the contribution margin, given the budgeted selling price and the standard variable costs. It is computed as the difference between the actual and the budgeted sales volume times the budgeted unit contribution margin. The budgeted unit contribution margin is the budgeted selling price minus the standard variable costs per unit:

$$net\ Var_{salevol} = (sVol_A - sVol_B) \cdot CM_{u\ bug}$$

$$\begin{array}{lcl}
\text{Net sales} & & \left(\begin{array}{cc}\text{Actual} & \text{Budgeted}\\ \text{sales} & - \text{sales}\\ \text{volume} & \text{volume}\end{array}\right) & \begin{array}{l}\text{Budgeted}\\ \times\ \text{unit contribution}\\ \text{margin.}\end{array}\\
\text{volume} & = \\
\text{variance} & &
\end{array}$$

The Meridian Clock Company's budgeted unit contribution margin is $15:

Budgeted unit selling price	$40
Standard unit variable costs	−25
Budgeted unit contribution margin	$15

Using the formula presented above, the net sales volume variance is computed as follows:

$$\text{Net sales volume variance} = [(11{,}000 - 10{,}000) \times \$15]$$
$$= \$15{,}000 \text{ F.}$$

In summary, as a profit center the Sales Department has responsibility for the sales price variance, the net sales volume variance, and any cost variances associated with its operations. The Meridian Clock Company's sales price variance was previously computed to be $11,000 U, the $1 reduction in selling price times the actual sales volume of 11,000 units. The net sales volume variance was determined to be $15,000 F, the 1,000 unit increase in sales volume times the budgeted unit contribution margin of $15. The cost variances assigned to the Sales Department net to $9,500 U, the difference between $74,500 in actual selling costs and $65,000 in selling costs allowed for the actual sales volume. As a profit center, the Sales Department's net variances are $5,500 unfavorable:

Sales price variance	$11,000 U
Net sales volume variance	15,000 F
Selling expense variances	9,500 U
Net Sales Department variances	$ 5,500 U

In an attempt to improve their overall performance, managers often commit themselves to unfavorable variances in some areas, believing these variances will be more than offset by other favorable variances. In the case above, it appears that the favorable net sales volume variance was not sufficient to offset the price reductions and the higher selling expenses. Also note that the more complete evaluation of the Sales Department as a profit center (with a $5,500 unfavorable variance) gives a very different impression than the evaluation of the Sales Department as a revenue center (with a $29,000 favorable variance) or as a dual revenue and cost center (with additional $9,500 unfavorable cost variances).

RECONCILING BUDGETED AND ACTUAL INCOME

It is possible to reconcile the difference between budgeted and actual net income for an entire organization. This can be done either by (1) assigning all costs and revenues to responsibility centers and summarizing the financial performance of each responsibility center or (2) developing a detailed reconciliation of actual and budgeted costs and revenues for the organization as a whole. Assume the Meridian Clock Company's budgeted and actual income statements, in a contribution format, for July 19x7 are as presented in Exhibit 7–5.

Following the first reconciliation approach, assume that the Meridian Clock Company contains three responsibility centers: a Production Department, a Sales Department, and an Administration Department. Further assume that the Production and the Administration Departments are cost centers and that the Sales Department is a profit center. The Production Department's variances, as item-

EXHIBIT 7–5   Budgeted and Actual Income Statements

Meridian Clock Company
Budgeted Income Statement
For the month of July, 19x7

Sales (10,000 units × $40)			$400,000
Less variable costs:			
Variable cost of goods sold:			
Direct materials (10,000 units × $10)	$100,000		
Direct labor (10,000 units × $6)	60,000		
Factory overhead (10,000 units × $4)	40,000	$200,000	
Selling (10,000 units × $5)		50,000	−250,000
Contribution margin			$150,000
Less fixed costs:			
Factory overhead		$ 50,000	
Selling		10,000	
Administrative		4,000	− 64,000
Net income			$ 86,000

Meridian Clock Company
Actual Income Statement
For the month of July, 19x7

Sales (11,000 units × $39)			$429,000
Less variable costs:			
Variable cost of goods sold:			
Direct materials	$108,000		
Direct labor	70,000		
Factory overhead	44,000	$222,000	
Selling		65,000	−287,000
Contribution margin			$142,000
Less fixed costs:			
Factory overhead		$ 51,000	
Selling		9,500	
Administrative		3,800	− 64,300
Net income			$ 77,700

ized in Exhibit 7–4, net to $3,000 U. The Sales Department's variances, as summarized on page 291, net to $5,500 U. The only variance for the Administration Department is the $200 difference between actual and budgeted fixed administrative costs ($3,800 actual — $4,000 budget). Because the Administration Department is a discretionary cost center, this variance is best identified as under budget. For consistency in the performance reports, however, it is labeled favorable. Assigning all previously computed variances to these three responsibility centers, the reconciliation of budgeted and actual income is as follows:

Budgeted net income		$86,000
Sales Department variances		
(a profit center)	$5,500 U	
Production Department variances		
(a standard cost center)	3,000 U	
Administration Department variances		
(a discretionary cost center)	200 F	− 8,300 U
Actual net income		$77,700

Following the second approach, a detailed reconciliation of budgeted and actual costs and revenues for the organization as a whole is presented in Exhibit 7–6. The actual results for the year are presented in column (1). The information in this column is based on the actual sales volume, the actual selling prices, and the actual costs. The original budget for the year is presented in column (7). The information in this column is based on the budgeted volume, the budgeted selling prices, and the budgeted costs. The three possible sources of variation between the original budget and the actual results (costs, selling prices, and volume) are analyzed in columns (2), (4), and (6).

The cost variances in column (2) reconcile the difference between the actual costs in column (1) and the costs allowed for the actual volume in column (3). Included in column (2) are the manufacturing cost variances (direct materials, direct labor, variable factory overhead, and fixed factory overhead, totaling $3,000 U), the selling expense variances (variable and fixed, totaling $9,500 U), and the administrative cost variances (all fixed, totaling $200 F). The sales revenues in columns (1) and (3) are based on actual volume at actual prices. Hence, no sales variances are included in column (2).

The sales price variance in column (4) reconciles the difference between the actual volume at actual selling prices in column (3) and the actual volume at budgeted selling prices in column (5). Note that the allowed costs for the actual volume, first computed in column (3), are restated in column (5). This means that column (5) is the flexible budget for both revenues and costs at the actual volume of production and sales. The differences between the actual results in column (1) and the flexible budget in column (5) are explained by the cost and price variances in columns (2) and (4).

EXHIBIT 7–6   Reconciliation of Budgeted and Actual Income

	(1) Actual Volume at Actual Selling Prices and Actual Costs (Actual results)	(2) Cost Variances	(3) Actual Volume at Actual Selling Prices and Standard Costs	(4) Sales Price Variance	(5) Actual Volume at Budgeted Selling Prices and Standard Costs (Flexible budget)	(6) Net Sales Volume Variance	(7) Budgeted Volume at Budgeted Selling Prices and Standard Costs (Original budget)
Volume (units)	11,000		11,000		11,000	1,000	10,000
Sales	$429,000		$429,000	$11,000 U	$440,000	$40,000	$400,000
Less variable costs:							
Direct materials	$108,000	$ 2,000 F	$110,000		$110,000	$10,000	$100,000
Direct labor	70,000	4,000 U	66,000		66,000	6,000	60,000
Factory overhead	44,000		44,000		44,000	4,000	40,000
Selling	65,000	10,000 U	55,000		55,000	5,000	50,000
Total	−287,000		−275,000		−275,000	−25,000	−250,000
Contribution margin	$142,000		$154,000		$165,000	$15,000 F	$150,000
Less fixed costs:							
Factory overhead	$ 51,000	1,000 U	$ 50,000		$ 50,000		$ 50,000
Selling	9,500	500 F	10,000		10,000		10,000
Administration	3,800	200 F	4,000		4,000		4,000
Total	− 64,300		− 64,000		− 64,000		− 64,000
Net income	$ 77,700	$12,300 U	$ 90,000	$11,000 U	$101,000	$15,000 F	$ 86,000

Finally, the net sales volume variance in column (6) reconciles the difference between the flexible budget for revenues and costs based on actual volume and the original budget for revenues and costs based on budgeted sales. The differential effects of the production and sales volume on revenues and costs are disclosed in this column and totaled to determine the net sales volume variance of $15,000 F.

SUMMARY

Responsibility accounting is the structuring of performance reports addressed to individual members of an organization in a manner that emphasizes the factors controllable by them. Each administrative unit for which performance reports are prepared is identified as a responsibility center. For the purpose of evaluating their financial performance, responsibility centers are classified as investment centers, profit centers, revenue centers, or cost centers. An investment center is responsible for the relationship between its profits and the total assets invested in the center. A profit center is responsible for the difference between revenues and costs. Although a revenue center is responsible for the generation of sales revenue, it is often assigned responsibility for the controllable costs incurred in generating revenues. If this is done, the revenue center has a dual responsibility as a revenue and cost center. If controllable costs are deducted from revenues, the center is, in fact, being treated as a profit center. A cost center is financially responsible only for the incurrence of costs and is often further classified as either standard or discretionary.

A standard cost center is a cost center that has clearly defined relationships between effort and accomplishment. The performance of a standard cost center is evaluated by comparing actual costs with the costs allowed in a flexible budget drawn up for the actual level of activity. A discretionary cost center is a cost center that does not have clearly defined relationships between activity and accomplishment. Discretionary cost centers are evaluated, for accounting purposes, by comparing the actual and budgeted costs for a given period. The difference is identified as over budget or under budget.

It is possible to reconcile the difference between budgeted and actual income for an entire organization. This can be done by (1) assigning all costs and revenues to responsibility centers and then summarizing the financial performance of each responsibility center or (2) developing a detailed reconciliation of all costs and revenues for the organization as a whole.

KEY TERMS

Cost center
Discretionary cost center
Flexible budget
Flexible budget variance
Investment center
Net sales volume variance
Order filling costs
Order getting costs
Profit center

Responsibility accounting
Responsibility center
Revenue center
Sales price variance
Sales volume variance
Standard cost
Standard cost center
Static budget

REVIEW QUESTIONS

7–1   Briefly describe the budgeting and performance evaluation cycle.

7–2   What is responsibility accounting? Why should noncontrollable costs be excluded from performance reports prepared in accordance with responsibility accounting?

7–3   Why are an organization's basic performance reports stated in terms of dollars?

7–4   Why does a production supervisor need more frequent performance measurements than the vice president of production?

7–5   Distinguish between investment and profit centers.

7–6   Why is a flexible budget rather than a static budget used to evaluate the financial performance of production departments?

7–7   Identify three alternative uses of standard costs.

7–8   What problems can result from the use of tight standards?

7–9   Distinguish between standard and discretionary cost centers.

7–10   Why are revenue center performance reports based on the original (static) budget?

7–11   How are the sales price and the sales volume variances computed?

7–12   Why are revenue centers often assigned responsibility for controllable costs?

7–13   Why is a sales department, when it is evaluated as a profit center, assigned responsibility for the standard variable cost of goods sold rather than the actual cost of goods sold?

7–14   How is the net sales volume variance computed?

7–15   Briefly describe two alternative approaches to reconciling the differences between budgeted and actual income.

REVIEW PROBLEM

Reconciling Budgeted and Actual Income

Presented are the budgeted and actual contribution income statements of the Well Read Publishing Company for April 19x7.

Well Read Publishing Company
Budgeted Contribution Income Statement
For the month of April, 19x7

Sales (22,000 × $8.50)		$187,000
Less variable costs:		
Variable cost of goods sold:		
Direct materials (22,000 × $0.75)	$16,500	
Direct labor (22,000 × $1.25)	27,500	
Factory overhead (22,000 × $1.50)	33,000	
Selling (22,000 × $2.50)	55,000	−132,000
Contribution margin		$ 55,000
Less fixed costs:		
Factory overhead	$20,000	
Selling	15,000	
Administration	10,000	− 45,000
Net income		$ 10,000

Well Read Publishing Company
Actual Contribution Income Statement
For the month of April, 19x7

Sales (21,000 × $9.00)		$189,000
Less variable costs:		
Variable cost of goods sold:		
Direct materials	$15,750	
Direct labor	25,000	
Factory overhead	32,500	
Selling	56,000	−129,250
Contribution margin		$ 59,750
Less fixed costs:		
Factory overhead	$17,500	
Selling	16,000	
Administration	12,000	− 45,500
Net income		$ 14,250

Well Read Publishing Company contains three responsibility centers: a Production Department, a Sales Department, and an Administration Department. The Production and Administration Departments are cost centers, and the Sales Department is a profit center.

Requirements

a) Prepare a performance report for the Production Department that compares actual and allowed costs.

b) Prepare a performance report for selling expenses that compares actual and allowed costs.

c) Determine the sales price and the net sales volume variances.

d) Prepare a report that summarizes the performance of the Sales Department.

e) Determine the amount by which the Administration Department was over or under budget.

f) Prepare a report reconciling budgeted and actual net income. Your report should focus on the performance of each responsibility center.

g) Prepare a detailed reconciliation of actual and budgeted costs, revenues, and income for the organization as a whole.

The solution to this problem is found at the end of the Chapter 7 exercises and problems.

EXERCISES

**7–1 Developing a
Flexible Budget**

Complete the following flexible budget for each level of activity.

	Flexible Budget Formula	Annual Production (units)		
		10,000	15,000	20,000
Direct materials	$ 4.00/unit			
Direct labor	10.00/unit			
Variable overhead:				
Indirect materials	0.75/unit			
Equipment maintenance	0.10/unit			
Utilities	0.50/unit			
Overtime	0.05/unit			
Fringe benefits	4.00/unit			
Fixed overhead:				
Depreciation	$220,000/year			
Supervision	40,000/year			
Insurance	25,000/year			
Property taxes	28,000/year			
Building maintenance	35,000/year			
Total				

7-2 Developing a Flexible Budget

Complete the following flexible budget for each level of activity.

	Flexible Budget Formula	Monthly Pages Typed		
		x_1 20,000	x_2 30,000	x_3 40,000
Direct materials	$0.05/page	y_1	y_2	y_3
Typist's fees	1.25/page			
Other variable costs:				
Indirect materials	0.02/page			
Pick-up & delivery	0.05/page			
Equipment maintenance	0.01/page			
Franchise fees	0.015/page			
Fixed costs:				
Supervision	$8,000/month			
Rent	5,000/month			
Advertising	3,000/month			
Insurance	1,500/month			
Telephone	800/month			
Electricity	750/month			
Total				

$$y_i = a + bx_i$$

7–3 Flexible Budgets and Performance Evaluation

Presented is the January 19x1 performance report for the production department of the Thompson Company.

Thompson Company
Production Department Performance Report
For the month of January, 19x1

	Actual	Budget	Variance
Volume	30,000	28,000	
Manufacturing costs:			
Direct materials	$ 89,600	$ 84,000	$ 5,600 U
Direct labor	165,000	140,000	25,000 U
Variable overhead	64,000	56,000	8,000 U
Fixed overhead	27,500	28,000	500 F
Total	$346,100	$308,000	$38,100 U

Requirements

a) Evaluate the performance report.

b) Prepare a more appropriate performance report.

7–4 Flexible Budgets and Performance Reports

Presented is the March 19x3 performance report for the Finishing Department of the Maple Chair Company.

Maple Chair Company
Finishing Department Performance Report
For the month of March, 19x3

	Actual	Budget	Variance
Volume	16,000	20,000	
Manufacturing costs:			
Direct materials	$ 35,000	$ 40,000	$ 5,000 F
Direct labor	150,000	200,000	50,000 F
Variable overhead	73,000	100,000	27,000 F
Fixed overhead	13,000	12,000	1,000 U
Total	$271,000	$352,000	$81,000 F

Requirements

a) Evaluate the performance report.

b) Prepare a more appropriate performance report.

7–5 Sales Revenue Variances

The following information is available regarding a product sold by the Maxell Company.

	Actual	Budget
Unit selling price	$ 85	$ 80
Unit sales	× 5,000	× 6,000
Revenue	$425,000	$480,000

Required: Compute the sales price and the sales volume variances. Use these variances to reconcile the difference between budgeted and actual revenues.

7–6 Sales Revenue Variances

The following information is available regarding a product sold by the Jones Company.

	Actual	Budget
Unit selling price	$ 26	$ 30
Unit sales	× 11,000	× 8,000
Revenue	$286,000	$240,000

Required: Compute the sales price and the sales volume variances. Use these variances to reconcile the difference between budgeted and actual revenues.

7–7 Sales Revenue Variances

The sales revenues of the Beach Company for the years 19x7 and 19x8 were as follows:

	19x7	19x8
Sales	$500,000	$583,000

Selling prices were 6 percent higher during 19x8.

Required: Treating 19x7 as the standard, compute the sales price and the sales volume variances for 19x8. Use these variances to reconcile the difference between 19x7 and 19x8 revenues.

7–8 Sales Variances

Presented is information pertaining to an item sold by the Winding Creek General Store.

	Actual	Budget
Unit sales	150	125
Unit selling price	$ 26	$ 25
Unit standard variable costs	− 20	− 20
Unit contribution margin	$ 6	$ 5
Revenues	$3,900	$3,125
Standard variable costs	−3,000	−2,500
Contribution margin at standard costs	$ 900	$ 625

Requirements

a) Compute the sales price and the sales volume variances.

b) Use the variances computed in requirement (a) to reconcile the budgeted and the actual revenues.

c) Compute the net sales volume variance.

d) Use the sales price and the net sales volume variances to reconcile the difference between the budgeted and the actual contribution margin at standard costs.

7–9 Sales Variances

Presented is information pertaining to a product of the Blue Mountain Supply Company.

	Actual	Budget
Unit sales	550	800
Unit selling price	$ 10	$ 8
Unit standard variable costs	− 5	− 5
Unit contribution margin	$ 5	$ 3
Revenues	$5,500	$6,400
Standard variable costs	−2,750	−4,000
Contribution margin at standard costs	$2,750	$2,400

Requirements

a) Compute the sales price and the sales volume variances.

b) Use the variances computed in requirement (a) to reconcile the budgeted and the actual revenues.

c) Compute the net sales volume variance.

d) Use the sales price and the net sales volume variances to reconcile the difference between the budgeted and the actual contribution margin at standard costs.

7–10 Reconciling Budgeted and Actual Gross Profit

The Bommer Company is a merchandising firm that buys and sells a single product. Presented is information from Bommer's 19x4 and 19x3 income statements.

	19x4	19x3
Unit sales	220,000	250,000
Sales revenue	$770,000	$750,000
Cost of goods sold	−506,000	−500,000
Gross profit	$264,000	$250,000

Requirements

a) Reconcile the variation in sales revenue using appropriate sales variances. Treat 19x3 as the base or standard.

b) Reconcile the variation in gross profit using appropriate sales and cost variances. Treat 19x3 as the base or standard.

7–11 Reconciling Budgeted and Actual Gross Profit

Garfield Company is a merchandising firm that buys and sells a single product. Presented is information from Garfield's 19x8 and 19x7 income statements.

	19x8	19x7
Unit sales	150,000	180,000
Sales revenue	$750,000	$720,000
Cost of goods sold	−525,000	−576,000
Gross profit	$225,000	$144,000

Requirements

a) Reconcile the variation in sales revenue using appropriate sales variances. Treat 19x7 as the base or standard.

b) Reconcile the variation in gross profit using appropriate sales and cost variances. Treat 19x7 as the base or standard.

(CPA Adapted)

7–12 Profit Center Performance Reports

The Record Rack is a store that specializes in the sale of recordings of classical music. Due to a recent upsurge in the popularity of J. S. Bach's works, the Record Rack has established a separate room, Bach's Concert Room, dealing only in recordings of Bach's music. The albums are purchased from a wholesaler for $4.25 each. Though the standard retail price is $7.75 per album, the manager of Bach's Concert Room may undertake price reductions and other sales promotions in an attempt to increase sales volume. With the exception of the cost of albums, the operating costs of Bach's Concert Room are fixed.

Presented are the budgeted and the actual August 19x3 contribution statements of Bach's Concert Room.

Record Rack: Bach's Concert Room
Budgeted and Actual Contribution Statements
For the month of August, 19x3

	Actual	Budget
Unit sales	4,200	4,000
Unit selling price	$ 7.25	$ 7.75
Sales revenue	$30,450	$31,000
Cost of goods sold	−17,850	−17,000
Gross profit	$12,600	$14,000
Operating costs	− 5,000	− 6,000
Contribution to corporate costs and profits	$ 7,600	$ 8,000

Required: Compute variances to assist in evaluating the performance of Bach's Concert Room as a profit center. Use these variances to reconcile the budgeted and actual contribution to corporate costs and profits.

7–13 Profit Center Performance Reports

Dip-In Donuts produces donuts in a central Chicago bakery and ships them to Dip-In Donut Shops throughout the Chicago area. Each shop is evaluated as a profit center. The shops purchase the Dip-In Donuts from the bakery at $1.50 per dozen. The standard retail price is $3.00 per dozen; however, individual shop managers may issue coupons and undertake other promotions to increase sales volume. With the exception of the cost of donuts, each shop's operating costs are fixed.

Presented are the budgeted and the actual May 19x6 contribution statements of the Wicker Park Shop.

Dip-In Donuts: Wicker Park Shop
Budgeted and Actual Contribution Statements
For the month of May, 19x6

	Actual	Budget
Unit sales (dozen)	15,500	14,000
Unit selling price (dozen)	$ 2.80	$ 3.00
Sales revenue	$43,400	$42,000
Cost of food sold	−23,250	−21,000
Gross profit	$20,150	$21,000
Operating costs	−19,500	−17,000
Contribution to corporate costs and profits	$ 650	$ 4,000

Required: Compute variances to assist in evaluating the performance of the Wicker Park Shop as a profit center. Use these variances to reconcile the budgeted and actual contribution to corporate costs and profits.

7–14 Discretionary Cost Center Performance Reports

Buggywhip Products had been extremely profitable at the turn of the century, but the company had been "whipped" in recent years by tough competition and a failure to introduce new consumer products. In 19x2 Tom Bright became head of Consumer Product Research (CPR) and began a number of product development projects. Although the group had several good ideas that led to the introduction of several promising products at the start of 19x6, Mr. Bright was criticized for poor cost control. The financial performance reports for CPR under Mr. Bright's leadership were consistently unfavorable. Management was quite concerned about cost control because profits were low and the company's cash budget indicated that additional borrowing would be required throughout 19x6 to cover out-of-pocket costs.

Because of his inability to exert proper cost control, Mr. Bright was relieved of his responsibilities in 19x6 and John Tight became head of Consumer Product Research. Mr. Tight vowed to improve the performance of CPR and scaled back CPR's developmental activities to obtain favorable financial performance reports.

By the end of 19x7, Buggywhip Products had improved its market position, profitability, and cash position. At this time the Board of Directors promoted Mr. Tight to President, congratulating him for the contribution CPR made to the revitalization of the company as well as his success in improving the financial performance of CPR. Mr. Tight assured the Board that the company's financial performance would improve even more in the future as he applied the same cost reducing measures that had worked so well in CPR to the company as a whole.

Requirements

a) For the purpose of evaluating financial performance, classify the Consumer Products Research department as a responsibility center. What unique problems are associated with evaluating the financial performance of this type of responsibility center?

b) Compare the performances of Mr. Bright and Mr. Tight in their role as head of Consumer Product Research. Did Mr. Tight do a much better job, thereby making him deserving of the promotion? Why or why not?

7–15 Discretionary Cost Center Performance Reports

The budget for the Literature Department of Classic University is set by the Dean of the School of Arts in consultation with the Chairperson of the Literature Department. It is a line item budget with separate appropriations for such things as faculty salaries, secretarial support, travel, research, equipment, and instructional supplies. The budget for each year is a function of the budget for the previous year, with an adjustment for certain items that were funded at an excess or inadequate level during the previous year.

While the Chairperson of the Literature Department has done a good job in controlling most departmental costs, the Dean is concerned about the Chairperson's inability to keep instructional supplies in line with the budget. Prior to meeting with the Dean to discuss the 19x8 departmental budget, the Chairperson developed the following summary of the financial performance of the Literature Department in controlling the cost of instructional supplies:

Classic University
Literature Department Summary of Financial Performance
for Instructional Supplies
For the years 19x3–19x7

	Student Enrollment	Actual	Budget	Budget Variance
19x3	4,500	$15,500	$12,000	$3,500 U
19x4	6,000	20,000	13,750	6,250 U
19x5	5,250	17,750	16,875	875 F
19x6	6,300	20,900	16,438	4,462 U
19x7	5,500	18,500	18,669	169 F

Required: Comment on the financial performance of the Literature Department. What budgetary planning and control problem is illustrated by the above data?

PROBLEMS

7–16 Evaluating Cost Center Performance Reports

Berwin Inc. is a manufacturer of small industrial tools with an annual sales volume of approximately $3.5 million. Sales growth has been steady during the year, and there is no evidence of cyclical demand. Production has increased gradually during the year and has been distributed evenly throughout each month. The company employs a sequential processing system with all production activities located in the same building. Fixed manufacturing overhead is applied to all products using a single rate.

Berwin has always been able to compete with other manufacturers of small industrial tools. However, its market has expanded only in response to product innovations. Thus, research and development is very important and has helped Berwin to expand as well as maintain demand.

Carl Viller, Controller, has designed and implemented a new budget system in response to concerns voiced by George Berwin, President. An annual budget that has been divided into 12 equal segments has been prepared to assist in the timely evaluation of monthly performance. Berwin was visibly upset upon receiving the May performance report for the Machining Department (reproduced below). Berwin exclaimed, "How can they be efficient enough to produce nine extra units every working day and still miss the budget by $300 a day?" Gene Jordan, Machining Department supervisor, could not understand "all the red ink" when he knew the department had operated more efficiently in May than it had in the preceding months. Jordan stated, "I was expecting a pat on the back and instead the boss tore me apart. What's more, I don't even know why!"

Berwin Inc.
Machining Department Performance Report
For the month ended May 31, 19x4

	Budget	Actual	(Over) Under Budget
Volume in units	3,000	3,180	(180)
Variable manufacturing costs:			
Direct materials	$24,000	$ 24,843	$ (843)
Direct labor	27,750	29,302	(1,552)
Factory overhead	33,300	35,035	(1,735)
Total	$85,050	$ 89,180	$(4,130)
Fixed manufacturing overhead:			
Indirect labor	$ 3,300	$ 3,334	$ (34)
Depreciation	1,500	1,500	
Taxes	300	300	
Insurance	240	240	
Other	930	1,027	(97)
Total	$ 6,270	$ 6,401	$ (131)
Corporate overhead:			
Research & development	$ 2,400	$ 3,728	$(1,328)
Selling & administration	3,600	4,075	(475)
Total	$ 6,000	$ 7,803	$(1,803)
Total costs assigned to department	$97,320	$103,384	$(6,064)

Requirements

a) Review the May performance report for the Machining Department. Based on the information presented in the report:

   1. Discuss the strengths of the new budget system in general.

   2. Identify the weaknesses of the performance report and explain how the report should be revised to eliminate each weakness.

b) Prepare a revised May performance report for the Machining Department.

(CMA Adapted)

7–17 Evaluating Cost Center Performance Reports with Behavioral Implications

Denny Daniels is Production Manager of the Alumalloy Division of WRT Inc. Alumalloy has limited contact with outside customers and has no sales staff. Most of its customers are other divisions of WRT. All sales and purchases with outside customers are handled by other corporate divisions. Therefore, Alumalloy is treated as a cost center for reporting and evaluation purposes rather than as a revenue or profit center.

Daniels perceives accounting as an historical number generating process that provides little useful information for conducting his job. Consequently, the entire accounting process is regarded as a negative motivational device that does not reflect how hard or how effectively he works as a production manager. Daniels tried to discuss these perceptions and concerns with John Scott, the Controller for the Alumalloy Division. Daniels told Scott, "I think the cost report is misleading. I know I've had better production over a number of operating periods, but the cost report still says I have excessive costs. Look, I'm not an accountant, I'm a production manager. I know how to get a good quality product out. Over a number of years, I've even cut the raw materials used to do it. But the cost report doesn't show any of this. Basically, it's always negative, no matter what I do. There's no way you can win with accounting or the people at corporate headquarters who use those reports."

Scott gave Daniels little consolation. The accounting system and the cost reports generated by headquarters, Scott stated, are just part of the corporate game and almost impossible for an individual to change. "Although these accounting reports are pretty much the basis for evaluating the efficiency of your division and the means corporate management uses to determine whether you have done the job they want, you shouldn't worry too much. You haven't been fired yet! Besides, these cost reports have been used by WRT for the last twenty-five years."

Daniels perceived from talking to the production manager of the Zinc Division that most of what Scott said was probably true. However, some minor cost reporting changes for Zinc had been agreed to by corporate headquarters. He also knew from the trade grapevine that the turnover of production managers was considered high at WRT, even though relatively few were fired. Most seemed to end up quitting, usually in disgust, because of beliefs that they were not being evaluated fairly. Typical comments of production managers who have left WRT are:

■ "Corporate headquarters doesn't really listen to us. All they consider are those misleading cost reports. They don't want them changed, and they don't want any supplemental information."

■ "The accountants may be quick with numbers, but they don't know anything about production. As it was, I either had to ignore the cost reports entirely or pretend they are important even though they didn't tell how good a job I had done. No matter what they say about not firing people, negative reports mean negative evaluations. I'm better off working for another company."

A recent copy of the cost report prepared by corporate headquarters for the Alumalloy Division is shown below. Daniels does not like this report because he believes it fails to reflect the division's operations properly, thereby resulting in an unfair evaluation of performance.

Alumalloy Division
Cost Report
For the month of April, 19x0

	Original Budget	Actual Cost	Excess Cost
Aluminum	$ 400,000	$ 437,000	$37,000
Labor	560,000	540,000	
Overhead	100,000	134,000	34,000
Total	$1,060,000	$1,111,000	

Requirements

a) Comment on Denny Daniels' perceptions of John Scott, the Controller; corporate headquarters; the cost report; and himself as a Production Manager. Discuss how his perceptions affect his behavior and probable performance as a production manager and employee of WRT.

b) Identify and explain three changes that could be made in the cost information presented to the production managers that would make the information more meaningful and less threatening to them.

(CMA Adapted)

7–18 Flexible Budget for Selling Expenses: Cost Estimation

Wielson Company employs flexible budgeting techniques to evaluate the performance of several of its activities. The selling expense flexible budgets for three representative monthly activity levels are shown as follows.

Wielson Company
Selling Expense Flexible Budget
For Representative Monthly Volumes

Activity measures:			
Unit sales volume	400,000	425,000	450,000
Dollar sales volume	$10,000,000	$10,625,000	$11,250,000
Number of orders	4,000	4,250	4,500
Number of sales personnel	75	75	75
Monthly expenses:			
Advertising & promotion	$1,200,000	$1,200,000	$1,200,000
Administrative salaries	57,000	57,000	57,000
Sales salaries	75,000	75,000	75,000
Sales commissions	200,000	212,500	225,000
Salesperson travel	170,000	175,000	180,000
Sales office expense	490,000	498,750	507,500
Shipping expense	675,000	712,500	750,000
Total	$2,867,000	$2,930,750	$2,994,500

The following assumptions were used to develop the budget:

- The average size of Wielson's sales force during the year was planned to be 75 people.
- Sales personnel are paid a monthly salary plus commission of gross dollar sales.
- The travel costs are best characterized as step-variable costs. The fixed portion is related to the number of sales personnel, whereas the variable portion tends to fluctuate with gross dollar sales.
- Sales office expense is a mixed cost with the variable portion related to the number of orders processed.
- Shipping expense is a mixed cost with the variable portion related to the number of units sold.

A sales force of 80 persons generated a total of 4,300 orders, resulting in a sales volume of 420,000 units during November 19x9. The gross dollar sales amounted to $10.9 million. The selling expenses incurred for November were as follows.

Monthly expenses:	
Advertising & promotion	$1,350,000
Administrative salaries	57,000
Sales salaries	80,000
Sales commissions	218,000
Salesperson travel	185,000
Sales office expense	497,000
Shipping expense	730,000
Total	$3,117,000

Required: Prepare a selling expense performance report for November that Wielson Company can use to evaluate its control over selling expenses. (CMA Adapted)

7–19 Multiple Product Flexible Budgets

Creative Products manufactures two models of cassette tape storage cases, Regular and Deluxe. Presented is standard cost information for each model:

	Regular	Deluxe
Direct materials:		
Lumber	2 board feet × $3 = $ 6.00	3 board feet × $3 = $ 9.00
Assembly kit	2.00	2.00
Direct labor	1 hour × $4 = 4.00	1.25 hours × $4 = 5.00
Variable overhead	1 labor hour × $2 = 2.00	1.25 labor hours × $2 = 2.50
Total	$14.00	$18.50

Budgeted fixed factory overhead is $15,000 per month.

During July 19x1 Creative Products produced 5,000 regular and 3,000 deluxe storage cases while incurring the following manufacturing costs:

Direct materials	$ 80,000
Direct labor	34,000
Variable overhead	16,000
Fixed overhead	17,500
Total	$147,500

Required: Prepare a flexible budget performance report for July 19x1 manufacturing activities.

7–20 Multiple Product Flexible Budget

Cozy Hearth manufactures two models of glass fireplace doors, Cozy I and Cozy II. Presented is standard cost information for each model:

	Cozy I	Cozy II
Direct materials:		
Frame	$10.00	$15.00
Glass	8.00	20.00
Installation kit	5.00	7.00
Direct labor:		
Class A:		
Cozy I (0.5 hour × $5)	2.50	
Cozy II (0.75 hour × $5)		3.75
Class B:		
Cozy II (0.25 hour × $8)		2.00
Variable overhead:		
Cozy I (0.5 labor hour × $4)	2.00	
Cozy II (0.75 labor hour × $4)		3.00
Total	$27.50	$50.75

Budgeted fixed factory overhead is $30,000 per month.

During August 19x3 Cozy Hearth produced 1,000 Cozy I and 800 Cozy II glass fireplace doors while incurring the following manufacturing costs:

Direct materials	$ 60,200
Direct labor	8,100
Variable overhead	4,900
Fixed overhead	29,000
Total	$102,200

Required: Prepare a flexible budget performance report for August 19x3 manufacturing activities.

7–21 Reconciling Budgeted and Actual Income

JK Enterprises sold 550,000 units during the first quarter ended March 31, 19x1. These sales represented a 10 percent increase over the number of units budgeted for the quarter. In spite of the sales increase, profits were below budget, as is shown in the condensed income statement presented below.

JK Enterprises
Income Statement
For the first quarter ended March 31, 19x1

	Budget	Actual
Sales	$2,500,000	$2,530,000
Variable expenses:		
Cost of goods sold	$1,475,000	$1,540,000
Selling	400,000	440,000
Total variable expenses	−1,875,000	−1,980,000
Contribution margin	$ 625,000	$ 550,000
Fixed expenses:		
Selling	$ 125,000	$ 150,000
Administration	275,000	300,000
Total fixed expenses	− 400,000	− 450,000
Income before taxes	$ 225,000	$ 100,000
Income taxes (40 percent)	− 90,000	− 40,000
Net income	$ 135,000	$ 60,000

The Accounting Department always prepares a brief analysis to explain the difference between budgeted net income and actual net income. This analysis, which has not yet been completed for the first quarter, is submitted to top management with the income statement.

Required: Prepare an explanation of the $125,000 unfavorable variance between the first quarter budgeted and actual before-tax income for JK Enterprises by calculating a single amount for each of the following:

1. Sales price variance.

2. Variable cost variance.

3. Net sales volume variance.

4. Fixed cost variance.

(CMA Adapted)

7–22 Reconciling Budgeted and Actual Income

Presented are the budgeted and actual contribution income statements of Queen's Encyclopedia, Limited, for October 19x8.

Queen's Encyclopedia, Limited
Budgeted Contribution Income Statement
For the month of October, 19x8

Sales (900 × $300)			$270,000
Less variable costs:			
Variable cost of goods sold:			
Direct materials (900 × $50)	$45,000		
Direct labor (900 × $20)	18,000		
Factory overhead (900 × $30)	27,000	$ 90,000	
Selling (900 × $70)		63,000	−153,000
Contribution margin			$117,000
Less fixed costs:			
Factory overhead		$ 40,000	
Selling		50,000	
Administration		10,500	−100,500
Net income			$ 16,500

Queen's Encyclopedia, Limited
Actual Contribution Income Statement
For the month of October, 19x8

Sales (1,000 × $320)			$320,000
Less variable costs:			
Cost of goods sold:			
Direct materials	$50,000		
Direct labor	22,000		
Factory overhead	35,000	$107,000	
Selling		100,000	−207,000
Contribution margin			$113,000
Less fixed costs:			
Factory overhead		$ 38,000	
Selling		65,000	
Administration		12,000	−115,000
Net income (loss)			$ (2,000)

Queen's Encyclopedia contains three responsibility centers: a Production Department, a Sales Department, and an Administration Department. The Production and Administration Departments are cost centers, and the Sales Department is a profit center.

Requirements

a) Prepare a performance report for the Production Department that compares actual and allowed costs.

b) Prepare a performance report for selling expenses that compares actual and allowed costs.

c) Determine the sales price and the net sales volume variances.

d) Prepare a report that summarizes the performance of the Sales Department.

e) Determine the amount by which the Administration Department was over or under budget.

f) Prepare a report reconciling budgeted and actual net income. Your report should focus on the performance of each responsibility center.

7–23 Reconciling Budgeted and Actual Income

The budgeted and the actual income statements of Queen's Encyclopedia, Limited, for October 19x8 are presented in Problem 7–22.

Required: Prepare a detailed reconciliation of actual and budgeted costs, revenues, and income for the organization as a whole.

7–24 Reconciling Budgeted and Actual Income

Presented are the budgeted and the actual income statements of the Jones Valve Company, for the year ended December 31, 19x2.

Jones Valve Company
Budgeted and Actual Income Statements
For the year ending December 31, 19x2

	Budget	Actual
Unit sales	20,000	18,000
Unit selling price	$ 18	$ 21
Sales	$360,000	$378,000
Less variable costs:		
Direct materials ($2 per unit standard)	$ 40,000	$ 45,000
Direct labor ($3 per unit standard)	60,000	54,000
Factory overhead ($3 per unit standard)	60,000	50,400
Selling ($1 per unit standard)	20,000	20,000
Total	−180,000	−169,400
Contribution margin	$180,000	$208,600
Less fixed costs:		
Factory overhead	$ 55,000	$ 56,000
Selling	60,000	54,000
Administration	40,000	47,500
Total	−155,000	−157,500
Net income	$ 25,000	$ 51,100

The Jones Valve Company contains three responsibility centers: a Production Department, a Sales Department, and an Administration Department. The Production and Administration Departments are cost centers, and the Sales Department is a profit center.

Requirements

a) Prepare a performance report for the Production Department that compares actual and allowed costs.

b) Prepare a performance report for selling expenses that compares actual and allowed costs.

c) Determine the sales price and the net sales volume variances.

d) Prepare a report that summarizes the performance of the Sales Department.

e) Determine the amount by which the Administration Department was over or under budget.

f) Prepare a report reconciling budgeted and actual net income. Your report should focus on the performance of each responsibility center.

7–25 Reconciling Budgeted and Actual Income

The budgeted and the actual income statements of the Jones Valve Company, for the year ended December 31, 19x2, are presented in Problem 7–24.

Required: Prepare a detailed reconciliation of actual and budgeted costs, revenues, and income for the organization as a whole.

7–26 Evaluating a Sales Compensation Plan

Betterbuilt Corporation manufactures a full line of windows and doors, including casement windows, bow windows, and patio doors. The bow windows and patio doors have a significantly higher gross profit per unit than casement windows, as is shown in the following schedule.

	Unit Price and Cost Data		
	Casement Windows	Bow Windows	Patio Doors
Sales price	$130	$250	$260
Manufacturing costs:			
Direct materials	$ 25	$ 40	$ 50
Direct labor	20	35	30
Variable overhead*	16	28	24
Fixed overhead†	24	42	36
Total manufacturing costs	− 85	−145	−140
Gross profit	$ 45	$105	$120

  * Variable manufacturing overhead is applied at the rate of 80 percent of direct labor cost.

  † Fixed manufacturing overhead is applied at the rate of 120 percent of direct labor cost.

The company sells almost entirely to general contractors of residential housing. Most of these contractors complete and sell fifteen to fifty houses per year. Each contractor builds tract houses that are similar, with some variations in exteriors and rooflines.

When contractors contact Betterbuilt, they are likely to seek bids for all the windows in the houses they plan to build in the next year. At this point, the Betterbuilt salespeople have an opportunity to influence the window configuration of these houses by suggesting patio doors or bow windows as variations for one or more casement windows for each of the several exteriors and rooflines built by the contractor.

The bow windows and patio doors are approximately twice as wide as the casement windows. A bow window or a patio door usually is substituted for two casement windows. Casement windows are usually ordered in pairs and placed side-by-side in those houses that could be modified to accept bow windows and patio doors.

Joseph Hite, President of Betterbuilt Corporation, is perplexed with the company's profit performance. In a conversation with his sales manager he declared, "Our total dollars sales volume is growing, but our net income has not increased as it should. Our unit sales of casement windows have increased proportionately more than the sale of bow windows or patio doors. Why aren't our salespeople pushing our more profitable products?" The sales manager responded with a sense of frustration, "I don't know what else can be done. The salespeople have been told which type of windows we want sold because of the greater profit margin. Furthermore, they have the best compensation plan in the industry, with $500 monthly draw against their commissions of 10 percent on sales dollars."

Requirements

a) Explain why Betterbuilt's present compensation program for its salespeople does not support the President's objectives to sell the more profitable units.

b) Identify and explain alternative compensation program(s) that may be more appropriate for motivating Betterbuilt Corporation's salespeople to sell the more profitable units.

(CMA Adapted)

7–27 Evaluating Alternative Sales Compensation Plans

Pre-Fab Corporation, a relatively large company in the manufactured housing industry, is known for its aggressive sales promotion campaigns. Pre-Fab's innovative advertising and sales strategies have resulted in generally satisfactory performance in the last few years.

One of Pre-Fab's objectives is to increase sales revenue by at least 10 percent annually. This objective has been attained. Return on investment is considered good and had increased annually until last year when net income decreased for the first time in nine years. The latest economic recession could be the cause of the change, but other factors, such as sales growth, discount this reason.

A significant portion of Pre-Fab's administrative expenses are fixed, but the majority of the manufacturing expenses are variable in nature. The increases in selling prices have been consistent with the 12 percent increase in manufacturing expenses. Pre-Fab has consistently been able to maintain a companywide contribution margin of approximately 30 percent. However, the contribution margin on individual product lines varies from 15 to 45 percent.

Sales commission expenses increased 30 percent over the past year. The prefabricated housing industry has always been sales oriented and Pre-Fab's management has believed in generously rewarding the efforts of its sales personnel. The sales force compensation plan consists of three segments:

- A guaranteed annual salary, which is increased annually at about a 6 percent rate. The salary is below industry average.
- A sales commission of 9 percent of total sales dollars. This is higher than the industry average.
- A year-end bonus of 5 percent of total sales dollars to each salesperson when their total sales dollars exceed the prior year by at least 12 percent.

The current compensation plan has resulted in an average annual income of $42,500 per sales employee, compared with an industry annual average of $30,000. However, the compensation plan has been effective in generating increased sales. Further, the sales department employees are satisfied with the plan. Management, however, is concerned about the financial implications of the current plan. They believe the plan has caused higher selling expenses and a lower net income relative to the sales revenue increase.

At the last staff meeting, the Controller suggested that the sales compensation plan be modified so that sales employees could earn an annual average income of $37,500. The Controller believed that such a plan still would be attractive to its sales personnel and, at the same time, allow the company to earn a more satisfactory profit.

The Vice President for sales voiced strong objection to altering the current compensation plan because employee morale and incentive would drop significantly if there were any change. Nevertheless, most of the staff believed that the area of sales compensation merited a review. The President stated that all phases of a company operation can benefit from a periodic review, no matter how successful they have been in the past.

Several compensation plans known to be used by other companies in the manufactured housing industry are:

- Straight commission as a percentage of sales.
- Straight salary.
- Salary plus compensation based on sales to new customers.
- Salary plus compensation based on contribution margin.
- Salary plus compensation based on unit sales volume.

Requirements

a) Discuss the advantages and disadvantages of Pre-Fab Corporation's current sales compensation plan with respect to (1) the financial aspects of the company and (2) the behavioral aspects of the sales personnel.

b) For each of the alternative compensation plans known to be used by other companies in the manufactured housing industry, discuss whether the plan would be an improvement over the current plan in terms of (1) the financial performance of the company and (2) the behavioral implications for the sales personnel.

(CMA Adapted)

7–28 Evaluating a Sales Compensation Plan

Prior to 19x3 the Carbon Chemical Company paid its sales representatives a straight salary plus selling expenses. In an attempt to better motivate them, the company changed their basis of compensation from salary to commissions based on gross sales. The commission rate was computed as 19x2 sales salaries divided by 19x2 gross sales revenues.

Early in 19x4 Martha Childs, the company President, was reviewing Carbon Chemical's 19x3 performance, as compared to its 19x2 performance. She is concerned that the commissions are not motivating the sales representatives to work in the company's best interest, and she wants your advice.

Presented is comparative 19x2 and 19x3 information.

	19x2	19x3
Gross sales	$648,000	$934,000
Less sales returns and allowances	− 8,000	− 34,000
Net sales	$640,000	$900,000
Variable costs:		
Cost of goods sold	$388,800	$560,400
Commissions	—	74,720
Total	−388,800	−635,120
Contribution margin	$251,200	$264,880
Fixed costs:		
Sales salaries	$ 51,840	$ —
Other selling	20,000	55,000
Administration	80,000	90,000
Total	−151,840	−145,000
Net income	$ 99,360	$119,880

Required: Evaluate the sales compensation plan, and suggest some alternative plans that might better motivate the sales representatives to work in the company's interest.

7–29 Evaluating a Companywide Performance Report

Mr. Micawber, the production supervisor, bursts into your office carrying the Crupp Company's 19x2 performance report:

There is villainy here, sir! And I shall get to the bottom of it. I will not stop searching until I have found the answer! Why is Mr. Heep so down on my department?

I thought we did a good job last year. But Heep claims I and my production people cost the company $31,500! I plead with you, sir, explain this performance report to me.

Trying to calm Mr. Micawber, you take the report from him and ask to be left alone for 15 minutes. The report is presented below.

Crupp Company, Limited
Performance Report
For the year 19x2

	Actual	*Budget*	*Variance*
Unit sales	7,500	5,000	
Sales	$262,500	$225,000	$37,500 F
Less manufacturing costs:			
Direct materials	$ 55,500	$ 47,500	$ 8,000 U
Direct labor	48,000	32,500	15,500 U
Factory overhead	40,000	32,000*	8,000 U
Total	−143,500	−112,000	−31,500 U
Gross profit	$119,000	$113,000	$ 6,000 F
Less selling and administrative expenses:			
Selling (all fixed)	$ 60,000	$ 40,000	$20,000 U
Administrative (all fixed)	55,000	50,000	5,000 U
Total	−115,000	− 90,000	−25,000 U
Net income	$ 4,000	$ 23,000	$19,000 U
Performance summary:			
Budgeted net income			$23,000
Sales department variances:			
Sales revenue	$ 37,500 F		
Selling expenses	20,000 U	$ 17,500 F	
Administration department variances		5,000 U	
Production department variances		31,500 U	19,000 U
Actual net income			$ 4,000

Handwritten annotations: "35" next to 7,500; "45" next to 5,000.

* Includes fixed factory overhead of $22,000.

Requirements

a) Evaluate the performance report. Is Mr. Heep correct? Or, is there "villainy here"?

b) Assume that the Sales Department is a profit center and that the Production and Administration Departments are cost centers. Determine the responsibility of each for cost, revenue, and income variances, and prepare a report reconciling budgeted and actual net income. Your report should focus on the performance of each responsibility center.

7–30 Evaluating Companywide Performance: The Case of Multiple Profit Centers

The Computeraid produces a variety of computer accessories. To improve financial incentives, the Production Department and the Sales Department are both treated as profit centers, with all goods produced in the Production Department being "sold" to the Sales Department at 150 percent of variable cost. The costs of the Administrative Department are allocated equally to the Production and Sales Departments. Presented are performance reports prepared for the Production and Sales Departments for the year 19x8:

Computeraid
Production Department Performance Report
For the year 19x8

	Actual	Budget	Variance
Unit sales	10,000	7,000	
Sales revenue	$241,500	$147,000	
Less variable manufacturing costs:			
Direct materials	$ 69,000	$ 35,000	
Direct labor	32,000	21,000	
Variable factory overhead	60,000	42,000	
Total	−161,000	− 98,000	
Contribution margin	$ 80,500	$ 49,000	
Less fixed costs:			
Fixed factory overhead	$ 24,000	$ 25,000	
Administration	15,000	10,000	
Total	− 39,000	− 35,000	
Manufacturing profit	$ 41,500	$ 14,000	$27,500 F

Computeraid
Sales Department Performance Report
For the year 19x8

	Actual	Budget	Variance
Unit sales	10,000	7,000	
Sales revenue	$310,000	$217,000	
Less variable costs:			
Cost of goods sold	$241,500	$147,000	
Selling & distribution	50,000	35,000	
Total	−291,500	−182,000	
Contribution margin	$ 18,500	$ 35,000	
Less fixed costs:			
Fixed selling & distribution	$ 8,000	$ 8,000	
Administration	15,000	10,000	
Total	− 23,000	− 18,000	
Selling profit (loss)	$ (4,500)	$ 17,000	$21,500 U

Management congratulated the Production Department supervisor for another outstanding performance and offered him a raise. The manager of the Sales Department, on the other hand, was called to a special meeting of the Board of Directors and told that unless she provided an adequate explanation of her department's performance, she would be terminated.

Required: Extremely concerned about her future with the organization, the manager of the Sales Department has asked you to (1) evaluate the 19x8 performance reports and (2) assist in preparing revised 19x8 performance reports for each department and Computeraid as a whole.

REVIEW PROBLEM SOLUTION

a) **Well Read Publishing Company**
Production Department Performance Report
For the month of April, 19x7

	Flexible Budget Formula	Actual	Flexible Budget	Flexible Budget Variance
Volume		21,000	21,000	
Manufacturing costs:				
Direct materials	$0.75/unit	$15,750	$15,750	$ -0-
Direct labor	1.25/unit	25,000	26,250	1,250 F
Variable overhead	1.50/unit	32,500	31,500	1,000 U
Fixed overhead	$20,000/month	17,500	20,000	2,500 F
Total		$90,750	$93,500	$2,750 F

b) **Well Read Publishing Company**
Selling Expenses Performance Report for Costs
For the month of April, 19x7

	Flexible Budget Formula	Actual	Flexible Budget	Flexible Budget Variance
Volume		21,000	21,000	
Selling expenses:				
Variable	$2.50/unit	$56,000	$52,500	$3,500 U
Fixed	$15,000/month	16,000	15,000	1,000 U
Total		$72,000	$67,500	$4,500 U

c)

Budgeted selling price		$8.50
Standard variable costs:		
Direct materials	$0.75	
Direct labor	1.25	
Factory overhead	1.50	
Selling	2.50	−6.00
Budgeted unit contribution margin		$2.50

Sales price variance = ($9.00 − $8.50) × 21,000 = $10,500 F

Net sales volume variance = (21,000 − 22,000) × $2.50 = $2,500 U

d)   **Well Read Publishing Company**
Sales Department Performance Report
For the month of April, 19x7

Sales price variance	$10,500 F
Net sales volume variance	2,500 U
Selling expense variances	4,500 U
Net sales department variances	$ 3,500 F

e)   Administrative department variance:

$12,000 actual − $10,000 budget = $2,000 U (over budget)

f)   **Well Read Publishing Company**
Reconciliation of Budgeted and Actual Net Income
For the month of April, 19x7

Budgeted net income		$10,000
Sales department variances	$3,500 F	
Production department variances	2,750 F	
Administrative department variances	2,000 U	4,250 F
Actual net income		$14,250

g)

Well Read Publishing Company
Reconciliation of Budgeted and Actual Income
For the month of April, 19x7

	(1) Actual Volume at Actual Selling Prices and Actual Costs (Actual results)	(2) Cost Variances	(3) Actual Volume at Actual Selling Prices and Standard Costs	(4) Sales Price Variance	(5) Actual Volume at Budgeted Selling Prices and Standard Costs (Flexible budget)	(6) Net Sales Volume Variance	(7) Budgeted Volume at Budgeted Selling Prices and Standard Costs (Original budget)
Volume (units)	21,000		21,000		21,000	1,000	22,000
Sales	$189,000		$189,000	$10,500 F	$178,500	$8,500	$187,000
Less variable costs:							
Direct materials	$ 15,750	$ 0	$ 15,750		$ 15,750	$ 750	$ 16,500
Direct labor	25,000	1,250 F	26,250		26,250	1,250	27,500
Factory overhead	32,500	1,000 U	31,500		31,500	1,500	33,000
Selling	56,000	3,500 U	52,500		52,500	2,500	55,000
Total	−129,250		−126,000		−126,000	−6,000	−132,000
Contribution margin	$ 59,750		$ 63,000		$ 52,500	$2,500 U	$ 55,000
Less fixed costs:							
Factory overhead	$ 17,500	2,500 F	$ 20,000		$ 20,000		$ 20,000
Selling	16,000	1,000 U	15,000		15,000		15,000
Administration	12,000	2,000 U	10,000		10,000		10,000
Total	− 45,500		− 45,000		− 45,000		− 45,000
Net income	$ 14,250	$3,750 U	$ 18,000	$10,500 F	$ 7,500	$2,500 U	$ 10,000

CHAPTER 8

Performance Evaluation of Standard Cost Centers

Upon completion of this chapter you should:

- Be familiar with the relationship between flexible budgeting and standard cost variance analysis.

- Understand the general model for analyzing variances between actual and flexible budget costs.

- Be able to apply the general variance analysis model to compute the following variable cost variances: materials price, materials quantity, labor rate, labor efficiency, variable overhead spending, and variable overhead efficiency.

- Know possible causes of favorable and unfavorable variances for each of the variances identified above.

- Understand why the total flexible budget variance for fixed overhead is usually not broken down into price and quantity variances for financial control purposes.

- Be able to identify major benefits and applications of standard cost variance analysis.

In Chapter 7 two types of cost centers were introduced, standard cost centers and discretionary cost centers. This chapter discusses standard cost centers in greater depth. You recall that standard cost centers are cost centers that have clearly defined relationships between effort (inputs) and accomplishment (outputs) that can be expressed in terms of standard costs per unit produced. These unit standards provide the basis for the budget formula used to prepare each period's flexible budget for the firm's actual production output. Manager performance, then, is evaluated by comparing actual costs incurred with flexible budget costs. Because of their role in determining flexible budget costs, standard costs are the basis for evaluating managers in standard cost centers.

The purpose of this chapter is to discuss how standard costs are established for direct materials, direct labor, and variable factory overhead,[1] and to show how they are used in evaluating standard cost centers. To use and interpret

---

[1] Standard unit costs ordinarily are not calculated for fixed factory overhead costs for performance evaluation purposes because these costs are incurred based on production capacity provided, not production capacity used. Accordingly, they are not controlled on a per unit of production basis.

standard cost variances properly, it is essential for managers to understand both the standard-setting process and the framework for computing and analyzing standard cost variances. In this chapter we focus on these aspects of standard cost planning and control systems.

BASIC VARIANCE ANALYSIS CONCEPTS

Standard cost variance analysis provides a system for examining the flexible budget variance, which is the difference between the *actual cost* and *flexible budget cost* of producing a given quantity of product or service. Flexible budget cost is computed as actual output times standard unit cost. Recall from Chapter 7 that standard unit cost represents what it should cost to produce a completed unit of product or service under efficient operating conditions. To determine standard unit cost, management establishes separate quantity and price (or rate) standards for each production component (materials, labor, and overhead). For example, the standard direct materials cost of manufacturing neckties might be $5 per necktie, consisting of $\frac{1}{3}$ yard standard quantity of fabric at a standard price of $15 per yard.

For the following general discussion of standard cost variance analysis, assume Wonderful Widgets, Inc., set its total standard cost of manufacturing widgets at $10 each. The company produced 250 widgets in July at an actual cost of $2,805; therefore, the total flexible budget variance was $305:

Actual cost to produce 250 widgets	$2,805
Less: Flexible budget cost for 250 widgets at $10 each	−2,500
Total flexible budget variance	$ 305 U

Since actual cost exceeded flexible budget cost, the variance was unfavorable (U).

Actual cost is based on actual *inputs*, and flexible budget cost is based on completed *outputs*. Actual cost is determined by multiplying actual quantities of materials, labor, and overhead inputs used in producing goods and services times the actual prices paid for the inputs. Flexible budget cost is determined by multiplying standard input quantities allowed for materials, labor, and overhead times the standard price per input unit. Standard cost variance analysis identifies the general causes for the total flexible budget variance by breaking it down into separate price and quantity variances for each production component. Two possible reasons why actual cost may differ from flexible budget cost for a given amount of output produced are: (1) there was a difference between the actual quantity and the standard quantity allowed for the production components and (2) there was a difference between actual and standard prices paid for the production components.

To simplify the Wonderful Widgets illustration, assume that widgets are manufactured from a single production component, called MLO, which contains all the normal elements of production—Materials, Labor, and Overhead. The actual cost of $2,805 (for the 250 widgets produced) consisted of 510 input units of MLO purchased at a price of $5.50 each. Also, assume the standards allow the use of two units of MLO, purchased at a standard price of $5, for each widget manufactured.

The following model shows the calculation of the total flexible budget variance using detailed quantity and price information for actual and flexible budget costs:

Flexible budget variance analysis

Input component: MLO		Output: 250 widgets	
Actual cost		**Flexible budget cost**	
Actual quantity	510	Standard quantity allowed	500*
Actual price	× $5.50	Standard price	× $5
Total	$2,805.00	Total	$2,500

Total flexible budget variance $305 U

*250 widgets × 2 units of MLO

Careful comparisons of actual quantity with standard quantity allowed and of actual price with standard price indicate that Wonderful Widgets had two variances in July that contributed to the total $305 unfavorable variance. They had a "quantity" variance that resulted from actually using 510 units of MLO instead of the standard quantity allowed of 500 units (two per widget). Also, they had a "price" variance that resulted from actually paying $5.50 for each unit of MLO, when the standard price was only $5. Therefore, the $305 un-favorable total flexible budget variance is explained by (1) the excess use of ten units of MLO and (2) the excess payment of 50 cents for each unit of MLO used during the period.

The graphs in Exhibit 8–1 show how quantity and price factors interrelate to produce total cost. Exhibit 8–1(a) shows the area representing total actual

EXHIBIT 8–1 Graphic Illustrations of Actual Costs, Standard Costs, and Basic Variances

Wonderful Widgets, Inc. for the month of July 19x4

(a) Actual cost of inputs

$2,805
(510 × $5.50)
Actual cost of inputs

(b) Standard cost of inputs allowed

$2,500
(500 × $5)
Standard cost of inputs allowed for outputs produced

(c) Total flexible budget variance

Total variance $305
($2,805 − $2,500)

(d) Price and quantity variances

Price variance $255
($2,805 − $2,550)

Quantity variance $50
($2,550 − $2,500)

cost of MLO used in making 250 widgets, calculated by multiplying the actual quantity of MLO used (510 units) times the actual price paid for MLO ($5.50). Exhibit 8–1(b) shows the area representing total flexible budget cost for 250 widgets, calculated by multiplying the standard quantity allowed for MLO (500 units) times the standard price for MLO ($5). When both *actual* cost and *flexible budget* cost are shown on the same graph (see Exhibit 8–1(c)), the $305 total variance between the actual cost and flexible budget cost of producing 250 widgets can be observed as being related to the difference between actual quantity and standard quantity allowed for MLO (510 units versus 500 units) and the difference between actual price and standard price paid for MLO ($5.50 versus $5).

To separate the $305 total flexible budget variance into detailed variances for price and quantity factors, a third value for production costs must be introduced; the standard cost of inputs, calculated as the actual quantity of inputs times the standard price per unit of input. We now have the following three possible production costs:

1. Actual cost

2. Standard cost of actual inputs

3. Flexible budget cost

Information about the standard cost of actual inputs enables the company to separately evaluate management's effectiveness in controlling both the prices paid for production inputs and the quantities of production inputs used. In our example, the standard cost of actual MLO inputs is $2,550, or 510 units times $5. The three costs calculated for Wonderful Widgets' production of 250 widgets, and the resulting standard cost variances, are summarized as follows:

	Quantity		Price		Total	
Actual cost	510 (actual)	×	$5.50 (actual)	=	$2,805	$255 difference equals price variance
Standard cost of actual inputs	510 (actual)	×	$5.00 (standard)	=	$2,550	$50 difference equals quantity variance
Flexible budget cost	500* (standard)	×	$5.00 (standard)	=	$2,500	

* (250 widgets × 2 units of MLO allowed per widget)

Note that in calculating the costs for determining the price variance, the quantity amounts are the same (actual/actual), but the prices are different (actual/standard); whereas, in calculating the costs for determining the quantity variance, the prices are the same (standard/standard), but the quantity amounts are different (actual/standard).

Wonderful Widgets actually paid $2,805 (or $5.50 per unit) for the 510 units of MLO used during the period; however, if management had paid the standard price of $5 for each unit of MLO used, the total amount spent for MLO would have been $2,550. Consequently, the $255 difference between actual cost and the standard cost of actual inputs represents the **price variance.** The price variance may also be calculated as the actual quantity used (AQ) times the difference between the actual price (AP) and standard price (SP):

$$\text{Price variance} = AQ(AP - SP)$$
$$= 510(\$5.50 - \$5)$$
$$= \$255 \text{ U.}$$

In Exhibit 8–1(d), the price variance is the horizontal portion of the total flexible budget variance area.

Using the standard cost of actual inputs, we can also determine the portion of the total flexible budget variance attributable to the quantity factor. Based on its standards, Wonderful Widgets allowed 2 units of MLO per widget completed, or 500 units of MLO, to complete 250 widgets. Instead, 510 units of MLO were used, representing 10 more units of MLO than the standards allowed. Even if the standard price of $5 had been paid for the actual units of MLO used, total actual cost would have exceeded total flexible budget cost by $50, or by the 10 excess units used times the $5 standard unit cost. This $50 difference between the standard cost of actual inputs ($2,550) and the flexible budget cost ($2,500) represents the **quantity variance.** The quantity variance may also be calculated as the standard price (SP) times the difference between the actual quantity (AQ) and standard quantity allowed (SQ):

$$\text{Quantity variance} = SP(AQ - SQ)$$
$$= \$5(510 - 500)$$
$$= \$50 \text{ U.}$$

In Exhibit 8–1(d), the quantity variance is represented by the vertical portion of the variance area of the total flexible budget variance. Another version of the model for calculating the price and quantity variances for Wonderful Widgets is presented below. This general model is used for standard cost variance analysis throughout the remainder of this chapter.

Standard cost variance analysis				
Input component: MLO				**Output: 250 widgets**
Actual cost		**Standard cost of actual inputs**		**Flexible budget cost**
Actual quantity (AQ)	510	Actual quantity (AQ)	510	Standard quantity allowed (SQ) 500*
Actual price (AP)	×$5.50	Standard price (SP)	× $5	Standard price (SP) × $5
	$2,805		$2,550	$2,500
		Price variance $255 U		Quantity variance $50 U
		Total flexible budget variance $305 U		

* 250 output units × 2 input units each

Before moving on to a more detailed standard cost variance analysis example, it should be emphasizd that standard cost variance analysis involves comparison of three different input cost values for a given amount of output. By comparing these values, we are able to isolate the total effect on actual costs of paying a price other than the standard price for actual inputs, and of using amounts other than the standard allowed quantity of inputs. Do not confuse the number of inputs with the number of outputs. In the Wonderful Widgets example, the actual inputs were 510 units of MLO, the actual outputs were 250 widgets, and the standard inputs allowed were 500 units of MLO (or two units of MLO per widget produced).

VARIANCE ANALYSIS FOR VARIABLE COSTS

In the Wonderful Widgets example, we assumed that each input unit contained some amount of materials, labor, and overhead. In an actual manufacturing situation, these three production components are acquired, used, and controlled separately—which is why these cost components are discussed separately in the following sections of this chapter. For each of these cost components, price and quantity variances are computed; however, these variances are ordinarily referred to by different names for direct labor and variable factory overhead. The commonly used names of the price and quantity variances for materials, labor, and variable overhead are as follows:

Cost Component	Price Variance Name	Quantity Variance Name
Direct materials	Materials price variance	Materials quantity variance
Direct labor	Labor rate variance	Labor efficiency variance
Variable overhead	Variable overhead spending variance	Variable overhead efficiency variance

To facilitate our discussion of materials, labor, and variable overhead variance analysis, we use the March 19x6 standard and actual cost information for Execupens, Inc., presented in Exhibit 8–2. Execupens manufactures gold casings for high-priced writing pens. Except for minor design differences, the casings are identical. Completed casings are sold to other manufacturers, who add their own writing element and a spring. Each casing has a standard cost of $68.

Note in Exhibit 8–2 that the $68 standard cost per unit includes only direct materials, direct labor, and variable overhead. These costs vary in total with the volume of production. As production increases, the flexible budget for the direct materials, direct labor, and variable overhead also increases. Fixed overhead is *excluded* from the unit standard cost because, within the relevant range of normal activity, it does not vary with the volume of production. For the purpose of internal planning and control, fixed costs are budgeted and evaluated for total capacity rather than on a per unit basis. Our focus in the body of this chapter is on internal planning and control. For external reporting, fixed overhead costs are normally assigned to products on a per unit basis. Also, to facilitate product costing, many organizations develop a standard fixed overhead cost per unit. Standard cost variances that arise under these circumstances are discussed in the appendix to this chapter.

The performance report showing the flexible budget variances for Execupens, Inc., is presented in Exhibit 8–3. In the following sections we analyze the flexible budget cost variances for each of the variable cost components and compute the appropriate price and quantity variances. Control of the fixed factory overhead flexible budget variance is also discussed.

EXHIBIT 8–2   Cost and Production Data

Execupens, Inc.
Cost and Production Data
For the month of March, 19x6

	Standard Quantity Allowed		Standard Price		Standard Cost (Flexible Budget Formula)
Standard cost per unit manufactured:					
Direct materials	6 grams	×	$ 8	=	$48
Direct labor	1 hour	×	$14	=	14
Variable overhead (based on direct labor)	1 hour	×	$ 6	=	6
Total standard cost per unit					$68
Budgeted fixed overhead per month					$198,000
Number of units manufactured during March, 19x6					20,000
Actual production costs:					
Direct materials	124,000 grams at $7.96				$ 987,040
Direct labor	19,200 hours at $14.84				284,928
Variable overhead					126,000
Fixed overhead					200,000
Total actual costs					$1,597,968

EXHIBIT 8–3   Performance Report

Execupens, Inc.
Production Department Performance Report
For the month of March, 19x6

	Flexible Budget Formula	Actual Costs	Flexible Budget Costs	Flexible Budget Variances
Volume		20,000	20,000	
Manufacturing costs:				
Direct materials	$48/unit	$ 987,040	$ 960,000	$27,040 U
Direct labor	$14/unit	284,928	280,000	4,928 U
Variable overhead	$6/unit	126,000	120,000	6,000 U
Fixed overhead	$198,000/month	200,000	198,000	2,000 U
Totals		$1,597,968	$1,558,000	$39,968 U

MATERIALS STANDARDS AND VARIANCES

There are two basic elements contained in the standards for direct materials—the *standard price* and the *standard quantity*. Materials standards indicate (1) how much should be paid for each unit of direct materials used and (2) the quantity of direct materials allowed to produce one unit of output. The standard price per unit of direct materials should include all reasonable costs necessary to acquire the materials. These costs include the invoice price of materials, less planned discounts, plus freight, insurance, special handling, and any other costs related to the acquisition of the materials.

The standard quantity represents the number of units of raw materials *allowed* for the production of one unit of finished product. The standard quantity of raw materials allowed to produce a unit of finished product should include the amount dictated by the physical characteristics of the process and the product, plus a reasonable allowance for normal spoilage, waste, and other inefficiencies. The quantity standard may be determined by engineering analysis, professional judgment, or by averaging the actual amount used for several periods. An average of actual past materials usage may not be a good standard because it includes excessive wastes and inefficiencies in the standard quantity. Execupens, Inc., has a direct materials quantity standard of 6 grams per finished unit produced. In fact, each unit may physically contain only 5 grams of raw materials, with the additional gram representing the amount allowed by the standards for normal spoilage, waste, and other inefficiencies.

Materials Variances Illustrated

Using the general variance analysis model introduced earlier, we can compute the materials price and quantity variances. The **materials price variance** is the difference between the actual materials cost and the standard cost of actual materials inputs. The **materials quantity variance** is the difference between the standard cost of actual materials inputs and the flexible budget cost for materials.

	Standard cost variance analysis		
Input component: direct materials			**Output: 20,000 casings**

Actual cost		**Standard cost of actual inputs**		**Flexible budget cost**	
Actual quantity (AQ)	124,000	Actual quantity (AQ)	124,000	Standard quantity allowed (SQ)	120,000*
Actual price (AP)	× $7.96	Standard price (SP)	× $8.00	Standard price (SP)	× $8.00
	$987,040		$992,000		$960,000

Materials price variance $4,960 F

Materials quantity variance $32,000 U

Total flexible budget materials variance $27,040 U

* 20,000 units × 6 grams per unit

Execupens, Inc., had a favorable materials price variance of $4,960 because the actual cost of materials used ($987,040) was less than the standard cost of actual materials used ($992,000). Stated another way, for the materials actually used, the total price paid was $4,960 less than the price allowed by the standards. The price variance can also be viewed as the actual quantity used times the difference between the actual price and the standard price. Execupens, Inc., paid 4 cents below the standard price for 124,000 grams of gold used, for a total savings of $4,960:

$$\text{Materials price variance} = AQ(AP - SP)$$
$$= 124,000\ (\$7.96 - \$8.00)$$
$$= 124,000 \times \$0.04$$
$$= \$4,960\ F$$

The unfavorable quantity variance of $32,000 occurred because the standard cost of actual materials used ($992,000) was greater than the flexible budget cost of materials ($960,000). A total of 120,000 grams of raw materials is allowed to produce 20,000 units of finished outputs. This is computed as 20,000 finished units times 6 grams of raw materials per unit. The materials quantity variance may also be computed as the standard price per gram times the difference between the number of grams actually used and the number of grams allowed. The use of 4,000 grams of gold more than the standard quantity allowed at a standard price of $8 per gram resulted in an additional cost of $32,000:

$$
\begin{aligned}
\text{Materials quantity variance} &= \text{SP(AQ} - \text{SQ)} \\
&= \$8.00\ (124{,}000 - 120{,}000) \\
&= \$8.00 \times 4{,}000 \\
&= \$32{,}000\ \text{U.}
\end{aligned}
$$

In the Execupens example, computation of the price variance was based on *materials actually used* during the period. However, since materials prices are ordinarily controlled at the point of purchase, rather than at the point of usage, many managers prefer to compute the materials price variance on the basis of *materials purchased* instead of materials used. If 125,000 grams of materials had been purchased at $7.96 but only 124,000 had been used, the materials variances would be computed as shown in the illustration at the top of page 335.

Note that now there are two actual quantities for materials. First, the actual quantity *purchased* is used to compute the materials price variance. The **materials purchased price variance** is the actual cost of materials purchased minus the standard cost of actual materials purchased. Second, the actual quantity *used* is utilized in computing the materials quantity variance. When the materials price variance is computed at the point of purchasing, all units of materials are charged to production at the standard price. Therefore, the materials price variance is not charged to production, and the flexible budget variance for materials consists entirely of the quantity variance.

Measuring the price variance at the point of materials purchases is desirable in situations where raw materials purchases vary substantially from the amount used during a given period. The purchasing manager needs to receive price variance information as soon as possible after the actual purchase of materials. If the price variance is measured when materials are used (which may be weeks or months after materials are purchased), the price variance information may be received too late to be useful in controlling materials prices. Also, timely reporting of price variance information is necessary for making pricing decisions, as it is for making other decisions based on current replacement costs.[2]

Interpreting Materials Variances

Accountants often overemphasize the computation of variances and forget that the main objectives of variance analysis are reporting and interpreting the variances. It is necessary to understand how variances are computed, but it is even more important to know what to do with the variances after they are computed.

---

[2] In working the exercises and problems in this chapter, assume (unless otherwise stated) that the production manager is responsible for raw materials purchases and that the quantity used equals the quantity purchased.

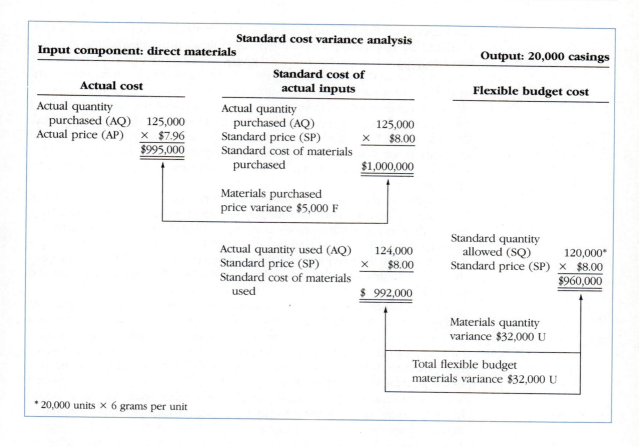

Standard cost variance analysis

Input component: direct materials   **Output: 20,000 casings**

Actual cost	**Standard cost of actual inputs**	**Flexible budget cost**
Actual quantity purchased (AQ) 125,000	Actual quantity purchased (AQ) 125,000	
Actual price (AP) × $7.96	Standard price (SP) × $8.00	
$995,000	Standard cost of materials purchased $1,000,000	

Materials purchased price variance $5,000 F

	Actual quantity used (AQ) 124,000	Standard quantity allowed (SQ) 120,000*
	Standard price (SP) × $8.00	Standard price (SP) × $8.00
	Standard cost of materials used $ 992,000	$960,000

Materials quantity variance $32,000 U

Total flexible budget materials variance $32,000 U

* 20,000 units × 6 grams per unit

A *favorable materials price variance* indicates that the manager responsible for materials purchases paid less per unit than the price allowed by the standards. This may result from receiving discounts for purchasing larger than normal quantities, effective bargaining by the manager, purchasing substandard quality materials, purchasing from a distress seller, or other factors. Ordinarily when a favorable price variance is reported, the manager's performance will be interpreted as favorable. However, if the favorable price variance resulted from the purchase of materials of lower than standard quality, or purchasing in larger than desirable quantities, the manager's performance would be questionable.

An *unfavorable materials price variance* means that the purchasing manager paid more per unit for materials than the price allowed by the standards. This may be caused by failure to buy in sufficient quantities to get normal discounts, failure to place materials orders on a timely basis thereby requiring a more expensive shipping alternative, uncontrollable price changes in the market for raw materials, failure to bargain for the best available prices, or other factors. It should be emphasized that the type of evaluation the purchasing manager receives depends on the reasons for the variance. An unfavorable variance does not always mean that the manager performed unfavorably, and a favorable variance does not always indicate favorable performance.

A *favorable materials quantity variance* means that the actual quantity of raw materials used was less than the quantity allowed for the units produced. This may result from factors such as less materials waste than allowed by the standards, better than expected machine efficiency, raw materials of higher quality than required by the standards, and more efficient use of raw materials by employees.

An *unfavorable materials quantity variance* occurs when the quantity of raw materials used exceeds the quantity allowed for the units produced. This may result from incurring more waste than provided for in the standards, poorly maintained machinery requiring larger amounts of raw materials, raw materials of lower quality than required by the standards, or poorly trained employees who were unable to use the materials at the level of efficiency required by the standards.

One possible cause for any standard cost variance (materials, labor, or overhead) is that the standard quantity or price used in computing the variance was too high or too low. A necessary consideration in evaluating any variance is that an inappropriate standard value may have been used in its computation. Thus, when investigating the causes for a given variance, always consider this possibility. If the standards are determined to be incorrect, they should be revised to reflect current efficient operating conditions. Higher level managers should always be eager to revise the standards to reflect changes in the environment not controllable by their subordinate managers. This attitude encourages responsibility center managers to have greater respect for both the reported variances and the entire performance evaluation system.

LABOR STANDARDS AND VARIANCES

Direct labor standards, like direct materials standards, consist of two components, *quantity* and *price*. The direct labor quantity standard is usually referred to as the labor efficiency, or usage, standard; the price standard is referred to as the labor rate standard. To evaluate management performance in controlling labor costs by using a standard cost system, it is necessary to determine the *standard labor time allowed* to produce a unit and the *standard labor rate* for each hour of labor allowed.

The standard labor time per unit can be determined by an engineering approach or an empirical observation approach. When using an engineering approach, industrial engineers ascertain the amount of labor required to produce a unit of finished product by applying time and motion methods or other available techniques. Normal operating conditions are assumed in arriving at the labor efficiency standard; therefore, allowances must be made for normal machine downtime, employee personal breaks, and so forth. Under the empirical approach, the long-run average time required in the past to produce a unit under normal operating conditions is used as a basis for the standard. By using normal operating conditions, inefficiencies such as machine downtime and employee breaks are automatically factored into the standard. The tightness of the standard can be adjusted by increasing or decreasing the observed average.

Setting labor rate standards may be quite simple or extremely complex, depending on the particular circumstances. If only one class of employees is used to make each product, and all employees have the same wage rate, determination of the standard cost is relatively easy: simply adopt the normal wage rate as the standard labor rate. If several different classes of employees are used in making each unit of product, separate efficiency and rate standards must be established for each class. For example, the standard direct labor cost per unit for making heavy machine components may be stated as follows:

Millwright labor (3 hrs at $15 per hr)	$ 45
Machinist labor (5 hrs at $12 per hr)	60
Standard labor cost per unit produced	$105

If wage rates vary for a given class of employees because of seniority or other differences, an average wage rate is ordinarily used for the labor rate standard. In these cases any variance caused by using an average rate should be negligible, unless there are large variations in wage rates within a particular employee class. To simplify our examples, we assume there is only one class of employees with all employees earning the same wage rate. As stated in Chapter 2, labor related fringe benefit costs are usually considered to be factory overhead and, therefore, are not included in the actual or standard labor rate.

Labor Variances Illustrated

Using the general variance model, we can compute the labor rate and efficiency variances. The **labor rate variance** is the difference between the actual labor cost and the standard cost of actual labor inputs. The **labor efficiency variance** is the difference between the standard cost of actual labor inputs and the flexible budget cost for labor.

Execupens' direct labor standards and labor usage data for March 19x6 are presented in Exhibit 8–2 on page 331. Note that the standards provide for 1 hour of direct labor time per unit at a cost of $14 per hour. During March 19x6, 19,200 hours were used at a cost of $14.84 per hour. Using these data, the labor rate (price) variance and labor efficiency (quantity) variance can be computed as shown in the following illustration.

Standard cost variance analysis

Input component: direct labor   **Output: 20,000 casings**

Actual cost		**Standard cost of actual inputs**		**Flexible budget cost**	
Actual hours (AH)	19,200	Actual hours (AH)	19,200	Standard hours allowed (SH)	20,000*
Actual rate (AR)	× $14.84	Standard rate (SR)	× $14.00	Standard rate (SR)	× $14.00
	$284,928		$268,800		$280,000

Labor rate variance $16,128 U

Labor efficiency variance $11,200 F

Total flexible budget labor variance $4,928 U

* 20,000 units × 1 hour per unit

The labor rate variance can also be computed as the actual hours used times the difference between the actual labor rate and the standard labor rate:

$$\text{Labor rate variance} = \text{AH}(\text{AR} - \text{SR})$$
$$= 19,200(\$14.84 - \$14.00)$$
$$= 19,200 \times \$0.84$$
$$= \$16,128 \text{ U.}$$

This computation of the labor rate variance shows that the company paid 84 cents above the standard rate for each of the 19,200 hours worked.

Since 20,000 units of product were finished during the period, and 1 hour of labor was allowed for each unit, the total standard hours allowed was 20,000. The labor efficiency variance can also be computed as the standard rate times the difference between the actual direct labor hours and the standard hours allowed for the output achieved:

$$\text{Labor efficiency variance} = \text{SR}(\text{AH} - \text{SH})$$
$$= \$14(19,200 - 20,000)$$
$$= \$14 \times 800$$
$$= \$11,200 \text{ F.}$$

This computation of the labor efficiency variance indicates that the company used 800 fewer direct labor hours than the budget permitted and that each of these hours saved $14, or a total of $11,200.

Interpreting Labor Variances

The possible explanations for labor rate variances are rather limited. An *unfavorable labor rate variance* may be caused by the use of higher skilled (and thus higher paid) laborers than provided for by the standards. Also, a new labor union contract increasing wages may have been implemented after the standards were set. In this case the standards should have been revised to account for the wage rate change. In a nonunion situation, where wages are not controlled by negotiated contract, there is the possibility that a manager may arbitrarily increase employee wages above the standard rate. This will also give rise to an unfavorable labor rate variance.

A *favorable labor rate variance* occurs if lower skilled (and thus lower paid) workers were used or if actual wage rates were below standard labor rates. As an example of falling wage rates, in the mid 1980s economic problems in the airline industry forced some union negotiators to relinquish previously awarded employee benefits. Such adjustments, however, should be reflected in the standards before the variances are reported.

Unfavorable labor efficiency variances occur whenever workers require more than the number of hours allowed by the standards to produce a given amount of product. This may be caused by a management decision to use poorly trained workers or poorly maintained machinery or by downtime resulting from the use of low-quality materials. Low employee morale, and generally bad working conditions, may also adversely affect the efficiency of workers, resulting in an unfavorable labor efficiency variance.

A *favorable labor efficiency variance* occurs when fewer labor hours are used than are allowed by the standards. This above normal efficiency may be caused by the company's use of higher skilled (and higher paid) workers, better machinery, or raw materials of higher quality than provided for by the standards. High employee morale, improved job satisfaction, or generally improved working conditions may also account for the above normal efficiency of the workers.

It is important to understand the potential interactive effect of the use of raw materials, direct labor, and machinery on the overall efficiency of the production process. These three factors must be combined efficiently to produce a unit of finished product of optimal quality. The quality of one factor usually affects the efficiency in using the other two components. For example, low-quality materials ordinarily reduces the efficiency of workers and machinery. Likewise, poorly maintained machinery reduces the efficiency of the workers and causes excessive waste of raw materials. And use of poorly trained workers often results in lower than normal output from the use of materials and machinery. Because of these interactive relationships, the interpretation of one variance is often interrelated with the interpretation of other variances. Seldom are there clear-cut and isolated explanations for each variance reported. Because of complexities of this sort, *using* variances is far more challenging than *computing* them.

VARIABLE OVERHEAD STANDARDS AND VARIANCES

Factory overhead costs are usually separated into fixed and variable elements for control purposes. Such a division is necessary because the variance between actual costs and expected costs is caused by different factors for fixed and variable costs. In this section we discuss the standards and variances related to variable overhead costs. Fixed overhead costs will be discussed in the next section.

In Chapter 2, factory overhead was defined as all manufacturing costs other than direct materials and direct labor. Variable factory overhead includes all variable manufacturing costs other than direct materials and direct labor. Examples of variable factory overhead are indirect materials and supplies, certain indirect labor, overtime costs, employee fringe benefits, utilities, and so forth.

Unlike direct materials and direct labor costs, which represent specific cost components, factory overhead represents a *group* of different costs. Consequently, setting standards is often more difficult for overhead costs than for materials or labor costs. Because of the difficulty of tracing overhead costs to the finished product, the engineering approach to setting overhead standards is seldom used. For mixed factory overhead costs (those that have variable and fixed components), an estimation technique, such as the high-low, least-squares, or scatter diagram method, is often used to separate the fixed and variable overhead components. These techniques were discussed in Chapter 3. If management believes the observations used in estimating variable costs reflect normal operating conditions, the estimate will probably be adopted as the standard variable cost.

Because it includes many heterogeneous costs, variable factory overhead poses a unique problem in measuring standard quantity and standard price. Direct materials have a natural physical measure of quantity such as tons, barrels, pounds, and meters. Similarly, direct labor is measurable in hours. However, no natural quantity measure is common to all variable overhead items. Variable overhead is a cost group that may include, at the same time, costs measurable in hours, pounds, grams, kilowatts, and gallons.

To deal with the problem of multiple quantity measures in variable factory overhead, most companies use an artificial, or substitute, measure of quantity for all items in the group. Typical substitute measures are *direct labor hours* and *machine hours*. The variable overhead standard then is stated in terms of this *common activity base,* and the amount of variable overhead budgeted is based on this artificial activity measure. To illustrate, assume that Execupens' standard variable overhead rate of $6 per direct labor hour consists of the following:

Variable Overhead Cost Item	Quantity Consumed per Direct Labor Hour	Standard Cost per Direct Labor Hour
Indirect materials:		
Silicon coating	2 fluid ounces	$0.25
Machine lubricants	3 centimeters	0.20
Cleaning supplies	3 grams	0.15
Indirect labor:		
Inspection	5 minutes	0.40
Fringe benefits	1 direct labor hour	3.50
Electricity	1 kilowatt hour	0.05
Machine depreciation	1 hour of machine time	1.45
Total variable factory overhead cost per direct labor hour		$6.00

Execupens, Inc., chose to measure variable factory overhead in terms of direct labor hours because a large portion of these costs is related to direct labor activity. Thus *direct labor hours worked* is better than *units of product finished* as a measure of how much variable overhead cost should be incurred because these costs tend to vary in relation to direct labor hours worked whether or not the workers are producing the standard one finished unit per direct labor hour. Also, if common facilities are used to produce two or more products that use unequal amounts of overhead, the same hourly overhead rate can be used to budget and charge different amounts of overhead for production of the products. For example, if one product required $\frac{1}{2}$ standard hour of direct labor and another required 1 hour, at a rate of $6 per direct labor hour, $3 of variable overhead would be allowed for making the first product, and $6 would be allowed for the second. The use of activity bases for allocating common costs, such as variable overhead, is discussed in greater depth in Chapter 12.

Variable Overhead Variances Illustrated

The general model for computing standard cost variances for materials and labor can also be used in computing variable overhead variances. However, the actual costs of inputs, such as indirect materials, indirect labor, and utilities, are ordinarily obtained directly from the accounting records rather than being computed as quantity times price.

The **variable overhead spending variance** is the difference between the actual variable overhead cost and the standard variable overhead cost for the actual activity base inputs (direct labor hours in this example). The **variable overhead efficiency variance** is the difference between the standard variable overhead cost for the actual activity base inputs and the flexible budget cost for variable overhead.

For Execupens, Inc., the actual variable overhead is given at $126,000. This represents the actual cost of indirect materials, variable indirect labor, utilities, and machine depreciation recorded during the period. Since actual variable overhead is expected to vary with labor hours, the standard cost of actual activity base inputs is calculated as 19,200 actual direct labor hours times the standard variable overhead rate of $6, or $115,200. The flexible budget cost for variable overhead allowed for the actual outputs is based on the 20,000 direct labor hours allowed for the units produced during the period (20,000 units × 1 hour). Consequently, the variable overhead flexible budget cost is 20,000 labor hours times the variable overhead rate of $6, or $120,000. Using these data, the variable overhead spending (price) variance and the variable overhead efficiency (quantity) variance are:

Standard cost variance analysis

Input component: variable overhead					Output: 20,000 casings

Actual cost		**Standard cost of actual inputs**		**Flexible budget cost**	
Actual hours (AH)	n/a*	Actual hours (AH)	19,200	Standard hours allowed (SH)	20,000†
Actual rate (AR)	× n/a	Standard rate (SR)	× $6.00	Standard rate (SR)	× $6.00
	$126,000		$115,200		$120,000

Variable overhead spending variance $10,800 U

Variable overhead efficiency variance $4,800 F

Total flexible budget variable overhead variance $6,000 U

* Not applicable

† 20,000 units × 1 hour per unit

Note that the spaces for actual hours and actual rate are left blank in the actual cost calculation. Since variable overhead is assumed to be incurred as direct labor hours are incurred, we could say that the actual quantity of inputs of variable overhead was 19,200 direct labor hours. Using 19,200 as the quantity of overhead inputs, the actual average variable overhead per labor hour can be determined as the actual variable overhead cost of $126,000 divided by 19,200 hours, or $6.56 per hour. Because variable overhead costs are not actually purchased in units of direct labor hours, it is probably less confusing to omit this computation. A more compelling reason for not making the computation is that it provides no benefit to management in controlling variable overhead costs.

An alternative to the computation of the variable overhead efficiency variance is as follows:

$$\text{Variable overhead efficiency variance} = \text{SR}(\text{AH} - \text{SH})$$
$$= \$6.00(19{,}200 - 20{,}000)$$
$$= \$6.00 \times 800$$
$$= \$4{,}800 \text{ F.}$$

This approach emphasizes that the 800 labor hours saved should have produced a variable overhead savings of $4,800, at the standard rate of $6 per direct labor hour.

Interpreting Variable Overhead Variances

The variable overhead spending variance measures the difference between actual variable overhead and the amount of overhead cost expected for the actual use of the activity base. Operating at 19,200 actual hours, with a standard rate of $6 per hour, management expected $115,200 (19,200 × $6) to be spent on variable overhead. Since actual costs were $126,000, management overspent, and a $10,800 unfavorable spending variance resulted.

Why did Execupens spend $10,800 too much? Was it caused by increasing prices for indirect materials, by higher than expected wage rates for indirect labor, or by higher than expected kilowatt rates for electricity? Or was it caused by workers' use of excessive quantities of indirect materials, indirect labor, and electricity for the actual direct labor hours worked? The answer is that the unfavorable spending variance could have resulted *both* from increasing prices for variable overhead goods and services used *and* from excessive consumption of these goods and services. Thus the term *spending* variance is used instead of the term *price* variance.

For variable overhead the *unfavorable spending variance* encompasses all factors that cause actual expenditures to exceed the amount expected for the actual labor hours, including consuming excessive quantities of variable overhead items, as well as paying too much for the variable overhead items consumed. Conversely, a *favorable spending variance* results when the actual expenditures are less than expected for the actual labor hours. This is caused by consuming fewer overhead items than expected, or by paying less than the expected amount for overhead items consumed, or by both of these.

The key to understanding the variable overhead spending variance is recognizing that the amount of variable overhead cost that can be incurred without exceeding the variable overhead spending budget is based on the actual level of the activity base chosen for budgeting variable overhead cost. For Execupens, actual direct labor hours determine the spending budget for variable overhead. Any deviation from this spending budget—due to mismanagement of variable overhead price or quantity variables—causes a spending variance to occur.

The variable overhead efficiency variance measures the difference between the standard variable overhead cost for the actual use of the activity base and the standard variable overhead cost for the allowed use of the activity base. This variance measures the amount of variable overhead that should have been incurred or saved because of the efficient or inefficient use of the activity base. It provides no information about the degree of efficiency in using variable overhead items such as indirect materials and indirect labor. This information is reflected in the spending variance. When overhead is being measured and budgeted on the basis of labor hours, it is logical to expect overhead costs to be affected by the degree of labor efficiency. This effect is measured by the variable overhead efficiency variance. Because of the connection of this variance to labor efficiency, it will always move in the *same direction* as the labor efficiency variance; when the labor efficiency variance is favorable, the variable overhead efficiency variance will be favorable, and vice versa.

In the Execupens illustration of variable overhead variances, the activity base selected for budgeting variable overhead cost was direct labor hours. Observations similar to those made for direct labor hours could also be made for other activity bases such as machine hours.

FIXED OVERHEAD STANDARDS AND VARIANCES

Because of the nature of fixed costs, the quantity of goods and services purchased by fixed expenditures does not change in proportion to changes in the level of production. For example, in the short run the production level does not affect the amount of depreciation on buildings, the number of fixed salaried employees, or the amount of real property subject to property taxes. Whether 20,000 or 30,000 units are produced, the same amount of fixed overhead is expected to be incurred so long as the production level is within the relevant range of activity provided by the current fixed overhead items. Therefore, a quantity or efficiency variance is ordinarily not computed for fixed overhead costs.

Even though the components of fixed overhead are not affected by the production activity level in the short run, the actual amount spent for fixed overhead items can differ from the amount budgeted by management. For example, higher than budgeted supervisors' salaries can be paid, extreme temperatures can cause heating or cooling costs to exceed budget, and price increases can cause the amounts paid for fixed property maintenance costs to be higher than expected. Fixed overhead costs in excess of the amount budgeted are reflected in the fixed overhead budget variance. The **fixed overhead budget variance** is the difference between budgeted and actual fixed overhead:

$$\text{Fixed overhead budget variance} = \text{Actual fixed overhead} - \text{Budgeted fixed overhead.}$$

Using the fixed overhead data in Exhibit 8–2 for Execupens, Inc., the fixed overhead budget variance is computed as $2,000 unfavorable, or $200,000 of actual fixed overhead costs minus $198,000 of budgeted fixed overhead costs. The fixed overhead budget variance is always the *same* as the total fixed overhead flexible budget variance. Because budgeted fixed overhead is the same for all outputs within the relevant range, the budget variance accounts for the total flexible budget variance between actual and allowed fixed overhead.

REPORTING STANDARD COST VARIANCES

Two critical factors in the operation of a responsibility accounting system are (1) the reporting of variances to the appropriate managers and (2) management's responding with explanations and control decisions. The method and format used to report variances to managers should be tailored to the specific needs of each situation. Exhibit 8–4 illustrates, for Execupens, one approach that is available for reporting performance results and standard cost variances for a standard cost center. This report is an expanded version of the flexible budget performance report presented in Exhibit 8–3. In this example, Execupen's production manager is assumed to be responsible for all raw materials purchases and the quantity used equals the quantity purchased. If purchases had been the

EXHIBIT 8–4   Standard Cost Performance Report

Execupens, Inc.
Production Department Standard Cost Performance Report
For the month of March, 19x6

	Actual Costs	Flexible Budget Cost	Flexible Budget Variances	Variance Analysis	
Direct materials	$ 987,040	$ 960,000	$27,040 U	$ 4,960 F	Materials price variance
				32,000 U	Materials quantity variance
Direct labor	284,928	280,000	4,928 U	16,128 U	Labor rate variance
				11,200 F	Labor efficiency variance
Variable factory overhead	126,000	120,000	6,000 U	10,800 U	Variable overhead spending variance
				4,800 F	Variable overhead efficiency variance
Fixed factory overhead	200,000	198,000	2,000 U	2,000 U	Fixed overhead budget variance
Totals	$1,597,968	$1,558,000	$39,968 U	$39,968 U	

responsibility of someone else, the materials price variance would not have been included in the production manager's performance report.

Managers receiving performance reports are usually required to respond to their immediate superiors within a designated period of time with explanations for variances that are significant in amount. Ordinarily, it is not economically feasible to investigate all variances. Each company must determine what constitutes a significant variance warranting managerial attention. All significant variances, both *unfavorable* and *favorable*, should be investigated. As stated before, a favorable variance does not necessarily indicate favorable managerial performance.

APPLICATIONS AND BENEFITS OF VARIANCE ANALYSIS

Standard costs are used primarily for performance evaluation, budgeting, and product costing. Throughout this chapter we have emphasized the performance evaluation aspect of standard costing. Closely related to the objective of performance evaluation is the objective of cost control, which is an important part of management responsibility that must be routinely evaluated. Although cost control is not a manager's only important responsibility, in a cost center it is a high priority with upper management. Standard costs provide a logical basis for evaluating a manager's performance. Standard cost reports are an important part of a responsibility reporting system for standard cost centers, and, as such, help to identify good and bad performers.

Standard cost reports can assist in formulating performance evaluations of managers by providing a beginning point, but serious consequences can result if standard cost reports are used exclusively to evaluate managers. Managers may learn quickly how to manipulate the system in order to generate favorable variances. For example, purchasing managers may buy substandard raw materials, and production managers may sacrifice quality for quantity, or sacrifice employee morale for higher productivity. Though these ploys may produce favorable variances in the short run, often they have negative effects on the organization in the long run. To avoid these types of manipulations, standard cost performance reports should be used as only *a part of an overall performance evaluation system* that considers all areas of manager performance.

Another use of standard costs discussed in Chapter 6 is to provide information useful in budgeting. If cost standards exist and are current, they can be used to budget manufacturing costs after sales and inventory requirements are budgeted. Having standard costs readily available significantly reduces the time and effort required to determine the budgeted costs for the planned production.

Standard costs are also useful in product costing. In a standard product costing system, manufactured inventory is always costed at standard allowed cost. Consequently, the cost of the finished inventory can be readily determined as the number of units in inventory times the standard cost per unit. This eliminates the product costing delays often associated with using actual costs for product costing. Product costing is considered in Chapter 11 and standard product cost systems are explained in an appendix to Chapter 11.

SUMMARY

Cost centers that have a predictable relationship between production inputs and outputs often use standard costs for controlling costs and evaluating manager performance. Standard cost systems require that cost standards be developed for each type of product produced (or service provided) and that they include standard unit costs for materials, labor, and overhead. Periodically, actual costs are compared with standard costs, and cost variances are reported to managers for possible corrective action.

Variance analysis involves breaking down flexible budget variances into specific variances caused by price and quantity departures from standards. Both price and quantity variances are reported for materials, labor, and overhead. Most companies measure the quantity of variable overhead consumed in terms of a substitute activity base, such as direct labor hours, rather than in terms of the quantity of overhead goods and services consumed. Therefore, the variable overhead efficiency variance measures the impact on overhead cost of the efficiency with which the activity base is used. The variable overhead spending variance measures the combined impact of price and quantity deviations from standards for variable overhead goods and services used.

For internal planning and control, fixed overhead is budgeted and reported in a lump sum and, therefore, is not affected by the level of activity achieved during the period. The fixed overhead budget variance is the difference between actual fixed overhead and budgeted fixed overhead. An additional fixed overhead variance is often computed when fixed overhead is applied to products on a unit basis for external reporting purposes. This variance is discussed in the following appendix.

APPENDIX
A CLOSER LOOK AT FIXED
OVERHEAD VARIANCES

The absorption cost method of external reporting treats all manufacturing costs as product costs. In Chapter 2 we indicated that most firms use a predetermined rate to assign factory overhead to products. This predetermined factory overhead rate is established at the start of the year by dividing the predicted overhead costs for the year by the predicted activity for the year. Many firms prefer to use separate overhead rates for fixed and variable overhead. When this is done, often variable overhead is assigned using the standard variable overhead rate, and fixed overhead is assigned using a separate *standard fixed overhead rate*.

The development of the variable overhead rate and its subsequent use in computing standard cost variances was considered in the body of this chapter. In this appendix we consider the development of a standard fixed overhead rate and its subsequent use in computing standard cost variances.

The motivation for using a standard fixed overhead rate is the same as the motivation for using a predetermined overhead rate, namely, more rapid product costing and smoothing the bookkeeping work load. Furthermore, the use of a standard fixed overhead rate results in identical fixed costs being assigned to identical products regardless of when they are produced during the year.

When a standard fixed overhead rate is used, *total fixed overhead* costs assigned to production behave as *variable* costs. As production increases, the total fixed overhead assigned to production increases. Because total budgeted fixed overhead does not vary, differences arise between budgeted and assigned fixed overhead, and managers often inquire about the cause of the differences.

The standard fixed overhead rate is computed as the *budgeted fixed costs* divided by some *budgeted standard level of activity*. Since budgeted fixed overhead is the same for all levels of output (within the relevant production range), the standard fixed overhead rate varies depending on the budgeted level of activity. In our example of Execupens, Inc. (see Exhibit 8–2), budgeted monthly fixed overhead is $198,000. To simplify the illustration, assume that Execupens develops their standard fixed overhead rate monthly, instead of annually, and that Execupens bases the rate on a budgeted activity level of 22,000 labor hours per month. The standard fixed overhead rate per direct labor hour is $9:

$$\text{Standard fixed overhead rate} = \frac{\text{Budgeted total fixed overhead}}{\text{Budgeted activity level}}$$

$$= \frac{\$198,000}{22,000 \text{ hours}}$$

$$= \$9.$$

The total fixed overhead assigned to production is computed as the standard rate of $9 multiplied by the standard hours allowed for the units produced. Therefore, the assigned fixed overhead equals the budgeted monthly fixed overhead only if the allowed activity is 22,000 hours. This is illustrated in Exhibit 8–5(a). If the company operates below the 22,000 budgeted hours, the fixed overhead assigned to production is less than the $198,000 budgeted; if it operates above the 22,000 budgeted hours, the fixed overhead assigned to production is more than the amount budgeted.

Even though total fixed overhead is not affected by producing below or above the standard activity level, the fixed overhead assigned to production increases at the rate of $9 per allowed labor hour. The difference between total budgeted fixed overhead and total standard fixed overhead assigned to pro-

EXHIBIT 8–5   Graphic Analysis of Fixed Overhead Costs and Variances

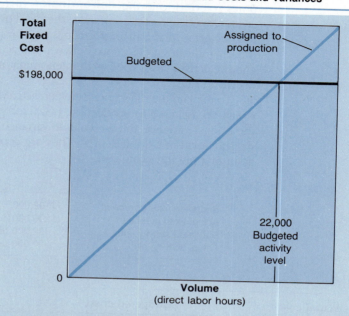

(a) Budgeted and assigned fixed overhead

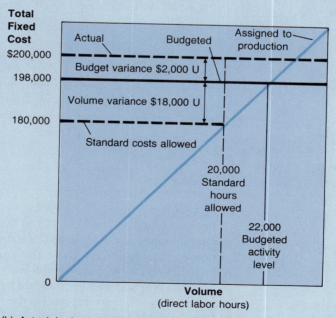

(b) Actual, budgeted, and assigned fixed overhead

duction is called the **fixed overhead volume variance.** This variance is some-times referred to as the **denominator variance,** a term that emphasizes the accounting origin of the variance. The fixed overhead volume variance indicates neither good nor bad performance by the production personnel. Instead, it merely indicates a difference between the activity allowed for the actual output and the activity level used as the denominator in computing the standard fixed overhead rate.

To explain the difference between actual fixed overhead and standard fixed overhead assigned to production, two fixed overhead variances are computed, the budget variance and the volume variance. These variances are illustrated in graphic form in Exhibit 8–5(b). They are computed below for Execupens, Inc., assuming the following data:

Budgeted fixed overhead	$198,000
Actual fixed overhead	$200,000
Budgeted activity level	22,000 units (or 22,000 hours)
Actual activity level	20,000 units (or 20,000 standard hours allowed)

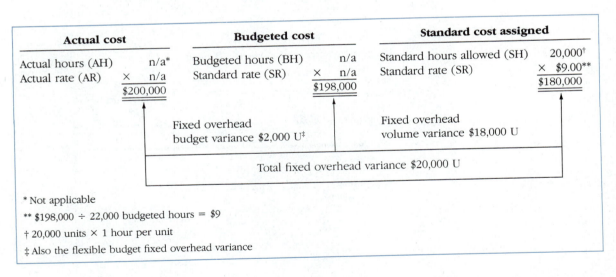

Because actual and budgeted fixed overhead do not vary for activity within the relevant range, their amounts are stated in total rather than computed as a function of some volume activity. The amount of fixed overhead assigned to production does vary with activity and is computed as the standard hours allowed for the actual outputs times the standard fixed overhead rate per hour. The fixed overhead budget variance represents the difference between actual fixed over-head and budgeted fixed overhead. The budget variance is caused by a combination of price and quantity factors related to the use of fixed overhead goods and services (e.g., heating or cooling costs, indirect labor, etc.). The $2,000 unfavorable budget variance for Execupens was caused either by using excessive quantities of fixed overhead goods and services, or by paying higher prices than expected for those items, or both.

The volume variance represents the difference between budgeted and assigned fixed overhead and is caused by a difference between the activity level allowed for the actual output and the budgeted activity used in computing the fixed overhead rate. The $18,000 unfavorable volume variance for Execupens means that the activity level allowed for the actual output was less than the budgeted activity level. As stated above, this variance ordinarily cannot be used to control costs. If the budgeted activity level is based on production capacity, this variance can be used only to alert management that facilities are under-utilized, or utilized above management's expectations.

KEY TERMS

Fixed overhead budget variance
Labor efficiency variance
Labor rate variance
Materials price variance
Materials purchased price variance
Materials quantity variance
Price variance

Quantity variance
Standard cost variance analysis
Variable overhead efficiency
  variance
Variable overhead spending
  variance

APPENDIX KEY TERMS

Denominator variance

Fixed overhead volume variance

REVIEW QUESTIONS

8–1 What is a standard cost variance, and what is the objective of variance analysis?

8–2 How do production inputs affect the cost of production outputs?

8–3 Standard cost variances can usually be broken down into two basic types of variances. Identify and describe these two types of variances.

8–4 What costs should be included in the determination of the standard materials price?

8–5 Identify two ways that materials standards can be determined. Which method is more precise?

8–6 Should the materials price variance be determined on the basis of materials purchased or materials used? Explain.

8–7 Identify possible causes for (1) a materials price variance and (2) a materials quantity variance.

8–8 Show two ways of computing the labor rate variance.

8–9   Explain how an unfavorable labor efficiency variance may be related to a favorable materials price variance.

8–10   What is the appropriate treatment in the standard cost system of a change in wage rates in the contract with the labor union?

8–11   How is the variable overhead spending variance computed, and what factors may cause it to occur?

8–12   If prices of indirect materials exceed the prices used in budgeting variable overhead, which variance is likely to be affected? Explain.

8–13   If the basic monthly rate for telephone service (not including long distance calls) increases beyond the amount budgeted, which variance will be affected?

8–14   Explain why only one variance is computed for fixed overhead for companies that use the contribution approach to internal reporting.

REVIEW PROBLEM

Standard Cost Variance Analysis

The flexible budget performance report for Teltek, Inc., for March 19x5 is presented below. Teltek manufactures PGX, its only product.

	Flexible Budget Formula	Actual Costs	Flexible Budget Costs	Flexible Budget Variances
Output volume		5,000	5,000	
Manufacturing costs:				
Direct materials	$20/unit	$104,125	$100,000	$4,125 U
Direct labor	$15/unit	82,400	75,000	7,400 U
Variable overhead	$12/unit	56,000	60,000	4,000 F
Fixed overhead	$30,000/month	32,000	30,000	2,000 U
Totals		$274,525	$265,000	$9,525 U

The standard unit cost for PGX is as follows:

Direct materials	4 pounds at $5 per pound	$20
Direct labor	1.5 hours at $10 per hour	15
Variable overhead	$8 per direct labor hour	12
Total standard cost per unit		$47

Actual cost of materials is based on 21,250 pounds of direct materials purchased and used, and actual cost of direct labor is based on 8,000 direct labor hours. Variable overhead is applied based on direct labor hours. The production supervisor is responsible for the purchase of all materials.

Requirements

a) Calculate all standard cost variances for direct materials, direct labor, and variable factory overhead.

b) Prepare a March 19x5 standard cost performance report for the Production Department.

The solution to this problem is found at the end of the Chapter 8 problems and exercises.

EXERCISES

8–1 Input/Output Analysis

Como Company manufactures a product called Powerpack. The standard input allowed for each unit of output is 8 units. Each unit of input has a standard cost of $5.00. During a recent period 9,000 units of input, acquired at a cost of $5.25 per unit, were used to manufacture 1,100 actual units of output.

Requirements

a) Determine the price variance.

b) Determine the quantity variance.

8–2 Graphical Representations

Prepare a graph depicting the variances computed in Exercise 8–1.

8–3 Materials Variances

Fisher Company uses standard costs to control materials costs. The standards call for 2 pounds of materials for each finished unit produced. The standard cost per pound of materials is $1.50. During May 4,800 finished units were manufactured and 8,800 pounds of materials were used. The price paid for the materials was $1.52 per pound. There were no beginning or ending materials inventories.

Requirements

a) Determine the flexible budget cost for the manufacture of 4,800 finished units.

b) Determine the actual materials cost incurred for the manufacture of 4,800 finished units, and compute the total materials variance.

c) How much of the difference between the answers to requirements (a) and (b) was related to the price paid for the purchase of materials?

d) How much of the difference between the answers to requirements (a) and (b) was related to the quantity of materials used?

8–4 Materials Price Variance Based on Purchases and on Usage

The Charleston Company manufactures decorative weather vanes that have a standard cost of $1.50 per pound for direct materials used in the manufacturing process. During September 11,000 pounds of materials were purchased for $1.55 per pound, and 10,000 pounds were actually used in making weather vanes. There were no beginning inventories.

Requirements

a) Determine the materials price variance assuming that materials costs are the responsibility of the materials purchasing manager.

b) Determine the materials price variance assuming that materials costs are the responsibility of the production manager.

c) Discuss the issues involved in determining the price variance at the point of purchase versus the point of consumption.

8–5 Direct Labor Variances

Dolex Company manufactures specialty electronic circuitry through a unique photo-electronic process. One of the primary products, Model ZX40, has a standard labor time of $\frac{1}{2}$ hour, and a standard labor rate of $13.50 per hour. During February the following activities pertaining to direct labor for ZX40 were recorded.

Direct labor hours used	2,200
Direct labor cost	$34,000
Units of ZX40 manufactured	4,600

Requirements

a) Determine the total flexible budget labor cost variance.

b) Determine the labor rate variance.

c) Determine the labor efficiency variance.

8–6 Variable Overhead Variances

Tea Bone Pickens Company bases standard variable overhead cost on direct labor hours. Standard variable overhead cost has been set at $15 per unit of output, based on $5 of variable overhead per direct labor hour for three hours allowed to produce one finished unit. Last month 4,300 direct labor hours were used and 1,400 units of output were manufactured. The following actual variable overhead costs were incurred.

Indirect materials	$ 4,500
Indirect labor	8,200
Utilities	5,800
Miscellaneous	3,500
Total variable overhead	$22,000

Requirements

a) Determine the variable overhead spending variance.

b) Determine the variable overhead efficiency variance.

c) How is the variable overhead efficiency variance related to labor efficiency?

d) If the company were to use smaller quantities of indirect materials than reflected in the standards, in which variance would the resulting cost savings be reflected? Explain.

8–7 Fixed Overhead Budget Variance

The Gainesville Company uses standard costs for cost control and internal reporting. Fixed costs are budgeted at $7,500 per month at a normal operating level of 10,000 units of production output. During October, actual fixed costs were $7,900, and actual production output was 9,500 units.

Requirements

a) Determine the fixed overhead budget variance.

b) Was the fixed overhead budget variance affected because the company operated below the normal activity level of 10,000 units? Explain.

8–8 Fixed Overhead Volume Variance (Appendix)

Assume that the Gainesville Company in Exercise 8–7 applied fixed overhead to inventory on a per unit basis.

Requirements

a) Determine the fixed overhead volume variance.

b) Explain the possible causes for the volume variance. How is reporting of the volume variance useful to management?

8–9 Causes for Variances

During January the May Company reported the following variances in the production of flagpoles, its only product.

1. Materials price variance

2. Materials quantity variance

3. Labor rate variance

4. Labor efficiency variance

5. Variable overhead spending variance

6. Variable overhead efficiency variance

7. Fixed overhead budget variance

Requirements

a) Identify the variances that are caused primarily by price factors.

b) Identify the variances that are caused primarily by quantity usage factors.

c) Identify the variances that are caused by both price and quantity factors.

8–10 Standard Costs of Services

The President of Guinnett Dekalb Bank has decided that his bank should be using a standard cost system to evaluate management's efficiency in controlling costs of various services that the bank performs for its customers.

Requirements

a) Identify five typical services that banks perform for their retail customers for which it would be practical to use standards costs.

b) What major obstacles is the bank likely to encounter in developing standard costs for its services and using them in performance evaluation and variance analysis?

PROBLEMS

8–11 Standard Costs and the Flexible Budget

The following performance report was prepared for a cost center in the Hoosier Company for March 19x2. The production volume was 1,800 units.

	Actual Costs	Flexible Budget Costs	Flexible Budget Variances
Direct materials	$ 8,200	$ 9,000	$800 F
Direct labor	5,550	5,400	150 U
Variable overhead:			
Supplies	680	630	50 U
Inspection	700	810	110 F
Indirect labor	900	990	90 F
Utilities	1,335	1,170	165 U
Fixed overhead:			
Depreciation	400	400	—
Supervision	950	900	50 U
Other	485	550	65 F
Totals	$19,200	$19,850	$650 F

Requirements

a) Determine the flexible budget formula for this cost center.

b) Determine the total variable standard cost per unit.

c) Assuming a production volume of 2,500 units, determine the flexible budget cost separately for direct materials, direct labor, and variable overhead.

8–12 Computation of Variable Cost Variances

Information pertaining to the standard costs and actual activity for the Tyler Company for September is presented below.

Standard cost per unit

Direct materials	4 units of material A at $2 per unit
	1 unit of material B at $3 per unit
Direct labor	3 hours at $8 per hour
Variable overhead	$1.50 per direct labor hour

Activity for September

Materials purchased:	
Material A	4,500 units at $2.05 per unit
Material B	1,100 units at $3.10 per unit
Materials used:	
Material A	4,150 units
Material B	1,005 units

There were no beginning raw materials inventories.

Direct labor used	2,950 hours at $8.20 per hour
Variable overhead costs incurred	$3,800
Production output	1,000 units

Requirements

a) Determine the materials price and quantity variances assuming materials purchases are the responsibility of the purchasing manager.

b) Determine the labor rate and efficiency variances.

c) Determine the variable overhead spending and efficiency variances.

8–13 Materials and Labor Variances; Alternative Computations; Interpretation of Variances

The Laxalt Company manufactures bookcases that have the following unit standard costs for direct materials and direct labor.

Direct materials—lumber (36 feet at $0.70 per foot)	$25.20
Direct labor (1 hour at $10 per hour)	10.00
Total standard direct cost per bookcase	$35.20

The following activities were recorded for March:

- 1,400 bookcases were manufactured.
- 51,200 feet of lumber costing $36,864 was purchased and used.
- $14,700 was paid for 1,500 hours of direct labor.

There were no beginning or ending work-in-process inventories.

Requirements

a) Compute the direct materials variances using two different computational techniques.

b) Compute the direct labor variances using two different computational techniques.

c) Give the possible reasons for the occurrence of each of the above variances.

8–14 Variance Computations: Performance Report

The Outdoor Company is a new firm that manufactures camping tents from a lightweight synthetic fabric. Each tent has a standard materials cost of $20, consisting of 4 yards of fabric at $5 per yard. The standards call for 2 hours of direct labor at $12 per hour and variable overhead at the rate of $2.50 per direct labor hour. Fixed costs are budgeted at $10,000 per month.

The following data were recorded for October 19x5, the first month of operations.

Fabric purchased	9,000 yards at $4.90 per yard
Fabric used in production of 1,700 tents	7,000 yards
Direct labor used	3,600 hours at $12.50 per hour
Variable overhead costs incurred	$8,900
Fixed overhead costs incurred	$13,000

Requirements

a) Compute all standard cost variances for variable costs (materials, labor, and overhead).

b) Determine the fixed overhead budget variance.

c) Determine the standard variable cost of the 1,700 tents produced, broken down into direct materials, direct labor, and variable overhead.

d) Prepare a standard cost performance report using the format illustrated in Exhibit 8–4. The production manager is not responsible for the materials price variance.

e) Give one possible reason for each of the variances computed above.

8–15 Determining Unit Costs: Variance Analysis and Interpretation

The Harmon Company, a manufacturer of dog food, produces its product in 1,000 bag batches. The standard cost of each batch consists of 8,000 pounds of direct materials at $0.30 per pound, 48 direct labor hours at $8.50 per hour, and variable overhead cost (based on machine hours) at the rate of $10 per hour for 16 machine hours per batch. The following variable costs were incurred for the last 1,000 bag batch produced.

Direct materials	8,200 pounds costing $2,378 were purchased and used
Direct labor	45 hours costing $450
Variable overhead	$200
Machine hours used	18

Requirements

a) Determine the actual and standard variable costs per bag of dog food produced, broken down into direct materials, direct labor, and variable overhead.

b) For the last 1,000 bag batch, determine the standard cost variances for direct materials, direct labor, and variable overhead.

c) Explain the possible causes for each of the variances determined in requirement (b).

8–16 Computation of Variances and Other Missing Data

The following data for the O'Keefe Company pertain to the production of 300 units of product X during December. Selected data items are omitted.

Direct materials (All materials purchased were used in current production.)
Standard cost per unit: ___(a)___ pounds at $3.20 per pound
Total actual cost: ___(b)___ pounds costing $5,673
Standard cost allowed for units produced: $5,760
Materials price variance: ___(c)___
Materials quantity variance: $96 U

Direct labor
　　Standard cost: 2 hours at $7.00
　　Actual cost per hour: $7.25
　　Total actual cost: ___(d)___
　　Labor rate variance: ___(e)___
　　Labor efficiency variance: $140 U

Variable overhead
　　Standard costs: ___(f)___ hours at $4 per direct labor hour
　　Actual cost: $2,250
　　Variable overhead spending variance: ___(g)___
　　Variable overhead efficiency variance: ___(h)___

　　Total units produced were 300.

Required: Fill in the missing amounts in the blanks lettered (a) through (h).

8–17 Computation of Missing Variances and Other Data

The following data pertaining to the production of the Dalko Company's primary product are for a recent month, with selected items omitted. Two thousand units of product were produced during the month, and the total flexible budget cost allowed was $100,000.

Direct materials
　　Standard cost per unit: 4 gallons at $7.90 per gallon
　　Total actual cost of materials used: ___(a)___ gallons at $8.00 per gallon
　　Total standard cost allowed: ___(b)___
　　Total flexible budget variance: ___(c)___
　　Materials price variance: ___(d)___
　　Materials quantity variance: $553 U

Direct labor
　　Standard cost per unit: 0.4 hour at $15 per hour
　　Total actual cost of labor: ___(e)___ hours at ___(f)___ per hour
　　Total standard cost allowed: ___(g)___
　　Total flexible budget variance: $485 F
　　Labor rate variance: $235 U
　　Labor efficiency variance: ___(h)___

Variable overhead
　　Standard cost per unit: ___(i)___ labor hours at $4 per hour
　　Actual cost: $4,200
　　Total standard cost allowed: ___(j)___
　　Total flexible budget variance: ___(k)___
　　Variable overhead spending variance: ___(l)___
　　Variable overhead efficiency variance: ___(m)___

Fixed overhead
　　Actual cost: ___(n)___
　　Budgeted cost: ___(o)___
　　Budget variance: $1,000 F

Required: Fill in the missing amounts in the blanks lettered (a) through (o).

8–18 Overhead Variances

The Grogan Coach Company controls variable overhead costs based on direct labor hours, and controls fixed costs on the basis of total budgeted costs. Each unit of output is allowed 10 standard direct labor hours. The standard variable overhead cost per unit of output, broken down by cost components, is presented below.

Indirect materials	$125
Indirect labor	90
Plant and facilities cost	60
Miscellaneous variable overhead	50
Standard variable overhead cost per unit of output	$325

Budgeted fixed costs per month are as follows:

Indirect labor	$ 8,000
Plant and facilities cost	3,000
Depreciation	2,500
Miscellaneous fixed costs	1,200
Total budgeted fixed costs	$14,700

During July 2,100 actual direct labor hours were worked, and the production output was 200 units. Actual costs incurred were as follows:

	Variable	Fixed
Indirect materials	$23,500	—
Indirect labor	19,000	$ 8,800
Plant and facilities	12,200	3,750
Depreciation	—	2,500
Miscellaneous	10,400	1,100
Total actual overhead costs	$65,100	$16,150

Required: Prepare a performance report that shows variable and fixed overhead variances broken down by cost items. Use the following column headings for your report.

				Variance Analysis	
Cost Item	Actual Costs	Standard Costs (Flexible Budget)	Total Variance	Spending or Budget	Efficiency
	$	$	$	$	$

8–19 Causes of Standard Cost Variances

Below are ten unrelated situations that would ordinarily be expected to affect one or more standard cost variances.

1. A salaried production foreman is given a raise, and no adjustment is made in the labor cost standards.

2. The materials purchasing manager gets a special reduced price on raw materials by purchasing a train carload. A warehouse had to be rented to accommodate the unusually large amount of raw materials. The rental fee was charged to rent expense, a fixed overhead item.

3. An unusually hot August caused the company to use 25,000 kilowatts more electricity than provided for in the variable overhead standards.

4. The local electric utility company raised the charge per kilowatt hour. No adjustment was made in the variable overhead standards.

5. The plant manager traded in his leased company car for a new Cadillac in July, increasing the monthly lease payment by $150.

6. A machine malfunction on the assembly line caused by using cheap and inferior raw materials resulted in decreased output by the machine operator and higher than normal machine repair costs. Repairs are treated as variable overhead costs.

7. The production maintenance supervisor decreased routine maintenance checks, resulting in lower maintenance cost and lower machine production output per hour. Maintenance costs are treated as fixed costs.

8. An announcement that vacation benefits had been increased resulted in improved employee morale. Consequently, raw materials pilferage and waste declined, and production efficiency increased.

9. The plant manager reclassified her secretary to administrative assistant and gave him an increase in salary.

10. A union contract agreement was signed calling for an immediate 5 percent increase in production worker wages. No changes were made in the standards.

Required: For each of the above situations indicate by letter which of the following standard cost variances would be affected. More than one variance will be affected in some cases.

a) Materials price variance

b) Materials quantity variance

c) Labor rate variance

d) Labor efficiency variance

e) Variable overhead spending variance

f) Variable overhead efficiency variance

g) Fixed overhead budget variance

8–20 Measuring the Effects of Decisions on Standard Cost Variances

Below are five unrelated situations that affect one or more standard cost variances for materials, labor, and overhead.

1. Lois Jones, a production worker, announced her intentions to resign in order to accept another job paying $1.20 per hour more. To keep from losing her, the

production manager agreed to raise her salary from $7.00 to $8.50 per hour. Lois works an average of 175 hours per month.

2. At the beginning of the month a supplier of a component used in our product notified us that, because of a minor design improvement, the price will be increased by 15 percent above the current standard price of $100 per unit. As a result of the improved design, we expect the number of defective components to decrease by 80 units per month. On the average 1,200 units of the component are purchased each month. Defective units are identified prior to use and are not returnable.

3. In an effort to meet a deadline on a rush order in Department A, the plant manager reassigned several higher skilled workers from Department B, for a total of 300 labor hours. The average salary of the Department B workers was $1.85 more than the standard $7.00 per hour rate of the Department A workers. Since they were not accustomed to the work, the average Department B worker was able to produce only 36 units per hour instead of the standard 48 units per hour. (Consider only the effect on Department A labor variances.)

4. Rob Celiba is an inspector who earns a flat salary of $700 per month plus a piece rate of 20 cents per bundle inspected. His company accounts for inspection costs as factory overhead. Because of a payroll department error in June, Rob was paid $500 plus a piece rate of 30 cents per bundle. He received gross wages totaling $1,100.

5. The materials purchasing manager purchased 5,000 units of component K2X from a new source at a price $12 below the standard unit price of $200. These components turned out to be of extremely poor quality with defects occurring at three times the standard rate of 5 percent. The higher rate of defects reduced the output of workers (who earn $8 per hour) from 20 units per hour to 15 units per hour on the units containing the discount components. Each finished unit contains one K2X component. To appease the workers, who were irate at having to work with inferior components, the production manager agreed to pay the workers an additional 25 cents for each of the components (good and bad) in the discount batch. Variable factory overhead is applied at the rate of $4 per direct labor hour. The defective units also caused a 20 hour increase in total machine hours. The actual cost of electricity to run the machines is $2 per hour.

Required: For each of the above situations determine which standard cost variance(s) will be affected, and compute the amount of the effect for one month on each variance. Indicate whether the effect is favorable or unfavorable. Assume the standards are not changed in response to these situations. (Round calculations to two decimal places.)

8–21 Developing Cost Standards for Materials and Labor

After several years of operating without a formal system of cost control, the Carlsen Company, a tools manufacturer, has decided to implement a standard cost system. The system will be established first for the department that makes lug wrenches for automobile mechanics. The standard production batch size is 100 wrenches. The actual materials and labor required for eight batches selected randomly from last year's production are as follows:

Batch	Materials Used (in pounds)	Labor Used (in hours)
1	504	10
2	508	9
3	506	9
4	521	5
5	516	8
6	518	7
7	520	6
8	515	8
Average	513.5	7.75

Management has obtained the following recommendations concerning what the materials and labor quantity standards should be.

- The manufacturer of the equipment used in making the wrenches advertises in the toolmakers' trade journal that the machine Carlsen uses can produce 100 wrenches with 500 pounds of raw materials and 5 labor hours. Carlsen's engineers believe the standards should be based on these data.

- The accounting department believes a more realistic standard would be 504 pounds and 5 hours.

- The production supervisor believes the standard should be 513.5 pounds and 7.75 hours.

- The production workers argue for standards of 515 pounds and 8 hours.

Requirements

a) State the arguments for and against each of the recommendations and the probable effects of each recommendation on the quantity variances for materials and labor.

b) Which recommendation provides the best combination of cost control and motivation to the production workers? Explain.

8–22 Variance Analysis for Services Costs

Atlantic Manufacturers Bank uses standard costs in its commercial loan department. The standard cost to process a loan has been determined as follows:

Direct materials (20 pages of forms at 10 cents per page)	$ 2
Direct labor (2 hrs at $8)	16
Variable overhead cost (2 hrs at $1 per labor hr)	2
Total standard variable cost per loan application	$20

Fixed costs in the commercial loan department are budgeted at $1,500 per month.

Last month 160 loan applications were processed, and the following costs were incurred.

Direct materials	3,500 pages of forms totaling $420
Direct labor	345 hrs at $8.20 per hr
Variable overhead	$400
Fixed overhead	$1,650

Requirements

a) Determine all standard variable cost variances discussed in this chapter for direct materials, direct labor, and variable overhead.

b) Determine the fixed overhead budget variance.

c) Identify some of the problems of using standard costing in a service oriented business.

8–23 Compiling and Reporting Standard Cost Variances

The Carberg Corporation manufactures and sells a single product. The cost system used by the company is a standard cost system. The variable standard cost per unit of product is shown below:

Material (1 lb of plastic at $2)	$ 2.00
Direct labor (1.6 hrs at $4)	6.40
Variable overhead cost	3.00
	$11.40

The overhead cost per unit was calculated from the following annual overhead cost budget for a 60,000 unit volume.

Variable overhead cost:		
Indirect labor (30,000 hrs at $4)	$120,000	
Supplies—oil (60,000 gals at $0.50)	30,000	
Utilities	30,000	$180,000
Fixed overhead costs:		
Supervision	$ 27,000	
Depreciation	45,000	
Other fixed costs	15,000	87,000
Total budgeted overhead costs for 60,000 units		$267,000

The charges to the manufacturing department for November, when 5,000 units were produced, are given as follows.

Materials (5,300 lbs at $2)	$10,600
Direct labor (8,200 hrs at $4.10)	33,620
Indirect labor (2,400 hrs at $4.10)	9,840
Supplies—oil (6,000 gals at $0.55)	3,300
Utilities	3,200
Supervision	2,475
Depreciation	3,750
Other fixed costs	1,250
Total	$68,035

The purchasing department normally buys about the same quantity as is used in production during a month. In November 5,200 pounds were purchased at a price of $2.10 per pound.

Requirements

a) Calculate the following variances from standard costs for the data given above.

   1. Materials purchased price variance

   2. Materials quantity variance

   3. Direct labor rate variance

   4. Direct labor efficiency variance

   5. Total flexible budget variance for each overhead item

b) The company has divided its responsibilities so that the purchasing department is responsible for the price at which materials and supplies are purchased, and the manufacturing department is responsible for the quantities of materials used. Does this division of responsibilities solve the conflict between price and quantity variances? Explain.

c) Prepare a report that details the flexible overhead budget variances. The report, which will be given to the manufacturing department manager, should display only that part of each variance that is the obvious responsibility of the manager. It should highlight the information in ways that would be useful to that manager in evaluating departmental performance and when considering corrective action. *Hint:* This part requires considerable thought, rather than technical analysis.

d) Assume that the department manager performs the timekeeping function for this manufacturing department. From time to time an analysis of overhead and direct labor variances has shown that the department manager has deliberately misclassified labor hours (e.g., listed direct labor hours as indirect labor hours, and vice versa) so that only one of the two labor variances is unfavorable. It is not feasible economically to hire a separate timekeeper. What should the company do, if anything, to resolve this problem?

(CMA Adapted)

8–24 Data Computations from Variance Information

On May 1, 19x5, Bovar Company began the manufacture of a new mechanical device known as "Dandy." The company installed a standard cost system in accounting for manufacturing costs. The standard costs for a unit of "Dandy" are as follows:

Raw materials (6 lbs at $1 per lb)	$ 6
Direct labor (1 hr at $4 per hr)	4
Overhead (75% of direct labor costs)	3
	$13

The following data were obtained from Bovar's records for May.

Actual production of "Dandy"	4,000 units
Unsold units of "Dandy"	2,500 units
Sales	$50,000
Purchases	$27,300
Materials purchased price variance	$ 1,300 U
Materials quantity variance	$ 1,000 U
Direct labor rate variance	$ 760 U
Direct labor efficiency variance	$ 800 F
Total overhead flexible budget variance	$ 500 U

Required: Compute each of the following items for Bovar for May.

1. Total standard quantity of raw materials allowed (in pounds)
2. Total actual quantity of raw materials used (in pounds)
3. Total standard labor hours allowed
4. Total actual hours worked
5. Actual direct labor rate per hour
6. Actual total overhead costs

(CPA Adapted)

8–25 Variance Analysis: Factory Overhead Based on Labor Cost

Armando Corporation manufactures a product with the following standard costs.

Direct materials (20 yds at $1.35 per yd)	$ 27
Direct labor (4 hrs at $9 per hr)	36
Variable factory overhead costs (based on $5 per labor hour)	20
Total variable standard cost per unit of output	$ 83
Total budgeted fixed factory overhead per month	$6,000

The following information pertains to July 19x1.

Direct materials purchased (18,000 yds at $1.38)	$24,840
Direct materials used (9,500 yds)	n/a
Direct labor (2,100 hrs at $9.15)	19,215
Total factory overhead ($6,800 fixed)	16,650
Total actual costs	$60,705

500 units of product were actually produced in July 19x1.

Requirements

a) Determine the standard variable overhead rate per direct labor hour.

b) Compute the following variances:

Materials purchased price variance
Materials quantity variance
Labor rate variance
Labor efficiency variance
Variable overhead spending variance
Variable overhead efficiency variance
Fixed overhead budget variance

c) Prepare a Production Department performance report showing actual costs, flexible budget costs, total flexible budget variances, and standard cost variances for July. The production manager is not responsible for the materials price variance.

(CPA Adapted)

8–26 Fixed Overhead Budget and Volume Variances (Appendix)

The Starling Company assigns fixed overhead costs to inventory for external reporting purposes by using a predetermined standard overhead rate based on direct labor hours. The standard rate is based on a normal (or denominator) activity level of 10,000 standard allowed direct labor hours per year. There are 5 standard allowed hours for each unit of output. Budgeted fixed overhead costs are $200,000 per year. During 19x8 the Starling Company produced 2,100 units of output, and actual fixed costs were $205,000.

Requirements

a) Determine the standard fixed overhead rate used to assign fixed costs to inventory.

b) Determine the amount of fixed overhead assigned to inventory in 19x8.

c) Determine the fixed overhead budget variance.

d) Determine the fixed overhead volume variance.

e) Even though the cost of security guards is controlled as a fixed cost, the number of hours worked by the guards may fluctuate somewhat. If the number of hours worked by the guards in 19x8 had been smaller, which fixed overhead variance would have been affected? Explain. If the wage rate for security guards had increased during the year (with no revision of the standard), which variance would have been affected? Explain.

f) What information does the fixed overhead volume variance computed above convey to management?

8–27 Variance Computations with Fixed Cost Assigned on a Unit Basis (Appendix)

The Terry Company manufactures a commercial solvent that is used for industrial maintenance. This solvent is sold by the drum and generally has a stable selling price. Because of a decrease in demand for this product, Terry produced and sold 60,000 drums in December 19x6, which is 50 percent of normal capacity. The following information is available regarding Terry's operations for December 19x6.

Standard costs per drum of product manufactured were as follows:

Materials:	
10 gallons of raw materials at $2 per gallon	$20
1 empty drum	1
Total materials cost	$21
Direct labor: 1 hour	$ 7
Variable factory overhead: per labor hour	$ 6
Fixed factory overhead: per labor hour	$ 6
(Fixed overhead is assigned to production based on a normal production volume of 120,000 allowed direct labor hours.)	

Costs incurred during December 19x6 were as follows:

Raw materials:	
600,000 gallons were purchased at a cost of $1,150,000.	
700,000 gallons were used.	
Empty drums:	
85,000 drums were purchased at a cost of $85,000.	
60,000 drums were used, and 60,000 drums	
of product were produced.	
Direct labor: 65,000 hours for a total of $470,000.	
Factory overhead:	
Variable factory overhead	$ 76,500
Supervision and indirect labor (contains $320,000 variable and	
$140,000 fixed)	460,000
Depreciation (fixed)	330,000
Total factory overhead	$866,500

Required: Compute the following variances.

1. Materials purchased price variance
2. Materials quantity variance
3. Labor rate variance
4. Labor efficiency variance
5. Variable overhead spending variance
6. Variable overhead efficiency variance
7. Fixed overhead budget variance
8. Fixed overhead volume variance

(CPA Adapted)

8–28 Sales, Flexible Budget, and Standard Cost Variances: Reconciliation of Actual and Budgeted Net Income

The Robson Company's Macon plant produces alloy ingots for industrial use. Andrew O'Brian, who was recently appointed general manager, just received the following income statement for his plant for May 19x6, his first month as manager.

	Actual	Budgeted	Variance
Units	5,500	6,000	500 U
Sales	$132,000	$120,000	$12,000 F
Less variable costs:			
Direct materials	$ 22,275	$ 23,400	$ 1,125 F
Direct labor	20,805	21,000	195 F
Factory overhead	15,860	16,500	640 F
Total variable costs	− 58,940	− 60,900	1,960 F
Contribution margin	$ 73,060	$ 59,100	$13,960 F
Less fixed manufacturing costs	− 26,500	− 25,000	− 1,500 U
Plant net income	$ 46,560	$ 34,100	$12,460 F

There were no beginning or ending inventories. The variable standard costs per unit are as follows:

Direct materials: $1\frac{1}{2}$ kilograms at $2.60 per kilogram
Direct labor: $\frac{1}{2}$ hour at $7.00 per hour
Variable overhead: $\frac{1}{2}$ direct labor hour at $5.50 per hour

The following actual data were collected.

Direct materials used: 8,250 kilograms
Direct labor hours used: 2,850 hours

Requirements

(*Note:* Parts (a) through (d) provide a review of material discussed in Chapter 7.)

a) Determine the amount of the plant net income variance traceable to the decision to raise the selling price. *Hint:* Compute the sales price variance.

b) Determine the amount of the plant net income variance traceable to selling 500 units below the budget. *Hint:* Compute the net sales volume variance.

c) Determine the amount of the plant net income variance traceable to manufacturing cost control factors. *Hint:* Compute the flexible budget variance for total manufacturing costs, including variable and fixed.

d) What does the sum of the answers to requirements (a) through (c) represent?

e) Determine the total flexible budget variance for direct materials and the appropriate standard cost variances.

f) Repeat requirement (e) for direct labor.

g) Repeat requirement (e) for variable factory overhead.

h) Determine the fixed factory overhead budget variance.

i) O'Brian feels very good about exceeding the original budgeted net income in spite of selling 500 fewer units of product than budgeted. From a cost control standpoint, does he have any reason to be pleased about his performance? Explain.

8–29 Evaluating Standard Costs

Comtech, Inc., which uses a simplified standard cost system, manufactures a lap-top computer that has a standard cost of $640 per unit broken down as follows:

Direct materials components (1 materials kit per unit)	$525
Direct labor (6¼ hours at $12)	75
Overhead ($6.40 per direct labor hour)	40
Total	$640

Direct materials consist of a kit of 5 component modules used in assembling the computers. All the modules are manufactured by either outside contractors or by other divisions of Comtech. Management is free to buy the components from any available source so long as the components meet the company engineering and quality standards. During October 19x9, the following report was prepared for the production department.

	Actual Costs	Flexible Budget Costs	Standard Cost Variances
Direct materials	$286,125	$262,500	$23,625 U
Direct labor	45,000	37,500	7,500 U
Overhead	20,875	20,000	875 U
Totals	$352,000	$320,000	$32,000 U

When asked to explain the flexible budget variances, the production manager argued that the report was not an accurate indication of his performance. He provided the following information to defend his claim that the standards were not appropriate.

1. Standard direct materials costs are based on the lowest prices available for the various components during the preceding period. Market prices during the current period are 2 percent higher than those of the previous period. Also, the standards did not allow for any defective parts that had to be scrapped or for any pilferage or other materials losses.

2. The standard direct labor cost of $12 per hour is a weighted average of all workers' wages on the production line during the preceding period. The manager maintains that, due to transfers of workers into the production department from other departments, there are more high-paid workers in the production department currently than when the standards were established. He also stated that skilled workers who

normally earn $15 per hour are being averaged with unskilled workers who earn $8 per hour.

3. The standard overhead cost includes a variable overhead cost of $5 per labor hour as well as a fixed overhead cost based on a budgeted capacity of 1,000 computers per month.

Requirements

a) Evaluate Comtech's standard cost system. Is the production manager's lack of confidence in the performance report justified? Explain.

b) Given the information provided, can quantity and price standard cost variances be determined for materials, labor, and overhead? If not, what additional information is needed for you to compute these variances?

c) Make recommendations for improving Comtech's standard cost variance analysis and reporting system. Create hypothetical data as necessary to illustrate your recommendations.

8–30 Behavioral Effects of Standard Costs

The Deleware Corp. has used a standard cost system for evaluating the performance of its responsibility center managers for three years. Top management feels that standard costing has not produced the cost savings or increases in productivity and profits promised by the accounting department. Large unfavorable variances are consistently reported for most cost categories and employee morale has fallen since the system was installed. To help pinpoint the problem with the system, top management asked for separate evaluations of the system by the plant department manager, the accounting department manager, and the personnel department manager. Their responses are summarized below:

Plant Manager: The standards are unrealistic. They assume an ideal working environment that does not allow materials defects or errors by the workers or machines. Consequently, morale has gone down and productivity has declined. Standards should be based on expected actual prices and recent past averages for efficiency. Thus, if we improve over the past, we receive a favorable variance.

Accounting Manager: The goal of accounting reports is to measure performance against an absolute standard and the best approximation of that standard is ideal conditions. Cost standards should be comparable to "par" on a golf course. Just as the game of golf uses a handicap system to allow for differences in individual players' skills and scores, it may be necessary for management to interpret variances based on the circumstances that produced the variances. Accordingly, in one case, a given unfavorable variance may represent poor performance; whereas, in another case, it may represent good performance. The managers are just going to have to recognize these subtleties in standard cost systems and depend on upper management to be fair.

Personnel Manager: The key to employee productivity is employee satisfaction and a sense of accomplishment. A set of standards that can never be met denies managers of this vital motivator. The current standards would be appropriate in a laboratory with a controlled environment, but not in the factory with its many variables. If we are to recapture our old "team spirit," we must give the managers a goal that they can achieve through hard work.

Required: Discuss the behavioral issues involved in the Deleware Corp.'s standard cost dilemma. Evaluate each of the three responses (pros and cons) and recommend a course of action.

REVIEW PROBLEM SOLUTION   a)

Standard cost variance analysis

Input component: direct materials   **Output: 5,000 units**

Actual cost		Standard cost of actual inputs		Flexible budget cost	
Actual quantity	21,250	Actual quantity	21,250	Standard quantity allowed	20,000*
Actual price	× $4.90	Standard price	× $5.00	Standard price	× $5.00
	$104,125		$106,250		$100,000

Materials price variance $2,125 F

Materials quantity variance $6,250 U

Total flexible budget materials variance $4,125 U

*Standard quantity of direct materials equals 5,000 units of PGX produced times 4 direct materials units allowed per PGX unit produced.

Standard cost variance analysis

Input component: direct labor   **Output: 5,000 units**

Actual cost		Standard cost of actual inputs		Flexible budget cost	
Actual hours	8,000	Actual hours	8,000	Standard hours allowed	7,500*
Actual rate	× $10.30	Standard rate	× $10.00	Standard rate	× $10.00
	$ 82,400		$ 80,000		$ 75,000

Labor rate variance $2,400 U

Labor efficiency variance $5,000 U

Total flexible budget labor variance $7,400 U

*Standard quantity of labor hours equals 5,000 units of PGX produced times 1.5 direct labor hours allowed per PGX unit produced.

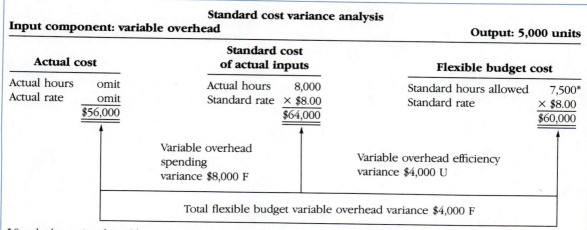

Standard cost variance analysis

Input component: variable overhead   **Output: 5,000 units**

Actual cost		Standard cost of actual inputs		Flexible budget cost	
Actual hours	omit	Actual hours	8,000	Standard hours allowed	7,500*
Actual rate	omit	Standard rate	× $8.00	Standard rate	× $8.00
	$56,000		$64,000		$60,000

Variable overhead spending variance $8,000 F

Variable overhead efficiency variance $4,000 U

Total flexible budget variable overhead variance $4,000 F

* Standard quantity of variable overhead in terms of direct labor hours equals 5,000 units of PGX produced times 1.5 direct labor hours allowed per PGX unit produced. Note that the standard hours allowed of variable overhead will always be the same as the standard direct labor hours when variable overhead has direct labor hours as an activity base.

b)

Toytek, Inc.
Production Department
Standard Cost Performance Report
For the month of March, 19x5

	Actual Costs	Flexible Budget Costs	Flexible Budget Variances	Variance Analysis	
Direct materials	$104,125	$100,000	$4,125 U	$2,125 F	Price Variance
				6,250 U	Quantity Variance
Direct labor	82,400	75,000	7,400 U	2,400 U	Rate Variance
				5,000 U	Efficiency Variance
Variable overhead	56,000	60,000	4,000 F	8,000 F	Spending Variance
				4,000 U	Efficiency Variance
Fixed overhead	32,000	30,000	2,000 U	2,000 U	Budget Variance
Totals	$274,525	$265,000	$9,525 U	$9,525 U	

Control of
Decentralized Operations

Upon completion of this chapter you should:

- Have a general understanding of the organizational theories of centralization and decentralization and be familiar with the advantages and disadvantages of each.

- Be able to compute the following ratios for a decentralized organizational unit: return on investment, investment turnover, and return on sales.

- Understand the problems in decentralized organizations related to defining the investment base and the investment center income.

- Be able to compute residual income for a decentralized organizational unit.

- Be familiar with the relative advantages of the residual income and return on investment methods for evaluating performance in decentralized units.

- Understand the concept of transfer pricing and be familiar with the major transfer pricing bases: market prices, variable costs, variable costs plus opportunity cost, absorption cost plus markup, negotiated prices, and dual prices.

- Understand when and how the use of transfer prices can lead to suboptimization for the organization as a whole.

Organizations that operate in several different industries, or widely dispersed geographic areas, are often segregated into quasi-independent parts. Although a centralized organizational structure is appropriate for many organizations, it has several limitations and is often replaced by a decentralized structure in diverse and complex organizations. The purpose of this chapter is to present techniques used to measure and evaluate the performance of segments of decentralized organizations. The various ways in which such operations can be evaluated, how they interact with each other, and the problems large organizations encounter when they have decentralized operations are all discussed.

The decentralized units normally become quasi-independent, often having their own controller function, computer system, and administrative and marketing staffs. When this occurs, the corporate office faces several problems in keeping the units properly functioning for the benefit of the entire organization. These problem areas are discussed in this chapter.

MANAGEMENT PHILOSOPHIES OF DECENTRALIZED OPERATIONS

To establish a proper framework for *decentralization,* it is necessary to examine some of the issues surrounding *centralization.* **Centralization** exists when the major functions of an organization (such as manufacturing, sales, accounting, computer operations, marketing, research and development, and management control) are controlled by top management. Reasons for centralization include the following:

- Economies of scale—Centralized resources can be more fully utilized than the same resources divided into smaller groupings.

- Sophistication of applications—By combining the firm's resources, greater efficiency may be achieved and more complex tasks performed.

- Improved control—Direct lines of authority provide better control of resources. Improved control permits the organization to rapidly shift resources to achieve changing corporate goals. Centralization also permits a greater perspective by top managers because they are in contact with a larger proportion of activities than if decentralized.

However, centralization does have its limitations, the most significant of which are given below:

- Span of control—After the size of a given function increases to a certain level, it becomes difficult to control from the top of an organization.

- Complexity—Combining activities into large centralized functions may create organizations of such complexity that they become unmanageable.

- Diseconomies of scale—When functions become too large, problems of control and efficiency begin to occur. Almost every organizational function has a point of diminishing returns where adding another employee, work task, or manager does little toward reaching the overall organizational objectives.

Decentralization is the delegation of decision-making authority to successively lower management levels in an organization. The lower in the organization the authority is delegated, the greater the decentralization. This approach offers several advantages that tend to counter the problems of centralization. The most compelling arguments for decentralization are based on the need for management to be more responsive to the various operating units and segments of the organization. The advantages of decentralization include the following:

- First-hand decision making—Personnel closely associated with problems and situations are allowed to make decisions. What's more, experience in decision making at low management levels results in trained managers when higher level positions become available.

- Faster decisions—Decisions are made locally without having to feed information up the chain of command and then wait for a response.
- Specialization—Corporate management can concentrate on strategic planning and policy, and divisional management can concentrate on operating decisions.
- Motivation—Managers who actively participate in decision making are more committed to the success of their programs and are more willing to accept responsibility for the consequences of their actions.

Before accepting decentralization as the answer to organizational problems, its disadvantages must be considered. The primary problems associated with this type of organizational structure are given below:

- Competent personnel—Division management may not be able to carry out and control its operations in accordance with company policy because of a lack of competent personnel.
- Performance measurement—It is difficult to keep all operating units on the same measurement system in a large organization. This includes reporting periods, methods of reporting, and consistency of data collection.
- Suboptimization—It is difficult to keep each unit operating for the benefit of the entire organization rather than for its own selfish benefit.

As organizations expand in size and complexity, centralized control becomes more difficult. Planning, organizing, and controlling may overwhelm top management in a large centralized organization. The solution to this problem is the decentralization of the organization into smaller operating units. With proper planning and staffing of each unit or division, the organization can often overcome the disadvantages of decentralization and improve overall organizational performance.

In most large decentralized organizations, the primary operating units are called divisions. Each division is largely autonomous, with the division manager being responsible for sales, production, and administration of the unit. Division managers frequently have control over all activities, although capital budgeting and long-range planning activities are often limited. These two activities are often centralized within corporate headquarters, with the various division managers given control over the investments once they are made. As generally organized, divisions are the most common example of investment centers.

A decentralized organizational structure is illustrated in Exhibit 9–1. The theory behind this structure is to delegate most responsibilities to each division and let each division operate as a quasi-independent business. You might want to contrast this with the centralized organizational chart in Exhibit 7–2.

The division management group usually includes managers from the computer center, personnel, marketing, controller's office, production, and other necessary functions. One potential problem of such a structure is the conflict

EXHIBIT 9–1   Decentralized Organizational Chart

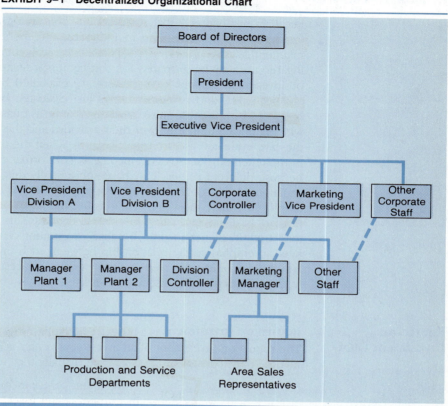

of two superiors. The dashed lines in Exhibit 9–1 represent each staff's responsibility to corporate headquarters, whereas the solid lines connect each staff to the division vice president who has day-to-day authority. For example, the controller has a dual responsibility: (1) to the divisional vice president who exercises line authority and (2) to the corporate controller who exercises functional authority. The divisional controller performs at the division level most of the controllership tasks outlined in Chapter 1. The divisional controller must follow certain firmwide accounting procedures specified by the corporate controller. Sometimes the divisional controller is regarded as an extension of the corporate controller or as a "front-office employee." In this case the divisional controller has a direct-line relationship with the corporate controller and a staff-line relationship with the division manager.

EVALUATION METHODS

Recall from Chapter 7 that responsibility accounting is the structuring of performance reports addressed to individual members of an organization in a manner that emphasizes the factors controllable by them. Responsibility accounting reports may be prepared for cost centers, revenue centers, profit centers, or investment centers. Cost centers are evaluated by comparing actual with allowed costs, and revenue centers are evaluated by comparing actual with budgeted revenues. Because divisions operate as quasi-independent businesses with significant authority over their activities and the size of their investments, they are evaluated as investment centers. When the investment center concept is implemented, the use of net income as a performance measure is not sufficient because different centers may have substantially different asset bases. In these situations net income does not properly reflect the efficient use of the assets employed. Today, most organizations use the *return on investment* ratio as the primary basis for evaluating investment centers. This concept is more relevant than traditional net income because investment center performance reports need to emphasize the relationship between each investment center's income and the size of its asset base. A closely related concept, *residual income,* is also frequently used and is discussed in a later section.

Return on Investment (ROI)

Return on investment is a measure of the earnings per dollar of investment.[1] The return on investment of an investment center is computed by dividing the income of the center by its asset base (usually total assets):

$$ROI = \frac{\text{Investment center income}}{\text{Investment center asset base}}.$$

It can also be computed as investment turnover times the return-on-sales ratio (also called margin, income percentage of revenue, and income-sales ratio):

$$ROI = \text{Investment turnover} \times \text{Return-on-sales ratio},$$

where,

$$\text{Investment turnover} = \frac{\text{Sales}}{\text{Investment center asset base}}, \text{ and}$$

$$\text{Return-on-sales ratio} = \frac{\text{Investment center income}}{\text{Sales}}$$

---

[1] Other similar concepts that are often used to supplement or replace ROI, but are not discussed here, include return on assets, return on net assets, and return on production assets.

When investment turnover is multiplied by the return-on-sales ratio, the product is the same as investment center income divided by investment center asset base:

$$\text{ROI} = \frac{\text{Sales}}{\text{Investment center asset base}} \times \frac{\text{Investment center income}}{\text{Sales}}$$

$$= \frac{\text{Investment center income}}{\text{Investment center asset base}}.$$

Once ROI is computed, it is compared to some previously identified performance criteria, such as the investment center's previous ROI, overall company ROI, the ROI of similar divisions, or the ROI of nonaffiliated companies that operate in similar markets, produce similar products, or provide similar services. The breakdown of ROI into investment turnover and return-on-sales ratio is useful in determining the source of variance in overall performance.

To illustrate the computation and use of ROI, the following information is available concerning the 19x3 operations of the Maine Division of North American Steel:

Sales	$1,200,000
Income	144,000
Investment base	800,000

From these facts ROI can be computed as

$$\text{ROI} = \frac{\text{Investment center income}}{\text{Investment center asset base}}$$

$$= \frac{\$144,000}{\$800,000}$$

$$= 0.18, \text{ or } 18 \text{ percent,}$$

or as

$$\text{ROI} = \frac{\text{Sales}}{\text{Investment center asset base}} \times \frac{\text{Investment center income}}{\text{Sales}}$$

$$= \frac{\$1,200,000}{\$800,000} \times \frac{\$144,000}{\$1,200,000}$$

$$= 1.5 \times 0.12$$

$$= 0.18, \text{ or } 18 \text{ percent.}$$

During 19x3, Maine Division earned a return on its investment base of 18 percent, consisting of an investment turnover of 1.5 times and a return-on-sales ratio of 0.12. Using such an analysis, the company has three measurement criteria with which to evaluate the performance of Maine Division: (1) ROI, (2) investment turnover, and (3) return-on-sales ratio.

For 19x3, North American chose to evaluate its divisions based on company ROI and its interrelated components of investment turnover and income-sales ratio. The information for each division is shown in Exhibit 9–2. Because each division is different in size, the company evaluation standard is not a simple average of the divisions but is based on desired levels of company sales, assets, and income.

Based on ROI, the Tijuana Division had the best performance, Alberta excelled in investment turnover, and Utah had the highest return-on-sales ratio. From Exhibit 9–2 it is obvious that Tijuana had the best year because it was the only division that exceeded each of the company's performance criteria. For 19x3, each division equaled or exceeded the minimum ROI established by the company, even though the component criteria of ROI were not always achieved. For example, Maine Division achieved the minimum ROI even though its return-on-sales ratio was below 0.15. It accomplished this by having an investment turnover that exceeded the minimum by 0.3 (1.5 less 1.2).

To properly evaluate each division the company should study the underlying components of ROI. For the Maine Division, management would want to know why the minimum investment turnover was exceeded while the return-on-sales ratio minimum was not. The Maine Division may have incurred unfavorable cost variances by producing inefficiently. As a result of inefficient production, the return-on-sales ratio declined to a point below the minimum desired level. It is difficult to evaluate a large operating division based on one financial figure. Management should select several key indicators of performance when conducting periodic reviews of its operating segments.

A similar analysis of ROI and its components can be made when planning for future periods. In developing plans for 19x4, management wants to know the possible effect of changes in the major elements of ROI for Maine Division. Sensitivity analysis can be used to predict the impact of changes in sales, the investment center asset base, or investment center income.

Assuming the investment base is unchanged, a projected ROI can be determined for Maine Division for a sales goal of $1,600,000 and an income goal of $160,000:

$$\text{ROI} = \frac{\text{Sales}}{\text{Investment center asset base}} \times \frac{\text{Investment center income}}{\text{Sales}}$$

$$= \frac{\$1,600,000}{\$800,000} \times \frac{\$160,000}{\$1,600,000}$$

$$= 2.0 \times 0.10$$

$$= 0.20, \text{ or } 20 \text{ percent.}$$

EXHIBIT 9–2   Division Evaluation Data

North American Steel
Performance Measures
For the year ended June 30, 19x3

		Performance Measures	
	ROI	Investment Turnover	Return-on-Sales Ratio
Operating unit:			
Maine division	0.18	1.5	0.12
Alberta division	0.24	3.0	0.08
Utah division	0.22	1.1	0.20
Tijuana division	0.27	1.5	0.18
Average	0.21	1.4	0.15
Company performance criteria:			
Projected minimums	0.18	1.2	0.15

Note that ROI increased from 18 to 20 percent, even though the return-on-sales ratio decreased from 12 to 10 percent. The change in turnover from 1.5 to 2.0 more than offset the reduced return-on-sales ratio.

Starting from Maine's 19x3 performance, now assume that projected operating efficiencies reduce expenses by $12,000, and that sales remain constant, thereby increasing income to $156,000. The ROI increases from 18 percent to 19.5 percent:

$$\text{ROI} = \frac{\text{Sales}}{\text{Investment center asset base}} \times \frac{\text{Investment center income}}{\text{Sales}}$$

$$= \frac{\$1,200,000}{\$800,000} \times \frac{\$156,000}{\$1,200,000}$$

$$= 1.5 \times 0.13$$

$$= 0.195, \text{ or } 19.5 \text{ percent.}$$

Sensitivity analysis may involve changing only one factor in the ROI model or a combination of factors. When more than one factor is changed, the user must be careful to properly analyze exactly how much change is caused by each factor.

Management may desire a minimum ROI. In this case the major elements of the ROI model can be manipulated to determine the best way to meet this minimum. If, for example, ROI is set at 24 percent, it may be obtained by changing only the investment base (from $800,000 to $600,000):

$$\text{ROI} = \frac{\text{Sales}}{\text{Investment center asset base}} \times \frac{\text{Investment center income}}{\text{Sales}}$$

$$= \frac{\$1,200,000}{\$600,000} \times \frac{\$144,000}{\$1,200,000}$$

$$= 2.0 \times 0.12$$

$$= 0.24, \text{ or } 24 \text{ percent.}$$

Or it may be obtained by changing a combination of the investment base (from $800,000 to $900,000) and income (from $144,000 to $216,000):

$$\text{ROI} = \frac{\text{Sales}}{\text{Investment center asset base}} \times \frac{\text{Investment center income}}{\text{Sales}}$$

$$= \frac{\$1,200,000}{\$900,000} \times \frac{\$216,000}{\$1,200,000}$$

$$= 1.333 \times 0.18$$

$$= 0.24, \text{ or } 24 \text{ percent.}$$

It may also be obtained by changing any combination of the three factors, together or separately.

Statistics such as ROI, investment turnover, and return-on-sales ratio mean little by themselves. They take on meaning only when compared with an objective, a trend, another division, a competitor, or an industry average. Many businesses establish minimum ROIs for each of their divisions, which are expected to attain or exceed this minimum return. The salaries, bonuses, and promotions of division managers may be tied directly to the ROI of their divisions. Without other evaluation techniques, managers often strive for ROI maximization, sometimes to the long-run detriment of the entire organization.

Investment Base. Despite the relevance and conceptual simplicity of ROI, a division's ROI cannot be computed until management determines how divisional investment and income are to be measured. Because the primary purpose for computing ROI is to evaluate the effectiveness of a division's operating management in using the assets entrusted to them, most organizations define investment as the average total assets of a division during the evaluation period.

For most companies the investment base is limited to each division's operating assets. These normally include those assets held for productive use as well as cash, accounts receivable, inventory, and plant and equipment. Nonproductive assets, such as land for a future plant site, would not be included in the investment base of a division, only for the company.

Corporate cash and receivables are sometimes held by corporate headquarters, which permits more efficiency in billings and collections. This enables the corporation to hold a smaller total amount of cash than would be required if each division had its own bank account. Although it is relatively easy to assign receivables held by corporate headquarters to divisions (on the basis of their origin) for ROI computations, the assignment of cash presents some problems. Because of operating economies, the total cash requirements of the entire organization are less than the cash requirements of all divisions acting as independent units. However, assigning cash on the basis of the division's independent cash needs is likely to raise objections. The best approach seems to be to allocate cash based on the amount of incremental cash needed to support each division as compared to the company as a whole; nevertheless, cash allocations are most frequently based on relative sales or cash expenditures.

The next problem relates to general corporate assets. It is not advisable to allocate the cost of physical assets utilized by corporate headquarters to the operating divisions. Though the divisions might need additional administrative facilities if they were truly independent, they have no control over the headquarter's facilities. Additionally, the joint nature and use of these facilities make any allocation arbitrary.

One of the problems with the comparisons of ROI among divisions is the difference in the historical cost of each division's assets. It is somewhat difficult to compare a division whose asset base is measured in 1985 dollars with one that has most of its asset base measured in 1974 dollars. To overcome this problem, many companies require all divisions to use some common dollar base.

Investment Center Income. Divisional income is equal to divisional revenues less divisional operating expenses. Except for service expenses that can be clearly identified with the activities of individual divisions (such as the variable costs of processing accounts receivable), the expenses of operating corporate headquarters should not be allocated to the division for ROI purposes. Some managers advocate not allocating even if the absence of corporate headquarters would cause divisions to incur additional expenses. In many decentralized operations, corporate general and administrative expenses are often allocated to divisions for internal reporting purposes, but they are excluded when computing divisional ROI.

Some companies allocate all expenses in determining ROI based on management's belief that these expenses represent the value of services rendered by the home office. Other managers believe that allocated expenses should not be included because division management has no control over the incurrence or allocation of headquarters' expenses. Also, the allocations are often for items of questionable value to the division, such as the corporation's legal costs.

Generally, such allocations are not included in the computation of divisional ROI. Only expenses directly associated with the division should be included in ROI computations. An example of a directly associated cost is the advertising expense of products only produced by the division. The amount of expenses allocated should be approximately the same as it would be if the division had incurred the services on its own. If allocated corporate costs are substantially greater than a division's independently incurred costs would be, costs are allocated in excess of benefits received, a very undesirable situation.

Asset Measurement.   Once divisional investment and income have been operationally defined and ROI computations have been made, the significance of the resulting ratios may still be questioned. Return on investment may be overstated in terms of constant dollars because inflation and arbitrary depreciation procedures cause an undervaluation of the inventory and fixed assets included in the investment center asset base. Asset measurement is particularly troublesome if inventories are valued at last-in, first-out (LIFO) cost and fixed assets were acquired many years ago. A division manager may hesitate to replace an old inefficient asset with a new efficient one because the replacement may lower income and ROI through an increased investment base and increased depreciation.

To improve the comparability between divisions' old and new assets, some firms value assets at original cost rather than at net book value (cost less accumulated depreciation) in ROI computations. This procedure does not reflect inflation, however. An old asset that cost $120,000 ten years ago is still being compared with an asset that costs $200,000 today. A better solution might be to value old assets at their replacement cost, although obtaining replacement cost data can be a problem. This raises issues about the cost and value of information and about whether or not the old asset would be replaced in kind at today's prices.

Residual Income

Residual income is an often-mentioned alternative for measuring investment center performance. **Residual income** is the excess of investment center income over the minimum return set by the corporation. The minimum return is computed as a percentage of the investment center's asset base. When residual income is the primary basis of evaluation, the management of each investment center is encouraged to maximize residual income rather than ROI.

To illustrate the computation, assume a company requires a minimum return of 12 percent on each division's investment base. The residual income of a division of the company that has an annual net operating income of $200,000 and an investment base of $1,500,000 is $20,000:

Division income	$200,000
Minimum return ($1,500,000 × 0.12)	−180,000
Residual income	$ 20,000

Many executives view residual income as a better measure of performance than ROI. They believe that residual income encourages managers to make profitable investments that would otherwise be rejected by managers who are being measured by ROI. To illustrate, assume that two divisions of Color Company have an opportunity to make an investment of $100,000 that will generate a return of 20 percent. The manager of Green Division is evaluated using ROI, and the manager of Orange Division is evaluated using residual income. The current ROI of each division is 24 percent, and each division has a current income of $120,000 and a minimum rate of 18 percent on invested capital. If each division has a current investment base of $500,000, the effect of the proposed investment on each division's performance is as follows:

	Current	+	Proposed	=	Total
Green division:					
Investment center income / Asset base	$120,000 / $500,000		$ 20,000 / $100,000		$140,000 / $600,000
ROI	0.24 or 24 percent		0.20 or 20 percent		0.233 or 23.3 percent
Orange division:					
Asset base	$500,000		$100,000		$600,000
Investment center income	$120,000		$ 20,000		$140,000
Minimum return (0.18 × base)	− 90,000		− 18,000		−108,000
Residual income	$ 30,000		$ 2,000		$ 32,000

Since the performance of the Green Division is being measured according to the best rate of return that can be generated, the manager will not want to make the new investment because it reduces the current ROI of 24 percent to 23.3 percent. This is true, even though the company's minimum return is only 18 percent. Not wanting to explain a decline in the division's ROI, the manager will probably reject the opportunity even though it may have benefited the company as a whole.

The Orange Division manager will probably be happy to accept the new project because it increases residual income by $2,000. Any investment that provides a return greater than the required minimum of 18 percent will be acceptable to the Orange Division manager. Given a profit maximization goal for the organization, the residual income method is preferred because it encourages division managers to accept all projects with returns above the 18 percent cutoff.

The primary disadvantage of the residual income method is that it measures performance in dollars. It cannot be used to compare the performance of divisions of different sizes; for example, the residual income of a multimillion dollar sales division would be expected to be larger than that of a half-million dollar sales division.

TRANSFER PRICING

Transfer pricing is used when products or services are exchanged between quasi-independent units of an organization. A **transfer price** is the internal value assigned a product or service that one division provides to another. Transfer-pricing transactions normally occur between profit or investment centers rather than between cost centers of an organization.

The objective of transfer pricing is to transmit financial data between departments or divisions of a company as they use each other's goods and services. Transfer-pricing systems are normally used in decentralized operations to determine whether organizational objectives are being achieved in each division. For division managers to be accountable for all transactions, both external and internal, transfer prices must be determined for the internal transfers of goods and services.

Management Considerations

The desire of the selling and buying divisions of the same company to maximize their individual performance measures often creates transfer-pricing problems. Acting as independent units, the divisions may take actions that are not in the best interest of the organization as a whole. The three examples that follow illustrate the need for the organization to maintain a corporate profit-maximizing viewpoint while attempting to allow divisional autonomy and responsibility.

Rex Manufacturing has five divisions that interchange products and product components with each other. Assume that Division 6 manufactures two products, Alpha and Beta. Alpha is sold externally for $50 per unit and Beta is transferred to Division 13 for $60 per unit. The costs associated with the two products are shown below:

	Product	
	Alpha	Beta
Direct materials	$15	$14
Direct labor	5	10
Variable manufacturing overhead	5	16
Fixed manufacturing overhead	6	15
Variable selling	4	—
Total	$35	$55

A proposal has just been received from another company to supply Division 13 with a substitute product similar to Beta at a price of $52. From the company's viewpoint, this is merely a make-or-buy decision. The relevant costs are the differential outlay costs of the alternative actions. If the fixed manufacturing costs of Division 6 cannot be reduced, the relevant costs are as follows:

Buy		$52
Make:		
Direct materials	$14	
Direct labor	10	
Variable manufacturing	16	−40
Difference favors making		$12

The decision for Division 13's management is basically one of cost minimization—buy from the source that charges the lowest price. If Division 6 cannot transfer at a price of $52 or less, the management of Division 13 may go to the external supplier so that the division's profits can be maximized. Although Division 13's managers are concerned about the cost of Beta, they are also concerned about the quality of the goods. If the $52 product is inferior in quality, Division 13's management may decide to buy from Division 6 at the higher price.

Prior to Division 13's receipt of the external offer to buy Beta for $52 per unit, Division 6 had been transferring Beta for $60. For Division 6 this is a decision to reduce the contribution margin of Beta and therefore lower divisional profits or find an alternative use of its resources. Of course, corporate management may intervene and require the internal transfer.

For the second example, assume that Division 6 can either transfer Beta to Division 13 or sell an equivalent amount externally for $60 per unit. Now the decision for Division 6's management is simple—sell to the buyer willing to pay the most.

To examine a slightly different transfer-pricing conflict, assume that Division 6 can sell all the Alpha that it can produce (it is operating at capacity). While there is no external market for Beta, there is a one-to-one trade-off between the production of Alpha and Beta. They both use equal amounts of the limited capacity of Division 6.

The corporation still regards this as a make-or-buy decision, but the costs of producing Beta have changed. Beta now includes an outlay cost and an opportunity cost. The outlay cost is the variable cost of $40 ($14 + $10 + $16) computed above. The opportunity cost is the net benefit forgone if the limited capacity of Division 6 is used to produce Beta rather than Alpha:

Selling price of Alpha		$50
Outlay costs of Alpha:		
Direct materials	$15	
Direct labor	5	
Variable manufacturing overhead	5	
Variable selling	4	−29
Opportunity cost of making Beta		$21

Accordingly, the relevant costs in the make-or-buy decision are as shown below:

Make:		
Outlay cost of Beta	$40	
Opportunity cost of Beta	21	$61
Buy		$52

Product Beta should be purchased from the outside supplier. If there were no outside suppliers, the relevant cost of manufacturing Beta would still be $61—which is another way of saying that Beta should not be produced and processed further in Division 13 unless the resultant revenues cover all outlay costs (including the $40 in Division 6) and provide a contribution of at least $21 ($61 − $40). *From the viewpoint of the corporation, the relevant costs in a make-or-buy decision are the external price, the outlay costs of manufacture, and the opportunity cost to manufacture.* The opportunity cost is zero if there is excess capacity.

Determining Transfer Prices

As illustrated above, the transfer price of goods or services may be subject to much controversy. Although a price must be agreed upon for each item or service transferred between divisions, the selection of the pricing method is dependent upon many factors. The conditions surrounding the transfer determines which of the alternative methods discussed below is selected.

In considering each method, observe that each transfer results in a revenue entry on the books of the supplier and a cost entry on the books of the receiver. Transfers may be considered as sales by the supplier and as purchases by the receiver. Although no method is likely to be ideal, one must be selected if the profit or investment center concept is used.

Market Price. When there is an existing market with established prices for an intermediate product and the transfer actions of the company will not affect prices, market prices are ideal transfer prices. If divisions are free to buy and sell outside the firm, the use of market prices preserves divisional autonomy and leads divisions to act in a manner that maximizes corporate goal congruence. Unfortunately, not all product transfers have equivalent external markets. Furthermore, the divisions should carefully evaluate whether the market price is competitive or controlled by one or two large companies.

When there are substantial selling expenses associated with outside sales, many firms specify the transfer price as market price less selling expenses. The internal sale may not require the incurrence of costs to get and fill the order.

To illustrate, assume that product Alpha of Division 6 can be sold competitively at $50 per unit or transferred to Division 24 for additional processing. Under most situations, Division 6 will never sell Alpha for less than $50, and Division 24 will likewise never pay more than $50 for it. However, if any variable expenses related to marketing and shipping can be eliminated by divisional transfers, these costs are generally subtracted from the competitive market price. In our illustration, where variable selling expenses are $4 for Alpha, the transfer price could be reduced to $46 ($50 − $4). A price between $46 and $50 would probably be better than either extreme price. To the extent that these transfer prices represent a near competitive situation, the profitability of each division can then be evaluated fairly.

Variable Costs. If there is excess capacity in the supplying division, establishing a transfer price equal to variable costs leads the purchasing division to act in a manner that is optimal from the corporation's viewpoint. The buying division has the corporation's variable cost as its own variable cost as it enters the external market. Unfortunately, establishing the transfer price at variable cost causes the supplying division to report zero profits or a loss equal to any fixed costs. If excess capacity does not exist, establishing a transfer price at variable cost may not lead to optimal action because the supplying division may have to forgo sales that include a markup for fixed costs and profits. If Beta could be sold externally for $60, Division 6 would not want to transfer Beta to Division 13 for a $40 transfer price based on the following variable costs:

Direct materials	$14
Direct labor	10
Variable manufacturing overhead	16
Total variable costs	$40

Division 6 would much rather sell outside the company for $60, which covers variable costs and provides for a profit contribution margin of $20:

Selling price of Beta	$60
Variable costs	−40
Contribution margin	$20

Variable Costs Plus Opportunity Costs. From the viewpoint of the corporation this is the optimal transfer price. Because all relevant costs are included in the transfer price, the purchasing division is led to act in an optimal manner regardless of whether or not excess capacity exists.

With excess capacity in the supplying division, the transfer price is the variable cost per unit. Without excess capacity the transfer price is the sum of the variable and opportunity costs. Following this rule in the above example, if Division 6 had excess capacity, the transfer price of Beta would be set at Beta's variable costs of $40 per unit. At this transfer price, Division 13 would buy Beta internally rather than externally at $52 per unit. If Division 6 cannot sell Beta externally, but can sell all the Alpha it can produce and is operating at capacity, the transfer price per unit would be set at $61, the sum of Beta's variable and opportunity costs ($40 + $21) computed previously. At this transfer price, Division 13 would buy Betas externally for $52. In both situations, the management of Division 13 has acted in accordance with the profit-maximizing goal of the organization.

However, there are two problems with this method. First, when the supplying division has excess capacity, establishing the transfer price at variable cost causes the supplying division to report zero profits or a loss equal to any fixed costs. Second, it is difficult to determine opportunity costs when the supplying division produces several products. If the problems with the previously mentioned transfer-pricing methods are too great, three other methods are available: absorption cost plus markup, negotiated prices, and dual prices.

Absorption Costs Plus Markup.   According to absorption costing, all variable and fixed manufacturing costs are product costs. Pricing internal transfers at *absorption cost* eliminates the supplying division's reported loss on each product that may occur using a variable cost transfer price. *Absorption cost plus markup* provides the supplying division with a contribution toward unallocated costs. In "cost plus" transfer pricing, "cost" should be defined as standard cost rather than actual cost. This prevents the supplying division from passing on the cost of inefficient operations to other divisions, and it allows the buying division to know its cost in advance of purchase. Even though cost plus transfer prices may not maximize company profits, they are widely used. Their popularity stems from several factors including ease of implementation, justifiability, and perceived fairness. Once everyone agrees on "absorption cost plus markup" pricing rules, internal disputes are minimized.

Negotiated Prices.   Negotiated transfer prices are used when the supplying and buying divisions independently agree on a price. Like market-based transfer prices, negotiated transfer prices are believed to preserve divisional autonomy. Negotiated transfer prices may lead to some suboptimal decisions, but this is regarded as a small price to pay for other benefits of decentralization. When negotiated transfer prices are used, some corporations establish arbitration procedures to help settle disputes between divisions. However, the existence of an arbitrator with any real or perceived authority reduces divisional autonomy.

Negotiated prices should have market prices as their ceiling and variable costs as their floor. Although frequently used where there is an external market for the product or component, the most common use of negotiated prices is where no identical-product external market exists. Negotiations may start with a floor price plus add-ons such as overhead and profit markups, or it may start with a ceiling price less adjustments for selling and administrative expenses and allowances for quantity discounts. Where no identical-product external market exists, the market price for a similar completed product may be used less the estimated cost of completing the product from the transfer stage to the completed stage.

Assume that service EDProcessing is transferred from Consulting Division to Auditing Division. There is no comparable external market, but Consulting Division provides a similar service, DPConsult, which is billed externally for $132 an hour. The cost to Consulting Division for service EDProcessing is as follows:

Direct labor	$35
Direct materials	10
Variable overhead	30
Direct costs	$75
Fixed overhead (estimated)	20
Total	$95

The managers of the Consulting and Auditing divisions decide to negotiate a fee for the service using a ceiling of $132. Consulting's management recognizes that the additional direct labor of service DPConsult is $12 per hour more than for service EDProcessing and thereby offers service EDProcessing for $120 per hour to Auditing. Auditing argues that the fixed overhead needs to be adjusted or maybe even eliminated. Consulting finally agrees to reduce the fixed overhead by 20 percent. The final transfer price (fee) of service EDProcessing to Auditing is $109 based on the following analysis:

Direct labor	$ 35
Direct materials	10
Variable overhead	30
Fixed overhead	16
Total costs	$ 91
Profit margin (20%)	18
Transfer price	$109

The transfer price of $109 is between the variable cost to produce, $75, and the adjusted external fee of $120. Auditing accepts the fee because it appears fair, and Consulting accepts the price because it exceeds variable costs and provides an adequate contribution margin. If the Consulting Division has idle capacity, Auditing should also argue that the fixed items be eliminated because they will not change if the service is provided.

Dual Prices. Dual prices exist when a company allows a difference in the supplier's transfer price and the receiver's transfer price for the same product. This method allegedly minimizes internal squabbles of division managers and problems of conflicting divisional goals. The supplier's price normally approximates market price, which allows the selling division to show a "normal" profit on items that it transfers internally. The receiver's price is usually variable cost or absorption cost. Dual prices eliminate the receiver's need for covering internally transferred profits when the final external price is established. The receiver is also allowed to make a profit from the final product that was transferred in.

Applying Transfer Pricing

Once transfer prices have been determined, they can be used to record interdivisional sales. Although most divisional income statements are very complex, the following illustrations concentrate only on the elements related to the transfer of goods and services. Leigh Ann's Fashions, a dress manufacturer, has two divisions, Sewing and Sales. The Sewing Division sells to the Sales Division and to other distributors. Sales buys from no one but Sewing. During the first quarter of 19x7 the Sewing Division incurred the following unit costs:

Direct materials	$ 8
Direct labor	5
Variable manufacturing overhead	3
Variable selling	1
Total	$17

Total production for the quarter was 30,000 dresses, of which 20,000 were sold to the Sales Division for $20 each. External sales were $25 for each dress. There were no beginning or ending inventories. Fixed manufacturing overhead for the quarter totaled $60,000.

After the Sales Division receives the dresses, they affix private labels where necessary and then package and ship to retail customers. The variable unit costs are $4, and the Sales Division incurs $40,000 in fixed costs each quarter. The Sales Division sold all dresses received during the first quarter for $30 each.

Exhibit 9–3 provides a simple illustration of how transfer pricing affects each division's income statement and the company as a whole. The 20,000 units transferred from Sewing to Sales shows up as $400,000 of internal sales for Sewing and as $400,000 of transferred-in cost to Sales. Note that both amounts are ignored for the overall company income statement. The reason for this elimination at the company level is the desire to provide external users of financial statements information related to economic activities with outside parties and not internal transfers.

Now assume Sales is allowed to buy from outside suppliers. An outside supplier has offered to sell the Sales Division dresses of similar style and quality for $18. The Sewing Division's management is offered the option of reducing its transfer price to $18, but it refuses even though Sewing has no other use for the production capacity. The Sales Division's management contends that Sewing

EXHIBIT 9–3   Divisional and Company Income Statements, Internal Transfer

Leigh Ann's Fashions
Divisional and Company Income Statements
First Quarter, 19x7

	Sewing Division	Sales Division	Company
Sales:			
External*	$250,000	$600,000	$850,000
Internal**	400,000	—	—
Total	$650,000	$600,000	$850,000
Variable costs:			
Incurred†	$510,000	$ 80,000	$590,000
Transferred-in‡	—	400,000	—
Total	−510,000	−480,000	−590,000
Contribution margin	$140,000	$120,000	$260,000
Fixed costs	− 60,000	− 40,000	−100,000
Net income	$ 80,000	$ 80,000	$160,000

* 10,000 units × $25 = $250,000, and 20,000 units × $30 = $600,000.

** 20,000 units × $20 = $400,000.

† 30,000 units × $17 = $510,000, and 20,000 units × $4 = $80,000.

‡ Transferred-in costs is the same as internal sales.

will have a markup of $2 on each dress because its variable selling cost is not necessary for internal sales, but Sewing's management disagrees. Note in Exhibit 9–4 that the company and the Sewing Division had a lower net income when the Sales Division purchased outside, but the Sales Division increased its income by $40,000 when it bought internally from the Sewing Division.

Finally, assume that Sewing is willing to negotiate a transfer price with Sales for $18. The resulting income statements for each division and the company as a whole are illustrated in Exhibit 9–5. Comparing Exhibits 9–3 and 9–5, the income to the company remains the same when there are internal transfers even though the transfer price changes from $20 to $18. However, the divisional incomes change by increasing one and reducing the other. No doubt the management of Sales is pleased to have the outside competition because its income increases under each alternative.

These examples illustrate that transfer prices affect the profitability of divisions and the evaluations of the division managers. By simply adjusting the transfer price, the Sewing Division's income is reduced from $80,000 to $40,000, a substantial difference for evaluation purposes.

EXHIBIT 9–4   Divisional and Company Income Statements, External Supplier

Leigh Ann's Fashions
Divisional and Company Income Statements
First Quarter, 19x7

	Sewing Division	Sales Division	Company
Sales:			
External*	$250,000	$600,000	$850,000
Internal	—	—	—
Total	$250,000	$600,000	$850,000
Variable costs:			
Incurred**	$170,000	$ 80,000	$250,000
External purchases†	—	360,000	360,000
Total	−170,000	−440,000	−610,000
Contribution margin	$ 80,000	$160,000	$240,000
Fixed costs	− 60,000	− 40,000	−100,000
Net income	$ 20,000	$120,000	$140,000

* 10,000 units × $25 = $250,000, and 20,000 units × $30 = $600,000.

** 10,000 units × $17 = $170,000, and 20,000 units × $4 = $80,000.

† 20,000 units × $18 = $360,000.

EXHIBIT 9–5   Divisional and Company Income Statements

Leigh Ann's Fashions
Divisional and Company Income Statements
First Quarter, 19x7

	Sewing Division	Sales Division	Company
Sales:			
External*	$250,000	$600,000	$850,000
Internal**	360,000	—	—
Total	$610,000	$600,000	$850,000
Variable costs:			
Incurred†	$510,000	$ 80,000	$590,000
Transferred-in‡	—	360,000	—
Total	−510,000	−440,000	−590,000
Contribution margin	$100,000	$160,000	$260,000
Fixed costs	− 60,000	− 40,000	−100,000
Net income	$ 40,000	$120,000	$160,000

* 10,000 units × $25 = $250,000, and 20,000 units × $30 = $600,000.

** 20,000 units × $18 = $360,000.

† 30,000 units × $17 = $510,000, and 20,000 units × $4 = $80,000.

‡ Transferred-in costs is the same as internal sales.

It is often necessary to determine the impact of transfer prices on a company to fully assess the results of decisions involving transfer pricing. Depending on how these types of decision are resolved, divisional managers are often very pleased or displeased with the reporting system and responsibility accounting.

SUBOPTIMIZATION

A transfer-pricing problem exists when divisions, acting in their own best interest, set transfer prices or make decisions based on transfer prices that are not in the best interest of the organization as a whole. The seriousness of the transfer-pricing problem depends on the extent to which the affairs of divisions are intertwined. When intermediate products have established markets and divisions are free to buy and sell outside the firm, the use of market prices avoids the transfer-pricing problem.

A potential transfer-pricing problem exists when divisions exchange goods or services for which there is not an established market. If the actual or potential amount of such transfers is relatively small, the use of cost-plus or negotiated prices seems most appropriate. The benefits of decentralization are believed to more than offset any loss of profit on individual products.

Though suboptimization may be tolerated on some products to obtain the benefits of decentralization, the transfer-pricing problem sometimes becomes so severe that cost and revenue centers should be used in place of investment or profit centers. Consider a single-product firm that attempts to operate its manufacturing and marketing activities as separate profit or investment centers. The affairs of these two divisions cannot be disentangled, and any attempt to do so will reduce the profits of the entire business.

The ideal solutions for the supplying division and for the buying division generally conflict. From the organization's perspective, the desired transfers may not occur because the division managers, pursuing their own best interests, could decide against a transfer. These conflicts sometimes are overcome by having a higher ranking manager impose a transfer price and insist that a transfer be made. But the managers of divisions in an organization that has a policy of decentralization often regard these orders as undermining their autonomy. So the imposition of a price may solve the goal congruence and incentive problem but exacerbate the autonomy problem. Transfer pricing thus becomes a problem with no ideal solutions.

It has been pointed out that there is seldom a single transfer price that will meet all the criteria for inducing top management's desired decisions. The best transfer price depends on the circumstances at hand. Furthermore, the optimal price for either division may differ from that employed for external needs, including tax requirements.

SUMMARY

When an organization expands in size, management must decide whether to adopt a centralized or decentralized structure. As individual units within an organization become large enough to be separately evaluated as quasi-independent businesses, management generally decides to decentralize its operations into investment centers. During such a change, sound practices of responsibility accounting must be developed.

The selection of the evaluation method to be used for each responsibility center is generally determined by what the center can realistically be responsible for in its operations. Centers that receive no revenues can hardly be labeled profit centers, but centers that have unique product lines sold externally can be considered profit or investment centers.

To properly evaluate each responsibility center, management must select some type of measurement system. The two most popular methods of evaluating investment center performance are return on investment (ROI) and residual income. In most situations, it is recommended that both methods be used if feasible.

Organizations that have internal transfers between profit or investment centers are faced with using transfer pricing and its related problems of goal congruence. Although there are no easy solutions to transfer-pricing problems, several workable alternatives were discussed in this chapter.

KEY TERMS

Centralization   Return on investment
Decentralization   Transfer price
Residual income

REVIEW QUESTIONS

9–1   What are the primary advantages of having a centralized organizational structure?

9–2   What are the primary advantages of having a decentralized organizational structure?

9–3   What criteria should management use when changing from one organizational structure to the other?

9–4   How can the problems of decentralization be minimized?

9–5   For what purpose do organizations use return on investment? Why is this measure preferred to net income?

9–6   How does residual income assist in the evaluation process?

9–7   List the elements in the ROI equation and tell how they are related.

9–8   How is an investment center's asset based determined?

9–9   How is overhead allocated to divisions using ROI? Why?

9–10   What information does residual income provide that ROI does not?

9–11   Should rates of return for each division using residual income be the same? Why? How are they determined?

9–12   In what types of organizations and for what purpose are transfer prices used?

9–13   What problems arise when transfer pricing is used?

9–14   From the viewpoint of the corporation, what is the best method of transfer pricing? What problems may limit the use of this method?

9–15   When do transfer prices lead to suboptimization? How can suboptimization be minimized? Can it be eliminated? Why or why not?

REVIEW PROBLEM

ROI and Residual Income

Parent Company, a decentralized organization, has three divisions, X, Y, and Z. Corporate management desires a minimum return of 15 percent on its investments.

The divisions' 19x8 results were as follows:

Division	Income	Investment
X	$30,000	$200,000
Y	50,000	250,000
Z	22,000	100,000

The company is planning an expansion project that will cost $50,000 and return $9,000 per year.

Requirements

a) Compute the ROI for each division for 19x8.

b) Compute the residual income for each division for 19x8.

c) Rank the divisions according to their ROI and residual income.

d) Assume other income and investments will remain unchanged. Determine the effect of adding the new project on each division's ROI and residual income.

The solution to this problem is found at the end of the Chapter 9 exercises and problems.

EXERCISES

9–1 ROI: Basic Computations

Salmon Company uses return on investment as one of the evaluation tools for division managers.
Selected operating data for three divisions of the company are given below.

	East Division	West Division	Central Division
Sales	$600,000	$750,000	$900,000
Operating assets	300,000	250,000	350,000
Net operating income	51,000	56,000	59,000

Requirements

a) Compute the return on investment for each division. (Round answers to three decimal places.)

b) Which divisional manager is doing the best job based on ROI? Why?

9–2 ROI: Basic Computations

Flexy Corporation allows its divisions to operate as autonomous units. The operating data for 19x4 are presented below:

	Lex Division	Rex Division	Tex Division
Sales	$4,500,000	$1,000,000	$9,600,000
Operating assets	2,000,000	800,000	3,500,000
Net operating income	440,000	120,000	980,000

Requirements

a) Compute each division's return on investment.

b) Which division has the best performance based on ROI?

c) What other factors should be considered in making an overall evaluation of the most effective division manager?

9–3 ROI and Residual Income: Basic Computations

The three divisions of the Atta Moore Company had the following results for 19x6:

	Division A	Division B	Division C
Sales	$60,000	$80,000	$100,000
Operating income	9,000	9,500	10,000
Investment base	60,000	61,000	62,000

The company has a minimum desired rate of return on investment of 15 percent.

Requirements

a) Compute each division's return on investment. (Round answers to three decimal places.)

b) Compute each division's residual income.

9–4 ROI and Residual Income: Basic Computations

The Firebird Division of Central Motors had an operating income of $90,000 and net assets of $400,000. Central Motors has a target rate of return of 16 percent.

Requirements

a) Compute the return on investment.

b) Compute the residual income.

9–5 ROI and Residual Income: Impact of a New Investment

From Exercise 9–4, Firebird has an opportunity to increase operating income by $20,000 with an investment in assets of $85,000.

Requirements

a) Compute the Firebird Division's return on investment if the project is undertaken. (Round your answer to three decimal places.)

b) Compute the Firebird Division's residual income if the project is undertaken.

9–6 ROI and Residual Income: Impact of a New Investment

The Aspirin Division of International Drugs reported an operating income of $2,100,000 for 19x3 with an investment of $9,000,000. The division manager desires to know the effect on the division's performance of an incremental investment of $6,000,000, which will increase annual operating income by $900,000 per year.

Required: Determine the impact of the new investment on ROI and residual income. Assume that an 18 percent return on investment is considered acceptable. (Round calculations to three decimal places.)

9–7 ROI: Fill in the Blanks

Provide the missing data in the following situations:

	Division K	Division L	Division M
Sales	$?	$5,000,000	$?
Net operating income	$100,000	$ 200,000	$144,000
Operating assets	$?	$?	$800,000
Return on investment	16%	10%	?
Return-on-sales ratio	0.04	?	0.12
Investment turnover	?	?	1.5

9–8 ROI: Fill in the Blanks

Provide the missing data in the following situations:

	Sun Division	Star Division	Moon Division
Sales	$4,000,000	$?	$900,000
Operating assets	$1,000,000	$?	$?
Net operating income	$?	$500,000	$180,000
Return-on-sales ratio	0.10	0.05	?
Investment turnover	?	2.0	?
Return on investment	?	?	0.20

9–9 ROI and Residual Income with Different Bases

Basic Company requires a return on capital of 12 percent. The following financial information is available for 19x8:

	Division 200 Value Base		Division 300 Value Base		Division 400 Value Base	
	Book	Current	Book	Current	Book	Current
Sales	$100,000	$100,000	$200,000	$200,000	$800,000	$800,000
Income	12,000	10,000	16,000	17,000	50,000	52,000
Assets	60,000	80,000	90,000	100,000	600,000	580,000

Requirements

a) Compute return on investment using both book and current values for each division. (Round answers to three decimal places.)

b) Compute residual income for both book and current values for each division.

c) Does book value or current value provide the better basis for performance evaluation? Which division do you consider the most successful?

9–10 ROI and Residual Income with Different Bases

Forward Trinket Company is considering evaluating its divisions on both a historical and replacement cost basis. The following information is available for 19x1:

	Assets		Income	
Division	Book Value	Replacement Value	Book Value	Replacement Value
Trinket	$ 600,000	$ 900,000	$120,000	$110,000
Gadget	700,000	700,000	120,000	120,000
Widget	1,000,000	1,400,000	200,000	180,000

The company has a minimum desired rate of 15 percent.

Requirements

a) Compute return on investment using book value and replacement value amounts for each division. (Round your answer to two decimal places.)

b) Compute residual income using book value and replacement value amounts for each division.

c) Does book value or replacement value provide the better basis for performance evaluation? Which division do you consider the most successful?

9–11 Transfer Pricing and Divisional Gross Profit

Leitch Consulting Company has two divisions, Tax Consultants and Financial Consultants. In addition to their external sales, each division performs work for the other division. The external fees earned by each division in 19x0 were $400,000 for Tax Consultants and $700,000 for Financial Consultants. Tax Consultants worked 3,000 hours for Financial Consultants and Financial Consultants worked 1,200 hours for Tax Consultants. The costs of services performed were $220,000 for Tax Consultants and $480,000 for Financial Consultants.

Requirements

a) Determine the gross profit for each division and for the company as a whole if the transfer price from Tax to Financial is $30 per hour and the transfer price from Financial to Tax is $25 per hour.

b) Determine the gross profit for each division and for the company as a whole if the transfer price from each division is $30 per hour.

c) What are the gross profit results for the divisions and the company as a whole if the two divisions net their hours and charge a transfer fee of $25 per excess hour? Which division manager would favor this arrangement?

9–12 Transfer Pricing and Divisional Gross Profit

Greenwood Paper Company has two divisions. The Pulp Division prepares the wood for processing. The Paper Division processes the pulp into paper. No inventories exist in either division at the beginning of 19x3. During the year, the Pulp Division prepared 40,000 cords of wood at a cost of $240,000. All the pulp was transferred to the Paper Division where additional operating costs of $5 per cord were incurred. The 400,000 pounds of finished paper were sold for $1,000,000.

Requirements

a) Determine the gross profit for each division and for the company as a whole if the transfer price from Pulp to Paper is, at cost, $6 per cord.

b) Determine the gross profit for each division and for the company as a whole if the transfer price is $5 per cord.

c) Determine the gross profit for each division and for the company as a whole if the transfer price is $7 per cord.

9–13 Internal or External Acquisition: No Opportunity Costs

The Van Division of the CP Corporation has offered to purchase 180,000 wheels from the Wheel Division for $52 per wheel. At a normal volume of 500,000 wheels per year, production costs per wheel for the Wheel Division are as follows:

Direct materials	$20
Direct labor	10
Variable overhead	6
Fixed overhead	20
Total	$56

The Wheel Division has been selling 500,000 wheels per year to outside buyers at $68 each. Capacity is 700,000 wheels per year. The Van Division has been buying wheels from outside suppliers at $65 per wheel.

Requirements

a) Should the Wheel Division manager accept the offer? Show computations.

b) From the standpoint of the company, will the internal sale be beneficial?

9–14 Appropriate Transfer Prices: Opportunity Costs

The Plains Peanut Butter Company recently acquired a peanut processing company that has a normal annual capacity of 4,000,000 pounds and that sold 2,800,000 pounds last year at a price of $2 per pound. The purpose of the acquisition is to furnish peanuts for the peanut butter plant. The peanut butter plant needs 1,600,000 pounds of peanuts per year. It has been purchasing peanuts from suppliers at the market price.

Production costs of the peanut processing company per pound are as follows:

Direct materials	$0.50
Direct labor	0.25
Variable overhead	0.12
Fixed overhead at normal capacity	0.20
Total	$1.07

Management is trying to decide what transfer price to use for sales from the newly acquired Peanut Division to the Peanut Butter Division. The manager of the Peanut Division argues that $2, the market price, is appropriate. The manager of the Peanut Butter Division argues that the cost price of $1.07 should be used—or perhaps even less, since fixed overhead costs should be recomputed.

Any output of the Peanut Division, up to 2,800,000 pounds, not sold to the Peanut Butter Division could be sold to regular customers at $2 per pound.

Requirements

a) Compute the annual gross profit for the Peanut Division using a transfer price of $2.00.

b) Compute the annual gross profit for the Peanut Division using a transfer price of $1.07.

c) What transfer price(s) will lead the manager of the Peanut Butter Division to act in a manner that will maximize company profits?

9–15 Negotiating a Transfer Price with Excess Capacity

The Weaving Division of Carolina Textiles, Inc., produces cloth that is sold to the Company's Dyeing Division and to outside customers. Operating data for the Weaving Division for 19x3 are as follows:

	To the Dyeing Division	To Outside Customers
Sales:		
300,000 yards at $5	$1,500,000	
200,000 yards at $6		$1,200,000
Variable expenses at $2	− 600,000	− 400,000
Contribution margin	$ 900,000	$ 800,000
Fixed expenses*	− 750,000	− 500,000
Net income	$ 150,000	$ 300,000

* Allocated on the basis of unit sales

The Dyeing Division has just received an offer from an outside supplier to supply cloth at $4.30 per yard. The manager of the Weaving Division is not willing to meet the $4.30 price. She argues that it costs her $4.50 per yard to produce and sell to the Dyeing Division, so she would show no profit on the Dyeing Division sales. Sales to outside customers are at a maximum, 200,000 yards.

Requirements

a) Verify the Weaving Division's $4.50 unit cost figure.

b) Should the Weaving Division meet the outside price of $4.30 for Dyeing Division sales? Explain.

c) Could the $4.30 be met and still show a profit for the Weaving Division sales to the Dyeing Division? Show computations.

9–16 Dual Transfer Pricing

The Greek Company has two divisions, Beta and Gamma. Gamma Division produces a product at a variable cost of $6 per unit and sells 150,000 units to outside customers at $10 per unit and 40,000 units to Beta Division at variable cost plus 40 percent. Under the dual transfer price system, Beta Division pays only the variable cost per unit. The fixed costs of Gamma Division are $250,000 per year.

Beta Division sells its finished product to outside customers at $23 per unit. Beta has variable costs of $5 per unit in addition to the costs from Gamma Division. The annual fixed costs of Beta Division are $170,000. There are no beginning or ending inventories.

Required: Prepare the income statements for the two divisions and the company as a whole. Why is the income for the company less than the sum of the profit figures shown on the income statements for the two divisions? Explain.

9–17 Transfer Pricing and Divisional Gross Profit

Century Company has two divisions. Division Jeff manufactures chocks and Division Sam finishes them. The unfinished chocks can be sold for $2.50 each or finished and sold for $3.00 each. After Jeff manufactures the chocks, some are sold to outsiders and some are transferred to Division Sam, which finishes them. The following information pertains to 19x7:

Manufacturing cost of Division Jeff to produce 2,000,000 units	$3,000,000
Sales revenue from 800,000 units sold by Jeff to outside market	2,000,000
Market value of 1,200,000 units when transferred to Sam	3,000,000
Sales revenue from 1,200,000 units processed by Sam and sold	3,600,000
Total additional processing cost of Sam	750,000

Required: Compute the gross profit for the company and for each division. Use market value as the transfer price.

9–18 Transfer Prices at Full Cost with Excess Capacity: Divisional Viewpoint

The Dairy Company has a Cheese Division that produces cheese that sells for $12 per unit in the open market. The cost of the product is $8 (variable manufacturing of $5 plus fixed manufacturing of $3). Total fixed manufacturing costs are $210,000 at the normal annual production volume of 70,000 units.

The Overseas Division has offered to buy 15,000 units at the full cost of $8. The Producing Division has excess capacity, and the 15,000 units can be produced without interfering with the current outside sales of 70,000 units. The total fixed cost of the Cheese Division will not change.

Required: Explain whether the Cheese Division should accept or reject the offer. Show calculations.

9–19 Transfer Pricing with Excess Capacity: Divisional and Corporate Viewpoints

The Boyett Art Company has a Print Division that is currently producing 100,000 prints per year but has a capacity of 150,000 prints. The variable costs of each print are $30, and the annual fixed costs are $900,000. The prints sell for $40 in the open market.

The Retail Division of the company wants to buy 50,000 prints at $28 each. The Print Division manager refuses the order because the price is below variable cost. The Retail Division manager argues that the order should be accepted because it will lower the fixed cost per print from $9 to $6.

Requirements

a) Should the order from Retail Division be accepted? Why or why not?

b) From the viewpoints of the Print Division and the company, should the order be accepted if the manager of the Retail Division intends to sell each print in the outside market for $42 after incurring additional costs of $10 per print?

c) What action should the company take assuming it believes in divisional autonomy?

PROBLEMS

9–20 Transfer Pricing

The International Building Company owns its own clay mine, which supplies clay for the Brick Division. The clay is charged to the Brick Division at market price. Income statements for 19x5 were as follows:

International Building Company
Divisional Income Statements
For the year ended December 31, 19x5

	Clay Mine	Brick Division
Sales	$800,000	$2,000,000
Production costs:		
Materials	$ —	$ 800,000
Labor	380,000	500,000
Overhead	160,000	300,000
Total	−540,000	−1,600,000
Gross profit	$260,000	$ 400,000
Selling and administrative costs	−120,000	− 300,000
Income of division	$140,000	$ 100,000

In 19x5 and 19x6 the clay mine sold 20,000 tons of clay. In 19x6 the market prices of clay increased 50 percent and conversion costs increased 10 percent, whereas the

Brick Division increased its price by 10 percent. Income statements for 19x6 were as follows:

International Building Company
Divisional Income Statements
For the year ended December 31, 19x6

	Clay Mine	Brick Division
Sales	$1,200,000	$2,200,000
Production costs:		
Materials	$ —	$1,200,000
Labor	418,000	550,000
Overhead	176,000	330,000
Total	− 594,000	−2,080,000
Gross profit	$ 606,000	$ 120,000
Selling and administrative costs	− 120,000	− 330,000
Income (loss) of division	$ 486,000	(210,000)

Corporate management is concerned about the Brick Division's 19x6 loss.

Requirements

a) Prepare income statements for the company in 19x5 and 19x6.

b) Evaluate the company's performance in 19x6.

c) What should be the transfer price for clay? Discuss.

9–21 ROI and Residual Income: Impact of a New Investment

Office Equipment, Inc., is a decentralized organization with four autonomous divisions. The divisions are evaluated on the basis of the change in their return on invested assets. Operating results in the Modern Division for 19x1 are given below:

Office Equipment, Inc.
Modern Division Income Statement
For the year ended December 31, 19x1

Sales	$2,500,000
Less variable expenses	−1,250,000
Contribution margin	$1,250,000
Less fixed expenses	− 900,000
Net operating income	$ 350,000

Operating assets for Modern Division currently average $1,800,000. The Modern Division can add a new product line for an investment of $300,000. Relevant data for the new product line are as follows:

Sales	$800,000
Variable expenses	0.60 of sales
Fixed expenses	$300,000

Requirements

a) Determine the effect on ROI of accepting the new product line. (Round calculations to three decimal places.)

b) If a return of 6 percent is the minimum that should be earned by any division, and residual income is used to evaluate managers, would this encourage the division to accept the new product line? Explain and show computations.

9–22 Transfer Pricing at Absorption Cost

Division 23 of Numbers Company produces large metal numbers that are sold to Division 86. This division uses numbers in constructing signs that are sold to highway departments of local governments.

Division 23 contains two operations, stamping and finishing. The unit variable cost of materials and labor used in the stamping operation is $100. The fixed stamping overhead is $800,000 per year. Current production of 20,000 units is at full capacity.

The variable cost of labor used in the finishing operation is $12 per number. The fixed overhead in this operation is $340,000 per year.

The company uses an absorption-cost transfer price. The price data for each operation presented to Division 86 by Division 23 are shown below:

Stamping:		
Variable cost per unit	$100	
Fixed overhead cost per unit ($800,000/20,000 units)	40	$140
Finishing:		
Labor cost per unit	$ 12	
Fixed overhead cost per unit ($340,000/20,000 units)	17	29
Total cost per unit		$169

An outside company has offered to lease Division 86 machinery that would perform the finishing part of the number manufacturing. The lease is $200,000 per year. With the new machinery, the labor cost per frame would remain at $12. If Division 23 transfers the units for $140, the following analysis can be made:

Current process:		
Finishing process costs (20,000 × $29)		$580,000
New process:		
Machine rental cost per year	$200,000	
Labor cost ($12 × 20,000 units)	240,000	−440,000
Savings		$140,000

The manager of Division 86 wants approval to acquire the new machinery.

Requirements

a) How would you advise the company concerning the proposed lease?

b) How could the transfer-pricing system be modified or the transfer-pricing problem eliminated?

9–23 Transfer Pricing with and without Capacity Constraints

The National Carpet Company has just acquired a new Backing Division. The Backing Division produces a rubber backing, which it sells for $2.00 per square yard. Sales are about 1,200,000 square yards a year. Since the Division has a capacity of 2,000,000 yards a year, top management is thinking that it might be wise for the company's Assembly Division to start purchasing from the newly acquired Backing Division.

The Assembly Division now purchases 600,000 square yards a year from an outside supplier at a price of $1.80 per square yard. That the current price is lower than the competitive $2.00 price is a result of the large quantity discounts.

The Backing Division's cost per square yard is shown below:

Direct materials	$1.00
Direct labor	0.20
Variable overhead	0.25
Fixed overhead (1,200,000 level)	0.10
Total cost	$1.55

Requirements

a) If both divisions are to be treated as investment centers, and their performance evaluated by the ROI formula, what transfer price would you recommend? Why?

b) What will be the effect on the profits of the company using your transfer price?

c) Based on your transfer price, would you expect the ROI in the Backing Division to increase, decrease, or remain unchanged? Explain.

d) What would be the effect on the ROI of the Assembly Division using your transfer price? Explain.

e) Assume that the Backing Division is now selling 2,000,000 square yards a year to retail outlets. What transfer price would you recommend? Explain what will happen between Backing and Assembly.

f) If the Backing Division is at capacity and decides to sell to the Assembly Division for $1.80 per square yard, what will be the effect on the profits of the company?

9–24 Transfer Pricing with and without Capacity Constraints

The Northern Clock Company is a decentralized organization containing three divisions. The Windup Division has asked the Dial Division, which is operating at capacity, to supply it with a large quantity of dials. The Dial Division sells dials outside for $2.50 each. The Windup Division, which is operating at 50 percent of capacity, wants to pay $2.00 each for the dials.

The Dial Division has a variable cost of production of $1.80. The current costs of the clock being built by the Windup Division are shown below:

Materials (except dials)	$30.00
Dials	2.00
Other variable costs	18.00
Fixed overhead	10.00
Total cost per clock	$60.00

The manager of the Windup Division believes that the $2.00 price from the Dial Division is necessary if the division is to compete with its competitor, Clockex.

Requirements

a) As division controller of the Dial Division, would you recommend that your division supply Windup Division as requested? Why?

b) If the Dial Division has excess capacity, would it be desirable for the Dial Division to supply the Windup Division with the fittings at $2.00 each? Explain.

c) Assuming the Dial Division has excess capacity, as the corporate controller, what would you advise?

9–25 Transfer Pricing and Special Orders

Atlantic Telephone Company has several manufacturing divisions. The Pacific Division produces a component part that is used in the manufacture of electronic equipment. The cost per part for July is as follows:

Variable cost	$ 90
Fixed cost (at 2,000 units per month capacity)	60
Total cost per part	$150

Some of Pacific Division's output is sold to outside manufacturers, and some is sold internally to the Electronics Division. The price per part is $175.

The Electronics Division's cost and revenue structure is shown below:

Selling price per unit		$1,000
Less variable costs per unit:		
Cost of parts from the Pacific Division	$175	
Other variable costs	400	
Total variable costs		− 575
Contribution margin per unit		$ 425
Less fixed costs per unit (at 200 units per month)		− 100
Net income per unit		$ 325

The Electronics Division received an order for 10 units. The buyer wants to pay only $500 per unit.

Requirements

a) From the perspective of the Electronics Division, should the $500 price be accepted? Explain.

b) If both divisions have excess capacity, would the Electronics Division's action benefit the company as a whole? Explain.

c) If the Electronics Division has excess capacity, but the Pacific Division does not, and can sell all its parts to outside manufacturers, what would be the advantage or disadvantage to the Electronics Division of accepting the 10 unit order at the $500 price?

d) To make a decision that is in the best interest of Atlantic Telephone, what transfer-pricing information is needed by the Electronics Division?

9–26 Transfer Pricing with an Outside Market

French Vision has four divisions, Frame, Glass, Plastic, and Assembly, that collectively produce protective industrial eyeglasses. The Frame, Glass, and Plastic Divisions supply parts to the Assembly Division, which produces the final product.

The monthly fixed outlay costs of all divisions, except the Plastic Division, are identical at $150,000 each. Plastic's monthly fixed outlay costs are $300,000. In addition, fixed costs that do not require the use of cash amount to $50,000 per month per division, except for Plastic, where these costs are $100,000. Average production is 50,000 eyeglasses per month.

The full costs of each component are shown below:

Division	Part	Variable Cost per Unit	+	Fixed Cost per Unit	=	Full Cost per Unit
Frame	Frame	$15		$4		$19
Glass	Glass	20		4		24
Plastic	Ear pieces	5		4		9
Plastic	Nose pieces	2		4		6

Full absorption-cost transfer prices are used. In the Assembly Division, the manager has authority to buy inside the company or to buy from an outside supplier. The outside prices vary somewhat throughout the year. For next month the outside prices are as follows:

Part	Outside Price
Frame	$20
Glass	26
Ear pieces	7
Nose pieces	6

The Assembly Division manager notices that the outside purchase price of ear pieces is $2 lower than the transfer price and places an order with an outside supplier. Consequently, the Plastic Division stops producing ear pieces, reallocates all its fixed cost to the remaining units of nose pieces, and adjusts the full cost transfer price.

Requirements

a) Reallocate the fixed cost in the Plastic Division, and determine the adjusted transfer prices for nose pieces. What action might the manager of the Assembly Division take? What are the likely consequences of this action?

b) What action might French Vision take in establishing transfer prices and organizing its operations to avoid similar problems in the future?

9-27 Evaluating ROI

The Independent Consulting Company has several decentralized divisions. Each division manager is responsible for service revenue, cost of operations, acquisition and financing of divisional assets, and working capital management.

The vice president of general operations is considering changing from annual to multiyear evaluations of division managers. Currently, a review of the performance, attitudes, and skills of management is undertaken annually. As a trial run, two managers will be selected for the new evaluation procedure. The selection has been narrowed to the managers of Divisions 11 and 14.

Both managers became division managers in 19x1. Their divisions have the following operating results for the last three years:

	Division 11			Division 14		
(in thousands)	19x1	19x2	19x3	19x1	19x2	19x3
Estimated industry sales	$1,000,000	$1,200,000	$1,300,000	$500,000	$600,000	$650,000
Division sales	$ 100,000	$ 110,000	$ 121,000	$ 45,000	$ 60,000	$ 75,000
Variable costs	$ 30,000	$ 32,000	$ 34,500	$ 13,500	$ 17,500	$ 21,000
Fixed operating costs	40,000	40,500	42,000	17,000	20,000	23,000
Fixed administrative costs	27,500	32,500	32,500	14,000	20,000	25,000
Total costs	− 97,500	− 105,000	− 109,000	− 44,500	− 57,500	− 69,000
Net income	$ 2,500	$ 5,000	$ 12,000	$ 500	$ 2,500	$ 6,000
Net assets	$ 22,700	$ 23,500	$ 24,500	$ 12,300	$ 14,000	$ 17,000
Return on investment	?	?	?	?	?	?

Requirements

a) Determine ROI for each year for each manager.

b) Is ROI an appropriate measurement for manager evaluation? Why?

c) What additional measures might be used?

d) Per year, which manager performed the best?

e) Over three years, which manager performed the best?

(CMA Adapted)

9–28 Decentralization and Autonomy

Edwin Hall, Chairman of the Board and President of Arrow Works Products Company, founded the company in the mid-1960s. He is a talented and creative engineer. Arrow Works was started with one of his inventions, an intricate die-cast item that required a minimum of finish work. The item was manufactured for Arrow Works by a Gary, Indiana, foundry. The product sold well in a wide market.

The company issued common stock in 1972 to finance the purchase of the Gary foundry. Additional shares were issued in 1975 when Arrow purchased a fabricating plant in Cleveland to meet the capacity requirement of a defense contract.

The company now consists of five divisions. Each division is headed by a manager who reports to Hall. The Chicago Division contains the product development and engineering department and the finishing (assembly) operation for the basic products. The Gary Plant and Cleveland Plant are the other two divisions engaged in manufacturing operations. All products manufactured are sold through two selling divisions. The Eastern Sales Division is located in Pittsburgh and covers the country from Chicago to the east coast. The Western Sales Division, which covers the rest of the country, is located in Denver. The Western Sales Division is the newest operation and was established just eight months ago.

Hall, who still owns 53 percent of the outstanding stock, actively participates in the management of the company. He travels frequently and regularly to all the company's plants and offices. He says, "Having a business with locations in five different cities spread over half the country requires all of my time." Despite his regular and frequent visits, he believes the company is decentralized with the managers having complete autonomy. "They make all the decisions and run their own shops. Of course they don't understand the total business as I do, so I have to straighten them out once in a while. My managers are all good men, but they can't be expected to handle everything alone. I try to help all I can."

The last two months have been a period of considerable stress for Mr. Hall. During this period, John Staple, manager of the fabricating plant, was advised by his physician to request a six-month sick leave to relieve the work pressures that had made him nervous and tense. This request had followed by three days a phone call in which Hall had directly and bluntly blamed Staple for the lagging production output and increased rework and scrap of the fabricating plant. Hall made no allowances for the pressures created by the operation of the plant at volumes in excess of normal and close to its maximum rated capacity for the previous nine months.

Hall thought Staple and he had had a long and good relationship before this event. Hall attributed his loss of temper in this case to his frustration with several other management problems that had arisen in the past two months. The sales manager of the Denver office had resigned shortly after a visit from Hall. The letter of resignation stated he was seeking a position with greater responsibility. The sales manager in Pittsburgh asked to be reassigned to a sales position in the field; he did not feel he could cope with the pressure of management.

Requirements

a) Explain the difference between centralized and decentralized management.

b) Is Arrow Works Products Company decentralized, as Edwin Hall believes? Explain your answer.

c) Could the events that have occurred over the past two months in Arrow Works Products Company have been expected? Explain your answer.

(CMA Adapted)

9–29 An Evaluation of Market Based Transfer Prices

A large, diversified corporation operates its divisions on a decentralized basis. Division A makes Product X, which can be sold either to Division B or to outside customers.

At current levels of production, the variable cost of making Product X is $1.40 per unit, the fixed cost is 30 cents, and the market price is $2.75 per unit.

Division B processes Product X into Product Y. The additional variable cost of producing Product Y is $1.00 per unit.

Top management is developing a corporate transfer pricing policy. The bases for setting transfer prices being reviewed are full absorption cost, total variable costs, and market price.

Requirements

a) In order to avoid waste and maximize efficiency up to the transfer point, which of the transfer price bases being reviewed should be used and why?

b) Which of the transfer price bases in the short run would tend to encourage the best use of the corporation's productive capacity? Why would this not be true in the long run?

c) Identify *two* possible advantages that Division B might expect if it purchased Product X from Division A at the current market price.

d) What possible disadvantage might accrue to Division A if it was committed to sell all its production of X to Division B at the current market price?

(CIA Adapted)

9–30 A Transfer Pricing Dispute

MBR Inc. consists of three divisions that formerly were three independent manufacturing companies. Bader Corporation and Roper Company merged in 19x5, and the merged corporation acquired Mitchell Company in 19x6. The name of the corporation was subsequently changed to MBR Inc., and each company became a separate division retaining the name of its former company.

The three divisions have operated as if they were still independent companies. Each division has its own sales force and production facilities. Each division management is responsible for sales, cost of operations, acquisition and financing of divisional assets, and working capital management. The corporate management of MBR evaluates the performance of the divisions and division managements on the basis of return on investment.

Mitchell Division has just been awarded a contract for a product that uses a component manufactured by the Roper Division as well as by outside suppliers. Mitchell used a cost figure of $3.80 for the component manufactured by Roper in preparing its bid for the new product. This cost figure was supplied by Roper in response to Mitchell's request for the average variable cost of the component and represents the standard variable manufacturing cost and variable selling and distribution expense.

Roper has an active sales force that is continually soliciting new prospects. Roper's regular selling price for the component Mitchell needs for the new product is $6.50. Sales of this component are expected to increase. However, the Roper management has indicated that it could supply Mitchell with the required quantities of the component at the regular selling price less variable selling and distribution expenses. Mitchell's management has responded by offering to pay standard variable manufacturing cost plus 20 percent.

The two divisions have been unable to agree on a transfer price. Corporate management has never established a transfer price policy because interdivisional transactions have never occurred. As a compromise, the corporate vice president of finance has suggested a price equal to the standard full manufacturing cost (i.e., no selling and distribution expenses) plus a 15 percent markup. This price has also been rejected by the two division managers because each considered it grossly unfair.

The unit cost structure for the Roper component and the three suggested prices are shown below:

Standard variable manufacturing cost	$3.20
Standard fixed manufacturing cost	1.20
Variable selling and distribution expenses	0.60
	$5.00
Regular selling price less variable selling and	
distribution expenses ($6.50 − $0.60)	$5.90
Standard full manufacturing cost plus 15% ($4.40 × 1.15)	$5.06
Variable manufacturing plus 20% ($3.20 × 1.20)	$3.84

Requirements

a) What should be the attitude of the Roper Division's management toward the three proposed prices?

b) Is the negotiation of a price between the Mitchell and Roper Divisions a satisfactory method of solving the transfer price problem? Explain your answer.

c) Should the corporate management of MBR Inc. become involved in this transfer price controversy? Explain your answer.

(CMA Adapted)

REVIEW PROBLEM SOLUTION

a)

$$\text{Return on investment} = \frac{\text{Investment center income}}{\text{Investment center asset base}}$$

$$\text{Division X} = \$30,000/\$200,000$$
$$= 0.15 \text{ or } 15 \text{ percent}$$

$$\text{Division Y} = \$50,000/\$250,000$$
$$= 0.20 \text{ or } 20 \text{ percent}$$

$$\text{Division Z} = \$22,000/\$100,000$$
$$= 0.22 \text{ or } 22 \text{ percent}$$

b)   Residual income = Investment center income − (Minimum return ×
Investment center asset base)

Division X = $30,000 − (0.15 × $200,000)
= $0.00

Division Y = $50,000 − (0.15 × $250,000)
= $12,500

Division Z = $22,000 − (0.15 × $100,000)
= $7,000

c) ROI ranks: Division Z First
Division Y Second
Division X Third

Residual income ranks: Division Y First
Division Z Second
Division X Third

Because the investments for each division are different, it is difficult to rank the divisions by residual income. Division Y had the largest residual income, but it also had the largest investment. Division Z's residual income was 56 percent of Division Y's income, but only 40 percent of the investment of Division Y. This fact, along with the best ROI ranking probably justifies Division Z being the best division of Parent Company.

d) Return on investment

Investment = $9,000/$50,000
= 0.18 or 18 percent

Division X = ($30,000 + $9,000)/($200,000 + $50,000)
= 0.156 or 15.6 percent

Division Y = ($50,000 + $9,000)/($250,000 + $50,000)
= 0.1967 or 19.67 percent

Division Z = ($22,000 + $9,000)/($100,000 + $50,000)
= 0.2067 or 20.67 percent

ROI will increase for Division X, but decrease for Divisions Y and Z even though the project's ROI of 18 percent exceeds the company's minimum return of 15 percent.

Residual income

Division X = ($30,000 + $9,000) − [0.15 × ($200,000 + $50,000)]
= $1,500

Division Y = ($50,000 + $9,000) − [0.15 × ($250,000 + $50,000)]
= $14,000

Division Z = ($22,000 + $9,000) − [0.15 × ($100,000 + $50,000)]
= $8,500

Because the project's ROI exceeds the company's minimum return, the residual income of all divisions will increase.

CHAPTER 10

Inventory Valuation Approaches and Segment Reporting

Upon completion of this chapter you should:

- Understand the basic difference between absorption costing and variable costing.
- Be able to compute ending inventory under absorption and variable costing and be able to reconcile the difference between the two.
- Be able to reconcile the difference between absorption costing net income and variable costing net income.
- Be familiar with the primary arguments for and against variable costing.
- Be able to describe segment reporting and know the primary purposes of segment reporting.
- Be familiar with the segment reporting format that provides contribution margin and segment margin for each segment, and net income for the company as a whole.
- Understand the difference between single-level and multilevel segment reporting.

A fundamental internal reporting decision that every manufacturing company makes is how to account for fixed factory overhead. The outcome of this decision affects inventory valuation and, thus, income measurement. Though the absorption costing procedures used for external reporting purposes treat fixed factory overhead as a product cost, an alternative concept, called variable costing, is often used for internal reporting. Variable costing procedures assign only variable manufacturing costs to products. All other costs, including fixed manufacturing overhead, are treated as period costs.[1]

One of the purposes of this chapter is to present an analysis of absorption and variable costing. Each method is defined and its effects on inventory valuation and income measurement are illustrated. The advantages and limitations of each procedure are also discussed.

Organizations with multiple products, multiple plants, or multiple markets for their products often find it desirable to report the profits of each segment of the organization separately. Segment reporting allows a company's internal profitability reports to be prepared by divisions, products, territories, or on some other basis. Basic issues in segment reporting include the definition of business segments and the assignment of costs and revenues to each segment.

---

[1] Recall from Chapter 2 that *product costs* are costs assigned to products. They are expensed when the products are sold. *Period costs* are expired nonproduct costs. They are treated as an expense in the period they are incurred.

Another purpose of this chapter is to illustrate the development of segment reports and to discuss their usefulness in internal decision making, especially the decision to continue or discontinue a segment. In our discussion, special attention is given to problems caused by costs that are common to several segments of a business.

ABSORPTION COSTING AND VARIABLE COSTING

Under **absorption costing,** also called **full costing,** all manufacturing costs are assigned to products. Direct materials, direct labor, variable factory overhead, and fixed factory overhead costs are assigned to inventory, whereas selling and administrative costs, both fixed and variable, are immediately expensed as period costs.

Under **variable costing,** also called **direct costing,** only variable manufacturing costs are assigned to products. Direct materials, direct labor, and variable factory overhead costs are assigned to inventory, whereas fixed factory overhead and both fixed and variable selling and administrative costs are immediately expensed as period costs. A summary of product and period costs under absorption costing and variable costing is presented in Exhibit 10–1.

The difference between absorption costing and variable costing is the inclusion or exclusion of fixed factory overhead as a product cost. Under absorption costing, fixed factory overhead is assigned to products and expensed as part of the cost of goods sold when inventories are sold. Under variable costing, fixed factory overhead is immediately expensed as a period cost.

EXHIBIT 10–1   A Comparison of Absorption and Variable Costing

Absorption Costing	Variable Costing
Product costs	
Direct materials	Direct materials
Direct labor	Direct labor
Variable factory overhead	Variable factory overhead
Fixed factory overhead	
Period costs	
Variable selling and administrative	Variable selling and administrative
Fixed selling and administrative	Fixed selling and administrative
	Fixed factory overhead

Inventory Valuations

The differing treatments of fixed factory overhead under absorption and variable costing result in different inventory valuations. To illustrate these differences, consider the following predicted cost data for the Morehart Company at a monthly volume of 4,000 units.

Direct materials	$7 per unit
Direct labor	$5 per unit
Variable factory overhead	$4 per unit
Total fixed factory overhead	$8,000 per month

To determine the unit cost of inventory using absorption costing, it is necessary to compute the average fixed overhead cost per unit by dividing the predicted monthly fixed overhead of $8,000 by the predicted monthly activity level of 4,000 units ($2 per unit). This per unit fixed overhead figure is essentially a predetermined factory overhead rate. Even though fixed factory overhead is not a variable cost, under absorption costing it is applied to inventory on a per unit basis the same as variable costs.

At a monthly volume of 4,000 units, Morehart's inventory costs per unit under variable and absorption costing are as shown below:

	Cost per Unit	
Costs Category	Variable Costing	Absorption Costing
Direct materials	$ 7	$ 7
Direct labor	5	5
Variable factory overhead	4	4
Fixed factory overhead		
($8,000/4,000 units)	—	2
Total unit costs	$16	$18

The $2 difference in unit cost results from assigning fixed costs to the product by the absorption method, but not by the variable method.

Assume that Morehart had no beginning inventory in March 19x4 but produced 4,000 units and sold 3,500 units. The March 31 ending inventories under absorption costing and variable costing are $9,000 and $8,000, respectively (see Exhibit 10–2).

The $1,000 difference in ending inventory between the two costing methods is due entirely to the treatment of fixed manufacturing costs. Under the variable costing method, all fixed manufacturing costs are treated as period costs and expensed. The difference can be explained as follows:

Inventory difference = Change in inventory units × Fixed costs per unit
= 500 units × $2
= $1,000.

EXHIBIT 10–2   Absorption and Variable Costing Inventory Valuation

March 19x4	Absorption Costing			Variable Costing		
	Units	Costs	Dollars	Units	Costs	Dollars
Beginning inventory	—		$ —	—		$ —
Product costs	4,000	$18	72,000	4,000	$16	64,000
Goods available for sale	4,000		$72,000	4,000		$64,000
Cost of goods sold	−3,500	$18	−63,000	−3,500	$16	−56,000
Ending inventory	500	$18	$ 9,000	500	$16	$ 8,000

Reconciliations of absorption costing and variable costing inventory valuations may be more complex where product costs vary from period to period, or if production volume differs from period to period. Variations in cost behavior or production volume require explicit considerations of the treatment of over- or underabsorbed overhead and inventory cost flow assumptions, such as LIFO, FIFO, or weighted average.

Income Determination

The different treatments of fixed factory overhead under absorption costing and variable costing require different income statement formats and often result in different net income amounts. Under absorption costing, variable and fixed manufacturing costs are mixed together in the cost of goods sold. Under variable costing, the cost of goods sold includes only variable manufacturing costs.

Income statements presented in a functional format are used in connection with absorption costing. In functional income statements, costs are classified according to business *function*, such as manufacturing, selling, or administration. Both variable and fixed costs are included within each category. Manufacturing costs (cost of goods sold) are subtracted from sales to determine gross profit, and selling and administration costs are subtracted from gross profit to obtain net income.

Income statements presented in the contribution format are ordinarily used in connection with variable costing. In contribution income statements, costs are classified according to *behavior*. The difference between revenues and variable costs is identified as the contribution margin—the amount contributed to cover fixed costs and provide for a profit. Accordingly, contribution margin minus fixed costs equals net income.

To compare functional and contribution income statements for variable and absorption costing, assume the following additional information is available for the Morehart Company.

Selling price	$30 per unit
Variable selling and administrative expenses	$3 per unit
Fixed selling and administrative expenses	$10,000 per month

Sales Varying and Production Constant. Assume production remains constant at 4,000 units per month during June, July, and August while sales are 4,000 units, 2,500 units, and 5,500 units, respectively. Previously, the unit cost at this production level was computed to be $18 under absorption costing and $16 under variable costing. Absorption costing and variable costing income statements for June, July, and August 19x4 are presented in Exhibit 10–3. A summary of unit inventory changes is presented at the bottom of the exhibit.

The first set of statements is prepared in a functional format using absorption costing. The second set of statements is prepared in a contribution format using variable costing.

In June, production and sales were equal, resulting in no deferral of costs in inventory. All current costs were deducted under both methods, as either product or period costs, resulting in the same net income under both methods.

In July, production exceeded sales (4,000 produced; 2,500 sold). Absorption costing results in deferring part of the current fixed overhead costs in the ending inventory of finished goods as product costs, whereas direct costing expenses all current fixed overhead costs as period costs. Consequently, absorption costing net income for July exceeded variable costing net income by $3,000, the increase in inventory (1,500 units) times the fixed overhead per unit ($2).

In August, sales exceeded production (4,000 produced; 5,500 sold). All production and all beginning inventory were sold. Consequently, under absorption costing, all the current period's fixed factory overhead and fixed factory overhead previously deferred in Finished Goods Inventory are expensed through cost of goods sold. Under variable costing, the prior period's ending inventory sold during August included only variable cost. The only fixed costs deducted on the August variable costing income statement are those incurred in August. As a result, expenses are greater and net income is smaller under absorption costing than under variable costing. The difference in net income of $3,000 is equal to the change in inventory (1,500 units) times the fixed overhead per unit ($2).

Sales Constant and Production Varying. Assume the sales remain constant at 4,000 units for the Morehart Company during October, November, and December 19x4. Production units were 4,000 for October, 5,000 for November, and 3,200 for December. Unlike the previous illustration where production was constant and fixed factory overhead costs were $2 per unit, this illustration (assuming an actual overhead rate is used) has the following fixed factory overhead costs per unit.

	October	November	December
Fixed factory overhead	$8,000	$8,000	$8,000
Units produced	÷4,000	÷5,000	÷3,200
Fixed costs per unit	$ 2.00	$ 1.60	$ 2.50

EXHIBIT 10–3   Absorption and Variable Costing Income (Production Constant)

Morehart Company
Absorption Costing Income Statements
For June, July, and August, 19x4

	Sales Equal Production	Production Exceeds Sales	Sales Exceed Production
	June	July	August
Unit sales	4,000	2,500	5,500
Sales (at $30 per unit)	$120,000	$75,000	$165,000
Cost of goods sold (at $18 per unit)	− 72,000	−45,000	− 99,000
Gross profit	$ 48,000	$30,000	$ 66,000
Selling and administrative expenses:			
Variable (at $3 per unit)	$ 12,000	$ 7,500	$ 16,500
Fixed	10,000	10,000	10,000
Total	− 22,000	−17,500	− 26,500
Net income	$ 26,000	$12,500	$ 39,500

Morehart Company
Variable Costing Income Statements
For June, July, and August, 19x4

	June	July	August
Unit sales	4,000	2,500	5,500
Sales (at $30 per unit)	$120,000	$75,000	$165,000
Variable expenses:			
Cost of goods sold (at $16 per unit)	$ 64,000	$40,000	$ 88,000
Selling and administrative (at $3 per unit)	12,000	7,500	16,500
Total	− 76,000	−47,500	−104,500
Contribution margin	$ 44,000	$27,500	$ 60,500
Fixed expenses:			
Factory overhead	$ 8,000	$ 8,000	$ 8,000
Selling and administrative	10,000	10,000	10,000
Total	− 18,000	−18,000	− 18,000
Net income	$ 26,000	$ 9,500	$ 42,500

Summary of Unit Inventory Changes

	June	July	August
Beginning inventory	—	—	1,500
Production	4,000	4,000	4,000
Total available	4,000	4,000	5,500
Sales	− 4,000	− 2,500	− 5,500
Ending inventory	—	1,500	—

As a result of this situation, the unit cost of inventory and, subsequently, the cost of goods sold, will vary each period. Given the variable unit costs of $16 from the previous illustration, the total unit manufacturing costs for these months are as follows:

	October	November	December
Variable costs per unit	$16.00	$16.00	$16.00
Fixed costs per unit	2.00	1.60	2.50
Total manufacturing costs per unit	$18.00	$17.60	$18.50

If sales remain the same over several periods, it is expected that income should be the same, especially if cost behavior is constant. However, as Exhibit

EXHIBIT 10–4   Absorption and Variable Costing Income (Sales Constant)

Morehart Company
Absorption Costing Income Statements
For October, November, and December, 19x4

	Sales Equal Production	Production Exceeds Sales	Sales Exceed Production
	October	November	December
Unit sales	4,000	4,000	4,000
Sales (at $30 per unit)	$120,000	$120,000	$120,000
Cost of goods sold:			
Beginning inventory	$ —	$ —	$ 17,600
Variable manufacturing costs	64,000	80,000	51,200
Fixed factory overhead	8,000	8,000	8,000
Cost of goods available	$ 72,000	$ 88,000	$ 76,800
Less: Ending inventory	— —	− 17,600	− 3,700
Cost of goods sold	− 72,000	− 70,400	− 73,100
Gross profit	$ 48,000	$ 49,600	$ 46,900
Selling and administrative expenses:			
Variable (at $3 per unit)	$ 12,000	$ 12,000	$ 12,000
Fixed	10,000	10,000	10,000
Total	− 22,000	− 22,000	− 22,000
Net income	$ 26,000	$ 27,600	$ 24,900

10–4 shows, absorption income varies even though sales and cost behavior remained constant. Under the variable costing method income remains constant when both sales and cost behavior are the same for different periods.

When sales equal production, the income under both methods is the same (see June in Exhibit 10–3, and October in Exhibit 10–4). All other things being equal, absorption income increases when production goes up and declines when production goes down.

Reconciliation of Income Differences

An examination of the previous illustrations reveals several important differences between absorption costing and variable costing.

■ When production equals sales, absorption costing net income equals variable costing net income.

Morehart Company
Variable Costing Income Statements
For October, November, and December, 19x4

	Sales Equal Production	Production Exceeds Sales	Sales Exceed Production
	October	November	December
Unit sales	4,000	4,000	4,000
Sales (at $30 per unit)	$120,000	$120,000	$120,000
Variable expenses:			
Cost of goods sold (at $16 per unit)	$ 64,000	$ 64,000	$ 64,000
Selling and administrative (at $3 per unit)	12,000	12,000	12,000
Total	− 76,000	− 76,000	− 76,000
Contribution margin	$ 44,000	$ 44,000	$ 44,000
Fixed expenses:			
Factory overhead	$ 8,000	$ 8,000	$ 8,000
Selling and administrative	10,000	10,000	10,000
Total	− 18,000	− 18,000	− 18,000
Net income	$ 26,000	$ 26,000	$ 26,000

Summary of Unit Inventory Changes

	October	November	December
Beginning inventory	—	—	1,000
Production	4,000	5,000	3,200
Total available	4,000	5,000	4,200
Sales	− 4,000	− 4,000	− 4,000
Ending inventory	—	1,000	200

- When production exceeds sales, absorption costing net income exceeds variable costing net income.
- When production is less than sales, absorption costing net income is less than variable costing net income.

For each period, the income differences between absorption and direct costing can be explained by analyzing the change in inventoried fixed factory overhead under absorption costing net income. In general,

$$\begin{array}{ccc} \text{Variable} & \text{Increase (or minus decrease)} & \text{Absorption} \\ \text{costing} & + \text{ in inventoried fixed} & = \text{costing} \\ \text{net income} & \text{factory overhead} & \text{net income.} \end{array}$$

This equation may be reversed to reconcile absorption costing net income to variable costing net income:

$$\begin{array}{ccc} \text{Absorption} & \text{Decrease (or minus increase)} & \text{Variable} \\ \text{costing} & + \text{ in inventoried fixed} & = \text{costing} \\ \text{net income} & \text{factory overhead} & \text{net income.} \end{array}$$

Exhibit 10–5 presents a set of reconciliations for June, July, and August, which reconciles from variable income to absorption income, as well as a set for October, November, and December, which reconciles in the reverse order.

EXHIBIT 10–5   Reconciliation of Absorption and Variable Costing Net Income

	June	July	August
Variable costing net income	$26,000	$ 9,500	$42,500
Change in inventoried fixed costs:			
Fixed overhead in ending inventory units	$ —	$ 3,000*	$ —
Less fixed overhead in beginning inventory	– —	– —	– 3,000†
Increase (decrease) in inventoried fixed costs	—	3,000	(3,000)
Absorption costing net income	$26,000	$12,500	$39,500

	October	November	December
Absorption costing net income	$26,000	$27,600	$24,900
Change in inventoried fixed costs:			
Fixed overhead in beginning inventory units	$ —	$ —	$ 1,600†
Less fixed overhead in ending inventory	– —	– 1,600**	– 500‡
Increase (decrease) in inventoried fixed costs	—	(1,600)	1,100
Variable costing net income	$26,000	$26,000	$26,000

* 1,500 units × $2.00 of fixed factory costs per unit.

** 1,000 units × $1.60 of fixed factory costs per unit.

† Ending of July is beginning of August and ending of November is beginning of December.

‡ 200 units × $2.50 of fixed factory costs per unit.

Note in the following totals for the three-month period (June to August) that total production equals total sales and total absorption costing net income equals total variable costing net income.

Month	Production	Sales	Absorption Costing Income	Variable Costing Income
June	4,000	4,000	$26,000	$26,000
July	4,000	2,500	12,500	9,500
August	4,000	5,500	39,500	42,500
Total	12,000	12,000	$78,000	$78,000

For any given time period, regardless of length, if total units produced equals total units sold, net income will be the same for absorption costing and variable costing, all other things being equal. Under absorption costing, all fixed factory overhead is released as a product cost through cost of goods sold when inventory is sold. Under variable costing, all fixed factory overhead is reported as a period cost and expensed in the period incurred. Consequently, over the life of a product the income differences within periods are offset since they are caused only by the timing of the release of fixed factory overhead to the income statement.

An Evaluation of Variable Costing

Few accounting topics have generated as much controversy as variable costing. The central theoretical issue in this controversy is whether or not the incurrence of fixed manufacturing costs adds value to products. Proponents of variable costing argue that the incurrence of these costs does not add value to a product. Fixed costs are incurred to provide the capacity to produce during a given period, and these costs expire with the passage of time regardless of whether the related capacity was used. Variable manufacturing costs, on the other hand, are incurred only if production takes place. Consequently, these costs are properly assignable to the units produced.

Proponents of variable costing also argue that inventories have value only to the extent that they avoid the necessity for incurring costs in the future. Having inventory available for sale does avoid the necessity of incurring some future variable costs, but the availability of finished goods inventory does not avoid the incurrence of future fixed manufacturing costs. They conclude that inventories should be valued at their variable manufacturing cost, and fixed manufacturing costs should be expensed as incurred.

When considering the accounting principle of matching, variable costing has an advantage over absorption costing because it matches revenues with the direct cost of producing the revenues. This results in net income varying only with sales and not with both sales and production, as is often found in absorption costing. In absorption costing, overproduction especially distorts net income during a period because the excess inventory is assigned fixed costs that would otherwise be assigned to the units produced and sold. Using absorption costing, a company may increase net operating income by simply producing more than it sells.

Opponents of variable costing argue that fixed manufacturing costs are incurred for only one purpose, namely, to manufacture the product. Because they are incurred to manufacture the product, they should be assigned to the product. It is also argued that in the long run all costs are variable. Consequently, by omitting fixed costs, variable costing understates long-run variable costs and misleads decision makers into underestimating true production costs.

On a pragmatic level, the central arguments for variable costing center around the fact that the use of variable costing facilitates the development of contribution income statements and cost-volume-profit analysis when production and sales are not equal. If all costs are accumulated on an absorption costing basis, contribution income statements are difficult to develop, and cost-volume-profit analysis becomes very complicated unless production and sales are equal.

Variable costing is now widely used for internal reporting. However, it is not acceptable for external reporting in published financial statements or for income tax determination. Consequently, accountants should routinely use variable costing for internal reports and absorption costing for external reports. The simultaneous use of variable and absorption costing is a prime example of the use of different costs for different purposes.

SEGMENT REPORTING

Most top-level managers must have more than cost reports to aid them in evaluating large operating units. Income statements are often a vital part of the evaluation process. In this section of the chapter, emphasis is on cost classifications and the evaluation of individual segments.

Segment reports are income statements that show operating results for portions or segments of a business. When the reporting of operating activities is presented for product lines, it is often labeled **product reporting.** Segment reporting is used primarily for internal purposes, although generally accepted accounting principles also require disclosure of segment information for some public corporations.

Segment reporting is very common in organizations where there are distinct divisions of product lines, geographic territories, or organizational units. The segments or products of the organization for which reports are prepared depend on the information needs of management. The four most common types of segment reports are as follows:

1. Income statements for each plant or division.

2. Income statements for each product line.

3. Income statements for each sales territory.

4. Cost reports for cost centers (segments without sales or revenue).

Segment reports usually include the costs of both manufacturing and nonmanufacturing activities. Divisional income statements and product reports include product costs and appropriate selling and administrative costs. A given report may often include operating data for several products or territories, which may require further segmentation.

The format and frequency of segment reports is limited only by the decision needs and willingness of management to pay for preparing the reports. Although there are many different types of segment reports, three functions basic to the preparation of every report are:

1. Identification of the reporting objective.

2. Assignment of direct costs to the reporting objective.

3. Allocation of indirect costs to the reporting objective.

Segment reporting requires careful control over data collection and storage because of the different reporting formats. To properly compute the income for each segment or product, all costs, fixed and variable, must be considered. To effectively report the activities of a business segment, management should use the contribution approach, which focuses on the contribution made by each segment to cover common costs and to provide for a profit. The contribution approach discussed in the first section of this chapter (and in Chapter 4) is used for detailed segment statements.

Reporting Objective

A company with a single product or a homogeneous activity has little difficulty defining the activities to be included in its operating report, but the reporting structure of a multisegment business is not so easily defined. For example, if management wants to know the profit contributed by a certain product in a particular sales region, cost determination may be complicated in that certain marketing efforts promote several products within the sales region, whereas others overlap different sales regions. Each reporting objective must be identified and described as precisely as possible to ensure that only relevant revenues and costs are assigned to each reporting segment.

Contribution Margin

In preparing segment income statements, management must decide whether to use the functional (absorption) approach or the contribution (variable) approach. Segment reports are more useful if they emphasize the segment's contribution to profit. To compute the contribution margin by segments, sales and variable expenses must be assigned to each reporting segment. Since records are generally kept by segments, the accumulation of these data is relatively easy.

Segment reporting is an excellent example of how the contribution margin approach can be used for evaluation purposes. It can be used for determining the effect on profit of certain types of short-run changes when other types are held constant. Examples include changes in sales volume, product mix, temporary changes in capacity, special orders, and product promotions. As sales volume changes in a particular segment, the impact on net income can be determined by multiplying the segment contribution margin per unit by the change in units sold, or by multiplying the contribution margin ratio by the changes in sales dollars. Many decisions relating to the short run involve only variable costs and sales.

Segment Report Configurations

The nature and extent of segmentation of operating reports depends on the organizational structure of the company. A highly decentralized multilevel organization with different levels of operation may use a reporting structure similar to that presented in Exhibit 10–6 for the Offshore Refining Company for 19x4. The benefits accruing to management from such a series of segment reports

---

EXHIBIT 10–6   Segment Report Configuration by Territory (in thousands)

Offshore Refining Company
Territory and Company Income Statements
For the year ended December 31, 19x4

| | Segments | | Company |
	Atlantic	Gulf	Totals
Sales	$150,000	$150,000	$300,000
Less: Variable manufacturing expenses	− 30,000	− 40,000	− 70,000
Manufacturing margin	$120,000	$110,000	$230,000
Less: Variable selling expenses	$ 14,000	$ 11,000	$ 25,000
Variable administrative expenses	25,000	30,000	55,000
Total	− 39,000	− 41,000	− 80,000
Contribution margin	$ 81,000	$ 69,000	$150,000
Less direct fixed expenses:			
Manufacturing	$ 30,000	$ 32,000	$ 62,000
Selling	9,000	11,000	20,000
Administrative	18,000	12,000	30,000
Total	− 57,000	− 55,000	−112,000
Territory margin	$ 24,000	$ 14,000	$ 38,000
Less common expenses:			
Manufacturing			$ 9,000
Selling			4,000
Administrative			2,000
Total			− 15,000
Net income			$ 23,000

are many. Segment reporting can aid in identifying trends, percentage relationships, and other income information that management uses to evaluate the performance of the various activities of the organization.

For the reports in Exhibit 10–6, the reporting objective was defined by territories. Sales and expense data are presented for the two reporting territories of Offshore Refining. The direct manufacturing costs (variable costs) are deducted from territory sales to determine the **manufacturing margin.** The variable expenses of nonmanufacturing activities are then deducted to obtain the contribution margin. All direct fixed expenses identifiable with each territory are subtracted from the contribution margin to arrive at the **territory margin,** which is the amount that each territory contributes toward covering common corporate expenses and generating corporate profits. Common corporate expenses include the general administrative expenses of operating the corporate offices and conducting corporate activities. These expenses are necessary in the operations of the company, but they are not identifiable with specific territories or divisions.

Multilevel Segment Report Configurations

The needs of large organizations are usually not met with just one segment report, whether segmented by territory, product, division, or other reporting objective. Exhibit 10–7 illustrates a set of multilevel reports for the Offshore Refining Company. Exhibit 10–7(a) segments the totals for the company in terms of divisions, Exhibit 10–7(b) further segments one of these divisions in terms of the product lines sold within the division, and Exhibit 10–7(c) divides one of these product lines into the areas where it is sold. As each segment is further divided, the report shows more detailed aspects of the company.

The *first-level statements* for Offshore Refining show the company totals and a set of income statements segmented by its major reporting objective, operating divisions. Sales and cost data are presented for Offshore's two divisions in Exhibit 10–7(a). The company totals column includes the same total sales and expenses as the company totals column in Exhibit 10–6, except that the fixed costs are allocated differently below the contribution margin level. All direct fixed expenses identifiable with each division are subtracted from the contribution margin to arrive at the **divisional segment margin,** which is the amount each division contributes toward covering common corporate expenses and generating corporate profits.

Second-level statements may be presented for each first-level reporting objective. In our illustration, a product line contribution statement is presented for each product of Division A. These reports, in Exhibit 10–7(b), are useful to management in making decisions related to product pricing, sales strategy, inventory levels, break-even analysis, and production scheduling. The decision to continue or discontinue a product may also be based, in part, on information provided by these statements.

In Exhibit 10–7(b), the computations of the manufacturing margin and the contribution margin follow the same format as the divisional contribution statement. However, the computation of the **product margin** (product sales less direct segment costs) is somewhat different from the computation of the divisional contribution. This difference occurs because some of the fixed expenses regarded as direct at the divisional segment level are not direct at the product level. These fixed expenses include such items as divisional office salaries and plant security, which pertain to the general operation of the division rather than to the products. Therefore, only part of the fixed expenses of the division is assigned to products, with the balance of $6,000,000 reported as common costs. These divisional expenses are similar to the common fixed expenses of the company in the divisional contribution statement.

The next set of reports, *third-level statements,* is a breakdown of a second-level reporting objective. Exhibit 10–7(c) shows the amount of contribution

---

EXHIBIT 10–7   Report Configurations Segmented by Division, Products of Division, and Territories of Product (in thousands)

(a) Segment margins by divisions of Offshore Refining Company (first level)

	Division A	Division B	Company Totals
Sales	$100,000	$200,000	$300,000
Less: Variable manufacturing expenses	− 20,000	− 50,000	− 70,000
Manufacturing margin	$ 80,000	$150,000	$230,000
Less: Variable selling expenses	$ 10,000	$ 15,000	$ 25,000
Variable administrative expenses	25,000	30,000	55,000
Total	− 35,000	− 45,000	− 80,000
Contribution margin	$ 45,000	$105,000	$150,000
Less direct fixed expenses:			
Manufacturing	$ 15,000	$ 50,000	$ 65,000
Selling	5,000	17,000	22,000
Administrative	10,000	18,000	28,000
Total	− 30,000	− 85,000	−115,000
Divisional margin	$ 15,000	$ 20,000	$ 35,000
Less common expenses:			
Manufacturing			$ 6,000
Selling			2,000
Administrative			4,000
Total			− 12,000
Net income			$ 23,000

The "Segments" header spans the Division A and Division B columns.

margin of Oil Products in Division A generated by each sales region. The territory margin is the contribution margin less direct fixed expenses associated with a given market area. The margins for the same product often vary because of different environments. For example, the company office that serves the Atlantic area may experience significantly higher marketing and distribution costs than the office serving the Gulf area. Though the Atlantic area is more populated, it is farther from the refineries. Additionally, the company may have a better reputation in the Gulf area, thereby making sales easier.

Note from Exhibit 10–7 that fewer fixed expenses are allocated to segments as the reporting process is separated into specific segments within segments of the business. Because the allocation would be very subjective, none of the fixed manufacturing expense is assignable to the sales territories in Exhibit 10–7(c), and smaller amounts of the selling and administrative expenses are allocated at this level. Each level has certain costs that can be defined as direct or indirect,

(b) Segment margins by products within Division A of Offshore Refining Company (second level)

	Segments		Division A Totals
	Oil Products	Gas Products	
Sales	$ 40,000	$ 60,000	$100,000
Less: Variable manufacturing expenses	− 5,000	− 15,000	− 20,000
Manufacturing margin	$ 35,000	$ 45,000	$ 80,000
Less: Variable selling expenses	$ 5,000	$ 5,000	$ 10,000
Variable administrative expenses	12,000	13,000	25,000
Total	− 17,000	− 18,000	− 35,000
Contribution margin	$ 18,000	$ 27,000	$ 45,000
Less direct fixed expenses:			
Manufacturing	$ 4,000	$ 8,000	$ 12,000
Selling	1,000	3,000	4,000
Administrative	4,000	4,000	8,000
Total	− 9,000	− 15,000	− 24,000
Product margin	$ 9,000	$ 12,000	$ 21,000
Less common expenses:			
Manufacturing			$ 3,000
Selling			1,000
Administrative			2,000
Total			− 6,000
Divisional margin			$ 15,000

(continued)

and at each subsequent level the total expenses are smaller because the indirect expenses are not carried forward from the previous level. This reduction is evident for the Atlantic and Gulf areas where the territorial margins totaled $14,500,000, whereas the total product margin was only $9,000,000.

Other Configurations

In addition to, or instead of, the segments shown in Exhibits 10–6 and 10–7, management may desire first-level statements for other reporting objectives. For example, Exhibit 10–8 illustrates how the company can be segmented into first-level reporting by products. The product segment report, when used as a first-level statement, includes the products of both Divisions A and B.

In Exhibits 10–6, 10–7(a), and 10–8, the same total costs and revenues are allocated and assigned through the contribution margin level. Because of differences in allocating fixed costs, the company's total fixed costs of $127,000,000 (direct plus common) are treated differently in each of the various first-level statements.

EXHIBIT 10–7   (Continued)

(c) Segment margins by territories of Oil Products within Division A of Offshore Refining Company (third level)

	Segments		Oil Products
	Atlantic	Gulf	Totals
Sales	$ 12,000	$ 28,000	$ 40,000
Less: Variable manufacturing expenses	− 1,500	− 3,500	− 5,000
Manufacturing margin	$ 10,500	$ 24,500	$ 35,000
Less: Variable selling expenses	$ 2,000	$ 3,000	$ 5,000
Variable administrative expenses	4,000	8,000	12,000
Totals	− 6,000	− 11,000	− 17,000
Contribution margin	$ 4,500	$ 13,500	$ 18,000
Less direct fixed expenses:			
Selling	$ 100	$ 400	$ 500
Administrative	1,000	2,000	3,000
Total	− 1,100	− 2,400	− 3,500
Territory margin	$ 3,400	$ 11,100	$ 14,500
Less common expenses:			
Manufacturing			$ 4,000
Selling			500
Administrative			1,000
Total			− 5,500
Product margin			$ 9,000

EXHIBIT 10–8   Alternative Reporting Examples (in thousands)

Segment margins by products
of Offshore Refining Company
(first level)

	Oil Products	Gas Products	Chemical Products	Saline Products	Company Totals
Sales	$40,000	$60,000	$120,000	$80,000	$300,000
Less: Variable manufacturing expenses	− 5,000	−15,000	− 35,000	−15,000	− 70,000
Manufacturing margin	$35,000	$45,000	$ 85,000	$65,000	$230,000
Less: Variable selling expenses	$ 5,000	$ 5,000	$ 14,000	$ 1,000	$ 25,000
Variable administrative expenses	12,000	13,000	22,000	8,000	55,000
Total	−17,000	−18,000	− 36,000	− 9,000	− 80,000
Contribution margin	$18,000	$27,000	$ 49,000	$56,000	$150,000
Less direct fixed expenses:					
Manufacturing	$ 4,000	$ 8,000	$ 24,000	$28,000	$ 64,000
Selling	1,000	3,000	5,000	6,000	15,000
Administrative	4,000	4,000	4,000	4,000	16,000
Total	− 9,000	−15,000	− 33,000	−38,000	− 95,000
Product margin	$ 9,000	$12,000	$ 16,000	$18,000	$ 55,000
Less common expenses:					
Manufacturing					$ 7,000
Selling					9,000
Administrative					16,000
Total					− 32,000
Net income					$ 23,000

In Exhibit 10–6, $112,000,000 of fixed costs is assigned to segments with $15,000,000 treated as common costs to both territories. For the division segment reports (Exhibit 10–7a), $115,000,000 of fixed costs is assigned and $12,000,000 is common. And for the product reports (Exhibit 10–8), $95,000,000 is assigned and $32,000,000 is common.

It is typical for the common costs to be different for each type of first-level segment report because cost traceability for each reporting objective is different. Because manufacturing expenses are assumed to occur at the divisional level, they should all be assigned to the division incurring them. Even though manufacturing expenses are incurred to produce the products, it is often difficult to assign every expense to a specific product. In Exhibit 10–6, only $62,000,000 is assigned to products, with $9,000,000 treated as common expenses; and in Exhibit 10–8, $64,000,000 is assigned to the territories, with $7,000,000 treated as common expenses.

Other segment configurations are used by organizations to meet different management needs. Although reports segmented by division, product line, and territory are the most common, segment reports can also be based on plants, single products, industries (for conglomerates), and domestic and foreign operations. Because segment reporting allows a company to examine itself from various perspectives, management will select the types of segment reports that are most beneficial for decision making.

Segment Margin

The **segment margin** represents the amount that a segment contributes toward the common (indirect) costs of the organization and toward profits.[2] It is generally considered one of the best gauges of profitability for a given segment of a company.

At the operating management level, segment margins are helpful in making decisions related to production, such as those pertaining to capacity changes and long-range pricing policies. The contribution margin is most useful in those situations involving short-run operating decisions, such as pricing of special orders, and accepting or rejecting special projects.

Direct Versus Common Segment Costs

It may be difficult to distinguish between direct and common costs. **Direct segment costs** are often defined as costs that would not be incurred if the segment being evaluated were to be discontinued. They are specifically identifiable with a particular segment. For example, if the Gas Products segment in Exhibit 10–8 were discontinued, Gas Product advertising would probably be discontinued; therefore, it should be classified as a direct cost of Gas Products. Other examples include equipment depreciation and segment management salaries. On the other hand, the Division A vice president would probably not be terminated even if Gas Products was discontinued. Therefore the vice president's salary is common to both product lines.

Common segment costs, also called **indirect segment costs,** are related to more than one segment and not directly traceable to a particular segment. These costs are referred to as common costs because they are incurred at one level for the benefit of two or more segments at a lower level. Nonmanufacturing activities often have numerous indirect costs. A large organization, for example, may provide a centralized computer operation to serve all its production and marketing activities. Other examples of common costs include salaries of corporate management, companywide sales promotion, and expenses of the corporate accounting department.

Note from Exhibit 10–7(a) that when segments are defined as divisions, Division A has $30,000,000 in direct fixed costs. In Exhibit 10–7(b), only $24,000,000 of this amount remains direct when the definition of a segment is

---

[2] Segment margin can also be used to assist in measuring the segment return on investment, a very popular evaluation tool in decentralized organizations. See Chapter 9 for a detailed discussion.

narrowed from divisions to that of product lines in a division. The other $6,000,000 becomes a common cost of Division A product lines.

There are several possible reasons that the $6,000,000 of direct fixed costs is a common cost when the division is broken down into product line segments; for example, the amount could include the monthly salary of the division manager. The division manager's salary is a direct cost when considering the division as a whole, but it is common to the separate product lines within the divisions. Other items that might be treated the same way include plant depreciation, security costs, computer costs, or office equipment.

The $24,000,000 of fixed costs that remain direct ($9,000,000 for Oil and $15,000,000 for Gas) after the division is separated into product line segments consists of items that can be assigned to the products. These might include product research, equipment rental, and product advertising.

Common segment costs should not be allocated; they should simply be deducted from the segment margin in total to arrive at the net income for the company or the segment income for the next higher level segment. Nothing is added to the usefulness of segment reports by allocating common costs to the various segments; in fact, allocations of this sort may significantly reduce the usefulness of the information. These arbitrary allocations will draw attention away from direct segment costs toward those items that are not directly traceable to a given segment.

Segment Decisions

Decisions to continue or drop a segment are frequently based on segment reports. A problem (similar to that previously discussed in comparing direct and common segment costs) arises when determining whether a cost is relevant to a segment or product being considered for continuation or noncontinuation. When a company is able to identify relatively small segments, accountants generally find that the smaller the segments used for reporting, the more the costs tend to be common and, therefore, irrelevant to most short-term decisions.

The isolation of direct costs is complicated in that accounting reports often show allocations of common costs among various segments as expenses in the segment reports. To illustrate, if common facilities are used by a dairy processor in the manufacture of various milk products, the income statement for each product would probably include a portion of the depreciation on these facilities. In Exhibit 10–9(a), Yogurt appears unprofitable, and management might be tempted to discontinue it. If the depreciation is $100,000 per year and a total of 1,000,000 liters of all products are made, each liter of product could be charged with $0.10. Suppose that Yogurt, with current sales of 200,000 liters, is dropped. The $20,000 depreciation expense now allocated to Yogurt will not be avoided, but the remaining 800,000 liters of the other products must be charged with $0.125 per liter. As a result, the apparent profitability of the remaining products would be reduced, and company profits would decline, as shown in Exhibit 10–9(b). In fact, the profit decline is due to the decision to drop

EXHIBIT 10-9   Continuing or Discontinuing a Product

(a) Current period product income statements (partial)

	Segments			Company Totals
	Cream	Ice Cream	Yogurt	
Sales (liters)	500,000	300,000	200,000	
	× $0.22	× $0.30	× $0.40	
	$110,000	$ 90,000	$ 80,000	$280,000
Variable costs	− 40,000	− 30,000	− 65,000	−135,000
Contribution margin	$ 70,000	$ 60,000	$ 15,000	$145,000
Depreciation expense	− 50,000	− 30,000	− 20,000	−100,000
Segment and company income	$ 20,000	$ 30,000	$ (5,000)	$ 45,000

(b) Pro forma product income statements (partial)

	Segments		Company Totals
	Cream	Ice Cream	
Sales	$110,000	$90,000	$200,000
Variable costs	− 40,000	−30,000	− 70,000
Contribution margin	$ 70,000	$60,000	$130,000
Depreciation expense	− 62,500	−37,500	−100,000
Segment and company income	$ 7,500	$22,500	$ 30,000

Yogurt. When a segment is dropped, there may be no short-run reduction in common costs. For this reason allocated common costs are generally irrelevant to a decision about whether a particular segment should be dropped. In making these decisions, managers must be wary of any sunk costs. Even if they are direct costs of a segment, they should be ignored in the decision analysis.

SUMMARY

Absorption costing and variable (sometimes called direct) costing are two alternative approaches to inventory valuation. The essential difference between absorption and variable costing is the inclusion, or exclusion, of fixed factory overhead as a product cost. Under absorption costing, fixed factory overhead is assigned to products and expensed as part of the cost of goods sold when inventories are sold. Under variable costing, fixed factory overhead is immediately expensed as a period cost.

Although absorption costing is generally accepted for external and income tax reporting, variable costing provides better information for use internally by management in evaluating the consequences of short-run decisions and in planning operations in the near term. Variable costing is superior primarily because it permits the development of contribution income statements, where costs are classified by behavior to assist management in understanding cost-volume-profit relationships.

Segment reports are income statements that show operating results for portions or segments of a business. The format and frequency of segment reports is limited only by management's needs and willingness to incur the cost for these reports.

The distinction between direct segment costs and indirect, or common, segment costs is very important in segment reporting. Direct segment costs are costs specifically identifiable with a particular segment of a business. By subtracting a segment's direct costs from its revenues, segment margin is obtained. Indirect, or common, segment costs are costs that are not directly traceable to a particular segment but are necessary to support the activities of two or more segments. Indirect segment costs may be allocated to segments for a variety of reporting purposes, but unavoidable indirect segment costs should not be allocated in internal reports that are to be used for management decisions such as whether to continue or discontinue a segment.

KEY TERMS

Absorption costing
Common segment costs
Direct costing
Direct segment costs
Divisional segment margin
Full costing
Indirect segment costs

Manufacturing margin
Product margin
Product reporting
Segment margin
Segment reports
Territory margin
Variable costing

REVIEW QUESTIONS

10–1 Explain the difference between product costs and period costs.

10–2 Can period costs exist under the absorption method? If so, give some examples.

10–3 How can full costing be a synonym for absorption costing?

10–4 Explain the basic difference between variable and absorption costing?

10–5 Is inventory more consistently valued using variable or absorption costing? Why?

10–6 What is the relationship between variable costing and the contribution income method?

10–7 How do you reconcile the differences in net income between the variable costing and absorption costing methods of inventory valuation?

10–8 What is the relationship between segment reports and product reports?

10–9 How are contribution margins and segment margins similar? How are they different?

10–10 What is a reporting objective? How is it determined?

10–11 How do you distinguish between direct and indirect segment costs?

10–12 Can a company have more than one type of first-level statements in segment reporting?

10–13 Explain the relationships between any two levels of statements in segment reporting.

10–14 What types of information are needed before management should decide on dropping a product?

REVIEW PROBLEM

Absorption and Variable Costing

Colorado Ski Company has just completed its first year of operation on December 31, 19x3. The President says she needs financial statements for both managerial review and external reporting purposes. The Controller informs the President that two sets of statements will be needed: one based on absorption costing and other based on variable costing. Although concerned about the cost of preparing two reports, the President agrees to let the Controller try it.

The following data are from the first year of operations:

Direct labor	$200,000
Direct materials	250,000
Variable manufacturing overhead	100,000
Fixed manufacturing overhead	130,000
Variable selling expenses	75,000
Fixed administrative expenses	112,000
50,000 pairs of skis were manufactured and 40,000 pairs sold at a price of $40.	

Requirements

a) Compute the cost of the inventory at the end of the year using (1) absorption costing and (2) variable costing.

b) Prepare income statements for 19x3 using both absorption and variable costing methods.

c) Reconcile the difference in the net incomes in part (b).

d) Explain to the President why both sets of statements are needed.

The solution to this problem is found at the end of the Chapter 10 exercises and problems.

EXERCISES

10–1 Absorption and Variable Costing Inventory Valuations

Piedmont Paper Company had the following information available for 19x8.

Direct labor	$750,000
Variable manufacturing overhead	400,000
Direct materials	600,000
Variable selling and administrative expenses	400,000
Fixed selling and administrative expenses	400,000
Fixed manufacturing overhead	800,000

For the period sales were 75,000 units, and production totaled 100,000 units.

Requirements

a) Compute the ending finished goods inventory under both absorption costing and variable costing.

b) Compute the cost of goods sold under both absorption and variable costing.

10–2 Absorption and Variable Costing Inventory Valuation

Automotive Electric Company projects the following costs for 19x1.

	Per Unit
Direct materials	$6
Direct labor	$8
Variable overhead	$2
Fixed overhead ($40,000 for 20,000 units)	$2

During May, 20,000 units were produced, but only 10,000 were sold. During June, 20,000 units were produced and sold. During July, 20,000 units were produced, and 24,000 units were sold. There was no inventory on May 1.

Required: Compute the amount of ending inventory and cost of goods sold under variable costing and absorption costing for each month.

10–3 Absorption and Variable Costing Income Statements

The Franklin Company sells its product at a unit price of $11.00. Unit manufacturing costs are direct materials, $2.00; direct labor, $3.00; and variable factory overhead, $1.50. Total fixed manufacturing costs are $30,000 per year. Selling and administrative expenses are $1.00 per unit variable and $10,000 per year fixed. Though 25,000 units were produced during 19x1, only 20,000 units were sold. There was no beginning inventory.

Requirements

a) Prepare an income statement using absorption costing.

b) Prepare an income statement using variable costing.

10–4 Absorption and Variable Costing Income Statements

Sky Company began the year 19x1 with great optimism. During 19x1 it had no sales, but there were $60,000 in variable manufacturing costs and $20,000 in fixed manufacturing costs. In 19x2 it sold half of the finished goods inventory from 19x1 for $50,000, but it had no manufacturing costs. In 19x3 it sold the remainder of the inventory for $60,000, did no manufacturing, and went out of business December 31. Selling and administrative expenses were all fixed at $10,000 each year.

Requirements

a) Prepare an income statement for each year using absorption costing.

b) Prepare an income statement for each year using variable costing.

10–5 Absorption and Variable Costing Income Statements

The Uncontrolled Profit Corporation was disappointed to find that increased sales volume in 19x2 did not result in increased profits. Both variable unit and total fixed manufacturing costs for 19x1 and 19x2 remained constant at $10 and $1,000,000, respectively.

In 19x1 the company produced 100,000 units and sold 80,000 units at a price of $25 per unit. There was no inventory at the beginning of 19x1. In 19x2 the company made 70,000 units and sold 90,000 units at a price of $25 per unit. Selling and administrative expenses, all fixed, were $50,000 each year.

Requirements

a) Prepare income statements for 19x1 and 19x2 using the absorption costing method.

b) Prepare income statements for 19x1 and 19x2 using the variable costing method.

c) Explain why the profit was different each year using the two methods. Show computations.

10–6 Absorption and Variable Costing Comparisons: Production Equals Sales

Hammond Catsup Company manufactures and sells 15,000 cases of catsup each quarter. The following data are available for the third quarter of 19x3.

Sales price per case	$ 25
Direct materials per case	12
Direct labor per case	4
Variable manufacturing overhead per case	3
Total fixed manufacturing overhead	30,000
Fixed selling and administrative expenses	10,000

Requirements

a) Compute the cost per case under both absorption costing and variable costing.

b) Compute net income under both absorption costing and variable costing.

c) Reconcile the income differences, if any. Explain.

10–7 Absorption and Variable Costing Comparisons: Production Exceeds Sales

Daniel Derma Company produces hand lotion which it sells in bulk to distributors who in turn bottle the product under private labels. The sales price per five-gallon container is $10. The production information for July 19x9 is as follows:

Fixed selling and administrative expenses	$20,000
Fixed manufacturing overhead	66,000
Variable manufacturing overhead per container	2
Direct labor costs per hour	12
Direct material costs per container	1

The average direct labor per container is 15 minutes. During July the company produced 30,000 containers of hand lotion, but sold only 28,000 containers. There was no beginning inventory on July 1, 19x9.

Requirements

a) Compute the cost per container under both absorption and variable costing.

b) Compute net income under both absorption and variable costing.

c) Compute the ending inventories under both absorption and variable costing.

10–8 Absorption and Variable Costing Comparisons: Sales Exceed Production

Goldberg Development sells commercial building lots. During 19x8 the company bought 1,000 acres of land for $5,000,000 and divided it into 200 sites of equal size. As the lots are sold, they are cleared at an average cost of $2,500. Storm drains and driveways are then installed at an average cost of $4,000 per site. Selling costs are 10 percent of sales price. Administrative costs are $425,000 per year. The average selling price per site was $80,000 during 19x8 when 50 sites were sold.

During 19x9 the company purchased and developed an identical 1,000 acres with all costs remaining constant. Sales totaled 300 sites in 19x9 at an average price of $80,000.

Required: Compute net income under both absorption costing and variable costing for 19x8 and 19x9.

10–9 Conversion from Absorption to Variable Costing Statements

The Greenville Company began operation on January 1, 19x1. The 19x1 income statement on an absorption costing basis is as follows:

Greenville Company
Absorption Costing Income Statement
For the year ended December 31, 19x1

Sales (15,000 units)		$450,000
Less cost of goods sold:		
Beginning inventory	$ —	
Cost of goods manufactured (20,000 units)	280,000	
Ending inventory (5,000 units)	− 70,000	−210,000
Gross profit		$240,000
Selling and administrative expenses		− 40,000
Net income		$200,000

All the selling and administrative expenses are fixed. Manufacturing costs include the following unit costs:

Direct materials	$ 4
Direct labor	5
Variable manufacturing overhead	2
Fixed manufacturing overhead	3
Total	$14

Required: Prepare a variable costing income statement for 19x1.

10–10 Conversion from Absorption to Variable Costing Statements

Blacksburg Company's absorption costing income statement for 19x6 was as follows:

Blacksburg Company
Absorption Costing Income Statement
For the year ended June 30, 19x6

Sales (8,000 units)			
Cost of goods sold:			
Beginning inventory		$ —	
Cost of goods manufactured (10,000 units)		400,000	
Less ending inventory		− 80,000	−320,000
Gross profit			$580,000
Selling expenses, 10% of sales		$ 90,000	
Administrative expenses		50,000	−140,000
Net income			$440,000

During 19x6 the direct labor totaled $100,000 and direct materials were $50,000. Variable costs were $2 per direct labor hour and 20,000 hours were worked. Administrative expenses were fixed.

Required: Prepare a variable costing income statement for 19x6.

10–11 Conversion from Variable to Absorption Costing Statements

The variable costing income statement for Sahota Company is as follows:

Sahota Company
Variable Costing Income Statement
For the year ended June 30, 19x7

Sales (9,000 units at $50)		$450,000
Variable expenses:		
Cost of goods sold (9,000 units at $24)	$216,000	
Selling (10% of sales)	45,000	−261,000
Contribution margin		$189,000
Fixed expenses:		
Manufacturing overhead	$100,000	
Administrative	45,000	−145,000
Net income		$ 44,000

Selected data for 19x7 concerning the operations of the company are as follows:

Beginning inventory	0 units
Units produced	10,000 units
Manufacturing costs:	
Direct labor	$12 per unit
Direct materials	9 per unit
Variable overhead	3 per unit

Required: Prepare an absorption costing income statement for 19x7.

10–12 Conversion from Variable to Absorption Costing Statements

The variable costing income statement for Friedberg Ltd. is as follows:

Friedberg Ltd.
Variable Costing Income Statement
For the year ended June 30, 19x4

Sales (4,000 units at $100)		$400,000
Variable expenses:		
Cost of goods sold (4,000 units at $30)	$120,000	
Selling (12% of sales)	48,000	−168,000
Contribution margin		$232,000
Fixed expenses:		
Manufacturing overhead	$100,000	
Administrative	60,000	−160,000
Net income		$ 72,000

Selected data for 19x4 concerning the operations of the company are as follows:

Beginning inventory	0 units
Units produced	5,000 units
Manufacturing costs:	
Direct labor	$16 per unit
Direct materials	10 per unit
Variable overhead	4 per unit

Required: Prepare an absorption costing income statement for 19x4.

10–13 Profit Planning with Absorption and Variable Costing

The Profit Control Corporation wants to ensure that its profits do not decline in proportion to sales declines. To prevent profits from decreasing, Profit Control plans to increase production above normal capacity. For 19x1 and 19x2 the following budget information is available:

	19x1	19x2
Sales volume estimates	500,000 units	400,000 units
Normal production capacity	500,000 units	500,000 units
Planned production	500,000 units	700,000 units
Fixed manufacturing overhead	$1,000,000	$1,000,000
Fixed selling and administrative expenses	$ 100,000	$ 100,000
Total variable manufacturing costs	$10 per unit	$10 per unit
Sales	$20 per unit	$20 per unit

Requirements

a) Prepare pro forma income statements using absorption costing for 19x1 and 19x2. (Round computations to the nearest dollar.)

b) Prepare pro forma income statements using variable costing for 19x1 and 19x2.

c) Can the company actually control profits? Explain.

10–14 Profit Planning with Absorption and Variable Costing

The Profit Planning Corporation wants to plan its production so that sales and production have a close relationship with each other. To accomplish this objective, the company depends on sales forecasts to alter the amount of its production during each year. For 19x5 and 19x6 the following budget information is available:

	19x5	19x6
Sales volume estimates	500,000 units	400,000 units
Normal production capacity	500,000 units	500,000 units
Planned production	500,000 units	400,000 units
Fixed manufacturing overhead	$1,000,000	$1,000,000
Fixed selling and administrative expenses	$ 100,000	$ 100,000
Total variable manufacturing costs	$10 per unit	$10 per unit
Sales	$20 per unit	$20 per unit

Requirements

a) Prepare pro forma income statements using absorption costing for 19x5 and 19x6.

b) Prepare pro forma income statements using variable costing for 19x5 and 19x6.

c) Was the company's objective reflected in the income statements? Which statement is the best indicator? Why?

10–15 Income Statements Segmented by Territory

The Dual Manufacturing Company has two product lines. The 19x1 income statements of each product line and the company are as follows:

Dual Manufacturing Company
Product Line and Company Income Statements
For the year ended December 31, 19x1

	Product Lines		
	Pens	Pencils	Total
Sales	$20,000	$30,000	$50,000
Less variable expenses	− 8,000	−12,000	−20,000
Contribution margin	$12,000	$18,000	$30,000
Less direct fixed expenses	− 8,000	− 7,000	−15,000
Product margin	$ 4,000	$11,000	$15,000
Less common fixed expenses			− 6,000
Net income			$ 9,000

The pens and pencils are sold in two territories, Alaska and Alabama, as follows:

	Alaska	Alabama
Pen sales	$12,000	$ 8,000
Pencil sales	9,000	21,000
Total sales	$21,000	$29,000

The common fixed expenses above are traceable to each territory as follows:

Alaska fixed expenses	$2,000
Alabama fixed expenses	3,000
Home office administration fixed expenses	1,000
Total common fixed expenses	$6,000

The direct fixed expenses of pens, $8,000, and of pencils, $7,000, cannot be identified with either territory.

Requirements

a) Prepare income statements segmented by territory for 19x1, and include a column for the entire firm.

b) Why are direct expenses of one type of segment reports not necessarily direct expenses of another type of segment reports?

**10–16 Income
Statements
Segmented by
Products**

Clayton Consulting Firm provides three types of client services. The income statement for 19x2 is as follows:

**Clayton Consulting Firm
Income Statement
For the year ended December 31, 19x2**

Sales		$800,000
Less variable costs		−535,000
Contribution margin		$265,000
Less fixed expenses:		
Service	$70,000	
Selling and administrative	65,000	−135,000
Net income		$130,000

The sales, contribution margin ratios, and direct fixed expenses for the three types of services are as follows:

	Service 14	Service 28	Service 33
Sales	$250,000	$250,000	$300,000
Contribution margin ratio	30%	40%	30%
Direct fixed expenses of services	$ 20,000	$ 18,000	$ 16,000

Required: Prepare income statements segmented by products, and include a column for the entire firm in the statement.

PROBLEMS

**10–17 Variable
Costing Income
Statement**

For the first three quarters of 19x4, Mustang Motor Company has had wide fluctuations in production and sales. Sales volume and the variable cost of production have increased with no increase in the selling price. Variable manufacturing costs per unit were as follows:

	Quarter		
	First	Second	Third
Direct materials	$1,500	$2,000	$2,500
Direct labor	2,000	2,000	3,000
Variable factory overhead	500	1,000	2,000

The motors sell for $10,000 each. The fixed manufacturing costs are $250,000,000 each quarter. The variable selling and administrative expenses are $600 for each unit sold, and the fixed selling and administrative expenses are $80,000,000 a quarter. Beginning motor inventory at the start of the first quarter, 20,000 units, was recorded at $110,000,000, including $30,000,000 of fixed costs. The company uses the FIFO inventory method. Production and sales data are as follows:

Quarter	Produced	Sold
First	150,000	140,000
Second	160,000	150,000
Third	160,000	170,000

Requirements

a) Prepare income statements for each quarter using variable costing.

b) Prepare income statements for each quarter using absorption costing.

c) Reconcile the incomes for each quarter between the two methods.

10–18 Absorption and Variable Costing Income Statements with Income Taxes

The operating data for the Silver Spoon Company are given below.

	19x1	19x2	19x3
Units manufactured	80,000	100,000	80,000
Units sold	70,000	90,000	100,000
Unit selling price	$10	$10	$10
Variable manufacturing costs per unit	$4	$4	$4
Fixed manufacturing cost	$200,000	$250,000	$300,000

There was no inventory on hand on January 1, 19x1. The company uses the FIFO method to maintain its inventories. Variable selling expenses are $1.20 per unit, and fixed selling and administrative expenses for each year are $60,000. Income tax is estimated at 30 percent of before-tax income.

Requirements

a) Prepare income statements for each year using absorption costing.

b) Prepare income statements for each year using variable costing.

c) Reconcile the income differences for each year between the two methods.

10–19 Variable Costing Income Statements with Income Taxes

The manager of a newly organized division of Brown Manufacturing does not understand why income went down when sales went up.

Information for the first and second quarters of 19x1 is given as follows for Arizona Division.

Brown Manufacturing Company
Absorption Costing Income Statements
For the first two quarters of 19x1

	First Quarter	Second Quarter
Units produced	20,000	15,000
Units sold	15,000	20,000
Sales	$300,000	$400,000
Cost of goods sold:		
Inventory, beginning of quarter	$ —	$ 75,000
Current production cost	300,000	275,000
Cost of merchandise available for sale	$300,000	$350,000
Less inventory, end of quarter	− 75,000	− —
Cost of goods sold	−225,000	−350,000
Gross profit	$ 75,000	$ 50,000
Selling and administrative expenses	− 25,000	− 25,000
Income before income taxes	$ 50,000	$ 25,000
Income tax (30%)	− 15,000	− 7,500
Net income	$ 35,000	$ 17,500

The company operated at normal capacity during the first quarter. Variable manu-facturing cost per unit was $5, and the fixed cost was $200,000. Selling and administrative expenses are all fixed.

Requirements

a) Revise the statement for each of the two quarters on the variable costing basis. *Hint:* Variable costing is not acceptable for tax purposes.

b) Explain the profit differences. How would variable costing help the manager avoid confusion?

10–20 Absorption Costing and Variable Costing Income Statements: All Fixed Costs

The Fixed Rock Company has only fixed costs. It built its building over a pile of rocks and simply sells them when customers visit the plant.

All employees of the plant are paid a fixed annual wage. There are no material costs and no variable overhead because the rocks came with the land and they do not need processing. They are washed in a creek that flows through the property. Costs are esti-mated as follows for 19x5 and 19x6.

Labor	$200,000
Depreciation	50,000
Insurance	20,000
Administration	40,000

Production capacity is 2,000 tons per year. Rocks sell for $200 per ton. Results for two years are as follows:

	19x5	19x6
Tons produced	1,600	2,000
Tons sold	1,500	2,100

Required: Prepare income statements for each year under both absorption costing and variable costing. Which method is better? Why?

10–21 Absorption and Variable Costing Comparisons

The March Manufacturing Company had two identical divisions, Left and Right. Their sales, production volume, and fixed manufacturing costs have been the same for both divisions for the last five years. These amounts for each division are as follows:

	19x1	19x2	19x3	19x4	19x5
Units produced	100,000	110,000	110,000	88,000	88,000
Units sold	90,000	90,000	100,000	100,000	100,000
Fixed manufacturing costs	$110,000	$110,000	$110,000	$110,000	$110,000

Left uses absorption costing, and Right uses variable costing. Both use FIFO inventory methods. Variable manufacturing costs are $5 per unit. Both have identical selling prices and selling and administrative expenses. There were no 1/1/x1 inventories.

Required: Which division reports the higher income in each year? Explain.

10–22 Absorption and Variable Costing Comparisons

Never Quit Shoe Company is concerned with changing to the variable costing method of inventory valuation for making internal decisions. The absorption statements of income for January and February are shown below.

Never Quit Shoe Company
Absorption Costing Income Statements
For January and February, 19x9

	January	February
Sales (8,000 units)	$160,000	$160,000
Cost of goods sold	− 99,200	−108,800
Gross profit	$ 60,800	$ 51,200
Selling and administrative expenses	− 30,000	− 30,000
Net income	$ 30,800	$ 21,200

Production data are as shown below.

	January	February
Production units	10,000	6,000
Variable costs per unit	$10	$10
Fixed overhead costs	$24,000	$24,000

Selling and administrative expenses above include variable costs of $1 per unit sold.

Requirements

a) Compute the absorption cost per unit manufactured in January and February.

b) Explain why the net income for January was higher than the net income for February when the same number of units was sold in each month.

c) Prepare income statements for both months using variable costing.

d) Reconcile the absorption costing and variable costing net income figures for each month. Start with variable costing net income.

10–23 Absorption and Variable Costing Comparisons

The Sweet Company manufactures peach jam. Because of bad weather, the crop was small. The following data have been gathered for the summer quarter of 19x3:

Beginning inventory, cases	—
Cases produced	10,000
Cases sold	9,600
Sales price per case	$50
Direct materials per case	$7
Direct labor per case	$6
Variable manufacturing overhead per case	$3
Total fixed manufacturing overhead	$400,000
Variable selling and administrative cost per case	$2
Fixed selling and administrative cost	$48,000

Requirements

a) Prepare an income statement for the quarter using absorption costing.

b) Prepare an income statement for the quarter using variable costing.

c) What is the value of ending inventory under absorption costing?

d) What is the value of ending inventory under variable costing?

e) Explain the difference in ending inventory under absorption costing and variable costing.

10–24 Conversion from Absorption to Variable Costing Statements

The income statement for Mug and Cup Company has been prepared on an absorption costing basis.

Mug and Cup Company
Absorption Costing Income Statement
For the month ended December 31, 19x1

Sales (5,000 units)		$25,000
Cost of goods sold:		
Inventory, beginning	$ 5,000	
Cost of goods manufactured	10,000	
Cost of products available for sale	$15,000	
Less inventory ending	− 2,500	12,500
Gross profit		$12,500
Selling and administrative expenses		− 3,000
Net income		$ 9,500

Variable unit costs have remained unchanged during the year. In 19x1 the monthly fixed factory overhead was $2,000. During December 4,000 units were manufactured.

Requirements

a) Recast the income statement for December to place it on a variable costing basis.

b) Reconcile the two statements.

10–25 Segment Reporting

Protection Company has provided you with the following information about its operations.

1. There are two products, umbrellas and hats.

2. There are two sales territories, Southeast and Northwest.

3. Monthly traceable direct fixed costs are $15,000 in the Southeast territory and $14,000 in the Northwest territory.

4. During January of 19x3, Southeast sold $40,000 of umbrellas and $20,000 of hats and Northwest sold $10,000 of umbrellas and $30,000 of hats.

5. Variable cost of sales and selling expenses total 40 percent for umbrellas and 70 percent for hats.

6. Of Northwest's direct fixed costs, $5,000 is traceable to umbrellas and $5,000 to hats.

7. Of Southeast's direct fixed costs, $4,000 is traceable to umbrellas and $2,000 to hats.

8. Total fixed costs of the Protection Company were $40,000 during January.

9. Total variable costs of the Protection Company were $55,000 during January.

Requirements

a) Prepare January 19x3 segment income statements for both territories, and include a column for the entire firm.

b) Prepare income statements segmented by product within each territory, and include a column for the entire firm.

10–26 Multiple Segment Reports

Ottawa Snow Company has two divisions: Snow and Ice. Because of increasing costs, the president wants to review overall operations by means of segment reporting. For 19x7 total revenue was $40,000,000: $14,000,000 for Snow and $26,000,000 for Ice. For Ice, $20,000,000 was generated by retail customers and $6,000,000 by manufacturing customers.

Total variable costs were $8,000,000 for Snow and $14,000,000 for Ice. For Ice, $11,500,000 was for retail customers and $2,500,000 for manufacturing customers. Total direct fixed costs were $2,000,000 for Snow and $10,000,000 for Ice. For Ice, $7,000,000 was for retail customers and $3,000,000 for manufacturing customers.

In addition to the above, there were common corporate fixed costs of $4,000,000 for selling and administrative facilities. Common corporate fixed costs of $1,000,000 were also incurred for administrative personnel and supplies. These costs are not allocated to divisions.

Requirements

a) Prepare segment income statements for the divisions, and include a column for the entire firm.

b) Prepare segment income statements for the separate parts of the Ice Division, and include a column for the entire division.

10–27 Multiple Segment Reports

Earth Products, Incorporated, sells throughout the world in three sales territories: Europe, the East, and the West. For July 19x3 all $50,000 of administrative expense are allocated, except $10,000, which is common to all units and cannot be traced to the sales territories. The percentage of product line sales made in each of the sales territories and the allocations of traceable fixed expenses are shown below.

| | Sales Territory | | | |
	Europe	East	West	Total
Cookware sales	40%	50%	10%	100%
China sales	40	40	20	100
Vases sales	20	20	60	100
Fixed administrative expense	$15,000	$15,000	$10,000	$ 40,000
Fixed selling expense	30,000	60,000	60,000	150,000

The manufacturing takes place in one large facility with three distinct manufacturing operations. Selected cost data are shown below.

| | Product Line | | | |
	Cookware	China	Vases	Total
Variable costs	$ 9	$ 9	$ 5	
Depreciation and supervision	15,000	15,000	12,000	$ 45,000*
Other factory overhead (common)				10,000
Fixed administrative expense				
(common)				50,000
Fixed selling expense (common)				150,000

* Includes common costs of $3,000.

The unit sales and selling price for each product are shown below.

	Unit Sales	Selling Price
Cookware	10,000	$10
China	20,000	15
Vases	15,000	20

Requirements

a) Prepare an income statement for July 19x3 segmented by product line, and include a column for the entire firm.

b) Prepare an income statement for July 19x3 segmented by sales territories and include a column for the entire firm.

10–28 Segment Reporting and Analysis

Neighborhood Bakery, Incorporated, bakes three products: donuts, pies, and cakes. It sells them in the cities of Irmo and Jackson. For March 19x4 the following absorption costing income statement was prepared.

Neighborhood Bakery, Inc.
Territory and Company Income Statements
For the month of March, 19x1

	Irmo	Jackson	Total
Sales	$2,100	$500	$2,600
Cost of goods sold	−1,500	−300	−1,800
Gross profit	$ 600	$200	$ 800
Selling and administrative expenses	− 400	−100	− 500
Net income	$ 200	$100	$ 300

Sales and selected variable expense data are as follows:

	Products		
	Donuts	Pies	Cakes
Fixed baking expenses	$200	$140	$100
Variable baking expenses as a percentage of sales	50%	50%	60%
Variable selling expenses as a percentage of sales	4%	4%	5%
City of Irmo, sales	$800	$900	$400
City of Jackson, sales	$200	$100	$200

The fixed selling expenses were $260 for March, of which $210 was a direct expense of the Irmo market and $50 a direct expense of the Jackson market. Fixed administrative expenses were $130, which management has decided not to allocate when using the contribution approach.

Requirements

a) Prepare a segment income statement for each sales territory for March, and include a column for the entire firm.

b) Prepare segment income statements for each product, and include a column for the entire firm.

c) Should any products or territories be dropped?

10–29 Segment Reporting and Analysis

The Hardback Book Company has prepared income statements segmented by divisions, but management is still uncertain about actual performance. Financial information for 19x8 is given as follows:

| | Segments | | |
	Textbook Division	Professional Division	Total Company
Sales	$180,000	$410,000	$590,000
Less variable expenses:			
Manufacturing	$ 32,000	$205,000	$237,000
Selling and administration	4,000	20,500	24,500
Total	− 36,000	−225,500	−261,500
Contribution margin	$144,000	$184,500	$328,500
Less direct fixed expenses	− 15,000	−220,000	−235,000
Net income	$129,000	$ (35,500)	$ 93,500

The Professional Division is of concern to management and needs additional analysis. Additional information regarding the 19x8 operations of the Professional Division is as follows:

	Accounting	Executive	Management
Sales	$140,000	$140,000	$130,000
Variable manufacturing expenses as a percentage of sales	60%	40%	50%
Other variable expenses as a percentage of sales	5%	5%	5%
Direct fixed expenses	$ 50,000	$ 75,000	$ 50,000

The professional accounting books are sold to auditors and controllers. The current information on these markets is as follows:

| | Sales Market | |
	Auditors	Controllers
Sales	$30,000	$110,000
Variable manufacturing expenses as a percentage of sales	60%	60%
Other variable expenses as a percentage of sales	16%	2%
Direct fixed expenses	$20,000	$ 25,000

Requirements

a) Prepare an income statement segmented by products of the Professional Division, and include a column for the division as a whole.

b) Prepare an income statement segmented by markets of the accounting books of the Professional Division.

c) Evaluate which accounting books the Professional Division should keep or
discontinue.

**10–30 Segment
Reports**

The Justa Corporation produces and sells three products. The three products, A, B, and
C, are sold in a local market and in a regional market. After the end of the first quarter
of 19x2, the following income statement was prepared.

**Justa Corporation
Territory and Company Income Statements
For the first quarter of 19x2**

	Local	Regional	Total
Sales	$1,000,000	$300,000	$1,300,000
Cost of goods sold	− 775,000	−235,000	−1,010,000
Gross profit	$ 225,000	$ 65,000	$ 290,000
Selling expenses	$ 60,000	$ 45,000	$ 105,000
Administrative expenses	40,000	12,000	52,000
Total	− 100,000	− 57,000	− 157,000
Net income	$ 125,000	$ 8,000	$ 133,000

Management has expressed special concern with the regional market because of
the extremely poor return on sales. This market was entered a year ago because of
excess capacity. It was originally believed that the return on sales would improve with
time, but after a year no noticeable improvement can be seen from the results as reported
in the above quarterly statement.

In attempting to decide whether to eliminate the regional market, the following
information has been gathered.

	Products		
	A	B	C
Sales	$500,000	$400,000	$400,000
Variable manufacturing expenses as a percentage of sales	60%	70%	60%
Variable selling expenses as a percentage of sales	3%	2%	2%

Sales by Markets

Product	Local	Regional
A	$400,000	$100,000
B	300,000	100,000
C	300,000	100,000

All administrative expenses and fixed manufacturing expenses are common to the
three products and the two markets and are fixed for the period. The remaining selling

expenses are fixed for the period and separable by market. All fixed expenses are based on a prorated yearly amount.

Requirements

a) Prepare the quarterly income statement showing contribution margins by markets (territories), and include a column for the company as a whole.

b) Assuming there are no alternative uses for the Justa Corporation's present capacity, would you recommend dropping the regional market? Why or why not?

c) Prepare the quarterly income statement showing contribution margins by products and include a column for the company as a whole.

d) It is believed that a new product can be ready for sale next year if the Justa Corporation decides to go ahead with continued research. The new product can be produced by simply converting equipment now used in producing Product C. This conversion will increase fixed costs by $10,000 per quarter. What must be the minimum contribution margin per quarter for the new product to make the change-over financially feasible?

(CMA Adapted)

**REVIEW PROBLEM
SOLUTION**

a)

	Cost per Unit	
	Absorption Costing	Variable Costing
Direct labor ($200,000/50,000)	$ 4.00	$ 4.00
Direct materials ($250,000/50,000)	5.00	5.00
Variable manufacturing overhead ($100,000/50,000)	2.00	2.00
Fixed manufacturing overhead ($130,000/50,000)	2.60	—
Total unit costs	$13.60	$11.00
Ending inventory units	10,000	10,000
Unit cost	× $13.60	× $11.00
Ending inventory value	$136,000	$110,000

b)   **Colorado Ski Company
Absorption Costing Income Statement
For the year ended December 31, 19x3**

Sales (40,000 units × $40)		$1,600,000
Cost of goods sold (40,000 units × $13.60)		− 544,000
Gross profit		$1,056,000
Selling and administrative expenses:		
Selling expenses	$ 75,000	
Administrative expenses	112,000	− 187,000
Net income		$ 869,000

Colorado Ski Company
Variable Costing Income Statement
For the year ended December 31, 19x3

Sales (40,000 units × $40)		$1,600,000
Variable expenses:		
Cost of goods sold (40,000 units × $11.00)	$440,000	
Variable selling	75,000	− 515,000
Contribution margin		$1,085,000
Fixed expenses:		
Manufacturing overhead	$130,000	
Administrative	112,000	− 242,000
Net income		$ 843,000

c) Reconciliation of absorption and variable costing net income

Absorption costing net income		$869,000
Change in inventoried fixed costs:		
Fixed overhead in beginning inventory units	$ —	
Less fixed overhead in ending inventory	−26,000	− 26,000
Variable costing net income		$843,000
Variable costing net income		$843,000
Change in inventoried fixed costs:		
Fixed overhead in ending inventory	$26,000	
Less fixed overhead in beginning inventory	− —	26,000
Absorption costing net income		$869,000

d) Generally accepted accounting principles require that absorption cost financial statements be used for external reporting. This includes all reports to creditors, stockholders, and governments. Absorption costing financial statements treat all manufacturing costs (fixed and variable) as product costs and assign them to the products produced, the premise being that all products should bear their share of all manufacturing costs. Although many companies use these statements for internal reporting, the analysis of operating results using absorption costing can be misleading because the various cost elements are not separated by fixed and variable behavior.

    For variable costing financial statements, the analysis of cost behavior is required, which in itself provides an additional component in the overall analysis of the operating results. The fixed manufacturing costs are treated as period costs and not assigned to inventories. Therefore variable costing provides a decision base for analysis, which includes a contribution margin (sales less variable costs) that permits an evaluation of costs that are directly related to the revenues.

Product Costing
and Cost Allocation

CHAPTER 11

Product Costing

Upon completion of this chapter you should:

- Know the three main types of manufacturing inventories and the three elements of manufacturing costs.
- Be able to prepare journal entries recording the flow of costs for a manufacturing organization.
- Understand the differences between job-order costing and process costing.
- Be familiar with the costing procedures used in recording cost data in a job-order cost system.
- Understand the use of predetermined factory overhead rates and how to dispose of underapplied or overapplied factory overhead.
- Be able to prepare basic process costing reports.

Product costing is the process of assigning costs to inventories as they are converted from raw materials into finished goods. Determining product costs is necessary for inventory valuations and expense measurement in general purpose financial statements, and it is useful for internal planning and control purposes, such as product pricing, operations budgeting, and profit planning.

The purpose of this chapter is to examine the two major product costing methods used in manufacturing organizations. These methods are *job-order costing* and *process costing*. We begin with a review of product costing systems introduced in Chapter 2.

MANUFACTURING INVENTORIES AND COSTS

Manufacturing organizations have three major inventory categories:

- *Raw materials* inventories contain the physically existing items that are to be converted into finished products.
- *Work-in-process* inventories contain the raw materials that are in the process of being converted into finished products.
- *Finished goods* inventories contain the manufactured products that are available for sale to customers.

The cost of manufacturing products from raw materials consists of three elements:

- *Direct materials* consist of the costs of primary raw materials used in processing finished goods. Examples of primary raw materials are lumber used in making furniture, crude oil used in refining petrochemicals, and fabric used in making garments.

- *Direct labor* consists of the wages earned by production employees for the time they actually spend working on the product. Examples include the wages paid to welders in an automobile assembly plant and to carpenters on a construction job.

- *Factory overhead* consists of all manufacturing costs other than direct materials and direct labor. It includes indirect materials (materials other than primary raw materials), indirect labor (all labor costs other than direct labor, such as wages paid for supervision, maintenance, and factory security), and other manufacturing costs (such as depreciation on factory buildings and equipment, insurance on factory facilities, and lubricants and cleaning supplies used).

Raw materials, work-in-process, and finished goods are the physical inventory categories for a manufacturing company, and the cost of these inventories is measured by the product costing system. Direct materials, direct labor, and factory overhead represent the cost components of inventory. The Raw Materials[1] inventory account includes only direct materials cost. In the processing stage, direct labor and factory overhead are added to direct materials; therefore, Work-in-Process and Finished Goods Inventory valuations include direct materials, direct labor, and factory overhead. As goods move through the typical manufacturing process, direct materials represents a progressively smaller proportion of total inventory cost, and direct labor and factory overhead represent a progressively larger proportion of total inventory cost.

MANUFACTURING COST FLOWS

Inventory costs in a manufacturing organization flow in a very logical pattern through the accounting system. Purchased raw materials are recorded initially in the Raw Materials account, and other incidental supplies are recorded as Manufacturing Supplies. As primary raw materials are requisitioned from materials stores to the factory, direct materials costs are assigned to Work-in-Process. Direct labor costs are added to Work-in-Process as labor hours are devoted to processing raw materials. As incurred, all other manufacturing costs are accumulated temporarily in an account called Factory Overhead. Periodically, factory overhead is assigned to Work-in-Process. In effect, Factory Overhead is a clearing

---

[1] As stated in Chapter 2, account titles are capitalized to distinguish them from physical items with the same name. For example, raw materials refers to the physical goods, whereas Raw Materials refers to the account.

account where all manufacturing costs, other than direct materials and direct labor, are collected until they are assigned to Work-in-Process.

When products are completed by the manufacturing department and transferred to the finished goods warehouse, the accumulated cost of processing these goods is transferred from Work-in-Process to Finished Goods Inventory. When the products are sold, the final transfer of product costs is from Finished Goods Inventory to Cost of Goods Sold. The general pattern of cost flows for a manufacturing organization is illustrated in T-accounts in Exhibit 11–1.

EXHIBIT 11–1   Manufacturing Cost Flows

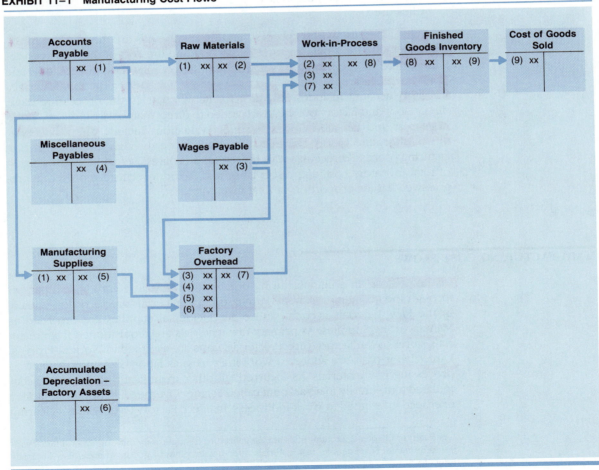

Journal entries

(1) Raw Materials	xx	
Manufacturing Supplies	xx	
Accounts Payable		xx
To record purchase of raw materials and manufacturing supplies on account.		
(2) Work-in-Process	xx	
Raw Materials		xx
To record requisition and transfer of raw materials to the factory from materials stores.		
(3) Work-in-Process	xx	
Factory Overhead	xx	
Wages Payable		xx
To assign direct labor cost incurred to Work-in-Process and indirect labor cost to Factory Overhead.		
(4) Factory Overhead	xx	
Miscellaneous Payables[2]		xx
To record incurrence of various factory overhead costs, such as repairs and maintenance, and property taxes.		
(5) Factory Overhead	xx	
Manufacturing Supplies		xx
To record supplies used in manufacturing.		
(6) Factory Overhead	xx	
Accumulated Depreciation—Factory Assets		xx
To recognize depreciation on factory assets.		
(7) Work-in-Process	xx	
Factory Overhead		xx
To assign factory overhead costs to Work-in-Process.		
(8) Finished Goods Inventory	xx	
Work-in-Process		xx
To record transfer of finished goods from work-in-process inventory to finished goods inventory.		
(9) Cost of Goods Sold	xx	
Finished Goods Inventory		xx
To record the cost of finished goods sold.		

The numbered journal entries posted to the accounts in Exhibit 11–1 are presented above with the appropriate explanations. Before the journal entries

---

[2] The account Miscellaneous Payables is used for convenience in this example to record any liability other than for wages and inventory purchases. Miscellaneous payables include utilities payable, taxes payable, and rent payable.

can be recorded, the supporting data must be collected and documented. These supporting data are provided by the **product costing system,** which consists of the records of manufacturing inventories and the records of manufacturing transactions.

JOB-ORDER COSTING AND PROCESS COSTING

Depending on the nature of the product, the cost of a unit of product transferred from Work-in-Process to Finished Goods Inventory will be determined by either a job-order or process cost system. These two cost systems can be distinguished based on their primary cost objectives and the length of the time period for which they account for costs.

Primary Cost Objective

Job-order costing is used when unique products are produced, or when products are produced in batches. In job-order costing, the primary cost objective for which manufacturing costs are accumulated is the job. Recall from Chapter 2 that cost objectives are the objects or activities to which costs are assigned. The job might be a single space satellite or a batch of identical pieces of furniture or clothing. Accordingly, the cost of a particular job is determined from the cost records maintained for that job. If the job consists of a batch of units, the cost of each unit is determined by dividing the total cost of the job by the number of units in the batch. For example, if 20 bookcases are manufactured in a batch at a total cost of $2,000, the cost per bookcase is $100.

Process costing is used when large quantities of a product are manufactured through a continuous process. The process might include the production of chemicals, newsprint, or cotton yarn. In process costing systems, the primary cost objective for which costs are accumulated is the manufacturing department, and the cost of a single unit is equal to the total accumulated product cost for the department divided by the number of units produced. For example, if a process manufacturing department produces 4,000 gallons of paint during the month at a total cost of $16,000, the cost per gallon is $4.

Time Period

Another important distinction between job-order and process costing is related to the time period used in accounting for manufacturing costs. In a job-order cost system, all job costs are accumulated on job cost records and in Work-in-Process inventory until the job is completed. A job is not considered completed until all units in the job are finished. For example, during July, 19x3, Brocks Brothers, Inc., a manufacturer of sport coats and suits for men and women, began work on 1,000 gray suits. Although some of the suits were finished at the end of July, the job was not completed until all suits were finished and transferred to finished goods. In a job-order cost system the job is a discrete production unit. The cost of the completed job (and the units in the job) is determined when the job is finished, which will not necessarily coincide with the end of an accounting period.

In a process costing system, the manufacturing process consists of a continuous stream of homogeneous goods entering and leaving the production process. During each accounting period the goods worked on usually consist of three groups: (1) goods started in the previous period and completed in the current period, (2) goods both started and completed in the current period, and (3) goods started but not completed in the current period. In a process cost system, costs are accumulated for each accounting period (e.g., month or year) and assigned to the units produced during the period. Since some goods are only partially processed during the period, it is necessary to determine the total production for the period in terms of the equivalent number of completed units. For example, if 200 units were started and completed through 50 percent of the process during the period, then the equivalent of 100 fully completed units were produced. The total number of equivalent units is divided into the total costs for the period to determine the average cost per unit.

To summarize, in a job-order costing system, costs are accumulated separately for each job, and unit production cost is determined when each job is completed. In process costing, manufacturing costs are accumulated for each department, and average unit production costs are determined each accounting period.

BASIC COST SYSTEM RECORDS

In any product cost system—job-order or process—several basic records must be maintained to support the system. These records can be classified as (1) *inventory records* and (2) *transaction records*. Separate inventory records must be maintained for raw materials, work-in-process, and finished goods inventories. In addition, records must be prepared to document transactions that increase or decrease the inventory balances. Exhibit 11–2 shows a typical raw materials inventory record used to record increases and decreases and the available balance for each type of raw material, a materials requisition form used to record transfers of direct materials from raw materials to work-in-process, and a direct labor ticket used to record direct labor hours and costs. These three records are virtually identical for job-order and process costing systems, except that in a process cost system the materials requisition form and direct labor ticket would indicate the department number instead of the job number.

Exhibit 11–2 also includes a typical finished goods inventory record. This record is maintained for each product in a process cost system; however, in a job-order system individual finished goods inventory records are required only when goods are produced for open stock. If products are manufactured for specific customers (which is often the case in companies that use job-order

EXHIBIT 11–2   Basic Cost System Records

Raw Materials Inventory Record

Inventory Number . . . .   Description . . . .

	Purchased			Issued			Balance		
Date	Units	Unit Cost	Total Cost	Units	Unit Cost	Total Cost	Units	Unit Cost	Total Cost

Materials Requisition Form

Requisition No. . . . .   Job No. . . . .

Date . . . .

Inventory Number	Quantity	Unit Cost	Total Cost

Issued by . . . .

Received by . . . .

Direct Labor Ticket

Employee No. . . . . . .   Job No. . . . .

Employee Name . . . .

Date . . . .

Time Work   Time Work
Started . . . .   Completed . . . .

Office Use		
Hours . . . . . Rate . . . . . Charge		

Finished Goods Inventory Record

Inventory No.   Description . . . .

	Received from Factory			Sold			Balance		
Date	Units	Unit Cost	Total Cost	Units	Unit Cost	Total Cost	Units	Unit Cost	Total Cost

systems), job cost records for completed but undelivered jobs provide the necessary detail and documentation for the balance in Finished Goods Inventory. The basic records illustrated in Exhibit 11–2 serve the dual purpose of keeping track of physical quantities and providing cost information for accounting transactions.

JOB-ORDER COSTING PROCEDURES

Job Cost Sheet

In job-order costing it is necessary to assign manufacturing costs simultaneously to (1) Work-in-Process and (2) specific jobs. Job cost sheets are used to accumulate the costs for specific jobs in process. As manufacturing costs are assigned to Work-in-Process, they are also recorded on the appropriate job cost sheets. The job cost sheets, therefore, constitute the subsidiary records for Work-in-Process. Each job cost sheet has a place for recording the different elements of manufacturing costs—direct materials, direct labor, and factory overhead. A typical job cost sheet is presented in Exhibit 11–3.

EXHIBIT 11–3   Job Cost Sheet

Job Cost Sheet

Job No. . . . .   Date Started. . . . .

Description . . . .   Target Completion Date . . . .

Number of Units in Job . . . .   Date Completed. . . . .

Date	Materials		Labor		Factory Overhead	
	Requisition Number	Amount	Hours	Amount	Rate per Hour	Amount
Totals						

Total Job Cost _____   Cost per Unit _____

Job-Order Costing Illustrated

To illustrate how manufacturing costs flow through the accounts in a job-order cost accounting system, the manufacturing transactions recorded by Brocks Brothers, Inc., in August 19x3 are presented below. Included are the transactions recorded in the general ledger and the procedures performed in the cost system records. Total inventories were $193,565 at the beginning of August and consisted of Raw Materials, $18,800; Work-in-Process, $97,315; and Finished Goods, $77,450. The components of these inventories are summarized below. In addition to these inventories, there was $1,200 in Manufacturing Supplies.

Raw Materials

Description	Quantity	Unit Cost	Total Cost
Gray fabric	800 yards	$10	$ 8,000
Blue fabric	500 yards	14	7,000
Brown fabric	200 yards	19	3,800
			$18,800

Work-in-Process		Finished Goods Inventory	
Job	Total Cost	Job	Total Cost
325	$55,245	323	$52,250
326	42,070	324	25,200
	$97,315		$77,450

The manufacturing transactions recorded by Brocks Brothers, Inc., for August are described below, along with the required *journal entries* and descriptions of the required product *cost system procedures.*

Cost system procedures consist of supporting documentation recorded in subsidiary accounts and other records related to recognizing changes in Raw Materials, Work-in-Process, and Finished Goods Inventory.

1. Purchased 1,000 yards of blue fabric at $14 per yard and 300 yards of brown fabric at $19 per yard.

Journal entry

Raw Materials	19,700	
Accounts Payable		19,700
To record purchase of fabrics.		

Cost system procedures

Record purchases on raw materials inventory records:
Blue fabric   1,000 yards @ $14 = $14,000
Brown fabric   300 yards @ $19 = $ 5,700

2. Requisitioned the following raw materials to the factory: 200 yards of gray fabric to Job 326 and 900 yards of blue fabric to Job 327, a new job started in August.

Journal entry

Work-in-Process	14,600	
Raw Materials		14,600
To record requisition of raw materials to factory.		

Cost system procedures

a) Prepare materials requisition forms.
b) Record materials issuances on raw materials inventory records:

   Gray fabric   200 yards @ $10 = $ 2,000
   Blue fabric   900 yards @ $14 = $12,600

c) Record direct materials cost on individual job cost sheets:
   Job 326 $ 2,000
   Job 327 $12,600

3. Manufacturing payroll for August is summarized below.

	Cost	Hours
Direct labor		
Job 325	$ 9,460	1,150
Job 326	16,845	2,100
Job 327	1,680	195
Total direct labor	$27,985	3,445
Indirect labor	7,200	
Total labor	$35,185	

Journal entry

Work-in-Process	27,985	
Factory Overhead	7,200	
Wages Payable		35,185
To record wages for the month and assign direct labor cost to Work-in-Process and indirect labor cost to Factory Overhead.		

Cost system procedures

a) Prepare labor tickets.

b) Record direct labor hours and costs on individual job cost sheets:

Job 325	1,150 hours	$ 9,460
Job 326	2,100 hours	$16,845
Job 327	195 hours	$ 1,680

4. Recorded the following factory overhead costs:

Manufacturing supplies used		$ 950
Factory depreciation		1,500
Other factory expenses:		
Maintenance and repairs	$1,740	
Property taxes	500	
Utilities	2,400	4,640
Total		$7,090

Journal entry

Factory Overhead	7,090	
Manufacturing Supplies		950
Accumulated Depreciation—Factory		
Assets		1,500
Miscellaneous Payables		4,640
To record actual factory overhead expenses incurred for August.		

Cost system procedures

None is required since the manufacturing inventory accounts are not affected by this transaction.

5. Applied factory overhead cost to Work-in-Process for August using a predetermined rate of $4 per direct labor hour.

Job Number	Direct Labor Hours		Overhead Rate		Applied Factory Overhead
325	1,150	×	$4	=	$ 4,600
326	2,100	×	$4	=	8,400
327	195	×	$4	=	780
	3,445				$13,780

Journal entry

Work-in-Process	13,780	
Factory Overhead		13,780
To apply factory overhead to Work-in-Process at the rate of $4 per direct labor hour.		

Cost system procedures

Record factory overhead applied on job cost sheets:
Job 325	$4,600
Job 326	$8,400
Job 327	$ 780

6. Completed Jobs 325 and 326, consisting of 1,500 and 1,000 units respectively.

Cost Summary	Job 325	Job 326
Total cost, beginning of month	$55,245	$42,070
Job costs assigned in August:		
Direct materials	—	2,000
Direct labor	9,460	16,845
Factory overhead	4,600	8,400
	$69,305	$69,315
Total cost of Jobs 325 and 326		$138,620

Journal entry

Finished Goods Inventory	138,620	
Work-in-Process		138,620
To record completion and transfer of Jobs 325 and 326 to finished goods inventory.		

Cost system procedures

Transfer job cost sheets for Jobs 325 and 326 from Work-in-Process subsidiary file to Finished Goods subsidiary file. Unit costs are computed as follows:

	Job 325	Job 326
a) Total job cost	$69,305	$69,315
b) Total units per job	1,500	1,000
Unit cost (a) ÷ (b)	$46.20	$69.32

7. Delivered the following jobs to customers:

	Total Cost
Job 323 (completed at beginning of month)	$ 52,250
Job 324 (completed at beginning of month)	25,200
Job 325 (completed in August; see transaction 6)	69,305
	$146,755

Journal entry	Cost of Goods Sold	146,755	
	Finished Goods Inventory		146,755
	To record delivery of Jobs 323, 324, and 325 to customers.		

Cost system procedures	Transfer job cost sheets for Jobs 323, 324, and 325 from Finished Goods subsidiary file to Completed and Delivered Jobs file.

Exhibit 11–4 shows the various manufacturing inventory accounts, Cost of Goods Sold, and the cost system records reflecting the above transactions. Note how the cost system records provide supporting documentation for the general ledger account balances.

ACCOUNTING FOR FACTORY OVERHEAD

In the illustration of Brocks Brothers, Inc., factory overhead was assigned to Work-in-Process and to specific jobs at the predetermined rate of $4 per direct labor hour. By using a predetermined overhead rate the total cost of a particular job can be determined as soon as the job is completed and the number of labor hours is tabulated. If actual overhead were assigned to jobs, total cost could not be determined until after the *end of the period* when total factory overhead is known.

The predetermined factory overhead rate is computed by dividing predicted total overhead for the year by the predicted activity for the year. Assuming Brocks Brothers, Inc., estimates total factory overhead cost for the year to be

EXHIBIT 11–4   General Ledger Accounts and Supporting Job-Order Cost System Records for Brocks Brothers, Inc.

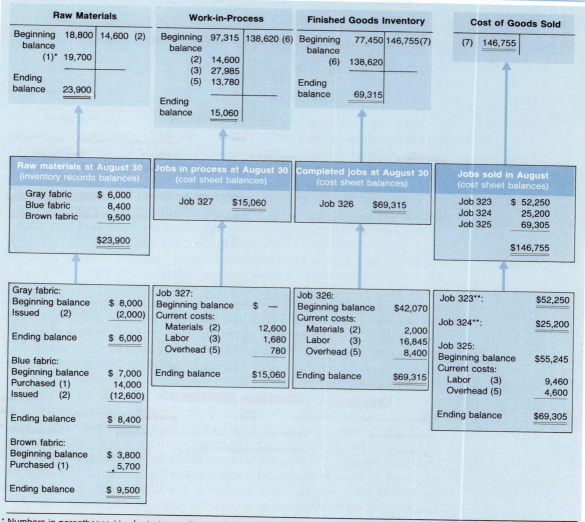

* Numbers in parentheses ( ) refer to transaction numbers.

** In Finished Goods at beginning of period.

$100,000 and total production activity (measured in terms of direct labor hours) to be 25,000 direct labor hours, the predetermined factory overhead rate is $4 per direct labor hour.

$$\text{Predetermined factory overhead rate} = \frac{\text{Predicted total overhead for the year}}{\text{Predicted total direct labor hours for the year}}$$

$$= \frac{\$100,000}{25,000 \text{ hours}}$$

$$= \$4.$$

Two important questions must be addressed whenever predetermined factory overhead rates are used: (1) What is the appropriate basis for overhead allocation, and (2) what disposition should be made of any underapplied or overapplied balance in factory overhead at the end of the period?

Basis for Overhead Allocation

In addition to direct labor hours, other common bases for overhead allocation include machine hours, direct labor dollars, and number of units produced. Examples of predetermined overhead rates using these bases are $2 per machine hour, 40 percent of direct labor, and $10 per unit completed.

A company, such as a clothing manufacturer, that has a labor-intensive manufacturing process would probably select a labor-related activity base, such as direct labor hours or direct labor dollars. Labor intensive companies usually find a close correlation between the amount of factory overhead incurred and the volume of labor-related activities. On the other hand, a company whose production is machine intensive, such as a chemical company, would probably use an activity base reflecting machine activity, such as machine hours. Companies that have more than one production department may use a different base for each department.

The primary goal in selecting an allocation base is to make sure that a logical association exists between the base and the significant factory overhead cost components. Also, the quantity of the base for each period, and for each job or department, should be fairly easy to measure. Direct labor hours is a widely used base because the annual prediction of direct labor hours is easily determined when the units of planned production and the number of plant employees are known. Moreover, the actual number of direct labor hours for each period, and for each job or department, is available in the product costing system.

Overapplied and Underapplied Overhead

Using the Brocks Brothers example (where predicted factory overhead for the year was $100,000, and direct labor hours were 25,000), assume that the company actually incurred $100,000 in factory overhead and that actual direct labor hours for the year were 25,000. Summary entries for actual and applied overhead are as follows:

Journal entry			
	Factory Overhead	100,000	
	Various balance sheet accounts		100,000
	To record actual factory overhead for the year.		
	Work-in-Process	100,000	
	Factory Overhead		100,000
	To apply factory overhead to Work-in-Process for 25,000 direct labor hours at the rate of $4 per direct labor hour.		

Because the actual cost recorded equals the applied cost, there is no balance in Factory Overhead at the end of the year. However, if either the actual overhead cost or the actual level of the production activity base differed from its predicted value, there would be a balance in Factory Overhead, representing overapplied or underapplied overhead.

Now assume that the prediction of 25,000 direct labor hours was correct but that actual overhead cost was $105,000. In this case, Factory Overhead shows a $5,000 debit balance representing underapplied factory overhead:

Factory Overhead

Actual 105,000	100,000	Applied
Underapplied factory overhead 5,000		

If actual factory overhead was only $98,000, Factory Overhead would be overapplied and show a $2,000 credit balance:

Factory Overhead

Actual 98,000	100,000	Applied
	2,000	Overapplied factory overhead

It is apparent from these examples that if the *prediction* of total factory overhead cost is not accurate, there will be an underapplied or overapplied balance in Factory Overhead at the end of the year. A similar result occurs when the actual production activity level is different from the predicted activity level used in computing the predetermined rate. Any balances in Factory Overhead during the year representing overapplied or underapplied overhead are usually allowed to accumulate from month to month. Any balance in Factory Overhead at the end of the year is usually disposed of by one of the two methods discussed in the following section.

Disposition of Factory Overhead Balances

To illustrate the disposition of a Factory Overhead balance at the end of the accounting period, assume the following year-end account balances (all debits) for a manufacturing company:

Work-in-Process	$300,000
Finished Goods Inventory	200,000
Cost of Goods Sold	500,000
Factory Overhead (underapplied)	8,000

A common method for disposing of the $8,000 debit balance in Factory Overhead at the end of the period is merely to write it off to Cost of Goods Sold by the following journal entry:

Journal entry

Cost of Goods Sold	8,000	
Factory Overhead		8,000

The effect of this entry is to close out the Factory Overhead account and to charge the underapplied balance to Cost of Goods Sold, thus increasing total expenses on the income statement and reducing net income. If Factory Overhead has a credit balance, representing overapplied overhead, Factory Overhead would be debited, and Cost of Goods Sold would be credited, reducing total expenses and increasing net income.

Another method of disposing of an end-of-period balance in Factory Overhead is to allocate it among Work-in-Process, Finished Goods Inventory, and Cost of Goods Sold. This allocation is frequently made on the basis of the relative total cost in each account at the end of the period. The following computations show how the $8,000 would be disposed of under the allocation method.

	Account Balance	Relative Portion of Total		Underapplied Factory Overhead		Allocation
Work-in-Process	$ 300,000	0.30	×	$8,000	=	$2,400
Finished Goods Inventory	200,000	0.20	×	8,000	=	1,600
Cost of Goods Sold	500,000	0.50	×	8,000	=	4,000
Total	$1,000,000	1.00				$8,000

The entry to record the assignment of the Factory Overhead balance to Work-in-Process, Finished Goods Inventory, and Cost of Goods Sold is shown in the following journal entry.

Journal entry	Work-in-Process	2,400	
	Finished Goods Inventory	1,600	
	Cost of Goods Sold	4,000	
	Factory Overhead		8,000

The rationale for writing the Factory Overhead balance off against Cost of Goods Sold is that it is convenient and simple. If the predicted amounts used in calculating the predetermined rate are relatively accurate, the underapplied or overapplied amount should be relatively small, thereby justifying the use of the most convenient method.

The allocation method, however, is more desirable if the Factory Overhead balance is relatively large. An overapplied or underapplied balance in Factory Overhead is always caused by the use of a predetermined overhead rate that differs from the actual overhead rate. If we waited until the end of the period to apply overhead, an accurate overhead rate based on actual cost could be used. Therefore it is logical to allocate the ending balance in Factory Overhead to the accounts affected by the inaccurate predetermined rate, that is, to Work-in-Process, Finished Goods Inventory, and Cost of Goods Sold. After the allocation, the balance in each account should be approximately the same as it would have been had an actual rate been used. An expanded discussion of factory overhead and other common cost assignments is provided in Chapter 12.

PROCESS COSTING PROCEDURES

Because many elements of process costing systems are similar to those discussed previously for job-order systems, only the concepts and procedures unique to process costing are emphasized in this section. Recall that process costing systems differ from job-order systems in two respects—the primary accounting unit for which costs are accumulated and the period of time for which costs are accumulated. In a *process costing system* costs are accumulated for each *department,* and the cost accumulation time period is the *accounting period.*

Process Costing with No Beginning Inventories

To illustrate process costing assume that Micro Systems Co. began business in 19x3 to manufacture memory chips for microcomputers. Sophisticated machinery has been purchased for manufacturing the chips in a one-step process. Each finished unit requires that one unit of raw materials be added at the beginning of the manufacturing process. The production and cost data for the first year of operations for Micro Systems are as follows:

Production Data	Units
Units started	20,000
Completed units transferred to finished goods	16,000
Units in process, end of period (75% converted)	4,000

Current Manufacturing Costs		Dollars
Raw materials transferred to processing		$ 80,000
Conversion costs:		
Direct labor for the period	$38,000	
Factory overhead applied		
(50% of direct labor cost)	19,000	57,000
Total costs for period		$137,000

The key to mastering process costing is understanding the **cost of production report,** which summarizes unit and cost data for each department. It consists of the following sections:

- Summary of units in process.
- Equivalent units.
- Total cost to be accounted for and cost per equivalent unit.
- Accounting for total cost.

The cost of production report for Micro Systems Co. is shown in Exhibit 11–5, and its four sections are discussed below.

Summary of Units in Process.   This section of the report provides a summary of all units in the department during the period. Units in process at the beginning of the period plus units started equals the total units in process during the period. Units in process during the period were either completed or still on hand at the end of the period.[3]

All units are treated the same in this section regardless of the amount of processing that took place on them during the period. The objective is to account for all the discrete units of product in process during the period. Note in Exhibit 11–5 that 20,000 individual units were in process during the period, 16,000 units were completed, and 4,000 units were still in process at the end of the period.

---

[3] In some processes units may be lost through spoilage or pilferage. These special situations are covered in advanced courses in cost accounting.

EXHIBIT 11-5   Process Costing without Beginning Inventories

Micro Systems Co.
Cost of Production Report
For the year ended December 31, 19x3

Summary of units in process

Beginning	—
Units started	20,000
In process	20,000
Completed	−16,000
Ending	4,000

Equivalent units in process

	Materials	Conversion
Units completed	16,000	16,000
Plus: equivalent units in ending inventory	4,000	3,000*
Equivalent units in process	20,000	19,000

Total cost to be accounted for and cost per equivalent unit in process

	Materials	Conversion	Total
Work-in-Process, beginning	$ —	$ —	$ —
Current cost	80,000	57,000**	137,000
Total cost in process	$80,000	$57,000	$137,000
Equivalent units in process	÷20,000	÷19,000	
Cost per equivalent unit in process	$ 4	$ 3	$ 7

Accounting for total cost

Transferred out (16,000 × $7)			$112,000
Work-in-Process, ending:			
Materials (4,000 × $4)		$16,000	
Conversion (3,000 × $3)		9,000	25,000
Total cost accounted for			$137,000

---

* 4,000 units 75% converted.
** Includes direct labor of $38,000 and applied factory overhead of $19,000.

Equivalent Units.   In this section of the cost of production report, the objective is to translate the number of units in process during the period into equivalent completed units. **Equivalent completed units** represents the number of completed units that is equal, in terms of production inputs, to a given number of partially completed units. For example, 80 units 50 percent completed in terms of processing costs are the equivalent of 40 completed units (80 × 0.50). Micro Systems Co. adds all materials at the beginning of the process, and all conversion costs—direct labor and factory overhead—are added evenly throughout the manufacturing process. Therefore, separate computations must be made for equivalent units of *materials* and equivalent units of *conversion*. Although the department worked on 20,000 units during the period, the total number of equivalent units completed with respect to conversion was only 19,000 units, 16,000 finished units plus 3,000 equivalent units (4,000 units 75 percent converted). All 20,000 units (16,000 finished and 4,000 in process) were completed with respect to materials.

Total Cost to Be Accounted for and Cost per Equivalent Unit. This section of the report summarizes the total cost assigned to the department during the period. The disposition of total cost is summarized in the next section of the report. Since there were no units in process at the beginning of the period, the only production cost that Micro Systems Co. had to account for during 19x3 was the current period's cost. Therefore, to compute the average cost per equivalent unit, the total cost charged to the department is divided by the equivalent units worked on during the period. Because the number of equivalent units in process differs for materials and conversion, separate computations of units cost are made for these cost components. The total cost per equivalent unit in process during the period is determined by adding together the unit materials and conversion costs.

Accounting for Total Cost. This section shows the disposition of the total cost charged to the department during the period. The general rule in assigning cost to units of production is that manufacturing cost follows the units worked on. Therefore the total cost to be accounted for is assigned to two groups of units: (1) the units completed during the period and (2) the units in process at the end of the period. The 16,000 units finished during the period are completed with respect to materials and conversion; hence, their total cost is $7 per unit— the unit materials cost of $4 plus the unit conversion cost of $3. The 4,000 units in ending work-in-process are assigned a full equivalent unit of cost for materials, or $4 per unit. However, for conversion costs only 3,000 equivalent units are assigned to ending Work-in-Process because the 4,000 units in process have gone through only 75 percent of the conversion (or manufacturing) process. Processing will be completed on these units in a subsequent period. The total costs accounted for should equal the total costs in process.

Journal Entries. The cost of production report summarizes the manufacturing costs assigned to Work-in-Process during the period and provides information for preparing the journal entry to record the cost of goods completed and transferred to finished goods inventory during the period. The journal entries and the supporting documents to record the assignment of costs to Work-in-Process are essentially the same as those discussed for job-order costing. The entries for Micro Systems Co. for 19x3 are as follows:

**Journal
entries**

(1)	Work-in-Process	80,000	
	Raw Materials		80,000
	To record materials requisitioned to factory.		
(2)	Work-in-Process	38,000	
	Wages Payable		38,000
	To record wages for the period.		
(3)	Work-in-Process	19,000	
	Factory Overhead		19,000
	To apply factory overhead at 50 percent of direct labor cost.		
(4)	Finished Goods Inventory	112,000	
	Work-in-Process		112,000
	To record transfer of completed units to finished goods.		

After the above entries are posted, Work-in-Process appears as follows:

Work-in-Process

(1)	Direct materials	80,000	112,000	(4)	To Finished Goods Inventory
(2)	Direct labor	38,000			
(3)	Factory overhead	19,000			
	Ending balance	25,000			

Note in Exhibit 11–5 that the $112,000 assigned to 16,000 units transferred out is equal to the amount credited to Work-in-Process for costs transferred to Finished Goods Inventory. Also, the $25,000 balance in Work-in-Process is equal to the amount assigned to ending work-in-process on the cost of production report.

Process Costing with Beginning Inventories

In the previous example, Micro Systems Co. was in its first year of operations and had no beginning inventories. Continuing the example into 19x4, the second year of operations, we can illustrate process costing procedures for a company that has both *beginning* and *ending* inventories. The pertinent information for 19x4 is summarized below.

Production Data	Units
Units in process, beginning of period (75% converted)	4,000
Units started	30,000
Completed and transferred to finished goods	29,000
Units in process, end of period (40% converted)	5,000

Current Manufacturing Costs		Dollars
Raw materials transferred to processing		$123,400
Conversion costs:		
Direct labor for the period	$62,200	
Factory overhead applied		
(50% of direct labor cost)	31,100	93,300
Total costs for period		$216,700

Whenever partially completed units in beginning inventory are carried forward from the previous period, the cost of these equivalent units is likely to be different from the cost of equivalent units processed in the current period. For costing purposes it is necessary in such cases to either (1) average the total cost of beginning inventory and current production over the total equivalent units in process, or (2) make a cost flow assumption, such as FIFO or LIFO, about the beginning inventory equivalent units and current production units. The weighted average method is discussed in the following section, and the FIFO (first-in, first-out) method is discussed in Appendix C at the end of this chapter.

Weighted Average Process Costing. In the **weighted average inventory method,** the costs of partially completed units in beginning work-in-process are combined with current manufacturing costs, and the total is assigned on an average basis to all equivalent units in process during the period. In this context, "in process" means being physically located in the production department at some time during the period. The weighted average method makes no cost distinction between beginning inventory units and units started during the current period. The total cost in process during the period is averaged over the total equivalent units in process during the period, making no distinction between the units started in the current period and the units started in the previous period.

Micro Systems' cost of production report for 19x4, prepared under the weighted average method, is shown in Exhibit 11–6. Note that the equivalent units of 34,000 for materials and 31,000 for conversion are called *equivalent units in process*. These amounts include the number of equivalent units in process during the period—partially completed units in beginning inventory plus equivalent units of work performed during the current period. Similarly, the cost computations of $139,400 and $102,300 are called *total costs in process* and include beginning Work-in-Process plus current manufacturing costs. Consequently, the unit cost figures represent the costs per equivalent unit in process. The total unit cost of $7.40 is assigned to all units transferred out during the period, whether they were started in the previous period or in the current period.

EXHIBIT 11–6 Weighted Average Process Costing with Beginning Inventories

Micro Systems Co.
Cost of Production Report
For the year ended December 31, 19x4

Summary of units in process

Beginning	4,000
Units started	30,000
In process	34,000
Completed	−29,000
Ending	5,000

Equivalent units in process	*Materials*	*Conversion*
Units completed	29,000	29,000
Plus: equivalent units in ending inventory	5,000	2,000*
Equivalent units in process	34,000	31,000

Total cost to be accounted for and cost per equivalent unit in process

	Materials	*Conversion*	*Total*
Work-in-Process, beginning	$ 16,000	$ 9,000	$ 25,000
Current cost	123,400	93,300†	216,700
Total cost in process	$139,400	$102,300	$241,700
Equivalent units in process	÷ 34,000	÷ 31,000	
Cost per equivalent unit in process	$ 4.10	$ 3.30	$ 7.40

Accounting for total cost

Transferred out (29,000 × $7.40)		$214,600
Work-in-Process, ending:		
Materials (5,000 × $4.10)	$ 20,500	
Conversion (2,000 × $3.30)	6,600	27,100
Total cost accounted for		$241,700

* 5,000 units 40% converted.
† Includes direct labor of $62,200 and applied factory overhead of $31,100.

SUMMARY

Product costing is the process of assigning costs to inventories as they flow through the manufacturing process. The total cost assigned to manufactured products establishes the values reported in the external financial statements for Work-in-Process and Finished Goods Inventories, and Cost of Goods Sold expense. Product cost information is also useful in many areas of internal management such as product pricing, profit planning, and cost control.

Job-order costing and process costing are the two primary product costing methods used by manufacturing organizations. Job-order costing involves accumulating costs by specific jobs, or batches of product, and is used primarily by companies that have a noncontinuous manufacturing process or that manufacture on a custom-order basis. Process costing involves accumulating costs by the departments that manufacture a product in a continuous process. When units worked on are not completely processed in one period, process costing uses the concept of equivalent units in computing unit costs for the period. Both job-order costing systems and process costing systems ordinarily assign factory overhead to the product on the basis of a predetermined overhead rate.

The weighted average method of process costing combines beginning inventory costs with current costs and computes an average cost per equivalent unit in process. The FIFO cost flow method is discussed in Appendix C at the end of the chapter.

APPENDIX A
NORMAL FACTORY OVERHEAD ACCOUNTING

Many companies use an accounting method for factory overhead, called **normal factory overhead accounting,** that does not close the balance in Factory Overhead at the end of the accounting period. As indicated earlier, total factory overhead tends to be rather stable from year to year because many of the components of factory overhead are not related to the level of production activity. Accordingly, predetermined overhead rates based on predicted activity for each year will vary if predicted production activity changes from year to year. For example, assume that a company predicts its total factory overhead to be fixed at $100,000 per year. When predicted activity is 25,000 direct labor hours, the factory overhead rate is $4; when predicted activity is 20,000 direct labor hours, the factory overhead rate is $5. This difference will affect gross profit for the product and may affect managers' evaluations of firm profitability.

Assume that it takes 1 direct labor hour to make 1 finished unit, and that combined direct materials and direct labor costs are $10 per unit. If the product sells for $18 per unit, the gross profit per unit decreases from $4 to $3 when direct labor hours (the factory overhead activity base) are decreased from 25,000 to 20,000:

	Overhead Based on Direct Labor Hours	
Direct labor hours	25,000	20,000
Selling price per unit	$18	$18
Direct materials and direct labor per unit	$10	$10
Factory overhead per unit (1 hr per unit)	4	5
Total cost per unit	−14	−15
Gross profit per unit	$ 4	$ 3

To illustrate further the impact of annual estimated factory overhead rates on reported profits, assume that the above company produced 25,000 units in 19x3 operating at a production level of 25,000 direct labor hours and produced 20,000 units in 19x4 operating at a production level of 20,000 direct labor hours. Also, assume that actual sales for each of the two years were 22,500 units. The gross profit for each of the two years is presented below.

	19x3	19x4
Sales (22,500 units at $18)	$405,000	$405,000
Cost of goods sold:		
(22,500 units at $14)	−315,000	—
(2,500 units at $14 left over from 19x3 plus 20,000 units at $15)	—	−335,000
Gross profit	$ 90,000	$ 70,000

In this example, gross profit varied by $20,000 in successive years that had the same amount of sales. The difference was caused entirely by the variation in the production level for the two years. In 19x4 the total fixed cost was spread over 5,000 fewer units, causing the cost per unit produced to be $1 higher than the units produced in 19x3. As discussed in Chapter 10, most managers feel that profits should not vary with the production activity level, but rather with changes in sales. A uniform unit cost from year to year will be achieved only if the production level is uniform and the factory overhead rate is based on annual predicted production activity. For the above company, the expected cost of producing a unit would be $15 each year only if it maintained its production level at 20,000 units each year.

In most manufacturing situations the operating level cannot be held constant. It is likely to vary from year to year because of fluctuating demand for the product, or other factors such as difficulty in obtaining raw materials, or the work force going on strike during the year. It would be infeasible, and in many cases impossible, to maintain production at a constant level just to keep product cost at a uniform level.

The effect of uniform production levels on unit production costs can be achieved by using a factory overhead rate based on a long-run normal production activity level. If the company in the example above normally operated at a level of 25,000 direct labor hours, under normal overhead accounting, $4 per unit would be used in costing the product, even in years when the production level was different from 25,000 direct labor hours. Using a normal factory overhead rate, the gross profit statements for 19x3 and 19x4 would appear as follows:

	19x3	19x4
Sales (22,500 units at $18)	$405,000	$405,000
Cost of goods sold (22,500 units at $14)	−315,000	−315,000
Gross profit	$ 90,000	$ 90,000

From the standpoint of profit measurement, the use of a normal overhead rate clearly overcomes the problem of fluctuating profits caused by fixed costs and fluctuating production levels. But how do normal overhead rates affect the entries in the cost system? In the example above, the normal rate was based on estimated factory overhead of $100,000 and normal production activity of 25,000 direct labor hours. In 19x3, when production activity was actually 25,000 direct labor hours and actual factory overhead was $100,000, the Factory Overhead account appeared as follows:

Factory Overhead

Actual 100,000 | 100,000 Applied

In 19x4, with a production activity of 20,000 direct labor hours and using the normal factory overhead rate of $4 per direct labor hour, applied factory overhead was $80,000, which produced a balance in Factory Overhead of $20,000, as shown below.

Factory Overhead

Actual 100,000 | 80,000 Applied

Underapplied
factory overhead 20,000 |

Unlike the treatment discussed in this chapter for disposing of the underapplied or overapplied factory overhead balance, when normal overhead rates are used, any balance left in Factory Overhead at the end of the period is not closed out. Because production activity is expected to fluctuate from time to time, it is anticipated that over a period of years the underapplied and overapplied factory overhead amounts will offset each other. Therefore, these balances are usually not closed out to Cost of Goods Sold or to the inventory accounts, but instead are reported as deferred items on the balance sheet. If the Factory Overhead balance is a material amount, generally accepted accounting principles do not permit it to be carried forward on the balance sheet for financial accounting purposes. In this case the balance should be allocated to Cost of Goods Sold and the inventory accounts.

APPENDIX B
PRODUCT COSTING USING STANDARD COSTS

In Chapter 8 we discussed the concept of standard cost and developed a model for computing standard cost variances. The main focus of that discussion was cost control and management performance evaluation. In addition, standard costs are often integrated into the product costing system in which they are used for inventory valuation. When this is done, the manufacturing accounts are charged with standard costs instead of actual costs, and the differences between standard costs and actual costs are recorded as standard cost variances. These variances are then disposed of in a manner similar to the disposition of under-applied and overapplied factory overhead, which was discussed in this chapter.

To illustrate, assume that Execupens, Inc. (discussed in Chapter 8) uses standard costs in costing its only product, gold casings for writing pens. For product costing purposes, standard costs usually include both variable costs and fixed costs. The standard product cost of one casing is $77, consisting of $68 of variable costs and $9 of assigned fixed costs:

Materials (6 gms at $8)	$48
Direct labor (1 hr at $14)	14
Variable overhead (1 hr at $6)	6
Total variable cost	$68
Fixed overhead (1 hr at $9)	9
Standard cost per unit	$77

The fixed overhead rate of $9 is computed by dividing budgeted fixed overhead of $198,000 by 22,000 standard direct labor hours allowed for a normal level of 22,000 units of output. Execupens' transactions for March 19x6, summarized from Chapter 8, were as follows:

- There were no beginning or ending units in process.
- 124,000 grams of materials were purchased by the production manager at $7.96 per gram for a total of $987,040.
- All 124,000 grams of materials were issued to processing.
- The direct labor payroll was $284,928 for 19,200 hours, an average of $14.84 per hour.
- Actual overhead costs were $126,000 variable and $200,000 fixed.
- 20,000 units were produced during the period.
- 16,000 units were sold.

Standard Cost Variances

The standard cost variances for Execupens, Inc., are summarized below. These variances were computed and discussed in Chapter 8.

Materials purchased price variance	$ 4,960 F
Materials quantity variance	32,000 U
Labor rate variance	16,128 U
Labor efficiency variance	11,200 F
Variable overhead spending variance	10,800 U
Variable overhead efficiency variance	4,800 F
Fixed overhead budget variance	2,000 U
Fixed overhead volume variance	18,000 U

Journal Entries

The cost of materials purchases are usually recorded at standard cost with any price variance recognized at the time of purchase. The entry to record Execupens' materials acquisitions at the time of purchase is as follows:

Journal entry

Raw Materials	992,000	
Materials Purchased Price Variance		4,960
Accounts Payable		987,040
To record at standard cost, $8, the purchase of 124,000 grams of gold.		

As units are transferred out of processing to finished goods inventory, the following entry is made.

Journal entry

Finished Goods Inventory	1,540,000	
Work-in-Process		1,540,000
To record completion of 20,000 units at the standard cost of $77.		

As units are sold, the following entry is made to record the cost of goods sold.

Journal entry

Cost of Goods Sold	1,232,000	
Finished Goods Inventory		1,232,000
To record the Cost of Goods Sold and decrease in Finished Goods Inventory at the standard cost of $77 for 16,000 units sold.		

At the end of the period when actual costs are known and standard cost variances are determined, the following entries are made to assign costs to Work-in-Process, to recognize actual costs, and to record standard cost variances. Work-in-Process is debited for the standard cost per unit for the 20,000 units produced in the following entries for materials, labor, variable overhead, and fixed overhead.

Journal entries

Work-in-Process (20,000 × $48)	960,000	
Materials Quantity Variance	32,000	
Raw Materials		992,000
To record raw materials cost assigned to Work-in-Process at standard cost.		
Work-in-Process (20,000 × $14)	280,000	
Labor Rate Variance	16,128	
Labor Efficiency Variance		11,200
Wages Payable		284,928
To record direct labor assigned to Work-in-Process at standard cost.		
Work-in-Process (20,000 × $6)	120,000	
Variable Overhead Spending Variance	10,800	
Variable Overhead Efficiency Variance		4,800
Factory Overhead		126,000
To record variable factory overhead assigned to Work-in-Process at standard cost.		
Work-in-Process (20,000 × $9)	180,000	
Fixed Overhead Budget Variance	2,000	
Fixed Overhead Volume Variance	18,000	
Factory Overhead		200,000
To record fixed factory overhead assigned to Work-in-Process at standard cost.		

Note in the journal entries that *unfavorable variances* are recorded as *debits* and *favorable variances* are recorded as *credits*. Unfavorable variances are viewed as current manufacturing costs incurred but not charged to processing, whereas favorable variances are viewed as excess charges of manufacturing costs to processing. At the end of the period after standard manufacturing costs and the cost variances have been recorded, it is necessary to dispose of the balances in the variance accounts. Probably the most common procedure for disposing of standard cost variances is to close them out with the net variance debited or credited to Cost of Goods Sold. Another method sometimes used is to allocate them pro rata among Work-in-Process, Finished Goods, and Cost of Goods Sold. This is the same procedure that was discussed earlier for allocating overapplied and underapplied factory overhead.

APPENDIX C
FIFO PROCESS COSTING

Under the **FIFO inventory method** of process costing, partially completed units held at the beginning of the period are not combined with currently produced units for costing purposes. Instead, the units in beginning inventory are costed as a separate group consisting of two components—the portion processed in the previous period is assigned the unit costs for that period, and the portion processed in the current period is assigned the current period's unit costs. For example, assume a company using the FIFO method had unit conversion costs of $5 in 19x3 and $6 in 19x4 and had one unit of inventory 60 percent converted at the end of 19x3. In 19x4 when the unit is completed, the conversion cost assigned to that unit would be $5.40:

Portion processed in 19x3:	$0.60 \times \$5.00 = \$3.00$
Portion processed in 19x4:	$0.40 \times \$6.00 = \underline{2.40}$
Total unit cost	$\underline{\underline{\$5.40}}$

This method of computing costs for units partially processed in two different periods is the distinguishing characteristic of the FIFO method of process costing. A FIFO cost of production report for 19x4 for the Micro Systems example developed earlier in this chapter is shown in Exhibit 11–7. Note in the computation of equivalent units that the FIFO method identifies the number of *equivalent units manufactured* during the current period by subtracting the partially completed equivalent units contained in beginning inventory from the equivalent units in process. In the weighted average method, the computation of equivalent units was based on total *equivalent units in process.*

In the FIFO method, the cost per equivalent unit manufactured consists of only *current manufacturing costs,* computed by dividing current costs (not total costs) by the equivalent units manufactured in the current period. This unit cost is then used to determine the cost of (1) currently completed units in beginning inventory, (2) units started and completed during the period, and (3) units started but not completed. Note in the last section of Exhibit 11–7 that the FIFO method assumes the units completed first are the units started in the previous period and completed in the current period. These units are assigned a cost based partially on the previous year's cost and partially on current unit costs. The next units completed are those that were both started and completed in the current period. These units are valued using only the current period's unit costs. The remaining units—those started but not completed—are assigned a full unit of current materials cost and a partial unit of current conversion cost based on their percentage of completion.

EXHIBIT 11–7   FIFO Process Costing with Beginning Inventories

Micro Systems Co.
Cost of Production Report
For the year ended December 31, 19x4

Summary of units in process

Beginning	4,000
Units started	30,000
In process	34,000
Completed	−29,000
Ending	5,000

Equivalent units manufactured	*Materials*	*Conversion*
Units completed	29,000	29,000
Plus: Equivalent units in ending inventory	5,000	2,000*
Equivalent units in process	34,000	31,000
Less: Equivalent units in beginning inventory	− 4,000	− 3,000**
Equivalent units manufactured	30,000	28,000

Total costs to be accounted for and cost per equivalent unit manufactured	*Materials*	*Conversion*	*Total*
Work-in-Process, beginning	omit †	omit †	$ 25,000
Current costs	$123,400	$ 93,300‡	216,700
Total costs in process	omit †	omit †	$241,700§
Equivalent units manufactured	÷ 30,000	÷ 28,000	
Cost per equivalent unit manufactured	$ 4.113	$ 3.332	$ 7.445

Accounting for total cost

Transferred out:			
Work-in-Process, beginning	$ 25,000		
Cost to complete (1,000 × $3.332)	3,332	$ 28,332	
Started and completed this period			
(25,000 × $7.445)		186,125	$214,457
Work-in-Process, ending:			
Materials (5,000 × $4.113)		$ 20,565	
Conversion (2,000 × $3.332)		6,664	27,229
Total costs accounted for			$241,686§

---

* 5,000 units 40% converted.

** 4,000 units 75% converted.

† Cost per equivalent unit manufactured is based on current costs only.

‡ Includes direct labor of $62,200 and applied factory overhead of $31,100.

§ Answer reflects $14 rounding error ($241,700 − $241,686).

In the case of Micro Systems Co., the difference in the cost valuations between the weighted average method and the FIFO method was only $129 ($27,100 − $27,229) for ending work-in-process and $143 ($214,600 − $214,457) for goods completed and transferred to finished goods. These *differences* in inventory cost valuations between weighted average and FIFO costing tend to be *small* if the change in unit manufacturing costs (materials, labor, and overhead) from one period to the next is small or if the equivalent units in beginning work-in-process represent a small percentage of the total equivalent units worked on during the year.

Under the weighted average method, the cost of goods completed was larger and the cost of ending work-in-process was smaller than under the FIFO method. These relationships between FIFO and weighted average will prevail as long as prices are rising from period to period. In times of falling prices, FIFO will produce a higher valuation for completed units and a lower valuation for units in process.

KEY TERMS

Cost of production report
Direct labor ticket
Equivalent completed units
Finished goods inventory record
Job cost sheet

Materials requisition form
Product costing system
Raw materials inventory record
Weighted average inventory method

APPENDIX KEY TERMS

FIFO inventory method

Normal factory overhead accounting

REVIEW QUESTIONS

11–1   How are the cost measurements that are generated by the product costing system used in financial accounting? In management accounting?

11–2   Name three types of inventories and three components of product cost in a manufacturing organization.

11–3   Trace the flow of manufacturing costs through the inventory accounts into Cost of Goods Sold.

11–4   Describe the difference between job-order and process costing in terms of the primary cost objective and time period for which costs are accumulated.

11–5   What is the function of job cost sheets, and what is their relationship to work-in-process inventory?

11–6   Name the job-order cost system records that provide supporting detail for each of the following general ledger accounts: Raw Materials, Work-in-Process, Finished Goods Inventory, and Cost of Goods Sold.

11–7   Which record in a process cost system provides cost data used to record the transfer of completed goods from work-in-process to finished goods?

11–8   Present the general equation for computing a predetermined factory overhead rate.

11–9   What are the primary benefits of using a predetermined factory overhead rate?

11–10 Briefly explain two methods for disposing of underapplied or overapplied factory overhead.

11–11 For each of the following examples of factory overhead rates, name the production activity base and describe the probable characteristics of the company's manufacturing process: $3 per direct labor hour, 25 percent of direct labor cost, and $0.80 per machine hour.

11–12 Under what circumstances will equivalent units in process be different for materials and conversion?

11–13 Describe the treatment of beginning work-in-process inventory under the weighted average method of process costing.

11–14 Present the general equation for computing cost per equivalent unit for the weighted average method.

11–15 Describe the calculation of the cost of units completed and transferred to finished goods under the weighted average method.

REVIEW PROBLEM

Weighted Average Process Costing: Journal Entries

Magnetic Media, Inc., manufactures magnetic data disks which are used in the computer industry. Since there is very little product differentiation between Magnetic's products, it uses a process costing system to determine inventory costs. Production and manufacturing cost data for 19x7 are as follows:

Production Data:		Units
Units in process, beginning of period (60% converted)		3,000,000
Units started		27,000,000
Completed and transferred to finished goods		25,000,000
Units in process, end of period (30% converted)		5,000,000
Manufacturing Costs:		Dollars
Work-in-Process, beginning of period		
(materials – $468,000; conversion – $252,000)		$ 720,000
Current manufacturing costs:		
Raw materials transferred to processing		6,132,000
Direct labor for the period		1,550,000
Actual factory overhead for the period:		
Manufacturing supplies used	$ 860,000	
Indirect labor	210,000	
Factory depreciation	1,400,000	
Maintenance and repairs	358,000	
Utilities	575,000	
Other	150,000	3,553,000

A predetermined factory overhead rate based on machine hours is used in costing inventory. Factory overhead cost and machine hours were estimated at $3.6 million and 300,000 machine hours, respectively. The factory operated 291,500 machine hours during 19x7. All materials are added at the start of the production process.

Requirements

a) Calculate the predetermined factory overhead rate and the over- or underapplied factory overhead balance at the end of 19x7.

b) Prepare a cost of production report for Magnetic Media, Inc., for 19x7 using the weighted average approach to process costing.

c) Prepare journal entries to record current manufacturing costs and inventory completed and transferred to finished goods during the period.

The solution to this problem is found at the end of the Chapter 11 exercises and problems.

EXERCISES

11–1 Job-Order Cost System and Predetermined Factory Overhead

The following information was taken from the job cost sheet for Job 101 for A-1 Cabinet Company.

Date started: December 27, 19x3
Date completed: January 13, 19x4

Date	Direct Materials	Direct Labor	Factory Overhead	Job Total
12–27–x3	$1,400			
12–30–x3		$ 370		
12–31–x3			$ 296	
1–04–x4	300	480		
1–11–x4		250		
1–13–x4		150	704	
Totals	$1,700	$1,250	$1,000	$3,950

Requirements

a) Prepare the journal entries to record the costs incurred for Job 101 in 19x4 for direct materials, direct labor, and factory overhead.

b) Prepare the journal entry to record the completion of Job 101.

c) Assume that A-1 Cabinet Company applies factory overhead costs at the end of each month and as jobs are completed on the basis of direct labor cost. What is its predetermined factory overhead rate?

11–2 Factory Overhead Account Entries

The December 31, 19x4, Factory Overhead account for Columbia Manufacturing Company is as follows:

Factory Overhead

265,000	275,000
	10,000

Requirements

a) How much was actual factory overhead?

b) How much factory overhead was applied to Work-in-Process?

c) What does the $10,000 balance represent?

d) Describe two alternatives that are available for disposing of the $10,000 balance.

e) Which of the alternatives in requirement (d) will result in the largest net income for the year? Explain.

11–3 Cost of Production Report: No Beginning Inventories

Rodeway Paving Products Company manufactures asphalt paving materials for highway construction through a single-step process in which all materials are added at the beginning of the process. During October 19x4, Rodeway accumulated the following data in its process costing system.

Production data:	
Work-in-process, October 1	0 tons
Raw materials transferred to processing	25,000 tons
Work-in-process, October 31 (75% converted)	5,000 tons
Cost data:	
Raw materials transferred to processing	$300,000
Conversion costs:	
Direct labor cost incurred	19,000
Factory overhead applied	?

Factory overhead is applied at the rate of $1 per equivalent unit (ton) processed.

Required: Prepare a cost of production report for October 19x4.

11–4 Equivalent Units Computations

During February 19x5, Apex Co. had 15,000 units of product in process in its Mixing Department, of which 3,000 were still in process (25 percent converted) at the end of the period.

Requirements

a) Determine the equivalent units in process for conversion costs assuming there was no beginning inventory.

b) Determine the equivalent units in process for conversion costs assuming that 2,800 of the 15,000 units were in beginning work-in-process, 30 percent converted, and that Apex uses weighted average costing.

c) Determine the equivalent units in process for conversion costs assuming that 2,800 of the 15,000 units were in beginning work-in-process, 30 percent converted, that 5,000 units were in ending inventory, 50 percent complete, and that Apex uses weighted average costing.

11–5 Job-Order Costing and Process Costing Applications

For each of the following situations indicate whether job-order or process costing is more appropriate and why.

a) A building contractor for residential dwellings.

b) A manufacturer of nylon yarn that sells to textile companies that make fabric.

c) A clothing manufacturer that makes suits in several different fabrics, colors, styles, and sizes.

d) A hosiery mill that manufactures one product that fits all sizes.

e) A vehicle battery manufacturer that has just received an order for 500,000 identical batteries to be delivered as manufactured over the next twelve months.

11–6 Costing Work-in-Process and Finished Goods Using Weighted Average Costing

King Manufacturing Company makes one product that is produced on a continuous basis in one department. All materials are added at the beginning of production. The total cost per equivalent unit in process in March 19x4 was $4.60, consisting of $3 for materials and $1.60 for conversion. During the month, 8,000 units of product were transferred to finished goods inventory, and on March 31, 4,000 units were in process, 10 percent converted. King uses weighted average costing.

Requirements

a) Determine the cost of goods transferred to finished goods inventory.

b) Determine the cost of the ending work-in-process inventory.

c) What was the total cost of the beginning work-in-process inventory, plus the current manufacturing costs?

11–7 Normal Factory Overhead (Appendix)

Sheraton Furniture Company predicted factory overhead to be $5 million for 19x6. Predicted production activity measured in direct labor hours was 400,000 hours. This level of activity is below the normal five-year average activity level of 500,000 hours. Planned production reductions for the year were made because of expected lower sales caused by a national economic recession. The recession is expected to end in a few months.

Requirements

a) If Sheraton uses a predetermined factory overhead rate based on predicted actual activity, what is the application rate?

b) If the predetermined factory overhead rate is based on long-term normal activity, what is the application rate?

c) If a normal factory overhead rate is used and the actual activity is 400,000 direct labor hours (as predicted), and if actual factory overhead is $5 million (as predicted), what is the balance in Factory Overhead at the end of the year?

d) What are the alternative methods of disposing of the balance determined in requirement (c)?

11–8 Equivalent Units: Weighted Average and FIFO Methods (Appendix)

Gerdons Refinery began December 19x4 with 5,000 barrels of inventory in process, 30 percent completed. During the period, 24,000 barrels were completed and transferred to the finished goods warehouse. Ending inventory consisted of 4,500 barrels, 85 percent completed.

Requirements

a) Calculate the equivalent units in process for conversion cost under the weighted average process cost method.

b) Calculate the equivalent units manufactured for conversion cost under the FIFO process cost method.

11–9 Accounting for Total Cost: FIFO Method (Appendix)

Arnoud Company had a cost per equivalent unit manufactured for January 19x7 of $4.56 for materials and $2.75 for conversion cost. During the period, 10,250 units were completed and transferred to finished goods. At the end of the month, 3,200 units were in work-in-process, 100 percent completed with regard to materials costs and 60 percent completed with regard to conversion costs. At the beginning of January, there were 1,500 units in process, 100 percent completed with regard to materials cost and 50 percent completed with regard to conversion cost. The beginning balance in Work-in-Process was $8,775. Arnoud uses FIFO process costing.

Requirements

a) Calculate the cost of the units completed and transferred to finished goods during January 19x7.

b) Calculate the cost of the units in work-in-process at the end of January 19x7.

11–10 Standard Cost Entries: Materials and Labor (Appendix)

Greenwich Clock Company manufactures clocks with movements purchased from a Swiss company and housings purchased from a British company. The standard materials and labor costs per unit for model AJ9 are $15 for the movement, $10 for the housing, and $8 for labor. Assembly line workers are paid $16 per hour. During January 19x2, Greenwich purchased 220 movements for $3,120 and 300 housings for $3,140 for Model AJ9. During January, workers were paid $1,701 for 105 hours to assemble 200 Model AJ9 clocks.

Requirements

a) Prepare the standard cost journal entries to record the purchase of Model AJ9 movements and housings during January.

b) Prepare the standard cost journal entry to record the wages for the assembly of Model AJ9 units during January.

PROBLEMS

11–11 Manufacturing Cost Flows: Journal Entries

Frankfort Manufacturing Co. completed the following transactions with respect to its manufacturing operations during November 19x5.

- Raw materials costing $60,000 and manufacturing supplies costing $9,000 were purchased on account.

- A total of $30,000 of raw materials were requisitioned to the factory for manufacturing operations conducted during November.

- Manufacturing payroll for the month consisted of 2,250 hours of direct labor and 400 hours of indirect labor, both at $12 per hour.

- Manufacturing supplies costing $3,000 were used.

- Depreciation on the factory building and equipment was $15,000.

- Miscellaneous factory overhead expenses totaled $3,600 for November.

- Factory overhead cost was applied to Work-in-Process at the rate of $10 per direct labor hour.

- Units of product with a total manufacturing cost of $45,000 were completed and transferred to the finished goods warehouse.

- Finished goods costing $36,000 were sold during November.

Requirements

a) Prepare journal entries for each of the transactions that occurred during November 19x5.

b) Prepare T-accounts for the ledger accounts used in recording the transactions in requirement (a), and post all entries to the appropriate accounts.

11–12 Job-Order Costing: Journal Entries

Tri-star Publishing Company prints sales fliers and catalogs for retail and mail-order companies. Production costs are accounted for using a job-order cost system. At the beginning of June 19x5, two jobs were in process: Job 425 with assigned costs of $13,750 and Job 426 with assigned costs of $1,800. The following information summarizes manufacturing activities for June.

- Raw materials costing $80,000 were purchased on account.

- Manufacturing supplies costing $9,000 were purchased on account.

- Raw materials and manufacturing supplies requisitioned during June were as follows:

Raw materials:	
Job 426	$ 2,600
Job 427	18,000
Job 428	14,400
Total direct materials	$35,000
Factory supplies	5,500
Total	$40,500

■ Salaries and wages were recorded as follows:

Direct labor (4,850 hrs at $10 per hr):	
Job 425	$ 5,000
Job 426	15,000
Job 427	20,500
Job 428	8,000
Total direct labor cost	$48,500
Indirect labor cost	5,000
Total payroll	$53,500

■ Depreciation of $5,000 was recorded on the plant and equipment.
■ Miscellaneous factory overhead costs of $8,750 were incurred on account.
■ Factory overhead was applied to production at the rate of $5 per direct labor hour.
■ Jobs 425, 426, and 427 were completed.

Requirements

a) Prepare journal entries to record the manufacturing activities for June 19x5.
b) Compute the balance in Work-in-Process at June 30. Show the job cost breakdown by individual jobs to support the balances in Work-in-Process and Finished Goods Inventory.

11–13 Job-Order Costing and Predetermined Factory Overhead: Journal Entries

United Fabricators accounts for production using a job-order cost system. Actual costs for direct materials and direct labor are assigned to the jobs; however, factory overhead costs are assigned using a predetermined rate based on machine hours. Annual factory overhead for 19x4 was predicted at the beginning of the year to be $400,000. Predicted machine hours for the year were 50,000. The following information is provided for the jobs worked on during November 19x4.

	Job 1007	Job 1008	Job 1009
Work-in-Process, November 1	$10,500	$8,000	$4,200
November production activity:			
Materials requisitioned (units)	1,200	1,400	1,600
Materials cost per unit	$4	$5	$3
Direct labor hours	250	1,800	400
Direct labor cost per hour	$8	$8	$8
Machine hours	1,250	2,000	1,500

Actual November factory overhead costs were $43,000.

Requirements

a) Prepare journal entries to record direct materials and direct labor assigned to production during November.

b) Compute the predetermined factory overhead rate.

c) Prepare the journal entry to apply factory overhead costs to Work-in-Process.

d) Assuming Jobs 1007 and 1008 were completed during November, what was the total cost for each job?

e) Assuming there was no November 1 balance in Factory Overhead, what was the balance at November 30? Does the balance represent overapplied or underapplied factory overhead?

11–14 Job-Order Costing: Journal Entries and Inventory Balances

Trimlawn Mower Company manufactures small gasoline-powered mowers for discount hardware and department stores. Trimlawn buys its three primary mower components (motors, chassis, and wheels) from several different suppliers depending on prices and availability. Trimlawn uses a job-order costing system and treats an order from each customer as a separate job. At the beginning of July, Trimlawn had the following inventories:

Raw Materials:		
Motors	1,200 at $30 =	$36,000
Chassis	850 at $12 =	10,200
Wheels	2,000 at $ 3 =	6,000
Total		$52,200

Work-in-Process:		
Job 365	500 mowers	$30,000
Job 366	300 mowers	16,500
Job 367	1,000 mowers	20,000
Job 368	600 mowers	9,000
Total		$75,500

Finished Goods:		
Job 363	800 mowers	$48,800
Job 364	570 mowers	33,915
Total		$82,715

During July, the following transactions were recognized in Trimlawn's costing system:

1. Purchased the following mower components:

Motors	$46,500
Chassis	18,000
Wheels	28,400

2. Requisitioned the following materials to the factory:

	Motors	Chassis	Wheels
Job 367	$ —	$ —	$6,000
Job 368	18,000	—	7,200
Job 369	21,000	8,400	8,400
Job 370	12,000	4,800	4,800
Job 371	7,500	3,000	3,000

3. Manufacturing payroll for the month of July is summarized below:

Direct labor:	
Job 365	$ 5,120
Job 366	3,200
Job 367	3,400
Job 368	4,160
Job 369	1,300
Indirect labor	3,436
Total	$20,616

4. The following factory overhead costs were incurred during July:

Manufacturing supplies purchased and used	$ 3,800
Utilities	2,600
Depreciation	5,000
Other	2,500
Total	$13,900

5. Factory overhead was applied to Work-in-Process using a predetermined rate based on annual estimated overhead of $180,000 and estimated direct labor of $200,000.

6. Jobs 365 through 368 were completed during the period.

7. At the end of July, finished goods inventory consisted of Job 367 which was awaiting shipment to the customer.

Requirements

a) Prepare the journal entries to record the above transactions.

b) What was Trimlawn's predetermined overhead rate? Show calculations.

c) Determine the balances in Trimlawn's Raw Materials, Work-in-Process, and Finished Goods Inventory accounts.

d) Prepare a statement of cost of goods manufactured and sold for Trimlawn for July. *Hint:* Review Chapter 2, if necessary, before completing this requirement.

11–15 Predetermined Factory Overhead: Determination of Rate and Disposition of Balance

The Norcross Company has decided to use a predetermined rate to assign factory overhead to production. Based on several years' experience the following predictions have been made for the current year, 19x4.

Predicted total factory overhead costs	$270,000
Predicted direct labor hours	30,000 hours
Predicted direct labor costs	$300,000
Predicted machine hours	45,000 hours

Requirements

a) Compute the predetermined factory overhead rate under three different bases: (1) direct labor hours, (2) direct labor costs, and (3) machine hours.

b) Assume that actual factory overhead was $268,000 and that Norcross elected to apply factory overhead to Work-in-Process based on direct labor hours. If actual direct labor was 32,000 hours for 19x4, was factory overhead overapplied or underapplied? By how much?

c) The Norcross Company follows the policy of writing off any under- or overapplied Factory Overhead balance to Cost of Goods Sold at the end of the year. Make the entry necessary at the end of 19x4 to dispose of the Factory Overhead balance determined in requirement (b).

11–16 Job-Order Costing with Predetermined Factory Overhead Rate

Avondale Foundries uses a job-order costing system and a predetermined factory overhead rate based on machine hours. For 19x4 predicted total factory overhead cost is $180,000 and predicted total machine usage is 30,000 hours. During the year the following activities were completed. There were no beginning inventories. Each ton of raw materials makes one ton of finished product.

- Purchased 2,000 tons of raw materials at $160 per ton.

- Purchased manufacturing supplies for $38,000.

- Issued to work-in-process 1,500 tons of raw materials and $32,000 in manufacturing supplies.

- Used 18,000 labor hours at $12 per hour and 22,000 machine hours. Ten percent of the total labor was indirect.

- Recorded the following manufacturing costs:

Depreciation	$32,500
Utilities	15,000
Maintenance and repairs	8,500
Miscellaneous	7,800
Total	$63,800

- Completed jobs with a total cost of $525,000 during 19x4.
- Jobs costing $495,000 were sold during 19x4.

Requirements

a) Prepare the journal entries to record the manufacturing activities for Avondale Foundries for 19x4.

b) Prepare a T-account for Factory Overhead showing the actual and applied factory overhead. Indicate whether the balance represents under- or overapplied factory overhead.

c) Prepare the journal entries to dispose of the under- or overapplied factory overhead under two separate assumptions:

  1. It is written off to Cost of Goods Sold.

  2. It is allocated to Work-in-Process, Finished Goods Inventory, and Cost of Goods Sold. (Round calculations to three decimal places.)

11–17 Disposition of Factory Overhead Balance

The Mouser Company had the following selected account balances at the end of 19x4.

Work-in-Process	$ 55,000 debit
Finished Goods Inventory	75,000 debit
Cost of Goods Sold	370,000 debit
Factory Overhead	32,000 credit

Requirements

a) Was factory overhead cost underapplied or overapplied in 19x4? Explain.

b) Prepare the journal entry to dispose of the Factory Overhead balance assuming it is written off to Cost of Goods Sold.

c) Prepare the journal entry to dispose of the Factory Overhead balance assuming it is allocated among Work-in-Process, Finished Goods Inventory, and Cost of Goods Sold.

d) Which method of disposing of under- or overapplied factory overhead cost is more accurate? Explain.

e) Does Mouser Company use a predetermined overhead rate or does it allocate actual overhead to Work-in-Process? Explain.

11–18 Selecting a Basis for Factory Overhead Application

Delicious Peach Company operates a peach processing and packing plant consisting of two departments, Grading and Packaging. The grading process is carried out primarily by an automated system that separates the fruit based on size and firmness. Packing the fruit is done primarily by hand. Delicious has decided to apply factory overhead costs to Work-in-Process using a predetermined rate. The following information has been collected for both departments at the beginning of 19x5.

	Grading	Packaging
Predicted factory overhead cost	$60,000	$ 50,000
Predicted direct labor hours	2,000	25,000
Predicted direct labor cost	$12,000	$120,000
Predicted machine hours	20,000	5,000

Requirements

a) Compute a predetermined factory overhead rate for each department for each of the following bases:

1. Direct labor costs

2. Direct labor hours

3. Machine hours

b) Which method (or methods) is probably the best suited for each department? Explain.

c) Discuss the effect on inventory valuation and income measurement of making an error in predicting (1) factory overhead cost or (2) the activity level of the overhead base.

11–19 Process Costing: No Beginning Inventories

Selected production and cost data for April 19x4, the first month of operations for Clark Manufacturing Company, are presented below:

Raw materials transferred to processing	8,500 units
Completed and transferred to finished goods	6,000 units
Direct materials cost debited to Work-in-Process	$29,750
Direct labor cost debited to Work-in-Process	$42,000

Each unit of production requires one unit of raw materials, which is added at the beginning of the process. Factory overhead is applied to Work-in-Process based on 50 percent of direct labor cost. Units in ending Work-in-Process were 40 percent converted.

Requirements

a) Determine the number of equivalent units in process for April for (1) materials and (2) conversion.

b) Determine the total cost per equivalent unit in process.

c) Determine the total cost of (1) units completed and transferred to finished goods and (2) units in process at the end of the month.

11–20 Process Costing: No Beginning Inventories: Production Report and Journal Entries

Fisk Manufacturing Company is a new company that produces newsprint paper through a special recycling process which uses scrap paper products. Production and cost data for October 19x7, the first month of operations for the company, are presented below.

Units of product started in process during October	90,000
Units completed and transferred to finished goods	75,000
Machine hours operated	10,000
Direct materials cost incurred	$243,000
Direct labor cost incurred	$95,265

Raw materials are added at the beginning of the process for each unit of product produced, and labor and factory overhead are added evenly throughout the manufacturing process. Factory overhead is applied to Work-in-Process at the rate of $12 per machine hour. Units in process at the end of the period were 65 percent converted.

Requirements

a) Prepare a cost of production report for Fisk Manufacturing Company for October 19x7.

b) Prepare the journal entries to record (1) raw materials transferred to processing during the month, (2) factory overhead applied to Work-in-Process during the month, and (3) the cost of units transferred to finished goods inventory during the month.

11–21 Process Costing: Computation of Manufacturing Costs

The Universal Company determined the cost per equivalent unit in process for materials to be $6 for August 19x5. There were no inventories at the beginning of August. There were 25,000 units finished during the period and ending work-in-process contained 5,000 units 80 percent converted. The combined cost of units finished and units in ending work-in-process was $299,625. Factory overhead is applied at the rate of 25 percent of direct labor cost. All materials are added at the beginning of the process.

Requirements

a) Determine the equivalent units in process for materials and conversion costs.

b) Determine the total current cost incurred for (1) direct materials, (2) direct labor, and (3) factory overhead.

c) Determine the cost per equivalent unit in process for materials and conversion costs.

11–22 Weighted Average Process Costing with Beginning Inventories: Production Report and Journal Entries

Chamblee Processing Company manufactures a product on a continuous basis in two departments, Processing and Finishing. All materials are added at the beginning of work on the product in the Processing Department. During December 19x5, the following events occurred in the Processing Department.

- Units started — 16,000 units
- Units completed and transferred to Finishing — 15,000 units
- Costs assigned to Processing:

Raw materials (one unit of raw materials for each unit of product started)	$142,000
Manufacturing supplies used	18,000
Direct labor costs incurred	51,000
Supervisors' salaries	12,000
Other production labor costs	14,000
Depreciation on equipment	6,000
Other production costs	18,000

Additional information:

- Chamblee uses weighted average costing and applies factory overhead to Work-in-Process at the rate of 100 percent of direct labor cost.

- Ending inventory in the Processing Department consists of 3,000 units that are one-third converted.

- Beginning inventory contained 2,000 units one-half converted, with a cost of $27,300 ($17,300 for materials and $10,000 for conversion).

Requirements

a) Prepare a cost of production report for the Processing Department for December.

b) Prepare all journal entries to record costs incurred by the Processing Department in December and to record the transfer of units to the Finishing Department. Overapplied or underapplied factory overhead is written off to Cost of Goods Sold at the end of each month.

11–23 Weighted Average Process Costing with Beginning Inventories: Production Report and Journal Entries

Hillsborough, Inc., processes its only product in a single process and uses weighted average process costing to account for inventory costs. The following inventory, production, and cost data are provided for June 19x8:

Production data:		
Beginning inventory (25 percent converted)	210,000 units	
Units started	650,000 units	
Ending inventory (50 percent converted)	180,000 units	

Manufacturing costs:		
Beginning inventory in process:		
Materials cost	$146,000	
Conversion cost	88,000	$234,000
Raw materials cost added at beginning of process		739,800
Direct labor cost incurred		410,000
Factory overhead applied		333,600

Requirements

a) Prepare a cost of production report for Hillsborough for June.

b) Prepare journal entries to record costs incurred during the month for raw materials and direct labor, and to record factory overhead applied. Also prepare the entry to record the cost of goods completed and transferred to finished goods inventory.

c) Prepare a cost of goods manufactured report for Hillsborough for June. *Hint:* Review Chapter 2, if necessary, to complete this requirement.

11–24 Cost of Production Report: FIFO and Beginning Inventories (Appendix)

Agrikill Chemical Co. manufactures a patented chemical product called WPK that is used by farmers to kill weeds and pests. WPK is produced through a continuous process, entirely in one department, with all materials added at the beginning of processing. Production and cost data for the company for February 19x8 are as follows:

Production data:	
In process, beginning of month (40% converted)	15,000 units
Started during February	95,000 units
Completed and transferred to finished goods	100,000 units
In process, end of month (50% converted)	10,000 units
Manufacturing costs:	
Work-in-process, beginning	$ 55,000
Raw materials transferred to processing	275,500
Conversion costs:	
Direct labor cost for February	82,170
Factory overhead (applied at the rate of $1 per equivalent unit for conversion cost)	?

Required: Prepare a cost of production report for February 19x8. Use FIFO process costing.

11–25 Process Costing: Work-in-Process Analysis: Weighted Average Costing

Karkare Products, Inc. manufactures automobile polish through a process involving two departments (Mixing and Bottling). All materials are added at the beginning of the Mixing Department process. Factory overhead is applied at the rate of 125 percent of direct labor costs. The Work-in-Process account for the Mixing Department for May 19x5 is presented below.

	Work-in-Process: Mixing		
May 1 balance (100,000 units, 40% converted)	260,200	(c) ?	Finished and transferred to Bottling Department (a) ? units
May costs assigned:			
Raw materials (400,000 units)	460,000		
Direct labor	(b) ?		
Factory overhead	100,000		
May 31 balance (60,000 units, 45% converted)	(d) ?		

The beginning Work-in-Process balance consists of materials, $140,000, and conversion cost, $100,200.

Required: Determine the values for the missing items lettered (a) through (d) in the Mixing Department Work-in-Process account. Assume the company uses weighted average costing. (*Hint:* You may want to prepare a cost of production report.)

11–26 Manufacturing Cost Flows: Standard Cost System: Journal Entries (Appendix)

Konrad Company uses a standard cost system in accounting for the production of its only product, a gadget called "de-slicer" that attaches to golf clubs to help golfers hit the ball straighter. The standard cost of producing one de-slicer has been determined to be $7.65. During a recent month the following activities occurred:

- Raw materials with a standard cost of $73,000 were purchased for $75,000.
- There were 20,000 units completed during the month.
- There were 18,500 units sold during the month.

At the end of the month, actual manufacturing activities were summarized as follows:

- Actual raw materials issued to processing had a standard cost of $71,000. There was an unfavorable materials quantity variance of $2,000.
- The direct labor flexible budget for the units produced during the period was $50,000, whereas actual direct labor was $47,500. The difference was caused by an unfavorable labor rate variance of $800 and a favorable labor efficiency variance of $3,300.
- Actual factory overhead was $38,000 and the flexible budget factory overhead for the units produced was $35,000.

Factory overhead standard cost variances were as follows:

Variable overhead spending variance	$1,200 U
Variable overhead efficiency variance	1,100 F
Fixed overhead budget variance	1,400 F
Fixed overhead volume variance	4,300 U

Required: Prepare journal entries to record (1) the purchase of raw materials; (2) the completion of finished goods; (3) the sale of finished goods; and (4) actual and standard costs for direct materials used, direct labor, and factory overhead.

11–27 Job-Order Costing: Preparation of Statement of Cost of Goods Manufactured

The Helper Corporation manufactures one product and accounts for costs by a job-order cost system. You have obtained the following information for the year ended December 31, 19x3, from the corporation's books and records.

- Total manufacturing cost added during 19x3 was $800,000, based on actual direct materials, actual direct labor, and applied factory overhead based on actual direct labor dollars.

- Cost of goods manufactured was $970,000, also based on actual direct material, actual direct labor, and applied factory overhead.

- Factory overhead was applied to Work-in-Process at 75 percent of direct labor dollars. Applied factory overhead for the year was 27 percent of the total manufacturing cost.

- Beginning Work-in-Process at January 1 was 225 percent of ending Work-in-Process at December 31.

Requirements

a) Prepare a formal statement of cost of goods manufactured for the year ended December 31, 19x3, for Helper Corporation. Use actual direct materials used, actual direct labor, and applied factory overhead. Show supporting computations.

b) Job 37, manufactured entirely in 19x3, had $2,500 of direct labor and $5,700 of direct materials. What was the total cost of manufacturing Job 37?

(CPA Adapted)

11–28 Multiple-Choice Questions: Job-order and Process Costing

1. Worrell Corporation has a job-order cost system. The following debits (credits) appeared in the general ledger account Work-in-Process for March 19x2.

March 1, balance	$ 12,000
March 31, direct materials	40,000
March 31, direct labor	30,000
March 31, factory overhead	27,000
March 31, to Finished Goods	(100,000)

Worrell applies overhead to production at a predetermined rate of 90 percent based on direct labor cost. Job No. 232, the only job still in process at the end of March 19x2, has been charged with factory overhead of $2,250. What was the amount of direct materials charged to Job No. 232?

a) $2,250

b) $2,500

c) $4,250

d) $9,000

2. Information for January 19x2 concerning Department A, the first stage of Ogden Corporation's production cycle, is as follows:

	Materials	Conversion
Work-in-Process, beginning	$ 8,000	$ 6,000
Current costs	40,000	32,000
Total costs	$ 48,000	$38,000
Equivalent units in process using weighted average method	100,000	95,000
Average unit costs	$ 0.48	$ 0.40
Goods completed	90,000 units	
Work-in-Process, ending	10,000 units	

Materials are added at the beginning of the process. The ending work-in-process inventory was 50 percent complete in conversion costs. How would the total costs accounted for be distributed using the weighted average method?

	Units Completed	Ending Work-in-Process
a)	$79,200	$6,800
b)	$79,200	$8,800
c)	$86,000	—
d)	$88,000	$6,800

3. Richardson Company computed the flow of physical units completed for Department M for March 19x2 as follows:

Units completed:	
From work-in-process on March 1, 19x2	15,000
From March production	45,000
Total	60,000

Materials are added at the beginning of the process. The 12,000 units of work-in-process at March 31, 19x2, were 80 percent complete in conversion costs. The work-in-process at March 1, 19x2, was 60 percent complete in conversion costs. Using the weighted average method, what were the equivalent units for March conversion costs?

a) 55,200

b) 57,000

c) 69,600

d) 63,600

4. Tooker Company adds materials at the beginning of the process in Department A. Information concerning the materials used in April 19x2 production is as follows:

Work-in-Process at April 1	10,000 units
Started during April	50,000 units
Completed and transferred to next	
department during April	36,000 units
Work-in-Process at April 30	24,000 units

Using the weighted average method, what are the equivalent units for the materials unit cost calculation for the month of April?

a) 52,000

b) 55,000

c) 57,000

d) 60,000

5. Roy Company manufactures product X in a two-stage production cycle in Departments A and B. Materials are added at the beginning of the process in Department B. Roy uses the weighted average method. Conversion costs for Department B were 50 percent complete in the 6,000 units in the beginning work-in-process and 75 percent complete in the 8,000 units in the ending work-in-process. During February 19x0, 12,000 units were completed and transferred out of Department B. An analysis of the Work-in-Process costs and production activity in Department B for February 19x0 is as follows:

	Transferred-in	Materials	Conversion
Work-in-Process, February 1	$12,000	$2,500	$1,000
February costs incurred	29,000	5,500	5,000

What was the total cost per equivalent unit of product X transferred out for February 19x0 (rounded to the nearest cent)?

a) $2.75

b) $2.78

c) $2.82

d) $2.85

(CPA Adapted)

11–29 Process Costing Production Reports for Two-Department Process: A Challenge Problem

The Dexter Production Company manufactures a single product. Its operations are a continuing process carried on in two departments—Machining and Finishing. In the production process, materials are added to the product in each department without increasing the number of units produced. For June 19x5, the company records indicated the following production statistics for each department.

	Machining	Finishing
Units in process, June 1	—	60,000
Units transferred from previous department	—	—
Units started in production	80,000	—
Units completed and transferred out	60,000	50,000
Units in process, June 30	20,000	10,000
Percent of completion of units in process at June 30:		
Materials	100%	100%
Conversion	50%	70%
Cost records showed the following charges for June:		
Materials	$240,000	$ 88,500
Labor	140,000	141,500
Overhead	65,000	25,700

Required: Prepare separate cost of production reports for the Machining and Finishing Departments for June 19x5. In preparing the report for the Finishing Department, the cost of the units transferred in from the Machining Department are treated the same as raw materials added at the beginning of the process. (Round calculations to three decimal places.)

(CPA Adapted)

11–30 Process Costing with Beginning Inventories: FIFO Method (Appendix)

Zeus Company has two production departments—Fabricating and Finishing. In the Fabricating Department, Polyplast is prepared from Miracle Mix and Bypro. In the Finishing Department, each unit of Polyplast is converted into six Tetraplexes and three Uniplexes. The Fabricating and Finishing Departments use process cost systems. Actual production costs are assigned monthly to Work-in-Process. Raw materials and work-in-process inventories are costed on a FIFO basis. The following data were taken from the Fabricating Department's records for December 19x1.

Quantities (units of Polyplast):	
In process, December 1	3,000
Started in process during the month	25,000
Total units to be accounted for	28,000
Transferred to Finishing Department	19,000
In process, December 31	9,000
Total units accounted for	28,000
Cost of work-in-process, December 1:	
Materials	$ 13,000
Labor	17,500
Overhead	21,500
Total	$ 52,000
Direct labor costs for December	$154,000
Factory overhead for December	$198,000

Polyplast work-in-process at the beginning and end of the month was partially completed as follows:

	Materials	Conversion
December 1	66⅔%	50%
December 31	100%	75%

The following data were taken from raw materials inventory records for December.

	Miracle Mix		Bypro	
	Quantity	Amount	Quantity	Amount
Balance, December 1	62,000	$62,000	265,000	$18,550
Purchases:				
December 12	39,500	$49,375		
December 20	28,500	$34,200		

The Fabricating Department used 83,200 units of Miracle Mix and 50,000 units of Bypro during the month.

Requirements

a) Compute the equivalent number of units of Polyplast manufactured during December, with separate calculations for materials and conversion.

b) Compute the following items to be included in the Fabricating Department's cost of production report for December 19x1, with separate calculations for materials and conversion. Prepare supporting schedules.

   1. Total costs to be accounted for.

   2. Unit costs for equivalent units manufactured. (Round calculations to three decimal places.)

   3. Transfers to Finishing Department during December and Work-in-Process at December 31. Reconcile your answer to requirement (b1).

(CPA Adapted)

REVIEW PROBLEM SOLUTION

a)

$$\text{Predetermined factory overhead rate} = \frac{\text{Predicted total overhead for the year}}{\text{Predicted total machine hours for the year}}$$

$$= \frac{\$3,600,000}{300,000}$$

$$= \$12 \text{ per machine hour.}$$

Actual overhead	$3,553,000
Less: Applied factory overhead	
(291,500 machine hours × $12)	3,498,000
Underapplied factory overhead	$ 55,000

b)   **Magnetic Media, Inc.**
Cost of Production Report
For the year ended December 31, 19x7

Summary of units in process

Beginning	3,000,000
Units started	27,000,000
In process	30,000,000
Completed	−25,000,000
Ending	5,000,000

Equivalent units in process	*Materials*	*Conversion*
Units completed	25,000,000	25,000,000
Plus: Equivalent units in ending inventory	5,000,000	1,500,000*
Equivalent units in process	30,000,000	26,500,000

Total cost to be accounted for and cost per equivalent unit in process	*Materials*	*Conversion*	*Total*
Work-in-Process, beginning	$ 468,000	$ 252,000	$ 720,000
Current cost	6,132,000	5,048,000**	11,180,000
Total cost in process	$ 6,600,000	$ 5,300,000	$11,900,000
Equivalent units in process	÷30,000,000	÷26,500,000	
Cost per equivalent unit in process	$0.22	$0.20	$0.42

Accounting for total cost

Transferred out		
(25,000,000 × $0.42)		$10,500,000
Work-in-Process, ending:		
Materials (5,000,000 × $0.22)	$ 1,100,000	
Conversion (1,500,000 × $0.20)	300,000	1,400,000
Total cost accounted for		$11,900,000

* 5,000,000 units 30% converted.

** Includes direct labor of $1,550,000 and applied factory overhead of $3,498,000.

c)

Work-in-Process		6,132,000	
Raw Materials			6,132,000
To record requisition of raw materials to factory.			
Work-in-Process		1,550,000	
Factory Overhead		210,000	
Wages Payable			1,760,000
To record wages for the month and assign direct labor cost to Work-in-Process and indirect labor cost to Factory Overhead.			
Factory Overhead		3,343,000	
Manufacturing Supplies			860,000
Accumulated Depreciation			1,400,000
Miscellaneous Payables			1,083,000
To record actual factory overhead expenses incurred for the period.			
Work-in-Process		3,498,000	
Factory Overhead			3,498,000
To apply factory overhead to Work-in-Process at the rate of $12 per machine hour.			
Finished Goods Inventory		10,500,000	
Work-in-Process			10,500,000
To record cost of goods manufactured			
Cost of Goods Sold		55,000	
Factory Overhead			55,000
To close underapplied factory overhead to Cost of Goods Sold.			

CHAPTER 12

The Assignment
of Common Costs

Upon completion of this chapter you should:

- Understand the nature of common costs.
- Understand the uses and limitations of common cost assignments.
- Understand the relationship between cost pools and cost objectives.
- Be familiar with alternative bases used for cost allocation.
- Be able to compute cost allocations for simple situations using the direct, step, and linear algebra allocation methods.
- Have a general understanding of the problems related to common cost allocation of nonmanufacturing costs, including home office costs and common costs in not-for-profit organizations.

In Chapter 2, *cost objectives* were defined as the objects or activities to which costs are assigned. All cost measurements involve assigning costs to cost objectives. Management may be concerned with determining the cost of constructing a building, manufacturing 500 units of inventory, or operating the personnel department. These are all examples of cost assignment.

In each of these examples, many costs can be directly associated with each specific cost objective. For example, the salary of the personnel manager is directly related to the personnel department. On the other hand, many other costs cannot be traced to a single cost objective and, therefore, must be assigned to the appropriate cost objectives through indirect measurement. For example, the cost of the electricity used by the personnel department (which occupies the third floor of the administrative office building) cannot be measured directly if there is only one electric meter for the whole building. In this case, it is necessary to make an indirect (or estimated) allocation of the total electricity cost for the building to each of the departments occupying the building.

The cost of electricity, which is a common cost of all the building occupants, may be allocated to the individual departments based on their relative quantities of floor space, electric lights and outlets, employees using electricity, or on some other basis. Regardless of the basis used for allocating the cost, there will be inherent weaknesses in the measurement of departmental costs because the allocations are only indirect estimates of electricity cost for the departments, not direct measurements of actual costs. To directly measure the actual cost for each department in the building, the company would have to rewire the building and install a separate meter in each department.

The purpose of this chapter is to discuss the nature and basic concepts, as well as uses and limitations, of common cost allocation. The special techniques and problems related to allocating manufacturing service department costs are also discussed. Finally, there are brief discussions of the cost assignment issues related to corporate home offices and not-for-profit organizations.

THE NATURE OF COMMON COSTS

As discussed in Chapter 7, in a responsibility accounting system, costs may be controlled at many different levels within an organization. For example, assume that manufacturing costs for Company X are incurred at the following levels: (1) plant administration (plant manager's costs), (2) plant services (maintenance, personnel, and cafeteria costs), (3) production departments (direct department costs), and (4) jobs (direct product costs). As shown in Exhibit 12–1 all manufacturing costs are directly assignable to a cost objective at some level. Therefore, when initially incurred, costs are charged, or assigned, to the cost objectives to which direct assignment can be made. For this reason, when raw materials are issued, their costs are assigned to specific departments and jobs, whereas the costs of cleaning supplies (which cannot be traced to specific jobs) are assigned to departments as overhead. Departmental overhead is then allocated, or reassigned, to the products using an overhead application rate. This is an example of common cost allocation.

EXHIBIT 12–1   Multilevel Cost Objectives

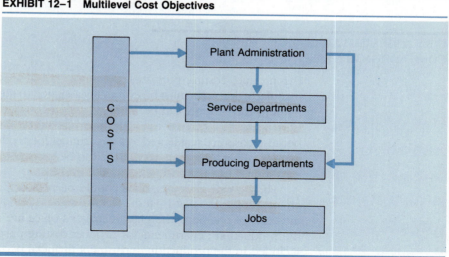

Common costs then are costs incurred at a given level for the benefit of two or more cost objectives to which direct assignment cannot readily be made. For the factory mentioned previously with four levels of cost objectives, three separate common cost allocations are required for *product costing purposes*. First, plant administration costs are allocated to the service and production departments that are supervised by the manager. Second, service department costs (including plant administration cost allocations) are allocated to the producing departments that receive the services. Third, all production department overhead costs (including allocated plant administration and service department costs) are applied to the product.

To summarize, at the point of incurrence all costs are directly assignable to some cost objective, even though the initial assignment may be to a general cost objective (such as factory overhead) that exists only for the purpose of facilitating reassignment to other cost objectives. When costs are incurred for the specific benefit of a given cost objective, the costs are said to be direct costs. Costs assigned to a cost objective by allocation from another cost objective are indirect costs. Hence, a **direct department cost** is a cost assigned to a department upon its incurrence, and an **indirect department cost** is a cost reassigned to a department from another cost objective. In the Company X example earlier, the plant manager's salary is a direct plant administration cost, and the reassigned plant administration costs are indirect department costs to the service departments. All service department costs are indirect department costs when reassigned to the production departments.

USES AND LIMITATIONS OF COMMON COST ASSIGNMENTS

For product costing purposes under the full absorption costing method, all manufacturing costs must be eventually assigned to the product. Full cost assignment to the product can be achieved only through the indirect assignment of all manufacturing costs not directly traceable to the product. However, just because costs are reassigned to a department for product costing purposes does not mean that these cost allocations can be used effectively for other purposes, such as cost control and performance evaluation.

For control purposes, costs should be reported at the level at which they are *controllable*—that is, at the *level of incurrence*. For example, even though the costs of operating the plant manager's office are appropriately allocated to the production departments for product costing purposes, they should not be included in the production department financial performance and cost control reports. Serious management morale problems may result if managers are held responsible for costs over which they have no control.

Indirect cost allocations may be made in some cases simply to inform managers of the cost of services they are receiving so that managers will not think the services are free. Such assignments, which are designed to provide information to managers, are often useful; however, they should not be used for performance evaluation purposes unless managers have some control over the amount of services received or over the costs incurred in providing the services. Managers will resist any cost allocations for services over which they have no control. When cost allocations can be justified for performance evaluation purposes, they should be based on the *standard cost* of services provided, not on the basis of *actual costs* incurred. Allocating standard costs prevents actual cost inefficiencies from being passed on to the users of the services.

In other cases, to encourage managers to take full advantage of service departments, the costs of services are intentionally not allocated to user departments. For example, if top management is trying to encourage managers to increase computer applications in their departments, computer center costs may intentionally not be allocated to users, or they may be allocated at arbitrarily very low rates.

Indirect department cost data should be used carefully when considering the overall profitability of a particular department or segment of a company. As discussed in Chapters 5 and 10, assigned costs that are unavoidable (and thus continue to be incurred whether or not the department is continued) should be disregarded in measuring the department's contribution to total company profits. To illustrate, assume that a department store's Toy Department reported a loss of $3,000 for the year, after deducting a cost allocation of $5,000 for the store manager's salary. The store manager's salary will be incurred whether or not the Toy Department continues; therefore, this cost should be ignored in a decision regarding continuation of the department. The department is contributing $2,000 (before the $5,000 unavoidable expense allocation) to the overall profitability of the store; therefore, overall profit will decline by that amount if the department is discontinued (assuming there is no alternative use for the space).

The key to using allocated common costs effectively is recognizing their uses and limitations. Allocated costs are fundamentally different from direct controllable costs and thus should be treated differently by users of cost information.[1]

---

[1] For a more complete discussion of the uses and limitations of common cost allocations, see "Allocation of Services and Administrative Costs," *Statement on Management Accounting Number 4B*, National Association of Accountants, 1985.

ALLOCATION OF COMMON COSTS

A major difference between direct cost assignments and indirect cost allocations is related to measurement precision. Initial cost assignment is a *direct measurement* of costs incurred for a specific cost objective, whereas subsequent indirect allocations are, at best, *estimates* of the costs incurred for the services provided to each cost objective.

To illustrate indirect cost allocation, assume that Company Y has a plant with two departments, A and B. Labor cost can be traced to a specific department for all employees except the plant manager, who earns $30,000 per year. If Company Y wants to assign all costs to the departments, the plant manager's salary must be reassigned to departments A and B using an allocation base. One possibility is to make the allocation according to the number of employees in each department, which is a reasonable basis if most of the plant manager's time is spent dealing with employee-related problems. If there are 20 employees in Department A and 30 employees in Department B, 40 percent (20 ÷ 50) of the plant manager's salary, or $12,000, would be allocated to Department A and 60 percent (30 ÷ 50), or $18,000, would be allocated to Department B.

Since common cost allocations are just estimates of the actual costs incurred for each cost objective, the amount assigned to a given cost objective is only as reliable as the allocation system used. Frequently, allocated costs are combined with direct costs (such as in product costing); therefore, any error in the allocation of common costs affects not only the allocated cost component but also the total cost for the cost objective.

For a better understanding of common cost allocation, it is necessary to examine further the basic components of common cost allocation systems. These basic components are as follows:

- Cost objectives
- Cost pools
- Allocation bases

In the example of Company Y, the two plant departments are the *cost objectives*, the plant manager's salary is the *cost pool*, and the number of employees in the departments is the *allocation base*.

COST OBJECTIVES

Before cost pools and allocation bases can be determined, it is necessary to know the objectives to which costs are to be allocated. In establishing cost objectives, management should consider potential allocation problems that may be encountered. Managers often feel that accountants have an unlimited ability to measure costs—that they can measure the cost of every activity, product, service, and operating component of the business. Although it is true that anything that has a cost is subject to cost measurement, consideration should always be given to the efforts and benefits of providing the cost measurement, as well as to the reliability of the cost information.

COST POOLS

A cost pool is a group of common costs, such as factory overhead, that is allocated to other cost objectives. As a practical matter it is not feasible in many situations to allocate each item of cost (such as the plant manager's salary) separately. Instead, several similar costs are combined into a cost pool, and the entire pool is allocated as a single item. Common costs are often pooled along departmental lines, such as payroll department costs, computer center costs, or maintenance department costs. Pooling all common labor-related costs or building-related costs, or the costs for any other natural function, is also frequently done. Sometimes these functional cost pools are referred to as departments even though they may not exist as such on the organization chart. For example, all building-related costs (depreciation, insurance, repairs, etc.) are often pooled together to form building department costs, which are then allocated to the departments that use the building.

The key consideration in establishing cost pools is that the items pooled together should be relatively homogeneous and have a logical *cause-and-effect* relation to the allocation base. For instance, a building cost pool would include all costs related to the maintenance and operation of the building and might be allocated on the basis of square footage occupied. The costs in this pool, such as insurance, property taxes, and depreciation, have a logical cause-and-effect relation to the amount of square footage provided. As the square footage increases, these costs are naturally expected to increase.

Within functional cost pools it may be useful to provide separate pools for fixed costs and variable costs. For example, fixed maintenance department costs might be accumulated in one pool, and variable maintenance department costs might be accumulated in another. Hence, the allocation basis may be different for fixed and variable costs.

To illustrate common cost allocation for fixed and variable costs, assume that Alco Manufacturing Company has one factory with three producing departments: Stamping, Assembly, and Inspection. There is also a Maintenance Department that provides services to the producing departments. Costs incurred by the Maintenance Department are allocated to the producing departments each period in separate pools for fixed costs and variable costs. Fixed costs consist of maintenance staff salaries, depreciation, insurance, and utilities on the maintenance shop facilities. Variable costs consist of supplies and parts used in performing maintenance services for the producing departments. Maintenance Department costs for 19x8 were as follows:

Fixed costs	$60,000
Variable costs	37,500
Total Maintenance Department costs	$97,500

Five hundred hours of service were performed for the three producing departments as follows:

Stamping Department	250
Assembly Department	200
Inspection Department	50
Total standard service hours	500

In setting up the Maintenance Department, Alco's management decided on a maintenance service *capacity* of 800 standard service hours per year. This capacity was based on a maximum need of 400 hours for the Stamping Department, and 200 hours each for the Assembly and Inspection Departments. It was also determined that *fixed costs* should be allocated to the producing departments on the basis of *capacity provided* for each department, and that *variable costs* should be allocated on the basis of *actual usage* of Maintenance Department services. Exhibit 12–2 shows the allocation computations for fixed and variable Maintenance Department costs. The fixed cost allocation percentages (50%, 25%, and 25%) reflect the cost of the capacity provided for each department, whereas the variable cost allocation percentages (50%, 40%, and 10%) reflect the variable costs actually incurred for each department during the period.

ALLOCATION BASES

The allocation base is the connecting link between cost objectives and cost pools. The **cost allocation base** is the factor, or characteristic, common to the cost objectives that determines how much of the cost pool is assigned to each cost objective. The allocation base selected varies depending on the nature of the common costs and the nature of the cost objectives. For example, labor-related costs may be allocated according to some measure (or estimate) of the labor time devoted to the various cost objectives, and depreciation and other building-related costs are often allocated on the basis of square footage occupied.

EXHIBIT 12–2   Allocation of Fixed and Variable Costs

Fixed cost allocation

Department	Capacity Provided			Total Fixed Cost		Fixed Cost Allocation
	Service Hours	Percent				
Stamping	400	50	×	$60,000	=	$30,000
Assembly	200	25	×	60,000	=	15,000
Inspection	200	25	×	60,000	=	15,000
Total	800	100				$60,000

Variable cost allocation

Department	Actual Service Hours		Variable Cost per Hour*		Variable Cost Allocation	Percent of Allocation
Stamping	250	×	$75	=	$18,750	50
Assembly	200	×	75	=	15,000	40
Inspection	50	×	75	=	3,750	10
Total	500				$37,500	100

Total maintenance department cost allocation

Department	Fixed Cost	Variable Cost	Total Allocation
Stamping	$30,000	$18,750	$48,750
Assembly	15,000	15,000	30,000
Inspection	15,000	3,750	18,750
Total	$60,000	$37,500	$97,500

* Variable cost per service hour:

Total variable cost $37,500	÷	Total hours 500	=	Variable cost per hour $75.

Other examples of common costs and frequently used allocation bases include the following:

Cost Category	Allocation Base
Employee health services	Number of employees or calls
Personnel	Number of employees or new hires
Plant and grounds	Square footage occupied
Maintenance repairs	Number of repair orders or service hours
Purchasing	Number of orders placed
Warehouse	Square footage used or value of materials stored.

The most important consideration in selecting an allocation base is making sure there is a logical cause-and-effect association between the base selected and the costs incurred. For instance, it is logical to allocate personnel department costs according to the number of employees because the function of the personnel department is to provide employee-related services to the various departments. Thus personnel costs are incurred as these services are provided. It follows that departments with a large number of employees should ordinarily receive a larger allocation of personnel department costs than departments with few employees.

Another consideration in selecting an allocation base is whether to reflect the service capacity provided or only the actual services used. Refer to Exhibit 12–2, where we use different bases for allocating fixed and variable costs. Fixed costs are allocated based on the capacity provided, and variable costs are allocated according to the actual services used. Basing fixed costs on capacity provided eliminates the possibility that the amount of the cost allocation to one department is affected by the level of services utilized by other departments. In Exhibit 12–2, the Assembly Department used 200 service hours during the year, equaling the capacity provided for it. The 200 hours represent 25 percent (200 hours ÷ 800 hours) of the total capacity of the service department, but they represent 40 percent (200 hours ÷ 500 total actual hours) of the total actual services rendered. If fixed costs had been allocated based on actual services used rather than on capacity provided, $24,000 (40 percent of the fixed costs), instead of $15,000, would have been allocated to the Assembly Department. This additional charge of $9,000 would have resulted from other producing departments failing to use the capacity provided for them. When fixed service department costs are allocated according to capacity provided, managers of producing departments are charged for the capacity provided whether they use it or not, and their use of services has no effect on the amount of costs allocated to other departments. A benefit of this allocation system is that it reduces the temptation for managers to avoid or delay services in order to minimize fixed cost allocations to their departments.

SERVICE DEPARTMENT COST ALLOCATION

A **service department** is a department that provides support functions primarily for one or more production departments. Examples of service departments are maintenance, personnel, payroll, cost accounting, internal audit, data processing, food services, and health services. These departments, which are considered essential elements in the overall manufacturing process, do not work directly on the "product," but they do provide auxiliary support to the producing departments. In addition to providing support for the various producing departments, some service departments also provide services to *other service departments*. For example, the payroll and personnel departments may provide services for all departments, both production and service; data processing may provide services only for other service departments; and cost accounting may provide services for the producing departments as well as limited services for food and health services. Services provided by one service department to other service departments are called **interdepartmental services.**

Three methods are discussed in this section for allocating service department costs: the *direct method,* the *step method,* and the *linear algebra method*. To illustrate each method we will allocate common service department costs for the Kona Kola Company for 19x8. Kona Kola has two producing departments, Mixing and Bottling, and three service departments. The service departments and their respective service functions and cost allocation bases are as follows:

Department	Service Functions	Allocations Base
Administrative Services	Accounting, audit, payroll, and inventory control	Total department capital investment
Human Resources	Personnel, training, and health services	Number of employees
Plant and Facilities	Maintenance, security, depreciation, and insurance	Square footage occupied

Kona Kola readily determined the appropriate allocation bases for the Human Resources Department and the Plant and Facilities Department; however, for Administrative Services the choice was much less clear. Because of the diversity of services provided by this department, no logical allocation base emerged as the obvious choice. After conducting correlation studies it was determined that the most equitable base for allocating Administrative Services costs was total capital investment in each department. Although this base does not correlate closely with each of the cost components incurred in the department, the company felt it represented a good compromise that should be acceptable to management at all levels and for all cost assignment purposes.

Difficulty in choosing an allocation base for service department costs is not uncommon. This example simply illustrates that when there is no obvious allocation base an effort should be made to find a substitute that is both *realistic and fair* in distributing costs to the various producing departments. *If an appropriate allocation base cannot be found, the decision to allocate the costs should be reconsidered.*

The data used to illustrate the service department cost allocations for Kona Kola Company for 19x8 are summarized as follows.

	Direct Department Costs	Number of Employees	Square Footage Occupied	Department Capital Investment
Service departments:				
Administrative Services	$ 27,000	15	4,000	$ 75,000
Human Resources	20,000	10	2,000	45,000
Plant and Facilities	10,000	5	3,000	50,000
Producing departments:				
Mixing	40,000*	24	11,000	180,000
Bottling	90,000*	56	33,000	270,000
Total	$187,000	110	53,000	$620,000

* Direct department overhead

Direct Allocation Method

The **direct allocation method** allocates all service department costs directly to the producing departments without any recognition of interdepartmental services. Exhibit 12–3 shows the flow of costs using the direct allocation method. Note that all arrows depicting the cost flows extend only from service departments to producing departments; there are no cost allocations between the service departments.

Exhibit 12–4 shows the service department cost allocations for the direct method. To explain the basic approach of the direct method, note the cost allocations of the Human Resources Department based on the number of

EXHIBIT 12–3   Flow of Costs—Direct Allocation Method

employees. Only the number of employees in the producing departments is considered in computing the allocation percentages—24 in the Mixing Department and 56 in the Bottling Department, for a total of 80 employees in the allocation base. Thirty percent (24 ÷ 80) of the producing department employees work in the Mixing Department; therefore, 30 percent of the Human Resources Department costs are allocated to the Mixing Department. Applying the same reasoning, 70 percent of the Human Resources Department costs are allocated to the Bottling Department. Similar logic is followed in computing the cost allocations for the Plant and Facilities Department and the Administrative Services Department.

The cost allocation summary at the bottom of Exhibit 12–4 shows that all service department costs have been allocated, increasing the producing department balances by the amounts of the respective allocations. Also note that total

EXHIBIT 12–4   Service Department Cost Allocations—Direct Allocation Method

	Total	Mixing	Bottling
Administrative Services Department:			
Allocation base (capital investment)	$450,000	$180,000	$270,000
Percent of total base	100%	40%	60%
Cost allocation	$ 27,000	$ 10,800	$ 16,200
Human Resources Department:			
Allocation base (number of employees)	80	24	56
Percent of total base	100%	30%	70%
Cost allocation	$ 20,000	$ 6,000	$ 14,000
Plant and Facilities Department:			
Allocation base (square footage occupied)	44,000	11,000	33,000
Percent of total base	100%	25%	75%
Cost allocation	$ 10,000	$ 2,500	$ 7,500

Cost Allocation Summary:

	Administrative Services	Human Resources	Plant and Facilities	Mixing	Bottling	Total
Departmental costs before allocations	$27,000	$20,000	$10,000	$40,000	$ 90,000	$187,000
Cost allocations:						
Administrative Services	(27,000)			10,800	16,200	—
Human Resources		(20,000)		6,000	14,000	—
Plant and Facilities			(10,000)	2,500	7,500	—
Departmental costs after allocations	$ —	$ —	$ —	$59,300	$127,700	$187,000

direct costs are not affected by the allocations—the total of $187,000 was merely redistributed so that all costs are assigned to the producing departments.

The total department costs of the producing departments after allocation of service costs are $59,300 for the Mixing Department and $127,700 for the Bottling Department. These amounts represent the total actual factory overhead costs for the producing departments for the period. If Kona Kola applies actual factory overhead costs to production, these amounts will be applied to the Mixing Department and Bottling Department Work-in-Process accounts at the end of the period. If the company uses a predetermined overhead rate, the difference between applied and actual overhead (after service department cost allocations) is the underapplied or overapplied Factory Overhead balance.

Step Allocation Method

Unlike the direct method, which gives no recognition to interdepartmental services, the **step allocation method** of allocating service department costs gives at least partial recognition to interdepartmental services among service departments. Under the step method, first management determines the service department that provides the most interdepartmental services. That department's total cost is then allocated to the other service departments and the producing departments. The service department allocated first receives no allocations from other service departments even though it may receive services from them. The service department allocated second (including costs received from the first department) is allocated to the remaining service departments (excluding the first department) and to the producing departments. The last service department to be allocated (including all costs received from other service departments) is allocated only to the producing departments.

Exhibit 12–5 shows the flow of service department costs for Kona Kola Company under the step allocation method. Note that Human Resources costs are allocated to the remaining two service departments and to the producing departments. Administrative Services costs are allocated to Plant and Facilities and to the producing departments. Plant and Facilities costs are allocated only to the producing departments.

Although there is no generally accepted rule for determining the order for allocating service department costs under the step method, as explained above, the department that provides the most services to other service departments is usually allocated first. Allocations of other service department costs follow in order based on their relative levels of *interdepartmental services*.

Exhibit 12–6 shows the computations for determining the sequence of cost allocations for Kona Kola's service departments. The measure of services provided by the service departments is stated in terms of the *allocation base*. For example, the services provided by the Administrative Services Department are measured in terms of total investment. The total investment in all departments other than Administrative Services is $545,000, and the total investment in other *service* departments is $95,000. Therefore, in terms of its allocation base, Administrative Services provided 17.4 percent ($95,000 ÷ $545,000) of its total services

EXHIBIT 12–5   Flow of Costs—Step Allocation Method

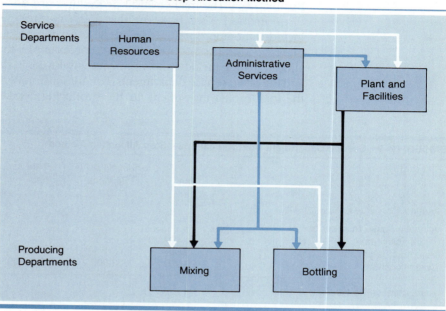

to other service departments. The total investment in all departments of $545,000 excludes the investment in Administrative Services, since only services to other departments are considered. Since interdepartmental services amounted to 20.0 percent for Human Resources and 12.0 percent for Plant and Facilities, the sequence of allocation of service department costs under the step method is Human Resources first, followed by Administrative Services and then Plant and Facilities.

EXHIBIT 12–6   Allocation Sequence for Step Allocation Method

	Administrative Services	Human Resources	Plant and Facilities
Allocation base	Capital investment	Number of employees	Square footage
(a) Total base for other service and producing departments	$545,000	100	50,000
(b) Total base for other service departments	$ 95,000	20	6,000
Percent of total services provided to other service departments [(b) ÷ (a)]	17.4%	20%	12%
Allocation sequence	Second	First	Third

Allocation of service department costs using the step method is shown in Exhibit 12–7. The mathematical procedures are essentially the same as in the direct method. Note, however, that under the step method the allocation base includes the appropriate base measure for the producing and service departments to which costs are allocated. For example, the Human Resources cost allocation base includes the number of employees in the producing departments and the other service departments. For Administrative Services, the base includes the total capital investment for the producing departments and the Plant and

EXHIBIT 12–7   Service Department Cost Allocations—Step Allocation Method

	Total	Administrative Services	Plant and Facilities	Mixing	Bottling
Human Resources Department:					
Allocation base (number of employees)	100	15	5	24	56
Percent of total base	100%	15%	5%	24%	56%
Cost allocation	$ 20,000	$3,000	$ 1,000	$ 4,800	$ 11,200
Administrative Services Department:					
Allocation base (capital investment)	$500,000		$50,000	$180,000	$270,000
Percent of total base	100%		10%	36%	54%
Cost allocation	$ 30,000		$ 3,000	$ 10,800	$ 16,200
Plant and Facilities Department:					
Allocation base (square footage occupied)	44,000			11,000	33,000
Percent of total base	100%			25%	75%
Cost allocation	$ 14,000			$ 3,500	$ 10,500

Cost Allocation Summary:	Human Resources	Administrative Services	Plant and Facilities	Mixing	Bottling	Total
Departmental costs before allocation	$20,000	$27,000	$10,000	$40,000	$ 90,000	$187,000
Cost allocations:						
Human Resources	(20,000)	3,000	1,000	4,800	11,200	—
Administrative Services		(30,000)	3,000	10,800	16,200	—
Plant and Facilities			(14,000)	3,500	10,500	—
Departmental costs after allocation	$ —	$ —	$ —	$59,100	$127,900	$187,000

Facilities Department. For Plant and Facilities, the base includes only the square footage for the producing departments since its costs are allocated to only these departments.

Note in Exhibit 12–7 that under the step method the total cost allocated from each service department includes the department's direct costs plus any costs received in previous allocations from other service departments. Since Human Resources costs are allocated first, they include only direct department costs. However, Administrative Services costs include $27,000 of direct department costs plus $3,000 of costs allocated from Human Resources. Plant and Facilities costs include $10,000 of direct department costs plus allocations of $1,000 from Human Resources and $3,000 from Administrative Services. These interdepartmental cost allocations are summarized at the bottom of Exhibit 12–7.

Linear Algebra Method

The *direct method* provides an easy way of allocating the service department costs to producing departments. Its primary weakness is that it does not recognize *any* interdepartmental services among service departments. This weakness is not crucial so long as all service departments are providing approximately the same level of services to all producing departments. When the quantity of services provided to the producing departments is significantly disproportionate, the service department cost allocations may be distorted using the direct method.

The *step method* recognizes interdepartmental services *only partially* because a service department cannot receive an allocation from other departments once its costs have been allocated. Although the step method overcomes much of the distortion inherent in direct allocations, significant distortions may remain under some circumstances. The only sure way of eliminating all distortions of this type is to recognize all interdepartmental services simultaneously.

The **linear algebra allocation method** allocates all service department costs simultaneously to service departments and to producing departments. To use this method, a linear algebraic equation is developed for each service and production department. Each equation represents total departmental costs, that is, direct department costs plus a percentage of service department costs. To illustrate the equations, assume a company has two service departments (S1 and S2) and two producing departments (P1 and P2). The percentage distribution of services is shown below for each department.

Services Provided from	Services Provided to				
	S1	S2	P1	P2	Total
S1	—	5%	40%	55%	100%
S2	10%	—	30%	60%	100%

Total direct department costs for the service and producing departments are as follows:

S1	$ 20,000
S2	$ 35,000
P1	$150,000
P2	$ 90,000

The algebraic equations expressing the total costs (direct and allocated) for each department are as follows:

$$S1 = 20,000 + 0.10 \ S2$$
$$S2 = 35,000 + 0.05 \ S1$$
$$P1 = 150,000 + 0.40 \ S1 + 0.30 \ S2$$
$$P2 = 90,000 + 0.55 \ S1 + 0.60 \ S2$$

Using the substitution method, these equations are solved as shown below.

Substituting S2 into S1:

$$S1 = 20,000 + 0.10(35,000 + 0.05 \ S1)$$
$$S1 = 20,000 + 3,500 + 0.005 \ S1$$
$$0.995 \ S1 = 23,500$$
$$S1 = 23,618.$$

Substituting the solution of S1 into S2:

$$S2 = 35,000 + 0.05(23,618)$$
$$S2 = 35,000 + 1,181$$
$$S2 = 36,181.$$

Substituting the solutions of S1 and S2 into P1:

$$P1 = 150,000 + 0.40(23,618) + 0.30(36,181)$$
$$P1 = 150,000 + 9,447 + 10,854$$
$$P1 = 170,301.$$

Substituting the solutions of S1 and S2 into P2:

$$P2 = 90,000 + 0.55(23,618) + 0.60(36,181)$$
$$P2 = 90,000 + 12,990 + 21,709$$
$$P2 = 124,699.$$

How do we interpret these solutions? First, note that the solutions to S1 and S2 consist of two components, their respective direct department costs plus the cost allocated from the other service department. For example, since the solved value for S1 is $23,618, the allocated costs from S2 are $3,618, or the difference between the value assigned to S1 after allocation and the S1 direct department costs. In a similar fashion, the solutions to P1 and P2 consist of three components. P1 consists of $150,000 plus $9,447 plus $10,854, and P2 consists of $90,000 plus $12,990 plus $21,709. For each of these producing department variables, the first component represents the *direct costs* of the department. The second component represents the allocation of S1 costs to the producing department after interdepartmental cost allocation, and the third component represents the allocation of S2 costs to the producing departments after interdepartmental cost allocation.

A summary of all cost allocations among service departments and producing departments is shown below, and a diagram of these allocations is provided in Exhibit 12–8.

	S1	S2	P1	P2	Total
Departmental costs before allocation	$20,000	$35,000	$150,000	$ 90,000	$295,000
S1 allocation	(23,618)	1,181	9,447	12,990	—
S2 allocation	3,618	(36,181)	10,854	21,709	—
Departmental costs after allocation	$ —	$ —	$170,301	$124,699	$295,000

The substitution method of simultaneously solving linear equations is inefficient except in the simplest of situations (such as our example). Where there are more than two service departments providing interdepartmental services, it is necessary to use matrix algebra for solving equations simultaneously. Using matrix algebra would also be very laborious were it not for the aid of computers. With a computer and appropriate software, solving matrix algebra problems is relatively easy. (A detailed discussion of matrix algebra is beyond the scope of this text.)

EXHIBIT 12–8   Flow of Costs—Linear Algebra Allocation Method

THE ALLOCATION OF NONMANUFACTURING COSTS

Many of the allocation concepts discussed in this chapter are often applied to nonmanufacturing costs in manufacturing organizations and to operating costs in service organizations, both for-profit and not-for-profit. Some of these applications are discussed below.

Home Office Expenses

Many top-level managers feel that all costs, including home office expenses, should be assigned for internal reporting purposes to the operating divisions of companies. **Home office expenses** consist of central corporate expenses, including the salaries of the president and other executive officers, public relations expenses (such as corporate advertising and corporate contributions), expenses of the legal and tax department, and corporate planning and development costs. The functions provided by these costs are vitally important to the operation of the organization, but some of these functions (such as the president's activities) are often not considered to directly benefit the operating divisions and profit centers. Because there is no direct association between profit producing functions and central home office functions, it is often difficult, if not impossible, to find a widely supported basis for allocating these costs to the divisions.

One of the most frequently used bases for allocating home office expenses is total revenues of the divisions. Using this basis, a division producing 30 percent of the company's total revenues is allocated 30 percent of all home office expenses, whereas another producing only 5 percent of total revenues is allocated just 5 percent. This allocation basis is often denounced by managers as a "soak the rich" approach that does not reflect an appropriate matching of effort and accomplishment. Managers of successful divisions argue that a disproportionate share of home office efforts is often devoted to struggling divisions and product lines, and to new or potential endeavors of the company, and not to the most successful divisions and product lines, which nevertheless carry the burden of cost allocation.

Despite the problems in making an equitable allocation of home office expenses, unfortunately many top managers feel that such allocations are important because they draw attention to the total cost of operating the business. Moreover, it is felt that home office cost allocation encourages managers to think in terms of total corporate profitability, not just of the profitability of their own areas. Allocation proponents emphasize that the company as a whole has not earned a profit until all costs, including home office costs, have been covered by revenues. Notwithstanding these alleged benefits, allocation of central corporate expenses is not the best means of achieving them unless division management perceives the allocation system to be fair and equitable. These favorable perceptions probably will not exist if top management uses broad, arbitrary allocation bases, such as total revenues or total profits. As in allocating manufacturing costs, the best results can be achieved only by relating the costs to the cost objectives on a logical cause-and-effect basis. For some home office costs, these bases may not exist.

Even if accurate and equitable allocations can be determined for home office costs, *imposed services* may still present a problem. Frequently, managers feel that the services received from corporate headquarters are not beneficial to their divisions but are imposed by top management, and given the opportunity, they would elect not to buy them at any price. Even if managers believe the services are needed, some would prefer to control the acquisition of the services by purchasing them from sources outside the company. When attitudes like these prevail among a company's managers, probably little is gained from home office cost allocation. Ordinarily, these kinds of negative attitudes are prevalent only in companies where home office costs are allocated to division managers for performance evaluation purposes.

Not-for-Profit Applications

So far we have discussed cost assignment and allocation only in for-profit organizations. Many of the concepts and procedures introduced, however, can be generalized for use in not-for-profit organizations. Historically, not-for-profit accounting has been based on the concept of stewardship (or fund) accounting, which emphasizes the reporting of funds received and their disposition. The use of accounting data to determine the cost of services and to evaluate manager performance has not been widely practiced in not-for-profit organizations.

As we have seen in our discussions of for-profit organizations, the assignment of costs to various cost objectives may be useful in certain circumstances. In not-for-profit organizations, cost allocations may play an even more significant role than in for-profit organizations. Cost allocations may actually reduce the funds available to an agency or operating unit to carry on its programs. For example, the fire department of a small local municipality may have an annual budget of $300,000; however, the cost allocations for general city services to the department may use up $20,000 of the budget, leaving disposable funds of only $280,000. An academic department in a university may have no choice but to obtain computer services from the university's central computer system at a cost substantially higher than comparable services received from outside sources. Charges for these internal services ordinarily are made against the operating funds of the departments.

Because the procedures for allocating costs in not-for-profit organizations are essentially the same as those discussed in for-profit organizations, we will not present a detailed discussion. The following is a summary of frequently allocated costs and allocation bases of selected not-for-profit organizations.

Organization	Common Costs	Allocation Base
Hospital	Administration Cafeteria Operating room	Patient days Meals served Actual time used

City government	Municipal building
	Tax assessment and
	  collection
	Accounting
		Space occupied
		Amount of budget
		  appropriation
		Number of transactions
		  processed

University	Classroom costs Computer services Academic administration	Class hours used Actual or CPU time used Student credit hours
Church	Buildings and grounds Printing and publicity Office and administration	Space occupied Actual services received Amount of budget appropriation

SUMMARY

Costs incurred for the benefit of two or more cost objectives (such as products, plants, departments, and territories) are called *common costs*. These costs are often assigned to specific cost objectives through the process of *cost allocation*. Allocation of service department costs to the producing departments allows manufacturing organizations to assign all manufacturing costs to products. Cost allocations are also used for other purposes such as internal reporting and performance evaluation of managers. However, these applications of cost allocation are often accompanied by severe limitations. Managers usually resist being evaluated on the basis of costs over which they have little or no control. When top management uses common cost allocations to evaluate managers, it is important that lower level managers understand and support the allocation system.

The basic cost allocation model consists of three components: cost pools, cost objectives, and allocation bases. Common costs are combined into homogeneous cost pools to prevent the need for separate allocation of similar costs. The allocation base relates the common costs to the cost objectives, and it provides a logical system for distributing the costs to the various cost objectives. Common costs may be fixed or they may vary with some measure of activity. Fixed common costs are often allocated on the basis of capacity provided, whereas variable costs are allocated according to actual benefits or services received.

Manufacturing organizations ordinarily have producing departments, in which the product is made, and service departments, such as personnel and maintenance, that provide support services to the producing departments. Since service departments are an essential part of the manufacturing process, their costs are usually allocated to the producing departments and included in factory overhead. The direct method allocates all service department costs to the producing departments without any recognition of interdepartmental services between the service departments. Whereas the *step method* gives only partial recognition to interdepartmental services, the *linear algebra method* provides *full recognition* of such services by using linear algebraic equations. Most of the cost allocation procedures discussed for manufacturing service departments can also be applied to nonmanufacturing costs and to common costs in non-manufacturing organizations, including not-for-profit organizations.

APPENDIX
JOINT PRODUCTS AND BY-PRODUCTS

Joint products are two or more products produced simultaneously by a common manufacturing process. The costs of producing joint products are called **joint costs.** An example of joint products is crude oil products (such as gasoline, diesel, and kerosene) that are produced by a common refining process. Similarly, various chemical products are often produced by a single process. A **by-product** is a product with insignificant value that is produced jointly with one or more other products.

Joint Product Cost Allocation

For product costing purposes, it is necessary to allocate joint product costs to the respective joint products. Joint cost allocation occurs at the split-off point in the production process. The **split-off point** is the point in the process where the joint products emerge as separate identifiable products. Any costs incurred in further processing of a joint product after split-off are specific product costs, *not joint costs.*

To illustrate joint cost allocation, assume Aem Enterprises manufactures two automotive fuel additives, Speedo and Econo, from a common manufacturing process. In August 19x3, Aem incurred joint costs of $24,000 in producing 8,000 pints of Speedo and 12,000 pints of Econo, as illustrated below.

Two methods available for allocating joint costs are the physical quantity method and the sales value method. Under the **physical quantity allocation method,** joint costs are allocated on the basis of relative quantities of a common physical characteristic possessed by the joint products. Physical characteristics used for joint cost allocation include the number of units of product, weight measures, and volume measures. For Aem Enterprises the unit measure (pint) is also a volume measure because 1 physical unit of product consists of 1 pint of volume measure. Under the physical quantity method, using pints of production as the allocation base, the allocated costs, $9,600 for Speedo and $14,000 for Econo, are computed as follows:

Product	Quantity (pints)	Relative Quantity		Joint Cost		Allocation
Speedo	8,000	0.40	×	$24,000	=	$ 9,600
Econo	12,000	0.60	×	$24,000	=	14,400
	20,000	1.00				$24,000

Each product has a cost of $1.20 per pint ($9,600 ÷ 8,000 and $14,400 ÷ 12,000). If Speedo sells for $3 per pint and Econo sells for $1 per pint, the gross profit for Speedo is $14,400, whereas Econo has a negative $2,400 gross profit.

	Speedo	Econo	Total
Unit sales (pints)	8,000	12,000	20,000
Sales price per unit	$3	$1	
Sales	$24,000	$12,000	$36,000
Cost of goods sold	- 9,600	-14,400	-24,000
Gross profit	$14,400	$ (2,400)	$12,000

Allocating joint costs on the basis of physical quantities produces a distortion in the gross profit computations any time the selling price per unit of quantity is not the same for all joint products. The reason for this distortion is that the physical quantity method assigns an *equal amount of cost* to each *unit of physical measure*—in this case to each pint—regardless of its selling price. If allocated on the basis of physical quantity, the cost per pint is $1.20 for both Speedo and Econo, but the selling price of Speedo is three times as much as Econo's selling price. Since together the products generate a total gross profit of $12,000, and one product cannot be produced without the other, it is unreasonable to assume that one is produced at a profit and the other is produced at a loss.

If selling prices vary significantly between the joint products, sales value is a more realistic basis for allocating joint costs. Under the **sales value allocation**

method each dollar of sales value for all products is assigned an equal amount of cost. The sales value method allocations for Speedo and Econo are as follows:

Product	Sales Value Computation	Sales Value Amount	Relative Sales Value		Joint Cost		Allocation
Speedo	8,000 × $3 =	$24,000	0.667	×	$24,000	=	$16,000
Econo	12,000 × $1 =	12,000	0.333	×	$24,000	=	8,000
		$36,000	1.000				$24,000

Speedo has a cost of $2 per pint ($16,000 ÷ 8,000), and Econo has a cost of $0.667 per pint ($8,000 ÷ 12,000).

Using the costs for Speedo and Econo determined by the sales value allocation method, the respective gross profits are $8,000 and $4,000, as shown in the partial income statements below.

	Speedo	Econo	Total
Units sales (pints)	8,000	12,000	20,000
Sales price per unit	$3	$1	
Sales	$24,000	$12,000	$36,000
Cost of goods sold	−16,000	− 8,000	−24,000
Gross profit	$ 8,000	$ 4,000	$12,000

Under the sales value method, the gross margin ratio is the same (one third of selling price) for both products.

Additional processing may be required after split-off on some joint products. In this case the sales value method must be modified to allocate joint costs on the basis of net realizable value at the point of split-off rather than on the basis of sales value for completed units. Net realizable value is computed as ultimate sales value less additional processing costs incurred beyond the split-off point. For example, if $4,000 of additional processing costs were required after split-off before the 8,000 pints of Speedo could be sold for $24,000, the joint cost allocation would be made on the basis of relative net realizable values of $20,000 ($24,000 − $4,000) for Speedo and $12,000 for Econo.

The decision of whether to continue with additional processing after split-off is unrelated to the cost allocation procedure. Sometimes additional processing is necessary before the product can be sold, in which case further processing ordinarily must be done. In other cases, the product may be sold either at split-off or after additional processing. The decision of whether to continue processing is based entirely on relevant cost analysis. If the additional revenue from processing exceeds the additional cost of processing, the product should be processed further; otherwise, the product should be sold at split-off. These relevant cost issues are discussed and illustrated in Chapter 5.

Accounting for By-products

A by-product is not treated as a joint product and therefore is not allocated costs in the joint cost allocation procedure. Production of by-products is not a major objective of the manufacturing process; it is a result of production of the main products. For example, a furniture factory primarily manufactures furniture, but it produces sawdust (which is saleable) as an inevitable and natural result.

If by-products do not generate revenues, which is the case for many waste by-products, there is no special accounting required other than recording any disposition costs as additional manufacturing expense. If by-products can be sold, and the selling price is insignificant, revenues from the sale of by-products are usually recorded either as other income or as a reduction of joint manufacturing costs. The remaining joint processing costs are then allocated to the joint products by either the physical quantity or sales value method. By costing by-products at selling price, no profit or loss is recognized when they are sold.

Products initially considered to be by-products may later become main products as new uses and applications for them are discovered. When this occurs, the accounting treatment should be revised to reflect a change in assumptions and to begin allocating costs to the products as joint products.

KEY TERMS

Common costs
Cost allocation base
Cost pools
Direct allocation method
Direct department costs
Home office expenses

Indirect department costs
Interdepartmental services
Linear algebra allocation method
Service department
Step allocation method

APPENDIX KEY TERMS

By-product
Joint costs
Joint products

Physical quantity allocation method
Sales value allocation method
Split-off point

REVIEW QUESTIONS

12–1   What are the primary purposes of cost assignment in a manufacturing organization?

12–2   Explain the difference between the terms cost assignment and cost allocation.

12–3   All costs are directly assignable to a cost objective at some level. Explain this statement.

12–4 Can a cost item be both a direct cost and a common cost at the same time? Explain.

12–5 Which type of cost assignment is more accurate, direct assignment or allocation? Explain.

12–6 Why are cost pools used in allocating common costs?

12–7 Describe two primary considerations in determining how common costs should be pooled.

12–8 What is the primary advantage of allocating fixed and variable common costs separately?

12–9 Give five examples of a cost objective.

12–10 What is the primary consideration in selecting a cost allocation base?

12–11 Indicate a likely basis for allocating the following types of common costs: cafeteria costs, utility costs, plant manager's salary, cost of annual employee picnic.

12–12 To what extent are interdepartmental services recognized under the direct, step, and linear algebra methods of service department cost allocation?

12–13 What is the major limitation of the linear algebra allocation method?

12–14 Allocation of home office expenses on the basis of sales revenue is often characterized as a soak-the-rich tactic. Explain.

12–15 Name three common costs that might require allocation if your college or university decided to compute the total cost of offering a section of management accounting.

REVIEW PROBLEM

Service Cost Allocations: Direct, Step, and Linear Algebra Methods

Cotswald's Clothiers, Inc., is organized into four departments: Women's Apparel, Men's Apparel, Administrative Services, and Facilities Services. The former two departments are the primary producing departments, and the latter two departments exist to provide services to the producing departments. Top management has decided that, for internal reporting purposes, the cost of service department operations should be allocated to the producing departments.

Administrative Services costs are allocated on the basis of the number of employees, and Facilities Services costs are allocated based on the number of floor square footage occupied. The service departments provide services to both producing departments as well as to each other. Data pertaining to the allocations for February 19x7 are as follows:

Department	Direct Department Cost	Number of Employees	Square Footage Occupied
Women's Apparel	$ 60,000	15	15,000
Men's Apparel	50,000	9	7,500
Administrative Services	18,000	3	2,500
Facilities	12,000	2	1,000
Total	$140,000	29	26,000

Required: Determine the amount of service department cost to be allocated to the producing departments under each of the following common cost allocation methods:

1. Direct method.

2. Step method (allocating first the service department with the greatest percentage of interdepartmental services).

3. Linear algebra method.

The solution to this problem is found at the end of the Chapter 12 exercises and problems.

EXERCISES

12–1 Selecting Cost Allocation Bases

Below is a list of service departments typically found in manufacturing and nonmanufacturing organizations.

Payroll	Personnel
Cafeteria	Building
Utilities	Maintenance
Computer Services	Security
Health Services	General Administration

Required: For each of the above service departments indicate the bases likely to be used to allocate costs to the producing departments.

12–2 Common Cost Allocation Computations

Sunset Strip Sign Company manufactures hotel signs through a process involving three departments—Molding, Fabrication, and Wiring. The following data were accumulated for 19x9 for these three departments.

	Molding	Fabrication	Wiring
Direct labor hours	10,000	38,000	2,000
Direct labor cost	$70,000	$400,000	$30,000
Number of employees	5	18	2
Square feet occupied	3,000	5,000	2,000

Total indirect costs incurred for the common benefit of all three departments in 19x9 were $150,000.

Required: Determine the common cost allocation for each department on the basis of the following:

1. Direct labor hours.

2. Direct labor cost.

3. Number of employees.

4. Square feet occupied.

12–3 Allocating Service Department Costs: Allocation Basis Alternatives

Clayton Glassworks has two producing departments, P1 and P2, and one service department, S1. Estimated direct overhead costs per month are as follows:

P1	$100,000
P2	200,000
S1	60,000

Other data:

	P1	P2
Number of employees	75	25
Production capacity (units)	50,000	30,000
Space occupied (sq ft)	2,500	7,500
Five-year average percent of S1's service output used	65%	35%

Required: For each of the following allocation bases, determine the total estimated overhead cost for P1 and P2 after allocating S1 cost to the producing departments.

1. Number of employees.

2. Production capacity in units.

3. Space occupied.

4. Five-year average percentage of S1 services used.

5. Estimated direct overhead costs. (Round your answer to the nearest dollar.)

12–4 Common Cost Allocation: Direct Method

The School of Business Administration of Alpha University consists of three academic departments and three service departments. The Dean of the School has asked you, his assistant, to compute the cost per student credit hour for each of the academic departments. Although the Dean gave no specific instructions on how to make the computations, you have decided that the service department costs should be allocated to the academic departments. You have accumulated the following data for the last school term to be used in the cost computations.

Department	Direct Cost	Allocation Base
Service:		
Administration	$150,000	Number of faculty
Student services	75,000	Number of students
Faculty services	60,000	Number of credit hours

	Direct Cost	Number of Faculty	Number of Students	Number of Credit Hours
Academic:				
Accounting/Finance	$380,000	20	350	4,500
Management/Marketing	440,000	25	250	3,000
Economics/Quantitative methods	350,000	15	150	1,500

Requirements

a) Prepare a schedule showing the allocation of service department direct costs to the academic departments.

b) Compute the total cost per student credit hour for each academic department.

c) Could the step method have been used with the information provided? Explain.

12–5
Interdepartmental Services: Step Allocation Method

O'Brian's Department Stores allocates the costs of the Personnel and Payroll Departments to three retail sales departments, Housewares, Clothing, and Furniture. In addition to providing services to the operating departments, Personnel and Payroll provide services to each other. O'Brian's allocates Personnel Department costs on the basis of the number of employees, and allocates Payroll Department costs on the basis of gross payroll. Cost and allocation information for June is as follows:

	Personnel	Payroll	Housewares	Clothing	Furniture
Direct department cost	$6,900	$3,200	$12,200	$20,000	$15,750
Number of employees	5	3	8	15	4
Gross payroll	$6,000	$3,300	$11,200	$17,400	$ 8,100

Requirements

a) Determine the percentage of total Personnel Department services that was provided to the Payroll Department.

b) Determine the percentage of total Payroll Department services that was provided to the Personnel Department.

c) Prepare a schedule showing Personnel Department and Payroll Department cost allocations to the operating departments assuming O'Brian's uses the step allocation method. (Round calculations to the nearest dollar.)

12–6 Service Department Cost Allocations: Direct Method

Portland Manufacturing Company has five operating departments, two of which are producing departments (P1 and P2), and three of which are service departments (S1, S2, and S3). All costs of the service departments are allocated to the producing departments. The table below shows the distribution of services from the service departments.

Services Provided from	Services Provided to				
	S1	S2	S3	P1	P2
S1	—	5%	25%	50%	20%
S2	10%	—	5%	45%	40%
S3	15%	5%	—	20%	60%

The direct operating costs of the service departments are as follows:

S1	$42,000
S2	80,000
S3	19,000

Required: Using the direct allocation method, prepare a schedule allocating the service department costs to the producing departments.

12–7 Service Department Allocations: Step Allocation Method

Refer to the data in Exercise 12–6. Using the step allocation method, prepare a schedule allocating the service department costs to the producing departments. (Round calculations to the nearest dollar.)

12–8 Common Cost Allocation: Determining Total Overhead

Springfield Manufacturing Company has two production departments, Melting and Molding. Common costs incurred for General Plant Management and for Plant Security benefit both production departments. Springfield allocates General Plant Management costs on the basis of the number of production employees, and Plant Security costs on the basis of space occupied by the production departments.

In November 19x5, the following costs were recorded.

Melting Department direct overhead	$125,000
Molding Department direct overhead	300,000
General plant management	90,000
Plant security	25,000

Other pertinent data are provided below.

	Melting	Molding
Number of employees	20	40
Space occupied (sq ft)	10,000	40,000
Machine hours	10,000	2,000
Direct labor hours	4,000	20,000

Requirements

a) Prepare a schedule allocating general plant management costs and plant security costs to the Melting and Molding Departments.

b) Determine the total departmental overhead costs for the Melting and Molding Departments.

c) Assuming the Melting Department uses machine hours and the Molding Department uses direct labor hours to apply overhead to production, calculate the overhead rate for each production department.

12–9 Service Department Allocations: Linear Algebra Method

Fargo Company's filament plant has two service departments (Administration and Maintenance) and two producing departments (Cutting and Assembling). Service and cost data for these departments are presented below:

Services Provided from	Services Provided to			
	Administration	Maintenance	Cutting	Assembling
Administration	—	30%	35%	35%
Maintenance	5%	—	60%	35%
Direct department costs:	$235,000	$126,500	$540,000	$360,000

Requirements

a) Prepare a schedule allocating the service department costs to the producing departments using the direct allocation method.

b) Prepare a schedule allocating the service department costs to the producing departments using the linear algebra allocation method.

c) Explain why the allocations to the producing departments are different under the direct and linear algebra allocation methods.

12–10 Service Cost Allocations: Direct, Step and Linear Algebra Methods

Brook Windshields, Inc., allocates Human Resources Department costs to the producing departments (Cutting and Welding) based on direct labor hours and allocates Facilities Department costs based on square footage occupied. Direct department costs, labor hours, and square footage data for the four departments for October 19x9 are as follows:

	Human Resources	Facilities	Cutting	Welding
Direct costs	$63,000	$90,000	$450,000	$600,000
Labor hours	2,000	2,000	8,000	10,000
Square footage	3,000	3,000	30,000	15,000

Requirements

a) Prepare a schedule showing the percentage of services provided from each service department to each of the service and producing departments.

b) Prepare a schedule showing the service department cost allocations using the direct allocation method.

c) Prepare a schedule showing the service department cost allocations using the step allocation method. Allocate in the order of greatest interdepartmental services.

d) Prepare a schedule showing the service department cost allocations using the linear algebra method. (Round allocations to nearest dollar.)

e) Discuss the relative advantages and disadvantages of the direct, step, and linear algebra methods of allocating service department costs.

PROBLEMS

12–11 Service Department Cost Allocation: Predetermined Overhead Rates

The Albany Company applies factory overhead in its two producing departments using a predetermined rate based on budgeted machine hours in the Stamping Department and based on budgeted labor hours in the Fabricating Department. The following data concerning next year's operations have been developed.

| | Service Departments | | Producing Departments | |
| | Human | Maintenance | | |
Budgeted costs	Resources	and Repairs	Stamping	Fabricating
Variable costs:				
Indirect materials	—	$16,000	$200,000	$ 80,000
Indirect labor	$60,000	50,000	140,000	200,000
Miscellaneous	—	—	28,000	30,000
Fixed costs:				
Miscellaneous	20,000	42,000	80,000	120,000
Other data:				
Direct labor hours (capacity)			20,000	30,000
Direct labor hours (budgeted)			14,000	20,000
Machine hours (capacity)			16,000	8,000
Machine hours (budgeted)			12,000	6,000
Number of employees (capacity)			20	30
Number of employees (budgeted)			12	18

Fixed Human Resources costs are allocated to the producing departments based on employee capacity and variable costs are allocated based on the budgeted number of employees. Fixed Maintenance and Repairs costs are allocated based on machine hour capacity, and variable costs are allocated based on the budgeted number of machine hours.

Requirements

a) Prepare a schedule showing the direct allocation of budgeted service department costs to the producing departments.

b) Determine the predetermined overhead rates for the producing departments.

12–12 Selecting Cost Allocation Bases

The Minot Company, a new company, has three producing departments, P1, P2, and P3, for which direct department costs are accumulated. In January, the following common costs of operation were incurred.

Plant manager's salary and office expense	$ 4,800
Plant security	1,200
Plant nurse's salary and office expense	1,500
Plant depreciation	2,000
Machine maintenance	2,400
Plant cafeteria cost subsidy	1,200
	$13,100

The following additional data have been collected for the three producing departments:

	P1	P2	P3
Number of employees	10	15	5
Space occupied (sq ft)	2,000	5,000	3,000
Direct labor hours	1,600	4,000	750
Machine hours	4,800	8,000	3,200
Number of nurse office visits	20	45	10

Requirements

a) Group the common cost items into cost pools based on the nature of the costs and their common basis for allocation. Identify the most appropriate allocation basis for each pool and determine the total January costs in the pool. *Hint:* A cost pool may consist of one or more cost items.

b) Allocate the cost pools directly to the three producing departments using the allocation bases selected in requirement (a).

12–13 Common Cost Allocation Bases and Computations

The Cheyenne Company has two service departments, Maintenance and Cafeteria, that serve two producing departments, Mixing and Packaging. The following data have been collected for these departments for the current year.

	Cafeteria	Maintenance	Mixing	Packaging
Direct department costs	$176,000	$112,000	$465,000	$295,000
Number of employees			50	30
Number of meals served			9,000	7,000
Number of maintenance hours used			800	600
Number of maintenance orders			180	170

Requirements

a) Using the direct method, compute the service department cost allocations under the following independent assumptions:

1. Cafeteria costs are allocated based on the number of employees, and Maintenance costs are allocated based on the number of maintenance hours.

2. Cafeteria costs are allocated based on the number of meals served, and Maintenance costs are allocated based on the number of maintenance orders.

b) Comment on the reasonableness of the bases used in the calculations in requirement (a). What considerations should determine which bases to use for allocating Cafeteria and Maintenance costs?

12–14 Direct Method of Service Department Cost Allocation: Determination of Overhead Rates

The Fresno Company, a commercial printer, uses a job-order cost system to compute its product costs. All costs other than direct job costs are accounted for as department overhead in either the producing departments (Office Products and Advertising) or the service departments (Administration and Facilities). Administration and Facilities costs are allocated to the producing departments on the basis of the number of employees and the space occupied, respectively. Overhead is applied to specific jobs on the basis of direct labor hours. The following data were collected for September 19x8.

	Administration	Facilities	Office Products	Advertising
Direct department costs	$2,500	$1,000	$3,200	$4,800
Number of employees	2	1	4	6
Space occupied (sq ft)	750	—	3,000	2,000
Direct labor hours	—	—	480	640

Requirements

a) Prepare a schedule allocating the service department costs to the producing departments using the direct allocation method.

b) Determine the overhead rate per direct labor hour for each of the producing departments. (Round answer to the nearest cent.)

c) Job 168 required 12 direct labor hours during the month in the Office Products Department. If the direct job cost was $850, how much was the total job cost?

12–15 Cost Allocation and Responsibility Accounting

The Austin Company uses a responsibility accounting system for evaluating its managers. Abbreviated performance reports for the company's three divisions for the month of March are presented below.

	Total	East	Central	West
Income before allocated costs	$165,000	$60,000	$75,000	$30,000
Less allocated costs:				
Computer Services	(66,000)	(22,000)	(22,000)	(22,000)
Personnel	(72,000)	(28,000)	(32,000)	(12,000)
Division income	$ 27,000	$10,000	$21,000	$ (4,000)

The manager of the West Division is very disturbed over his performance report and recent rumors that his division may be abolished because of its failure to report a profit in recent periods. He feels that the reported profit figures do not fairly present operating results because his division is being unfairly burdened with service department costs. He is particularly concerned over the amount of Computer Services costs charged to his division. He feels that it is inequitable for his division to be charged with one third of the total cost when it is using only 20 percent of the services. He feels that the Personnel Department's use of the Computer Services Department should also be considered in the cost allocations.

Cost allocations were based on the following distributions of services provided.

| | | Services Provided to | | | |
Services Provided from	Personnel	Computer Services	East	Central	West
Computer Services	40%	—	20%	20%	20%
Personnel	—	10%	35%	40%	15%

Requirements

a) What method is the company using to allocate Personnel and Computer Service costs?

b) Recompute the cost allocations using the step method. (Round calculations to the nearest dollar.)

c) Revise the performance reports to reflect the cost allocations computed in requirement (b).

d) Comment on the complaint of the manager of the West Division.

12–16 Common Cost Allocation: Predetermined Overhead Rate

The Gervais Company has one plant with two producing departments, Assembly and Testing. All manufacturing overhead costs that are not directly traceable to these departments are accumulated in one cost pool called General Service Department costs. General Service costs are, then, allocated to the producing departments based on direct labor hours. In the process of establishing predetermined overhead rates for 19x5, the chief cost accountant obtained the following data:

	General Service	Assembly	Testing
Budgeted variable overhead costs per direct labor hour	—	$4	$8
Budgeted fixed department overhead	$30,000	$15,000	$30,000

Gervais's operations for 19x5 are budgeted at 6,000 direct labor hours in Assembly and 1,500 direct labor hours in Testing.

Requirements

a) Prepare a budget of total overhead costs for 19x5 for the producing departments showing both direct department costs and allocated indirect department costs.

b) Determine the predetermined overhead rates for 19x5 for the Assembly and Testing Departments. (Round to the nearest cent.)

c) Assuming that Job 146 processed in 19x5 required 75 direct labor hours in Assembly and 5 direct labor hours in Testing, determine the amount of factory overhead that should be applied to the job.

12–17 Common Cost Allocations: Linear Algebra Method

Hannibal, Inc., has two service departments (S1 and S2) and two producing departments (P1 and P2). The distribution of services provided by the service departments is as follows:

Services Provided from	Services Provided to			
	S1	S2	P1	P2
S1	—	10%	40%	50%
S2	20%	—	55%	25%

Total department costs for the service and producing departments are as follows:

S1	$ 45,000
S2	30,000
P1	180,000
P2	260,000
Total	$515,000

Requirements

a) Set up algebraic equations expressing the total cost for each department reflecting simultaneous allocation of service department costs to all departments receiving services.

b) Solve the equations in requirement (a) using the substitution method or any other method that you may have learned for simultaneously solving linear equations, including use of a computer. (Round calculations to the nearest dollar if the substitution method is used.)

c) How much cost is allocated between S1 and S2? How much S1 and S2 cost is allocated to P1 and P2?

12–18 Allocation of Common Fixed Costs

The Maintenance Department of Plattsburg Mills provides services to two producing departments, Spinning and Weaving. Maintenance services used are measured by the standard maintenance labor time for the various services provided. The following data are available for the first three months of 19x2 concerning the standard hours for the actual services provided.

	Standard Hours Used	
	Spinning Department	Weaving Department
January	8,000	12,000
February	6,000	12,000
March	4,000	12,000

The Maintenance Department facilities and staff size were established based on expected maintenance needs of 8,000 service hours by the Spinning Department and 12,000 hours by the Weaving Department.

Requirements

a) If fixed Maintenance Department costs were $54,000 per month for January through March, how much should be allocated for each month to Spinning and Weaving under the following independent assumptions: (1) that fixed maintenance cost is allocated based on actual service hours; and (2) that fixed maintenance cost is allocated based on the capacity provided?

b) Which method of allocation is most appropriate? Explain.

12–19 Step Allocation: Determination of Cost Reimbursement

Community Clinic is a not-for-profit outpatient facility that provides medical services to both fee paying and low-income government supported patients. Reimbursement from the government is based on total actual costs of services provided, including both direct cost of patient services and indirect operating costs. Patient services are provided through two producing departments, Medical Services and Ancillary Services (includes X-ray, therapy, etc.). In addition to the direct costs of these departments, the clinic incurs common costs accumulated in two service departments, Administration and Facilities. Administration costs are allocated based on the number of full-time employees, and Facilities costs are allocated on the basis of space occupied. Costs, and related data, for the current month are as follows:

	Administration	Facilities	Medical Services	Ancillary Services
Direct costs	$9,000	$2,000	$60,700	$24,800
Number of employees	5	4	12	8
Space occupied (sq ft)	1,500	—	8,000	2,000
Number of patient visits	—	—	4,000	1,500

Requirements

a) Using the step allocation method, prepare a schedule allocating the common service department costs to the producing departments.

b) Determine the amount to be reimbursed from the government for each low-income patient visit.

12–20 Common Cost Allocation in a Not-for-Profit Organization

Dunwoody Community Church is organized into four operating divisions: Education, Benevolence, Community Services, and Recreation. Direct costs for each division for the year are as follows:

Education	$ 85,000
Benevolence	230,000
Community Services	125,000
Recreation	50,000
Total	$490,000

Other data pertaining to church operations are as follows:

	Building Space Occupied	Participants Served during Year	Number of Employees
Education	15,000	10,000	8
Benevolence	1,000	2,500	5
Community Services	4,000	7,500	3
Recreation	5,000	5,000	4
Totals	25,000	25,000	20

The common indirect costs of operating the church and the allocation bases are as follows:

	Cost	Allocation Base
Building and utilities	$ 60,000	Space occupied
General administration	45,000	Number of employees
Miscellaneous supplies and costs	25,000	Participants served
Total common costs	$130,000	

Requirements

a) Using the direct method, prepare a schedule allocating each common cost to the operating divisions.

b) Determine the total cost of each operating division broken down into direct and indirect costs.

12–21 Budgeted Service Department Cost Allocation: Pricing a New Product

Trimco Products Company is adding a new diet food concentrate called Body Trim to its line of body building and exercise products. A plant is being built for manufacturing the new product. Management has decided to price the new product based on a 100 percent markup on total manufacturing costs. A direct cost budget for the new plant projects that direct department costs of $2,100,000 will be incurred in producing an expected normal output of 700,000 pounds of finished product. In addition, common costs for Human Resources and Computer Services will be shared by the Body Trim Division with the two exercise products divisions, Commercial Products and Retail Products. Budgeted annual data to be used in making the allocations are summarized below.

	Human Resources	Computer Services	Commercial Products	Retail Products	Body Trim
Number of employees	5	5	50	30	20
Computer time (hrs)	500	—	1,500	1,250	750

Direct costs are budgeted at $90,000 for the Human Resources Department and $160,000 for the Computer Services Department.

Requirements

a) Using the step allocation method determine the total direct and indirect costs of Body Trim.

b) Determine the selling price per pound of Body Trim. (Round calculations to the nearest cent.)

12–22 Allocation of Home Office Costs

Megacorp, Inc., is a large conglomerate holding company with five major divisions. Home office costs are substantial and top management insists on allocating these costs to the five operating divisions. As corporate controller you are considering alternative allocation bases including sales revenue, number of employees, and total assets of the subsidiaries. Your assistant has collected the following data for you to use in making the allocations:

Total Home Office Costs	$ 20 million
Sales Revenue:	
Division A	$100 million
Division B	100 million
Division C	400 million
Division D	500 million
Division E	900 million
Number of Employees:	
Division A	1,500
Division B	1,200
Division C	2,000
Division D	2,500
Division E	2,800
Total Assets:	
Division A	$ 20 million
Division B	30 million
Division C	30 million
Division D	50 million
Division E	170 million

Requirements

a) Discuss the reasons why top management of Megacorp would want to allocate home office costs to the operating divisions. Are any of these reasons valid? Explain.

b) Calculate the home office cost allocation to each of the operating divisions for each of the bases under consideration.

c) What are some of the primary criticisms the division managers are likely to have of top management's decision to allocate home office costs to the divisions?

12–23 Allocation of Home Office Costs: Aggregate Versus Detail

Partial income statements for the three divisions of International Computer Company are presented as follows (in thousands).

	Microcomputer Division	Software Division	Mainframe Division	Total
Income before home office costs	$25,000	$5,000	$45,000	$75,000
Home office costs	−10,000	−2,000	−18,000	−30,000
Net income	$15,000	$3,000	$27,000	$45,000

Home office costs are allocated based on income before the home office cost deduction. The manager of the microcomputer division is distressed over her division's net income, and she feels that a major reason for the poor showing is the arbitrary and inequitable method by which home office costs are being allocated. She believes that much of the company's home office efforts in the past year have been directed at getting the new Software Division started and that the allocations do not reflect the relative benefits received by the divisions from home office activities.

She further suggests that home office costs should not be allocated in total but should be broken down into cost components with each component allocated on the basis that best reflects the services received by the three divisions. Corporate accounting reports show that home office costs consist of the following cost categories:

Administration	$ 6 million
Planning and Development	10 million
Legal and regulatory	12 million
Personnel relations and communications	2 million
	$30

The following data have been prepared for possible use in allocating home office costs:

Cost	Allocation Base	Microcomputer Division	Software Division	Mainframe Division
Administration	Total sales (millions)	$100	$25	$275
Planning and Development	New products in development	20	75	5
Legal and regulatory	Legal department hours used	1,000	4,000	1,000
Personnel relations	Number of employees	500	100	400

Requirements

a) Assuming all of the home office costs are controlled at the home office level and that the performance of services by the home office is determined solely by the home office staff, is it reasonable to include home office costs in performance evaluation reports for the division managers? Explain.

b) Discuss the pros and cons of allocating home office costs in total versus allocating them by individual cost components. Are division managers likely to be more receptive of home office cost allocation if costs are allocated by components instead of in the aggregate?

c) Revise the division income statements to reflect home office cost allocations by individual cost components. Is this revised statement a reasonable basis for evaluating performance by the division managers? Discuss.

12–24 Joint Cost Allocation: Physical Quantity Method (Appendix)

Chemco, Inc., processes two products, Bugoff and Weedout, used in the control of weeds and pests in lawn care. These products begin from a unique joint refining process in batches of 10,000 liters of mixture. At split-off, one fourth of the mixture emerges as Bugoff and three fourths as Weedout. Both products require further processing after split-off. The following cost and production data for August 19x1 were determined.

Total joint costs per batch	$15,000
Cost of further processing of Bugoff	5,000
Cost of further processing of Weedout	10,000
Beginning inventories	none

Requirements

a) Determine the joint cost allocation per batch for each product using the physical quantity method.

b) Determine the total cost per liter for each product. (Round answer to the nearest cent.)

c) Assuming that Bugoff and Weedout both sell for $8 per liter, prepare a schedule of gross profit per batch for each product line. Compute the gross profit percentage on each batch. Comment on the appropriateness of the allocation system used.

12–25 Joint Cost Allocation: Physical Quantity and Relative Sales Methods (Appendix)

Hills and Dales Farms is a large poultry producer that processes and sells various grades of packaged chicken to grocery chains. Chickens are grown and accounted for in groups of 50,000. At the end of the standard growing period, the chickens are separated and sold by grades. Grades A and B are sold to grocery chains, and grades C and D are sold for other uses. For costing purposes, Hills and Dales treats each batch of newly hatched chicks as a joint product. The following data pertain to the last batch of 50,000 chicks.

Grade	Number of Chickens	Average Pounds per Chicken	Selling Price per Pound
A	25,000	4	$0.50
B	15,000	3	0.40
C	6,000	$2\frac{1}{2}$	0.30
D	4,000	$1\frac{1}{4}$	0.20

Total joint costs for this batch were $40,000.

Requirements

a) Determine the cost, gross profit, and gross profit percent per pound for each grade of chickens assuming the physical quantity method of joint cost allocation is used, and the quantity is measured in terms of the number of chickens.

b) Repeat requirement (a) assuming the physical quantity is measured in terms of pounds. (Round calculations to two decimal places.)

c) Repeat requirement (a) assuming the relative sales value method of joint cost allocation is used. (Round calculations to three decimal places.)

12–26 Service Department Cost Allocation: Direct and Step Methods

The Parker Manufacturing Company has two production departments (Fabrication and Assembly) and three service departments (General Factory Administration, Factory Maintenance, and Factory Cafeteria). The costs of the General Factory Administration Department, Factory Maintenance Department, and Factory Cafeteria are allocated to the production departments on the basis of direct labor hours, square footage occupied, and number of employees, respectively. A summary of costs and other data for each department prior to allocation of service department costs for the year ended June 30, 19x3, appears below.

	Fabrication	Assembly	General Factory Administration	Factory Maintenance	Factory Cafeteria
Direct labor costs	$1,950,000	$2,050,000	$90,000	$82,100	$87,000
Direct materials costs	$3,130,000	$950,000	—	$65,000	$91,000
Manufacturing overhead costs	$1,650,000	$1,850,000	$70,000	$56,100	$62,000
Direct labor hours	562,500	437,500	31,000	27,000	42,000
Number of employees	280	200	12	8	20
Square footage occupied	88,000	72,000	1,750	2,000	4,800

Requirements

a) Assuming that Parker elects to distribute service department costs directly to production departments without recognizing interdepartmental services, how much Factory Maintenance Department costs would be allocated to the Fabrication Department?

b) Assuming the same method of allocation as in requirement (a), how much General Factory Administration Department costs would be allocated to the Assembly Department?

c) Assuming that Parker elects to distribute service department costs to other service departments (starting with the service department with the greatest total costs) as well as to the production departments, how much Factory Cafeteria Department costs would be allocated to the Factory Maintenance Department?

d) Assuming the same method of allocation as in requirement (c), how much Factory Maintenance Department costs would be allocated to the General Factory Administration Department?

(CPA Adapted)

12–27 Whether or Not to Allocate: Selecting Bases for Allocation

Bonn Company recently reorganized its computer and data processing activities. The small installations located within the accounting departments at its plants and subsidiaries have been replaced with a centralized data processing department at corporate headquarters responsible for the operations of a newly acquired large-scale computer system. The new department has been in operation for two years and has been regularly producing reliable and timely data for the past twelve months. Because the department has focused its activities on converting applications to the new system and producing reports for the plant and subsidiary managements, little attention has been devoted to the costs of the department. Now that the department's activities are operating relatively smoothly, company management has requested that the departmental manager recommend a cost accumulation system to facilitate cost control and the development of suitable rates to charge users for service. For the past two years, the departmental costs have been recorded in one account. The costs have been allocated to user departments on the basis of computer time used. The schedule below reports the costs and charging rate for 19x5.

(1) Salaries and benefits	$ 622,600
(2) Supplies	40,000
(3) Equipment maintenance contract	15,000
(4) Insurance	25,000
(5) Heat and air conditioning	36,000
(6) Electricity	50,000
(7) Equipment and furniture depreciation	285,400
(8) Building improvements depreciation	10,000
(9) Building occupancy and security	39,300
(10) Corporate administrative charges	52,700
Total costs	$1,176,000
Computer hours for user processing	2,750
Hourly rate ($1,176,000/2,750)	$ 428 (rounded)
Use of available computer hours:	
Testing and debugging programs	250
Setup of jobs	500
Processing jobs	2,750
Downtime for maintenance	750
Idle time	742
Total	4,992

The department manager recommends that the department costs be accumulated by five activity centers within the department: Systems Analysis, Programming, Data Processing, Computer Operations (processing), and Administration. He then suggests that the costs of the Administration activity should be allocated to the other four activity centers before a separate rate for charging users is developed for each of the first four activities. After reviewing the details of the accounts, the manager made the following observations regarding the charges to the several subsidiary accounts within the department.

1. Salaries and benefits—records the salary and benefit costs of all employees in the department.

2. Supplies—records punch card costs, paper costs for printers, and a small amount for miscellaneous other costs.

3. Equipment maintenance contracts—records charges for maintenance contracts; all equipment is covered by maintenance contracts.

4. Insurance—records cost of insurance covering the equipment and furniture.

5. Heat and air conditioning—records a charge from the corporate Heating and Air Conditioning Department estimated to be the incremental costs to meet the special needs of the computer department.

6. Electricity—records the charge for electricity based on a separate meter within the department.

7. Equipment and furniture depreciation—records the depreciation for all owned equipment and furniture within the department.

8. Building improvements depreciation—records amortization of the depreciation of all building improvements required to provide proper environmental control and electrical service for the computer equipment.

9. Building occupancy and security—records the Computer Department's share of the depreciation, maintenance, heat, and security costs of the building; these costs are allocated on the basis of square feet occupied.

10. Corporate administrative charges—records the Computer Department's share of the corporate administrative costs; they are allocated on the basis of the number of employees.

Requirements

a) For each of the ten cost items, state whether or not it should be allocated to the five activity centers, and for each cost item that should be allocated, recommend the basis upon which it should be allocated. Justify your conclusion in each case.

b) Assume that the costs of the Computer Operations (processing) activity will be charged to the user departments on the basis of computer hours. Using the analysis of computer utilization shown above, determine the total number of hours that should be employed to determine the charging rate for Computer Operations (processing). Justify your answer.

(CMA Adapted)

12–28 Joint Cost Allocation: Physical Quantity and Sales Value Methods (Appendix)

Vreeland, Inc., manufactures products X, Y, and Z from a joint process. Joint product costs were $120,000 during September. Additional information is as follows:

Product	Units Produced	Sales Value at Split-Off	Sales Value and Additional Costs if Processed Further	
			Sales Value	Additional Costs
X	6,000	$40,000	$55,000	$9,000
Y	4,000	35,000	45,000	7,000
Z	2,000	25,000	30,000	5,000

Requirements

a) Determine the amount of joint product costs to be allocated to each of the products during September assuming the company uses the physical quantity method of joint cost allocation.

b) Determine the amount of joint product costs to be allocated to each of the products during September assuming the company uses the sales value method of joint cost allocation. (Round calculations to four decimal places.)

c) Should any of the products be processed further? Explain.

(CPA Adapted)

12–29 Joint Cost Allocation: Net Realizable Sales Value Method (Appendix)

Doe Corporation grows, processes, cans, and sells three main pineapple products— sliced pineapple, crushed pineapple, and pineapple juice. The outside skin is cut off in the Cutting Department and processed as animal feed. The skin is treated as a by-product. Doe's production process is as follows:

■ Pineapples are first processed in the Cutting Department. The pineapples are washed, and the outside skin is cut away. Then the pineapples are cored and trimmed for slicing. The three main products (sliced, crushed, and juice) and the by-product (animal feed) are recognized after processing in the Cutting Department. Each product is then transferred to a separate department for final processing.

■ The trimmed pineapples are forwarded to the Slicing Department, where the pine-apples are sliced and canned. Any juice generated during the slicing operation is packed in the cans with the slices.

■ The pieces of pineapple trimmed from the fruit are diced and canned in the Crushing Department. Again, the juice generated during this operation is packed in the can with the crushed pineapple.

- The core and surplus pineapple generated from the Cutting Department are pulverized into a liquid in the Juicing Department.
- The outside skin is chopped into animal feed in the Feed Department.

The Doe Corporation uses the relative sales value method (based on net realizable value) to assign costs of the joint process to its main products. The by-product is inventoried at its market value. A total of 270,000 pounds were entered into the Cutting Department during May. The schedule below shows the costs incurred in each department, the proportion by weight transferred to the four final processing departments, and the selling price of each product.

Department	Costs Incurred	Percent of Product by Weight Transferred to Departments	Selling Price per Pound of Final Product
Cutting	$60,000	—	None
Slicing	4,700	35	$0.60
Crushing	10,580	28	0.55
Juicing	3,250	27	0.30
Animal feed	700	10	0.10
Total	$79,230	100	

Requirements

a) Calculate the number of pounds of pineapple that result as output for pineapple slices, crushed pineapple, pineapple juice, and animal feed.

b) Calculate the net realizable value at the split-off point of the three main products.

c) Calculate the amount of the cost of the Cutting Department assigned to each of the three main products and to the by-product in accordance with corporate policy. (Round calculations to four decimal places.)

d) Calculate the gross profits for each of the three main products.

(CMA Adapted)

12–30 Cost Allocation and Performance Evaluation

The Village Branch of Citizens and Northern Bank is managed by Ron Short who has full responsibility for the bank's operations. The Village Branch is treated as a profit center within the company's responsibility accounting system and, according to rumors throughout the company, if the Village Branch does not become more profitable it is likely to be closed. Ron is upset with the corporate accounting department because of the number of different indirect costs which are allocated to his branch each period. He feels that many of these costs provide no direct benefits to his branch and that they are not relevant to an evaluation of his performance or that of the Village Branch. An income statement for the Village Branch is presented below for February 19x4.

Branch revenues		$145,000
Direct branch costs		− 90,000
Branch margin		$ 55,000
Allocated costs:		
Computer Operations Department	$ 4,500	
Personnel Department	5,000	
Payroll Department	3,800	
Maintenance Department	6,000	
Accounting Department	5,200	
Legal and Audit Department	4,200	
Transportation Department	9,000	
Administrative Overhead	12,000	− 49,700
Branch Net Income		$ 5,300

An investigation of Mr. Short's complaint by the controller's office provided the following additional information:

■ Computer operations costs are billed based on actual CPU and computer connect time used by the branch.

■ Personnel and payroll costs are primarily fixed and are allocated to the various operating departments based on the number of employees in each division.

■ Maintenance costs are charged to the operating departments based on the standard hours actually worked in each department plus the actual cost of materials and supplies used.

■ Accounting costs are allocated based on the number of transactions processed by the computer for each branch.

■ Legal and audit costs are allocated based on total revenues of the operating departments. The Village Branch has been involved in only one lawsuit which was about five years ago. Mr. Short gets a copy of the company audit report each year but seldom reads it.

■ Transportation costs consist primarily of the costs of operating the company helicopter and the company airplane. The helicopter is used to deliver checks to the local clearing center and for local executive transportation and the airplane is used primarily for executive travel out of town. Transportation costs are allocated to the operating departments based on revenues. Mr. Short has never flown in the corporate airplane.

■ Administrative overhead consists of all other administrative costs including home office salaries and office expenses. These costs are allocated to the operating departments based on revenues. Mr. Short seldom ever sees anyone from the home office.

Requirements

a) Evaluate each of the cost allocations to determine whether it seems appropriate to allocate it to the operating divisions. Also evaluate the basis upon which each cost is allocated to the operating departments.

b) Prepare a revised income statement for the Village Branch based on your evaluations in requirement (a).

c) Do you agree with Mr. Short's complaint? How do the cost allocations affect the decision to continue or discontinue the Village Branch?

REVIEW PROBLEM SOLUTION

1. Direct Method

	Total	Women's	Men's
Administrative Services Department:			
Allocation base (number of employees)	24	15	9
Percent of total base	100%	62.5%	37.5%
Cost allocation	$18,000	$11,250	$6,750
Facilities Services Department:			
Allocation base (square footage)	22,500	15,000	7,500
Percent of total base	100%	66.7%	33.3%
Cost allocation	$12,000	$8,000	$4,000

Cost allocation summary:

	Administrative	Facilities	Women's	Men's	Total
Departmental costs before allocation	$18,000	$12,000	$60,000	$50,000	$140,000
Cost allocations:					
Administrative	(18,000)	—	11,250	6,750	-0-
Facilities	—	(12,000)	8,000	4,000	-0-
Departmental costs after allocation	$ -0-	$ -0-	$79,250	$60,750	$140,000

2. Step Method

Allocation sequence:

Allocation Base	Administrative Number of Employees	Facilities Square Footage
Total base for other service and producing departments (a)	26	25,000
Total base for other service departments (b)	2	2,500
Percent of total services provided to other service departments (b)/(a)	7.7%	10.0%
Order of allocation	Second	First

Step allocations:

	Total	Administrative	Women's	Men's
Facilities Services Department:				
Allocation base (square footage)	25,000	2,500	15,000	7,500
Percent of total base	100%	10%	60%	30%
Cost allocation	$12,000	$1,200	$7,200	$3,600
Administrative Services Department:				
Allocation base (number of employees)	24	—	15	9
Percent of total base	100%	—	62.5%	37.5%
Cost allocation	$19,200	—	$12,000	$7,200

Cost allocation summary:

	Facilities	Administrative	Women's	Men's	Total
Departmental costs before allocation	$12,000	$18,000	$60,000	$50,000	$140,000
Cost allocations:					
Facilities	(12,000)	1,200	7,200	3,600	-0-
Administrative	—	(19,200)	12,000	7,200	-0-
Departmental costs after allocation	$ -0-	$ -0-	$79,200	$60,800	$140,000

3. Linear Algebra Method

Legend:

A = Administrative Services Department
F = Facilities Services Department
W = Women's Apparel Department
M = Men's Apparel Department

Summary of services:

Services Provided from	Services Provided to			
	A	*F*	*W*	*M*
A	—	2/26 = 7.7%	15/26 = 57.7%	9/26 = 34.6%
F	2,500/25,000 = 10%	—	15,000/25,000 = 60%	7,500/25,000 = 30%

Total cost equations:

$$A = 18,000 + 0.10F$$
$$F = 12,000 + 0.077A$$
$$W = 60,000 + 0.577A + 0.60F$$
$$M = 50,000 + 0.346A + 0.30F$$

Solutions to equations using substitution method:

$$A = 18,000 + 0.10(12,000 + 0.077A)$$
$$A = 18,000 + 1,200 + 0.0077A$$
$$0.9923A = 19,200$$
$$A = 19,349 \text{ (or \$18,000 direct cost plus \$1,349 allocated from F)}$$

$$F = 12,000 + 0.077(19,349)$$
$$F = 12,000 + 1,490$$
$$F = 13,490 \text{ (or \$12,000 direct cost plus \$1,490 allocated from A)}$$

$$W = 60,000 + 0.577(19,349) + 0.60(13,490)$$
$$W = 60,000 + 11,164 + 8,094$$
$$W = 79,258 \text{ (or \$60,000 direct cost plus \$11,164 allocated from A}$$
$$\text{and \$8,094 allocated from F)}$$

$$M = 50,000 + 0.346(19,349) + 0.30(13,490)$$
$$M = 50,000 + 6,695 + 4,047$$
$$M = 60,742 \text{ (or \$50,000 direct cost plus \$6,695 allocated}$$
$$\text{from A and \$4,047 allocated from F)}$$

Cost allocation summary:

	Administrative	Facilities	Women's	Men's	Total
Departmental costs before allocation	$18,000	$12,000	$60,000	$50,000	$140,000
Cost allocations:					
Administrative	(19,349)	1,490	11,164	6,695	-0-
Facilities	1,349	(13,490)	8,094	4,047	-0-
Departmental costs after allocation	$ -0-	$ -0-	$79,258	$60,742	$140,000

PART IV

Selected Topics
for Further Study

CHAPTER 13

Relevant Costs for Quantitative Models

Upon completion of this chapter you should:

- Understand the nature of quantitative models and their use in aiding decision making.
- Understand the issues involved in developing relevant cost data for use in quantitative models.
- Be able to apply the economic order quantity model to determine the most economic inventory order quantity and reorder point.
- Be able to apply the safety stock assumptions to determine the minimum amount of safety stock required to prevent stockouts.
- Have a general understanding of the basic elements of the linear programming model and be able to solve a simple linear programming model using the graphical approach.
- Be able to prepare payoff tables as an aid in evaluating decision alternatives that have different risk levels.
- Understand what is meant by the value of perfect information and why a decision maker might find this concept useful.

A **model** is a simplified representation of some real-world phenomenon. Models are used to learn about the related phenomenon and to quickly and inexpensively determine the effect of some proposed action. Children learn by playing with model houses, boats, cars, and horses. Museums and libraries contain educational models of buildings, drilling platforms, spaceships, prehistoric animals, and ecosystems. Airframe manufacturers study the aerodynamics of model planes in wind tunnels. Captains of supertankers learn how to pilot their craft using models in small lakes. These are all examples of **physical models,** scaled down versions or replicas of physical reality.

Managers and other decision makers also use **quantitative models** that are simply a series of algebraic relationships. Quantitative models can be further classified into **descriptive models** that merely specify the relationships between a series of independent and dependent variables and **optimizing models** that suggest a specific choice between decision alternatives. Cost-volume-profit relationships, contribution income statements, and operating budgets are all descriptive models.

The purposes of this chapter are to illustrate the usefulness of optimizing models as decision aids and to discuss the proper use of accounting data in optimizing models. Attention is focused on three models that are widely used by managers and accountants: the economic order quantity, linear programming, and payoff tables. The models introduced in this chapter are not accounting models per se, but they often use accounting data. Consequently, the accuracy and relevance of accounting data is critical to their proper use.

QUANTITATIVE MODELS ARE DECISION AIDS

Quantitative, especially optimizing, models are often criticized as being over-simplistic, unrealistic, and prone to "make" incorrect decisions. It is true that models are a simplified representation of reality, but this is also one of their strengths. The use of a model helps management focus on the few variables that are most critical to a decision. Furthermore, the assumptions that underlie a model can be specified and evaluated.

All quantitative models, descriptive and optimizing, are intended to *assist* managers in decision making. Managers cannot relinquish their decision-making responsibility to models that are merely intended to be decision support systems. In the final analysis, *managers, not models, make decisions.* Managers must carefully evaluate the data used in the model, the assumptions underlying the model, and the output of the model. If everything appears satisfactory, a manager may implement the action suggested by an optimizing model. If a manager suspects faulty data, an oversimplistic assumption, or changed circumstances that invalidate the model, the suggested action should not be implemented. Instead, the manager should undertake further analysis or make a decision based on professional judgment.

Optimizing models, like many other aspects of a business, should be managed using the principle of exception. When everything is going according to plan, management implements the action suggested by the model. If any invalidating circumstances are suspected, management should intervene. Properly used as decision aids, models increase the speed and quality of management's decisions.

ECONOMIC ORDER QUANTITY

The operating budget (discussed in Chapter 6) specifies the number of units to be purchased or manufactured during a period of time. In merchandising organizations, for example, the number of units to be purchased is computed, for each inventory item, as the total needs for current sales, plus the desired ending inventory, less the expected beginning inventory. The operating budget does not specify the order quantity or the reorder point. The **order quantity** is the quantity of inventory ordered *at one time,* and the **reorder point** is the inventory level at which an order for additional units is placed.

Consider the order quantity. If budgeted 19x4 purchases of inventory item B-25 are 2,400 units, management might place one order for 2,400 units, three orders for 800 units, 2,400 orders for 1 unit, or some other combination of number of orders and order size.

Assume that the demand for item B-25 is constant throughout the year and that new orders are timed to arrive just as the previous order is exhausted. In this case, an order quantity of 800 units might produce the variations in inventory level illustrated in Exhibit 13–1. The maximum inventory level is reached just as a new order is received. Subsequent to the receipt of an order, the inventory level falls at a constant rate per unit of time, and another order is received just as the inventory level falls to zero. With a maximum inventory of 800 units, a minimum inventory of 0 units, and a constant rate of decline per unit of time, the average inventory of item B-25 is 400 units $[(800 + 0)/2]$.

Inventory Costs

A variety of costs are associated with inventory, including the costs of the units purchased, of ordering inventory, of carrying inventory, and of insufficient inventory. Several costs in each of these categories are listed in Exhibit 13–2. Management's objective is to determine the **economic order quantity** (EOQ), the order quantity that results in the minimum total annual inventory costs. Because only costs that vary with the order quantity are relevant to this decision, each of the cost categories in Exhibit 13–2 is examined to identify the relevant and the irrelevant costs.

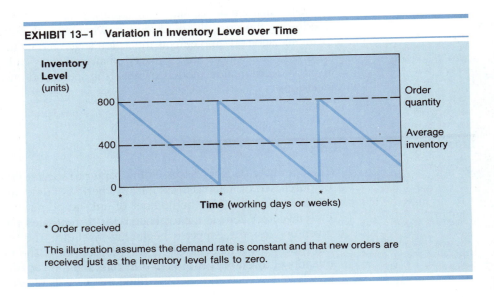

EXHIBIT 13–1   Variation in Inventory Level over Time

* Order received

This illustration assumes the demand rate is constant and that new orders are received just as the inventory level falls to zero.

EXHIBIT 13–2 Inventory Costs for Purchased Goods Intended for Resale*

Costs of units purchased

Unit price
Transportation-in

Costs of carrying inventory

Insurance
Personal property taxes
Storage space costs
Deterioration and obsolescence
Opportunity cost of money invested in
     inventory

Costs of ordering inventory

Processing the order
Receiving and inspecting the order
Processing payment for the order

Costs of insufficient inventory

Lost contribution from missed sales
Lost customer goodwill
Cost of special orders
Cost of processing backorders

---

* In the case of manufactured goods, variable manufacturing costs are substituted for the unit price and the cost of ordering inventory includes machine set-up costs. If goods are to be processed further in a subsequent department, the costs of insufficient inventory include the costs of excessive idle time and the costs of expediting production once the goods are available.

In the absence of quantity discounts, the total annual costs of the units purchased vary only with total units purchased, not with the order quantity or the number of orders. Consequently, the total annual costs of the units purchased are irrelevant to determining the order quantity and are excluded from order quantity models.

The total annual costs of ordering inventory are computed as follows:

$$\begin{array}{l}\text{Total annual} \\ \text{ordering costs}\end{array} = \begin{array}{l}\text{Cost of placing} \\ \text{an order}\end{array} \times \begin{array}{l}\text{Number of orders} \\ \text{per year.}\end{array}$$

Because the number of orders per year is computed as the annual demand divided by the order size, the total annual costs of ordering inventory vary with the order size. As the order size increases, the number of orders per year decreases, and the total annual ordering costs decrease. Conversely, as the order size decreases, the number of orders per year increases, and the total annual ordering costs increase.

Assume that the cost of placing an order for part B-25 is $25. If the order quantity is 800 units, the total annual ordering costs are $75 [$25 × (2,400/800)]. A decrease in the order size to 600 units would increase the total available ordering costs to $100 [$25 × (2,400/600)].

As might be suspected, the costs of carrying inventory also vary with the order size. Increasing the order size increases the average inventory and the total annual costs of carrying inventory. Conversely, decreasing the order size reduces the average inventory and the total annual carrying costs.

Note that the cost of carrying inventory includes an opportunity cost for the money invested in inventory. The interest rate on borrowed money is frequently used to estimate this opportunity cost. However, the rate of return management desires to earn on inventory investments is a better choice. The issues involved in determining this rate are discussed in financial management textbooks; one possible rate is the organization's cost of capital (discussed in Chapter 14).

Carrying costs are often expressed as a percentage of the unit purchase price. Assume the carrying costs for part B-25 are 25 percent of the unit purchase price. If the unit purchase price is $12 and the order size is 800 units, the cost of carrying 1 unit in inventory for 1 year is $3 ($12 × 0.25), and the total annual carrying costs are $1,200 [$3 × (800/2)].

Operations research textbooks sometimes contain sophisticated models that allow stockouts and backorders to occur. These models then include stockout costs in the determination of the economic order quantity. We shall assume that management does not intentionally allow stockouts to occur. Consequently, the costs of insufficient inventory are irrelevant to the determination of our economic order quantity.

In summary, only the costs of ordering and carrying inventory are relevant to determining the economic order quantity, and these costs vary inversely with each other. As the order size increases, total annual ordering costs decrease and total annual carrying costs increase. As the order size decreases, total annual ordering costs increase and total annual carrying costs decrease. The total relevant costs for determining the economic order quantity are computed as follows:

$$\begin{array}{c} \text{Total annual ordering} \\ \text{and carrying costs} \end{array} = \left(\begin{array}{c} \text{Cost of placing} \\ \text{an order} \end{array} \times \frac{\text{Annual demand}}{\text{Order quantity}} \right)$$
$$+ \left(\begin{array}{c} \text{Unit carrying} \\ \text{costs per year} \end{array} \times \frac{\text{Order quantity}}{2} \right).$$

Determining the Economic Order Quantity

There are two basic approaches to determining the economic order quantity (EOQ): (1) a trial and error tabular approach and (2) a formula approach. Both approaches are based on the following assumptions.

1. The demand rate is known and uniform.

2. There are no quantity discounts.

3. Ordering costs are a known function of the number of orders.

4. Carrying costs are a known function of average inventory.

5. Stockouts are not intentionally permitted.

Though these assumptions are seldom completely valid, the EOQ model is useful because if often produces lower total annual inventory costs than order quantities based on professional judgment.

Trial and Error Approach. Recall that the annual demand for inventory part B-25 is 2,400 units, the cost of placing an order is $25, and the cost of carrying 1 unit in inventory for 1 year is $3. If management orders 800 units at a time, the total annual ordering and carrying costs are $1,275 (see Exhibit 13–3).

Also tabulated in Exhibit 13–3 are the total annual ordering and carrying costs for several additional order sizes. The information tabulated in Exhibit 13–3 is graphed in Exhibit 13–4. Both exhibits illustrate that *the minimum annual costs occur at the order size where the annual ordering costs equal the annual carrying costs,* 200 units in this example. The essence of the trial and error approach is to find the order size where these two costs are equal by repeated trial and error.

Even though the EOQ model suggests that an order size of exactly 200 units is most economical, management might order in other lot sizes because of quantity discounts, warehouse capacity constraints, limited shelf life of an inventory item, or a variety of other factors. An examination of Exhibit 13–4 reveals that small deviations from the economic order quantity are not very costly. The total cost curve is high at both ends but relatively low between 100 and 300 units. The existence of this wide low-cost area near the EOQ, with high costs at order quantities far from the EOQ, is what makes this model so valuable despite its restrictive assumptions. Even if the model is not completely accurate, it helps management get into the low-cost area.

EXHIBIT 13–3   Relevant Annual Costs for Determining the Economic Order Quantity

Order quantity (units)	20	50	150	200	300	800	1,200	2,400
Number of orders (annual demand ÷ order quantity)	120	48	16	12	8	3	2	1
Average inventory (order quantity divided by two)*	10	25	75	100	150	400	600	1,200
Relevant annual costs:								
Ordering (number of orders × $25)	$3,000	$1,200	$400	$300	$200	$ 75	$ 50	$ 25
Carrying (average inventory × $3)	30	75	225	300	450	1,200	1,800	3,600
Total	$3,030	$1,275	$625	$600**	$650	$1,275	$1,850	$3,625

* This assumes that the demand rate is constant and that the inventory level is zero when the new order is received.
** Minimum annual ordering and holding costs.

EXHIBIT 13–4   Behavior of Inventory Ordering and Carrying Costs

Formula Approach.   By setting annual ordering costs equal to annual carrying costs, and solving for the order quantity, the economic order quantity formula is derived.

Annual Ordering Costs	=	**Annual Carrying Costs**

$$\text{Cost of placing an order} \times \frac{\text{Annual demand}}{\text{Order quantity}} = \text{Unit carrying costs per year} \times \frac{\text{Order quantity}}{2}$$

$$\text{Economic order quantity} = \sqrt{\frac{2 \times \text{Annual demand} \times \text{Cost of placing an order}}{\text{Unit carrying cost per year}}}$$

For part B-25, the economic order quantity is once again determined to be 200 units:

$$\text{EOQ} = \sqrt{\frac{2 \times 2{,}400 \times \$25}{\$3}}$$

$$= 200 \text{ units.}$$

Reorder Point

The reorder point is the inventory level at which an order for additional units is placed. The reorder point must allow sufficient inventory to cover demand during the **lead time,** the time between the placement and the receipt of an order. Assuming demand takes place evenly throughout a year containing n work days, the equation for daily demand is

$$\text{Daily demand} = \text{Annual demand}/n.$$

If the lead time required to fill an order is known and certain, the reorder point that results in a new order arriving just as the previous order is exhausted is computed as

$$\frac{\text{Reorder}}{\text{point}} = \frac{\text{Daily}}{\text{demand}} \times \frac{\text{Lead}}{\text{time.}}$$

Assume the organization using part B-25 operates 240 days per year and that the lead time for this item is 5 days. Under these circumstances the reorder point for B-25 is 50 units:

$$\text{Daily demand} = 2{,}400 \text{ units}/240 \text{ days}$$
$$= 10 \text{ units per day.}$$

$$\text{Reorder point} = 10 \text{ units per day} \times 5 \text{ days}$$
$$= 50 \text{ units.}$$

Management places an order whenever the inventory level falls to 50 units.

Safety Stocks

Safety stocks are extra units of inventory carried to prevent stockouts due to variations in the demand for units during the lead time. Stockouts can occur because of delays in the receipt of an order or increases in the daily demand for an inventory item. If management desires to avoid stockouts, and daily demand or lead time or both are uncertain, they must carry safety stocks.

Safety stocks can be computed as the difference between the maximum lead time demand and the reorder point without safety stocks. Safety stocks do not increase the economic order quantity; they do, however, increase the reorder point. Assume the maximum daily demand for part B-25 is 12 units, and the maximum lead time is 8 days. Under these circumstances, the safety stock for this item would be set at 46 units:

Maximum demand per day	12 units
Maximum lead time	× 8 days
Maximum lead time demand	96 units
Reorder point without safety stocks	−50 units
Safety stock	46 units

Safety stocks can be viewed as a base inventory. If the safety stocks for part B-25 are never used, they will have an annual carrying cost of $138, computed as the $3 carrying costs per unit per year times 46 units of safety stock.

The economic order quantity for part B-25 will remain at 200 units, but the reorder point will increase to 96 units, computed as the reorder point without safety stocks plus the safety stock. Possible patterns for part B-25's inventory level with safety stocks and variations in lead time demand are illustrated in Exhibit 13–5. Note that the presence of the base inventory layer increases the maximum inventory to 246 units.

Economic Lot Size

The economic order quantity has been discussed in the context of a merchandising firm. Assuming that production is in batches and no units are available until the batch is complete, the model is also applicable to manufacturing. In this case, variable manufacturing costs are substituted for the unit price, and the cost of ordering inventory includes machine setup costs. With these substitutions, the model is used to compute an economic lot (batch) size that results in the minimum ordering and carrying costs.

In recent years, the application of the EOQ model to manufacturing has been criticized by proponents of "just-in-time production" or "zero inventories," who argue that management should try to minimize inventories rather than try

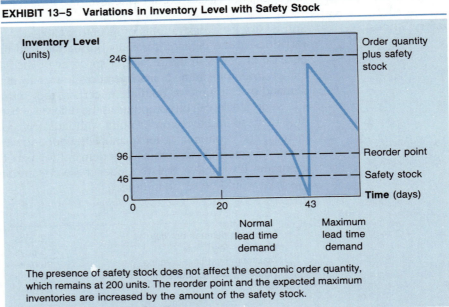

EXHIBIT 13–5   Variations in Inventory Level with Safety Stock

The presence of safety stock does not affect the economic order quantity, which remains at 200 units. The reorder point and the expected maximum inventories are increased by the amount of the safety stock.

to optimize the batch size. This is done with a batch size of one unit. Proponents of zero inventories believe total production and inventory costs are reduced when management focuses its attention on balancing production operations and producing good units in batches of one rather than on producing batches of units in accordance with the EOQ model.

Others believe that the EOQ model is a useful management tool and that managers who properly use it should achieve more satisfactory results for their organization. However, like the just-in-time inventory and other models, if the EOQ model is inappropriately applied to situations in which its assumptions are invalid, the results will not be satisfactory.

Managers sometimes spend too much time trying to optimize production and minimize costs for the current cost structure when better results would be achieved by trying to reduce the cost structure. An analysis of the economic lot size (order quantity) formula reveals that a reduction in the cost of placing an order will reduce the economic lot size. In recent years, many managers have worked to reduce ordering costs by reducing the number of suppliers of raw materials and establishing closer relationships with the remaining suppliers in order to achieve more timely delivery, more dependable delivery, lower prices, and more uniform quality. The installation of computer aided manufacturing and automated assembly lines has also reduced machine setup times and costs. All these actions reduce the economic lot size.

Managers cannot shift the blame for bad decisions to a model. Managers, not models, make decisions. The economic lot size (order quantity) model is intended for batch production. If it is inappropriately applied to situations in which continuous production is more appropriate, the results will be less than optimal. The model assumes that the demand rate is known and uniform. If the demand rate is uncertain or variable, use of the model may result in excess inventory or inventory stockouts.

The EOQ model is intended to optimize for a given cost structure. If managers fail to minimize ordering and setup costs, their firm will be less competitive, even if they use the model properly. Managers of competitive firms must strive to reduce their firm's cost structure and make appropriate use of quantitative models as decision aids.

LINEAR PROGRAMMING

Linear programming is an optimizing model used to assist managers in making decisions under constrained conditions when linear relationships exist between all variables. This model may be applied to a variety of business decisions, including product mix, raw materials mix, production scheduling, transportation scheduling, and cash management. The objective in linear programming is to determine the action that will maximize profits or minimize costs. The constraints can represent limited resources (such as labor hours, machine hours, raw materials, or money), limited consumer demand, or required physical characteristics of the final product (such as a minimum percentage of protein or a maximum percentage of fat).

Although the concepts underlying linear programming are straightforward, the actual solution to linear programming problems can be extremely complex. Fortunately, the availability of computers and modeling specialists has resulted in situations where the manager need not be concerned about the detailed operation of the solution technique. The manager should, of course, have a general understanding of how the solution is determined (the model's assumptions) and be able to evaluate both the data used and the suggested solution.

Assumptions and Uses of Accounting Data

As its name implies, the most critical linear programming assumption is that linear relationships exist between all variables. The total contribution from the sale of products X and Y, for example, must be of the form $aX + bY$, where a is the unit contribution of product X, and b is the unit contribution of product Y. Curvilinear relationships, such as $aX - 0.05X^2 + bY - 0.0002bY^3$ are not allowed. Another assumption of linear programming is that fractional production is permitted. The suggested solution to a linear programming problem might, for example, specify the production and sale of 25.2 units of X and 32.7 units of Y.

When these assumptions are not valid, the manager might elect to use other models. Alternatively, if it seems appropriate, the manager might use professional judgment to adjust the suggested linear programming solution; for example, the production of X might be rounded to 25 units, and the production of Y might be rounded to 32 units.

Every linear programming model includes an **objective function,** or goal to be maximized or minimized. Accounting data are often used in the objective function. *If the objective is to maximize profits, the coefficients of the variables in the objective function should be unit contribution margins.* If the objective is to minimize costs, the coefficients should be unit variable costs. The total contribution margin or variable costs of each product will vary in proportion to changes in volume. Profit and cost measures that include an allocation of fixed costs should not be used in the objective function. They do not vary in direct proportion to changes in production; hence their use violates the linearity assumption.

Graphic Analysis of Product Mix Decisions

We use graphic analysis to illustrate the solution of linear programming problems. Though graphic analysis can be used to solve problems containing only two variables, it provides the general understanding necessary to evaluate more complex problems containing three or more variables. The following steps are involved in graphic analysis.

1. *Develop an equation for the objective function* indicating how each variable affects the profit maximization or cost minimization goal.

2. *Develop an equation for each constraint* indicating how each variable affects the total use of the constraint.

3. *Graph the constraints.*

4. *Identify the feasible solutions* that are bounded by the constraints.

5. *Determine the optimal solution* that maximizes or minimizes the value of the objective function.

Assume the Martin Company produces two products, A and B, in two departments, Assembly and Finishing. Product A has a unit contribution margin of $50, and product B has a unit contribution margin of $40. The demand for each product exceeds Martin's capacity to produce. Production information is as follows:

	Labor Hours per Unit		Total Labor Hours Available per Week
	A	B	
Assembly Department	20	20	600
Finishing Department	20	10	400

Martin can only obtain raw materials sufficient to produce 25 units of B each week. Management desires the product mix that will maximize the weekly contribution of products A and B toward fixed costs and profits. Using the five steps, the problem is solved as follows:

1. *Objective function.* The objective is to maximize the total weekly contribution of products A and B. Given information on the unit contribution margin, Martin's objective function is

$$\text{Maximize } \$50A + \$40B.$$

2. *Constraints.* There are constraints for maximum assembly hours, maximum finishing hours, and maximum production of product B. Because each constraint indicates an upper limit on the use of some resource, the less than or equal to symbol is used in each:

$$20A + 20B \leq 600 \text{ Assembly Department hours,}$$
$$20A + 10B \leq 400 \text{ Finishing Department hours,}$$
$$B \leq 25 \text{ units.}$$

The assembly hours constraint indicates that any combination of A and B can be produced, providing it does not require more than 600 assembly hours. The finishing hours constraint indicates that any combination of A and B can be produced, providing it does not require more than 400 finishing hours. Finally, because of raw materials limitations, no more than 25 units of B can be produced.

To be technically precise, two more constraints are added to indicate that negative production is prohibited:

$$A \geq 0,$$
$$B \geq 0.$$

Hence the production of A and the production of B must be greater than or equal to zero.

3. *Graph.* One axis must be designated to represent each variable. In Exhibit 13–6, the horizontal axis is labeled product A, and the vertical axis is labeled product B. The opposite could also have been done.

The set of all feasible A and B values is determined by solving each constraint for its maximum A and B values, assuming all production was devoted to that product, and drawing lines on graph paper connecting, for each constraint, the maximum value of each product. The maximum values of A and B, for each constraint, are computed as follows:

	Maximum Values	
	Product A	Product B
Assembly hours	600/20 = 30	600/20 = 30
Finishing hours	400/20 = 20	400/10 = 40
Raw materials		25

The lines connecting these maximum values are illustrated in Exhibit 13–6. Because the raw materials constraint affects only product B, it does not intersect the horizontal axis for product A. Instead, it is drawn parallel to the horizontal axis. The nonnegativity constraints are represented by the horizontal and vertical axes.

4. *Feasible solutions.* After the lines representing each constraint are drawn, the **feasible region,** representing all possible production volumes and mixes, is depicted by the area between the vertical and horizontal axes and the first set of enclosing lines that represent constraints (this is the area enclosed by the solid lines from points 1–2–3–4–5 in Exhibit 13–6). The firm can produce anywhere within the feasible region; however, it is likely that one product mix will provide a higher total contribution than any other mix.

EXHIBIT 13–6   Graphic Approach to Linear Programming

5. *Optimal solution.* In linear programming, the **optimal solution** is the feasible solution that maximizes or minimizes the value of the objective function, depending on management's goal. An important characteristic of linear programming is that *if there is a single optimal solution, it is found at a corner point where the lines representing two or more constraints intersect.* Knowing this, it is only necessary to evaluate the solutions represented by corner points. In Exhibit 13–6, there are five corner points, which, for convenience, are numbered 1 through 5. The value of the objective function at each corner point is computed in Exhibit 13–7. The maximum optimal solution, represented by

EXHIBIT 13–7   Evaluation of Alternative Corner Solutions

Corner	Value of A	Value of B	Value of Objective Function $\$50A + \$40B =$
1	0	0	$ —
2	0	25	1,000
3	5	25	1,250
4	10*	20*	1,300
5	20	0	1,000

* Optimal solution

corner 4, calls for a weekly production of 10 units of product A and 20 units of product B. This solution will provide a weekly contribution of $1,300. Fixed costs, of course, would be deducted from this amount to determine the weekly profit.

The Corner Solution

The reason that the unique solution is always found at a corner point can be illustrated by drawing a line representing some arbitrary value for the objective function. In the case of the Martin Company, the end points for an objective function with a value of $500 are 10 units of product A and 12.5 units of product B. In general,

Desired contribution ÷ Unit contribution = End point.

For A,

$$\$500 \div \$50 = 10 \text{ units.}$$

For B,

$$\$500 \div \$40 = 12.5 \text{ units.}$$

Drawing this line in Exhibit 13–6, observe that 10 units of A or 12.5 units of B or any combination along this line will provide a weekly contribution of $500. An objective function having a higher value would be drawn farther from the origin, parallel to the first line. To maximize the value of the objective function, additional lines are drawn parallel to the first line, but farther from the origin, until only one point on a line touches the feasible solution. This one unique point will be a corner point; corner 4 in this case. You may draw these additional lines as an exercise.

Simplex Method

Though it is possible to solve two variable problems with the aid of graphic analysis, linear programming problems containing three or more variables must be solved by a mathematical solution technique known as the **simplex method.** The mechanics of the simplex method are far from simple, even though the method arrives at a solution by comparing objective function values at multi-dimensional corner points, just as was done earlier with the graphic approach. To solve the Martin Company's product mix problem, the same set of equations would be used as in the previous illustration. Software packages are available to solve linear programming problems on most computers.

PAYOFF TABLES

Certainty means the probability of an event's occurring is 100 percent, whereas **uncertainty** means the probability of an event's occurring is less than 100 percent. When the outcome of a decision alternative is uncertain, managers often desire information on the expected value of that alternative. A decision alternative's **expected value** is simply the weighted average of the possible cash flows associated with that alternative. Identifying each possible cash flow as an outcome, the expected value of a decision alternative is computed as follows:

$$\text{Expected value} = \Sigma \,(\text{Outcome})\,(\text{Probability of outcome}),$$

where Σ is a summation sign indicating that the product of each cash flow multiplied by its related probability is to be summed.

Assume a particular investment has the following possible outcomes.

Outcome	Net Cash Flow	Probability
1	$2,000	0.50
2	5,000	0.20
3	8,000	0.30
		1.00

This investment has three possible outcomes, and, because one of them will occur, the associated probabilities sum to 1.00, or 100 percent. The expected value of this investment is $4,400:

$$\text{Expected value} = (\$2,000)(0.50) + (\$5,000)(0.20) + (\$8,000)(0.30)$$
$$= \$4,400.$$

The expected cash flow of $4,400 is the weighted average of the possible cash flows of $2,000, $5,000, and $8,000. A cash flow of exactly $4,400 will not occur, but this weighted amount is a better *summary measure* of the project's cash flows than any one of the three possible outcomes. The advantages of expected value as a summary measure increase with the number of possible outcomes. With only three possible outcomes the situation is fairly simple, but imagine a situation where there are ten or fifteen possible outcomes; here a summary measure of possible outcomes would be welcome.

Constructing Payoff Tables

Expected value is frequently employed as a decision criterion when a manager must select one of several alternative actions, with the outcomes of each subject to uncertainty. A **payoff table** is often used to enumerate the alternative actions management may take and the possible monetary outcomes of each action. Each monetary outcome results from the joint effect of management's action and an event that can occur. Once the payoff table is constructed, the outcome and probability information in it are used to compute each action's expected value. The following example illustrates the relationship between actions, events, and outcomes, as well as the construction and use of payoff tables.

On Saturdays during July and August, Janet Gaines sells hotdogs at a Long Island beach. She acquires the precooked and prepackaged hotdogs for $0.60 each and sells them for $1.00. She must order her hotdogs in lots of 100 on Thursdays. Past daily demand has varied between 200 and 500 units with the following probability distribution.

Event	Probability Distribution
200 units demanded	0.20
300 units demanded	0.30
400 units demanded	0.40
500 units demanded	0.10

Janet wants to know how many hotdogs to order each Thursday to maximize the expected value of hotdog sales. Unsold hotdogs are donated to a local orphanage.

The payoff table for this particular decision is presented in Exhibit 13–8. The decision alternatives are the order sizes listed in the left column. The possible events are the levels of demand listed across the top (along with the related probability of each event). The outcomes, resulting from the joint effect of the order size and the demand, are presented in the center of the table. These outcomes range from a loss of $100 if 500 units are ordered but only 200 are sold to a profit of $200 if 500 units are ordered and sold. Sample computations for other outcomes are presented below the table.

EXHIBIT 13–8   Payoff Table Illustrated

Action	Event				Expected Value of Action
	Demand (probability)				
Order Size	200 (0.20)	300 (0.30)	400 (0.40)	500 (0.10)	
200	$ 80*	$ 80	$ 80	$ 80	$ 80
300	20	120	120	120	100 maximum
400	(40)**	60	160	160	90†
500	(100)	—	100	200	40

* Example of computation: ($1 × 200) − ($0.60 × 200) = $80.
** Example of computation: ($1 × 200) − ($0.60 × 400) = $(40).
† Example of computation: ($−40)(0.20) + ($60)(0.30) + ($160)(0.40) + ($160)(0.10) = $90.

The expected values, shown in the right column, are computed for each action as the sum of each outcome times the related probability. The probability of an outcome is the same as the probability of the event that results in that outcome, given an action. In this example, an order size of 300 units has the highest expected value; therefore, using expected value as the decision criterion, Janet Gaines should order 300 hotdogs each Thursday.

Value of Perfect Information

A manager sometimes has an opportunity to acquire additional information before making a decision, but because information is seldom free, the manager should evaluate the potential benefits of the additional information and the cost of obtaining it. The potential benefits are derived from the ability to make decisions that result in increased cost savings, increased revenues or net cash inflows. The cost of information includes the cost of resources used in obtaining it and the cost of delaying a decision. The **value of perfect information** is the maximum amount a manager would be willing to pay for additional information. It is computed as the difference between the expected profits with perfect information and the current expected profits. Though perfect information is seldom available, a manager might still desire to know its value because the value of perfect information serves as an upper limit on the amount he or she would pay for additional information.

If Janet Gaines had perfect information, she would always order the number of hotdogs she could sell. Ordering less would result in lost sales, and ordering more would result in excess costs. A payoff table with perfect information is shown in Exhibit 13–9. The expected value *with* perfect information is $136. This value is computed for the entire set of actions, rather than for each action, because the order size varies with demand. She will order 200 units 20 percent

EXHIBIT 13–9   Payoff Table for Perfect Information

Action	Event				
	Demand (probability)				
Order Size	200 (0.20)	300 (0.30)	400 (0.40)	500 (0.10)	Weighted Value
200	$80				$ 16*
300		$120			36
400			$160		64
500				$200	20
Expected value with perfect information					$136

* Example of computation: ($80 × 0.20) = $16.

of the time, 300 units 30 percent of the time, and so forth. The expected value *of* perfect information is $36:

Expected profits with perfect information	$136
Current expected profits	−100
Expected value of perfect information	$ 36

Knowing the expected value of perfect information, Janet is in a better position to bargain with someone who offers her any additional information, perfect or imperfect.

Attitudes Toward Risk

The previous discussion assumed that management is completely indifferent toward risk and makes decisions solely on the basis of expected value. Obviously, this is not true. Few managers would be indifferent to the following investment alternatives.

Investment	Outcome	Probability
A	$ (10,000)	0.90
	240,000	0.10
B	$ 5,000	0.50
	25,000	0.50

Both investments have an expected value of $15,000.

$$\text{Expected value (A)} = (\$-10{,}000 \times 0.90) + (\$240{,}000 \times 0.10)$$
$$= \$15{,}000.$$

$$\text{Expected value (B)} = (\$5,000 \times 0.50) + (\$25,000 \times 0.50)$$
$$= \$15,000.$$

Yet investment A has a 90 percent probability of a $10,000 loss, whereas investment B has all positive outcomes. Most decision makers would prefer investment B.

In addition to information on each action's expected value, management should obtain information on the variability of an action's outcome. This information might be the range of possible outcomes, the probability of negative outcomes, or statistical measures such as the standard deviation or the coefficient of variation. Statistical measures are discussed in introductory statistics textbooks. With information on expected values and variability, managers can make whatever trade-offs between return and risk they believe are appropriate.

SUMMARY

A model is a simplified representation of some real-world phenomenon. Managers and other decision makers often use optimizing models, such as the economic order quantity, linear programming, and payoff tables that suggest a specific choice among decision alternatives. These models are decision aids; they do not make decisions. Before implementing a decision suggested by a model, a manager should carefully evaluate the data used in the model, the assumptions underlying the model, and the output of the model. If the manager suspects any problems, the suggested action should not be implemented. Instead, the manager should undertake further analysis or make a decision based on professional judgment. When the outcome of an action is subject to uncertainty, the manager should not act only on the basis of expected value but should obtain information on the outcome's variability and make whatever trade-offs between return and risk he or she believes are appropriate.

APPENDIX
VARIANCE INVESTIGATION DECISIONS

Managers responsible for certain types of processes must often decide whether or not to shut down the process for inspection and adjustment, if necessary. In general, management wants to shut down the process only when it is out-of-adjustment. However, there is no way of knowing for certain whether the process is in-adjustment or out-of-adjustment except by shutting it down and performing an inspection. Obviously, if the process is in-adjustment, no further action is necessary, and if the process is out-of-adjustment, it is necessary to adjust it.

If the managers do not shut the process down for inspection, they may incur excess operating costs if the process is, in fact, out-of-adjustment. Conversely, there will be no excess operating costs if it is in-adjustment.

EXHIBIT 13–10 Payoff Table for Variance Investigation

| | Event (probability) | | |
Action	In-Adjustment (0.80)	Out-of-Adjustment (0.20)	Expected Cost of Action
Inspect and adjust if necessary	$200	$ 500*	$260**
Do not inspect	0	2,000	400†

* Inspection costs of $200 + adjustment costs of $300
** ($200)(0.80) + ($500)(0.20)
† ($0)(0.80) + ($2,000)(0.20)

In summary, there are two possible actions: (1) Inspect and adjust if necessary, and (2) do not inspect. There are also two possible events (or states): (1) The process is in-adjustment, and (2) the process is out-of-adjustment. Payoff tables are often used to summarize the outcomes of these alternative actions and events.

Assume management is trying to determine whether or not to inspect an automatic production process. There is an 80 percent probability that the process is in-adjustment and a 20 percent probability that it is out-of-adjustment. Relevant costs are as follows:

Inspection	$ 200
Adjustment, if necessary	300
Excess operating costs if out-of-adjustment	2,000

The payoff table for this decision is presented in Exhibit 13–10. Since the objective is to minimize expected costs, the best action here is to inspect and adjust if necessary.

KEY TERMS

Certainty
Descriptive model
Economic order quantity
Expected value
Feasible region
Lead time
Linear programming
Model
Objective function
Optimal solution

Optimizing model
Order quantity
Payoff table
Physical model
Quantitative model
Reorder point
Safety stocks
Simplex method
Uncertainty
Value of perfect information

REVIEW QUESTIONS

13–1 Distinguish between descriptive and optimizing models, and give three examples of each.

13–2 Do optimizing models make decisions? Discuss.

13–3 Once management has decided on the number of units to order during a period of time, what inventory ordering decisions remain?

13–4 What is the relationship between order size, total annual ordering costs, and total annual carrying costs?

13–5 Present a formula to compute the total annual ordering and carrying costs of inventory.

13–6 Identify five assumptions that underlie the economic order quantity model presented in this text.

13–7 Present the economic order quantity formula.

13–8 What adjustments are necessary before the economic order quantity formula can be applied to manufacturing firms?

13–9 What is the objective of linear programming?

13–10 What is the most critical assumption underlying linear programming? What are the implications of this assumption for accounting data used in linear programming?

13–11 Identify the steps involved in solving a linear programming problem with graphic analysis.

13–12 In graphic analysis, if there is a single optimal solution, where is it found?

13–13 How is the expected value of a decision alternative computed?

13–14 For what purpose is a payoff table used? What two factors determine the outcomes included in a payoff table?

13–15 How is the value of perfect information computed?

REVIEW PROBLEM

Economic Order Quantity by Trial and Error and Formula

Presented is information pertaining to an imported plant sold by a florist shop in a major city:

Annual demand	900 units
Unit cost	$20.00
Cost of placing an order	$200.00
Carrying cost as a percent of unit cost	20%

Requirements

a) Prepare a table, similar to that in Exhibit 13–3, of the relevant annual costs for determining the economic order quantity. Complete the table for lot sizes of 100, 200, 300, 400, 600, and 900 units.

b) Prepare a graph, similar to that in Exhibit 13–4, for the behavior of inventory ordering and carrying costs.

c) Based on requirements (a) and (b), what can be said about ordering and carrying costs at the economic order quantity?

d) Use the economic order quantity formula to determine the optimal order size.

The solution to this problem is found at the end of the Chapter 13 exercises and problems.

EXERCISES

13–1 Determining Order Quantity, Reorder Point, and Safety Stock

The annual demand for inventory item T-20 is 1,000 units, the cost of placing an order is $100, and the cost of carrying one unit in inventory for one year is $5.

Requirements

a) Use the economic order quantity formula to determine the optimal order size.

b) Assuming a lead time of 10 days and a work year of 250 days, determine the reorder point.

c) Assuming the maximum lead time is 15 days and the maximum daily demand is 6 units, determine the safety stock required to prevent stockouts.

13–2 Determining Order Quantity, Reorder Point, and Safety Stock

The annual demand for inventory item Q-7 is 5,000 units, the cost of placing an order is $160, and the cost of carrying one unit in inventory for one year is $10.

Requirements

a) Use the economic order quantity formula to determine the optimal order size.

b) Assuming a lead time of 15 days and a work year of 250 days, determine the reorder point.

c) Assuming the maximum lead time is 20 days and the maximum daily demand is 25 units, determine the safety stock required to prevent stockouts.

13–3 Impact of Deviations from EOQ

Faced with a cash surplus, the Loveday Department Store *increased* the size of several inventory order quantities that had previously been determined using the EOQ model. Use the words "increase," "decrease," or "no change" to indicate the impact of management's decision on each of the following:

1. Average inventory.

2. Number of orders per year.

3. Total annual carrying costs.

4. Total annual ordering costs.

5. Total annual carrying and ordering costs.

6. Cost of goods sold.

13–4 Impact of Deviations from EOQ

Faced with a cash shortage, the Arnold Discount Store *reduced* the size of several inventory order quantities that had previously been determined using the EOQ model. Use the words "increase," "decrease," or "no change" to indicate the impact of management's decision on each of the following:

1. Average inventory.
2. Number of orders per year.
3. Total annual carrying costs.
4. Total annual ordering costs.
5. Total annual carrying and ordering costs.
6. Cost of goods sold.

13–5 Cost Savings with Economic Order Quantity: Shelf Life

The Pleasant View Hospital places orders for a particular inventory item in lot sizes of 25 units. Additional information about this inventory item is as follows:

Annual demand	720 units
Ordering costs	$25 per order
Purchase price	$100 per unit

Annual inventory carrying costs are estimated to be 40 percent of the unit cost.

Requirements

a) Determine the economic order quantity.

b) Determine the annual cost savings if Pleasant View changes from an order size of 10 units to the economic order quantity.

c) The shelf life of this item is limited. Assuming that shelf life is based on the number of days it may be used after it is placed in inventory, determine the optimal lot size under each of the following circumstances. Assume a 360-day year.
   1. Shelf life = 20 days.
   2. Shelf life = 10 days.

Hint: Determine how many days an order will last.

13–6 Cost Savings with Economic Order Quantity: Quantity Discounts

The Mason Company currently purchases a particular item in sizes of 1,250 units. Mason's annual use of this item is 6,250 units. Ordering costs are $200 per order, and carrying costs are $10 per unit per year.

Requirements

a) Determine the economic order quantity.

b) Determine the amount of the annual cost savings if Mason changes from an order size of 1,250 units to the economic order quantity.

c) The supplier offers a discount of $2 per unit off of the purchase price of orders in lots of 625 units or more. What action do you recommend? *Hint:* Compare the annual cost savings from the discount to the increased total annual ordering and carrying costs required to qualify for the discount.

13–7 Graphic Analysis

The graph presents a series of maximum production constraints.

The objective function is:

$$\text{Maximize } \$40J + 50I$$

Required: Determine the optimal solution and the corresponding value of the objective function with the aid of graphic analysis.

13–8 Graphic Analysis

Presented are the objective function and the constraints for a linear programming problem:

$$\text{Maximize } \$6A + \$8B$$

Constraints:

$$1A + 2B \leq 12$$
$$1A + 1B \leq 8$$
$$A \geq 0$$
$$B \geq 0$$

Required: Determine the optimal solution and the corresponding value of the objective function with the aid of graphic analysis.

13–9 Linear Programming with Graphic Analysis

The Menz Company produces two products, X and Y, in one department. Product X has a unit contribution margin of $40, and product Y has a unit contribution margin of $70. The demand for product X exceeds Menz's production capacity, which is limited by available labor and machine hours. The maximum demand for product Y is 8 units per week. Product information follows:

	Hours per Unit		Total Hours
	X	Y	Available per Week
Labor	12	18	180
Machine	6	4	60

Management desires the product mix that will maximize the weekly contribution toward fixed costs and profits.

Requirements

a) Formulate the objective function and constraints necessary to determine the optimal product mix.

b) Determine the optimal solution and the corresponding value of the objective function with the aid of graphic analysis.

13–10 Linear Programming with Graphic Analysis

The Old Salt Desk Company produces two styles of desks, Captain's and Mate's, in two departments, Assembly and Finishing. The Captain's desks have a unit contribution margin of $200, and Mate's desks have a unit contribution margin of $150. The demand for Captain's desks exceeds Old Salt's production capacity, which is limited by the available hours in each department. The demand for Mate's desks is 80 units per month. Production information follows:

	Hours per Unit		Total Hours
	Captain	Mate	Available per Month
Assembly Department	10	10	1,500
Finishing Department	40	20	4,000

Management desires the product mix that will maximize the monthly contribution toward fixed costs and profits.

Requirements

a) Formulate the objective function and constraints necessary to determine the optimal product mix.

b) Determine the optimal solution and the corresponding value of the objective function with the aid of graphic analysis.

13–11 Computing Expected Values and Evaluating Risk

Presented is information on the possible outcomes of two investment alternatives.

Investment I		Investment II	
Outcome	Probability	Outcome	Probability
$(22,000)	0.50	$2,000	0.30
0	0.20	4,000	0.40
50,000	0.30	6,000	0.30

Requirements

a) Compute the expected value of each investment.

b) Indicate which you prefer and why you prefer it.

13–12 Computing Expected Values and Evaluating Risk

Presented is information on the possible outcomes of three investment alternatives.

Investment I		Investment II		Investment III	
Outcome	Probability	Outcome	Probability	Outcome	Probability
$10,000	1.00	$10,000	0.30	$−30,000	0.30
		12,000	0.40	0	0.10
		14,000	0.30	10,000	0.20
				47,500	0.40

Requirements

a) Compute the expected value of each investment.

b) Indicate which investment you prefer and why you prefer it.

13–13 Payoff Tables and the Value of Perfect Information

The Wild Kat Oil Company prospects for oil in the mountains of Pennsylvania. Currently, the cost of drilling an oil well is $40,000. If oil is found, the well is sold for $800,000. If oil is not found, the well is worthless. At each drilling site, Wild Kat has two possible actions: (1) drill, or (2) do not drill. At each drilling site there are two possible states or events: (1) oil is present, or (2) oil is not present. In a particular area of the mountains, the probability of finding oil is 8 percent, and the probability of not finding oil is 92 percent.

Requirements

a) With the aid of a payoff table, determine the expected value of each action for each site.

b) A new testing service can determine in advance whether or not oil will be found at a drilling site. Determine the value of perfect information for each site.

13–14 Payoff Tables and the Value of Perfect Information

The operator of a Chalmette newsstand must determine the number of copies of the *Bourbon Street Journal* to stock each day. The operator buys the *Journal* for $0.50 per copy and sells it for $0.75 per copy. Unsold papers are worthless at the end of the day. Past daily demand has varied between 200 and 400 copies with the following probabilities.

Event	Probability
200 copies demanded	0.25
300 copies demanded	0.50
400 copies demanded	0.25

Requirements

a) With the aid of a payoff table determine whether the operator should order 200, 300, or 400 copies.

b) Determine the value of perfect information.

13–15 Variance Investigation (Appendix)

The cost of inspection is $500; the cost of adjustment, if necessary, is $900; the excess operating cost if out-of-adjustment equipment is not corrected is $5,000. The probability that the equipment is in-adjustment is 80 percent, and the probability that the equipment is out-of-adjustment is 20 percent.

Required: With the aid of a payoff table, determine if the equipment should be inspected and adjusted if necessary.

13–16 Variance Investigation (Appendix)

The cost of inspection is $300; the cost of adjustment, if necessary, is $800; the excess operating cost if out-of-adjustment equipment is not corrected is $1,400. The probability that the equipment is in-adjustment is 75 percent, and the probability that the equipment is out-of-adjustment is 25 percent.

Required: With the aid of a payoff table, determine if the equipment should be inspected and adjusted if necessary.

13–17 Variance Investigation (Appendix)

The Bilco Oil Company currently sells three grades of gasoline: regular, premium, and "regular plus," which is a mixture of regular and premium. Regular plus is advertised as being "at least 50 percent premium." Although any mixture containing 50 percent or more premium gas could be sold as "regular plus," it is less costly to use exactly 50 percent. The amount of premium gas in the mixture is determined by one small valve in the blending machine. If the valve is properly adjusted, the machine provides a mixture that is 50 percent premium and 50 percent regular. Assume that if the valve is out-of-adjustment, the machine provides a mixture that is 60 percent premium and 40 percent regular. Once the machine is started it must continue until 100,000 gallons of "regular plus" have been mixed.

Available cost data are as follows:

Cost per gallon:	
Premium	$ 0.64
Regular	$ 0.60
Cost of checking the valve	$80.00
Cost of adjusting the valve	$40.00

Subjective estimates of the probabilities of the valve's condition are estimated to be:

Condition	Probability
Valve in-adjustment	0.70
Valve out-of-adjustment	0.30

Required: With the aid of a payoff table, determine if the valve should be checked, and adjusted if necessary, before each batch of 100,000 gallons of "regular plus" is mixed.

(CMA Adapted)

PROBLEMS

13–18 Economic Order Quantity by Trial and Error and Formula

The Mountain Shop sells 240 Mt. Washington sleeping bags each year. Mt. Washington sleeping bags retail for $175 and wholesale for $100. The Mountain Shop's ordering and carrying costs are as follows:

Cost of placing each order	$50
Annual carrying costs as a percentage of unit cost	15%

Requirements

a) Prepare a table, similar to that in Exhibit 13–3, of the relevant annual costs for determining the economic order quantity. Complete the table for lot sizes of 10, 20, 30, 40, 50, and 60 units. Identify the economic order quantity.

b) Prepare a graph, similar to that in Exhibit 13–4, for the behavior of inventory ordering and carrying costs.

c) Based on requirements (a) and (b), what can be said about ordering and carrying costs at the economic order quantity?

d) Use the economic order quantity formula to determine the optimal order size.

13–19 Economic Lot Size by Trial and Error and Formula

The Designer Phone Company manufactures telephones, in a variety of styles, for residential use. Presented is information about the Classic Touch, one of Designer's models.

Annual sales	500 units
Variable manufacturing costs per unit	$80
Set-up and ordering costs per batch	$50

Carrying costs per year as a percentage of variable manufacturing costs are:

Insurance	2.0%
Personal property taxes	0.5
Storage space	3.0
Deterioration and obsolescence	4.5
Opportunity cost of money invested in inventory	15.0
Total	25.0%

Requirements

a) Prepare a table, similar to that in Exhibit 13–3, of the relevant annual costs for determining the economic lot size. Complete the table for lot sizes of 10, 20, 40, 50, 80, and 100 units. Identify the economic lot size.

b) Prepare a graph, similar to that in Exhibit 13–4, for the behavior of inventory ordering and carrying costs.

c) Based on requirements (a) and (b), what can be said about ordering and carrying costs at the economic lot size?

d) Use the economic order quantity formula to determine the optimal lot size.

13–20 Plotting Variations in Inventory Levels with Safety Stocks

An inventory item with an average daily demand of 5 units and a maximum daily demand of 10 units has an economic order quantity of 100 units. In the absence of safety stocks, the item's reorder point is 25 units. Safety stocks are set at 75 units.

Requirements

a) Determine each of the following:

   1. Reorder point with safety stocks.

   2. Maximum inventory level.

   3. Average lead time.

   4. Maximum lead time.

b) Graph the variations in inventory levels over a period of 60 days. Start at the beginning of day 1 (time 0) with maximum inventory. Assume that daily demand is normal during the first inventory cycle and that inventory is replenished at the end of the first cycle without the use of safety stocks. Assume that daily demand is normal during the second cycle until inventory is reordered. Assume maximum daily demand and lead time until the second order is received. Continue the graph through the end of 60 days with normal daily demand and lead times.

13–21 Economic Order Quantity and Reorder Point: Missing Data

Supply the missing data in each case. Assume that all costs and quantities are optimal, according to the EOQ formula.

	Case 1	Case 2	Case 3	Case 4
Annual demand	250	?	200	?
Economic order quantity	?	?	?	200
Average inventory	?	50	?	?
Orders per year	?	30	5	?
Working days per year	250	?	?	?
Average daily demand	?	12	0.8	?
Lead time in days	10	?	5	8
Reorder point	?	60	?	80
Annual ordering costs	$?	$?	$?	$?
Annual carrying costs	?	1,500	?	?
Total	$?	$?	$?	$?
Cost of placing an order	$100	?	$ 20	$ 80
Annual unit carrying costs	$ 20	?	?	$ 10

Hint: For cases 2 and 3, costs are equal at the EOQ; for case 4, work backward from the EOQ.

13–22 Estimating Inventory Ordering and Carrying Costs

Evans, Inc., is a large wholesale distributor that deals exclusively in baby shoes. Because of the substantial costs related to ordering and storing the shoes, the company has decided to employ the economic order quantity (EOQ) model to help determine the optimum quantities of shoes to order from the different manufacturers.

    Before Evans, Inc., can employ the EOQ model, it needs to develop values for two of the cost parameters—ordering costs and carrying costs. As a starting point, management has decided to develop the values for the two cost parameters by using cost data from the most recent fiscal year, 19x5.

The company placed 4,000 purchase orders during 19x5. The largest number of orders placed during any one month was 400 orders in June, and the smallest number of orders placed was 250 in December. Selected cost data for these two months and the year for the Purchasing, Accounts Payable, and Warehouse Departments appear below.

The Purchasing Department is responsible for placing all orders. The costs listed for the Accounts Payable Department relate only to the processing of purchase orders for payment. The Warehouse Department's costs reflect two operations—receiving and shipping. The receiving clerks inspect all incoming shipments and place the orders in storage. The shipping clerks are responsible for processing all sales orders to retailers.

The company leases space in a public warehouse. The rental fee is priced according to the square feet occupied during the month. The annual charges during 19x5 totaled $34,500. Annual insurance and property taxes on the shoes vary with the value of the average monthly inventory. In 19x5 they amounted to $5,700 and $7,300, respectively. The company's opportunity cost of inventory investments is 20 percent.

	Costs for High Activity Month (June: 400 Orders)	Costs for Low Activity Month (December: 250 Orders)	Annual Costs
Purchasing Department:			
Purchasing manager	$ 1,750	$ 1,750	$ 21,000
Buyers	2,500	1,900	28,500
Clerks	2,000	1,100	20,600
Supplies	275	150	2,500
Accounts Payable Department:			
Clerks	2,000	1,500	21,500
Supplies	125	75	1,100
Data processing	2,600	2,300	30,000
Warehouse Department:			
Supervisor	1,250	1,250	15,000
Receiving clerks	2,300	1,800	23,300
Receiving supplies	50	25	500
Shipping clerks	3,800	3,500	44,000
Shipping supplies	1,350	1,200	15,200
Freight-out	1,600	1,300	16,800
	$21,600	$17,850	$240,000

The inventory balances tend to fluctuate during the year depending on the demand for baby shoes. The average monthly inventory during 19x5 was $190,000.

The boxes in which the baby shoes are stored are all approximately the same size. Consequently, the shoes all occupy about the same amount of storage space in the warehouse.

Required: Using the 19x5 data, determine estimated values appropriate for (1) the cost of placing an order and (2) the annual carrying costs per dollar of inventory investment.

(CMA Adapted)

13–23 Accounting Inputs to Linear Programming: Graphic Analysis

The Smile Camera Company manufactures two popular cameras, Little Smile and Big Smile. Recent increases in demand have pushed Smile Camera to the limits of their production capacity. The president is a former engineer who knows that linear programming can be used to determine the optimal product mix. However, he needs your assistance in formulating the objective function coefficients and in determining the profit implications of the optimal solution.

The following information is available from the accounting records.

	Little Smile	Big Smile
Unit selling price	$150	$220
Unit manufacturing costs:		
Direct materials	$ 38	$ 54
Direct labor	30	30
Factory overhead	48	80
Total	$116	$164

Production employees are paid $10 per direct labor hour. A total of 450 direct labor hours is available each month. Factory overhead is applied at the rate of $16 per machine hour. Seventy-five percent of the overhead rate is for variable costs, and 25 percent is for fixed costs. A total of 750 machine hours is available each month. The factory overhead rate is based on the full utilization of 750 machine hours each month.

Additional information:

- Because of insufficient raw materials, only 100 Big Smile Cameras can be produced each month.
- Variable selling and administrative expenses are $6 per unit of either product.
- Fixed selling and administrative expenses are $2,300 per month.

Requirements

a) Formulate the objective function and constraints necessary to determine the optimal monthly production mix.

b) Determine the optimal solution and the corresponding value of the objective function with the aid of graphic analysis.

c) Determine the Smile Camera Company's expected monthly profit.

13–24 Accounting Inputs to Linear Programming: Graphic Analysis

Kyoto Electric produces two video cassette recorders, a manual model that does not contain an automatic timer, and an automatic model that does. Though demand for the automatic model is only 75 units per month, Kyoto has been unable to satisfy the demand for the lower priced manual model. The following information is available from the accounting records.

	Manual	Automatic
Unit selling price	$200	$329
Unit manufacturing costs:		
Direct materials	$105	$190
Conversion:		
Department 1	24	24
Department 2	45	90
Total	$174	$304

The conversion costs include direct labor, variable overhead, and fixed overhead. In Department 1, conversion costs are assigned at the rate of $20 per hour. Fifty percent is for variable costs, and 50 percent is for fixed costs. A total of 180 hours is available each month in Department 1. In Department 2, conversion costs are assigned at the rate of $30 per hour. Eighty percent is for variable costs, and 20 percent is for fixed costs. A total of 300 hours is available each month in Department 2. The fixed overhead rates, as a portion of total conversion costs, are based on the full utilization of production capacity.

Additional information:

■ Variable selling and administrative expenses are $10 per unit of either product.

■ Fixed selling and administrative expenses are $1,200 per month.

Requirements

a) Formulate the objective function and the constraints necessary to determine the optimal monthly production mix.

b) Determine the optimal solution and the corresponding value of the objective function with the aid of graphic analysis.

c) Determine Kyoto Electric's expected monthly profit.

13–25 Formulating Objective Function and Constraints

Presented is unit information about three products manufactured and sold by Camden Products, Inc.

	Product X	Product Y	Product Z
Selling price	$110	$130	$200
Direct materials	35	40	50
Direct labor	32	24	48
Variable factory overhead	25	30	40
Fixed factory overhead	20	24	32
Variable selling and administrative expenses	8	6	10

Additional information:

- Fixed selling and administrative expenses are $60,000 per year.
- The direct labor rate is $16 per hour.
- Variable factory overhead is applied at the rate of $10 per machine hour, and fixed factory overhead is applied at the rate of $8 per machine hour.
- A total of 120,000 direct labor hours and 125,000 machine hours are available each year.
- The fixed overhead rate is based on total available machine hours.
- Management desires to produce a minimum of 10,000 units of product X and a maximum of 20,000 units of product Z each year.
- The demand for products X and Y exceeds production capacity.

Requirements

a) Formulate the objective function and the constraints necessary to determine the optimal yearly production mix.

b) Determine the expected annual profit if Camden produces 10,000 units of X, 4,000 units of Y, and 20,000 units of Z.

13–26 Formulating Objective Function

A processing department of the East Orange Chemical Company can vary the production mix of two products, Compound B1 and Compound B2. Because of the high demand for these products, a chemical engineer has been requested to determine the optimal monthly volumes of each product. The engineer has formulated all the constraints needed to determine the optimal mix with the aid of linear programming and has asked you to assist in developing the objective function coefficients. The engineer has provided you with the following production information.

	Per Two-Liter Bottle*	
	Compound B1	Compound B2
Raw materials:		
C25	1 liter	2 liters
D80	3 liters	1 liter
MA5	—	1 liter
Bottle	1	1
Direct labor	0.4 hours	0.6 hours

* The difference between total inputs and outputs is due to shrinkage, waste, and evaporation.

You obtain the following information from an analysis of the accounting records.

Selling prices:	
Compound B1	$12.20/bottle
Compound B2	18.00/bottle
Raw materials costs:	
C25	$ 0.80/liter
D80	0.40/liter
MA5	0.65/liter
Bottles	0.50/each
Direct labor rate	$ 9.00/hour

Monthly factory overhead = $20,000 + 0.40 direct labor dollars
Monthly selling and administrative costs = $15,000 + 0.25 sales revenue

Required: Formulate the objective function necessary to determine the optimal monthly production in bottles.

13–27 Evaluating and Formulating Objective Function and Constraints

The Elon Co. manufactures two industrial products, X-10, which sells for $90 a unit, and Y-12, which sells for $85 a unit. Each product is processed through both of the company's manufacturing departments. The limited availability of labor, material, and equipment capacity has restricted the ability of the firm to meet the demand for its products. The plant manager believes that linear programming can be used to routinize the production schedule for the two products.

The following data are available to the plant manager.

	Amount Required per Unit	
	X-10	Y-12
Direct materials:		
Weekly supply limited to 1,800 pounds at $12 per pound	4 pounds	2 pounds
Direct labor:		
Department 1—weekly supply limited to 10 people at 40 hours each at an hourly rate of $6	$\frac{2}{3}$ hour	1 hour
Department 2—weekly supply limited to 15 people at 40 hours each at an hourly rate of $8	$1\frac{1}{4}$ hour	1 hour
Machine time:		
Department 1—weekly capacity limited to 250 hours	$\frac{1}{2}$ hour	$\frac{1}{2}$ hour
Department 2—weekly capacity limited to 300 hours	0 hours	1 hour

The overhead costs for Elon are accumulated on a plantwide basis. The overhead is assigned to products on the basis of the number of direct labor hours required to manufacture the product. This base is appropriate for overhead assignment because most of the variable overhead costs vary as a function of labor time. The estimated overhead cost per direct labor hour is as follows:

Variable overhead cost	$ 6
Fixed overhead cost	6
Total overhead cost per direct labor hour	$12

The plant manager formulated the following equations for the linear programming statement of the problem.

$$A = \text{number of units of X-10 to be produced.}$$
$$B = \text{number of units of Y-12 to be produced.}$$

Objective function to minimize costs:

Minimize $85A + 62B$

Constraints:

Material
$$4A + 2B \le 1,800 \text{ pounds}$$
Department 1 labor
$$\tfrac{2}{3}A + 1B \le 400 \text{ hours}$$
Department 2 labor
$$1\tfrac{1}{4}A + 1B \le 600 \text{ hours}$$
Nonnegativity
$$A \ge 0, \qquad B \ge 0.$$

Requirements

a) The formulation of the linear programming equations as prepared by the plant manager of Elon Co. is incorrect. Explain what errors have been made in the formulation prepared by the plant manager.

b) Formulate and label the proper equations for the linear programming statement of Elon's production problem.

(CMA Adapted)

13–28 Expected Values for Alternative Actions

The Jon Co. has just agreed to supply Arom Chemical, Inc., with a substance critical to one of Arom's manufacturing processes. Because of the critical nature of this substance, Jon Co. has agreed to pay Arom $1,000 for any shipment that is not received by Arom on the day it is required.

Arom establishes a production schedule that enables it to notify Jon Co. of the necessary quantity 15 days in advance of the required date. Jon can produce the substance in 5 days. However, capacity is not always readily available, which means that Jon may not be able to produce the substance for several days. There may be occasions when there are only one or two days available to deliver the substance. *When the substance is completed by Jon Co.'s manufacturing department and released to its shipping department, the number of days remaining before Arom Chemical, Inc., needs the substance will be known.*

Jon Co. has undertaken a review of delivery reliability and costs of alternative shipping methods. The results are presented in the following table.

Shipping Method	Costs per Shipment	Probability That the Shipping Will Take This Number of Days					
		1	2	3	4	5	6
Motor freight	$100	—	—	0.10	0.20	0.40	0.30
Air freight	$200	—	0.30	0.60	0.10	—	—
Air express	$400	0.80	0.20	—	—	—	—

Required: Prepare a decision table that can be used by the shipping clerk of Jon Co. to decide which delivery alternative to select. The decision table should specify the shipping method to use as a function of the days, 1 through 6, until the shipment is needed by Arom. Use the expected monetary value decision criterion as the basis for constructing the table. *Hint:* Compute the expected cost of shipping by each method for each alternative number of days until the shipment is needed by Arom.

(CMA Adapted)

13–29 Potpourri of Quantitative Analysis

1. A spindle manufacturer used about 200 cases of raw wood per month. It pays a broker $50 to locate a supplier and handle the ordering and delivery arrangements. Storage and handling costs are $0.02 per case per month. If each case costs $0.78, the most economical order quantity, rounded to the next whole number, is:

   a) 884 cases.

   b) 1,133 cases.

   c) 625 cases.

   d) 1,000 cases.

   e) Some amount other than those given above.

2. A company would use the economic order quantity model to:

   a) Minimize the unit purchase price of inventory.

   b) Minimize the number of orders placed during the year.

   c) Minimize the cost of placing orders.

   d) Minimize the combined costs of placing orders and carrying inventory.

   e) Minimize the required amount of safety stock.

3. The calculation of the reorder point in units requires the:

   a) Purchase price per month.

   b) Annual demand for units.

   c) Daily demand for units.

d) Storage cost per unit.

e) Warehouse capacity.

4. The process of evaluating the effect of changes in variables such as sales prices or labor wage rates on the optimum solution in a linear programming application is called:

a) Simplex method analysis.

b) Iterative analysis.

c) Regression analysis.

d) Sensitivity analysis.

e) Matrix analysis.

5. One limitation of the linear programming technique is that it is effective only for:

a) Two product situations.

b) Manufacturing resource constraint situations.

c) Straight-line relationship situations.

d) Income maximization situations.

e) Cost minimization situations.

6. A small company makes only two products with the following two production constraints representing two machines and their maximum availability:

$$2X + 3Y \le 18$$
$$2X + 1Y \le 10,$$

where:

X = the units of the first product
Y = the units of the second product.

If the profit equation is $Z = \$4X + \$2Y$, the maximum possible profit is:

a) $20.

b) $21.

c) $18.

d) $24.

e) Some profit other than those given above.

7. The Tyson Company is considering hiring several new employees to handle an overload from a new contract. If the new people are not hired, there will be delays in contract work. The following payoff table has been prepared for analyzing whether new people are needed.

	Hire New People	Do Not Hire People
Retain new customers	$100,000	$75,000
Lose new customers	25,000	50,000

Based on past experience, the company expects to retain 75 percent of the new customers with no new hires. The expected profit for the "no hire" decision is:

a) $81,250.

b) $131,250.

c) $68,740.

d) $31,250.

e) Some amount other than those given above.

8. Carson Airways has experienced the following number of breakdowns in its automated reservation process system during the last year:

Number of Breakdowns in the Month	Number of Months
0	3
1	3
2	6
3 or more	0

Each breakdown costs Carson Airways $300. Carson can purchase a maintenance contract for $200 per month that will cover the costs of all breakdowns in excess of one in each individual month. The net cost advantage (disadvantage) per month of the maintenance contract for the past year would have been:

a) $100.

b) $(600).

c) $25.

d) $(50).

e) Some amount other than those given above.

9. The Ajax Construction Company has won a contract to repair several public buildings. The jobs require completion by a specific date or a lump sum payment must be forfeited. Ajax wants to know if insurance for completion would be worthwhile. They have estimated that 80 percent of their jobs are completed on time. A company analyst has calculated the following payoff table:

	Insure	Do Not Insure
On time	$15,000	$20,000
Late	17,000	2,000

The probability of being on time such that Ajax would be indifferent between insuring and not insuring is:

a) 0.95.

b) 0.80.

c) 0.75.

d) 0.50.

e) Some probability other than those given above.

(CMA Adapted)

13–30 Variance Investigation and the Value of Perfect Information (Appendix)

Cillia Company manufactures a line of women's handbags. An analysis of the operations of Cillia's Cutting Department for May 19x4 revealed that excess materials were used. Donna Cook, Cutting Department Supervisor, gathered the following information to use in deciding whether or not the excess use of materials should be investigated:

Predicted cost of investigating	$ 4,000
Predicted cost of making the necessary changes if the Cutting Department is operating improperly	8,000
Predicted cost of future excess usage that would be saved by making the necessary changes if the Cutting Department is operating improperly	40,000
Estimated probability that the Cutting Department is operating properly	0.90

Requirements

a) Recommend whether or not Cillia Company should investigate the excess use of materials. Support your recommendation by preparing a payoff table for use in making the decision computing the expected value of the cost of each possible action.

b) Donna Cook is uncertain about the probability estimate that the Cutting Department is operating properly. Determine the estimated probability that the Cutting Department is operating properly that would cause Cillia Company to be indifferent between the two possible actions.

c) Assume a consultant is available to advise Cillia Company and is able to accurately determine the state of the Cutting Department operations. Compute the expected value of perfect information.

(CMA Adapted)

REVIEW PROBLEM SOLUTION

a)

Order quantity (units)	100	200	300	400	600	900
Number of orders (Annual demand / order quantity)	9	4.5	3	2.25	1.5	1
Average inventory (Order quantity/2)	50	100	150	200	300	450
Relevant annual costs:						
Ordering	$1,800	$ 900	$ 600	$ 450	$ 300	$ 200
Carrying	200	400	600	800	1,200	1,800
Total	$2,000	$1,300	$1,200	$1,250	$1,500	$2,000

b) Total Annual Costs

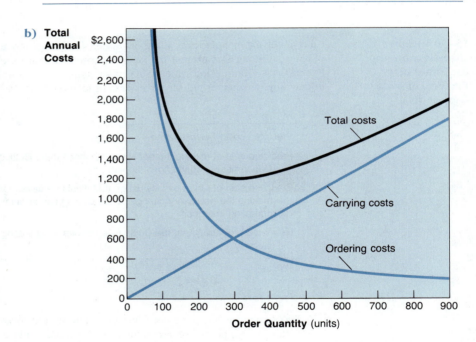

Order Quantity (units)

c) Annual ordering and carrying costs are equal at the economic order quantity.

d) Economic order quantity $= \sqrt{\dfrac{2 \times 900 \times \$200}{\$20 \times 0.20}}$

$= \underline{\underline{300}}$ units.

CHAPTER 14

Capital Budgeting

Upon completion of this chapter you should:

- Understand the role of capital budgeting in long-range planning.
- Be able to identify cost and revenue data relevant to capital expenditure decisions and be able to properly organize the data for use in capital budgeting models.
- Be able to use capital budgeting models, such as net present value and internal rate of return, that consider the time value of money.
- Be able to use capital budgeting models, such as payback and accounting rate of return, that do not consider the time value of money.
- Be able to evaluate the strengths and weaknesses of alternative capital budgeting models.
- Understand the importance of management's judgment and attitude toward risk in finalizing capital expenditure decisions.
- Understand the differences between a total cost approach and a differential analysis approach to organizing project cash flows.

The emphasis in most of this text is on short-range planning and control, where we assume the organization's basic facilities and products or services do not change. In this chapter we relax this assumption and turn our attention to a portion of long-range planning that deals with the identification and evaluation of major investment proposals to expand or change the organization's activities or facilities.

Capital expenditures involve investment of significant financial resources in projects to develop or introduce new products or services, to expand current production or service capacity, or to change current production or service facilities. Changes in current facilities might, for example, be intended to achieve lower operating costs, lower levels of environmental pollution, or make operating conditions safer. Investments in the financial securities of another entity are not capital expenditures.

Capital budgeting is a process that involves the identification of potentially desirable projects for capital expenditure, the subsequent evaluation of capital expenditure proposals, and the selection of proposals that meet certain criteria. A number of quantitative models have been developed to assist managers in evaluating capital expenditure proposals. The purpose of this chapter is to introduce important capital budgeting concepts and models and to discuss the proper use of accounting data in these models.

The best capital budgeting models are similar in many respects to the short-range planning models used in Chapters 5, 6, and 13. They all emphasize cash flows and focus on future costs (and revenues) that differ between competing alternatives. The major difference is that capital budgeting models involve cash flows over several years, whereas short-range models involve only single-year cash flows. When the cash flows associated with a proposed activity extend over several years, an adjustment should be made to make the future cash flows comparable.

The time value of money concept explains why monies received or paid at different points in time must be adjusted to make them comparable. The time value of money is introduced in the appendix to this book. If you have not previously studied the time value of money, or feel you would benefit from a review of time value concepts, read the appendix to this book before continuing this chapter.

LONG-RANGE PLANNING AND CAPITAL BUDGETING PROCEDURES

Most organizations plan not only for operations in the current period, but also for the longer term, perhaps five to ten or even twenty years in the future. Most planning beyond the next budget year is called *long-range planning*.

Increased uncertainty and an increased number of alternatives makes planning more difficult as the planning horizon increases. Nevertheless, the fact that long-range planning is difficult and involves uncertainties does not relieve management of long-range planning and capital expenditure decisions. Capital expenditure decisions will be made; the question is how will they be made? Will they be made on the basis of the best information available? Will care be taken to ensure that capital expenditure decisions are in line with the organization's long-range goals? Will the potential consequences, both good and bad, of capital expenditures be considered? Will important alternative uses of the organization's limited financial resources be considered in a systematic manner? Will managers be held accountable for the results of major capital expenditure programs they initiate? The alternative to a systematic approach to capital budgeting is the haphazard expenditure of significant resources on the basis of hunch, immediate need, and persuasion—without accountability by the person(s) making the capital expenditure decisions.

A basic requirement for a systematic approach to capital budgeting is a well-formulated set of long-range goals the organization hopes to achieve over a multiyear period. These goals serve as a guideline, thereby reducing the types of capital expenditure decisions considered by management. If, for example, Swift Clippers' primary goal is to become the largest chain of hair stylists in the nation, its management should not consider a proposal to construct and operate a meat packing plant.

Procedures should also be developed for the review, evaluation, approval, and post-audit of capital expenditure proposals. Central to these procedures in a large organization is a capital budgeting committee that provides guidance to managers in the formulation of capital expenditure proposals. This committee also reviews, analyzes, and approves or rejects major capital expenditure proposals. Very significant projects may also require the approval of top management and even the board of directors. The capital budgeting committee should include persons knowledgeable of capital budgeting models, financing alternatives and costs, production techniques, cost estimation and prediction methods, research and development efforts, overall organization strategy, and the expectations of the organization's stockholders or owners. A management accountant—who is generally expert in data collection, retrieval, and analysis—is normally part of the capital budgeting committee.

Not all capital expenditure proposals will require committee approval. With the approval of top management, the committee may provide guidelines to line managers at each level of the organization, indicating the type and dollar amount of capital expenditures they can make without committee approval. Typically, managers at higher levels have greater discretion in making capital expenditures. In a college or university, for example, a department chairman may have authority to purchase office and instructional equipment with a maximum limit of $3,000 per year; a dean may have authority to renovate offices or classrooms with a maximum limit of $20,000 per year; but the formal review of a capital budgeting committee and final approval of the board of trustees may be required to convert the power plant from fuel oil to wood chips at a cost of $225,000.

The post-auditing of approved capital expenditure proposals is an important part of a well-formulated approach to capital budgeting. Such a post-audit involves the development of project performance reports comparing planned and actual results. Project performance reports should be provided to the manager who initiated the capital expenditure proposal, to the manager assigned responsibility for the project (if a different person), to the project manager's supervisor, and to the capital budgeting committee. These reports help keep the project on target, help identify the need to reevaluate the project if the initial analysis was in error or significant environmental changes occur, and help improve the quality of investment proposals. When managers know they will be held accountable for the results of projects they initiate, they are likely to put more care into the development of capital expenditure proposals and take a greater interest in approved projects.

A post-audit review of approved projects also helps the capital budgeting committee do a better job in evaluating new proposals. The committee may learn how to adjust proposals for the biases of individual managers; learn of new factors that should be considered in evaluating proposals; and avoid the routine approval of projects that appear desirable by themselves, but are related to larger projects that are not working out.

CAPITAL BUDGETING MODELS THAT CONSIDER THE TIME VALUE OF MONEY

The capital budgeting models presented in this chapter have gained wide acceptance by for-profit and not-for-profit organizations. All managers should have at least a rudimentary knowledge of the operation of these models and their strengths and weaknesses. Our primary focus is on the net present value and internal rate of return models, which are superior because they consider the time value of money. Later discussions in the chapter consider more traditional capital budgeting models, such as payback and the accounting rate of return, which, although useful under certain circumstances, do not consider the time value of money. Also, the cost of financing capital expenditures is briefly considered; however, a detailed treatment of this topic, as well as a detailed examination of the sources of funds for financing investments, is left to books on financial management.

Organizing Expected Cash Flows

The focus of capital budgeting models that consider the time value of money is on future cash receipts and future cash disbursements that differ under decision alternatives. It is often convenient to distinguish between three phases of a project's cash flows:

- Initial investment
- Operation
- Disinvestment

All cash expenditures necessary to begin operations are classified as part of the project's initial investment. Expenditures to acquire property, plant, and equipment are clearly part of the initial investment. Less obvious, but equally important, are expenditures to acquire working capital such as inventories and to recruit and train employees. Although the initial investment phase often extends over many years, in most textbook examples and problems we assume that the initial investment takes place at a single point in time.

Cash receipts from sales of goods or services, as well as normal cash expenditures for materials, labor, and other operating expenses, occur during the operation phase. The operation phase is typically broken down into one-year periods. For each period, operating cash expenditures are subtracted from operating cash receipts to determine the net operating cash inflow or outflow for the period.

The disinvestment phase occurs at the end of the project's life when assets are disposed of and any initial investment of working capital is recovered. Although this phase may also extend over many years, in textbook examples and problems we assume disinvestment takes place at a single point in time.

To illustrate the analysis of a project's cash flows, assume the management of Mobile Yogurt Shoppes is considering a capital expenditure proposal to operate a new Mobile Yogurt Shoppe in a resort community in the Ozark Mountains. Each Mobile Yogurt Shoppe is located in a specially constructed motor vehicle that moves on a regular schedule, such as that of a bus, throughout the community it serves. The predicted cash flows associated with the project, which has an expected life of five years, are presented in Exhibit 14–1.

Net Present Value

A project's **net present value,** usually computed as of the time of the initial investment, is the present value of the project's net cash inflows from operations and disinvestment less the amount of the initial investment. In computing a project's net present value, the cash flows occurring at different points in time are adjusted for the time value of money using a **discount rate** that is the minimum rate of return required for the project to be acceptable. Projects whose net present values are positive, or at least equal to zero, are acceptable, and projects whose net present values are negative are unacceptable. Assuming management uses a 12 percent discount rate, the net present value of the proposed investment in a Mobile Yogurt Shoppe is shown in Exhibit 14–2 to be $20,400. Since the net present value is greater than zero, the investment in the Mobile Yogurt Shoppe is expected to be profitable, even when adjusted for the time value of money.

EXHIBIT 14–1   Analysis of a Project's Predicted Cash Flows

Initial investment:		
Vehicle and equipment		$ 90,554
Inventories and other working capital		4,000
Total		$ 94,554
Operation (per year for five years):		
Sales		$175,000
Cash expenditures:		
Food	$47,000	
Labor	65,000	
Supplies	9,000	
Fuel and utilities	8,000	
Advertising	4,000	
Miscellaneous	12,000	−145,000
Net annual cash inflow		$ 30,000
Disinvestment (at the end of five years):		
Sale of vehicle and equipment		$ 8,000
Recovery of investment in inventories and other working capital		4,000
Total		$ 12,000

EXHIBIT 14–2   Net Present Value Analysis of a Project's Predicted Cash Flows

	Predicted Cash Inflows (Outflows) (A)	Year(s) of Cash Flows (B)	12% Present Value Factor (C)	Present Value of Cash Flows (A) × (C)
Initial investment	$(94,554)	0	1.000	$ (94,554)
Operation	30,000	1–5	3.605	108,150
Disinvestment	12,000	5	0.567	6,804
Net present value of all cash flows				$ 20,400

As an exercise, you should verify the amounts and computations in Exhibit 14–2. Start by tracing the cash flows back to Exhibit 14–1. Next verify the 12 percent present values factors in Tables 1 and 2 found in the appendix at the back of the book. Note that the initial investment is assumed to occur at a single point in time, identified as time zero, the start of the project. In net present value computations, all cash flows are restated in terms of their value at time zero. Hence, time zero cash flows have a present value factor of one. To simplify computations, all other cash flows are assumed to occur at the end of years one through five, even if they occurred during the year. Although further refinements could be made to adjust for the fact that cash flows occur throughout each year rather than at the end of the year, such adjustments are seldom necessary. Observe that the net operating cash inflows are treated as an annuity, whereas the cash flows for the initial investment and the disinvestment are treated as lump-sum amounts. If the net operating cash flows varied from year to year, we would have to treat each year's cash flow as separate amounts.

Internal Rate of Return

"break even" discount rate

The **internal rate of return** (IRR), often called the **time adjusted rate of return,** is the discount rate that equates the present value of a project's cash inflows with the present value of the project's cash outflows. It may also be stated as:

1. The minimum rate that could be paid for the money invested in a project without losing money, or

2. The discount rate that results in a project's net present value equaling zero.

Computing IRR with Equal Cash Inflows. An investment proposal's internal rate of return is relatively easy to compute in simple situations involving a single investment and a series of equal annual net cash inflows. In general, the relationship between the initial investment and the equal annual cash inflows can be expressed as follows:

$$\underset{\text{investment}}{\text{Initial}} = \underset{\text{for an annuity of \$1}}{\text{Present value factor}} \times \underset{\text{cash inflow.}}{\text{Annual net}}$$

We can solve for the appropriate present value factor as follows:

$$\underset{\text{for an annuity of \$1}}{\text{Present value factor}} = \frac{\text{Initial investment}}{\text{Annual net cash inflows}}.$$

Once the present value factor is calculated, we enter Table 2 and go across the row corresponding to the expected life of the project until we find a table factor equal to the present value factor computed for the project. The corresponding percentage for the present value factor is the proposal's internal rate of return. If a table factor does not exactly equal the proposal's present value factor, a more accurate answer can be obtained by interpolation.

To illustrate, assume the Mobile Yogurt Shoppes' proposed investment has a zero disinvestment value. Using all information in Exhibit 14–1, except that for disinvestment, the proposal's present value factor is 3.152:

$$\underset{\text{for an annuity of \$1}}{\text{Present value factor}} = \frac{\text{Initial investment}}{\text{Annual net cash inflows}}$$

$$= \frac{\$94,554}{\$30,000}$$

$$= \underline{3.152}.$$

Entering Table 2, and going across the row for five periods, the closest table factor is 3.127, which corresponds to an internal rate of return of 18 percent. Because the proposal's present value factor is slightly larger than 3.127, a more accurate answer can be obtained by interpolation:

	Present Value Factors	
16 percent	3.274	3.274
Internal rate of return	−3.152	
18 percent		−3.127
Difference	0.122	0.147

$$\underset{\text{rate of return}}{\text{True internal}} = 0.16 + \left(\frac{0.122}{0.147} \times (0.18 - 0.16) \right)$$

$$= \underline{0.1766}$$

Hence, the proposal's internal rate of return, ignoring any disinvestment value, is 17.66 percent.

The calculated internal rate of return should be compared to the discount rate established by management to evaluate investment proposals. If the proposal's IRR is greater than or equal to the discount rate, the project is acceptable; if the proposal's IRR is less than the discount rate, the project is unacceptable. Because Mobile Yogurt Shoppes has a 12 percent discount rate, the project is acceptable using the IRR model.

Computing IRR with Unequal Cash Inflows. If periodic cash flows subsequent to the initial investment are unequal, the simple procedure of determining a present value factor and looking up the closest corresponding factor in Table 2 cannot be used. Instead, a trial-and-error approach is used to determine the internal rate of return.

The first step is to select a discount rate estimated to be close to the proposal's IRR and compute the proposal's net present value. If the resulting net present value is zero, the selected discount rate is the actual rate of return. However, it is unlikely that the first rate selected will be the proposal's IRR. If the resulting net present value is positive, this indicates that the actual IRR is greater than the initially selected rate. In this case, the next step is to compute the proposal's net present value using a higher rate. If the second computation produces a negative net present value, the actual IRR is less than the selected rate. Therefore, the actual IRR is between the first and the second rates. This trial-and-error approach continues until a discount rate is found that equates the proposal's cash inflows and outflows. For the Mobile Yogurt Shoppes' investment proposal outlined in Exhibit 14–1, the details of the trial-and-error approach are presented in Exhibit 14–3.

Note in Exhibit 14–3 that the first rate produced a negative net present value, indicating that the proposal's IRR is less than 24 percent. To produce a positive net present value, a smaller rate was selected for the second trial. Since the second rate produced a positive net present value, the proposal's true IRR must be between 16 and 24 percent. The 20 percent rate selected for the third trial produced a net present value of zero, indicating that this is the proposal's IRR.

Although manual calculation of an investment proposal's IRR can be tedious, accurate results are easily obtained with the aid of a computer and appropriate software. Furthermore, many hand calculators contain IRR calculation functions. All the user must do is enter the predicted cash flows for each period. This computational ease does, however, increase the opportunity for inappropriate use. Being able to plug numbers into a computer or calculator and obtain a number labeled IRR may mislead the unwary user into believing it is easy to use this capital budgeting model. This simply is not true. Training and professional judgment are required to identify relevant costs, implement procedures to obtain relevant cost information, and make a good decision on the basis of IRR information.

EXHIBIT 14–3   Computations of Internal Rate of Return with Unequal Cash Flows

First trial with a 24 percent discount rate:

	Predicted Cash Inflows (Outflows) (A)	Year(s) of Cash Flows (B)	24% Present Value Factor (C)	Present Value of Cash Flows (A) × (C)
Initial investment	$(94,554)	0	1.000	$(94,554)
Operation	30,000	1–5	2.745	82,350
Disinvestment	12,000	5	0.341	4,092
Net present value of all cash flows				$ (8,112)

Second trial with a 16 percent discount rate:

	Predicted Cash Inflows (Outflows) (A)	Year(s) of Cash Flows (B)	16% Present Value Factor (C)	Present Value of Cash Flows (A) × (C)
Initial investment	$(94,554)	0	1.000	$(94,554)
Operation	30,000	1–5	3.274	98,220
Disinvestment	12,000	5	0.476	5,712
Net present value of all cash flows				$ 9,378

Third trial with a 20 percent discount rate:

	Predicted Cash Inflows (Outflows) (A)	Year(s) of Cash Flows (B)	20% Present Value Factor (C)	Present Value of Cash Flows (A) × (C)
Initial investment	$(94,554)	0	1.000	$(94,554)
Operation	30,000	1–5	2.991	89,730
Disinvestment	12,000	5	0.402	4,824
Net present value of all cash flows				$ 0

Cost of Capital

When discounting models are used to evaluate capital expenditure proposals, management must determine the discount rate (1) used to compute a proposal's net present value or (2) used as the standard for evaluating a proposal's IRR. An organization's cost of capital is often used as this discount rate.

The cost of capital is the average cost of obtaining the resources necessary to make investments. The cost of capital is the average rate an organization must pay for invested funds. This average rate takes into account such items as interest paid on notes or bonds, the effective dividend rate on preferred stock, and the discount rate that equates the present value of all dividends expected on common stock over the life of the organization to the current market value of the organization's common stock. Investing in a project that has an internal rate of return equal to the cost of capital should not affect the market value of the firm's securities. Investing in a project that has a return greater than the cost of capital should increase the market value of a firm's securities. If, however, a firm invests in a project that has a return of less than the cost of capital, the market value of the firm's securities should fall.

The cost of capital is the minimum return that is acceptable for investment purposes. Any investment proposal not expected to yield this minimum rate should normally be rejected. Because of difficulties encountered in determining the cost of capital, many organizations adopt a discount rate or target rate of return without complicated mathematical analysis.

CAPITAL BUDGETING MODELS THAT DO NOT CONSIDER THE TIME VALUE OF MONEY

Until recent years, capital budgeting models that do not consider the time value of money were more widely used than discounting models. Although their popularity has declined, nondiscounting models remain popular, especially as an initial screening device. Two nondiscounting models, payback and accounting rate of return, are considered.

Payback Period

The payback period is the time required to recover the initial investment in a project from its operations. The payback method decision rule states that acceptable capital expenditure proposals must have less than some maximum payback period designated by management. The payback method emphasizes management's concern with liquidity and the need to minimize risk through a rapid recovery of the initial investment.

When a proposal is expected to have equal annual operating cash inflows, its payback period is computed as follows:

$$\text{Payback period} = \frac{\text{Initial investment}}{\text{Annual operating cash inflows}}.$$

For the Mobile Yogurt Shoppes' investment proposal, outlined in Exhibit 14–1, the payback period is 3.15 years:

$$\text{Payback period} = \frac{\$94,554}{\$30,000}$$

$$= \underline{\underline{3.15}}.$$

Determining the payback period for an investment proposal that has unequal cash flows is slightly more complicated. Assume the Alderman Company is evaluating a capital expenditure proposal that requires an initial investment of $50,000 and has the following expected cash inflows:

Year	Cash Inflow
1	$15,000
2	25,000
3	40,000
4	20,000
5	10,000

To compute the payback period, the net unrecovered amount must be determined as of the end of each year. In the year of full recovery, the cash inflows are assumed to occur evenly and are prorated based on the unrecovered investment at the start of the year. Full recovery of the Alderman Company's investment proposal is expected to occur in year 3:

Year	Cash Inflow	Unrecovered Investment
0	$ 0	$50,000
1	15,000	35,000
2	25,000	10,000
3	40,000	

Therefore, $10,000 of $40,000 is needed in year 3 to complete the recovery of the initial investment. This provides a proration of 0.25 ($10,000/$40,000) and a payback period of 2.25 years (2 years plus 0.25 of year 3). If management specified a maximum payback period of 3 years, this proposal would be acceptable. Note that the cash inflows of years 4 and 5 are ignored.

The bail-out period is an often used variation of the payback period. The bail-out period is the time required to recover the initial investment in a project from any source of funds. Unlike the payback method, which recognizes only operating cash inflows, the bail-out method recognizes cash inflows from either operations or early disposal.

Assume that the Baker Company is considering a capital expenditure proposal requiring an initial investment of $50,000. The net cash inflows from operations are estimated to be $10,000 per year for eight years. The disposal value of the investment is $30,000 during the first year, and it declines by $5,000 during the second year and each subsequent year. As shown in the following table, the bail-out period of the investment proposal is three years, and the payback period is five years.

Year	(1) Disposal Value	(2) Cumulative Operating Inflows	(1) + (2) Total Recovery
1	$30,000	$10,000	$40,000
2	25,000	20,000	45,000
3 Bail-out	20,000	30,000	**50,000**
4	15,000	40,000	55,000
5 Payback	10,000	**50,000**	60,000
6	5,000	60,000	65,000

The bail-out period indicates how soon an organization can get out of a project and recover all its initial investment. It provides additional information to assist management in making investment decisions.

Accounting Rate of Return

The accounting rate of return, sometimes called the simple rate of return, is computed as the average annual increase in net income that results from acceptance of a capital expenditure proposal divided by either the initial investment or the average investment in the project:

$$\text{Accounting rate of return} = \frac{\text{Average annual increase in net income}}{\text{Initial investment}}$$

or

$$\text{Accounting rate of return} = \frac{\text{Average annual increase in net income}}{\text{Average investment}}.$$

This method differs from all other capital budgeting models discussed in this chapter in that it focuses on accounting income rather than cash flow. In most capital budgeting applications, accounting net income is computed as net cash inflow from operations minus expenses not requiring the use of cash, such as depreciation.

Consider the Mobile Yogurt Shoppes' capital expenditure proposal, whose cash flows are outlined in Exhibit 14–1. The vehicle and equipment cost $90,554 and have a disposal value of $8,000 at the end of five years, resulting in an average annual increase in net income of $13,489.20:

Annual net cash inflow from operations	$30,000.00
Less average annual depreciation [($90,554 − $8,000)/5]	−16,510.80
Average annual increase in net income	$13,489.20

Taking the investment in inventories and other working capital into account, the initial investment is $94,554 ($90,554 + $4,000), and the accounting rate of return on initial investment is 14.27 percent:

$$\text{Accounting rate of return} = \frac{\$13,489.20}{\$94,554.00}$$

$$= \underline{\underline{0.1427}}.$$

The average investment, computed as the initial investment plus the expected value of any disinvestment, all divided by two, is $53,277 [($94,554 + $12,000)/2]. The accounting rate of return on average investment is 25.32 percent:

$$\text{Accounting rate of return} = \frac{\$13,489.20}{\$53,277}$$

$$= \underline{\underline{0.2532}}.$$

When using the accounting rate of return, management specifies some minimum acceptable rate of return. Capital expenditure proposals with a lower accounting rate of return are rejected, whereas acceptable proposals have an accounting rate of return greater than or equal to the minimum.

EVALUATION OF CAPITAL BUDGETING MODELS

As a single criterion for evaluating capital expenditure proposals, capital budgeting models that consider the time value of money are superior to capital budgeting models that do not consider the time value of money. The payback model is merely concerned with how long it takes to recover the initial investment from a project. Yet, investments are not made with the objective of merely getting the investment back. Indeed, not investing has a payback period of zero. Investments are made to earn a profit. Hence, what happens after the payback period is just as important as the payback period itself. The payback model, when used as the sole investment criterion, has a fatal flaw in that it fails to consider cash flows after the payback period.

The accounting rate of return is superior to the payback period in that it does consider the profitability of a capital expenditure proposal. Using the accounting rate of return, a project that merely returns the initial investment will have an average annual increase in net income of zero and an accounting rate of return of zero. The problem with the accounting rate of return is that it fails to consider the timing of cash flows. All cash flows within the life of an investment proposal are treated equally, despite the fact that cash flows early in a project's life are more valuable than cash flows late in a project's life. Early period cash flows can earn additional profits by being invested elsewhere. Consider the two investment proposals summarized in Exhibit 14–4, both of which have an accounting rate of return of 5 percent. Yet, Proposal A is superior to Proposal B because most of its cash flows occur in the first two years.

EXHIBIT 14–4   The Accounting Rate of Return Illustrated with Differences in the Timing of Cash Flows

	Project A	Project B
Predicted net cash inflow from operations		
Year 1	$ 50,000	$ 10,000
Year 2	50,000	10,000
Year 3	10,000	50,000
Year 4	10,000	50,000
Total	$120,000	$120,000
Total depreciation	−100,000	−100,000
Total net income	$ 20,000	$ 20,000
Project life	÷4 years	÷4 years
Average annual increase in net income	$ 5,000	$ 5,000
Initial investment	÷100,000	÷100,000
Accounting rate of return on initial investment	0.05	0.05

The net present value and internal rate of return models both consider the time value of money and project profitability. They almost always provide the same evaluation of individual projects whose acceptance or rejection will not affect other projects.[1] There are, however, two basic differences between the net present value and the internal rate of return models that often lead to differences in the evaluation of competing investment proposals:

1. The net present value model gives explicit consideration to investment size. The internal rate of return model does not.

2. The net present value model assumes that all net cash inflows are reinvested at the discount rate, whereas the internal rate of return model assumes that all net cash inflows are reinvested at the project's internal rate of return.

These differences are considered later when we discuss mutually exclusive investments.

ADDITIONAL ASPECTS OF CAPITAL BUDGETING

Screening and Selection

The capital budgeting models discussed above do not make investment decisions. Rather, they help managers separate capital expenditure proposals that meet certain criteria from those that do not. Managers then focus additional attention on those proposals that pass the initial screening performed using the

---

[1] An exception often occurs when periods of net cash outflows are mixed with periods of net cash inflows. Under these circumstances, an investment proposal may have multiple internal rates of return. For a further discussion of this point, consult a financial management textbook.

capital budgeting models. In performing this initial screening, management may use a single capital budgeting model, or they may use multiple models, including some we have not discussed. Management might specify that proposals must be in line with the organization's long-range goals, have a maximum payback period of three years, have a positive net present value when discounted at 14 percent, and have an initial investment of less than $500,000. The maximum payback period might be intended to reduce risk, the present value criterion might be to ensure an adequate return to investors, and the maximum investment size might reflect the resources available for investment.

Nonquantitative factors are apt to play a decisive role in management's final decision to accept or reject a capital expenditure proposal that has passed the initial screening. Very important at this point are management's attitudes toward risk and financing alternatives, their confidence in the professional judgment of managers making investment proposals, their beliefs about the future direction of the economy, and their evaluation of alternative investments. In the remaining portion of this chapter, we focus on the evaluation of risk, the evaluation of investment alternatives, and an approach to the differential analysis of project cash flows.

Evaluating Risk

All capital expenditure proposals involve many sources of risk, including risk related to:

- The cost of the initial investment.
- The time required to complete the initial investment and begin operations.
- Whether or not the new facilities will operate as planned.
- The life of the facilities.
- The customers' demand for the product or service.
- The final selling price.
- Operating costs.
- Disposal values.

Projected cash flows, such as those summarized for the Mobile Yogurt Shoppes' proposal in Exhibit 14–1, are based on management's best prediction as to what will happen. Although these predictions are likely to reflect the professional judgment of economists, marketing personnel, engineers, and accountants, they are far from certain.

Many techniques have been developed to assist in the analysis of the risks inherent in capital budgeting. Suggested approaches include the following:

- The discount rate for individual projects may be adjusted based on management's perception of the risks associated with a project. A project perceived as being almost risk free may be evaluated using a discount rate of 12 percent; a project perceived as having moderate risk may be evaluated using a discount rate of 16 percent; and a project perceived as having high risk may be evaluated using a discount rate of 20 percent.

- Several internal rates of return and/or net present values may be computed for a project. For example, a project's net present value might be computed three times: first, assuming the most optimistic projections of cash flows; second, assuming the most likely projections of cash flows; and third, assuming the most pessimistic projections of cash flows. The final decision then is based on management's attitudes toward risk.

- A capital expenditure proposal may be subject to sensitivity analysis, which was defined in Chapter 4 as a study of the responsiveness of a model's dependent variable(s) to changes in one or more of its independent variables. Management might want to know, for example, the minimum annual net cash inflows that will provide an internal rate of return of 12 percent, other cost and revenue projections being as expected.

Consider the situation presented in Exhibit 14–1 and analyzed using net present value and internal rate of return models in Exhibits 14–2 and 14–3. This proposal has a positive net present value when its cash flows are discounted at 12 percent and it has an expected IRR of 20 percent. Assuming Mobile Yogurt Shoppes has a 12 percent discount rate, management might wish to know the minimum annual net cash inflow that will meet this criterion.

In Exhibit 14–2, disinvestment cash inflows have a net present value of $6,804. When this amount is subtracted from the initial investment, $87,750 ($94,554 − $6,804) of the initial investment must be recovered from operations. If this amount is to be recovered over a five-year period, with equal annual net cash inflows, and a 12 percent discount rate, the factor 3.605 (see Table 2) must equate the annual net cash inflows with the portion of the initial investment to be recovered from operations. Hence, the minimum annual net cash inflows must be $24,341.19:

$$\text{Minimum annual net cash inflow} = \frac{\$87,750}{3.605}$$

$$= \$24,341.19.$$

If management could then predict the probability of annual net cash inflows being greater than or equal to $24,341.19, they would have the probability of this project meeting a 12 percent discount rate. Again, the ultimate decision to accept or reject the proposal rests with management and their attitudes toward risk.

It is interesting to note the similarity of the analysis here, determining the minimum annual net cash inflows, and the determination of the break-even point in Chapter 4. In effect, $24,341.19 in annual net cash inflows is a time-adjusted break-even point.

Total Cost and Differential Analysis of Cash Flows

All the examples presented so far assume that the capital expenditure proposal will produce additional net cash inflows. This is not always the case. Units of government and not-for-profit organizations may provide services that do not produce any cash inflows. For-profit organizations may be required to make capital expenditures to maintain product quality or bring facilities up to environmental or safety standards. In these situations, it is impossible to compute a project's payback period, accounting rate of return, or internal rate of return. It is possible, however, to compute the present value of all costs associated with alternative ways of providing the service or meeting the environmental or safety standard. Here, the alternative with the smallest negative net present value is preferred.

Capital expenditure proposals to reduce operating costs by upgrading facilities may not have any incremental cash inflows associated with them. Again, we may use a **total cost approach** and calculate the present value of the costs associated with each alternative, with the low-cost alternative being preferred. Alternatively, we may perform a differential analysis of cash flows and, treating any reduced operating costs as if they were cash inflows, compute the net present value or the internal rate of return of the cost reduction proposal. Basically, a **differential analysis** focuses on the differences between the cash flows of the current operating conditions and the future alternative management is considering. Once the amounts are netted out, the differences can be adjusted for the time value of money. To illustrate the differential approach, we will consider an example first introduced in Chapter 5.

The Ace Stamping Company uses a Model I stamping machine to produce 10,000 widgets per year. Widgets sell for $15 each. Ace's variable and fixed costs are as follows:

Variable:	
Direct materials	$3 per unit
Direct labor	4 per unit
Factory overhead	1 per unit
Selling and administrative	1 per unit
Fixed:	
Factory overhead other than depreciation	$19,000 per year
Depreciation on Model I stamping machine	15,000 per year
Selling and administrative	12,000 per year

The Model I stamping machine is two years old and has a remaining useful life of four years. It cost $90,000 and has an estimated salvage value of zero dollars at the end of its useful life. Its current book value (original cost less accumulated depreciation) is $60,000, but its current disposal value is only $35,000.

Management is evaluating the desirability of replacing the Model I stamping machine with a new Model II stamping machine. The new machine costs $80,000, has a useful life of four years, and a predicted salvage value of zero dollars at the end of its useful life. Although the new machine would have the same productive capacity as the old machine, its operating costs would be lower because it would require only one operator rather than the two needed by the old machine. Furthermore, it has fewer moving parts, so it would require less maintenance and use less power. The new labor and overhead costs would be as follows:

Direct labor	$2.00 per unit
Variable factory overhead	0.80 per unit
Fixed overhead other than depreciation	$16,000 per year

A differential analysis of the cash flows associated with this cost reduction proposal, broken down into the three phases of the project's life, are presented in Exhibit 14–5. Because the proposal does not have a disposal value, this portion

EXHIBIT 14–5 Differential Analysis of Predicted Cash Flows

	Differential Analysis of Predicted Cash Flows		
	Keep Old Model I Machine	Replace with New Model II Machine	Difference (Effect of Replacement on Cash Flow
	(A)	(B)	(A) − (B)
Initial investment:			
Cost of new machine		$80,000	$80,000
Disposal value of old machine		(35,000)	(35,000)
Net initial investment			$45,000
Annual operating cash savings:			
Direct labor:			
Old (10,000 × $4)	$40,000		
New (10,000 × $2)		20,000	$20,000
Variable overhead:			
Old (10,000 × $1)	10,000		
New (10,000 × $0.80)		8,000	2,000
Fixed overhead:			
Old	19,000		
New		16,000	3,000
Net annual cash savings			$25,000
Disinvestment at end of life:			
Old	$ 0		
New		$ 0	$ 0

of the analysis could have been omitted. Readers interested in a detailed explanation of the relevant costs included in this analysis are referred to Exhibit 5–1 and the accompanying Chapter 5 discussion of relevant costs. Assuming Ace Stamping has a discount rate of 16 percent, the proposal's net present value, computed in Exhibit 14–6, is $24,950. The proposal is acceptable.

Mutually Exclusive Investments

Two or more capital expenditure proposals are **mutually exclusive investments** if the acceptance of one automatically causes the rejection of the other(s). When faced with mutually exclusive investments, management must determine which one to accept. The decision is relatively easy if only one of the proposals meets the organization's investment criteria. If, however, two or more proposals pass the initial screening performed by the investment criterion, management is faced with the task of selecting the best of the acceptable proposals. To help determine the best investment proposal, management may request that the proposals be ranked on the basis of some criterion, such as net present value or internal rate of return. Unfortunately, although these models almost always lead to identical decisions when used to evaluate individual investment proposals, they frequently produce different rankings of acceptable proposals. Consider the three investment proposals summarized in Exhibit 14–7.

Assuming the organization has a 12 percent cost of capital, all projects have positive net present values and all projects have an internal rate of return in excess of 12 percent. Therefore, all are acceptable. The problem is to determine which of these acceptable proposals is most desirable. Ranking the proposals by their net present value indicates that Proposal B is best, whereas ranking by IRR indicates that Proposal C is best.

An often-stated criticism of net present value, when used to rank investment proposals, is that it fails to adjust for the size of the proposed investment. To overcome this difficulty, managers may rank projects on the basis of each project's **present value index,** which is computed as the present value of the project's

---

EXHIBIT 14–6   Net Present Value Analysis of Differential Cash Flows

	Predicted Cash Inflows (Outflows)	Year(s) of Cash Flows	16% Present Value Factor	Present Value of Cash Flows
	(A)	(B)	(C)	(A) × (C)
Initial investment	$(45,000)	0	1.000	$(45,000)
Operation	25,000	1–5	2.798	69,950
Disinvestment	0	5	0.552	0
Net present value of all cash flows				$ 24,950

EXHIBIT 14–7   Ranking Capital Budgeting Proposals

	Proposal A	Proposal B	Proposal C
Predicted cash flows:			
Initial investment	$(26,900)	$(55,960)	$(30,560)
Operation:			
Year 1	10,000	20,000	20,000
Year 2	10,000	20,000	20,000
Year 3	10,000	20,000	0
Year 4	10,000	20,000	0
Disinvestment	0	0	0
Investment criterion:			
Net present value at 12%	$ 3,470	$ 4,780	$ 3,240
Internal rate of return	18%	16%	20%
Present value index	1.129	1.085	1.106
Ranking by investment criterion:			
Net present value	2	1	3
Internal rate of return	2	3	1
Present value index	1	3	2

subsequent cash flows divided by the initial investment:

$$\text{Present value index} = \frac{\text{Present value of subsequent cash flows}}{\text{Initial investment}}.$$

For Proposal A, the present value of the subsequent cash flows, discounted at 12 percent, is $30,370 ($10,000 × 3.037), and the present value index is 1.129:

$$\text{Present value index} = \frac{\$30,370}{\$26,900}$$

$$= \underline{1.129}.$$

Using this criterion, projects that have a present value index of 1.0 or greater are acceptable, and the project with the highest present value index is preferred. Ranking the proposals in Exhibit 14–7 on the basis of their present value index results in Proposal A being ranked number 1.

    We now have three acceptable proposals, three criteria, three different rankings, and the task of selecting only one of the three proposals. Many managers would select Proposal C because it has the highest IRR or Proposal A because it has the highest present value index. Either selection provides a satisfactory, but not an optimal, solution to the dilemma. If the true cost of capital is 12 percent and other investment opportunities only return 12 percent, the net present value criterion provides the proper choice. This is illustrated in Exhibit 14–8 by evaluating the additional return earned on the difference between Proposals B and A, and Proposals B and C.

EXHIBIT 14–8   Analysis of Incremental Investments

	Proposal B	Proposal A	Difference B − A
Predicted cash flows:			
Initial investment	$(55,960)	$(26,900)	$(29,060)
Operation:			
Year 1	20,000	10,000	10,000
Year 2	20,000	10,000	10,000
Year 3	20,000	10,000	10,000
Year 4	20,000	10,000	10,000
Disinvestment	0	0	0
Net present value of difference			$ 1,310

	Proposal B	Proposal C	Difference B − C
Predicted cash flows:			
Initial investment	$(55,960)	$(30,560)	$(25,400)
Operations:			
Year 1	20,000	20,000	0
Year 2	20,000	20,000	0
Year 3	20,000	0	20,000
Year 4	20,000	0	20,000
Disinvestment	0	0	0
Net present value of difference			$ 1,540

The difference in the net present value and internal rate of return rankings results from differences in their reinvestment assumptions. The net present value model assumes that all net cash inflows from a project are reinvested at the discount rate, whereas the internal rate of return model assumes that all net cash inflows from a project are reinvested at the project's internal rate of return. If unlimited funds are available at the discount rate, marginal investments are made at this rate and the assumption underlying the net present value model is the correct one. Returning to Exhibit 14–8, if all funds not invested in the chosen project and all funds recovered from the chosen project can only earn the discount rate, the firm is $1,540 better off selecting Proposal B rather than Proposal C.

The present value index eliminates the impact of size from net present value computations. However, size is an important consideration in evaluating invest-ment proposals, especially if all funds not invested in a project can only earn the discount rate. In Exhibit 14–8, we can see that if all funds not invested in the chosen project can only be invested at the discount rate, the firm is $1,310 better off by selecting Proposal B rather than Proposal A.

SUMMARY

Capital budgeting involves the identification of potentially desirable projects for capital expenditures, the subsequent evaluation of capital expenditure proposals, and the selection of proposals that meet certain criteria. In this chapter we have studied a number of capital budgeting models that are used to assist managers in evaluating capital expenditure proposals. We concluded that capital budgeting models that consider the time value of money, such as net present value and internal rate of return, are superior to capital budgeting models that do not consider the time value of money, such as the payback period and the accounting rate of return.

It is important to remember that capital budgeting models do not make investment decisions. Rather, they help managers separate capital expenditure proposals that meet certain criteria from those that do not. In making the final decision to accept or reject a capital expenditure proposal that has passed the initial screening, nonquantitative factors, such as management's attitude toward risk, are apt to play a decisive role.

In the latter portion of this chapter, we outlined some suggested approaches to analyzing risk, saw how differential analysis can aid in evaluating capital expenditure proposals that do not produce additional cash inflows, and studied the problems involved in selecting from among mutually exclusive investments. The impact of taxes on capital budgeting is considered in Chapter 15, and the impact of price level changes on capital budgeting is considered in Chapter 17.

KEY TERMS

Accounting rate of return
Bail-out period
Capital budgeting
Capital expenditures
Cost of capital
Differential analysis
Discount rate
Internal rate of return

Mutually exclusive investments
Net present value
Payback period
Present value index
Simple rate of return
Time adjusted rate of return
Total cost approach (to capital budgeting)

REVIEW QUESTIONS

14–1   What is the relationship between long-range planning and capital budgeting?

14–2   What tasks are often assigned to the capital budgeting committee?

14–3   What purposes are served by a post-audit of approved capital expenditure proposals?

14–4   Into what three phases are a project's cash flows organized?

14–5   State three alternative definitions or descriptions of the internal rate of return.

14–6   Why is the cost of capital an important concept when discounting models are used for capital budgeting?

14–7   Distinguish between the payback period and the bail-out period.

14–8   In what way does the accounting rate of return differ from all other capital budgeting models discussed in this chapter.

14–9   What weakness is inherent in the payback period when it is used as the sole investment criterion?

14–10   What weakness is inherent in the accounting rate of return when it is used as an investment criterion?

14–11   Why are the net present value and the internal rate of return models superior to the payback and accounting rate of return models?

14–12   State two basic differences between the net present value and internal rate of return models that often lead to differences in the evaluation of competing investment proposals.

14–13   Identify several nonquantitative factors that are apt to play a decisive role in the final selection of projects for capital expenditures.

REVIEW PROBLEM

Survey of Capital Budgeting Models

Consider the following investment proposal:

Initial investment:	
Depreciable assets	$27,740
Working capital	3,000
Operation (per year for four years):	
Cash receipts	$25,000
Cash expenditures	15,000
Disinvestment:	
Salvage value of plant and equipment	$ 2,000
Recovery of working capital	3,000

Required: Determine each of the following:

1. Net present value at a 10 percent discount rate.

2. Internal rate of return.

3. Payback period.

4. Accounting rate of return on initial investment and on average investment.

Round calculations to four decimal places.

The solution to this problem is found at the end of the Chapter 14 exercises and problems.

EXERCISES

14–1 Time Value of Money: Basics (Book Appendix)

Remember that money is of the prolific, generating nature. Money can beget money and its offspring can beget more, and so on. Five shillings turned is six; turned again it is seven and threepence, and so on until it is a hundred pounds. The more there is of it the more it produces every turning, so that the profits rise quicker and quicker.

Benjamin Franklin

Required: Using the equations and tables in the appendix to this text, determine the answers to each of the following independent situations.

1. The future value in two years of $1,000 deposited in a savings account with interest compounded annually at 8 percent.

2. The present value of $9,000 to be received in five years, discounted at 12 percent.

3. The present value of an annuity of $2,000 per year for five years discounted at 16 percent.

4. An initial investment of $32,010 is to be returned in eight equal, annual payments. Determine the amount of each payment if the interest rate is 10 percent.

5. A proposed investment will provide cash flows of $20,000; $8,000; and $6,000; at the end of years 1, 2, and 3, respectively. Using a discount rate of 20 percent, determine the present value of these cash flows.

6. Find the present value of an investment that will pay $5,000 at the end of years 10, 11, and 12. Use a discount rate of 14 percent.

14–2 Time Value of Money: Basics (Book Appendix)

Required: Using the equations and tables in the appendix to this text, determine the answers to each of the following independent situations:

1. The future value in two years of $3,000 deposited in a certificate of deposit with interest compounded annually at 10 percent.

2. The present value of $8,000 to be received in five years, discounted at 8 percent.

3. The present value of an annuity of $10,000 per year for four years discounted at 12 percent.

4. An initial investment of $14,740 is to be returned in six equal, annual payments. Determine the amount of each payment if the interest rate is 16 percent.

5. A proposed investment will provide cash flows of $6,000; $8,000; and $20,000; at the end of years 1, 2, and 3, respectively. Using a discount rate of 18 percent, determine the present value of these cash flows.

6. Find the present value of an investment that will pay $6,000 at the end of years 8, 9, and 10. Use a discount rate of 14 percent.

14–3 NPV, IRR: Equal Annual Net Cash Inflows

The Sharp Company is evaluating a capital expenditure proposal that requires an initial investment of $8,002 and has predicted cash inflows of $2,000 per year for 15 years, with no salvage value.

Requirements

a) Using a discount rate of 14 percent, determine the net present value of the investment proposal.

b) Determine the proposal's internal rate of return.

14–4 NPV, IRR: Equal Annual Net Cash Inflows

The Tack Company is evaluating a capital expenditure proposal that requires an initial investment of $28,590 and has predicted cash inflows of $7,500 per year for seven years, with no salvage value.

Requirements

a) Using a discount rate of 16 percent, determine the net present value of the investment proposal.

b) Determine the proposal's internal rate of return.

14–5 IRR, Equal Cash Flows: Interpolation

The Midway Company is evaluating a capital expenditure proposal that requires an initial investment of $26,400 and has predicted cash inflows of $10,000 per year for four years, with no salvage value.

Required: Determine the proposal's internal rate of return. Interpolate if necessary. Round all calculations to four decimal places.

14–6 IRR, Equal Cash Flows: Interpolation

The Inn Between Company is evaluating a capital expenditure proposal that requires an initial investment of $142,925 and has predicted cash inflows of $25,000 per year for 13 years, with no salvage value.

Required: Determine the proposal's internal rate of return. Interpolate, if necessary. Round all calculations to four decimal places.

14–7 NPV, IRR: Unequal Annual Net Cash Inflows

The Lake Ski Company is evaluating a capital expenditure proposal that has the following predicted cash flows:

Initial investment	$(42,580)
Operation:	
Year 1	18,000
Year 2	25,000
Year 3	20,000
Salvage	0

Requirements

a) Using a discount rate of 12 percent, determine the net present value of the investment proposal.

b) Determine the proposal's internal rate of return.

14–8 NPV, IRR: Unequal Annual Net Cash Inflows

The Alpine Ski Company is evaluating a capital expenditure proposal that has the following predicted cash flows:

Initial investment	$(40,860)
Operation:	
Year 1	20,000
Year 2	30,000
Year 3	10,000
Salvage	0

Requirements

a) Using a discount rate of 14 percent, determine the net present value of the investment proposal.

b) Determine the proposal's internal rate of return.

14–9 Payback, Accounting Rate of Return

Presented is information pertaining to three capital expenditure proposals:

	Proposal A	Proposal B	Proposal C
Initial investment:			
Depreciable assets	$50,000	$100,000	$70,000
Working capital	0	0	10,000
Net cash inflow from operations			
(per year for four years)	20,000	35,000	25,000
Disinvestment:			
Depreciable assets	0	20,000	10,000
Working capital	0	0	10,000

Requirements

a) Determine each proposal's payback period.

b) Determine each proposal's accounting rate of return on:

   1. Initial investment.

   2. Average investment.

Round calculations to three decimal places.

14–10 Payback, Accounting Rate of Return

Presented is information pertaining to three capital expenditure proposals:

	Proposal X	Proposal Y	Proposal Z
Initial investment:			
Depreciable assets	$90,000	$60,000	$95,000
Working capital	0	0	5,000
Net cash inflow from operations			
(per year for four years)	37,500	20,000	40,000
Disinvestment:			
Depreciable assets	0	10,000	15,000
Working capital	0	0	5,000

Requirements

a) Determine each proposal's payback period.

b) Determine each proposal's accounting rate of return on:

1. Initial investment.

2. Average investment.

Round calculations to three decimal places.

14–11 Survey of Capital Budgeting Models

Consider the following investment proposal:

Initial investment:	
Depreciable assets	$18,293
Working capital	2,000
Operation (per year for five years):	
Cash receipts	$ 8,000
Cash expenditures	3,000
Disinvestment:	
Salvage value of plant and equipment	$ 2,000
Recovery of working capital	2,000

Required: Determine each of the following:

1. Net present value at a 14 percent discount rate.

2. Internal rate of return.

3. Payback period.

4. Accounting rate of return on initial investment and on average investment.

Round calculations to four decimal places.

14–12 Survey of Capital Budgeting Models

Consider the following investment proposal:

Initial investment:	
Depreciable assets	$36,000
Working capital	4,000
Operation (per year for seven years):	
Cash receipts	$15,500
Cash expenditures	7,000
Disinvestment:	
Salvage value of plant and equipment	$ 4,880
Recovery of working capital	4,000

Required: Determine each of the following:

1. Net present value at a 12 percent discount rate.

2. Internal rate of return.

3. Payback period.

4. Accounting rate of return on initial investment and on average investment.

Round calculations to four decimal places.

14–13 Bail-Out, Payback, IRR, Minimum Cash Flows

The management of Low Risk, Limited, is currently evaluating the following investment proposal:

	Time 0	Year 1	Year 2	Year 3	Year 4
Initial investment	$120,000				
Disposal value during year		$60,000	$40,000	$20,000	$ 0
Net operating cash inflows		50,000	50,000	50,000	50,000

Requirements

a) Determine the proposal's bail-out period.

b) Determine the proposal's payback period.

c) Determine the proposal's internal rate of return. Do not interpolate.

d) Given the amount of the initial investment, determine the minimum annual net cash inflow required to obtain an internal rate of return of 18 percent. Round the answer to the nearest dollar.

14–14 Bail-Out, Payback, IRR, Minimum Cash Flows

The management of Limited Risk, Inc., is currently evaluating the following investment proposal:

	Time 0	Year 1	Year 2	Year 3	Year 4
Initial investment	$270,000				
Disposal value during year		$150,000	$100,000	$ 50,000	$ 0
Net operating cash inflows		100,000	100,000	100,000	100,000

Requirements

a) Determine the proposal's bail-out period.

b) Determine the proposal's payback period.

c) Determine the proposal's internal rate of return. Do not interpolate.

d) Given the amount of the initial investment, determine the minimum annual net cash inflow required to obtain an internal rate of return of 14 percent. Round the answer to the nearest dollar.

14–15 Ranking Investment Proposals with Payback, Accounting Rate of Return, and Net Present Value

Presented is information pertaining to the cash flows of three mutually exclusive investment proposals:

	Proposal A	Proposal B	Proposal C
Initial investment	$60,000	$60,000	$60,000
Operation:			
Year 1	30,000	20,000	50,000
Year 2	30,000	20,000	5,000
Year 3		20,000	5,000
Year 4		20,000	20,000
Disinvestment	0	0	0
Life	2 years	4 years	4 years

Requirements

a) Rank these investment proposals using the payback, the accounting rate of return on initial investment, and the net present value criteria. Assume that the organization's cost of capital is 10 percent. Round calculations to four decimal places.

b) Explain the difference in rankings. Which investment would you recommend?

14–16 Ranking Investment Proposals with Payback, Accounting Rate of Return, and Net Present Value

Presented is information pertaining to the cash flows of three mutually exclusive investment proposals:

	Proposal X	Proposal Y	Proposal Z
Initial investment	$45,000	$45,000	$45,000
Operation:			
Year 1	40,000	22,500	45,000
Year 2	5,000	22,500	
Year 3	22,500	22,500	
Disinvestment	0	0	0
Life	3 years	3 years	1 year

Requirements

a) Rank these investment proposals using the payback, the accounting rate of return on initial investment, and the net present value criteria. Assume that the organization's cost of capital is 14 percent. Round calculations to four decimal places.

b) Explain the difference in rankings. Which investment would you recommend?

14–17 Ranking Investment Proposals Using NPV and Present Value Index

The Megabite Dog Food Company is considering the replacement of its traditional canned dog food with dog food packaged in either resealable plastic containers or in disposable foil-lined pouches. Although either alternative will produce significant cost savings and marketing benefits, limitations on available shelf space in stores requires management to select only one alternative. Cash flow information on each alternative is presented below:

	Plastic Containers	Lined Pouches
Initial investment in necessary equipment	$50,000	$150,000
Increase in annual net cash flows	$20,000	$56,000
Life of equipment	5 years	5 years
Disposal value of equipment	$10,000	$12,000

Megabite has a 10 percent cost of capital.

Requirements

a) Evaluate the investment alternatives using the net present value and the present value index criteria.

b) Explain the difference in rankings. Which investment would you recommend?

14–18 Ranking Investment Proposals Using NPV and Present Value Index

The Sea Breeze Cat Sand Company is considering the replacement of its traditional bag packaging of "cat sand" with either reuseable plastic pails or reuseable aluminum pails. Customers would make a refundable deposit on the container each time they purchased "cat sand." Because the pails would be reuseable, the net cost of "cat sand" to customers who returned the pail for a refund would be lower than the cost of "cat sand" sold in bags. Cash flow information on each alternative is presented below:

	Plastic	Aluminum
Initial investment	$80,000	$68,000
Increase in annual net cash flows	$35,000	$30,000
Life of equipment	4 years	4 years
Disposal value of equipment	$8,000	$9,000

Sea Breeze has a 16 percent cost of capital.

Requirements

a) Evaluate the investment alternatives using the net present value and the present value index criteria.

b) Explain the difference in rankings. Which investment would you recommend?

PROBLEMS

14–19 Payback, IRR: Computational Relationships

Supply the missing data for each of the following investment proposals:

	Proposal A	Proposal B	Proposal C
Initial investment	(a)	$31,475	$113,000
Annual net cash inflow	$30,000	(c)	(e)
Economic life in years	10	6	10
Salvage value	$0	$5,000	$0
Payback period in years	(b)	(d)	5.650
Internal rate of return	12%	24%	(f)

Assume that the annual net cash inflows are equal. Round computations to four decimal places.

14–20 Accounting Rate of Return, NPV: Computational Relationships

Supply the missing data for each of the following investment proposals:

	Proposal D	Proposal E	Proposal F
Initial investment	$40,000	(c)	$80,000
Annual net cash inflow	(a)	$20,000	$30,000
Economic life in years	4	5	6
Salvage value	$0	$14,000	(e)
Accounting rate of return on initial investment	(b)	10%	(f)
Cost of capital	18%	12%	14%
Net present value	$13,800	(d)	$45,790

Assume that the annual net cash inflows are equal. Round computations to four decimal places.

14–21 NPV Analysis of Equipment Replacement Decision

DuBose Manufacturing is planning on purchasing a new machine that costs $45,000. If the new machine is purchased, an old machine will be sold for $5,000. Management is convinced that the new machine can produce the following annual cost savings:

Materials and supplies	$7,500
Maintenance	4,500

The new machine will require about $2,200 more labor annually to operate than the old machine. It will also require an overhaul, predicted to cost $6,000, at the end of six years' use. The new machine has an estimated life of eight years and a predicted salvage value of $3,000. The old machine will not have a disposal value in eight years. DuBose's cost of capital is 14 percent.

Required: Determine the net present value of purchasing the new machine. Is the replacement an acceptable investment using the net present value criterion?

14–22 NPV Analysis of Equipment Replacement Decision

The Gamma Company is interested in replacing a stamping machine with a new, improved model. The old machine has a salvage value of $10,000 now and a predicted salvage value of $2,000 in six years. If the old machine is kept, it must be rebuilt in one year at a predicted cost of $20,000.

The new machine costs $80,000 and has a predicted salvage value of $12,000 at the end of six years. If purchased, the new machine will allow cash savings of $20,000 for each of the first three years and $10,000 for each year of its remaining six-year life.

The Gamma Company's cost of capital is 14 percent.

Required: Determine the net present value of purchasing the new machine. Is the new machine an acceptable investment using the net present value criterion?

14–23 NPV Total and Differential Analysis of Replacement Decision

Gusher Petro is evaluating a proposal to purchase a new processor that would cost $120,000 and have a salvage value of $12,000 in five years. It would provide annual operating cash savings of $15,000, as detailed below:

	Old Processor	New Processor
Salaries	$34,000	$44,000
Supplies	6,000	5,000
Utilities	13,000	6,000
Cleaning and maintenance	22,000	5,000
Total cash expenditures	$75,000	$60,000

If the new processor is purchased, the old processor will be sold for its current salvage value of $30,000. If the new processor is not purchased, the old processor will be disposed of in five years at a predicted scrap value of $2,000. The old processor's present book value is $50,000. If kept, in one year the old processor will require repairs predicted to cost $40,000.

Gusher's cost of capital is 16 percent.

Requirements

a) Use the total cost approach to evaluate the alternatives of keeping the old processor and purchasing the new processor. Indicate which alternative is preferred.

b) Use the differential cost approach to evaluate the desirability of purchasing the new processor.

14–24 NPV Total and Differential Analysis of Replacement Decision

The White Snow Automatic Laundry must either have a complete overhaul of its current dry cleaning system or purchase a new one. White Snow's accountant has developed the following cost projections:

	Present System	New System
Purchase cost new	$40,000	$50,000
Remaining book value	15,000	
Overhaul needed now	20,000	
Annual cash operating costs	35,000	20,000
Current salvage value	10,000	
Salvage value in five years	2,500	10,000

If White Snow keeps the old system, the system will have to be overhauled immediately. With the overhaul, the old system will have a useful life of five more years. White Snow has a cost of capital of 20 percent.

Requirements

a) Use the total cost approach to evaluate the alternatives of keeping the old system and purchasing the new system. Indicate which alternative is preferred.

b) Use the differential cost approach to evaluate the desirability of purchasing the new system.

14–25 NPV Differential Analysis of Replacement Decision

The management of Essen Manufacturing Company is currently evaluating a proposal to purchase a new and innovative drill press as a replacement for a less efficient piece of similar equipment, which would then be sold. The cost of the equipment including delivery and installation is $175,000. If the equipment is purchased, Essen will incur costs of $5,000 in removing the present equipment and revamping service facilities. The present equipment has a book value of $100,000 and a remaining useful life of ten years. Because of new technical improvements that have made the present equipment obsolete, it now has a disposal value of only $40,000.

Management has provided you with the following tabulation of comparative manufacturing costs:

	Present Equipment	New Equipment
Annual production (units)	400,000	400,000
Annual costs:		
Direct labor	$0.075/unit	$0.05/unit
Overhead:		
Depreciation (10% of asset book value)	$20,000	$17,500
Other	$48,000	$20,000

Additional information:

- Management believes that if the current equipment is not replaced now, it will have to wait ten years before replacement is justifiable.

- Both pieces of equipment are expected to have a negligible salvage value at the end of ten years.

- Management expects to sell the entire annual production of 400,000 units.
- Essen's cost of capital is 14 percent.

Required: Evaluate the desirability of purchasing the new equipment.

14–26 Potpourri of Capital Budgeting

Select the letter corresponding to the best answer in each of the following independent cases.

1. The discount rate (hurdle rate) must be determined in advance for the:

   a) Payback period method.

   b) Time adjusted rate of return method.

   c) Internal rate of return method.

   d) Net present value method.

2. Which of the following capital budgeting techniques consider(s) cash flow over the entire life of the project?

	Internal rate of return	**Payback**
a)	Yes	Yes
b)	Yes✓	No
c)	No	Yes
d)	No	No✓

3. It is assumed that cash flows are reinvested at the rate earned by the investment in which of the following techniques?

	Internal rate of return	**Net present value**
a)	Yes	Yes
b)	Yes	No
c)	No	No
d)	No	Yes

4. On May 1, 19x5, a company purchased a new machine, which it did not have to pay for until May 1, 19x7. The total payment on May 1, 19x7, includes both principal and interest. Assuming interest at a 10 percent rate, the cost of the machine would be the total payment multiplied by what time value of money concept?

   a) Future amount of an annuity of $1.

   b) Future amount of $1.

   c) Present value of an annuity of $1.

   d) Present value of $1.

5. At December 31, 19x4, Zar Co. had a machine with an original cost of $84,000, accumulated depreciation of $60,000, and an estimated salvage value of zero. On December 31, 19x4, Zar was considering the purchase of a new machine having a five-year life, costing $120,000, and having an estimated salvage value of $20,000 at the end of five years. In its decision concerning the possible purchase of the new machine, how much should Zar consider as sunk cost at December 31, 19x4?

   a) $120,000.

   b) $100,000.

c) $24,000.

d) $4,000.

6. Womark Company purchased a new machine on January 1, 19x1, for $90,000 with an estimated useful life of five years and a salvage value of $10,000. The machine will be depreciated using the straight-line method. The machine is expected to produce cash inflows from operations, net of income taxes, of $36,000 a year in each of the next five years. The payback period would be:

a) 2.2 years.

b) 2.5 years.

c) 4.0 years.

d) 4.5 years.

7. Hamilton Company invested in a two-year project having an internal rate of return of 12 percent. The project is expected to produce cash flow from operations, net of income taxes, of $60,000 in the first year and $70,000 in the second year. How much will the project cost?

a) $103,610.

b) $109,370. $(\$60,000)(.893) + 70,000\ (0.797)$

c) $116,090.

d) $122,510.

8. Axel Corp. is planning to buy a new machine with the expectation that this investment should earn a discounted rate of return of at least 15 percent. This machine, which costs $150,000, would yield an estimated net cash flow of $30,000 a year for ten years, after income taxes. In order to determine the net present value of buying the new machine, Axel should first multiply the $30,000 by which of the following factors?

a) 20.304 (Future amount of an ordinary annuity of $1).

b) 5.019 (Present value of an ordinary annuity of $1).

c) 4.046 (Future amount of $1).

d) 0.247 (Present value of $1).

Items 9 and 10 are based on the following data:

Amaro Hospital, a nonprofit institution not subject to income taxes, is considering the purchase of new equipment costing $20,000 in order to achieve cash savings of $5,000 per year in operating costs. The equipment's estimated useful life is ten years, with no net residual value. Amaro's cost of capital is 14 percent.

9. What factor contained in or developed from the above information should be used in computing the internal rate of return for Amaro's investment in the new equipment?

a) 5.216.

b) 4.000.

c) 1.400.

d) 0.270.

10. How much is the accounting rate of return based on Amaro's initial investment in the new equipment?

a) 27 percent.

b) 25 percent.

c) 15 percent.

d) 14 percent.

(CPA Adapted)

14–27 NPV Analysis of Replacement and Expansion: Relevant Costs

Illinois Products Company manufactures several different products. One of the firm's principal products sells for $20 per unit. The sales manager of Illinois Products has stated repeatedly that he could sell more units of this product if they were available. In an attempt to substantiate his claim, the sales manager conducted a market research study last year at a cost of $44,000 to determine potential demand for this product. The study indicated that Illinois Products could sell 18,000 units of this product annually for the next five years.

The equipment currently in use has the capacity to produce 11,000 units annually. The variable production costs are $9 per unit. The equipment has a book value of $60,000 and a remaining useful life of five years. The salvage value is negligible now and will be zero in five years.

A maximum of 20,000 units could be produced annually on a new machine, which could be purchased for $300,000. The new machine has an estimated life of five years and no salvage value. Illinois Products' production manager has estimated that the new equipment would produce production efficiencies that would reduce the variable production costs to $7 per unit.

The sales manager felt so strongly about the need for additional capacity that he attempted to prepare an economic justification for the equipment even though this was not part of his responsibilities. His analysis, presented below, disappointed him because it did not justify acquiring the equipment.

Required investment:	
Purchase price of new equipment	$300,000
Loss on disposal of old equipment	60,000
Cost of market research study	44,000
Total investment	$404,000
Annual returns:	
Contribution from product:	
Using new equipment [20,000($20 − $7)]	$260,000
Using existing equipment [11,000($20 − $9)]	−121,000
Increase in contribution	$139,000
Less depreciation ($300,000/5 years)	− 60,000
Increase in income	$ 79,000
Less 20% cost of capital on additional required investment	
(0.20 × $404,000)	− 80,800
Net annual return of proposed investment in new equipment	$ (1,800)

Illinois Products Company has a 20 percent cost of capital.

Requirements

a) The controller of Illinois Products Company plans to prepare a discounted cash flow analysis of this investment proposal and has asked you to prepare correct calculations of:

1. The required investment in the new equipment.

2. The recurring annual cash flows.

Explain the treatment of each item you treat differently from the original analysis prepared by the sales manager.

b) Calculate the net present value of the proposed investment in the new equipment and indicate whether the investment proposal is acceptable.

(CMA Adapted)

14–28 Project Screening and Evaluation with Risk: Multiple Criteria

Transhemisphere uses a capital budgeting committee to evaluate and approve capital expenditure proposals. Because the committee is composed of busy executives, a staff has been assigned to assist the committee in the mechanical aspects of proposal evaluation. As a member of this staff you have been requested to evaluate five mutually exclusive capital expenditure proposals.

Transhemisphere uses multiple criteria in the evaluation of capital expenditure proposals. The criteria are designed to consider the time period monies invested in a project are unavailable for other purposes, the maximum possible time-adjusted loss on a project, and the time-adjusted relative profitability of a project. To assist in monitoring accepted proposals, the committee also requests information regarding the minimum annual cash flows required for time-adjusted break-even. The criteria are applied on a sequential basis, with only proposals that meet the earlier criteria receiving further evaluation.

Specific procedures you are to follow are as follows:

1. Determine the expected payback and bail-out period of each proposal. Only proposals having an expected bail-out and/or payback period of three years or less are subject to further evaluation.

2. Evaluate the net present value of the pessimistic cash flows associated with each project using Transhemisphere's cost of capital of 16 percent. Projects whose pessimistic cash flows have a net negative present value of $50,000 or more are eliminated from further consideration.

3. Rank the remaining projects on the basis of the internal rate of return of their expected cash flows.

4. For the highest ranked project, determine the minimum annual net cash inflows needed to obtain an internal rate of return equal to the company's cost of capital.

Information pertaining to the five capital expenditure proposals you have been asked to evaluate is presented as follows in thousands of dollars (000):

Proposal	Initial Investment	Disposal Value at End of Year			Pessimistic		Expected	
		One	Two	Three	Annual Cash Flow	Life	Annual Cash Flow	Life
A	$196	$150	$100	$-0-	$ 40	7 years	$ 50	10 years
B	500	400	350	-0-	75	10 years	110	12 years
C	400	300	100	-0-	40	8 years	50	10 years
D	420	250	200	150	100	7 years	100	10 years
E	250	150	75	-0-	15	9 years	75	12 years

The nature of the investments is such that none of them has a disposal value after the end of their third year.

Requirements

a) Following Transhemisphere's capital budgeting procedures, evaluate the five proposals.

b) Regardless of Transhemisphere's procedures, which proposal do you recommend and why?

Round calculations to the nearest dollar. Do not interpolate.

14–29 Post-Audit and Reevaluation of Investment Proposal: NPV

The Anthony Company's capital budgeting committee is evaluating a capital expenditure proposal for the production of a stereo tuner to be sold as an add-on feature for television sets not equipped for stereophonic sound. The proposal calls for an independent contractor to construct the necessary facilities by 12/31/x0 at a total cost of $250,000. Payment for all construction costs will be made on that date and an additional $50,000 in cash will be made available on 12/31/x0 for working capital to support sales and production activities.

Management anticipates that the stereo tuner has a limited market life because of the high probability that by 19x7 all quality television sets will have built-in stereo tuners. Accordingly, the proposal specifies that production will cease on 12/31/x6. The investment in working capital will be recovered on that date, and the production facilities will be sold for $30,000. Predicted net cash inflows from operations for 19x1 through 19x6 are as follows:

19x1	$100,000
19x2	100,000
19x3	100,000
19x4	40,000
19x5	40,000
19x6	40,000

The Anthony Company has a time value of money of 16 percent. For capital budgeting purposes all cash flows are assumed to occur at the end of each year.

Requirements

a) Evaluate the capital expenditure proposal using the net present value method. Should Anthony accept the proposal?

b) Assume the capital expenditure proposal is accepted, but that construction delays caused by labor unrest and difficulties in obtaining the necessary construction permits delay the completion of the project. Payments totaling $200,000 were made to the construction company on 12/31/x0 for 19x0 construction. However, completion is now scheduled for 12/31/x1, and an additional $100,000 will be required to complete construction. If the project is continued, the additional $100,000 will be paid on 12/31/x1 and the plant will begin operations on 1/1/x2.

   Because of the cost overruns, the capital budgeting committee requests a reevaluation of the project in early 19x1, before agreeing to any additional expenditures. After much effort, the following revised predictions of net operating cash inflows are developed:

19x2	$120,000
19x3	100,000
19x4	40,000
19x5	40,000
19x6	40,000

   The working capital investment and disinvestment and the plant salvage values are not changed, except that the cash for working capital would now be made available on 12/31/x1.

   Use the net present value method to reevaluate the initial decision to accept the proposal. Given the currently available information about the project, should it have been accepted in 19x0? *Hint:* Determine the net present value as of 12/31/x0, assuming management has not committed Anthony to the proposal.

c) Given the situation that exists in early 19x1, should management continue or cancel the project? Assume the facilities have a current salvage value of $50,000. *Hint:* Assume the decision is being made on 1/1/x1.

14–50 Post-Audit and Reevaluation of Investment Proposal: IRR

Throughout his four years in college, Ronald King worked at the local Beef Burger Restaurant in College City. Although the working conditions were good and the pay was not bad, Ron believed he could do a much better job of managing the restaurant than the current owner-manager. In particular, Ron felt that the proper use of marketing campaigns and sales incentives, such as selling a second burger for a 25 percent discount, could increase annual sales by 50 percent.

Just before graduation in 19x2, when Ron inherited $500,000 from his great-uncle, he decided to give serious consideration to buying the restaurant. It seemed like a good idea because he liked the town and its college atmosphere, knew the business, and always wanted to work for himself. He also knew that the current owner wanted to sell the restaurant and retire to Florida.

As part of a small business management course, Ron developed the following income statement for the restaurant's 19x1 operations:

Beef Burger Restaurant: College City
Income Statement
For the year ended December 31, 19x1

Sales:		$450,000
Expenses:		
✓ Cost of food	$150,000	
✓ Supplies	20,000	
Employee expenses	140,000	
Utilities	28,000	
Property taxes	20,000	
Insurance	10,000	
Advertising	8,000	
Depreciation	60,000	−436,000
Net income		$ 14,000

non cash (handwritten annotation pointing to Depreciation)

Ron believed the cost of food and supplies were all variable, the employee expenses and utilities were half variable and half fixed in 19x1, and all other expenses were fixed.

If Ron purchased the restaurant and followed through on his plans, he believed there would be a 50 percent increase in unit sales volume and all variable costs. Of the fixed costs, only advertising would increase, by $12,000. The use of discounts and special promotions would, however, limit the increase in sales revenue to only 40 percent even though sales volume increased 50 percent.

Requirements

a) Determine:

Deprec. (handwritten)

1. The current annual net cash inflow. → 14,000 + 60,000 = $74,000 (handwritten)

2. The predicted annual net cash inflow if Ron executes his plans and his assumptions are correct. → take into acct fixed & var. costs & ↑ sales Rev. (handwritten)

b) Ron believes his plan would produce equal net cash inflows during each of the next 15 years, the period remaining on a long-term lease for the land the restaurant is built on. At the end of that time, the restaurant would have to be demolished at a predicted net cost of $80,000. Assuming Ron would otherwise invest the money in bonds expected to yield 12 percent, determine the maximum amount he could pay for the restaurant. *need to subtract 80,000 at end.* (handwritten)

c) Assume Ron accepts an offer from the current owner to buy the restaurant for $400,000. Unfortunately, although the expected increase in sales volume does occur, customers make much more extensive use of the promotions than Ron had anticipated. As a result, total sales revenues are 8 percent below projections. Furthermore, to improve employee attitudes, Ron gave a 10 percent raise immediately after purchasing the restaurant.

Reevaluate the initial decision using the actual sales revenue and the increase in labor costs, assuming conditions will remain unchanged over the remaining life of the project. Was the investment decision a wise one? Round calculations to the nearest dollar.

d) Ron can sell the restaurant to a large franchise operator for $300,000. Alternatively, he believes that additional annual marketing expenditures and changes in promotions costing $20,000 per year can bring the sales revenues up to their original projections. Should Ron sell the restaurant, or keep it and make the additional expenditures? Round calculations to the nearest dollar. *Hint:* Ron has just bought the restaurant.

REVIEW PROBLEM SOLUTION

Basic computations:

Initial investment:	
Depreciable assets	$27,740
Working capital	3,000
Total	$30,740
Operation:	
Cash receipts	$25,000
Cash expenditures	−15,000
Net cash inflow	$10,000
Disinvestment:	
Sale of depreciable assets	$ 2,000
Recovery of working capital	3,000
Total	$ 5,000

a) Net present value at a 10 percent discount rate:

	Predicted Cash Inflows (Outflows)	Year(s) of Cash Flows	10% Present Value Factor	Present Value of Cash Flows
Initial investment	$(30,740)	0	1.000	$(30,740)
Operation	10,000	1–4	3.170	31,700
Disinvestment	5,000	4	0.683	3,415
Net present value of all cash flows				$ 4,375

b) Internal rate of return:

Because the proposal has a positive net present value when discounted at 10 percent, its internal rate of return must be greater than 10 percent. Through a trial-and-error approach, the internal rate of return is determined to be 16 percent.

	Predicted Cash Inflows (Outflows)	Year(s) of Cash Flows	16% Present Value Factor	Present Value of Cash Flows
Initial investment	$(30,740)	0	1.000	$(30,740)
Operation	10,000	1–4	2.798	27,980
Disinvestment	5,000	4	0.552	2,760
Net present value of all cash flows				$ 0

c) Payback period $= \dfrac{\$30,740}{\$10,000}$

$\qquad\qquad\qquad = \underline{3.074}$ years

d) Accounting rate of return on initial and average investments:

Annual net cash inflow from operations	$10,000
Less average annual depreciation [($27,740 − $2,000)/4]	− 6,435
Average annual increase in net income	$ 3,565

Average investment $\quad = \dfrac{\$30,740 + \$5,000}{2}$

$\qquad\qquad\qquad\qquad = \underline{\$17,870}$

$\begin{array}{l}\text{Accounting rate of return} \\ \text{on initial investment}\end{array} = \dfrac{\$3,565}{\$30,740}$

$\qquad\qquad\qquad\qquad = \underline{0.1160} \quad \text{or} \quad \underline{11.60\%}$

$\begin{array}{l}\text{Accounting rate of return} \\ \text{on average investment}\end{array} = \dfrac{\$3,565}{\$17,870}$

$\qquad\qquad\qquad\qquad = \underline{0.1995} \quad \text{or} \quad \underline{19.95\%}$

CHAPTER 15

Impact of Taxes on Capital Budgeting and Other Management Decisions

Upon completion of this chapter you should:

- Be able to describe the four primary types of taxes.
- Be familiar with the general tax computation model for a corporation.
- Understand the major effects of taxes on capital budgeting decisions.
- Be able to determine the net present value of capital expenditure proposals taking tax effects into consideration.
- Be able to identify the four major types of organizational forms and describe generally the tax treatment of each.
- Be aware of the tax considerations affecting the selection of an organizational form and tax entity.
- Be familiar with several major areas in which alternative tax treatments are available.

It is important for managers to be able to determine the economic impact of *taxes* on business decisions. Because cash outlays for all expenses adversely affect profitability and liquidity, planning and control measures should apply to all costs, including taxes. A primary consideration of the manager in tax planning is tax avoidance. Unlike *tax evasion* (which is the illegal nonpayment of taxes), tax avoidance is the reduction of taxes through legitimate means. For example, failure to report a gain on the sale of assets constitutes tax evasion, whereas planning the disposition of assets through a nontaxable exchange for other assets is a legitimate means of tax avoidance.

In situations where tax avoidance is not an available or feasible option, the manager should consider deferring the payment of taxes. Tax deferral refers to the planning and timing of transactions so that the taxpayer qualifies for delays in the payment of taxes. Because of the time value of money, delaying tax payments into the future reduces their present value. Therefore, the objective in tax deferral is to plan transactions within the provisions of the tax law so that the present value of present and future tax payments is minimized.

The purpose of this chapter is to provide an overview of the major types of taxes that affect management decisions. The specific effects of taxes on capital budgeting and other management decisions are also discussed. Because of the complexity of this subject, our objective is to expose the reader only to the general significance of taxes in business decision making. For specific applications of tax laws, managers should ordinarily consult the advice of experts in the field of taxation.

TYPES OF TAXES

The types of taxes that affect business enterprises may be classified into four categories: income taxes, property taxes, excise taxes, and foreign taxes.

Income Taxes

An **income tax** is any tax that is based on income. Some examples of income that is taxed are the incomes of individuals, corporations, estates, and trusts. The income of proprietorships or partnerships is not taxed directly; instead, it is passed through to the owners who must pay taxes on the business income based on their individual tax status. The federal government and most states and several large cities collect income taxes from individuals and corporations.

Property Taxes

A **property tax** is a tax based on the ownership of property and is usually determined by multiplying a statutory tax rate (often referred to as the tax millage) times the assessed value of the property. The assessed value is usually a specified percentage of estimated fair market value. Tangible property taxes are levied on real property (land and buildings) and tangible personal property (such as equipment and inventories). Intangible personal property taxes are levied on property such as investment securities and receivables. There is no federal property tax, tangible or intangible; however, state and local governments rely heavily on property taxes.

Excise Taxes

An **excise tax** is a tax on an activity performed by, or a privilege granted to, the taxed party. Excise taxes are the broadest form of taxes and include many different types of taxes, such as sales taxes, licenses to do business, cigarette and alcohol taxes, gasoline and other fuel taxes, telephone taxes, import duties, and gift taxes. Excise taxes are levied by government authorities at federal, state, and local levels.

Foreign Taxes

Businesses that operate in foreign countries or conduct transactions with foreign enterprises may be affected by taxes imposed by foreign governments. Most of the types of taxes discussed above can also be found in various foreign countries. In addition, several European countries have adopted a value added tax.

Under a **value added tax,** manufacturers pay taxes based on the value added to goods that they produce during the period. For example, if a manufacturer of electric motors purchases component parts for $25 and sells assembled motors for $45, the value added is $20. The value added tax would be $20 times the tax rate. An appliance manufacturer purchasing the motors for $45, and adding other parts and supplies costing $105, pays value added tax only on the excess of its selling price over $150 ($45 plus $105). Under a value added system, the total value of the final consumable product is taxed as the product moves through the manufacturing and distribution process, but without any duplication of taxes. Several members in the U.S. Congress have advocated the adoption of a value added tax as a partial or total substitute for business income taxes. Many foreign countries, however, have both value added and income taxes.

MEASURING TAXES

For all types of taxes two basic variables determine the amount of taxes owed—the tax base and the tax rate. A **tax base** is a monetary measurement of the conditions or activities subject to taxes. Examples of tax bases are taxable income for income taxes, assessed value of property for property taxes, and total sales for sales taxes. A **tax rate** is a percentage that is multiplied times the tax base to determine total taxes.

For most taxes, the tax base is either provided directly by the taxing authority or is easily determined; however, computing the tax base for income taxes is usually somewhat difficult. Federal and other income taxes are administered under a self-assessment system where the party being taxed has the responsibility of measuring the tax base and computing the taxes due. The general procedure for computing the tax base for corporate income taxes is as follows:

Total revenues earned	$xx	
Less: Nontaxable revenues	xx	
Gross income		$xx
Total expenses and deductions	$xx	
Less: Nondeductible expenses	xx	
Allowable deductions		−xx
Taxable income		$xx

Income tax rates are normally *graduated*; that is, the tax rate increases as taxable income increases. For example, federal income taxes on corporations are computed as follows:

- 15 percent on the first $50,000 of taxable income,
- 25 percent on the next $25,000 of taxable income, and
- 34 percent on all taxable income in excess of $75,000.[1]

Higher tax rates are applied only to *marginal,* or additional, taxable income; therefore, a corporation that has $100,000 of taxable income pays taxes at the 34 percent rate on only the last $25,000 of taxable income. On taxable income of $100,000, total federal income taxes are $22,250, computed as follows:

---

[1] An additional 5 percent tax is imposed on income between $100,000 and $335,000, which in effect creates a flat tax of 34 percent for corporations with taxable income of $335,000 or more.

15% of $50,000	$ 7,500
25% of 25,000	6,250
34% of 25,000	8,500
Total taxes	$22,250

TAXES IN CAPITAL BUDGETING DECISIONS

Capital budgeting was discussed in Chapter 14 as a process for evaluating the desirability of alternative capital expenditure proposals. Using present value techniques, alternative capital investment projects can be reduced to a common basis for making relative comparisons. All future cash outflows and inflows are converted to present value equivalents using a predetermined discount rate. Cash flows from capital expenditures usually affect cash outflows for income taxes.

Cash flows related to capital expenditures may affect taxes in several different ways:

- Operating income[2] generated by capital expenditures increases income taxes.

- Reduced operating costs resulting from capital expenditures increase income taxes.

- Depreciation of capital assets reduces income taxes.

- A gain on the sale of capital assets increases income taxes, whereas a loss on the sale of capital assets decreases income taxes.

Increased Revenues

A capital expenditure that is expected to generate annual cash flows of $10,000 before taxes will not produce net annual cash flows of $10,000 unless the revenue from the project is nontaxable. Ordinarily, taxes must be paid on a capital project's net revenue, thus reducing the net cash inflow. Assuming a 34 percent tax rate,[3] the annual after-tax cash flow is $6,600:

After-tax cash flow = Pretax cash flow − (Pretax cash flow × Tax rate),
After-tax cash flow = $10,000 − ($10,000 × 0.34)
                              = $6,600.

Most managers prefer to use the following variation of the above equation:

After-tax cash flow = Pretax cash flow × (1 − Tax rate),
After-tax cash flow = $10,000 × (1 − 0.34)
                              = $6,600.

---

[2] Operating income equals revenues less the expenses generated by a capital expenditure.

[3] Throughout this chapter, unless otherwise stated, the maximum corporate tax rate of 34 percent is used to illustrate the impact of taxes on management decisions.

The after-tax cash flow amount is multiplied times the appropriate discount factor to determine the present value of after-tax cash flows.

Decreased Costs

Many capital outlays have the objective of reducing costs rather than increasing revenues. Cost reduction measures decrease the amount of tax deductible expenses, increase taxable income, and increase income taxes. The after-tax effect of cost reductions can be computed using the equation discussed previously. For example, if a capital project is expected to save $8,000 per year in costs, the after-tax cost savings, assuming a 34 percent tax rate, are $5,280 [$8,000 × (1 − 0.34)].

Depreciation

Depreciation is a systematic procedure for allocating the acquisition cost of a capital asset over its useful life. The annual depreciation allocation is not accompanied by a cash outlay; however, it is an expense deduction in computing taxable income. Therefore, depreciation does provide an indirect inflow of cash from the reduction of taxes that it produces. This reduction of income taxes is often referred to as the **depreciation tax shield.** Since the income tax law does not allow capital expenditures to be fully deducted from income when they are made, it is only logical that depreciation deductions should be allowed.

The current tax rules governing the depreciation deduction represent a combination of rules under two previous tax laws—the 1969 Act and the 1981 Act. The 1969 Act established the **Asset Depreciation Range (ADR)** guidelines for determining the appropriate useful life for depreciable assets. The ADR guidelines provide estimated useful lives for many different types of assets, including assets related to specialized industries. The 1981 Act created the **Accelerated Cost Recovery System (ACRS)** and assigned all depreciable assets to one of four broad asset classifications, which were subject to highly accelerated rates of cost recovery. As originally designed, ACRS depreciation periods recovered cost over a period much shorter than an asset's estimated useful life.

Current depreciation rules, which are based on the Tax Reform Act of 1986, require two steps in determining the depreciation deduction. First, the ADR guidelines are used to determine the estimated useful lives of depreciable assets. Second, based on their ADR lives, assets are assigned to ACRS classes, which determine the allowable depreciation period and depreciation method. Typically, the ACRS depreciation life is shorter than the ADR estimated useful life. For example, if an asset has an ADR estimated useful life of four years, it is classified into a three-year ACRS classification and is depreciated using the 200 percent declining balance method. The result is that most assets are depreciated over a shorter period for tax purposes than for accounting purposes.

There are eight different ACRS classes, six for personal property and two for real property. Exhibit 15–1 presents a summary of these eight classes, their related ADRs and depreciation methods, and examples of assets in each class. Note that personal property may be depreciated over periods ranging from

EXHIBIT 15–1   Tax Depreciation Asset Lives and Calculation Methods

ADR Asset Lives	ACRS Life	Depreciation Method	Examples
Personal property:			
4 years or less	3 years	200% declining balance	Specialized tools, certain breeding stock
More than 4 but less than 10 years	5 years	200% declining balance	Automobiles, computers, private airplanes
10 or more but less than 16 years	7 years	200% declining balance	Single-purpose agricultural or horticultural structures, office furniture and fixtures, and most machinery and equipment
15 or more but less than 20 years	10 years	200% declining balance	Railroad cars, barges, tugs
20 or more but less than 25 years	15 years	150% declining balance	Telecommunication distribution-plant equipment
25 years or more	20 years	150% declining balance	Municipal sewers, hydroelectric plants
Real property:			
All residential	27.5 years	Straight-line	Apartments and other rental housing
All nonresidential	31.5 years	Straight-line	Offices, warehouses

three years to twenty years using the 200 percent or 150 percent declining balance depreciation methods, whereas real property may be depreciated over 27.5 or 31.5 years using only the straight-line depreciation method. Assets for which an ADR has not been provided are depreciated in the seven-year ACRS class. For personal property, the depreciation method may be switched to straight-line at the point where it provides higher depreciation deductions than the declining balance method. This will always occur in the year in which the straight-line rate, based on the remaining life, is greater than the original declining balance depreciation rate.

To avoid having to recognize various short periods of depreciation in the years of acquisition and retirement, most depreciation calculations for tax purposes must assume a midyear convention, which treats property as if it were placed in service at midyear in the year of acquisition and retired at midyear in the last year of its depreciable life. The midyear convention in effect causes the depreciation deductions for an asset to be spread over one year more than the number of years represented by its ACRS classification. For example, an asset in the three-year ACRS classification would be attributed one-half year's depreciation in years 1 and 4, and a full year's depreciation in years 2 and 3, resulting in the equivalent of three full years of depreciation spread over four years.

An alternative to the ACRS method of depreciation is also available. It allows taxpayers to depreciate assets over their ADR estimated lives using the straight-line method. For this alternative calculation, assets for which there is no ADR life are depreciated over 12 years and real property is depreciated over 40 years, except for low-income housing, which is depreciated over 27.5 years.

To illustrate the present value of the depreciation tax shield, assume that machinery purchased in 19x1 has an ADR estimated useful life of four years and a depreciable cost of $15,000. The amount of the annual depreciation tax shield will vary depending on whether the taxpayer elects to use the ACRS class life of three years with 200 percent double declining depreciation or the alternative straight-line depreciation for the four-year ADR useful life. Under both options, one-half year's depreciation would be recognized in the first and last years of the depreciation period.

The annual ACRS depreciation deductions calculated using the 200 percent declining balance method, and the related tax savings are as follows:

Year	(1) Depreciation Base*	(2) Depreciation Rate**	(3) (1) × (2) Annual Depreciation	(4) Tax Rate	(5) (3) × (4) Tax Shield
1	$15,000	$\frac{1}{2} \times \frac{2}{3}$	$ 5,000	0.34	$1,700
2	10,000	$\frac{2}{3}$	6,667	0.34	2,267
3	3,333	$\frac{2}{3}$	2,222	0.34	755
4	1,111	$\frac{1}{1}$	1,111	0.34	378
			$15,000		$5,100

* Under declining balance depreciation, the depreciation base is the book value (cost − accumulated depreciation) of the asset at the beginning of the year. When a company switches to the straight-line method (as this company did in year 4), the depreciation base for the remaining life of the asset is the book value of the asset at the beginning of the year in which the switch occurred.

** The depreciation rate is 200 percent times the straight-line rate of $\frac{1}{3}$, or $\frac{2}{3}$. Applying the midyear convention, the depreciation in the first year is one-half the normal first year depreciation. At the end of year 3, the depreciation method is switched to straight-line, which results in writing off 100 percent of the book value balance in the first half of year 4.

The annual straight-line depreciation deductions using the ADR asset life of four years and the related tax savings are as follows:

Year	(1) Cost	(2) Depreciation Rate	(3) (1) × (2) Annual Depreciation*	(4) Tax Rate	(5) (3) × (4) Tax Shield
1	$15,000	$\frac{1}{2} \times \frac{1}{4}$	$ 1,875	0.34	$ 637.50
2	15,000	$\frac{1}{4}$	3,750	0.34	1,275.00
3	15,000	$\frac{1}{4}$	3,750	0.34	1,275.00
4	15,000	$\frac{1}{4}$	3,750	0.34	1,275.00
5	15,000	$\frac{1}{2} \times \frac{1}{4}$	1,875	0.34	637.50
			$15,000		$5,100.00

* Applying the midyear convention, the depreciation amounts for years 1 and 5 are equal to one-half the normal full-year straight-line amount. Consequently, even though the ACRS life is four years, it takes five years to recognize four full years of depreciation.

Using a 12 percent discount rate, the present values of the depreciation tax shields for ACRS and straight-line depreciation are summarized below.

Year	(1) 12 Percent Present Value Factor	ACRS Rates (2) Tax Shield	(3) (1) × (2) Present Value of Tax Shield	Straight-Line Rates (4) Tax Shield	(5) (1) × (4) Present Value of Tax Shield
1	0.893	$1,700	$1,518	$ 637.50	$ 569
2	0.797	2,267	1,807	1,275.00	1,016
3	0.712	755	538	1,275.00	908
4	0.636	378	240	1,275.00	811
5	0.567	—	—	637.50	361
		$5,100	$4,103	$5,100.00	$3,665

Note that both depreciation methods produce $5,100 of tax shield over the life of the capital project. However, because of the differences in the timing of these reductions, the present value of the depreciation tax savings is greater using the ACRS 200 percent declining balance method than using the alternative straight-line method. As long as there is taxable income to be absorbed by depreciation, the method that provides the most accelerated recovery of capital asset cost will also provide the highest present value of the tax shield.

Gain or Loss on Sale of Capital Assets

To determine the total net present value of a capital expenditure, it is necessary to include as cash inflow any expected proceeds from the sale of the asset at the end of its useful life. If a taxable gain is realized on the sale of an asset, the gain increases income taxes, which reduces the net cash generated by the sale. On the other hand, a loss on the sale of an asset is deducted in computing taxable income and, therefore, reduces income taxes. In this case the tax reduction represents additional cash inflow generated by the asset. This cash savings is added to the selling price of the asset to determine the net cash generated by the sale.

To illustrate, assume an asset has a book value (cost less accumulated depreciation) of $5,000 and is sold before the end of its useful life for $7,000. The sale results in a taxable gain of $2,000 ($7,000 − $5,000). Cash generated directly by the sale is $7,000, but the $2,000 gain increases taxes by $680 ($2,000 × 0.34); therefore, the net cash generated by the sale of the asset is $6,320 ($7,000 − $680). If the asset sells for only $3,000, there is a tax deductible loss of $2,000 ($3,000 − $5,000) that reduces taxes by $680 ($2,000 × 0.34). In this case the net cash generated is $3,680, the selling price of $3,000 plus the tax savings of $680.

The tax effects of gains and losses related to asset dispositions must also be taken into consideration in a capital budgeting decision that involves replacing an asset currently in use. The gain or loss on the sale of the old asset increases or decreases both taxes and the net cash generated by the sale.

Capital Budgeting with Taxes Illustrated

To illustrate how the various effects of income taxes enter into the capital budgeting analysis, assume that Willoughby's Courier Service is considering purchasing a small delivery truck that costs $12,000 and is predicted to generate cash revenues of $6,000 per year net of operating costs. Willoughby's predicts that it can be sold for $2,500 after six years of use. Willoughby's has a $500 offer from one of its customers for the old truck, which is fully depreciated. The new truck qualifies for ACRS five-year 200 percent declining balance depreciation. Willoughby's capital investment policy requires new capital expenditures to produce a positive net present value using a 12 percent discount rate. The analysis of the proposal, including tax effects, is presented in Exhibit 15–2.

Exhibit 15–2 shows that Willoughby's can expect a positive net present value of $8,458 on the investment after considering all cash flows, including those related to income taxes. Although this alternative might appear to be a desirable investment, Willoughby's should consider all other feasible alternatives before making a decision, including purchasing other trucks, leasing possibilities, and even the alternative of keeping the old truck. In each case, the analysis of cash flows should include the cash flow effects of taxes.

EXHIBIT 15–2   Analysis of Capital Expenditure Including Tax Effects

Cash Flow Item*	(1) Actual Cash Inflows (Outflows)	(2) Year(s) of Cash Flows	(3) 12% Present Value Factor	(4) (1) × (3) Present Value of Cash Flows
Purchase of new truck	$(12,000)	0	1.000	$(12,000)
Sale of old truck	500	0	1.000	500
Taxes on gain on sale of old truck				
($500 × 0.34)	(170)	0	1.000	(170)
Annual operating income generated by truck	6,000	1–6	4.111	24,666
Taxes on annual operating income				
($6,000 × 0.34)	(2,040)	1–6	4.111	(8,386)
Tax savings on depreciation**				
Year 1	816	1	0.893	729
Year 2	1,306	2	0.797	1,041
Year 3	783	3	0.712	557
Year 4	470	4	0.636	299
Year 5	470	5	0.567	266
Year 6	235	6	0.507	119
Sale of new truck	2,500	6	0.507	1,268
Taxes on gain on sale of new truck†				
($2,500 × 0.34)	(850)	6	0.507	(431)
New present value of all cash flows				$ 8,458

* All cash flows occur at the end of the year.

** Depreciation cash flow computations:

Year	Depreciation Base		Depreciation Rate*		Annual Depreciation	Tax Rate		Cash Savings
1	$12,000	×	$\frac{1}{2} \times \frac{2}{5}$	=	$2,400	× 0.34	=	$ 816
2	9,600	×	$\frac{2}{5}$	=	3,840	× 0.34	=	1,306
3	5,760	×	$\frac{2}{5}$	=	2,304	× 0.34	=	783
4	3,456	×	$\frac{2}{5}$	=	1,382	× 0.34	=	470
5	2,074	×	$1 \div 1\frac{1}{2}$	=	1,382	× 0.34	=	470
6	2,074	×	$\frac{1}{2} \div 1\frac{1}{2}$	=	692	× 0.34	=	235

* Depreciation based on five-year ACRS class and the 200 percent declining balance method. Switched to the straight-line method after year four and depreciated the remaining book value of $2,074 over the remaining 1.5 years (year five and one-half of year six).

† The gain on the sale of the truck is equal to the selling price since the truck is fully depreciated on the date of its expected sale.

FORMS OF ORGANIZATION AND TAXES

The income tax consequences of management decisions are often affected by the legal form under which a business is organized. The basic forms of business organization are *proprietorships, partnerships,* and *corporations*. As discussed earlier, the general model for computing taxes includes a tax base and the appropriate tax rates. To evaluate the differences in taxes for the three alternative business forms, it is necessary to analyze differences in their respective income tax bases and tax rates. The following discussion is limited to federal income tax considerations.

Sole Proprietorships

A **sole proprietorship** is an unincorporated business owned by one individual. Legally, a proprietorship is not a separate entity; therefore, business transactions of a proprietorship are taxed as transactions of the individual taxpayer. All business revenues increase and all business expenses reduce the proprietor's individual income tax base. A proprietor combines business net income with all other types of income (such as salaries, interest, and dividends) in determining total taxable income.

Tax rates for individuals range from 15 percent to 28 percent. Under the Tax Reform Act of 1986, single individuals, for years after 1987, pay taxes at the 28 percent rate on all taxable income exceeding $17,850. Married individuals filing joint tax returns reach the 28 percent tax bracket at taxable income of $29,750.

Partnerships

A **partnership** is an unincorporated business owned by two or more individuals.[4] These businesses are required to report taxable income to the Internal Revenue Service (IRS); however, they do not pay taxes on their income. Instead, *the income of partnerships is allocated to the individual partners* who include their pro rata share of partnership income in their individual taxable income. All income of the partnership is allocated to the partners whether or not an equal amount of cash or other assets is distributed to the partners. Consequently, partners may be required to pay taxes on income that they actually have not received during the period. Partnership income is taxed to the individual partners at rates applicable to the partners' income, that is, at a maximum rate of 28 percent for individuals and 34 percent for corporations.

Corporations

A **corporation** is a legally recognized entity created by an act of the state and empowered to conduct business activities within the provisions of a corporate charter issued by the government of the state of incorporation. As a separate

---

[4] Although partners are ordinarily individuals, other entities may also form a partnership. For example, the partners of a partnership may consist of a combination of individuals, corporations, trusts, and even other partnerships.

legal entity, a corporation is not dependent on its owners for legal recognition. It can conduct in its own name almost any transaction that an individual can conduct.

Unlike proprietorships and partnerships, a corporation is a separate taxable entity that must pay taxes on its taxable income. In addition, any dividends distributed by a corporation to its owners (shareholders) must be included in the income tax base of the individual owners. Consequently, *dividend income received by corporate stockholders is subject to double taxation*—corporate taxes and individual taxes. To illustrate the potential impact of double taxation, assume that a corporation distributes a $66,000 dividend, representing the amount remaining after subtracting corporate taxes at 34 percent on $100,000 of earnings. Assuming the stockholders receiving the dividends are in the 28 percent tax bracket, they pay $18,480 taxes on the dividends received. The income available to the stockholders after taxes is only $47,520 (or $66,000 less $18,480). As shown below, of the $100,000 in corporate taxable income, corporate taxes of $34,000 and individual taxes of $18,480 are paid for a total of $52,480, leaving only $47,520 to the stockholders after the payment of corporate and individual income taxes.

Corporate income providing dividends	$100,000
Less: Corporate income taxes (34%)	− 34,000
Total dividend distributed	$ 66,000
Less: Individual income taxes (28%)	− 18,480
Income to stockholders after corporate and individual income taxes	$ 47,520

Salaries paid to corporate employees who are also stockholders are deductible business expenses of the corporation in computing taxable income. The income used to pay salaries to stockholders, therefore, avoids corporate taxes and is taxed only to the stockholders. In the example above, if the $100,000 of corporate income that provided the dividends had been distributed as salaries, no corporate income taxes would have been paid. The employee-stockholders would have received the full $100,000 as salaries and would have paid $28,000 ($100,000 × 0.28) in individual taxes, leaving them $72,000 after taxes. By paying salaries instead of dividends, total taxes decrease from $52,480 to $28,000, and total after-tax income available to the employee-shareholders increases from $47,520 to $72,000. Distributions to shareholders cannot be arbitrarily designated as salaries to avoid double taxation. According to the federal tax law, salary payments must be commensurate with services provided by the stockholders to the corporation. Otherwise, the Internal Revenue Service will disallow the salary deduction to the corporation and treat the distribution as a dividend.

Subchapter S Corporations

A **subchapter S corporation** is a business that is legally organized as a corporation, but has opted under a special provision of the tax law to be taxed as a partnership. A subchapter S corporation enjoys the legal advantages of incorporation (such as limited liability and unlimited life), without the disadvantages of corporate taxation. Like a partnership, the income of a subchapter S corporation is allocated to the owners and included in their taxable income whether or not it is actually distributed to them. The corporate income is allocated in proportion to the ownership percentages of the stockholders.

To qualify for subchapter S tax treatment, a corporation must (1) have no more than 35 stockholders; (2) have only one class of stock; (3) have no stockholders other than individuals, estates, and trusts; (4) have the approval of all stockholders for the tax option treatment; and (5) receive no more than 25 percent of its gross receipts from passive sources such as dividends, interest, rents, royalties, and gains on stocks or other securities.

SELECTING A TAX ENTITY

Selection of an organizational form and tax entity is an easy decision for most large business enterprises. Clearly, the majority of all large organizations find it advantageous and necessary to operate and be taxed as *corporations*. The advantages of incorporation for large businesses are related to the following:

- The ease with which capital funds can be generated through the issuance of publicly traded securities.

- The ease with which ownership can be readily transferred through the sale of shares of stock.

- The limitation of liability for owners of corporate stock to the amounts of their investments.

- The unlimited life of corporate organizations.

Although examples are not as numerous, some very large businesses operate as partnerships. For example, most public accounting firms are organized as partnerships; several of them have more than 1,000 partners and generate more than $1 billion in revenues annually. The relatively small number of owners and the low turnover of ownership make the partnership alternative feasible for these organizations. Most large corporations, however, have thousands (in some cases millions) of different owners, and changes in ownership occur daily as shares of capital stock are purchased and sold. The corporate form is the only feasible alternative for these organizations.

Organizations that are not constrained by their large size to operate as corporations may base the organizational decision to a large extent on tax considerations. Although there are no clear-cut rules for determining which organizational form and tax entity should be adopted, there are several tax-related variables discussed below that should be considered.

Utilization of Income

Business income can be either distributed to the owners or reinvested into the business for operating or expansion purposes. If the owners anticipate distribution of profits, incorporation poses the potential problem of double taxation. Even if earnings are not distributed, incorporation probably produces the highest taxes since the maximum corporate rate is higher than the maximum individual rate (34 percent versus 28 percent).

Utilization of Operating Losses

If a business has a negative taxable income (that is, expenses exceed revenues), the result is an **operating loss.** Obviously, in this situation no income taxes are due on current business operations; however, in some cases the taxpayer may be able to offset current business losses against profits or gains from other sources, or even against the organization's profits from other years. From the standpoint of operating losses, it is generally desirable to use the losses to offset profits from other sources. For example, if an individual has two businesses and one has taxable income of $10,000, whereas the other has an operating loss of $10,000, the taxpayer would prefer not to pay any taxes since the combined net income is zero. Operating losses of one business can be offset against profits of another business owned by the taxpayer only if the businesses are organized as proprietorships, partnerships, or subchapter S corporations. The income or loss of a regular corporation ordinarily cannot be combined with that of another corporation, except for corporations that qualify for consolidated tax reporting.

All types of tax entities are permitted to apply operating losses to reduce taxable income for the previous three years and the following fifteen years. When losses are used to reduce taxable income of previous years, the taxes that were paid in those years are refunded. Losses applied to future periods merely reduce taxable income and taxes due for those years. When applying current operating losses to other years, the losses must first be carried back to the third preceding year. If all the loss is not absorbed by the income of that year, the remainder is applied to the second preceding year, then to the first preceding year, and then to the fifteen years following the current period. With the carryback and carryover provisions, most operating losses are usually eventually used, but it may take as long as fifteen years to realize the total tax benefits from the current period's losses.

Employee Benefits

As explained earlier, a stockholder of a corporation may be an employee of the company and receive salary payments that are deductible as expenses by the corporation in computing its taxable income. The concept of owner-employee does not apply to proprietorships and partnerships because these businesses are inseparable from their owners. If a proprietorship or partnership deducts payments to its owners as salaries, these deductions are offset by the salaries received, which are included in the owners' taxable incomes.

All businesses are allowed under the tax law to deduct the cost of qualified fringe benefits provided for their employees, including medical insurance, certain death benefits, certain meals and lodging, recreation, and deferred compensation benefits. These expense deductions are available even for benefits paid to employees who are also stockholders of the corporations. Because proprietors and partners cannot be employees of their own companies, these tax deductible employee benefits are not available to proprietorships or partnerships. However, the tax laws allow individuals who are proprietors or partners to take a personal deduction for certain contributions to qualified retirement plans. There is no provision for individuals to deduct costs associated with the other employee benefits named above.

Dividends Received Deduction

A *dividends received deduction* is a deduction from gross income granted to *corporations* based on a percentage of dividends received from investments in other corporations. Corporations are permitted to deduct 80 percent of the dividends received from other domestic corporations, thus paying taxes on only 20 percent of the dividends. Proprietorships, partnerships, and subchapter S corporations are not allowed this deduction.

If a business receives dividends that are expected to be reinvested in the business, the corporate dividends deduction may be a significant advantage related to the corporate form. However, if the dividends received are distributed, the owner-stockholders are required to include them in their taxable incomes.

Capital Gains and Losses

A **capital asset** is generally defined for tax purposes as an asset held for investment gain; it, therefore, excludes assets such as inventory, accounts receivables, and assets used in the business such as land, buildings, and equipment. A gain or loss on the sale of a capital asset is called a **capital gain or loss.** The excess of capital gains over capital losses is a net capital gain. Conversely, the excess of capital losses over capital gains is a net capital loss.

Corporations and individuals are required to include net capital gains in taxable income subject to taxes at ordinary income rates. Corporations are not permitted to deduct net capital losses from other taxable income. Net capital losses by corporations can be carried back three years and forward five years and used to reduce capital gains for those years. Individuals are permitted to deduct capital losses in the current year from other taxable income up to an annual limit of $3,000 with any excess carried forward indefinitely to reduce future capital gains or to be deducted against future taxable income.

From the above discussion it is obvious that there is no clear answer to the question of which organizational form provides the greatest tax advantage. On certain points incorporation is preferred, whereas on other points a noncorporate form (proprietorship or partnership) is more desirable. Each business situation must be evaluated based on its particular circumstances to determine the most desirable organizational structure from the standpoint of taxes.

OTHER TAX CONSIDERATIONS FOR MANAGEMENT

In tax accounting, just as in financial accounting, there are several areas where alternative methods and treatments are available for measuring taxable revenues and deductible expenses. In most cases the alternative selected for financial accounting purposes does not necessarily have to be the same method chosen for tax purposes. The alternative chosen for *financial accounting purposes* should be dictated by the company's particular circumstances and management's desire to present fairly the company's financial picture. For *tax purposes* the choice among alternative treatments is a management decision that should be aimed at minimizing taxes and maximizing the net present value of future cash flows. Economically, the tax alternative decision is similar to a product pricing decision or a capital budgeting decision. Several tax-related areas where management decisions are often required are discussed below.

Depreciation Alternatives

Before 1981, the costs of assets used in a trade or business were recoverable, for tax purposes, through depreciation using straight-line, sum-of-years'-digits, or declining balance depreciation. The laws restricted the applicability of these methods based on the types of assets in use and their expected useful lives.

The Economic Recovery Tax Act of 1981 replaced traditional depreciation methods (sum-of-the-years'-digits and declining balance) with the *Accelerated Cost Recovery System*. Initially, the ACRS provided for the recovery of asset costs over shortened time periods using statutory depreciation rates that approximate declining balance depreciation during the earlier years and sum-of-the-years'-digits depreciation during the remainder of the recovery period. The Tax Reform Act of 1986 generally lengthened the depreciation period and replaced the ACRS statutory rates with 200 percent or 150 percent declining balance depreciation for personal property and straight-line depreciation for real property. The alternative of using straight-line depreciation and longer asset lives is also available under the 1986 law for all depreciable assets.

All depreciation methods provide an absolute tax shield equal to the cost of the depreciable asset times the tax rate. However, as observed in the capital budgeting discussion, *because of variations in the timing of the tax shield, accelerated depreciation rates produce the greatest present value of the future tax benefits from depreciation.*

Inventory Costing Alternatives

Whenever a company has inventory on hand at the end of the year, the total cost of goods available for sale during the year must be allocated between goods that were sold during the year and goods that are on hand at the end of the year. In some cases, it is appropriate to determine by specific identification the costs of units sold and units still on hand. In many cases it is necessary for organizations to use an arbitrary cost flow method in making the allocation.

Even if specific costs can be determined, it may be advantageous to use a cost flow method to gain maximum benefit from the provisions in the tax law. For tax purposes, a company may use either a specific cost or a cost flow method based on a first-in, first-out (FIFO), last-in, first-out (LIFO), or average cost assumption. FIFO assigns the cost of the earliest acquired units to cost of goods sold, and the cost of the latest acquired units to ending inventory. LIFO assigns the cost of the latest acquired units to cost of goods sold, and the cost of the earliest acquired units to ending inventory. The average method assigns the average cost of all units available during the period to both units sold and units in ending inventory.

During *inflationary periods* FIFO produces the lowest cost of goods sold, the highest taxable income, and the highest taxes, whereas LIFO results in the highest cost of goods sold, the lowest taxable income, and the lowest taxes. The average cost method results in amounts for cost of goods sold, taxable income, and taxes between the two extremes of FIFO and LIFO. The net economic difference between FIFO and LIFO during an inflationary period is illustrated in Exhibit 15–3. For each of the three years, there are 200 units in both beginning and ending inventory, and 800 units are both purchased and sold. At the beginning of the first year, inventory is valued at $1 per unit, and the purchase price of inventory is $2 in the first year, $3 in the second year, and $4 in the third year. Goods are sold at twice the current purchase price.

Note in Exhibit 15–3 that under FIFO, ending inventory is $200 greater than beginning inventory for each of the three years, whereas under LIFO, beginning and ending inventory are the same. The number of units in beginning and ending inventory is the same for each period; therefore, LIFO is charging all costs of purchases to cost of goods sold. Since the purchase price of units increased by $1 per unit each year, FIFO charges $200 ($1 times 200 units) more to ending inventory each period than for the previous period. Consequently, cost of goods sold is $200 less each year for FIFO than for LIFO, FIFO taxable income for each period is $200 more than LIFO taxable income, and taxes are $68 ($200 × 0.34) more for FIFO than LIFO each year. The obvious conclusion is that *as long as prices are increasing, LIFO costing minimizes taxable income and taxes.*

Revenue Recognition Alternatives

For financial accounting purposes, revenues generally may be reported either as cash is collected (*cash basis*) or as the right to receive the cash is realized (*accrual basis*). Ordinarily, a company must report income for tax purposes on the same basis used for financial reporting purposes. If inventory transactions represent a significant part of a company's operations, sales and cost of goods sold are required for tax and financial accounting purposes to be reported on the accrual basis. An exception to this general rule is available for reporting installment sales for tax purposes. Although most sales made on installment are fully recognized as revenues in the financial statements at the time the sales are

EXHIBIT 15–3 Comparison of Tax Effects of FIFO and LIFO Inventory Costing Methods

	Year 1		Year 2		Year 3	
FIFO inventory method	*Units*	*Cost*	*Units*	*Cost*	*Units*	*Cost*
Beginning inventory	200 at $1	$ 200	200 at $2	$ 400	200 at $3	$ 600
Purchases	800 at $2	1,600	800 at $3	2,400	800 at $4	3,200
Goods available for sale	1,000	$1,800	1,000	$2,800	1,000	$3,800
Ending inventory	− 200 at $2	− 400	− 200 at $3	− 600	− 200 at $4	− 800
Goods sold	800	$1,400	800	$2,200	800	$3,000
Sales	800 at $4	$3,200	800 at $6	$4,800	800 at $8	$6,400
Cost of goods sold		−1,400		−2,200		−3,000
Taxable income		$1,800		$2,600		$3,400
Taxes (at 34%)		$ 612		$ 884		$1,156
LIFO inventory method	*Units*	*Cost*	*Units*	*Cost*	*Units*	*Cost*
Beginning inventory	200 at $1	$ 200	200 at $1	$ 200	200 at $1	$ 200
Purchases	800 at $2	1,600	800 at $3	2,400	800 at $4	3,200
Goods available for sale	1,000	$1,800	1,000	$2,600	1,000	$3,400
Ending inventory	− 200 at $1	− 200	− 200 at $1	− 200	− 200 at $1	− 200
Goods sold	800	$1,600	800	$2,400	800	$3,200
Sales	800 at $4	$3,200	800 at $6	$4,800	800 at $8	$6,400
Cost of goods sold		−1,600		−2,400		−3,200
Taxable income		$1,600		$2,400		$3,200
Taxes (at 34%)		$ 544		$ 816		$1,088
LIFO tax savings						
Excess of taxes under FIFO over taxes under LIFO		$ 68		$ 68		$ 68

made, in some cases, for tax purposes, revenue recognition may be deferred until the cash payments are collected.

To illustrate the *installment sales method,* assume that in 19x4 a company sells $100,000 of merchandise that was purchased for $65,000. The $100,000 is to be collected in five equal annual payments. The total gross profit on the sale is $35,000, or 35 percent of sales. Under the accrual basis the full $35,000 of gross profit is recognized in 19x4; however, under the installment method only the gross profit on the portion of the revenues collected, that is, $7,000 ($20,000 × 0.35), is included in taxable income in 19x4. The taxable income and taxes due in 19x4 under the accrual and installment methods are summarized as follows. Operating expenses are assumed to be $5,000 for the year.

Accrual Method		Installment Method	
Sales	$100,000	Installment collections	$20,000
Cost of goods sold	− 65,000	Gross profit on collections	
Gross profit (35%)	$ 35,000	($20,000 × 35%)	$ 7,000
Operating expenses	− 5,000	Operating expenses	− 5,000
Taxable income	$ 30,000	Taxable income	$ 2,000
Taxes ($30,000 × 0.34)	$ 10,200	Taxes ($2,000 × 0.34)	$ 680

The current tax savings from electing the installment method was $9,520 ($10,200 − $680). In reality this is not a tax savings but rather a tax deferral. The company still has $28,000 of unreported gross profit ($35,000 − $7,000). As the $80,000 balance in unpaid installments is collected, $28,000 ($80,000 × 0.35) of additional gross profit will be reported as taxable income resulting in taxes of $9,520 ($28,000 × 0.34).

The primary benefit in adopting the installment method is related to the time value of the deferred tax payment. By investing the $9,520 tax deferral, additional income can be earned. This income is the economic benefit resulting from the tax deferral. Another potential benefit for smaller companies, whose marginal tax rates are near or below the maximum tax rate, is that by spreading gross profit over several years the marginal tax rate may be lowered resulting in a direct tax savings. This benefit is in addition to the time value benefit realized on the deferral of the tax payment.

Capital Funding Alternatives

As previously stated, corporations are not permitted to deduct dividends paid on equity capital in computing taxable income. Interest expense on borrowed capital, however, is a deductible expense. *Because of the interest expense deduction, debt capital may be less expensive to a company than equity capital.* To illustrate, assume that a company plans to acquire a new building costing $1,000,000 and that the funds can be obtained either by selling 12 percent long-term bonds (debt capital) or by selling 12 percent preferred stock (equity capital). In both cases the annual outlay to service the capital funds is $120,000 ($1,000,000 × 0.12). However, since interest payments are deductible, the annual after-tax cost of the bonds is only $79,200 [$120,000 × (1 − 0.34)], and the annual cost of the bonds after taxes as a percent of the funds obtained is 7.92 percent ($79,200 ÷ $1,000,000), compared to 12 percent for the preferred stock.

Investment Alternatives

When evaluating alternatives for investing excess funds, an important tax consideration is the taxability of the income received on the investment. The tax treatment of periodic income is not the same for all investments. Corporations are allowed an 80 percent special deduction on dividends received from investments in other corporations. Another tax break on investment income available to all taxpayers (corporate and noncorporate) involves interest received on *municipal bonds* issued by government agencies other than the federal government. The federal constitution prohibits the IRS from taxing income on municipal bonds; therefore, the after-tax return for these bonds is the same as the stated interest rate. Taxpayers in the 34 percent tax bracket investing in 10 percent municipal bonds pay no taxes on the interest received, and their after-tax yield on the investment is 10 percent. In contrast, if these taxpayers invest in 12 percent corporate bonds, the interest is taxable and the after-tax yield is only 7.92 percent [$0.12 \times (1 - 0.34)$]. In this case, taking taxes into consideration, the municipal bonds offer a higher return to the investor. Ordinarily, the interest rate on municipal bonds is considerably lower than that on comparable corporate bonds; however, for a taxpayer in a high tax bracket the return on municipal bonds is often higher than the after-tax return on corporate bonds.

SUMMARY

The effects of taxes on business enterprises represent one of the most important considerations in management decision making. Effective management of resources generally requires that efforts be undertaken to avoid or defer taxes through legally available means. Probably the most important category of taxes is income taxes; however, most businesses must also contend with property and excise taxes. Taxes are exacted against businesses by the federal government as well as by state, local, and even foreign governments.

Understanding taxes is particularly important in capital budgeting. Taxes affect capital budgeting decisions through (1) the reduction of operating profits, (2) the depreciation tax shield, and (3) the tax on the sale of assets. Income taxes also play an important role in the selection of the organizational form for a business. Sole proprietorships and partnerships merely serve as conduits through which profits flow into the tax returns of the business owners. Corporations, however, are separate taxable entities whose profits are taxed directly. Corporate profits that provide dividends suffer a double tax burden; they are taxed first to the corporation and then to the stockholders.

The income tax laws provide numerous choices in reporting various types of revenues and expenses for tax purposes. Through careful planning and the effective utilization of alternative tax treatments, management can minimize the adverse effect of taxes on the firm.

KEY TERMS

Accelerated Cost Recovery System (ACRS)
Asset Depreciation Range (ADR)
Capital asset
Capital gain
Capital loss
Corporation
Depreciation tax shield
Excise tax
Income tax

Operating loss
Partnership
Property tax
Sole proprietorship
Subchapter S corporation
Tax avoidance
Tax base
Tax deferral
Tax rate
Value added tax

REVIEW QUESTIONS

15-1 Define and differentiate the following three types of taxes: income taxes, property taxes, and excise taxes.

15-2 Many European countries have a value added tax. Explain how a value added tax works.

15-3 What are the two basic components in determining the amount of any tax?

15-4 Assuming the entire pretax cash flow is subject to taxes, complete the following equation:

$$\text{After-tax cash flow} = \underline{\ ?\ } \times (1 - \underline{\ ?\ }).$$

15-5 Explain the concept of depreciation as an income tax shield.

15-6 What is the absolute amount of the depreciation income tax shield provided by an asset costing $10,000 if the tax rate is 34 percent? Explain.

15-7 Why does ACRS declining balance depreciation usually provide a greater tax shield in real terms than straight-line depreciation?

15-8 Why is it desirable to switch from the declining balance method to the straight-line method before the end of an asset's life?

15-9 Describe generally how the following tax entities are treated for income tax purposes under the federal income tax law: proprietorships, partnerships, and corporations.

15-10 One of the major disadvantages of corporations is the problem of double taxation of dividends paid to shareholders. Explain.

15-11 What is an operating loss? How are operating losses treated for tax purposes?

15-12 Compare the tax treatment of net capital losses between corporations and individuals.

15-13 During a period of rising prices, which inventory method minimizes the present value of present and future taxes? Explain.

15-14 The installment sales method of revenue recognition provides for tax deferral, not tax avoidance. Explain the difference.

15-15 How can lower interest municipal bonds sometimes produce a higher after-tax return to the investor than higher interest corporate bonds?

REVIEW PROBLEM

Capital Budgeting with Tax Considerations

Roberds Supply Company is considering replacing its computer system with a more up-to-date system. The new system would cost $60,000 and would have an ADR estimated life of six years even though Roberds would expect to use the computer for at least seven years. The old computer, which is fully depreciated, can be sold for $5,000. Roberds estimates that the annual benefit in cost savings of having the new computer would be approximately $15,000 for seven years, after which it would be sold for approximately $5,000. The company's marginal income tax rate is 34 percent, and its required minimum return on new capital investments is 14 percent.

Requirements

a) Compute the present value of the depreciation tax shield for the new computer assuming Roberds uses ACRS 200 percent declining balance depreciation, with a switch to straight-line depreciation at the most advantageous time. *Hint:* Refer to Exhibit 15–1 to find the computer's ACRS life.

b) Compute the present value of the depreciation tax shield for the new computer assuming Roberds uses the alternative straight-line depreciation method.

c) Compute the net present value of the investment assuming Roberds uses the ACRS accelerated depreciation method.

d) Compute the net present value of the investment assuming Roberds uses the alternative straight-line depreciation method.

e) Which of the answers computed in requirements (c) and (d) represents the appropriate net present value of the investment for capital budgeting purposes? Explain.

The solution to this problem is found at the end of the Chapter 15 exercises and problems.

EXERCISES

15–1 Corporate Tax Computation: Marginal Tax Rate

Ajax Corporation reported taxable income of $82,000 in 19x5.

Requirements

a) Using the federal corporate tax rates given in the chapter, compute the total tax liability for Ajax Company for 19x5.

b) What was Ajax's marginal tax rate?

15–2 Computation of After-Tax Cash Flows

Rustin Company has an opportunity to purchase a machine that will generate annual pretax cash inflows and additional taxable income of $50,000 before depreciation. Rustin has a marginal tax rate of 34 percent.

Required: Compute Rustin's predicted after-tax net cash flows from the purchase of the machine. Ignore depreciation.

15–3 Depreciation Tax Shield

The Statesboro Company purchased a new machine costing $20,000 at the beginning of 19x1. For tax purposes, the machine can be depreciated over its ADR life of six years on a straight-line basis, or it can be depreciated under ACRS for five years using the 200 percent declining balance method. Statesboro's marginal tax rate is 34 percent.

Requirements

a) Compute the absolute amount of the total tax shield over the life of the machine under both depreciation alternatives.

b) Compute the real amount of the total tax shield under both depreciation alternatives using a present value rate of 12 percent. (Round calculations to the nearest dollar.)

15–4 Depreciation Tax Shield

Lakeland Refinery Company is evaluating a possible investment in a new storage facility that would cost $250,000. For tax purposes, assume the capital investment has an ADR expected useful life of 15 years and qualifies for ten-year ACRS depreciation. The company is in the maximum corporate tax bracket of 34 percent.

Requirements

a) Compute the absolute amount of the total tax shield over the life of the machine assuming the company elects to use ACRS accelerated depreciation.

b) Compute the absolute amount of the total tax shield over the life of the machine assuming the company elects to use the alternative straight-line method.

c) Compute the real amount of the total tax shield under both depreciation alternatives using a present value rate of 12 percent. (Round calculations to the nearest dollar.)

d) For capital budgeting purposes, which depreciation method should the company assume will be used?

15–5 After-Tax Investment Costs

Jim Grant is considering purchasing a new machine for his business which would cost $10,000 and qualify for five-year ACRS accelerated depreciation.

Requirements

a) Compute the after-tax cost of the investment in present dollars, assuming a 12 percent discount rate and taking into account the depreciation tax shield. Assume Jim operates his business as a proprietorship and is in the 15 percent tax bracket.

b) Repeat requirement (a) assuming now that Jim is in the 28 percent tax bracket.

c) Repeat requirement (a) assuming now that Jim operates his business as a corporation and has a tax rate of 34 percent.

d) What conclusions can be drawn from this exercise?

15–6 Capital Budgeting with Tax Effects

Toco Hills Shoe Repair Shop recently purchased a new electric shoe repair machine at a cost of $5,000. Depreciation has been recorded on the machine for one year using seven-year ACRS accelerated depreciation. The owner of the shop has just returned from an equipment trade show where a new computerized shoe repair machine was introduced. This new model, which can be purchased for $7,500, has an expected useful life of ten years, and qualifies for seven-year ACRS depreciation. The manufacturer predicts that it will increase revenues by 20 percent per year without any significant increase in operating costs.

Requirements

a) Since the old repair machine is only one year old, should the owner even consider replacing it with the new computerized model? Explain.

b) What are the relevant items to be considered from a capital budgeting standpoint in replacing the old machine with the new model?

c) Which of the relevant items have related tax effects?

15–7 Capital Budgeting with Tax Effects

Colombia Coffee Cafe is considering the purchase of a new cash register to replace the wooden drawer that has been in use since the cafe opened a few months ago. The cash register is likely to have little if any direct effect on operating revenues and expenses. It would be acquired primarily for the convenience of the manager. The cash register, which can be purchased for $1,200, qualifies for five-year ACRS accelerated depreciation. A friend of the owner of the cafe told him that, because of tax considerations, the real cost of the cash register was not really $1,200 but something less.

Requirements

a) Since the purchase of the cash register could not produce a profit, should it even be evaluated as a capital budgeting expenditure? Explain.

b) Explain why the real cost of the cash register is less than $1,200.

c) Assuming the company is in the 34 percent tax bracket, compute the real cost of the cash register.

15–8 Alternative Capital Budgeting Methods with Tax Effects

Systek Corporation has a capital investment opportunity that would cost $100,000. It would generate estimated net cash inflows before taxes and depreciation of $30,000 per year for six years and would qualify for five-year ACRS accelerated depreciation. The investment would have no recoverable value at the end of six years. The company has a 34 percent tax rate.

Requirements

a) Calculate the net cash inflows after depreciation and taxes from the investment for each of the six years.

b) Compute the payback period for the investment.

c) Compute the accounting rate of return for the investment.

d) Assuming a cost of capital of 12 percent, compute the net present value of the investment.

15–9 Capital Budgeting Cash Flows

Douglas Company is considering purchasing a new machine that has a cost of $35,000. The machine qualifies for seven-year ACRS depreciation. Management predicts that the new machine would increase revenues by $5,000 per year for fifteen years and would reduce operating costs by $2,500 per year. At the end of its useful life it can be sold for $2,500.

Required: Prepare a list of the cash flow items that are relevant to Douglas Company's capital budgeting decision concerning the purchase of the machine. Do not attempt to compute the amount of each cash flow item.

15–10 Capital Funding Alternatives

Jordan Company, a soft drink producer, is engaged in negotiations for the acquisition of a company that manufactures aluminum cans. Jordan's management believes that the company can be purchased for $10 million and paid for by issuing either 15 percent long-term bonds or 15 percent preferred stock. Jordan Company has a marginal tax rate of 34 percent.

Requirements

a) Compute the annual after-tax cost of the funds used to acquire the can company assuming long-term bonds are issued.

b) Compute the annual after-tax cost of the funds used to acquire the can company assuming preferred stock is issued.

15–11 Taxability of Investment Income

To help finance future expansion, the Baldwin Company is investing a substantial portion of its excess cash resources in an expansion fund consisting of low-risk securities. At the end of 19x5 the corporate treasurer was instructed to purchase another $100,000 of securities for the fund. The following securities are being considered.

- Acme Corporation common stock, expected to pay annual dividends of $10,000 with no significant market appreciation over the next five years.

- Bilkko Corporation bonds, bearing interest at the rate of 10 percent per year, maturing in five years.

- Central County municipal bonds, bearing interest at the rate of 7 percent per year, maturing in five years.

Requirements

a) Compute the annual after-tax income from each of the securities under consideration assuming the full $100,000 is invested in the same security and the company is in a 34 percent tax bracket.

b) Repeat requirement (a) assuming the company is in a 25 percent tax bracket.

15–12 Carryback and Carryover of Operating Losses

Because of poor weather conditions, Bob Moore's Ski Shop had a 19x5 operating loss of $30,000. The company earned an operating profit of $5,000 in 19x4, $15,000 in 19x3, and $6,000 in 19x2.

Requirements

a) Explain specifically how Bob Moore may use the 19x5 operating loss to reduce taxes in other years if his store is operated as a proprietorship.

b) How may Bob Moore use the 19x5 operating loss if his business is incorporated?

15–13 Organization Form and Taxation of Income

John Devoe owns a hardware store which he has operated as a proprietorship since it opened several years ago. Now that it is profitable, he is considering whether he should incorporate the business. He expects profits to be about $75,000 per year for the foreseeable future. If incorporated, a reasonable salary for himself would be about $50,000 per year. Without regard to his business income, he is already in a 28 percent tax bracket. For purposes of this problem, assume a flat corporate tax rate of 34 percent.

Requirements

a) Compute the annual income taxes on the income from the store assuming John does not incorporate the business.

b) Compute the annual income taxes on the income from the store (both corporate and individual) assuming John does incorporate the business and pays all business net income out to himself as a dividend.

c) Compute the annual income taxes on the income from the store (both corporate and individual) assuming John does incorporate the business and retains all net income in the business for future expansion and pays no dividends to himself.

15–14 Taxation of Capital Gains and Losses

Robert Rowe has a nondepreciable capital asset which cost $15,000 but now is worth only $10,000. His net taxable income for the current year from other sources is $40,000.

Requirements

a) Compute the amount of the capital loss that will be realized if Robert sells the capital asset.

b) How much of the capital loss can be deducted from other taxable income assuming Robert is taxed as an individual? What disposition would be made of the remainder of the capital loss?

c) How much of the capital loss can be deducted from other taxable income assuming Robert is taxed as a corporation? What disposition would be made of the remainder of the capital loss?

15–15 Inventory Costing Methods and Taxes

Brunswik Wire Company is a new company that distributes a newly developed coaxial cable for use by the cable television industry. Because of increasing demand for the product, the prices have increased several times during the year. Purchases of cable by Brunswik during its first year of operations were as follows:

100 rolls at $200 per roll
250 rolls at $225 per roll
300 rolls at $240 per roll
400 rolls at $250 per roll

Brunswik has sales of $450,000 during the year (950 rolls) and other operating expenses of $75,000. Assume a flat income tax rate of 34 percent.

Requirements

a) Compute the income taxes for Brunswik for the year assuming it uses the FIFO inventory method.

b) Compute the income taxes for Brunswik for the year assuming it uses the LIFO inventory method.

c) How would the relative taxes under the FIFO and LIFO methods differ if the price of cable had been declining during the year? Explain.

15–16 Alternative Taxation of Installment Sales

Corner Food Shoppe decided to sell a vacant lot next to its store which had been acquired ten years ago for planned expansion at a cost of $30,000. The owners have been offered $100,000 for the lot from potential buyers who can pay for it at $20,000 per year for five years plus interest at the current prime rate. Corner Food Shoppe pays taxes at the maximum corporate rate of 34 percent.

Requirements

a) Compute the total income taxes on the sale of the lot in the year of sale assuming the sale is reported for tax purposes on the accrual basis.

b) Compute the total income taxes on the sale of the lot in the year of the sale and in each of the subsequent four years assuming the sale is reported for tax purposes on the installment sales basis.

c) Which method should the Corner Food Shoppe use if it wants to minimize the present value of the total taxes on the sale of the lot? Explain.

15–17 Selecting an Organizational Form

Sharon and Janice plan to open a new gifts and antiques shop in a mountain resort location. They have sought your advice on whether they should organize their business as a partnership or as a corporation. Sharon's other taxable income places her in the maximum tax bracket already, but Janice has no other income. Sharon will be working half time in the shop, and Janice will be working full time refinishing furniture and managing the shop. The anticipated profits of $50,000 per year will be divided as follows:

	Sharon	Janice	Total
Remuneration for services	$10,000	$20,000	$30,000
Division of remaining profits	10,000	10,000	20,000
Totals	$20,000	$30,000	$50,000

Requirements

a) Identify and explain the issues involved in the selection of a tax entity for this new business.

b) Which alternative tax entity do you recommend for this business based on the limited information available to you? Explain the reasons for your recommendation.

15–18 Tax Considerations in Capital Budgeting

Johnstown Company is evaluating a potential capital investment in a machine that would generate an increase in annual operating revenues of $10,000. The machine would cost $40,000 and last six years and would have no expected salvage value at the end of that period. It would qualify for five-year ACRS accelerated depreciation.

Requirements

a) Ignoring all income tax effects, compute the payback period, the accounting rate of return, and the net present value of the investment. Assume a 14 percent discount rate.

b) Considering all relevant income tax effects and assuming a 34 percent corporate tax rate, calculate the payback period, the accounting rate of return, and the net present value of the investment. Assume a 14 percent discount rate.

PROBLEMS

15–19 Capital Budgeting Decisions with Tax Considerations

J.R.'s Painting Company, a residential and commercial paint contractor, is considering expanding into industrial painting and related services, including sandblasting. This expansion would require purchasing sandblasting equipment costing about $50,000. The equipment has an ADR life of nine years; therefore, it could be depreciated under ACRS over five years. After nine years, J.R.'s expects to be able to sell the equipment for about $1,200. Predicted income and expenses related to sandblasting services are as follows:

	Year 1	Year 2	Year 3	Years 4–9 (per year)
Revenues	$20,000	$30,000	$40,000	$50,000
Expenses:				
Labor	$18,000	$18,000	$18,000	$18,000
Sand	5,000	7,500	10,000	12,500
Repairs	500	1,000	1,500	2,000
Total	−23,500	−26,500	−29,500	−32,500
Income before depreciation	$ (3,500)	$ 3,500	$10,500	$17,500

J.R.'s tax rate is 34 percent, and the required return on new investments is 16 percent.

Required: Compute the net present value of the investment in the sandblasting equipment. Should J.R.'s purchase the equipment? (Round calculations to the nearest dollar.)

15–20 Capital Budgeting with Tax Considerations

Jones, Jones, and Jones, a medium-sized law firm, currently has five secretaries employed in its secretarial pool. An office equipment salesperson recently told the Joneses that a word processing system would improve the efficiency and effectiveness of their clerical department and should save the cost of one secretary's salary each year. The proposed system would cost $15,000 and has an estimated useful life of seven years, after which it can be sold for an estimated $1,000. By adding word processing, the attorneys believe that only four secretaries will be needed—three doing conventional typing and one operating the word processor. The total cost of employing a secretary is $15,000 per year; however, word processing secretaries usually earn about 20 percent more than conventional secretaries. The annual maintenance contract on the word processing equipment would be $1,000. The equipment qualifies for five-year ACRS depreciation, and the company has a 34 percent marginal tax rate.

Requirements

a) Compute the net present value of the investment in the word processing equipment assuming a present value rate of 14 percent. (Round calculations to the nearest dollar.)

b) Was the salesperson correct in claiming that the word processing system would save the cost of one secretary?

15–21 Net Present Value Method

Delk Printing Company is considering the purchase of a coin-operated photocopy machine that will cost $3,000 and will generate estimated gross income of $1,200, $1,600, and $2,500 over a three-year period. Maintenance costs are estimated to be $150, $250, and $500 for the three years, respectively. Even though Delk will keep the machine only three years, after which it will be sold for an estimated $900, the tax code requires the machine to be depreciated on the basis of its five-year ACRS classification. Consequently, it will not be fully depreciated at the time it is sold. Delk pays income taxes at the 34 percent corporate rate and requires a return of 30 percent on machinery of this type.

Requirements

a) Compute the net present value of the investment. Should Delk proceed with the purchase of the photocopier? Explain.

b) Compute the net present value of the investment, assuming Delk is an individual paying taxes at a 28 percent rate. Should Delk proceed with the purchase of the photocopier? Explain.

15–22 Purchase versus Lease Costs

Paran Productions is considering whether to purchase or lease a high-quality telepro-duction camera that can be purchased for $250,000 or leased for six years for $50,000 per year. The company estimates that the camera would have a useful life of six years and could be sold at the end of the six-year period for $50,000. Assume that lease payments are deductible when incurred for tax purposes and that, if purchased, the camera could be depreciated under five-year ACRS depreciation. Also, assume that Paran's income tax rate is 34 percent and its cost of capital rate is 12 percent.

Requirements

a) Compute the present value of the cost of leasing the camera reflecting tax considerations.

b) Compute the present value of the cost of purchasing the camera reflecting tax considerations.

15–23 Selection of Organizational Form

Bob Allen and Joyce Baker, two college professors specializing in environmental science, own a consulting firm to which they devote time during their evenings, weekends, and vacations. The firm also employs four other full-time professionals. Currently, Allen and Baker are each in a 28 percent marginal tax bracket, not including their consulting business income. In 19x6, the business had net income before owners' salaries and income taxes of $80,000. Allen and Baker believe that the time they put into their firm would justify an annual salary of $25,000 each if the business were operated as a corporation.

Requirements

a) How would the $80,000 of business income be taxed if the business operated as a partnership? How much total taxes would be paid by the partners on the business income?

b) How would the $80,000 of business income be taxed if the business operated as a regular corporation and only normal salaries were distributed to the owners? How much total taxes would be paid on the business income by the corporation and the owners?

c) Repeat requirement (b) assuming the remainder of the business income after taxes is distributed to the owners as dividends.

d) How would the $80,000 of business income be taxed if the business operated as a subchapter S corporation? How much total taxes would be paid by the corporation and the owners on the business income?

15–24 Impact of Inventory Costing Methods on Taxes

Marco Company, a regional distributor of a new microcomputer called Comp-10, has just completed its third year of operations. Purchases and sales data for each of the first three years are given as follows.

	Year 1	Year 2	Year 3
Purchases (units)	1,500	2,750	4,000
Cost per unit	$120	$100	$ 90
Sales (units)	1,450	2,720	3,980
Selling price per unit	$300	$250	$225
Tax rate	34%	34%	34%
Operating expenses (as a percent of gross profit)	50%	50%	50%

Requirements

a) Compute total income taxes for each year assuming FIFO inventory costing is used.

b) Repeat requirement (a) assuming LIFO inventory costing is used.

c) Comment on the tax effects of inventory costing methods (FIFO versus LIFO) in times of (1) falling prices and (2) rising prices.

15–25 Deferred Income Taxes: Installment Sales

Druid Corporation is selling some of its excess land that is no longer needed in operations. The land was purchased fifteen years ago for $25,000 and now is worth $100,000. Any gain on its sale will be taxed at a maximum tax rate of 34 percent. A prospective buyer has offered to purchase the land with a $25,000 down payment and three payments of $25,000 at the end of each of the next three years.

Requirements

a) Compute the total amount of income taxes that will be paid on the sale of the land assuming it is reported for tax purposes all in the year of sale.

b) Repeat requirement (a) assuming the sale is reported on the installment basis.

c) Which method of tax reporting is preferred? Explain.

d) If the company had the option of a cash sale for $100,000, should it be rejected in order to qualify the sale for the installment sales method?

15–26 Timing the Payment of Taxes

The Burdock Company's transactions are summarized below for 19x5, its first year of operations. Recognizing the company's critical shortage of cash, the president instructed the controller (who is also the tax manager) to consider all options in the tax law that might reduce tax payments for the current year.

1. Purchased equipment in September at a cost of $20,000. The equipment qualifies for five-year cost recovery under ACRS.

2. A total of 400 units of product were sold during the year. The following purchases of inventory were made during the year.

   50 units at $40
   200 units at $45
   200 units at $50
   50 units at $55

3. The 400 units were sold (all on installment accounts) for a total of $50,000. During the year, $20,000 was collected on the accounts. (Assume this sale qualifies for the installment method.)

4. Operating expenses paid during the year totaled $9,000. An additional $4,000 of expenses was accrued but unpaid at the end of the year. The only other expense was depreciation on the equipment.

Requirements

a) For each of the four items listed above, indicate the alternative tax treatments that are available to the Burdock Company.

b) Assuming there were no other transactions during the year, compute the minimum tax liability for the company for 19x5. Burdock Company is organized as a regular (not subchapter S) corporation.

15–27 Effect of Inventory Alternatives on Taxes

The management of Stark Products Company has asked its accounting department to describe the effect on income taxes of accounting for inventories on the LIFO rather than the FIFO basis during 19x4 and 19x5. The accounting department is to assume that the change to LIFO would have been effective on January 1, 19x4, and that the initial LIFO inventory was the ending 19x3 FIFO inventory.

Presented below are selected data for the years 19x4 and 19x5 during which the FIFO method was employed.

	19x3	19x4	19x5
Inventory (December 31)	$69,000	$ 75,000	$ 84,000
Sales		$540,000	$617,500
Less: Cost of goods sold		$294,000	$355,000
Other expenses		135,000	154,000
Total		−429,000	−509,000
Net income before income taxes		$111,000	$108,500
Less: Income taxes (34%)		− 37,740	− 36,890
Net income		$ 73,260	$ 71,610

Additional information:

▪ Inventory on hand at 12/31/x3 consisted of 30,000 units valued at $2.30 each.

▪ Sales (all units sold at the same price throughout the year):

19x4—120,000 units at $4.50 each
19x5—130,000 units at $4.75 each

▪ Purchases (all units purchased at the same price throughout the year):

19x4—120,000 units at $2.50 each
19x5—130,000 units at $2.80 each

▪ Income taxes at the effective rate of 34 percent are paid on December 31 each year.

Required: If inventories had been valued using LIFO, determine the values for 19x4 and 19x5 for ending inventories, net income before income taxes, income taxes, and net income.

(CMA Adapted)

15–28 Capital Budgeting and Funding Alternatives

LeToy Company produces a wide variety of children's toys, most of which are manufactured from stamped parts. The Production Department recommended that a new stamping machine be acquired. The Production Department further recommended that the company consider using the new stamping machine for only six years. Top management concurs with the recommendation and has assigned Ann Mitchum of the Budget and Planning Department to supervise the acquisition and analyze the alternative financing available. After careful analysis and review, Mitchum has narrowed the financing of the project to the two following alternatives.

1. The first alternative is a lease agreement with the manufacturer of the stamping machine. The manufacturer is willing to lease the equipment to LeToy for six years even though it has an economically useful life of ten years. The lease agreement calls for LeToy to make annual payments of $62,000 at the beginning of each year. The manufacturer (lessor) retains the title to the machine, and there is no purchase option at the end of six years. The lease payments would be deductible as operating expense for tax purposes.

2. The second alternative would be for LeToy to purchase the equipment outright from the manufacturer for $240,000. LeToy can recover the cost under ACRS over five years. The asset would be sold for $45,000 at the end of six years.

All maintenance, taxes, and insurance are the same under both alternatives and are paid by LeToy. LeToy has an average cost of capital of 12 percent and is in a 34 percent tax bracket.

Requirements

a) Calculate the net-of-tax present value cost of acquiring the stamping machine through the leasing alternative. (Round computations to the nearest dollar.)

b) Calculate the net-of-tax present value cost of acquiring the stamping machine through the purchase alternative.   (CMA Adapted)

15–29 Tax Considerations in Using Payback, Accounting Rate of Return, and Net Present Value

The Baxter Company manufactures toys and other short-lived faddish items. The Research and Development Department came up with an item that would make a good promotional gift for office equipment dealers. Aggressive and effective effort by Baxter's sales personnel has resulted in almost firm commitments for this product for the next five years. It is expected that the product's appeal will be exhausted by that time. In order to produce the quantity demanded, Baxter will need to buy additional machinery and rent some additional space. It appears that about 25,000 square feet will be needed; 12,500 square feet of presently unused, but leased, space is available now. (Baxter's present lease with ten years to run costs $3 a square foot.) There is another 12,500 square feet adjoining the Baxter facility, which Baxter will rent for five years at $4 per square foot per year if it decides to make this product. The equipment will be purchased for $720,000. It will require $30,000 in modifications, $60,000 for installation, and $90,000 for testing; all these activities will be done by a firm of engineers hired by Baxter. All the expenditures will be paid for on January 1, 19x3. The equipment will be depreciated over five years under ACRS using the 200 percent declining balance method. At the end of the five years, the asset is expected to be sold for $180,000. The following estimates of revenues and expenses (other than depreciation and taxes) for this product for the five years have been developed. The company pays income taxes at the 34 percent corporate rate.

	19x3	19x4 & 19x5	19x6 & 19x7
Sales	$1,000,000	$1,600,000	$800,000
Materials, labor, and overhead outlays	400,000	750,000	350,000
Allocated general overhead	40,000	75,000	35,000
Rent	87,500	87,500	87,500

Requirements

a) Prepare a schedule that shows the incremental after-tax cash flows for this project.

b) If the company requires a three-year payback period for its investment, would this project be undertaken?

c) Calculate the after-tax accounting rate of return on initial investment for the project. (Round answer to three decimal places.)

d) A newly hired business school graduate recommends that the company consider the use of the net present value method to study this project. If the company sets a required rate of return of 24 percent after taxes, will this project be accepted? (Round calculations to the nearest dollar.)

(CMA Adapted)

15–30 Selecting Tax Alternatives to Minimize Taxes

The Janeski Service Corporation has just completed its first year of operations. The income statement (on an accrual basis) for the year prepared by the bookkeeping department is as follows:

Sales	$325,000
Gain on sale of land	32,000
Interest income	1,000
Total revenues	$358,000
Materials and supplies	$128,000
Wages and benefits	43,000
Depreciation (straight-line)	7,000
Bad debts	500
Interest	5,500
Administrative services	11,000
Other expenses	5,000
Total expenses	−200,000
Net income	$158,000

Mr. Janeski has made the following preliminary calculation of the corporation's tax liability.

Tax on first $50,000 at 15%	$ 7,500
Tax on next $25,000 at 25%	6,250
Tax on next $83,000 at 34%	28,220
	$41,970

You have just been hired by Janeski as an accountant, and he indicates that the company is in a "cash-squeeze" position. As your first task, he asks you to review the tax computation to determine if this year's tax liability might be reduced. In reviewing the firm's records, you assemble the following information.

1. There are no ending inventories.

2. Accounts receivable at year end amount to $18,000, and accounts payable and other current payables are $4,000.

3. New equipment costing $60,000 was purchased early in the year. In the bookkeeper's depreciation calculation, salvage value was estimated to be $4,000, and the useful life of the equipment was estimated at eight years. You determined that the equipment qualified for five-year ACRS depreciation.

4. A tract of land, acquired in January as a building site at a cost of $12,000, was sold in November when a new shopping plaza was constructed on adjoining land. The land was sold for $44,000, of which $33,000 will be received in future years.

Required: Present a revised determination of taxable income and total taxes that takes advantage of all available means (discussed in this chapter) to reduce this year's taxes. Explain any items where your presentation differs from the income statement given above.

(CMA Adapted)

REVIEW PROBLEM SOLUTION

a) Using ACRS 200 percent declining balance depreciation, the computer would be written off over the five-year period from the midpoint of year 1 to the midpoint of year 6. The depreciation method would be switched to straight-line at the beginning of year 5 to maximize the present value of the depreciation tax shield.

	(1)	(2)	(3) (1) × (2)	(4)	(5) (3) × (4)	(6)	(7) (5) × (6)
Year	Depreciation Base	Depreciation Rate	Annual Depreciation	Tax Rate	Tax Shield	Present Value Factor	Present Value of Tax Shield
1	$60,000	$\frac{1}{2} \times \frac{2}{5}$	$12,000	0.34	$ 4,080	0.877	$ 3,578
2	48,000	$\frac{2}{5}$	19,200	0.34	6,528	0.769	5,020
3	28,800	$\frac{2}{5}$	11,520	0.34	3,917	0.675	2,644
4	17,280	$\frac{2}{5}$	6,912	0.34	2,350	0.592	1,391
5	10,368*	$1 \div 1\frac{1}{2}$	6,912	0.34	2,350	0.519	1,220
6	10,368*	$\frac{1}{2} \div 1\frac{1}{2}$	3,456	0.34	1,175	0.456	536
			$60,000		$20,400		$14,389

* Represents asset book value at the point where the depreciation method switched to straight-line.

b) Using the alternative straight-line depreciation, the computer would be written off over six years from the midpoint of year 1 to the midpoint of year 7.

	(1)	(2)	(3) (1) × (2)	(4)	(5) (3) × (4)	(6)	(7) (5) × (6)
Year	Depreciation Base	Depreciation Rate	Annual Depreciation	Tax Rate	Tax Shield	Present Value Factor	Present Value of Tax Shield
1	$60,000	$\frac{1}{2} \times \frac{1}{6}$	$ 5,000	0.34	$ 1,700	0.877	$ 1,491
2	60,000	$\frac{1}{6}$	10,000	0.34	3,400	0.769	2,615
3	60,000	$\frac{1}{6}$	10,000	0.34	3,400	0.675	2,295
4	60,000	$\frac{1}{6}$	10,000	0.34	3,400	0.592	2,013
5	60,000	$\frac{1}{6}$	10,000	0.34	3,400	0.519	1,765
6	60,000	$\frac{1}{6}$	10,000	0.34	3,400	0.456	1,550
7	60,000	$\frac{1}{2} \times \frac{1}{6}$	5,000	0.34	1,700	0.400	680
			$60,000		$20,400		$12,409

c)

	(1)	(2)	(3)	(4) (1) × (3)
Cash Flow Items	Actual Cash Inflows (Outflows)	Year(s) of Cash Flows	12% Present Value Factor	Present Value of Cash Flows
Purchase of new computer	$(60,000)	0	1.000	$(60,000)
Sale of old computer	5,000	0	1.000	5,000
Taxes on gain on sale of old computer ($5,000 × 0.34)	(1,700)	0	1.000	(1,700)
Annual operating income from new computer	15,000	1–7	4.288	64,320
Taxes on annual operating income ($15,000 × 0.34)	(5,100)	1–7	4.288	(21,869)
Plus present value of depreciation tax shield (see requirement a)				14,389
Sale of new computer	5,000	7	0.400	2,000
Taxes on gain on sale of new computer ($5,000 × 0.34)	(1,700)	7	0.400	(680)
Net present value of all cash flows				$ 1,460

d)

Cash Flow Items	(1) Actual Cash Inflows (Outflows)	(2) Year(s) of Cash Flows	(3) 12% Present Value Factor	(4) (1) × (3) Present Value of Cash Flows
Purchase of new computer	$(60,000)	0	1.000	$(60,000)
Sale of old computer	5,000	0	1.000	5,000
Taxes on gain on sale of old computer ($5,000 × 0.34)	(1,700)	0	1.000	(1,700)
Annual operating income from new computer	15,000	1–7	4.288	64,320
Taxes on annual operating income ($15,000 × 0.34)	(5,100)	1–7	4.288	(21,869)
Plus present value of depreciation tax shield (see requirement a)				12,409
Sale of new computer	5,000	7	0.400	2,000
Taxes on gain on sale of new computer ($5,000 × 0.34)	(1,700)	7	0.400	(680)
Net present value of all cash flows				$ (520)

e) For capital budgeting purposes, the depreciation alternative that produces the most favorable net present value of the investment should normally be used in evaluating the investment. Hence, in evaluating the computer investment, Roberds should use the net present value calculated using ACRS depreciation (requirement c) which indicates that the investment meets the required 14 percent minimum return.

CHAPTER 16

Financial Statement Analysis and the Statement of Resource Flows

LEARNING OBJECTIVES

Upon completion of this chapter you should:

- Understand why it is important for managers to analyze their firm's financial statements.
- Be able to evaluate a firm's solvency by preparing and interpreting selected financial statement ratios.
- Be able to evaluate a firm's overall performance by preparing and interpreting selected financial statement ratios.
- Understand the role of the statement of resource flows in reporting the financial activities of a business.
- Be able to prepare simple statements of working capital flows and cash flows.
- Be able to convert an accrual basis income statement to a cash basis income statement.
- Be able to evaluate the significance of the information contained in a statement of resource flows.

General purpose financial statements are designed to provide information to a large and diverse group of users, including stockholders, creditors, and managers. Because of the broad objectives of financial statements, they do not include certain financial measures often needed by specific user groups. Through financial analysis, however, individual users are able to generate a considerable amount of additional useful information from the statements.

Financial statement analysis is the process of interpreting and evaluating financial statements by using data contained in them to produce additional financial measures. Financial statement analysis involves comparing financial statements for the current period with those of previous periods, studying the internal composition of the financial statements, and studying relationships within and between the financial statements.

The purpose of financial statement analysis is to give the user an understanding of the firm and its operations beyond that provided by merely reading the statements. A large amount of useful information is tapped through analysis that otherwise is not immediately obvious to the user. For example, creditors can evaluate the likelihood that the company will make its interest and principal payments on time, stockholders can evaluate the profitability of the firm's assets and the return on investment to various equity holders, and managers can evaluate their overall effectiveness in using the resources entrusted to them by creditors and stockholders.

The primary purpose of this chapter is to discuss the benefits of financial analysis to managers and to illustrate several analytical measures that provide information useful to managers. The second part of this chapter discusses the statement of resource flows. This statement, the income statement, and balance sheet together constitute the basic financial statement package. To gain maximum benefit from financial statements, all three statements should be utilized.

FINANCIAL STATEMENT ANALYSIS BY MANAGERS

One of the most important reasons for managers to analyze their firm's financial statements is to evaluate the overall performance of the firm. Managers should be aware of total company performance, not just the performance of their particular areas of responsibility. By analyzing the financial statements for the company as a whole, managers gain a perspective on how the organization is performing.

General purpose financial statements provide the only overall measure of the firm's performance available to some managers. The internal reporting system is often limited to reporting component performances, with no report of overall performance provided to managers below the top levels.

By evaluating the overall performance of the organization, managers are able to compare their firm with similar firms and identify potential weaknesses that may be worthy of management attention. For example, if a firm has a return on equity of 8 percent while the industry norm is 15 percent, this comparison might signal an existing problem requiring management attention. In fact, there may be good reasons for the below-average return; without financial analysis, however, management may not even be aware of the deficiency, or the conditions causing it. Since internal reports of other companies are not available, the only basis for making comparisons with those companies is through their external financial statements and other published materials.

Financial analysis is also necessary for managers whose firms have lending agreements that impose financial restrictions on the organization. Analysis of the financial statements is often necessary to determine if restrictions are being met. For example, an agreement may require the debt-to-equity ratio to be maintained at a specified level. Failure to comply could result in a call for immediate liquidation of the debt and could damage the firm's credit rating and its ability to obtain borrowed capital in the future.

A more subtle, but no less important, reason for managers to analyze financial statements is to see their firm as outsiders see it. The financial statements are, in effect, the only window through which outsiders may view the firm. By evaluating the firm's financial statements, managers can better understand the behavior and attitudes of outsiders toward the firm and thereby develop a more realistic view of the firm themselves.

THE NEED FOR EVALUATIVE STANDARDS

Information obtained directly from the financial statements, and analytical measures derived from the statements, have little usefulness standing alone. To be interpreted effectively, this information must be evaluated against some *standard*. Depending on managers' objectives, several different standards may be used. The most common financial analysis standards are (1) the firm's financial measures for previous periods, (2) financial measures for other firms and industry averages, and (3) budgeted measures for the firm for the period under evaluation.

An important aspect of financial analysis is tracking the firm's progress over time, which is done by comparing the firm's performance for the current period with several previous periods. To get an indication of future performances, it is useful for managers to compare the firm's current performance to its past performances. This comparison, however, should not be the only standard used because it tends to encourage mediocrity if the only objective is to improve on previous periods' performances.

Evaluating financial measures against comparable measures for other firms in the same industry is also beneficial to managers, especially in heavily competitive industries. Several financial information organizations (including Dun and Bradstreet, Standard and Poors, and Moody's) publish averages for commonly used financial measures for all major industries. Failure to perform close to industry norms could signal difficulties in competing with other firms in the future.

When comparing a firm's financial measures with those of other firms, it is necessary to consider any material differences that might exist between the firms. For example, if one firm is located farther from major suppliers than other firms in the industry, higher freight costs and possibly lower profits may occur. Differences in accounting practices must also be taken into account in comparing firms; for example, allowances must be made in comparing two firms that use different methods of inventory valuation. Although there are limitations in making intercompany comparisons, looking at other firms' performances is a useful indicator of relative performance.

From management's perspective, probably the most realistic standard of performance is the firm's budgeted performance. Chapter 6 discussed operating budgets and pro forma financial statements, which represent management's most realistic expectations for the period. Analytical measures taken from these statements should be compared with the same measures derived from the actual financial statements for the period. For performance evaluation purposes, this comparison is likely to provide managers the most useful evaluation of current financial statements.

PROCEDURES FOR FINANCIAL STATEMENT ANALYSIS

Financial statement analysis measures may be divided into two groups: measures of *solvency* of the firm and measures of *performance*. The 19x4 and 19x3 balance sheets and income statements for Dunfield's, Inc., are provided in Exhibit 16–1 as a basis for illustrating these two groups of analytical measures. Financial statements for two successive periods are presented because several of the ratios require averages to be computed for the period. To obtain average information, the beginning and ending balances are summed and divided by 2. Normally, averages computed from values for only two points during the year (beginning and ending) should be used only if monthly or quarterly data are not available. In the following discussion, each analytical measure is presented in general form along with an example of the measure for Dunfield's for 19x4.

Measures of Solvency

Solvency refers to the ability of a firm to pay its debts as they become due. The primary measures of *short-term solvency* are the current ratio, acid test ratio, inventory turnover, and number of days receivables outstanding. The debt-to-equity ratio and the times-interest-earned measure are useful in assessing *long-term solvency*.

EXHIBIT 16–1 Comparative Financial Statements

Dunfield's, Inc.
Comparative Income Statements
For the years ended December 31, 19x4 and 19x3
(*in thousands*)

	19x4	19x3
Sales	$9,734	$8,028
Cost of goods sold	−6,085	−4,843
Gross profit	$3,649	$3,185
Operating expenses:		
Selling	$1,030	$ 891
General and administrative	602	527
Total	−1,632	−1,418
Operating income	$2,017	$1,767
Other revenues and expenses:		
Interest income	$ 90	$ 84
Interest expense	(345)	(314)
Total	− 255	− 230
Income before income taxes	$1,762	$1,537
Provision for income taxes (34%)	− 599	− 523
Net income	$1,163	$1,014
Earnings per share	$ 2.88	$ 2.51

EXHIBIT 16–1 *(cont.)*

Dunfield's, Inc.
Comparative Balance Sheets
December 31, 19x4 and 19x3
(*in thousands*)

Assets	*19x4*	*19x3*
Current assets:		
Cash	$1,335	$1,341
Marketable securities	250	200
Accounts receivable	1,678	1,386
Inventories	1,703	1,439
Other current assets	280	156
Total current assets	$5,246	$4,522
Property, plant, and equipment	$6,861	$6,041
Less: Accumulated depreciation	−3,426	−3,080
Net	3,435	2,961
Other assets	73	72
Total assets	$8,754	$7,555

Liabilities and stockholders' equity		
Current liabilities:		
Accounts payable	$1,564	$1,228
Taxes payable	482	336
Other current liabilities	202	178
Total current liabilities	$2,248	$1,742
Long-term debt	1,208	1,192
Deferred taxes payable	271	230
Total liabilities	$3,727	$3,164
Stockholders' equity:		
Common stock ($1 par, 404,000 shares outstanding)	$ 404	$ 404
Premium on common stock	270	270
Retained earnings	4,353	3,717
Total stockholders' equity	5,027	4,391
Total liabilities and stockholders' equity	$8,754	$7,555

Current Ratio. The **current ratio** measures the relationship between current assets and current liabilities. The general equation for the current ratio and the computation for Dunfield's, as of December 31, 19x4, are as follows:

$$
\begin{aligned}
\textit{General equation:} \qquad \text{Current ratio} &= \frac{\text{Current assets}}{\text{Current liabilities}} \\[6pt]
\textit{Example:} \qquad\qquad\quad &= \frac{\$5{,}246}{\$2{,}248} \\[6pt]
&= 2.33
\end{aligned}
$$

Current assets represent cash and other assets that will be converted into cash (either directly or indirectly) through operations within a reasonably short period of time. Under normal operating conditions, cash is generated by sales of inventory and collection of accounts receivable. Current liabilities are financial obligations that will become due within a relatively short period of time and will be paid from cash currently on hand and from the pool of cash generated from current assets. Therefore, comparing current assets to current liabilities indicates the extent to which current assets are available to cover current liabilities. Dunfield's current ratio of 2.33 implies that the company has $2.33 of current assets for each $1 of current liabilities.

There is no universal guideline for evaluating the current ratio. Although a current ratio of 2.0 is often considered to be the norm, using an artificial guideline like this may lead to erroneous conclusions. For example, a current ratio of 2.0 is inadequate for a firm that has 90 percent of its total current assets tied up in obsolete or slow-moving inventory, while most of its current liabilities are due in the near term. The adequacy of a particular current ratio depends on (1) the composition of the current assets and how quickly they will convert to cash and (2) how soon current liabilities must be paid.

The current asset and current liability accounts are often referred to as *current operating,* or *current working,* accounts because assets and liabilities related to operating revenues and expenses normally flow in and out of the balance sheet through these accounts. The difference between current assets and current liabilities may be viewed as the net amount of working funds available in the short run. This fund is referred to as **working capital.** Dunfield's December 31, 19x4 working capital is computed as follows:

$$
\begin{array}{ccccc}
\text{Current assets} & - & \text{Current liabilities} & = & \text{Working capital,} \\[4pt]
\$5{,}246 & - & \$2{,}248 & = & \$2{,}998.
\end{array}
$$

The concept of working capital as a pool of operating funds is discussed in greater detail later in this chapter.

Acid Test Ratio. Current liabilities are usually paid with cash, not with other current assets. The **acid test ratio** is more specific than the current ratio as a test of short-term solvency. It measures the availability of cash, and other current monetary assets that can be quickly converted into cash, to pay current liabilities. *Current monetary assets* include cash, marketable securities, and current receivables. The general equation for the acid test ratio and the computation for Dunfield's, as of December 31, 19x4, are as follows:

General equation: Acid test ratio $= \dfrac{\text{Cash} + \begin{array}{c}\text{Marketable}\\\text{securities}\end{array} + \begin{array}{c}\text{Current}\\\text{receivables}\end{array}}{\text{Current liabilities}}$

Example: $= \dfrac{\$1,335 + \$250 + \$1,678}{\$2,248}$

$= 1.45$

Dunfield's acid test ratio indicates that it has $1.45 of current monetary assets for each $1 of current liabilities. This ratio is also referred to as the **quick ratio** because it shows the amount of cash that can be obtained relatively quickly for each $1 of current liabilities outstanding. Many analysts consider an acid test ratio of 1.0 to be adequate for most businesses; however, as stated earlier in discussing the current ratio, the composition of the ratio components must be considered before deciding what is an adequate ratio. When evaluating the current and acid test ratios, the manager must consider other factors, such as seasonal characteristics of the business, the availability of short-term credit lines, the collection terms for accounts receivables, and the payment terms of accounts payable.

As a follow-up to the current ratio and the acid test ratio, most analysts evaluate the liquidity of the primary assets in the cash flow stream—namely, inventory and accounts receivable. The inventory turnover and days receivables outstanding are the measures ordinarily used for this purpose.

Inventory Turnover. **Inventory turnover** indicates the approximate number of times the average stock of inventory was sold and replenished during the year. Inventory turnover is computed as the total cost of the inventory sold during the year divided by the average inventory on hand during the year.

General equation: Inventory turnover $= \dfrac{\text{Cost of goods sold}}{\text{Average inventory}}$

Example: $= \dfrac{\$6,085}{(\$1,703 + \$1,439)/2}$

$= 3.87 \text{ times}$

During 19x4, Dunfield's sold inventory costing $6,085, and the average inventory for the year was $1,571 [($1,703 + $1,439)/2]; therefore, the average stock of inventory was sold and replenished 3.87 times during the year. Assuming a 365-day year, the average number of days required for each turnover of inventory was 94.3 days (365 days ÷ 3.87). That is, during the year the average inventory on hand was sufficient to meet the average sales needs for 94.3 days. Since ending inventory is somewhat higher than the average inventory for the year, inventory at year-end is sufficient to supply somewhat more than 94.3 days' average sales.

What constitutes an appropriate inventory turnover ratio varies from industry to industry. Obviously, a fast food restaurant should have a high inventory turnover, whereas a jewelry store ordinarily has a low inventory turnover. The nature of the firm's supply sources, the use of inventory display in selling merchandise, the quickness with which inventory must be delivered to customers, and information on industry norms all should be considered in interpreting the inventory turnover ratio.

Days Receivables Outstanding. Next to cash and marketable securities, receivables are the most liquid assets. They are converted directly into cash in the normal course of business. The **days receivables outstanding** ratio measures the number of days, on the average, it took to generate the sales uncollected at the year end. It is computed as ending receivables divided by average daily sales.

$$\text{General equation:} \quad \text{Days receivables outstanding} = \frac{\text{Ending receivables}}{\text{Average daily sales}}$$

$$\text{Example:} \qquad\qquad\qquad\qquad\qquad\quad = \frac{\$1,678}{\$9,734/365}$$

$$= 62.9 \text{ days}$$

At the end of 19x4, Dunfield's had receivables on hand equal to the average sales for 62.9 days. In evaluating this measure, management should consider the terms under which credit sales are made. For example, if Dunfield's sells goods and services on 30-day credit terms, a ratio of 62.9 days probably indicates serious receivables collection problems. This ratio, which is a broad average, is a reliable indicator only if the amount of daily sales was fairly even throughout the year. For more precise information, management should conduct a detailed analysis of year-end receivables to determine their ages and probable collection periods.

Long-term solvency is a separate matter from that of short-term solvency. Obviously, all long-term debts must eventually be paid in some future current period; however, solvency is a matter that should be monitored both for the near term and the extended future. The debt-to-equity ratio and the times-interest-earned measure are useful in analyzing long-term solvency.

Debt-to-Equity Ratio. Most business enterprises have two basic sources of capital—*debt* and *equity*. The balance between the amounts of capital provided by creditors and owners is important in evaluating the long-term solvency of a business. Creditors regard equity as a cushion against future operating losses and bankruptcy. The larger the percentage of total assets financed by equity capital, the more secure are the creditors. Aggressive, growth-oriented organizations tend to rely more heavily on debt than equity, whereas stable, conservative organizations tend to have a larger proportion of equity. The **debt-to-equity ratio** is computed as total liabilities divided by total stockholders' equity.

$$\text{General equation:} \quad \text{Debt-to-equity ratio} = \frac{\text{Total liabilities}}{\text{Total stockholders' equity}}$$

$$\text{Example:} \qquad\qquad\qquad = \frac{\$3,727}{\$5,027}$$

$$= 0.74$$

Dunfield's December 31, 19x4 debt-to-equity ratio of 0.74 indicates that the creditors have provided $0.74 of capital for each $1 provided by the stockholders. Stated another way, for each $1.74 of asset book values, the company could suffer a $1 loss and still have total assets on the books equal to total liabilities. In evaluating the debt-to-equity ratio, it is necessary to recognize the possible understatement or overstatement of assets and owners' equity. For example, if a company purchased land for $1 million that has a fair market value of $10 million, the company in effect has $9 million of unrecorded assets and owners' equity. Although the debt-to-equity ratio is useful as a general indicator of the adequacy of long-term solvency, the amount of long-term debt that a company can justify is primarily related to its ability to repay the funds plus interest.

Times Interest Earned. Because a financially sound business normally pays interest obligations out of current earnings, creditors are interested in the adequacy of earnings to provide payment of interest charges. **Times interest earned,** a measure of interest paying ability, shows the relationship between earnings available to pay interest and total interest expense.

$$\text{General equation:} \quad \text{Times interest earned} = \frac{\text{Net income} + \text{Interest expense} + \text{Income taxes}}{\text{Interest expense}}$$

$$\text{Example:} \qquad\qquad\qquad = \frac{\$1,163 + \$345 + \$599}{\$345}$$

$$= 6.11 \text{ times}$$

In the numerator, interest expense and income taxes are added to net income to determine the pool of earnings from which interest expense is paid. Since interest expense is deducted in computing taxable income, the earnings pool from which interest is paid is income before deductions for interest and taxes. For Dunfield's this pool of earnings for 19x4 is 6.11 times the amount of the current year's interest charge on debt.

Measures of Performance

Operating performance is related to the broad objective of profitability. The basic activities that characterize a typical for-profit organization are as follows:

- Generating capital (equity and debt).
- Acquiring assets with capital.
- Using assets to generate sales and profits.
- Using profits to pay the cost of capital.

The measures discussed below assist managers in evaluating their performance of these activities.

Asset Turnover. The **asset turnover** ratio measures the ability of the firm to use its assets to generate sales. It is computed as sales divided by average total assets.

$$\text{General equation:} \quad \text{Asset turnover} = \frac{\text{Sales}}{\text{Average total assets}}$$

$$\text{Example:} \qquad\qquad = \frac{\$9,734}{(\$8,754 + \$7,555)/2}$$

$$= 1.19 \text{ times}$$

For Dunfield's, the asset turnover of 1.19 times indicates that on the average each $1 of assets generated $1.19 of sales during 19x4. The interpretation of this measure depends largely on the nature of the business. Organizations that are capital intensive, such as utilities or heavily automated manufacturers, typically have a lower asset turnover than organizations that are primarily dependent on labor, such as a garment manufacturer. Also, firms that generate a small amount of sales with each dollar of assets usually must earn a higher percentage of profit on each sales dollar than firms that produce a high amount of sales with each invested asset dollar.

Return on Sales. The ability of a firm to generate sales with available assets is important; to be profitable, however, these sales must exceed the cost of generating them. **Return on sales** is a measure of the ability of the firm to generate profits from sales produced by the firm's assets; it is computed by dividing the sum of net income and net-of-tax interest expense by sales.

$$\text{General equation:} \quad \text{Return on sales} = \frac{\text{Net income} + \text{Net-of-tax interest expense}}{\text{Sales}}$$

$$\text{Example:} \quad = \frac{\$1,163 + \$345(1 - 0.34)}{\$9,734}$$

$$= 0.143, \text{ or } 14.3\%$$

Interest expense is added to net income because it is not considered an expense of using assets, but rather a cost of providing the capital invested in assets. Since interest expense reduces taxes, it is adjusted for taxes at the current tax rate of 34 percent. On the average, 14.3 percent of each $1 of Dunfield's 19x4 sales remained as profit after covering all expenses other than interest.

Return on Assets. The **return on assets** ratio combines the asset turnover and return on sales ratios to measure directly the ability of the firm to use its assets to generate profits. The return on assets computation is derived from the asset turnover and return on sales ratios as follows:

$$\text{Return on assets} = \text{Asset turnover} \times \text{Return on sales}$$

$$= \frac{\text{Sales}}{\text{Average total assets}} \times \frac{\text{Net income} + \text{Net-of-tax interest expense}}{\text{Sales}}$$

$$\text{General equation:} \quad = \frac{\text{Net income} + \text{Net-of-tax interest expense}}{\text{Average total assets}}$$

$$\text{Example:} \quad = \frac{\$1,163 + \$345(1 - 0.34)}{(\$8,754 + \$7,555)/2}$$

$$= 0.171, \text{ or } 17.1\%$$

The 19x4 return on assets for Dunfield's may also be approximated by multiplying the asset turnover of 1.19 times the return on sales of 14.3 percent. From the previous analyses it can be concluded that on the average each dollar of assets generated $1.19 of sales and $0.171 of income, and each dollar of sales resulted in $0.143 of income. Return on assets is an important indicator of the overall performance of management because it measures management's effectiveness in using the total capital entrusted to them by both the creditors and the stockholders. A variation of this ratio (return on investment), discussed in

Chapter 9, is commonly used for evaluating the performance of divisions in decentralized organizations.

The return on assets ratio measures profitability before deducting capital costs (interest and dividends); therefore, the adequacy of the profitability indicated by this ratio depends on the cost of debt and the return expected by the stockholders on their investments.

Return on Equity. **Return on equity** measures the profits attributable to the shareholders as a percentage of their equity in the firm. This measure is more specific than the return on assets ratio in measuring performance because it focuses only on *stockholders'* profits and investment. The profits available to stockholders consist of net income after deducting all costs and expenses, including interest expense. Return on equity is computed as net income divided by average stockholders' equity.[1]

$$General\ equation{:}\quad \text{Return on equity} = \frac{\text{Net income}}{\text{Average stockholders' equity}}$$

$$Example{:}\qquad\qquad = \frac{\$1,163}{(\$5,027 + \$4,391)/2}$$

$$= 0.247, \text{ or } 24.7\%$$

The 19x4 return attributable to Dunfield's shareholders was 24.7 percent, compared to a return on assets of 17.1 percent. The return to the shareholders is higher than the return on assets as a result of financial leverage. **Financial leverage** refers to the use of capital that has a fixed interest or dividend rate. Any time capital can be acquired at a fixed rate,[2] and the return on assets is higher than that fixed rate, the return to the common shareholders is increased through *favorable financial leverage.* Conversely, if the fixed cost of capital is greater than the return it generates, the shareholders are subsidizing the cost of debt or other fixed rate capital, and there is *unfavorable financial leverage.* Dunfield's favorable financial leverage occurred because the return on assets

---

[1] If there is more than one class of capital stock outstanding, the return on equity is computed as the return on common equity. In computing return on equity, net income must be reduced by the amount of annual dividends on preferred stock, and stockholders' equity must be reduced by the book value of preferred stock.

[2] In an unstable money market the actual interest rate on a loan may change from period to period as the prime rate changes. These are called *variable rate loans*. Even in these situations the interest rate is fixed for a short period of time, and management's ability to generate favorable leverage varies inversely with changes in the applicable interest rate.

was 17.1 percent, whereas the interest rate as a percent of average total liabilities was only 10 percent, computed as follows:

$$\text{Average interest rate} = \frac{\text{Interest expense}}{\text{Average total liabilities}}$$

$$= \frac{\$345}{(\$3,727 + \$3,164)/2}$$

$$= 0.10, \text{ or } 10.0\%.$$

The total debt required a return of only $345 (or 10 percent); therefore the return above 10 percent on the assets acquired with debt increased the return to the shareholders to 24.7 percent.

Earnings per Share. For external reporting purposes, earnings per share amounts are disclosed on the face of the income statement. If a company has gains or losses from extraordinary sources such as a natural disaster, or from other unusual and infrequent events, income and earnings per share figures must be presented separately for income before extraordinary items and for net income. Note on Dunfield's income statement in Exhibit 16–1 that reported earnings per share are $2.88 in 19x4 and $2.51 in 19x3. Since there were no extraordinary items, earnings per share amounts were presented only for net income.

Earnings per share for companies with simple capital structures is computed as net income divided by the average number of shares outstanding for the period. A simple capital structure is one consisting only of common stock. The computations are more difficult for companies with more complex capital structures that include preferred stock, convertible bonds, or other types of equity securities. Since financial statements already include earnings per share figures, the manager does not have to compute these figures.

Earnings per share measures are used extensively by investors as a basis for evaluating the overall profitability of the firm. The advantage of the earnings per share measure is that it is reported on the same basis as capital stock prices— that is, on an individual share basis. Investors often use the **price earnings ratio,** which compares the current market price with earnings per share of the stock, to arrive at a multiple of earnings represented by the selling price.

Managers also may use earnings per share as a broad measure of overall performance; however, it should not be relied on too heavily, nor should it be substituted for other more detailed profitability ratios. Changes in the capital structure during the year make it more difficult to compare earnings per share from year to year. The other profitability measures discussed above are likely to be more beneficial to managers in evaluating overall management performance. Another reason why managers should monitor earnings per share figures is to be familiar with the measure used extensively by investors in making decisions about the company's capital stock.

STATEMENT OF RESOURCE FLOWS

The *balance sheet* presents a picture of an organization's financial position at a specific point in time. It summarizes all resources (assets) owned by an organization and the sources of those resources, which include investments by creditors and stockholders as well as earnings retained in the business. The only reason a company's balance sheet changes is that the company engages in transactions involving resource inflows and outflows. Otherwise the balance sheet would be static.

Revenue and expense transactions summarized on the *income statement* constitute a major portion of all resource flows. By definition, revenues represent the inflow of resources generated from the sale of goods and services, and expenses represent the outflow of resources necessary to generate revenues. As illustrated in the first part of this chapter, many significant decisions of investors, creditors, and managers are based on information obtained from the income statement.

In addition to resource flows reported on the income statement, many other significant transactions generate and use resources. Information about these transactions is also important for decision making. This information—which relates primarily to questions about increases and decreases in debt and equity and major asset acquisitions and dispositions—has significant long-run implications on the firm's operations.

An overall summary of the major transactions that cause the balance sheet to change between two balance sheet dates is normally presented in a separate financial statement. This statement includes information about operating (revenue and expense), investing (noncurrent asset), and financing (long-term debt and equity) transactions. Balance sheet changes occur because of resource inflows and outflows related to operating, investing, and financing transactions. Hence, this statement could be called a **statement of resource flows.**

The Basis for Measuring Resource Flows

There are several possible ways to measure resources and their inflows and outflows. Resources are received by a business in a variety of forms, such as cash, receivables, equipment, and other assets. Likewise, resources flow out of a business in a variety of forms, such as cash, inventory, and other assets.

Because a substantial amount of resource flows occur in the form of cash and because maintaining adequate cash is vital to the continuation of any business, many managers prefer to analyze resource inflows and outflows in terms of cash. When this approach to resource flow analysis is used, the primary objective of the statement of resource flows is to identify all the major categories of transactions that generated and used cash during the period. Thus, the statement is called a **statement of cash flows.**

Another approach to preparing the statement of resource flows is based on working capital instead of cash. Earlier in this chapter working capital was defined as current assets minus current liabilities. Managers commonly view working capital as a pool of relatively liquid resources available to the company in the short run. In this sense, current liabilities are viewed as negative working capital rather than as debt, and the difference between current assets and current liabilities is regarded as net available liquid funds in the short term. Many transactions, such as rendering services on account, increase working capital even though they do not increase cash. Conversely, many transactions, such as accruing salaries payable, decrease working capital even though they do not decrease cash. When the working capital approach to resource flow analysis is used, the primary objective of the statement of resource flows is to identify all the major categories of transactions that generated and used working capital during the period. Thus, the statement is called a **statement of working capital flows.**

Whether a company uses the cash approach or the working capital approach to resource flow analysis, significant transactions that affected the company's overall resources but did not directly affect its cash or working capital should be reported on the statement of resource flows. For example, the acquisition of land by issuing common stock represents a significant resource transaction that did not affect either cash or working capital. As discussed later, under either approach, this transaction would be reported as a supplemental item.

Traditionally, when interest rates are low, managers tend to be less concerned about actual cash on hand and more concerned about their working capital position than when interest rates are high. However, in recent years, during both periods of high and low interest rates, the cash approach to resource flow analysis has been gaining in use. For external reporting purposes, most companies are required to include a statement of cash flows in their general purpose financial statements. However, because some managers still use the working capital approach for internal analysis of resource flows, both methods are illustrated in the following sections.

STATEMENT OF WORKING CAPITAL FLOWS

The primary objective in preparing the statement of working capital flows is to identify all transactions that increased or decreased working capital during the period. The basic accounting (or balance sheet) equation can be used to illustrate the types of transactions that increase and decrease working capital. By modifying the equation to show working capital isolated on the left side, the types of transactions that increase and decrease working capital can be readily identified:

$$\underset{\text{assets}}{\text{Current}} + \underset{\text{assets}}{\text{Noncurrent}} = \underset{\text{liabilities}}{\text{Current}} + \underset{\text{liabilities}}{\text{Long-term}} + \underset{\text{equity}}{\text{Owners}}$$

$$\overbrace{\underset{\text{assets}}{\text{Current}} - \underset{\text{liabilities}}{\text{Current}}}^{\text{Working capital}} = \underset{\text{liabilities}}{\text{Long-term}} + \underset{\text{equity}}{\text{Owners'}} - \underset{\text{assets.}}{\text{Noncurrent}}$$

The left side of the second equation represents working capital; therefore, only transactions that increase the net amount of the left side of this equation increase working capital, and only transactions that decrease the net amount of the left side of this equation decrease working capital. Since the equation must balance, working capital is increased or decreased only by transactions that affect both sides of the equation. If a transaction affects only the left side of the equation, the result is offsetting changes in the working capital accounts but no change in total working capital. Examples of transactions affecting only the left side of the equation are (1) paying a $200 account payable with cash, (2) purchasing $500 of supplies with cash, (3) purchasing $750 of inventory on account, and (4) paying a $400 account payable by issuing a six-month note payable.

If a company has total current assets of $5,000 and total current liabilities of $2,100 before completing the four transactions above, its total working capital is $2,900 both before and after the transactions. The calculations are illustrated below.

	Current Assets	−	Current Liabilities	=	Working Capital
Beginning balances	$5,000		$2,100		$2,900
(1) Paid $200 account payable with cash	(200)		(200)		—
Balances	$4,800		$1,900		$2,900
(2) Purchased $500 of supplies with cash	500*				
	(500)		—		—
Balances	$4,800		$1,900		$2,900
(3) Purchased $750 of inventory on account	750		750		—
Balances	$5,550		$2,650		$2,900
(4) Paid $400 account payable by			(400)**		
issuing a six-month note payable	—		400		—
Ending balances	$5,550		$2,650		$2,900

* Increased one current asset and decreased another.

** Increased one current liability and decreased another.

From the analysis above it is apparent that any transaction affecting only working capital accounts does not change the total amount of working capital. These transactions, therefore, do not constitute sources or uses of working capital. *For working capital to be increased or decreased, there must be changes in the nonworking capital components of the balance sheet equation;* that is, there must be a change in long-term liabilities, owners' equity, or noncurrent assets. The most common changes in these components can be summarized as follows:

Component	Type of Change in Component	Effect on Working Capital	Common Increases and Decreases in Working Capital	Type of Transaction(s)
Long-term liabilities	Increase	Increase	Borrowing on long-term debt	Financing
	Decrease	Decrease	Repayment of long-term debt	Financing
Owners' equity	Increase	Increase	Sale of capital stock	Financing
			Operating at a profit	Operating
	Decrease	Decrease	Purchase of treasury stock	Financing
			Operating at a loss	Operating
			Payment of dividends	Financing
Noncurrent assets	Increase	Decrease	Purchase of noncurrent assets	Investing
	Decrease	Increase	Sale of noncurrent assets	Investing

Net Income and Working Capital

One of the most important causes of increased working capital for a well-managed company is its normal operating activities. These activities generate revenues, expenses, and the resulting net income, all of which are reported on the income statement. Since operations are expected to be a major source of working capital, this category of resource flows is reported first on the statement of resource flows. To measure the effects of operations on working capital, it is usually necessary to make one or more adjustments to net income. Seldom is net income, as reported on the accrual basis income statement, equal to the change in working capital caused by operating transactions.

Although most revenues and expenses on the income statement increase or decrease working capital, some revenues and expenses have no effect on working capital. Consequently, to determine the effects of operations on working capital, it is necessary to convert net income as computed on the income statement to a working capital basis. This conversion involves making adjustments to net income to remove any items reflected in net income that have no effect on working capital. The adjustment for depreciation expense is the one most often required. Depreciation is recorded in the accounting records by the following journal entry.

Journal entry	Depreciation Expense		xx	
	Accumulated Depreciation			xx

The effect of the debit in this entry is to decrease net income, and the effect of the credit is to decrease noncurrent assets. Depreciation Expense and Accumulated Depreciation are both nonworking capital accounts; therefore, this entry does not increase or decrease working capital. To adjust net income to reflect only expenses that decreased working capital, depreciation expense must be removed from the net income computation as follows:

Net income (accrual basis)	$xx
Plus: Expenses that did not affect working capital	
(depreciation expense)	xx
Net income (working capital basis)	$xx

Other examples of transactions that require adjustments to net income are listed below:

- Amortization of intangible assets.
- Depletion of natural resources.
- Amortization of premium or discount on long-term debt.
- Amortization of premium or discount on long-term investments.
- Increases or decreases in deferred (long-term) tax liabilities.

This list includes the most common income statement items that do not affect working capital. The general rule is that any revenue or expense that is recorded without an offsetting increase or decrease in a working capital account will necessitate an adjustment to net income to determine the amount of working capital generated by operations.

Illustration of Statement of Working Capital Flows

The comparative balance sheets for Omega Corporation presented in Exhibit 16–2 are used to illustrate the statement of working capital flows. Because changes in working capital are always accompanied by changes in nonworking capital accounts, *the procedure for identifying transactions that cause changes in working capital involves analyzing the nonworking capital accounts to identify changes in them that increased or decreased total working capital.* This procedure is much easier than the alternative of analyzing every transaction in each working capital account. The majority of the transactions recorded in the working capital accounts usually have no effect on total working capital. Therefore, examining the mass of transactions recorded in the working capital accounts to identify transactions that affected total working capital would ordinarily be an enormous task and an inefficient method of identifying them.

The information obtained by analyzing the transactions entered in the nonworking capital accounts for Omega Corporation, including an indication of how each change affected working capital and cash, is summarized as follows.

EXHIBIT 16–2   Comparative Balance Sheets

Omega Corporation
Comparative Balance Sheets
December 31, 19x5 and 19x4

Assets	19x5	19x4
Current assets:		
Cash	$ 700	$ 800
Accounts receivable (net)	5,055	2,100
Inventory	6,800	7,500
Prepaid insurance	150	450
Total	$12,705	$10,850
Land	25,000	15,000
Building	40,000	40,000
Accumulated depreciation (building)	(9,000)	(8,000)
Equipment	23,000	18,000
Accumulated depreciation (equipment)	(7,700)	(6,500)
Total assets	$84,005	$69,350
Liabilities and stockholders' equity		
Current liabilities:		
Accounts payable	$ 2,400	$ 3,600
Notes payable	—	5,000
Dividends payable	1,000	—
Total	$ 3,400	$ 8,600
Mortgage note payable	34,250	35,000
Total liabilities	$37,650	$43,600
Stockholders' equity:		
Common stock ($1 par value)	$30,000	$10,000
Premium on common stock	2,200	2,000
Retained earnings	14,155	13,750
Total stockholders' equity	46,355	25,750
Total liabilities and stockholders' equity	$84,005	$69,350

Later we will use the information pertaining to changes in cash to prepare a statement of cash flows.

Land. The $10,000 increase in land was caused by the issuance of 10,000 shares of Omega common stock in exchange for five acres of land to be used for plant expansion. This transaction had no effect on either working capital or cash; however, it represented offsetting financing (issuance of common stock) and investing (acquisition of land) transactions that should be shown as supplemental information on the statement of working capital flows and on the statement of cash flows.

Building. No transactions.

Accumulated Depreciation—Building. Depreciation expense of $1,000 was recorded on the building. The acquisition of a building is treated as a decrease in working capital or cash; however, using the building has no effect on these resources. Therefore, depreciation expense decreased net income but had no effect on working capital or cash. This $1,000 must be added to net income in determining the effect of operations on both working capital and cash.

Equipment. Equipment costing $5,000 was purchased for cash. This was an investing transaction that decreased both working capital and cash.

Accumulated Depreciation—Equipment. Depreciation expense of $1,200 was recorded on the equipment. This transaction decreased net income but had no effect on working capital or cash. This $1,200 will be added to net income in determining the effect of operations on working capital and in determining the effect of operations on cash.

Mortgage Note Payable. A $6,000 payment was made on the note. Of this amount, $5,250 was applied to interest expense, and $750 reduced the principal amount of the note. The effect of the interest expense was to decrease net income, working capital, and cash. The payment of principal reduced both working capital and cash by $750. Thus, the interest expense was an operating transaction reflected in net income, and the payment of the principal was a financing transaction.

Common Stock. Two transactions were recorded in the common stock account. First, 10,000 shares of common stock were issued at par value in exchange for land, causing a $10,000 increase in common stock. (See the above explanation for land for the effects on working capital and cash.) Second, 10,000 shares were issued for $10,200 cash, including $10,000 in par value and $200 in excess of par value. This financing transaction increased both working capital and cash by $10,200.

Premium on Common Stock. See previous explanation.

Retained Earnings. This account was increased by net income of $1,405 and decreased by a dividend declaration of $1,000. Net income of $1,405 must be adjusted for nonworking capital expenses (depreciation on building and equipment) to determine the amount of working capital provided by operations. The dividend declaration was recorded by a debit to Retained Earnings and a credit to Dividends Payable, a current liability account. This financing transaction decreased working capital by $1,000 but had no effect on cash.

Note that the above analysis of working capital accounts is presented in the same order in which the accounts are presented in the balance sheet. This approach provides an orderly procedure for gathering the data for preparing the statement of resource flows. The changes in working capital explained above are summarized in the statement of working capital flows in Exhibit 16–3.

EXHIBIT 16–3   Statement of Working Capital Flows

Omega Corporation
Statement of Working Capital Flows
For the year ended December 31, 19x5

Working capital flows from operating activities:		
Net income	$ 1,405	
Nonworking capital expenses included in net income:		
Depreciation expense	2,200	
Net working capital provided by operating activities		$ 3,605
Working capital inflows (outflows) from investing activities:		
Purchase of equipment	$ (5,000)	
Net working capital used by investing activities		(5,000)
Working capital inflows (outflows) from financing activities:		
Proceeds from issuance of common stock	$10,200	
Payment of mortgage note principal	(750)	
Declaration of cash dividend	(1,000)	
Net working capital provided by financing activities		8,450
Net increase in working capital		$ 7,055

Schedule of nonworking capital investing and financing activities:

Common stock issued to acquire land	$10,000

Schedule of changes in working capital:

Working Capital Accounts	Working Capital December 31 19x5	Working Capital December 31 19x4	Working Capital Increase (Decrease)
Cash	$ 700	$ 800	$ (100)
Accounts Receivable (net)	5,055	2,100	2,955
Inventory	6,800	7,500	(700)
Prepaid Insurance	150	450	(300)
Accounts Payable	(2,400)	(3,600)	1,200
Notes Payable	—	(5,000)	5,000
Dividends Payable	(1,000)	—	(1,000)
Total	$ 9,305	$ 2,250	$ 7,055

The statement of working capital flows consists of three separate parts: (1) working capital flows from operating, investing, and financing activities; (2) the schedule of nonworking capital investing and financing activities; and (3) the schedule of changes in working capital. Note in Exhibit 16–3 that net income is $1,405, whereas working capital provided by operations is $3,605. This difference between net income and the amount of working capital provided by operations consists of one expense item (depreciation expense) deducted in computing net income that did not reduce working capital. To show the effects of operations on working capital, this item must be removed from the computation of net income. Because most revenue and expense items produce a direct effect on total working capital, ordinarily very few of these adjustments are required.

All significant inflows and outflows of resources that do not directly affect working capital are shown in a separate schedule in the second part of the statement of working capital flows. Note in Exhibit 16–3 that this schedule includes only the information about the exchange of common stock for land. This transaction represented important offsetting financing and investing activities that had no effect on working capital.

Finally, the statement of working capital flows includes a schedule that shows the specific working capital account changes that make up the total change in working capital for the period. For Omega Corporation, the $7,055 net increase in working capital was reflected in the working capital accounts as a $100 decrease in cash, a $2,955 increase in net accounts receivable, and so forth. The changes in working capital accounts shown in this schedule resulted from the operating, investing, and financing transactions summarized in the first part of the statement. These account changes also reflect the transactions (such as a collection of an account receivable) that affect the working capital accounts but have no effect on the net amount of working capital.

STATEMENT OF CASH FLOWS

The primary focus of the statement of cash flows is on transactions that increased or decreased cash during the period. One way to identify these transactions is to conduct a detailed analysis of each of the many cash receipts and disbursements recorded during the period. A more efficient approach, however, is to analyze the accounts other than Cash, since every debit or credit to Cash must be offset by a debit or credit to some other account.

Adjusting Net Income to Cash Basis

To determine the effects of operations on cash, it is necessary to adjust accrual net income as reported on the income statement to the cash basis. Two types of adjustments are required: (1) revenues and expenses that did not affect working capital accounts and (2) changes in working capital accounts other than cash. For the first group the same adjustments made to net income in the statement of working capital flows are required in the statement of cash flows. If a revenue or expense item does not affect a working capital account, it obviously does not affect cash either, since cash is part of working capital.

The adjustments in the second group are necessary to eliminate from net income the effects of increases and decreases in the current noncash accrual accounts. If a company were using a strict cash basis of accounting for net income, revenues and expenses would be recognized only upon the receipt and payment of cash. Therefore Accounts Receivable, Inventory, and Prepaid Expenses would not be recognized.[3] Similarly, there would be no recognition of liabilities for Accounts Payable and Accrued Expenses Payable. *Increases and decreases in these working capital accounts result entirely from applying accrual concepts in measuring net income.* The types of adjustments required to convert accrual net income to a cash basis are described below. These adjustments for changes in working capital accounts are in addition to the nonworking capital revenue and expense adjustments (such as depreciation) made in the statement of working capital flows.

Accounts Receivable. Under accrual basis accounting, revenues are equal to total sales; under cash basis accounting, revenues are equal to collections from sales. Therefore, if sales exceed collections, resulting in *increased* Accounts Receivable, accrual revenues will exceed cash revenues. Conversely, if collections exceed sales, resulting in decreased Accounts Receivable, *accrual* revenues will be less than cash revenues. To convert net income to a cash basis, increases in Accounts Receivable are subtracted from accrual net income, and decreases are added to accrual net income.

Inventory. Under the accrual basis of measuring net income, inventory is recognized as an asset when purchased, and it is recorded as an expense when sold. Under the cash basis, inventory purchases are recorded immediately as expenses. If the amount of inventory sold is less than the amount purchased, resulting in an increase in inventory, cost of goods sold will be less and net income will be greater on the accrual basis than on the cash basis. To adjust to the cash basis increases in inventory are deducted from net income. Conversely, if the amount of inventory sold exceeds the amount purchased, thereby resulting in an inventory decrease, cost of goods sold will be greater and net income will be less on the accrual basis than on the cash basis. To adjust to the cash basis decreases in inventory are added to net income.

Prepaid Expenses. Under accrual accounting, prepayments for supplies, insurance, rent, and other expenses are recognized as assets and deducted as expenses when the items are consumed; on the cash basis, however, these items are expensed when cash payments are made. Increases in prepaid expense accounts during the period indicate that payments for these items exceeded the amounts deducted on the income statement. This increase is subtracted from net income to adjust to the cash basis. Conversely, decreases in prepaid expense accounts represent excess expenses over cash payments, which are added back to net income to adjust to the cash basis.

---

[3] Even on a strict cash basis, a business would, of course, need to keep records outside the formal ledger accounts on its receivables and payables.

Accounts Payable and Accrued Payables. The balances in Accounts Payable and Accrued Payables represent liabilities for inventory purchases and other expenses that have been incurred but not paid. If either Accounts Payable or Accrued Payables increases during the period, the expense deduction on the income statement is greater than the amount paid during the year for the related expenses. These increases are added to net income to adjust to the cash basis. Conversely, net income must be reduced by the amount of any decreases in Accounts Payable or Accrued Payables, since these decreases represent cash payments made during the period that were not recorded as expenses.

To summarize, in adjusting accrual net income to determine cash flows from operating activities, it is necessary to make the following adjustments to net income.

1. Adjustments for revenues and expenses not affecting working capital:

   ▪ Subtract revenues (such as amortization of long-term unearned revenues) that were not accompanied by increases in working capital accounts.

   ▪ Add expenses (such as depreciation) that were not accompanied by decreases in working capital accounts.

2. Adjustments for changes in working capital accounts other than cash:

   ▪ Subtract *increases* in current accrual asset accounts, such as Accounts Receivable, Inventory, and Prepaid Expenses.

   ▪ Add *decreases* in current accrual asset accounts, such as Accounts Receivable, Inventory, and Prepaid Expenses.

   ▪ Add *increases* in current accrual liability accounts, such as Accounts Payable and Accrued Payables.

   ▪ Subtract *decreases* in current accrual liability accounts, such as Accounts Payable and Accrued Payables.

The adjustments to net income in the first group are required on both the statements of working capital and cash flows, whereas the second group of adjustments is required only on the statement of cash flows.

After determining the amount of cash generated by operations, all other sources and uses of cash are determined by analyzing the nonworking capital accounts and any working capital accounts (such as short-term notes payable) that were not analyzed in making the adjustments to net income. The presentation of the statement of cash flows is very similar to the statement of working capital flows. Omega Corporation's statement of cash flows is presented in Exhibit 16–4.

Comparison of Exhibits 16–3 and 16–4 reveals some interesting differences between the working capital and cash statements. Omega reported $1,405 in *net income* on its income statement prepared in accordance with accrual

EXHIBIT 16–4   Statement of Cash Flows

Omega Corporation
Statement of Cash Flows
For the year ended December 31, 19x5

Cash flows from operating activities:		
Net income	$ 1,405	
Noncash expenses and revenues included in net income:		
Depreciation expense	2,200	
Increase in Accounts Receivable	(2,955)	
Decrease in Inventory	700	
Decrease in Prepaid Insurance	300	
Decrease in Accounts Payable	(1,200)	
Net cash provided by operating activities		$ 450
Cash inflows (outflows) from investing activities:		
Purchase of Equipment	$ (5,000)	
Net cash used by investing activities		(5,000)
Cash inflows (outflows) from financing activities:		
Payment of short-term note payable	$ (5,000)	
Proceeds from issuance of common stock	10,200	
Payment of mortgage note principal	(750)	
Net cash provided by financing activities		4,450
Net decrease in cash		$ (100)
Schedule of noncash investing and financing activities:		
Dividends declared but not paid		$ 1,000
Common stock issued to acquire land		$10,000

accounting concepts. *Working capital* provided by operations was $3,605, whereas *cash* provided by operations was $450. Although the company reported a $7,055 *increase* in working capital, it had a $100 *decrease* in cash. On the working capital statement, the declared dividend entered into the primary computation of resource changes, but on the cash basis it was reported as a noncash financing item. The reason for this difference is that the dividend declaration decreased working capital but had no effect on cash. The decrease in cash for the dividend will be shown as a use of cash in the period when the dividend is paid.

Note in Exhibit 16–4 that the statement of cash flows consists of only two primary parts: the summary of cash flows from operating, investing, and financing activities and the schedule of noncash investing and financing activities. In the first part of the statement, cash provided by operations is computed by adjusting net income to eliminate items that increased or decreased net income but did not affect cash. The effect of these adjustments is to convert net income from an accrual basis to a cash basis.

A more direct approach to determining cash basis net income is to prepare a cash basis income statement by making the necessary adjustment to each item on the income statement. Although this approach is seldom used in preparing the statement of cash flows, it may be useful to managers and other financial statement users because it shows not only the net amount of cash provided by operations, but also how each component of net income increased or decreased cash. Exhibit 16–5 illustrates the conversion of the complete income statement for Omega Corporation from the accrual basis to the cash basis.

EXHIBIT 16–5 Conversion of Income Statement from Accrual Basis to Cash Basis

Omega Corporation
Accrual and Cash Basis Income Statements
For the year ended December 31, 19x5

	Accrual Basis	Increase	Decrease	Cash Basis
Sales	$58,000		$2,955(a)	$55,045
Cost of goods sold:				
Beginning inventory	$ 7,500			
Plus purchases	31,300			
Less ending inventory	(6,800)			
Total	−32,000	1,200(b)	700(c)	−32,500
Gross profit	$26,000			$22,545
Operating expenses:				
Salaries expense	$12,000			$12,000
Bad debts expense	545			545
Insurance expense	300		300(d)	—
Depreciation expense	2,200		2,200(e)	—
Interest expense	5,750			5,750
Other expenses	3,800			3,800
Total	−24,595			−22,095
Net income	$ 1,405			$ 450

(a) To remove sales related to the increase in Accounts Receivable that increased Sales but did not affect cash.

(b) To include in Cost of Goods Sold the decrease in Accounts Payable paid in cash during the current period.

(c) To remove from Cost of Goods Sold the decrease in Inventory acquired in a previous period that had no effect on cash in the current period.

(d) To remove the decrease in Prepaid Insurance expensed in the current period but paid for in the previous period.

(e) To remove Depreciation Expense that did not affect cash.

INTERPRETING THE STATEMENT OF RESOURCE FLOWS

Techniques like those illustrated earlier in this chapter for analyzing the balance sheet and income statement are not available for analyzing the statement of resource flows. There are no widely used ratios for examining this statement and its relationship to the other financial statements. Despite the lack of uniform analytical procedures, the statement of resource flows is important in communicating useful financial information. Whether the working capital or cash approach is used, this statement often provides the best available report of the company's overall performance. Unlike the income statement, which reports primarily operating activities, the statement of resource flows summarizes management's operating, investing, and financing activities for the period. It tells where capital came from, where capital was invested, and how profitable past company investments were during the period.

Many important questions that investors, creditors, and managers have about a company can be answered with information obtained from the statement of resource flows. Some of these questions are listed below.

- Were capital investments compatible with the sources of capital?
- Did management use short-term capital to finance long-term investments?
- Was the decision to raise dividends consistent with the level of resources generated by operations?
- Why did short-term liquidity deteriorate even though earnings increased?
- Were the increases in working capital (or cash) generated primarily by operations, by long-term capital sources, or by liquidating investments in long-term assets?
- How much was invested in new capital assets during the year?
- What happened to funds generated by the sale of common stock or long-term bonds, or generated by the disposition of a division or other segment of the business?

Managers should give close attention to the statement of resource flows because if often portrays a different picture of management's performance than that revealed in the income statement and balance sheet. For example, if long-term financial stability were sacrificed during the period for current liquidity and profitability, this development would probably be apparent in the statement of resource flows. The assessment of a company's overall performance is not completed until the manager, or other user, has read and interpreted all financial statements, including the income statement, the balance sheet, and the statement of working capital or cash flows.

SUMMARY

Financial statement analysis is the process of using financial statement data to generate additional financial information. Investors and creditors, as well as managers, can benefit from financial analysis. In this chapter the primary focus was on analytical measures that benefit managers.

Measures for analyzing financial statements can be classified into solvency and performance measures. For evaluating short-term solvency, the current ratio and acid test ratio are used to determine the sufficiency of current assets to satisfy current liabilities. Other short-term solvency measures aimed at evaluating the liquidity of current assets are inventory turnover and the number of days receivables outstanding. Long-term solvency can be evaluated by computing the debt-to-equity ratio and the times interest earned multiple. These measures indicate the overall riskiness of the creditors' investment in the firm and the ability of the firm to meet its continuing interest requirements.

To evaluate current performance, several measures are available that focus both on the ability of the assets to generate sales and profits and on the profit returns attributable to creditors and stockholders. The productivity of the firm's assets is measured by the asset turnover multiple, the return on sales ratio, and the return on assets ratio. The profitability of the shareholders' investment is measured by the return on equity ratio. The favorable or unfavorable use of financial leverage can be determined by comparing return on assets with return on equity. Favorable leverage exists when the return on equity exceeds the return on assets; unfavorable leverage exists when the return on equity is less than the return on assets. Earnings per share may be helpful in assessing overall company performance, although it should be used with caution.

Historically, the income statement and the balance sheet have been the primary financial statements used to evaluate a company. The statement of resource flows, however, contains a substantial amount of useful information not found in these other statements. Though the income statement summarizes changes in the balance sheet related to operating transactions, the statement of resource flows reports all material changes in the balance sheet. Complete information about financing and investing transactions is found only in the statement of resource flows.

The statement of resource flows summarizes balance sheet changes in terms of resource inflows and outflows from operating, investing, and financing activities. Two methods for measuring resource flows are the working capital basis and the cash basis. Although, historically, most companies used the working capital basis in their published financial statements, most companies are now required to use the cash approach for external reporting purposes. However, for internal use, the working capital approach may still be used.

KEY TERMS

Acid test ratio	Quick ratio
Asset turnover	Return on assets
Current ratio	Return on equity
Days receivables outstanding	Return on sales
Debt-to-equity ratio	Solvency
Earnings per share	Statement of cash flows
Financial leverage	Statement of resource flows
Financial statement analysis	Statement of working capital flows
Inventory turnover	Times interest earned
Price earnings ratio	Working capital

REVIEW QUESTIONS

16–1 What is the general purpose for conducting ratio analysis of financial statements?

16–2 Name three reasons why managers should analyze their firm's financial statements.

16–3 What is the purpose of evaluation standards in financial analysis?

16–4 What types of standards are probably most relevant for financial analysis by managers?

16–5 Explain and differentiate the terms "solvency evaluation" and "performance evaluation."

16–6 Explain the difference between the current ratio and the acid test ratio.

16–7 Why is it useful to compute the inventory turnover and the days receivables outstanding? How is each of these measures computed?

16–8 What are the primary measures of long-term solvency? How are they computed?

16–9 Which financial statement analysis measure provides information concerning the sales output produced by a firm's assets?

16–10 Why is interest expense added in the numerator in computing return on assets?

16–11 Explain the concept of financial leverage. What causes financial leverage to be favorable? Unfavorable?

16–12 What is the general purpose of a statement of resource flows? What is its relationship to the income statement and the balance sheet?

16–13 Why is depreciation expense added to net income in measuring resources generated by operations on the working capital basis? On the cash basis?

16–14 Name three major sources and three major uses of working capital.

16–15 How would net income be adjusted for the following account changes in preparing a statement of cash flows: increase in Accounts Receivable, decrease in Inventory, increase in Prepaid Insurance, and increase in Accounts Payable?

**REVIEW
PROBLEM**

**Ratio Analysis and
Statement of Cash
Flows**

Comparative 19x7 and 19x8 financial statements for O'Keefe's, Inc., are presented below.

O'Keefe's, Inc.
Comparative Income Statements
For the years ended December 31, 19x7 and 19x8
(*in thousands*)

	19x8	19x7
Sales	$3,000	$2,500
Cost of goods sold	−2,600	−2,300
Gross profit	$ 400	$ 200
Operating expenses:		
Selling	$ 125	$ 105
General and administrative	70	60
Total	− 195	− 165
Operating income	$ 205	$ 35
Other revenues and expenses:		
Interest income	$ 10	$ 5
Interest expense	(40)	(20)
Total	− 30	− 15
Income before income taxes	$ 175	$ 20
Provision for income taxes (34%)	− 60	− 7
Net income	$ 115	$ 13
Earnings per share	$ 1.28	$ 0.19

O'Keefe's, Inc.
Comparative Balance Sheets
December 31, 19x7 and 19x8
(*in thousands*)

Assets	19x8	19x7
Current assets:		
Cash	$ 300	$ 270
Marketable securities	75	45
Accounts receivable	325	280
Inventories	400	350
Other current assets	60	55
Total current assets	$1,160	$1,000
Property, plant, and equipment	$1,500	$1,300
Less: Accumulated depreciation	− 800	− 750
Net	700	550
Other assets	15	12
Total assets	$1,875	$1,562

Liabilities and stockholders' equity

Current liabilities:		
Accounts payable	$ 435	$ 330
Taxes payable	45	5
Other current liabilities	50	45
Total current liabilities	$ 530	$ 380
Long-term debt	300	250
Total liabilities	$ 830	$ 630
Stockholders' equity:		
Common stock ($1 par)	$ 90	$ 70
Premium on common stock	15	10
Retained earnings	940	852
Total stockholders' equity	1,045	932
Total liabilities and stockholders' equity	$1,875	$1,562

Additional information:

- During 19x8, Cost of Goods Sold and Operating Expenses included a total of $50,000 in depreciation expense.
- Dividends of $27,000 were declared and paid during 19x8.
- Common stock of $15,000 was issued at par for cash in 19x8.
- Equipment costing $200,000 was acquired during 19x8 by paying cash of $190,000 and issuing 5,000 shares of common stock worth $10,000.
- During 19x8, long-term debt of $20,000 was paid off in cash and new long-term debt of $70,000 was issued for cash.
- The company extended a loan of $3,000 to the president during 19x8.

Requirements

a) Prepare a complete ratio analysis for 19x8 including measures of solvency and measures of performance.

b) Prepare a statement of cash flows for 19x8.

EXERCISES

16–1 Short-Term Solvency Ratios

Windover, Inc., had the following current assets and current liabilities in its end-of-year financial statements for 19x1 and 19x0.

Current assets	*19x1*	*19x0*
Cash	$ 1,700	$ 1,500
Accounts receivable	16,200	6,900
Marketable securities	2,000	2,500
Inventory	8,300	7,400
Total	$28,200	$18,300

Current liabilities

Accounts payable	$ 5,600	$ 3,700
Notes payable	1,000	1,000
Accrued expenses payable	5,400	4,300
Total	$12,000	$ 9,000

Additional data:

	19x1	19x0
Sales	$195,000	$220,000
Cost of goods sold	132,000	158,000
Inventory, beginning of 19x0		6,800

Required: Compute the following ratios for 19x1 and 19x0. (Round calculations to two decimal places.)

1. Current ratio.

2. Acid test ratio.

3. Inventory turnover.

4. Days receivables outstanding.

16–2 Short-Term Solvency Ratios

The following items (listed alphabetically) were taken from the 19x7 year-end financial statements of Monteray Corporation.

Accounts payable	$ 27,500
Accounts receivable	32,000
Cash	4,800
Cost of goods sold	195,000
Inventory, beginning	80,000
Inventory, ending	65,000
Marketable securities	15,750
Other current payables	8,200
Sales	325,000

Required: Compute the following ratios. (Round calculations to two decimal places.)

1. Current ratio.

2. Acid test ratio.

3. Inventory turnover.

4. Days receivables outstanding.

16–3 Long-Term Solvency Ratios

Selected financial statement data for 19x5 are given below for Vail Construction Company.

Income taxes	$ 36,018
Interest expense	4,000
Net income	48,178
Total assets	399,363
Total liabilities	133,121

Requirements (Round calculations to two decimal places.)

a) Compute the debt-to-equity ratio.

b) Compute the ratio of times interest earned.

16–4 Short-Term Solvency Ratios

The financial data given below were obtained from the end-of-year financial statements of York Company for 19x2, 19x1, and 19x0.

	19x2	19x1	19x0
Accounts receivable	$ 153,000	$ 165,000	$ 150,000
Cost of goods sold	1,680,000	1,450,000	1,600,000
Current assets	750,000	600,000	675,000
Current liabilities	525,000	450,000	500,000
Inventory	375,000	275,000	325,000
Sales	1,850,000	2,000,000	1,750,000

Requirements

a) Compute the following financial ratios for 19x2 and 19x1. (Round calculations to two decimal places.)

   1. Current ratio.

   2. Acid test ratio.

   3. Inventory turnover.

   4. Days receivables outstanding.

b) Comment on the short-term solvency of York Company for 19x1 and 19x2. Did the company's short-term solvency improve or deteriorate during 19x2? Explain.

16–5 Long-Term Solvency Ratios

Summaries of the end-of-year financial statements of Palo Alto Company for 19x6 are given as follows.

Income statement:

Sales		$8,000,000
Less: Cost of goods sold	$3,425,000	
Selling expenses	625,000	
Administrative expenses	525,000	
Interest expense	1,475,300	
Income tax expense	50,250	−6,100,550
Net income		$1,899,450

Balance sheet:

Total assets	$850,000	Total liabilities	$600,000
		Stockholders' equity	250,000
		Total	$850,000

Requirements

a) Compute the ratio of times interest earned. (Round computations to two decimal places.)

b) Compute the debt-to-equity ratio.

16–6 Effects of Financing Decisions

Provo, Inc., has total assets of $2,500,000 and total liabilities of $2,000,000. Provo is considering two alternatives for acquiring additional warehouse space. Under the first alternative the building would be purchased for $300,000 and financed by issuing long-term bonds. Under the other alternative the building would be rented on an annual lease of $30,000 per year.

Requirements

a) Compute the current debt-to-equity ratio.

b) What effect will the addition of the warehouse space have on the debt-to-equity ratio (1) assuming the building is purchased by issuing bonds and (2) assuming the building is rented on an annual lease?

16–7 Ratio Analysis: Measures of Performance

The following selected data were obtained from the end-of-year financial statements of Nelox Corporation for 19x9 and 19x8.

	19x9	19x8
Total assets	$7,349,000	$6,553,000
Interest expense	115,000	102,000
Long-term liabilities	1,220,000	1,239,000
Net income	619,000	563,000
Sales	8,196,000	6,996,000
Stockholders' equity	3,624,000	3,221,000

Requirements

a) Compute the following performance measurement ratios for 19x9. (Round computations to three decimal places. Ignore income taxes.)

   1. Asset turnover.

   2. Return on sales.

   3. Return on assets.

   4. Return on equity.

b) Is Nelox Company using financial leverage? If so, is the leverage favorable or unfavorable? Explain.

16–8 Schedule of Changes in Working Capital

Roswell Company's current assets and current liabilities at the end of 19x6 and 19x5 are as follows:

	19x6	19x5
Current assets		
Cash	$ 8,500	$ 6,400
Accounts receivable	17,000	20,200
Inventory	41,000	44,000
Prepaid expenses	800	950
Total	$67,300	$71,550
Current liabilities		
Accounts payable	$15,500	$17,200
Notes payable	10,000	7,500
Taxes payable	1,500	1,250
Total	$27,000	$25,950

Required: Prepare a schedule of changes in working capital for 19x6.

16–9 Effects of Operations on Working Capital

Bob's Big Pizza Restaurant had the following income statement for 19x9.

Bob's Big Pizza Restaurant
Income Statement
For the year 19x9

Sales		$88,000
Less costs and expenses:		
Cost of food	$25,000	
Wages	21,000	
Utilities	6,000	
Rent	18,000	
Depreciation	1,500	
Miscellaneous	3,500	−75,000
Net income		$13,000

Requirements

a) Indicate for each item on the income statement which working capital accounts were most likely affected by the revenue or expense transaction and whether total working capital was increased or decreased.

b) Adjust net income from the accrual basis to the working capital basis.

16–10 Changes in Working Capital

Below is a list of typical financing, investing, and operating transactions.

1. Sold capital stock for cash.
2. Purchased a building for cash.
3. Declared cash dividends.
4. Issued long-term bonds payable.
5. Recorded a net loss for the period.
6. Purchased a building site by issuing long-term bonds.
7. Sold equipment with a five-year remaining life for an amount equal to book value.
8. Sold treasury stock for cash.
9. Borrowed cash on a long-term note.
10. Sold a fully depreciated piece of equipment.

Required: For each of the above transactions indicate whether working capital increased, decreased, or was not affected. Also indicate whether the change in working capital was accompanied by a change in noncurrent assets, long-term liabilities, or owners' equity.

16–11 Effects of Transactions on Working Capital

Fastdata, Inc., had the following account balances at June 30, 19x1.

Accounts Payable	$ 7,500
Accounts Receivable	12,600
Cash	3,000
Inventory	18,000
Notes Payable	3,000
Supplies	300
Wages Payable	1,325

In July the following transactions were recorded.

- Collected $7,000 of accounts receivable.
- Paid the balance of wages payable.
- Paid $4,250 on accounts payable.
- Negotiated a six-month extension on a $3,000 account payable, and issued a note payable for that amount.
- Purchased $2,500 of inventory for cash and $6,300 on account.

Requirements

a) Compute working capital at June 30, 19x1.

b) Prepare a schedule showing the effect of each of the July transactions on working capital and showing the July 31 working capital. Compute the net change in working capital during July.

16–12 Effects of Transactions on Working Capital

Hendrix Company reported current assets of $45,000 and current liabilities of $31,500 on its December 31, 19x5 balance sheet. During January, 19x6 the following transactions were recorded.

- Purchased $3,000 in inventory on account.
- Purchased land for $15,000 paying a $2,500 cash down payment and issuing a long-term note for the balance.
- Sold merchandise costing $5,000 for $9,250.
- Paid $4,500 on accounts payable.
- Paid cash expenses of $1,800.
- Purchased supplies for $250 cash.

Requirements

a) Compute Hendrix Company's working capital at December 31, 19x5.

b) Prepare a schedule showing the effect of each of the January transactions on working capital and showing the January 31 working capital.

16–13 Working Capital and Cash Flows from Operations

Conn Publishing Company had the following current assets and current liabilities for the years ending December 31, 19x7 and 19x6:

Current assets	19x7	19x6
Cash	$ 5,000	$ 2,500
Accounts Receivable	42,000	53,000
Inventory	92,000	81,000
Prepaid Expenses	8,500	6,000
Due from Officers	10,000	10,000
Current liabilities		
Accounts Payable	$28,000	$32,000
Salaries Payable	10,000	16,000
Interest Payable	4,500	-0-
Taxes Payable	15,000	11,500
Notes Payable (for bank loan)	25,000	12,500

Additional information:

During 19x7, Conn Publishing Company recorded depreciation expense of $22,000 and had net income of $67,500.

Requirements

a) Compute Conn's working capital at the end of 19x7 and 19x6 and the change in working capital during 19x7.

b) Identify the working capital accounts that resulted from using the accrual basis of income measurement.

c) Compute the amount of working capital provided by operations in 19x7.

d) Compute the amount of cash provided by operations in 19x7.

16–14 Cash Provided by Operations

The following information about changes in selected accounts for Warren Company has been provided to you for the year ended December 31, 19x3:

Accounts Payable	$35,000 increase
Accounts Receivable	20,000 increase
Accumulated Depreciation	16,500 increase
Accrued Expenses Payable	14,800 decrease
Cash	27,000 increase
Depreciation Expense	16,500 increase
Inventory	22,000 decrease
Notes Payable—Bank	15,000 increase
Retained Earnings	32,000 increase
Supplies	3,400 decrease
Wages Payable	8,000 decrease

Dividends of $20,000 were declared and paid during 19x3.

Requirements

a) Based only on the information provided above, compute the amount of net income reported for 19x3.

b) Based only on the information provided above, compute the amount of cash provided by operations in 19x3.

PROBLEMS

16–15 Financial Leverage

The following data have been determined for McClellan Company and McDonough Company for 19x5.

	McClellan	McDonough
Net income	$ 270,000	$ 405,000
Interest expense	120,000	112,500
Total assets, beginning of 19x5	3,750,000	6,375,000
Total assets, end of 19x5	4,042,500	6,847,500
Stockholders' equity, beginning of 19x5	1,594,500	3,703,500
Stockholders' equity, end of 19x5	1,689,000	3,832,500

Requirements

a) Compute the following ratios for McClellan and McDonough Companies at the end of 19x5. (Ignore taxes and round calculations to three decimal places.)

1. Return on assets.

2. Return on equity.

b) Comment on the use of financial leverage by these two companies. Which company is the most highly leveraged? Which company's stockholders are benefiting the most from the use of leverage?

16–16
Comprehensive Ratio
Analysis

Rocky Mountain Company's financial statements are presented below.

Rocky Mountain Company
Comparative Balance Sheets
December 31, 19x4 and 19x3

Assets	19x4	19x3
Cash	$ 243,000	$ 270,000
Accounts receivable	1,147,000	1,120,000
Inventory	637,000	556,000
Total current assets	$2,027,000	$ 1,946,000
Property, plant, and equipment (net)	7,587,000	6,952,000
Total assets	$9,614,000	$ 8,898,000

Liabilities and stockholders' equity	19x4	19x3
Accounts payable	$ 297,000	$ 256,000
Accrued expenses payable	607,000	594,000
Total current liabilities	$ 904,000	$ 850,000
Long-term debt	1,350,000	1,282,000
Total liabilities	$2,254,000	$ 2,132,000
Common stock	$5,200,000	$ 5,200,000
Retained earnings	2,160,000	1,566,000
Total stockholders' equity	7,360,000	6,766,000
Total liabilities and stockholders' equity	$9,614,000	$ 8,898,000

Rocky Mountain Company
Income Statement
For the year ended December 31, 19x4

Sales		$11,677,000
Cost of goods sold		− 6,513,000
Gross profit		$ 5,164,000
Less operating expenses:		
Depreciation	$ 567,000	
Other expenses	2,882,000	− 3,449,000
Income from operations		$ 1,715,000
Less interest expense		− 94,000
Income before income taxes		$ 1,621,000
Less income taxes		− 486,000
Net income		$ 1,135,000

Requirements (Round all calculations to three decimal places.)

a) Prepare a short-term solvency ratio analysis for Rocky Mountain Company for 19x4.

b) Prepare a long-term solvency ratio analysis for 19x4.

c) Prepare a performance ratio analysis for 19x4.

16–17
Comprehensive
Financial Analysis

Comparative income statements and balance sheets for Seneca Company are presented below for 19x9 and 19x8.

Seneca Company
Comparative Income Statements
For the years ended December 31, 19x9 and 19x8

	19x9	19x8
Sales	$11,778,070	$11,241,498
Cost of goods sold	− 6,615,148	− 6,395,466
Gross profit	$ 5,162,922	$ 4,846,032
Less selling and administrative expenses	− 3,565,750	− 3,363,722
Operating income	$ 1,597,172	$ 1,482,310
Other revenues and expenses:		
Interest revenue	141,264	80,198
Interest expense	(76,698)	(70,204)
Other expenses	(47,230)	(18,850)
Income before income taxes	$ 1,614,508	$ 1,473,454
Income taxes	− 720,368	− 660,818
Net income	$ 894,140	$ 812,636

Seneca Company
Comparative Balance Sheets
December 31, 19x9 and 19x8

Assets	19x9	19x8
Cash	$ 241,816	$ 259,370
Marketable securities	437,268	202,802
Accounts receivable	966,982	1,046,246
Inventory	1,501,438	1,620,470
Prepaid expenses	124,988	115,618
Total current assets	$ 3,272,492	$ 3,244,506
Investments and other assets	774,836	604,368
Property, plant, and equipment (net)	2,818,912	2,681,680
Trademarks and other intangibles	263,322	281,362
Total assets	$ 7,129,562	$ 6,811,916

Liabilities and stockholders' equity

Notes payable	$ 179,294	$ 175,174
Current maturities of long-term debt	10,030	15,056
Accounts payable and accrued expenses	1,822,326	1,932,930
Total current liabilities	$ 2,011,650	$ 2,123,160
Long-term debt	556,368	539,280
Total liabilities	$ 2,568,018	$ 2,662,440
Common stock	$ 124,778	$ 124,744
Additional paid-in capital	228,388	226,344
Retained earnings	4,208,378	3,798,388
Total stockholders' equity	4,561,544	4,149,476
Total liabilities and stockholders' equity	$ 7,129,562	$ 6,811,916

Requirements

a) Prepare a comprehensive financial analysis of Seneca, Inc., for 19x9, including (1) short-term solvency ratios, (2) long-term solvency ratios, and (3) performance measurement ratios. (Round all calculations to three decimal places.)

b) Comment on the financial condition of Seneca, Inc., with respect to short-term solvency, long-term solvency, and performance.

16–18 Working Capital and Cash Provided by Operations

The current assets and current liabilities for Macon Company are summarized below for 19x1 and 19x0.

Current assets	19x1	19x0
Cash	$ 230,000	$ 147,000
Accounts receivable	523,000	435,000
Inventory	810,000	670,000
Prepaid expenses	58,000	52,000
Total	$1,621,000	$1,304,000

Current liabilities		
Accounts payable	$ 733,000	$ 577,000
Notes payable	88,000	104,000
Accrued expenses	164,000	199,000
Current portion of long-term debt	8,000	4,000
Total	$ 993,000	$ 884,000

Additional information:

■ Net income for 19x1 was $444,000.

■ Depreciation expense for 19x1 was $134,000.

■ Amortization expense on intangible assets for 19x1 was $38,000.

Requirements

a) Compute the amount of working capital provided by operations in 19x1.

b) Compute the amount of cash provided by operations in 19x1.

16–19 Conversion of Net Income: Working Capital Basis and Cash Basis

Ferguson Company has the following changes in selected current asset, current liability, and other accounts during 19x4.

1. Decrease in Accounts Receivable—$15,000
2. Increase in Accumulated Depreciation—$12,000
3. Increase in Accumulated Amortization on Intangible Assets—$3,000
4. Decrease in Wages Payable—$3,500
5. Decrease in Prepaid Expenses—$1,250
6. Increase in Inventory—$4,500
7. Decrease in Accounts Payable—$75
8. Decrease in Discount on Bonds Payable—$400
9. Decrease in Interest Payable—$350
10. Increase in Cash—$5,250

Additional information:

- Net income for 19x4 was $43,250.
- There were no acquisitions or dispositions of fixed or intangible assets during the year.
- Bonds payable were not issued or retired during the year.

Requirements

a) Prepare a schedule showing the adjustment to net income (increase or decrease) for each of the ten items above in computing the amount of working capital provided by operations.

b) Prepare a schedule showing the adjustment to net income (increase or decrease) for each of the ten items above in computing the amount of cash provided by operations.

16–20 Statement of Working Capital Flows

Comparative balance sheets for Arnold's Computer Repair, Inc., for 19x7 and 19x6 are given below.

Arnold's Computer Repair, Inc.
Comparative Balance Sheets
December 31, 19x7 and 19x6

Assets	19x7	19x6
Cash	$ 1,200	$1,550
Supplies	850	600
Prepaid insurance	450	375
Total current assets	$ 2,500	$2,525
Land	$15,000	$ —
Tools and testing equipment	8,750	8,750
Less accumulated depreciation	(4,375)	(3,500)
Total fixed assets	19,375	5,250
Total assets	$21,875	$7,775

Liabilities and owners' equity

Accounts payable	$ 650	$ 488
Interest payable	563	—
Total current liabilities	$ 1,213	$ 488
Notes payable (equipment)	$ 4,000	$5,000
Notes payable (land)	15,000	—
Total long-term liabilities	19,000	5,000
Common stock	$ 1,000	$1,000
Retained earnings	662	1,287
Total stockholders' equity	1,662	2,287
Total liabilities and stockholders' equity	$21,875	$7,775

Additional information:

- Net income was $21,850.
- Land was acquired by issuing a ten-year note payable.
- Dividends were paid during the year to Arnold, the company's only stockholder.

Requirements

a) Prepare a statement of working capital flows showing all significant changes in resources.

b) Prepare a schedule of changes in working capital.

16–21 Statement of Cash Flows

Using the information provided in Problem 16–20, prepare a statement of cash flows for Arnold's Computer Repair, Inc., for 19x7.

16–22 Statement of Working Capital Flows

Financial statements for Instaprint Corporation are given below.

Instaprint Corporation
Comparative Balance Sheets
December 31, 19x9 and 19x8

Assets	19x9	19x8
Cash	$ 530,000	$ 192,000
Accounts receivable	606,000	578,000
Inventories	792,000	822,000
Prepaid expenses	108,000	152,000
Total current assets	$2,036,000	$1,744,000
Land, buildings, and equipment	$1,606,000	$1,500,000
Less accumulated depreciation	(852,000)	(756,000)
Total fixed assets	754,000	744,000
Patents	100,000	—
Total assets	$2,890,000	$2,488,000

Liabilities and stockholders' equity

Accounts payable	$ 342,000	$ 382,000
Accrued expenses payable	112,000	70,000
Short-term notes payable	146,000	200,000
Total current liabilities	$ 600,000	$ 652,000
Long-term debt	248,000	—
Total liabilities	$ 848,000	$ 652,000
Common stock and paid-in capital	$ 410,000	$ 310,000
Retained earnings	1,632,000	1,526,000
Total stockholders' equity	2,042,000	1,836,000
Total liabilities and stockholders' equity	$2,890,000	$2,488,000

Instaprint Corporation
Income Statement
For the year ended December 31,19x9

Sales	$2,902,000
Cost of goods sold	−1,662,000
Gross profit	$1,240,000
Less operating expenses	− 968,000
Operating income	$ 272,000
Other income (interest and gain on sale of land)	50,000
Other expense (interest)	(34,000)
Income before taxes	$ 288,000
Income taxes	− 118,000
Net income	$ 170,000

Additional information:

- Depreciation expense for the year was $96,000.
- Cash dividends of $64,000 were declared and paid during the year.
- Land acquired for $20,000 ten years ago was sold during the year for $50,000.
- Equipment costing $126,000 was acquired during the year.
- A patent was acquired in 19x9 in exchange for common stock.

Requirements

a) Prepare a statement of working capital flows for Instaprint Corporation for 19x9.
b) Prepare a schedule of changes in working capital.

16–23 Statement of Cash Flows

Using the financial statements and other information on the Instaprint Corporation provided in Problem 16–22, prepare a statement of cash flows.

16–24 Working Capital and Cash Provided by Operations: Cash Basis Income Statement

Parks Company's income statement for 19x5 is given below.

Parks Company
Income Statement
For the year ended December 31, 19x5

Sales		$98,000
Cost of goods sold:		
Beginning inventory	$18,000	
Plus purchases	62,000	
Less ending inventory	(23,500)	−56,500
Gross profit		$41,500
Operating expenses:		
Salaries	$14,000	
Insurance	500	
Depreciation	1,250	
Interest	900	
Supplies	450	
Other	2,500	−19,600
Net income		$21,900

Current assets and current liabilities for Parks Company at the end of 19x5 and 19x4 were as follows:

	19x5	19x4
Current assets		
Cash	$ 1,200	$ 800
Accounts receivable	4,900	6,000
Inventory	23,500	18,000
Prepaid insurance	525	500
Supplies	750	1,100
Total current assets	$30,875	$26,400
Current liabilities		
Accounts payable	$ 8,200	$ 8,500
Wages payable	1,150	950
Interest payable	325	400
Total current liabilities	$ 9,675	$ 9,850

Requirements

a) Compute the amount of working capital provided by operations.

b) Compute the amount of cash provided by operations.

c) Prepare a schedule converting Parks Company's income statement from the accrual basis to the cash basis. *Hint:* Use format in Exhibit 16–5.

16–25 Ratio Analysis   Presented below are the 19x1 balance sheet and income statement for MND Corporation.

MND Corporation
Balance Sheet
As of December 31, 19x1

Assets

Cash		$ 7,500,000
Accounts receivable		12,000,000
Inventory		9,000,000
Property, plant, and equipment	$48,400,000	
Less: Accumulated depreciation	−11,900,000	36,500,000
Total assets		$65,000,000

Liabilities and stockholders' equity

Accounts payable	$10,700,000
Notes payable (short term)	5,300,000
Mortgage bonds (due in 19x4)	9,500,000
Common stock ($10 par value,	
4,500,000 shares authorized, 2,500,000 shares	
issued and outstanding)	25,000,000
Paid in capital in excess of par value	5,000,000
Retained earnings	9,500,000
Total liabilities and stockholders' equity	$65,000,000

MND Corporation
Income Statement
For the year ended December 31, 19x1

Cash sales		$10,000,000
Credit sales		60,000,000
Total sales		$70,000,000
Cost of goods sold:		
Beginning inventory of finished goods	$ 4,000,000	
Cost of goods manufactured	50,000,000	
Goods available	$54,000,000	
Ending inventory of finished goods	− 5,000,000	−49,000,000
Gross profit		$21,000,000
Operating expenses:		
Selling	$ 3,000,000	
General	10,800,000	−13,800,000
Operating income		$ 7,200,000
Interest expense		− 1,000,000
Income before income taxes		$ 6,200,000
Income taxes (34%)		− 2,108,000
Net income		$ 4,092,000

Requirements

a) Compute the following solvency ratios for MND Corporation for the fiscal year 19x1. (Round calculations to three decimal places.)

   1. Current ratio.

   2. Acid test ratio.

   3. Days receivables outstanding (based on credit sales).

   4. Finished goods inventory turnover.

   5. Debt-to-equity.

   6. Times interest earned.

b) Compute the following performance ratios. (Round calculations to three decimal places.)

   1. Asset turnover.

   2. Return on sales.

   3. Return on assets.

   4. Return on equity.

(CMA Adapted)

16–26 Interpreting Financial Analysis Ratios

Thorpe Company is a wholesale distributor of professional equipment and supplies. The company's sales have averaged about $900,000 annually for the three-year period 19x3–19x5. The firm's total assets at the end of 19x5 amounted to $850,000. The president of Thorpe Company has asked the controller to prepare a report that summarizes the financial aspects of the company's operations for the past three years. This report will be presented to the Board of Directors at their next meeting. In addition to comparative financial statements, the controller has decided to present a number of relevant financial ratios to assist in the identification and interpretation of trends. At the request of the controller, the accounting staff has calculated the following ratios for the three-year period 19x3–19x5.

	19x3	19x4	19x5
Current ratio	2.00	2.13	2.18
Acid test ratio	1.20	1.10	0.97
Days receivables outstanding	37.60	42.60	51.20
Inventory turnover	5.25	4.80	3.80
Debt-to-equity ratio	0.79	0.69	0.61
Asset turnover	1.75	1.88	1.99
Sales as a percentage of 19x3 sales	1.00	1.03	1.06
Gross profit percent	40.00	38.60	38.50
Return on sales	7.8%	7.8%	8.0%
Return on assets	8.5%	8.6%	8.7%
Return on equity	15.1%	14.6%	14.1%

In the preparation of his report, the controller has decided first to examine the financial ratios independently of any other data to determine if the ratios themselves reveal any significant trends over the three-year period.

Requirements

Answer the following questions. Indicate in each case which ratio(s) you used in arriving at your conclusion.

a) The current ratio is increasing, whereas the acid test ratio is decreasing. Using the ratios provided, identify and explain the contributing factor(s) for this apparently divergent trend.

b) In terms of the ratios provided, what conclusion(s) can be drawn regarding the company's use of financial leverage during the 19x3–19x5 period?

c) Using the ratios provided, what conclusion(s) can be drawn regarding the company's ability to generate sales and profits from the assets available to management?

(CMA Adapted)

16–27 Statement of Cash Flows

The schedule shown below presents the net changes in the balance sheet accounts as of December 31, 19x2, as compared to December 31, 19x1, for the Lock Company. Lock's statement of cash flows has not yet been prepared for the year ended December 31, 19x2. Additional information regarding Lock's operations during 19x2 follows the schedule.

Debit balance accounts	Net Change Increase (Decrease)
Cash	$ (340,000)
Accounts Receivable	1,040,000
Inventories	580,000
Property, Plant, and Equipment	1,800,000
Total	$3,080,000

Credit balance accounts	
Allowance for Bad Debts	$ 600,000
Accumulated Depreciation	950,000
Accounts Payable	1,250,000
Notes Payable (current)	(150,000)
Bonds Payable	(2,000,000)
Common Stock, $10 par value	9,000,000
Paid in Capital in Excess of Par Value	1,300,000
Retained Earnings	(7,870,000)
Total	$3,080,000

Additional information:

1. Lock Company incurred a net after-tax loss from regular operations of $500,000 for the year. In addition, Lock had an extraordinary gain from the sale of condemned

land of $1,400,000 net of $600,000 taxes. The condemned land had a book value of $2,500,000.

2. Accounts receivable of $650,000 were written off during 19x2 by debiting Allowance for Bad Debts. The provision for bad debts expense for the year was $1,250,000.

3. Machinery acquired five years earlier at a cost of $2,000,000 was sold for $550,000 during 19x2. The machinery had a book value of $350,000 at the date of sale.

4. A new parcel of land with a market value of $6,300,000 was purchased in April, 19x2, and was paid for with cash of $1,500,000 plus 400,000 shares of Lock's common stock.

5. Two million dollars of bonds issued at par value ten years ago were retired during 19x2.

6. A 5 percent stock dividend was declared on January 15, 19x2, on 10,000,000 shares of Lock common stock. The market value of the stock on that date was $11 per share.

7. A cash dividend of $0.30 per share of common stock was declared on December 31, 19x2, payable on January 15, 19x3.

Requirements

a) Prepare a statement of cash flows for Lock Company for the year ended December 31, 19x2 including all significant noncash resource flows.

b) Prepare a schedule of changes in working capital.

(CMA Adapted)

16–28 Financial Statement Analysis: Statement of Cash Flows

You have been assigned by the acquisitions committee of Control Group, Inc., to examine a potential acquisition, Retailers, Inc. This company is a merchandising firm that appears to be available because of the death of its founder and principal shareholder. Recent financial statements of Retailers, Inc., are shown below.

Retailers, Inc.
Comparative Balance Sheets
December 31, 19x1 and 19x2

	19x1	19x2
Cash	$ 120,000	$ 130,000
Accounts receivable	370,000	430,000
Inventory	400,000	400,000
Property, plant, and equipment	800,000	900,000
Less: Accumulated depreciation	(250,000)	(325,000)
Total assets	$1,440,000	$1,535,000
Accounts payable	$ 260,000	$ 300,000
Long-term note payable	280,000	280,000
Common stock	690,000	690,000
Retained earnings	210,000	265,000
Total equities	$1,440,000	$1,535,000

Retailers, Inc.
Income Statement
For the year ended December 31, 19x2

Sales	$2,943,000
Less expenses:	
Cost of goods sold	$2,200,000
Wages expense	350,000
Supplies expense	42,600
Depreciation expense	100,000
Interest expense	22,400
Loss on sale of fixed assets	75,000
Total	−2,790,000
Net income before taxes	$ 153,000
Income taxes (34%)	− 52,020
Net income	$ 100,980

Retailers, Inc.
Statement of Working Capital Flows
For the year ended December 31, 19x2

Working capital flows from operating activities:		
Net income	$ 100,980	
Nonworking capital expenses included in net income:		
Depreciation expense	100,000	
Nonoperating loss on sale of equipment	75,000	
Net working capital provided by operating activities		$ 275,980
Working capital inflows (outflows) from investing activities:		
Purchase of property, plant, and equipment	$ (250,000)	
Sale of equipment	50,000	(200,000)
Working capital inflows (outflows) from financing activities:		
Declaration of cash dividend		(45,980)
Net increase in working capital		$ 30,000

Requirements

a) Calculate the following ratios for 19x2. (Round calculations to three decimal places.)

1. Current ratio.

2. Acid test.

3. Inventory turnover.

4. Days receivables outstanding.

5. Debt-to-equity.

6. Times interest earned.

7. Asset turnover.

8. Return on sales.

9. Return on assets.

10. Return on equity.

b) Prepare a statement of cash flows for 19x2.

c) Explain why working capital was generated by the sale of equipment, even though there was a loss on the sale.

d) What is your recommendation regarding the acquisition of Retailers, Inc.?

(CMA Adapted)

16–29 Statement of Working Capital Flows

The following information was gathered from the records of Butler Butcher Shop for 19x4:

1. Current assets were $47,000 at the beginning of the year and $39,000 at the end of the year. Current assets included Cash of $10,000 at the beginning of the year and $12,500 at the end of the year. Other current assets included Accounts Receivable, Inventory, and Prepaid Expenses. Current liabilities consisted of Accounts Payable and Accrued Expenses Payable.

2. Current liabilities were $26,000 at the beginning of the year and $31,000 at the end of the year.

3. Common stock with a par value of $25,000 was sold for cash during the year for $75,000.

4. Long-term notes payable of $60,000 were paid off during the year.

5. Purchased land for $50,000, paying 25 percent down payment and financing the balance on a five-year note payable.

6. Depreciation expense for the year was $15,000.

7. Purchased treasury stock for cash at a cost of $10,000.

8. Acquired equipment by issuing a $35,000 note to be paid in 18 months.

9. The 19x4 net income (loss) was $(20,500).

Requirements

a) Compute the amount of working capital provided by operations in 19x4.

b) Compute the amount of net income for 19x4.

c) Prepare a statement of working capital flows in good form for 19x4.

16–30 Cash Flow Statement

Using the information provided in Problem 16–29, prepare a statement of cash flows in good form for 19x4. *Hint:* Pool all noncash working capital accounts.

**REVIEW PROBLEM
SOLUTION**

a) Solvency measures:

$$\text{Current ratio} = \frac{\text{Current assets}}{\text{Current liabilities}}$$

$$= \frac{\$1,160}{\$530}$$

$$= \underline{\underline{2.19}}$$

$$\text{Acid test ratio} = \frac{\text{Cash} + \text{Marketable securities} + \text{Current receivables}}{\text{Current liabilities}}$$

$$= \frac{\$300 + \$75 + \$325}{\$530}$$

$$= \underline{\underline{1.32}}$$

$$\text{Inventory turnover} = \frac{\text{Cost of goods sold}}{\text{Average inventory}}$$

$$= \frac{\$2,600}{\dfrac{\$350 + \$400}{2}}$$

$$= \underline{\underline{6.93}} \text{ times}$$

$$\text{Days receivable outstanding} = \frac{\text{Ending receivables}}{\text{Average daily sales}}$$

$$= \frac{\$325}{\dfrac{\$3,000}{365}}$$

$$= \underline{\underline{39.54}} \text{ days}$$

$$\text{Debt-to-equity} = \frac{\text{Total liabilities}}{\text{Total stockholders' equity}}$$

$$= \frac{\$830}{\$1,045}$$

$$= \underline{\underline{0.79}}$$

$$\text{Times interest earned} = \frac{\text{Net income} + \text{Interest expense} + \text{Income taxes}}{\text{Interest expense}}$$

$$= \frac{\$115 + \$40 + \$60}{\$40}$$

$$= \underline{\underline{5.38}} \text{ times}$$

Performance measures:

$$\text{Asset turnover} = \frac{\text{Sales}}{\text{Average total assets}}$$

$$= \frac{\$3,000}{\dfrac{\$1,562 + \$1,875}{2}}$$

$$= \underline{\underline{1.75}} \text{ times}$$

$$\text{Return on sales} = \frac{\text{Net income} + \text{Net-of-tax interest expense}}{\text{Sales}}$$

$$= \frac{\$115 + \$40(1 - 0.34)}{\$3,000}$$

$$= \underline{\underline{0.047}} \quad \text{or} \quad \underline{\underline{4.7\%}}$$

$$\text{Return on assets} = \frac{\text{Net income} + \text{Net-of-tax interest expense}}{\text{Average total assets}}$$

$$= \frac{\$115 + \$40(1 - 0.34)}{\dfrac{\$1,562 + \$1,875}{2}}$$

$$= \underline{\underline{0.082}} \quad \text{or} \quad \underline{\underline{8.2\%}}$$

$$\text{Return on equity} = \frac{\text{Net income}}{\text{Average stockholders' equity}}$$

$$= \frac{\$115}{\dfrac{\$932 + \$1,045}{2}}$$

$$= \underline{\underline{0.116}} \quad \text{or} \quad \underline{\underline{11.6\%}}$$

b)   **O'Keefe's, Inc.**
Statement of Cash Flows
For the year ended December 31, 19x8
(*in thousands*)

Cash flows from operating activities:	
Net income	$115
Noncash expenses and revenues included in net income:	
Depreciation expense	50
Increase in accounts receivable	(45)
Increase in inventory	(50)
Increase in other current assets	(5)
Increase in accounts payable	105
Increase in taxes payable	40
Increase in other current liabilities	5
Net cash provided by operating activities	$215

Cash inflows (outflows) from investing activities:		
Acquisition of equipment	$(190)	
Net cash used by investing activities		(190)
Cash inflows (outflows) from financing activities:		
Common stock issued for cash	$ 15	
Long-term debt issued for cash	70	
Payments on long-term debt	(20)	
Loan to President of company	(3)	
Dividends paid	(27)	
Net cash provided by financing activities		35
Net increase in cash and cash equivalents		
(marketable securities)		$ 60
Equipment acquired by issuance of common stock		$ 10

CHAPTER 17

The Impact of Changing Prices

Upon completion of this chapter you should:

- Be familiar with the use of price indexes as a means of reporting the effects of inflation and deflation on monetary values.
- Be able to prepare a constant dollar balance sheet and income statement.
- Be able to compute the purchasing power gain or loss from holding monetary claims and obligations during periods of changing prices.
- Understand the fundamental difference between constant dollar and current cost accounting.
- Be familiar with selected applications of price level adjusted data, including: cost behavior analysis, budgeting, performance evaluation, and capital budgeting.

A **price index** is a standardized measure of the amount of money needed to purchase a standard package or basket of goods and services. In the United States, the **Consumer Price Index** (CPI), prepared by the U.S. Department of Commerce, Bureau of Labor Statistics, is a widely used measure of the cost of living for the typical consumer household. The CPI, for a particular time period, is computed by comparing the cost of a standard package of goods and services during that period with the cost during some base period. The base period, currently 1967, is assigned an index of 100 and the index of any other period is expressed as a multiple of 100. The 1986 index of 330.7 indicates that the cost of the standard package increased 230.7 percent between 1967 and 1986, when $330.70 was required to buy what $100 would buy in 1967.

The purchasing power of money varies inversely with prices. During periods of **inflation,** the purchasing power of money declines as prices rise. Conversely, during periods of **deflation,** the purchasing power of money increases as prices fall. Inflation and deflation cause dollar measurements to become a rubber meterstick that expands and contracts over time. The dollars spent to purchase land in 19x5 have a different purchasing power than the dollars spent to purchase inventory in 19x8. Yet, dollars spent in both years are treated as identical measures in traditional accounting reports. This variability creates problems for managers who use accounting data to plan and control activities. The severity of the problem depends on the rate of inflation or deflation and the length of management's planning period. During the late 1970s and early 1980s, when annual inflation exceeded 10 percent in the United States and many other nations, ignoring inflation was folly. Even a small rate of inflation can have a significant impact on the evaluation of multiyear capital expenditure proposals.

Managers of leading corporations have responded to inflation in a variety of ways, including those listed below.

- Using replacement costs rather than historical costs in pricing decisions.
- Including an allowance for inflation during the budgeting process.
- Updating standard costs more frequently.
- Adjusting performance reports to separately identify variances caused by inflation.
- Changing the hurdle or discount rates used for capital budgeting.
- Adjusting financial ratio analysis.
- Placing increased emphasis on the statement of resource flows.

The purpose of this chapter is to indicate how the usefulness of management accounting data and reports can be enhanced by adjusting them for changing prices. To provide a framework for the discussion of management accounting applications, we begin with an illustration of how general purpose financial statements are adjusted for changes in the general price level. Next we consider the uses and limitations of general price level adjusted financial statements and identify some alternative approaches that might be used to prepare financial statements during periods of changing prices. Finally, we focus on price level adjustments to management accounting data and reports.

CONSTANT DOLLAR FINANCIAL INFORMATION

Nominal dollars are the dollar amounts actually recorded in historical cost accounting records and presented in traditional financial statements. The nominal dollar amounts assigned to assets acquired in different years may not represent dollars of uniform purchasing power. **Constant dollars** are dollars of uniform purchasing power. **Constant dollar accounting** involves restating the nominal dollar amounts presented in financial statements into dollars of uniform purchasing power. This is accomplished by multiplying the nominal dollars actually paid for an asset by a conversion ratio computed as

$$\text{Conversion ratio} = \frac{\text{Price index on the date being adjusted to}}{\text{Price index on the date being adjusted from}}.$$

Assume that land was purchased for $50,000 in 19x3, when the price index was 120. If management is preparing constant dollar financial statements as of December 31, 19x5, when the price index was 150, the constant dollar amount paid for the land is computed as follows:

$$\text{Constant dollars} = \text{Nominal dollars} \times \text{Conversion ratio,}$$
$$\text{Constant dollars} = \$50,000 \times (150/120)$$
$$= \$62,500.$$

In terms of *general* purchasing power, $62,500 is required on 12/31/x5 to have the same buying power as $50,000 in 19x3. The price index is based on the overall cost of a specific package of goods and services. Changes in the index represent changes in the overall cost of the package. The prices of individual items in the package and the prices of items not included in the package may change at different rates. Consequently, if an organization were to buy or sell this *specific* asset on 12/31/x5, its actual price would likely be something other than $62,500.

In preparing constant dollar financial statements, an important distinction is made between monetary and nonmonetary items. **Monetary items** are assets and liabilities whose values are fixed in terms of nominal dollars, for example, cash, accounts receivable, accounts payable, and bonds payable. Cash represents current purchasing power. The number of dollars a firm will receive to settle its accounts receivable or pay to settle its liabilities is not affected by changes in the price level. **Nonmonetary items** are assets and equities whose values are not fixed in terms of nominal dollars, for example, inventory, land, buildings, equipment, and total stockholders' equity. The number of dollars land can be sold for is likely to be affected by changes in the price level.

Constant Dollar Balance Sheet

Assume that the December 31, 19x6, historical cost balance sheet of Custard Park Lodge, presented in Exhibit 17–1, is to be restated in terms of the December 31, 19x6, price level. Because the dollar amounts assigned monetary assets and liabilities represent December 31, 19x6, purchasing power, they are not restated. The amounts assigned the nonmonetary assets represent purchasing power as of the date each asset was acquired. Accordingly, to prepare a constant dollar balance sheet in terms of the December 31, 19x6, price level, the nonmonetary assets must be restated using the appropriate conversion ratios.

Although it is possible to restate all the elements of stockholders' equity in terms of December 31, 19x6, purchasing power, this would require a complex analysis of all the increments to retained earnings. Instead, total stockholders' equity is computed as the residual amount, that is, total constant dollar assets minus total constant dollar liabilities.[1]

To prepare constant dollar financial statements, information is needed regarding (1) the current price index, (2) the price index when all currently owned nonmonetary assets were acquired, and (3) the average price index of

---

[1] If Custard Park Lodge had preferred stock outstanding, it would normally be treated as a monetary liability.

EXHIBIT 17–1   Historical Cost Balance Sheet

Custard Park Lodge
Balance Sheet
December 31, 19x6

Assets

Cash		$ 14,400
Accounts receivable		1,000
Inventories		4,500
Property, plant, and equipment	$250,000	
Less: Accumulated depreciation	− 60,000	190,000
Total assets		$209,900

Liabilities and stockholders' equity

Liabilities:		
Accounts payable	$ 2,500	
Long-term debt	100,000	$102,500
Stockholders' equity:		
Common stock ($5 par; 10,000 shares		
outstanding)	$ 50,000	
Premium on common stock	35,400	
Retained earnings	22,000	107,400
Total liabilities and stockholders' equity		$209,900

all periods included in the statements. Presented below is all the price level information needed to prepare constant dollar financial statements for Custard Park Lodge.

Date or Period	Price Index
1/1/x3	120
8/1/x5	145
1/1/x6	150
5/1/x6	157
Average 19x6	160
12/31/x6	165

Only three of these indexes are used in preparing Custard Park Lodge's constant dollar balance sheet. The ending inventory was acquired on 5/1/x6 when the price index was 157. The plant, property, and equipment was acquired on 1/1/x3 when the price index was 120. The 12/31/x6 price index is 165. The remaining indexes will be used to prepare a constant dollar income statement. Custard Park Lodge's constant dollar balance sheet is presented in Exhibit 17–2.

EXHIBIT 17–2   Nominal and Constant Dollar Balance Sheets

Custard Park Lodge
Nominal and Constant Dollar Balance Sheets
December 31, 19x6

	(1) *Nominal Dollars*	(2) *Conversion Ratio*		(3) *Constant Dollars*
Cash	$ 14,400	M		$ 14,400
Accounts receivable	1,000	M		1,000
Inventories*	4,500 ×	165/157	=	4,729
Property, plant, and equipment**	250,000 ×	165/120	=	343,750
Less: Accumulated depreciation**	(60,000) ×	165/120	=	(82,500)
Total assets	$209,900			$281,379
Accounts payable	$ 2,500	M		$ 2,500
Long-term debt	100,000	M		100,000
Stockholders' equity	107,400	R		178,879
Total liabilities and stockholders' equity	$209,900			$281,379

M = Monetary item, already stated in terms of 12/31/x6 dollars.
R = Residual interest of stockholders, computed as total constant dollar assets less total liabilities.
* The ending inventories were acquired on 5/1/x6 when the price level was 157.
** The property, plant, and equipment was acquired on 1/1/x3 when the price level was 120.

Comparing the nominal amounts with the constant dollar amounts, we see that the use of constant dollars (rather than nominal dollars) can have a significant impact on financial statement analysis. The debt-to-equity ratio (computed as total liabilities divided by total stockholders' equity), for example, changes from 0.95 under nominal dollars to 0.57 under constant dollars:

$$\text{Nominal dollar debt-to-equity ratio} = \frac{\$100,000 + \$2,500}{\$107,400}$$
$$= 0.95,$$

$$\text{Constant dollar debt-to-equity ratio} = \frac{\$100,000 + \$2,500}{\$178,879}$$
$$= 0.57.$$

The constant dollar ratio indicates that creditors have provided a significantly smaller portion of capital than the nominal dollar ratio would suggest. The firm's financial position appears stronger using constant dollars.

Constant Dollar Income Statement

Assume Custard Park Lodge's nominal dollar income statement for the year ended December 31, 19x6 (presented in column (1) of Exhibit 17–3) is to be restated in terms of the December 31, 19x6, price index. It is necessary to restate all transactions in terms of the December 31, 19x6, price index. To simplify computations assume all transactions, except those pertaining to inventory and fixed asset acquisition, occurred evenly throughout 19x6 at an average price index of 160. The costs assigned to supplies expense include costs of supplies acquired on 8/1/x5 when the price index was 145 and on 5/1/x6 when the price index was 157. The depreciation assigned to 19x6 is for assets acquired on 1/1/x3 when the price index was 120.

Each of the nominal dollar amounts in column (1) of Exhibit 17–3 is multiplied by a conversion ratio in column (2) to obtain the constant dollar amount presented in column (3). Again, the use of constant dollars, rather than nominal dollars, can have a significant impact on financial statement analysis. The income tax rate, for example, is 18.4 percent under constant dollars ($5,863/$31,776), but it is only 15.0 percent under nominal dollars ($5,685/$37,900). Many people point to constant dollar financial statements and ratios to argue that profits are not as large as they appear, and effective tax rates are higher than they appear.

EXHIBIT 17–3   Nominal and Constant Dollar Income Statements

Custard Park Lodge
Nominal and Constant Dollar Income Statements
For the year ended December 31, 19x6

	(1) Nominal Dollars	(2) Conversion Ratio	(3) Constant Dollars
Sales*	$170,000	165/160	$175,313
Less expenses:			
Supplies (FIFO):			
Purchased 8/1/x5	$ 3,600	165/145	$ 4,097
Purchased 5/1/x6	2,500	165/157	2,627
Salaries*	90,000	165/160	92,813
Depreciation	20,000	165/120	27,500
Miscellaneous*	4,000	165/160	4,125
Total	−120,100		−131,162
Operating income	$ 49,900		$ 44,151
Less: Interest expense*	− 12,000	165/160	− 12,375
Income before income taxes	$ 37,900		$ 31,776
Provision for income taxes*	− 5,685	165/160	− 5,863
Net income	$ 32,215		$ 25,913

* These items occur evenly throughout 19x6 at an average price level of 160.

Return on sales (computed as net income plus net-of-tax interest expense divided by sales) also changes, from 24.95 percent under nominal dollars to 20.54 percent under constant dollars:

$$\frac{\text{Nominal dollar}}{\text{return on sales}} = \frac{\$32,215 + \$12,000(1 - 0.15)}{\$170,000}$$

$$= 0.2495, \text{ or } 24.95\%;$$

$$\frac{\text{Constant dollar}}{\text{return on sales}} = \frac{\$25,913 + \$12,375(1 - 0.184)}{\$175,313}$$

$$= 0.2054, \text{ or } 20.54\%.$$

The constant dollar percent indicates that expenses other than interest absorb a higher portion of revenues than the nominal dollar percent suggests.

Purchasing Power Gains and Losses

Holding monetary assets produces losses as purchasing power falls during inflationary periods and gains as purchasing power rises during deflationary periods. Conversely, owing monetary liabilities produces gains during inflationary periods and losses during deflationary periods. These gains and losses, due entirely to changes in the purchasing power of money, are called **purchasing power gains and losses.** Because inflation is more common than deflation, the effects of holding monetary assets and owing monetary liabilities during inflationary periods are the ones emphasized in this chapter.

Assume that Thomas Lee held $10,000 in cash throughout 19x4, as the price index rose from 200 to 240. Because the $10,000 declined in purchasing power, he sustained a loss, the amount of which can be computed in terms of the price level at the beginning of the year, the end of the year, or any other time. Managers are likely to prefer that amounts be stated in terms of the more current end-of-year dollars. The general approach is to restate the nominal dollars held at the beginning of the year, and any nominal dollar changes that took place during the year, into constant end-of-year dollars. The number of constant end-of-year dollars needed to avoid a loss is then computed as the beginning balance in constant dollars, plus any increases in constant dollars, or minus any decreases in constant dollars. If fewer nominal dollars are actually held at the end of the year, the difference is a purchasing power loss. If more nominal dollars are held, the difference is a purchasing power gain. Thomas Lee's loss from holding cash is computed as follows:

	Nominal Dollars	Conversion Ratio	Constant Dollars
Cash balance, 1/1/x4	$10,000	240/200	$12,000
Change	—		—
Cash balance, 12/31/x4	$10,000		$12,000
Purchasing power loss (L)	$ 2,000 L		

A total of 12,000 end-of-year dollars are required to have the same purchasing power as 10,000 beginning-of-year dollars. Thomas Lee lost $2,000 in purchasing power by holding $10,000 in cash throughout 19x4.

If Thomas Lee owed a $20,000 note throughout 19x4, he would have had a purchasing power gain. The dollars owed at the end of the period were cheaper than the dollars owed at the beginning. The purchasing power gain, in terms of constant end-of-year dollars, is $4,000:

	Nominal Dollars	Conversion Ratio	Constant Dollars
Note payable, 1/1/x4	$20,000	240/200	$24,000
Change	—		—
Note payable, 12/31/x4	$20,000		$24,000
Purchasing power gain (G)	$ 4,000 G		

These examples illustrate why, other things being equal, debtors prefer inflation and creditors prefer price stability or deflation. However, other things are seldom equal. The gains from owing monetary liabilities and the losses from holding monetary assets can be reduced or eliminated by abnormally high interest rates. Treasurers should take inflationary expectations and interest rates into consideration when planning their organizations' mix of monetary assets and liabilities. Information on purchasing power gains and losses can be useful in evaluating the success of these plans.

It is customary to disclose purchasing power gains and losses in constant dollar financial statements. To do this for Custard Park Lodge, the following additional information is needed regarding the beginning and ending balances, and changes, in monetary accounts.

	19x6		
	Beginning Balance	Change	Ending Balance
Cash	$ 4,000	$+10,400	$ 14,400
Accounts Receivable	2,000	−1,000	1,000
Accounts Payable	5,000	−2,500	2,500
Notes Payable	100,000	—	100,000

The purchasing power gains and losses for each monetary item are computed in Exhibit 17–4. For simplicity, assume all changes took place evenly throughout the year at an average price level of 160. The gain or loss on each item is computed as the difference between expected constant dollars and actual nominal dollars at the end of 19x6. Custard Park Lodge had a net purchasing power gain of $9,528 during 19x6.

EXHIBIT 17–4   Purchasing Power Gains and Losses on Monetary Items

Custard Park Lodge
Schedule of Purchasing Power Gains and Losses
For the year ended December 31, 19x6

	Nominal Dollars	Conversion Ratio	Constant Dollars	Gain (G) or Loss (L)
Cash:				
Beginning, 1/1/x6	$ 4,000	165/150	$ 4,400	
Change	10,400	165/160	10,725	
Ending, 12/31/x6	$ 14,400		$ 15,125*	$ 725 L
Accounts receivable:				
Beginning, 1/1/x6	$ 2,000	165/150	$ 2,200	
Change	− 1,000	165/160	− 1,031	
Ending, 12/31/x6	$ 1,000		$ 1,169*	169 L
Accounts payable:				
Beginning, 1/1/x6	$ 5,000	165/150	$ 5,500	
Change	− 2,500	165/160	− 2,578	
Ending, 12/31/x6	$ 2,500		$ 2,922*	422 G
Notes payable:				
Beginning, 1/1/x6	$100,000	165/150	$110,000	
Change	—	165/160	—	
Ending, 12/31/x6	$100,000		$110,000*	10,000 G
Purchasing power gain				$ 9,528 G

* This is the expected account balance in the absence of purchasing power gains or losses.

Selecting the Price Index

Once the mechanics are mastered, the preparation of constant dollar financial statements is straightforward. More troublesome are the selection of an appropriate price index and the interpretation of the resulting financial statements.

The Consumer Price Index is the most widely known index, and it is prescribed by the Financial Accounting Standards Board as the index to use in preparing any required constant dollar financial information. The CPI is based on the cost of food, clothing, shelter, fuel, transportation, doctors' services, and other items that a typical consumer household buys for day-to-day living. The exact manner in which the prices of specific items enter into the determination of the CPI and the scope of the CPI are subject to criticism. Individual consumers are affected by the cost of the items they buy rather than the cost of the items included in the index. Before the elements of the index were changed in 1982, for example, it was based on the assumption that individual consumers participated in the purchase of a new house every month. Many managers also argue that the CPI is so oriented to consumers that it does not adequately capture the changing costs of items their organizations purchase in their daily operations.

Although some businesses use the CPI in preparing certain constant dollar financial information distributed to outsiders, they are free to select another price index for internal use. The use of such an index would have to be justified on the basis of costs and benefits. Possible alternatives include the Gross National Product Implicit Price Deflator and a variety of specific industry and firm indexes.

The **Gross National Product Implicit Price Deflator,** published by the U.S. Department of Commerce, is a broad-based index that encompasses the entire U.S. economy. Because it is more comprehensive, many managers prefer it to the CPI. However, it is prepared quarterly, whereas the CPI is prepared monthly. During periods of high inflation, managers may prefer the more frequently available CPI.

A specific price index might be prepared to track the cost of items of particular interest to an industry or firm. Inland Steel, for example, prepares an internal construction cost index for use in long-range planning.[2] Specific indexes are useful for valuing specific assets, and for internal planning and control, but they are not useful for evaluating changes in general purchasing power.

Alternative Approaches to Price Level Adjustments

The two basic approaches to adjusting for changes in the price level are constant dollar accounting and current cost accounting. Constant dollar accounting does not involve a new basis for accountability. Historical dollars are still accounted for using standard accounting procedures; however, the resulting financial data are adjusted for changes in general purchasing power. Constant dollar costs are not intended to measure the replacement cost or the sales value of nonmonetary assets, such as inventory, land, buildings, and equipment. Managers interested in these amounts often request current cost information.

Current cost accounting updates balance sheet asset items to their current value and then adjusts the income statement to reflect these changes. Current cost accounting involves a departure from historical dollars and standard accounting procedures. Alternative approaches to current cost accounting are based on replacement costs (sometimes called entry values or input values) and sales values (sometimes called liquidation values, exit values, or output values). A **replacement cost** is the current cost to purchase or reproduce an asset or its productive capacity. Replacement cost information is useful in pricing decisions, in which managers try to price products so that their selling prices exceed their purchase or current reproduction costs. Replacement cost information might be developed using current labor rates and materials costs, price lists for used or new equipment, engineering studies, and specific price indexes, such as Inland Steel's internal construction cost index. Sales values for fixed assets can be developed in a similar manner. Sales value information would be par-

---

[2] Allen H. Seed, III, *The Impact of Inflation on Internal Planning and Control* (New York: National Association of Accountants, 1981), pp. 117–121.

ticularly relevant to a decision to continue or discontinue some aspect of operations. If a plant's net sales value exceeds the present value of its future operating
cash flows, management should consider selling the plant.

PRICE LEVEL ADJUSTMENTS FOR MANAGEMENT ACTION

In the preceding sections we mentioned or illustrated how management might
use price level adjusted information for ratio analysis, financial planning and
performance evaluation, product pricing, and the decision to continue or discontinue some aspect of operations. In this section we will focus on some
additional uses of price level adjusted information, namely, cost behavior analysis, budgeting, performance evaluation, and capital budgeting.

Cost Behavior Analysis

Changes in prices reduce the comparability of costs incurred in different time
periods, making it more difficult to analyze cost behavior. In Chapter 3 we
suggested that one response to this problem is to use something other than
cost as the dependent variable. Direct labor hours might be substituted for labor
dollars, kilowatt hours might be substituted for the cost of electricity, and so
forth. In budgeting, the use of these variables could be predicted and then
multiplied by their predicted unit cost. One disadvantage of this approach is
that it is necessary to implement it on a very disaggregated basis. An alternative
approach, if an appropriate price index is available or can be developed, is to
analyze cost behavior in constant, rather than nominal, dollars. Consider the
following data:

Observation	Unit Volume	Total Cost (Nominal Dollars)
Y1	500	$2,450
Y2	300	2,000
Y3	400	2,700
Y4	200	2,000

Plotting these data on a scatter diagram (see Exhibit 17–5a) does not reveal
an obvious cost behavior pattern. There are at least three possible explanations:
(1) There is no distinct relationship between unit volume and total cost, (2)
there have been technological changes in the product or the production process,
or (3) there have been changes in the price level. Perhaps management believes
there should be a positive relationship between volume and costs, and that
technology is constant. This leaves changes in the price level as the most logical
explanation of the lack of a relationship.

EXHIBIT 17–5   Cost Estimation with Changing Prices

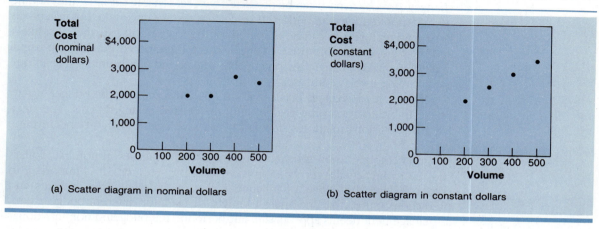

(a) Scatter diagram in nominal dollars

(b) Scatter diagram in constant dollars

Assume that an industry price index is available and management is able to obtain the following information:

Observation	Price Index
Y1	154
Y2	176
Y3	198
Y4	220

All costs can now be restated in terms of the price index at observation Y4:

Observation	Unit Volume	Total Cost (Nominal Dollars)	Conversion Ratio		Total Cost (Constant Dollars)
Y1	500	$2,450	× 220/154	=	$3,500
Y2	300	2,000	× 220/176	=	2,500
Y3	400	2,700	× 220/198	=	3,000
Y4	200	2,000	× 220/220	=	2,000

Plotting the constant dollars in Exhibit 17–5(b) reveals a cost behavior pattern with a high positive correlation between unit volume and total costs. Based on this information, an equation can be developed for total costs using any of the methods discussed in Chapter 3. The cost estimation equation will, of course, only be valid for the price level at observation Y4. If the price level is expected to increase to 230, the cost estimating equation should be adjusted using a conversion ratio of 230/220 before cost predictions are made.

Budgeting

The accuracy of predictions for revenues and expenditures is affected by price changes. If such changes can be predicted with reasonable certainty, they should be incorporated into the budget. If price changes are uncertain, but potentially large, budget forecasts can be prepared for the lowest possible, the most likely, and the highest possible price changes. These three-tiered budgets are useful in alerting management to the potential problems and opportunities that accompany varying levels of inflation.

If price level changes occur that are not allowed for in the budget, it may be desirable to revise the budget and any related standard costs. The need for such revisions might be signaled by an investigation of cost and revenue variances.

In attempting to budget future revenues and expenses in nominal dollars (dollars to be actually recorded in the accounting records), it is important to recognize that the effects of inflation will vary. Different price indexes and predictions (subjective and analytic) might be used for different budget items, as management deems appropriate. Furthermore, the budgeted nominal dollar depreciation on fixed assets acquired in prior periods will not be affected by subsequent price changes.[3] No future cash flows are associated with sunk costs.

Performance Evaluation

Theoretically, standard costs should be continually updated to reflect current prices. If this were done, performance reports would always be based on the prices in effect during the evaluation period, and it would not be necessary to make explicit adjustments for changing prices in performance reports.

Because of the time and cost of updating standard costs, especially when they are used for inventory valuation, many firms prefer to update standards only once a year, or once every six months. Under these circumstances, if significant price changes occur, it is desirable to make a special allowance for price changes in performance reports. Two frequently mentioned approaches to making such allowances involve the use of (1) planned variances or (2) price level adjusted flexible budgets.

Under the planned variance approach, standard costs for each input are based on the average prices predicted for the coming year, or other budget period. If management expects costs to rise throughout the year, they will plan on favorable variances during the early portions of the year and unfavorable variances during the later portions of the year. Though inventory could then be valued on the basis of the unadjusted standard costs, budgets for the year and performance reports prepared during the year would also reflect the planned variances.

---

[3] If management were attempting to price products to provide for the replacement of fixed assets, they should consider the replacement cost rather than the historical cost of the asset. This is an example of the use of different costs for different purposes.

A price level adjusted flexible budget[4] is prepared by adjusting a regular flexible budget for changes in the price level that were not allowed for in the standard costs. The adjustment is for changes in the *price level* rather than changes in the *costs of specific inputs* acquired. The appropriate managers may still be held responsible for any additional deviations between the price level adjusted cost of inputs and the actual cost of inputs. In subsequent analysis these additional deviations would be included in the materials price variance, the labor rate variance, the variable overhead spending variance, and the fixed overhead budget variance.

Capital Budgeting

The profitability of long-term investments in plant and equipment is significantly affected by changes in the price level, even if the annual price level changes are quite small. An annual inflation rate of 5 percent, for example, will amount to a 63 percent increase in prices when compounded annually over ten years. If inflation might affect future cash receipts and disbursements to this extent, management most certainly should consider it in evaluating capital expenditure proposals. Two methods are used to allow for inflation in such evaluations:

1. Predict future cash receipts and disbursements in constant dollars that reflect the current price level, and evaluate these constant dollar cash flows using a discount rate that does not include an allowance for inflation.

2. Predict cash receipts and disbursements in nominal dollars that reflect expected changes in the price level, and evaluate these nominal dollar cash flows using a discount rate that includes an allowance for inflation.

In the first method, inflation is eliminated from the predicted cash flows by using constant dollars at the current price level, rather than expected, actual, nominal dollars. An advantage of this method is that many managers find it easier to think in terms of constant, current prices. Projections of large future nominal dollar cash flows may be as confusing as they are enlightening. A problem with this method is the determination of a discount rate that excludes an allowance for inflation. If financial markets reflect inflationary expectations, the cost of capital will include an allowance for inflation that must be estimated and deducted to determine the discount rate.

When taxes are an important consideration, the first method also requires an adjustment of the depreciation tax shield from nominal dollars to constant dollars. The depreciation tax savings, realized in periods subsequent to acquisition, are based on the unadjusted historical cost of an asset. Because inflation causes purchasing power to fall, these future tax savings have less purchasing power than current dollars. Accordingly, when the first method is used, the

---

[4] Seed, pp. 86–87. D.I. MacGibbon, "Why Not Price Adjust Your Budget?" *The Australian Accountant,* November 1979, pp. 686–687.

depreciation tax savings must be adjusted from nominal dollars to constant dollars. The effect of taxes on capital budgeting with changing prices is illustrated in the appendix to this chapter.

In the second method, inflation is incorporated into the predicted cash flows by using nominal dollars, which are the expected, actual, cash receipts and disbursements. These nominal dollars are often predicted on the basis of current prices adjusted for expected future changes in the price level. The inflation adjusted present value of $1 to be received in n periods is a function of both the unadjusted time value of money and the rate of inflation. It is computed as

$$iapv\,\$1 = \frac{1}{(1 + r)^n} \times \frac{1}{(1 + i)^n},$$

where $iapv\,\$1$ = inflation adjusted present value of $1,
r = unadjusted discount rate,
i = rate of inflation,
n = number of periods.

If the unadjusted discount rate is 12 percent and the expected rate of inflation is 8 percent, the present value of $1 to be received in one year is computed, using factors found in Table 1 in the appendix (see p. 804), to be $0.827:

$$pv\,\$1 = (0.893)(0.926)$$
$$= 0.827.$$

An organization's cost of capital may already include an allowance for expected inflation. If this is so, management might use the cost of capital percent as the adjusted discount rate.

To illustrate the first method, assume that the Downtown Hotel is evaluating a proposal to install vending machines in an empty storage room. The machines cost $12,000 and have an estimated life of six years. In current dollars, management believes the machines will produce $4,000 in annual operating cash inflows and $1,000 in salvage value. The hotel's discount rate of 12 percent does not include an allowance for inflation.

Exhibit 17–6 presents the computation of the project's net present value using constant dollars and a 12 percent discount rate that excludes an allowance for inflation. The project's net present value is $4,951.

To illustrate the second method, assume management believes annual inflation will be 8 percent over the life of the project. The project is reevaluated in Exhibit 17–7 using nominal dollars and inflation adjusted discount factors, which are computed at the bottom of the exhibit. Annual nominal dollar cash flows, also computed at the bottom of Exhibit 17–7, assume that operating cash inflows will increase at the inflation rate of 8 percent each year. The second method indicates the project's net present value is $4,948. The difference between the net present values using the first and second methods is due to rounding errors. The choice of the method to use is a matter of personal preference.

EXHIBIT 17–6   Capital Budgeting with Constant Dollars and a Discount Rate That Excludes Inflation

Cash flow item:	Predicted Cash Inflows (Outflows)	Year(s) of Cash Flow	12 Percent Present Value Factor	Present Value of Cash Flows
Acquisition cost	$(12,000)	0	1.000	$(12,000)
Annual operating cash inflow	4,000	1–6	4.111	16,444
Disposal value	1,000	6	0.507	507
Net present value of all cash flows				$ 4,951

EXHIBIT 17–7   Capital Budgeting with Nominal Dollars and a Discount Rate That Includes Inflation

Cash flow item:	Predicted Cash Inflows (Outflows)	Year(s) of Cash Flow	12 Percent Present Value Factor**	Present Value of Cash Flows
Acquisition cost	$(12,000)	0	1.000	$(12,000)
Annual operating cash inflow*				
Year 1	4,320	1	0.827	3,573
Year 2	4,666	2	0.683	3,187
Year 3	5,039	3	0.565	2,847
Year 4	5,442	4	0.467	2,541
Year 5	5,877	5	0.386	2,269
Year 6	6,347	6	0.319	2,025
Disposal value ($1,000 × 1.08⁶)	1,587	6	0.319	506
Net present value of all cash flows				$ 4,948

* Schedule of annual nominal dollar cash inflows:

	Year 1	Year 2	Year 3	Year 4	Year 5	Year 6
Constant dollar operating cash inflows	$4,000	$4,000	$4,000	$4,000	$4,000	$4,000
Conversion to nominal dollars	$\times 1.08$	$\times 1.08^2$	$\times 1.08^3$	$\times 1.08^4$	$\times 1.08^5$	$\times 1.08^6$
Nominal dollar operating cash flows	$4,320	$4,666	$5,039	$5,442	$5,877	$6,347

** Computation of inflation adjusted present value factors:

	Year 1	Year 2	Year 3	Year 4	Year 5	Year 6
Unadjusted factor for 12% discount rate	0.893	0.797	0.712	0.636	0.567	0.507
Factor for 8% rate of inflation	×0.926	×0.857	×0.794	×0.735	×0.681	×0.630
Adjusted present value factor	0.827	0.683	0.565	0.467	0.386	0.319

SUMMARY

The purchasing power of money varies inversely with prices. During periods of inflation, the purchasing power of money declines as prices rise. Conversely, during periods of deflation, the purchasing power of money increases as prices fall. This variability creates problems for investors as they attempt to interpret accounting data presented in general purpose financial statements, and for managers who use accounting data to plan and control firm activities.

In an attempt to make general purpose financial statements more useful, many large corporations prepare constant dollar financial data to supplement traditional financial statements that use nominal dollars. The managers of leading corporations have responded to price level changes by using replacement costs rather than historical costs in pricing decisions, building an allowance for inflation into budgets, updating standards more frequently, adjusting performance reports to separately identify variances caused by inflation, increasing the hurdle or discount rates used for capital budgeting, adjusting ratio analysis for inflation, and placing increased emphasis on the statement of changes in financial position.

Managers often ignore the impact of changing prices during periods of relative price level stability. However, the profitability of long-term investments in plant and equipment is significantly affected by changes in the price level, even if the annual price level changes are quite small. Two methods of allowing for inflation in the evaluation of capital expenditure proposals were presented in this chapter. With the first method, future cash receipts and disbursements are predicted in constant dollars that reflect the current price level, and these constant dollar cash flows are then evaluated using a discount rate that does not include an allowance for inflation. With the second method, future cash receipts and disbursements are predicted in nominal dollars that reflect expected price level changes, and these nominal dollar cash flows are then evaluated using a discount rate that includes an allowance for inflation. The effect of taxes on capital budgeting with changing prices is considered in the appendix to this chapter.

APPENDIX
PRICE INDEXING, TAXES, AND CAPITAL BUDGETING

Because capital budgeting is a long-term activity of business, it needs to include adjustment factors not only for inflation and deflation, but also for income taxes. In evaluating the results of a capital budgeting decision the after-tax cash flows may be substantially different from the before-tax cash flows. Because each year will have its own inflation or deflation rate and related taxes, it is very difficult to compare different years without distorting the evaluation procedure. Likewise, it is difficult to compare different projects unless constant dollars are used for each project, along with the related taxes.

Note also that during periods of inflation, a company's tax liability may increase even though its constant dollar before-tax net income remains the same. To illustrate, assume that the Sigma Company has a tax rate of 34 percent for both 19x3 and 19x4. During this period, inflation caused the price index to move from 300 to 312, while before-tax net income increased by a corresponding amount, from $400,000 to $416,000.

	19x3	19x4
Nominal income before taxes	$400,000	$416,000
Taxes (34 percent)	− 13,600	− 14,144
Nominal income after taxes	$386,400	$401,856
Constant income before taxes	$416,000*	$416,000
Taxes (based on nominal income		
as required by current tax laws)	− 13,600	− 14,144
Constant income after taxes	$402,400	$401,856

* $400,000 × 312/300 = $416,000, assuming all revenues and costs occur at a price index of 300.

If a one-year change can actually cause a decrease in real income (from $402,400 to $401,856), imagine what can happen in a capital budgeting decision, which usually impacts a company's income over several years. Ignoring such inputs for a capital budgeting decision can have devastating results.

To properly evaluate the effects of both inflation and taxation on capital budgeting, management should integrate them into the decision model. To illustrate a comprehensive example, the first method discussed in this chapter's section on capital budgeting is used. In this method, predicted future cash flows are stated in constant dollars that reflect the current price level, and these constant dollar cash flows are evaluated using a discount rate that does not allow for inflation. The key to the proper use of this method is to restate the nominal dollar depreciation tax savings into constant dollars.

Assume that Computer Consultants is evaluating a proposal to install a minicomputer with terminals that clients can use on demand for certain types of programs and problems. Fees will be charged for the computer time and any assistance that is required. The estimated constant dollar operating cash inflows from the new system are shown in Exhibit 17–8. The minicomputer installation, including terminals and hookups, will cost $35,000. After six years the company will sell the system for a projected nominal dollar salvage value of $8,000. Straight-line depreciation with a five-year life and the required half-year convention will be used for tax purposes. The company's marginal tax rate is 34 percent. Using a discount rate that does not allow for inflation, the company requires a return of 12 percent on new investments. The predicted inflation rate is 8 percent. As shown in Exhibit 17–8, management should accept the proposal because it has a net present value, including inflation, of $10,633.

EXHIBIT 17–8   Capital Budgeting, Including Taxes, with Constant Dollars and a Discount Rate That Excludes Inflation

Cash flow item:	Predicted Cash Inflows (Outflows)	Year(s) of Cash Flow	12 Percent Present Value Factor	Present Value of Cash Flows
Acquisition cost	$(35,000)	0	1	$(35,000)
Annual operating cash flows				
Year 1	14,000	1	0.893	12,502
Year 2	17,800	2	0.797	14,187
Year 3	19,900	3	0.712	14,169
Year 4	12,000	4	0.636	7,632
Year 5	8,000	5	0.567	4,536
Year 6	4,000	6	0.507	2,028
Taxes on cash inflows (34%)				
Year 1	(4,760)	1	0.893	(4,251)
Year 2	(6,052)	2	0.797	(4,823)
Year 3	(6,766)	3	0.712	(4,817)
Year 4	(4,080)	4	0.636	(2,595)
Year 5	(2,720)	5	0.567	(1,542)
Year 6	(1,360)	6	0.507	(690)
Tax savings on depreciation*				
Year 1	1,190	1	0.893	1,063
Year 2	2,380	2	0.797	1,897
Year 3	2,380	3	0.712	1,695
Year 4	2,380	4	0.636	1,514
Year 5	2,380	5	0.567	1,349
Year 6	1,190	6	0.507	603
Disposal value ($8,000/1.08^6)	5,041	6	0.507	2,556
Tax on disposal ($8,000 × 0.34)	(2,720)	6	0.507	(1,379)
Net present value of all cash flows				$ 10,633

* Tax savings on depreciation:

Year	Depreciation Base	Depreciation Rate	Annual Depreciation	Tax Rate	Cash Savings
1	$35,000	$\frac{1}{2} \times \frac{1}{5}$	$3,500	0.34	$1,190
2	35,000	$\frac{1}{5}$	7,000	0.34	2,380
3	35,000	$\frac{1}{5}$	7,000	0.34	2,380
4	35,000	$\frac{1}{5}$	7,000	0.34	2,380
5	35,000	$\frac{1}{5}$	7,000	0.34	2,380
6	35,000	$\frac{1}{2} \times \frac{1}{5}$	3,500	0.34	1,190

KEY TERMS

Constant dollar accounting
Constant dollars
Consumer Price Index
Current cost accounting
Deflation
Gross National Product Implicit
   Price Deflator

Inflation
Monetary items
Nominal dollars
Nonmonetary items
Price index
Purchasing power gains and losses
Replacement cost

REVIEW QUESTIONS

17–1 How is the Consumer Price Index computed for a particular time period?

17–2 What is the relationship between prices and purchasing power?

17–3 Identify some of the ways managers respond to inflation.

17–4 A ratio is used to convert nominal dollars to constant dollars. How is this conversion ratio computed?

17–5 Provide examples of monetary items and nonmonetary items.

17–6 How can an organization have a purchasing power loss during an inflationary period? How can it have a purchasing power gain during an inflationary period?

17–7 Why do managers sometimes criticize the Consumer Price Index?

17–8 Identify and distinguish between the two basic approaches to adjusting for changes in the price level.

17–9 Give two examples of decisions for which managers might prefer current cost information to constant dollar information.

17–10 In budgeting, how might management evaluate the potential impact of uncertain, but potentially large, price changes?

17–11 When might management use a price level adjusted flexible budget?

17–12 When a price level adjusted flexible budget is used for performance evaluation, are managers relieved of all responsibility for variations in input costs?

17–13 Why are even low rates of inflation important in capital budgeting?

17–14 Briefly describe two alternative approaches to allowing for inflation in the evaluation of capital expenditure proposals.

REVIEW PROBLEM

Price Level Capital Budgeting

The president of Newproducts, Inc., became very concerned about the impact inflation was having on the profitability of the company. She requested that all capital budgeting decisions include a consideration for inflation. After an extensive study, the company's executive committee determined that an inflation rate of 6 percent be used for all capital budgeting decisions until further notice. Newproducts' current discount rate of 10 percent does not include an allowance for inflation.

The shipping department has requested the purchase of a $25,000 binding machine to increase the efficiency of the packing process. In constant dollars the machine would save the company an estimated $5,000 per year by reducing overtime wages and minimizing damage that occurs during the packing process. The machine would last six years and have an estimated salvage value in constant dollars of $4,000.

Requirements

a) Determine the net present value of the machine purchase and related savings using constant dollars and the unadjusted discount rate.

b) Determine the net present value of the machine purchase and related savings using nominal dollars and an inflation adjusted discount rate.

c) Should the company accept the proposal by the shipping department?

The solution to this problem is found at the end of the Chapter 17 exercises and problems.

EXERCISES	Presented below is information on the total cost of a standard package of goods during each of five years.
17–1 Constructing a Price Index	

Year	Cost
19x2	$272
19x3	320
19x4	384
19x5	416
19x6	480

Required: Treating the 19x3 price level as the base period, develop a price index for each year. *Hint:* The base year price level is assigned an index of 100. Determine the cost in other years as a ratio of the base year cost and multiply this ratio by 100.

17–2 Constructing a Price Index

A manufacturer that produces a variety of goods from three raw materials has asked you to construct a materials price index. The index is to be based on the total standard costs. Presented is cost information for each of five years.

| | Unit Price of Material | | | Total Cost of |
Year	1	2	3	Standard Package
19x3	$135	$245	$208	$588
19x4	150	250	200	600
19x5	168	275	217	660
19x6	180	295	233	708
19x7	210	325	245	780

Requirements

a) Treating the price level as the base period, develop a price index for each year. *Hint:* The base year price level is assigned an index of 100. Determine the cost in other years as a ratio of the base year cost and multiply this ratio by 100.

b) Determine if the price index computed in requirement (a) is equally useful in tracking the cost of each material. Present supporting calculations. *Hint:* One approach is to construct a price index for each material.

17–3 Price Level Adjusted Salary

Eleanor Frost studied hard in school and worked hard at her job. She was pleased with her annual salary increases, regarding them as both a reward and an incentive. Yet, her money did not seem to go as far as when she started working. Information on Eleanor's salary and the price level follows:

	19x1	19x2	19x3	19x4	19x5
Salary	$24,000	$26,400	$31,000	$33,200	$36,000
Price index	120	135	150	170	190

Required: Evaluate Eleanor's salary in constant 19x5 dollars. Round calculations to the nearest dollar.

17–4 Price Level Adjusted Sales

Harold "Hot" Aire, the sales manager of Big Time Shoes, was on his way to an executive committee meeting to argue for a salary increase. He brought the following sales data as justification for the increase.

	19x2	19x3	19x4	19x5	19x6
Sales revenue	$440,000	$460,000	$510,000	$525,000	$540,000

Though the president was impressed with the sales figures, he asked you to perform some additional analysis of Big Time's sales record. You obtain the following price level information.

	19x2	19x3	19x4	19x5	19x6
Price index	120	160	180	200	240

Required: Evaluate Big Time's sales revenue in constant 19x6 dollars.

17–5 Price Level Adjusted Sales

In 19x1 the vice-president of marketing set a five-year sales goal of 80 percent above the current sales level. The nominal sales and average price level indexes for each year were as follows:

Year	Sales	Price Index
19x1	$100,000	128
19x2	120,000	134
19x3	144,000	144
19x4	160,000	140
19x5	178,000	148
19x6	190,000	160

Requirements

a) Evaluate the five-year sales goal in terms of nominal dollars.

b) Evaluate the five-year sales goal in terms of price level adjusted dollars.

17–6 Constant Dollar Balance Sheet Items

The following balances are taken from the Collins Company accounts as of December 31, 19x8.

Cash	$146,000
Accounts receivable	256,000
Inventory, raw materials	400,000
Buildings, book value	800,000
Equipment	580,000
Notes payable	440,000

The price indexes on the dates of the transactions affecting these items are as follows:

Transaction/date	Price Index
Accounts receivable, all current	200
Inventory, LIFO method, base year 19x4	140
Buildings, acquired 19x2	120
Equipment, one-half 19x2, one-half 19x3	
Notes payable, issued 19x4	140
19x2	120
19x3	125
19x5	144
12/31/19x8	210

Required: Determine the amount of each item in constant dollars as of December 31, 19x8.

17–7 Constant Dollar Balance Sheet Items

Presented is information taken from the nominal dollar balance sheet of the Brantford Machine Shop, as of December 31, 19x9.

Cash	$ 7,500
Inventory	18,000
Buildings, net of accumulated depreciation	120,000
Land	90,000
Bonds payable	250,000

The price indexes on the dates of transactions affecting these items are as follows:

Transaction	Price Index
Acquired land, 2/1/x2	150
Issued bonds, 1/15/x3	160
Completed construction of building, 6/1/x4	175
Acquired current inventory, 9/15/x9	300

The price index as of December 31, 19x9, was 280.

Required: Determine the amount of each item in constant dollars as of December 31, 19x9.

17–8 Constant Dollar Balance Sheet

The balance sheet for Bender Home Builders as of December 31, 19x6, is presented below in nominal dollars.

Bender Home Builders
Balance Sheet
December 31, 19x6

Assets

Cash		$ 25,000
Accounts Receivable		112,000
Inventories, LIFO, base year 19x1		350,000
Finished units, two		220,000
Equipment, net of depreciation		180,000
Total assets		$887,000

Liabilities and owner's equity

Liabilities:		
Accounts payable	$ 15,000	
Notes payable	90,000	$105,000
Owner's equity:		
Bender Capital	$953,000	
Bender Drawing	(171,000)	782,000
Total liabilities and owner's equity		$887,000

The price indexes on the dates of significant transactions affecting these items are as follows:

Transaction/date	Price Index
Organized, 19x1	110
Finished units built during 19x6	200
Equipment purchased in 19x4	160
Notes payable issued in 19x5	166
Accounts receivable acquired in July 19x6	178

Required: Prepare a constant dollar balance sheet as of December 31, 19x6, when the price index is 220.

17–9 Constant Dollar Balance Sheet

Presented is the nominal dollar balance sheet of the Rapid City Supply Company, as of December 31, 19x7.

Rapid City Supply Company
Balance Sheet
December 31, 19x7

Assets

Cash		$ 27,000
Accounts receivable		30,000
Inventories (FIFO)		45,000
Property, plant, and equipment	$240,000	
Less: Accumulated depreciation	−60,000	180,000
Total assets		$282,000

Liabilities and stockholders' equity

Liabilities:		
Accounts payable	$ 25,000	
Notes payable	140,000	$165,000
Stockholders' equity:		
Common stock ($1 par; 30,000 shares outstanding)	$ 30,000	
Premium on common stock	25,000	
Retained earnings	62,000	117,000
Total liabilities and stockholders' equity		$282,000

The price indexes on the dates of significant transactions affecting these items are as follows:

Transaction	Price Index
Issued common stock, 1/15/x1	127
Acquired property, plant, and equipment, 6/1/x4	140
Issued notes payable, 6/1/x4	140
Acquired ending inventory, 10/1/x7	200

Required: Prepare a constant dollar balance sheet as of December 31, 19x7. The December 31, 19x7, price index is 210.

17–10 Constant Dollar Income Statement

Presented is the Jones Company's nominal dollar income statement for the year ended December 31, 19x7.

Jones Company
Income Statement
For the year ended December 31, 19x7

Sales		$600,000
Cost of goods sold:		
From beginning inventory	$ 56,000	
From current purchases	240,000	−296,000
Gross profit		$304,000
Other expenses:		
Salaries	$180,000	
Depreciation	21,000	
Miscellaneous	30,000	−231,000
Income before income taxes		$ 73,000
Provision for income taxes		− 24,000
Net income		$ 49,000

The beginning inventory was acquired when the price index was 280. The fixed assets were acquired when the price index was 240. All other acquisitions, revenues, and expenditures, including taxes, took place evenly throughout 19x7 at an average price index of 300. The December 31, 19x7, price index is 320.

Required: Prepare a constant dollar income statement.

17–11 Constant Dollar Income Statement

Presented is the Krueger Company's nominal dollar income statement for the year ended December 31, 19x5.

Krueger Company
Income Statement
For the year ended December 31, 19x5

Sales		$510,000
Cost of goods sold:		
From beginning inventory	$ 20,000	
From current purchases	210,000	−230,000
Gross profit		$280,000
Other expenses:		
Salaries	$120,000	
Depreciation	100,000	
Miscellaneous	24,000	−244,000
Income before income taxes		$ 36,000
Provision for income taxes		− 8,000
Net income		$ 28,000

The beginning inventory was acquired when the price index was 160. The fixed assets were acquired when the price index was 80. All other acquisitions, revenues, and expenditures took place evenly throughout 19x5 at an average price index of 180. The December 31, 19x5 price index is 210.

Required: Prepare a constant dollar income statement.

17–12 Purchasing Power Gains and Losses

Presented is information regarding two monetary accounts.

Account	Balance 1/1/x7	Change 19x7	Balance 12/31/x7	Change 19x8	Balance 12/31/x8
Accounts Receivable	$45,000	$9,000	$54,000	−$12,000	$42,000
Taxes Payable	30,000	−8,100	21,900	6,000	27,900

Additional information:

Date	Price Index
1/1/x7	240
Average 19x7	288
12/31/x7	320
Average 19x8	300
12/31/x8	280

All changes in account balances took place evenly throughout each year at the year's average price index.

Requirements

a) Determine the 19x7 purchasing power gain or loss for each item. Present your answer in terms of the 12/31/x7 price level.

b) Determine the 19x8 purchasing power gain or loss for each item. Present your answer in terms of the 12/31/x8 price level.

c) Explain your answers to requirements (a) and (b).

17–13 Purchasing Power Gains and Losses

Presented is information regarding two monetary accounts.

Account	Balance 1/1/x3	Change 19x3	Balance 12/31/x3	Change 19x4	Balance 12/31/x4
Cash	$28,000	$8,000	$36,000	−$11,000	$25,000
Accounts Payable	16,380	−1,380	15,000	8,800	23,800

Additional information:

Date	Price Index
1/1/x3	210
Average 19x3	200
12/31/x3	180
Average 19x4	220
12/31/x4	240

All changes in account balances took place evenly throughout each year at the year's average price index.

Requirements

a) Determine the 19x3 purchasing power gain or loss for each item. Present your answer in terms of the 12/31/x3 price level.

b) Determine the 19x4 purchasing power gain or loss for each item. Present your answer in terms of the 12/31/x4 price level.

c) Explain your answers to requirements (a) and (b).

17–14 Cost Behavior Analysis

Sirrine Industries had the following utility expenses during a period of rising prices.

Month	Kilowatt Hours	Amount	Price Index
April	500,000	$2,200	140
May	550,000	2,700	150
June	520,000	2,600	160
July	560,000	3,200	168

The plant manager has questioned why there is not a more constant relationship between usage and costs.

Requirements

a) Plot each month's cost using historical dollars.

b) Plot each month's cost using constant dollars in terms of the July price level.

c) Evaluate the concerns expressed by the plant manager.

17–15 Cost Behavior Analysis

Until recently the lumber costs for Columbus Cabinets had always exhibited a linear relationship with board feet purchased. The quarterly purchases for 19x5 were as follows:

Quarter	Board Feet	Total Cost	Price Index
First	620,000	$403,000	240
Second	720,000	475,200	250
Third	680,000	476,000	280
Fourth	630,000	434,700	300

Requirements

a) Plot each quarter's cost and volume using historical dollars.

b) Plot each quarter's cost and volume using constant dollars in terms of the fourth quarter price level.

c) Which method shows a linear relationship?

17–16 Sale of Fixed Assets

Riggman Construction Company bought a piece of equipment for $40,000 in January 19x1. The equipment had a five-year life with no estimated salvage value. The company used the straight-line depreciation method. The equipment was sold in December of 19x3 for $20,000. The price indexes for each period were as follows:

Period/year	Price Index
January 19x1	300
19x1 average	309
19x2 average	315
19x3 average	321
December 19x3	324
19x4 average	327
19x5 average	336

Requirements

a) Calculate the depreciation expense on a constant dollar basis for each year.

b) Determine the gain or loss on the sale of equipment using both the nominal and constant dollar methods.

17–17 Sale of Fixed Assets

Dave's Copying bought two identical copiers for $30,000 each in January 19x3. The equipment had a six-year life with no estimated salvage value. The company used the straight-line depreciation method. Copier A was sold in December 19x5 for $15,500 and the other, Copier B, was sold in December 19x7 for $8,000. The price indexes for each period were as follows:

Period/year	Price Index
January 19x3	400
19x3 average	404
19x4 average	412
19x5 average	416
December 19x5	420
19x6 average	428
19x7 average	430
December 19x7	432
19x8 average	436

Requirements

a) Calculate the depreciation expense on a constant dollar basis for each year.

b) Determine the gain or loss on the sale of each piece of equipment using both the nominal and constant dollar methods.

17–18 Inflation and Taxes (Appendix)

John and Jean had a combined taxable income in 19x8 of $80,000. In 19x9 their combined taxable income was $88,000. During this period the price index increased from 400 to 416. Their tax rate is 20 percent.

Requirements

a) What was their after-tax income in nominal and constant dollars?

b) Explain how much better or worse they were in 19x9.

17–19 Inflation and Taxes (Appendix)

Klassic Kola has increased its sales and net income before taxes consistently during the last few years, but for some reason the financial condition has not improved. The president believes that the company is paying too much in taxes in relation to its growth. The following information is available for the last three years.

Year	Taxable Income	Price Index
19x5	$432,000	300
19x6	460,000	320
19x7	500,000	340

The company's tax rate is 34 percent.

Requirements

a) Compute the nominal income after taxes for all years.

b) Compute the constant dollar income after taxes for all years.

c) Evaluate the president's concern that taxes are increasing faster than real income.

PROBLEMS

17–20 Price Level Adjusted Flexible Budget

The Frame Company's budgeted monthly production costs are as follows:

Direct materials	$ 9 per unit
Direct labor	10 per unit
Variable overhead	6 per unit
Fixed overhead:	
Depreciation	$22,000 per month
Other	40,000 per month

During May 19x3, Frame produced 22,000 units and incurred the following production costs.

Direct materials	$196,000
Direct labor	250,000
Variable overhead	148,500
Fixed overhead:	
Depreciation	22,000
Other	46,000

All materials and other supplies are purchased and paid for in the month of use. Except for depreciation, the budgeted costs are based on a price index of 160. Depreciation is based on a price index of 80. The price index during May was 180.

Requirements

a) Prepare a traditional (nominal dollar) performance report based on a budget drawn up for the actual level of activity.

b) Prepare a price level adjusted performance report in constant May 19x3 dollars. This performance report should also be based on the actual level of activity. *Hint:* Actual depreciation must be restated.

17–21 Price Level Adjusted Flexible Budget

Presented is the April 19x2 performance report for the production department of the Kiger Company.

Kiger Company
Production Department Performance Report
For the month of April, 19x2

	Actual	*Budget*	*Variance*
Volume	12,000	10,000	
Manufacturing costs:			
Direct materials	$ 63,000	$ 50,000	$13,000 U
Direct labor	74,000	60,000	14,000 U
Variable overhead	52,000	40,000	12,000 U
Fixed overhead:			
Depreciation	20,000	20,000	—
Other	31,000	30,000	1,000 U
Total	$240,000	$200,000	$40,000 U

All materials and other supplies are purchased and paid for in the month of use. Except for depreciation, the original budget was based on a price index of 120. Depreciation is based on a price index of 100. The average price index during April 19x2 was 126.

Requirements

a) Prepare a traditional (nominal dollar) performance report based on a budget drawn up for the actual level of activity.

b) Prepare a price level adjusted performance report in constant April 19x2 dollars. This performance report should also be based on the actual level of activity. *Hint:* Actual depreciation must be restated.

17–22 Price Level Adjusted Cost Estimation and Cost Prediction

The following information is available concerning unit production volume, materials costs, and a specific price index for materials costs.

Observation	*Unit Volume*	*Materials Cost*	*Price Index*
19x1	25,000	$594,000	220
19x2	15,000	405,000	250

Requirements

a) Develop a cost estimating equation in terms of the 19x2 price index. Use the high-low method.

b) Management expects to produce 24,000 units in 19x3. The predicted 19x3 price index is 275. Adjust the equation developed in requirement (a), and then use it to predict the 19x3 materials costs.

c) Compare the equation developed in requirement (a) to one developed using nominal dollars. What cost prediction error would likely occur if an equation based on nominal dollars were used to predict 19x3 materials costs?

17–23 Price Level Adjusted Cost Estimation and Cost Prediction

The following information is available concerning unit production volume and maintenance costs.

Year	Unit Volume	Maintenance Costs
19x2	5,000	$54,250
19x3	3,500	42,400
19x4	4,000	51,625
19x5	3,000	47,500
19x6	4,500	67,000

Management has asked you to assist in developing an equation to predict 19x7 maintenance costs.

Requirements

a) Plot the volume and cost data on a scatter diagram. Does there appear to be a high correlation between volume and maintenance costs?

b) Assume the Accounting Department has developed the following specific price index for maintenance costs.

	19x2	19x3	19x4	19x5	19x6
Price index	310	320	350	380	400

Restate all maintenance costs in terms of the 19x6 price index, and plot the adjusted volume and cost data on a scatter diagram. Does there appear to be a high correlation between volume and maintenance costs?

c) Use the high-low method to develop a cost estimating equation at the 19x6 price level.

d) The predicted 19x7 production volume and price index are 4,200 units and 410, respectively. Predict the 19x7 maintenance costs in 19x7 nominal dollars.

17–24 Trend Analysis of Constant Dollar Income Statements

Presented are comparative nominal dollar income statements for Quebec Computer Services for the years ending December 31, 19x1 through 19x5.

Quebec Computer Services
Comparative Income Statements
For the years ending December 31, 19x1 through 19x5

	19x1	19x2	19x3	19x4	19x5
Sales	$200,000	$250,000	$275,000	$350,000	$400,000
Less expenses:					
Salaries	$150,000	$160,000	$180,000	$210,000	$240,000
Depreciation	30,000	30,000	30,000	30,000	30,000
Other	6,000	7,200	7,500	9,000	11,000
Total	−186,000	−197,200	−217,500	−249,000	−281,000
Income before income taxes	$ 14,000	$ 52,800	$ 57,500	$101,000	$119,000
Provision for income taxes	− 4,700	− 17,000	− 19,000	− 34,000	− 40,000
Net income	$ 9,300	$ 35,800	$ 38,500	$ 67,000	$ 79,000

Quebec Computer Services began operations on April 1, 19x1, by acquiring property, plant, and equipment costing $250,000. Sales and profits have increased every year since then. In late 19x5, Quebec's management offered to sell the firm to Canadian Computing, Ltd., for $500,000. This price is relatively low given Quebec's earnings record and projected earnings growth. The primary reason for the sale is a need for cash to replace old computer equipment.

As part of its evaluation procedures, Canadian Computing has asked you to prepare comparative constant dollar income statements. You have acquired the following information.

	Price Index
April 1, 19x1	100
Average, 19x1	120
Average, 19x2	140
Average, 19x3	150
Average, 19x4	180
Average, 19x5	175
Average, 19x6	200
December 31, 19x6	210

Requirements

a) Prepare comparative constant dollar income statements in terms of the December 31, 19x6, price index.

b) Evaluate Quebec Computer Services' constant dollars earnings record.

17–25 Price Level Adjusted Capital Budgeting

Megabucks Incorporated's management became increasingly concerned about the impact of inflation on the profitability of capital expenditures. In response to this concern, the capital budgeting committee passed a resolution stating that inflation was to be given explicit consideration in the evaluation of all capital expenditures, by increasing the discount rate from 12 to 20 percent, to allow for expected annual inflation. No other adjustments were recommended, and projected cash flows continued to be stated in current dollars.

Following adoption of the resolution, the profitability of accepted projects increased, but Megabucks found itself with a large amount of excess cash to invest in short-term securities. Of more concern was that the overall profitability and stock prices were actually falling, whereas liquid assets were increasing. Megabucks was becoming a prime candidate for a corporate takeover.

Requirements

a) Explain how management's attempt to cope with inflation may have contributed to Megabucks' problems.

b) Suggest two alternative methods of allowing for inflation in the evaluation of capital expenditure proposals.

c) Determine the present value of the following project with the inflation adjusting approach used by Megabucks and each of the methods suggested in requirement (b).

Initial investment	$2,800,000
Life	4 years
Salvage value	none
Annual operating cash inflow	$1,000,000

17–26 Price Level Adjusted Capital Budgeting

Potsdam Package Company is evaluating the desirability of purchasing a small packaging machine for $12,000. Use of the machine would save Potsdam $5,000 in operating expenses during each of the next four years. The machine has a salvage value of $1,500 at the end of its four-year life. All dollar amounts are stated at the current price level. Potsdam's discount rate of 10 percent does not allow for inflation.

Requirements

a) Determine the machine's net present value using constant dollars and the unadjusted discount rate.

b) Assume that management expects inflation of 6 percent during each of the next four years. Determine the machine's net present value using nominal dollars and an inflation adjusted discount rate. (Round calculations to the nearest dollar.)

17–27 Price Level Adjusted Capital Budgeting

Kwick Kopies is evaluating the desirability of opening a new photocopy service center on College Avenue. Kwick Kopies would sign a six-year nonrenewable lease and invest $100,000 in the building and photocopy equipment. Management expects the center to provide operating cash inflows of $25,000 during each year. The photocopy equipment has an expected salvage value of $10,000 at the end of six years. All dollar amounts are stated at the current price level. Kwick Kopies' discount rate of 12 percent does not allow for inflation.

Requirements

a) Determine the project's net present value using constant dollars and the unadjusted discount rate.

b) Assume management expects inflation of 8 percent during each of the next six years. Determine the project's net present value using nominal dollars and an inflation adjusted discount rate. (Round all calculations to the nearest dollar.)

17–28 Price Level Capital Budgeting with Taxes (Appendix)

Refer to Problem 17–26. Assume that management expects inflation of 6 percent during each of the next four years. Also assume that Potsdam Package Company has a marginal tax rate of 34 percent and that the packaging machine qualifies for three-year straight-line depreciation. The depreciable cost of the asset produces the following tax savings.

Year	Costs		Depreciation Rate		Annual Depreciation		Tax Rate		Tax Savings
1	$12,000	×	$\frac{1}{2} \times \frac{1}{3}$	=	$2,000	×	0.34	=	$ 680
2	12,000	×	$\frac{1}{3}$	=	4,000	×	0.34	=	1,360
3	12,000	×	$\frac{1}{3}$	=	4,000	×	0.34	=	1,360
4	12,000	×	$\frac{1}{2} \times \frac{1}{3}$	=	2,000	×	0.34	=	680

Requirements

a) Determine the net present value of purchasing the machine and its related savings using constant dollars and the unadjusted discount rate.

b) Determine the net present value of the machine using nominal dollars and an inflation adjusted discount rate. (Round calculations to the nearest dollar.)

17–29 Price Level Capital Budgeting with Taxes (Appendix)

Refer to Problem 17–27. Assume management expects inflation of 8 percent during each of the next six years. Also assume that Kwick Kopies has a marginal tax rate of 34 percent and that the project qualifies for five-year straight-line depreciation. The depreciable cost of the asset produces the following tax savings.

Year	Cost		Depreciation Rate		Tax Rate		Tax Savings
1	$100,000	$\times$	$\frac{1}{2} \times \frac{1}{5}$	$\times$	0.34	=	$3,400
2	100,000	$\times$	$\frac{1}{5}$	$\times$	0.34	=	6,800
3	100,000	$\times$	$\frac{1}{5}$	$\times$	0.34	=	6,800
4	100,000	$\times$	$\frac{1}{5}$	$\times$	0.34	=	6,800
5	100,000	$\times$	$\frac{1}{5}$	$\times$	0.34	=	6,800
6	100,000	$\times$	$\frac{1}{2} \times \frac{1}{5}$	$\times$	0.34	=	3,400

Requirements

a) Determine the project's net present value using constant dollars and the unadjusted discount rate.

b) Determine the project's net present value using nominal dollars and an inflation adjusted discount rate. (Round calculations to the nearest dollar.)

17–30
Comprehensive Price Level and Capital Budgeting with Taxes (Appendix)

Catix Corporation permits each division to make capital expenditures up to $200,000 without approval of the corporate headquarters. The corporate controller has determined that the cost of capital for Catix Corporation is 12 percent. This rate does not allow for inflation, which is expected to occur at an average rate of 8 percent over the next five years. Catix pays income taxes at the rate of 34 percent.

The Electronics Division of Catix is considering the purchase of an automated assembly and soldering machine for use in the manufacture of its printed circuit boards. The machine would be placed in service in early 19x1. The divisional controller estimates that if the machine is purchased, two positions will be eliminated, yielding a cost savings for wages and employee benefits. However, the machine would require additional supplies and more power would be required to operate the machine. The cost savings and additional costs in current 19x0 prices are as follows:

Wages and employee benefits of the two positions eliminated ($25,000 each)	$50,000
Cost of additional supplies	4,000
Cost of additional power	10,000

The new machine would be purchased and installed at the end of 19x0 at a net cost of $80,000. Straight-line depreciation will be used. The machine will become technologically obsolete in four years and will have no salvage value at that time. A three-year class life with straight-line depreciation will be used for tax purposes.

The Electronics Division compensates for inflation in capital expenditure analyses by adjusting the expected nominal dollar cash flows by an estimated price level index. The adjusted after-tax cash flows are then discounted using the appropriate discount rate. The estimated year-end index values for each of the next five years are as follows:

Year	Year-end Price Index
19x0	1.00
19x1	1.08
19x2	1.17
19x3	1.26
19x4	1.36
19x5	1.47

The Plastics Division of Catix compensates for inflation in capital expenditure analyses by adding the anticipated inflation rate to the cost of capital and then uses the inflation adjusted cost of capital to discount the projected nominal dollar cash flows. The Plastics Division recently rejected a project with cash flows and economic life similar to those associated with the machine under consideration by the Electronics Division. The Plastics Division's analysis of the rejected project was as follows:

Annual pre-tax cost savings, net	$ 36,000
Less incremental depreciation expenses	− 20,000
Increase in taxable income	$ 16,000
Increase in income taxes (34%)	− 5,440
Increase in after-tax income	$ 10,560
Add back noncash expense (depreciation)	20,000
Net after-tax annual cash inflow unadjusted for inflation	$ 30,560
Present value of net cash inflows using the sum of the cost of capital (12%) and the inflation rate (8%) or a minimum required return of 20% (factor of 2.589).	$ 79,120
Investment required	(80,000)
Net present value	$ (880)

Requirements

a) Using the price index provided, prepare a schedule showing the net nominal dollar after-tax annual cash flows adjusted for inflation for the automated assembly and soldering machine under consideration by the Electronics Division.

b) Without prejudice to your answer to requirement (a), assume that the net nominal dollar after-tax annual cash flows adjusted for inflation for the project being considered by the Electronics Division are as follows:

	19x1	19x2	19x3	19x4
Nominal dollar after tax cash flows	$30,000	$35,000	$37,000	$40,000

For the Electronic Division's project, calculate the net present value that will be meaningful to management.

c) Evaluate the methods used by the Plastics Division and the Electronics Division to compensate for expected inflation in capital expenditure analyses.

(CMA Adapted)

**REVIEW PROBLEM
SOLUTION**

a)

Cash flow item:	Predicted Cash Inflows (Outflows)	Year(s) of Cash Flow	10 Percent Present Value Factor	Present Value of Cash Flows
Acquisition cost	$(25,000)	0	1.000	$(25,000)
Annual savings	5,000	1–6	4.355	21,775
Disposal value	4,000	6	0.564	2,256
Net present value of all cash flows				$ (969)

b)

Cash flow item:	Predicted Cash Inflows (Outflows)	Year(s) of Cash Flow	10 Percent Present Value Factor**	Present Value of Cash Flows
Acquisition cost	$(25,000)	0	1.000	$(25,000)
Annual savings*				
Year 1	5,300	1	0.857	4,542
Year 2	5,618	2	0.735	4,129
Year 3	5,955	3	0.631	3,758
Year 4	6,312	4	0.541	3,415
Year 5	6,691	5	0.464	3,105
Year 6	7,093	6	0.398	2,823
Disposal value ($4,000 × 1.06^6)	5,674	6	0.398	2,258
Net present value of all cash flows				$ (970)

* Schedule of annual nominal dollar savings:

	Year 1	Year 2	Year 3	Year 4	Year 5	Year 6
Constant dollar savings flows	$5,000	$5,000	$5,000	$5,000	$5,000	$5,000
Conversion to nominal dollars	× 1.06	× 1.06^2	× 1.06^3	× 1.06^4	× 1.06^5	× 1.06^6
Nominal dollar savings flows	$5,300	$5,618	$5,955	$6,312	$6,691	$7,093

** Computation of inflation adjusted present value factors:

	Year 1	Year 2	Year 3	Year 4	Year 5	Year 6
Unadjusted factor for 10% discount rate	0.909	0.826	0.751	0.683	0.621	0.564
Factor for 6% rate of inflation	×0.943	×0.890	×0.840	×0.792	×0.747	×0.705
Adjusted present value factor	0.857	0.735	0.631	0.541	0.464	0.398

c) No. The company should reject the shipping department proposal to purchase a $25,000 binding machine. The constant dollar cash flows have a negative net present value when discounted at 10 percent and the nominal dollar cash flows have a negative net present value when discounted at an inflation adjusted rate. The $1 difference between the solutions to parts (a) and (b) is due to rounding.

In this problem it was necessary to compute the inflation adjusted discount rate and the nominal dollar cash flows. In practice, a company's cost of capital will already include an allowance for inflation. Predicted cash flows, on the other hand, are likely to be stated in constant dollars. If constant dollar cash flows are evaluated using an inflation adjusted discount rate, an acceptable project may be erroneously rejected. In practice, it is likely that predicted cash flows will have to be restated from constant dollars to nominal dollars while no adjustment will be required for the discount rate.

Appendix:
Time Value of Money

The concept of time value of money explains why an amount of money received today is worth more than the same amount received at some future date. Because money can be invested to earn interest, a given amount of money today will accumulate to a greater amount in the future. Stated another way, for a given value one must have more money in the future than today to maintain the same value. Conversely, a sum of money to be received in the future is worth less in the present.

Future value is the amount a current sum of money earning a stated rate of interest will accumulate to at the end of a future period. Suppose you deposit $500 in a savings account at a financial institution that pays interest at the rate of 10 percent per year. At the end of the first year the original deposit of $500 will have grown to $550 ($500 × 1.10). If you leave the $550 for another year, the amount will grow to $605 ($550 × 1.10). It can be stated that $500 today has a future value in one year of $550, or conversely, that $550 one year from today has a present value of $500. Note that interest of $55 ($605 − $550) was earned in the second year, whereas interest of only $50 was earned in the first year. The reason for the increased amount is that interest during the second year has been earned on the principal plus interest from the first year ($550). When periodic interest is computed on principal plus prior period's accumulated interest, the interest is said to be compounded.

To determine future values at the end of each period, multiply the beginning amount by 1 plus the interest rate. Where multiple periods are involved, the future value is determined by repeatedly multiplying the beginning amount times 1 plus the interest rate for each period. When $500 is invested for two years at an interest rate of 10 percent per year, its future value is computed as $500 × 1.10 × 1.10. In general,

$$fv = pv(1 + r)^n,$$

where fv = future value amount,
pv = present value amount,
r = interest rate per period,
n = number of periods.

For the above situation the equation becomes

$$
\begin{aligned}
fv \text{ of } \$500 &= pv\,(1 + r)^n \\
&= \$500\,(1 + 0.10)^2 \\
&= \$605.
\end{aligned}
$$

From the general future value equation the compound amount, or future value, of $1.00 can be derived any time the interest rate and number of periods is known. Once the future value for $1.00 is determined, this amount may be multiplied by any present value amount to determine its future value.

Present value is the current worth of a specified amount of money to be received at some future date at some interest rate. Present value, then, is the inverse of future value. Solving for *pv* in the future value equation, the new *pv* equation can be determined as

$$fv = pv \, (1 + r)^n$$

$$pv = \frac{fv}{(1 + r)^n}.$$

The present value equation is often expressed as the future value amount times the present value of $1.00:

$$pv = fv \times \frac{\$1}{(1 + r)^n}.$$

Using the first equation, the present value of $8,800 to be received in one year, discounted at 10 percent, is computed as follows:

$$pv \text{ of } \$8,800 = \frac{\$8,800}{(1 + 0.10)^1}$$

$$= \frac{\$8,800}{1.10}$$

$$= \$8,000.$$

This amount can also be computed by multiplying $8,800 times the present value of $1.00:

$$pv \text{ of } \$8,800 = \$8,800 \times \frac{\$1}{(1 + 0.10)^1}$$

$$= \$8,800 \times 0.909$$

$$= \$8,000.$$

Thus when the time value of money is 10 percent, the present value of $8,800 to be received one period from now is $8,000.

The present value of $8,800 two periods from now is $7,273 [$8,800/(1.10)^2]. The computation can also be expressed as $8,800 × $1/(1.10)^2. Although these factors can be computed by hand, this approach is quite time-consuming for multiperiod problems. Tables providing the present value of $1.00 have been prepared for various interest rates and time periods to facilitate computations. Table 1 in this appendix can be used to determine the present values of future amounts. Using the factors in Table 1 (see p. 804) for the present value of $1.00, the present values of any future amount can be determined. For example, with an interest rate of 10 percent, the present value of the following future amounts to be received in one period are as shown below.

Future Value Amount		Present Value Factor of $1.00		Present Value
$ 100	×	0.909	=	$ 90.90
628	×	0.909	=	570.85
4,285	×	0.909	=	3,895.07
9,900	×	0.909	=	9,000.00

To further illustrate the use of Table 1, consider the following application. Alert Company wants to invest its surplus cash at 12 percent in order to have $10,000 to pay off a long-term note due at the end of five years. Table 1 shows that the present value factor for $1.00, discounted at 12 percent per year for five years, is 0.567. Multiplying $10,000 by 0.567, the present value is determined to be $5,670:

$$pv \text{ of } \$10,000 = fv \times pv \text{ of } \$1 \text{ factor}$$
$$= \$10,000 \times 0.567$$
$$= \$5,670.$$

Therefore, if Alert invests $5,670 today, it will have $10,000 available to pay off its note in five years.

Present value tables are also used to make investment decisions. Assume that the Monroe Company can make an investment that will provide a cash flow of $12,000 at the end of eight years. If the company demands a rate of return of 14 percent per year, what is the most it will be willing to pay for this investment? From Table 1 we find that the present value factor for $1.00, discounted at 14 percent per year for eight years, is 0.351:

$$pv \text{ of } \$12,000 = fv \times pv \text{ of } \$1 \text{ factor}$$
$$= \$12,000 \times 0.351$$
$$= \$4,212.$$

If the company demands an annual 14 percent return, the most it would be willing to invest today is $4,212.

ANNUITIES

Not all investments provide a single sum of money. Many investments provide periodic cash flows called annuities. An **annuity** is a series of equal cash flows received or paid over equal intervals of time. Suppose that $100 will be received at the end of each of the next three years. If the time value of money is 10 percent, the present value of this annuity can be determined by summing the present value of each receipt:

$$\text{Year 1} \quad \$100 \times \frac{\$1}{(1 + 0.10)^1} = \$\ 90.90$$

$$\text{Year 2} \quad \$100 \times \frac{\$1}{(1 + 0.10)^2} = \quad 82.65$$

$$\text{Year 3} \quad \$100 \times \frac{\$1}{(1 + 0.10)^3} = \quad \underline{75.13}$$

$$\text{Total} \qquad\qquad\qquad\qquad\qquad \underline{\underline{\$248.68}}$$

Alternatively, the following equation can be used to compute the present value:

$$pva = \frac{a}{r}\left(1 - \frac{1}{(1 + r)^n}\right),$$

where pva = present value of an annuity of \$1.00 (also called the annuity factor),
r = prevailing rate per period,
n = number of periods,
a = annuity amount.

This equation is used to compute the factors presented in Table 2. The present value of an annuity of \$1.00 per period for three periods, discounted at 10 percent per period, is as follows:

$$pva \text{ of } \$1 = \frac{\$1}{0.10}\left(1 - \frac{1}{(1 + 0.10)^3}\right)$$

$$= 2.4868.$$

Using this factor, the present value of a \$100 annuity can be computed by multiplying \$100 × 2.4868, which yields \$248.68. To determine the present value of an annuity of any amount, the annuity factor of \$1.00 can be multiplied by the annuity amount:

$$pva = a \times (pva \text{ of } \$1).$$

As an additional illustration of the use of Table 2, assume that the Red Kite Company is considering an investment in a piece of equipment that will produce net cash inflows of $2,000 at the end of each year for five years. If the company's desired rate of return is 12 percent, an investment of $7,210 will provide such a return:

$$pva \text{ of } \$2,000 = \$2,000 \times (pva \text{ of } \$1)$$
$$= \$2,000 \times 3.605$$
$$= \$7,210.$$

Here the $2,000 annuity is multiplied by 3.605, the factor for an annuity of $1.00 for five periods, discounted at 12 percent per period. This factor is found in Table 2.

Another use of Table 2 is to determine the amount that must be received annually to provide a desired rate of return on an investment. Assume the Burnsville Company invests $33,550 and desires a return of the investment plus interest of 8 percent in equal payments at the end of each year for ten years. The minimum amount that must be received each year is determined by solving the equation for the present value of an annuity:

$$pva = a \times (pva \text{ of } \$1)$$
$$a = pva/(pva \text{ of } \$1).$$

From Table 2 we see that the 8 percent factor for ten periods is 6.710. When the investment of $33,550 is divided by 6.710, the required annuity is computed to be $5,000:

$$a = \$33,550/6.710$$
$$= \$5,000.$$

UNEQUAL FLOWS

Many investment situations do not produce equal periodic cash flows. When this occurs, the present value for each cash flow has to be determined independently because the annuity table can be used only for equal periodic cash flows. Table 1 is used to determine the present value of each future amount separately. To illustrate, assume the Atlantic Sabers wishes to acquire the contract of a popular baseball player who is known to attract large crowds. Management believes this player will return incremental cash flows to the team at the end of each of the next three years in the amounts of $25,000, $40,000, and $15,000. After three years, the player anticipates retiring. If the team's owners require a minimum return on their investment of 14 percent, how much would they be willing to pay for the player's contract?

To solve this problem, it is necessary to determine the present value of the expected future cash flows. Here we use Table 1 to find the $1.00 present value factors at 14 percent for periods 1, 2, and 3. The cash flows are then multiplied by these factors:

Year	Present Value at 14 Percent		Annual Cash Flow		Present Value Amount
1	0.877	×	$25,000	=	$21,925
2	0.769	×	40,000	=	30,760
3	0.675	×	15,000	=	10,125
Total					$62,810

The total present value of the cash flows for the three years, $62,810, represents the maximum amount the team would be willing to pay for the player's contract.

DEFERRED RETURNS

Many times organizations make investments for which no cash is received until several periods have passed. The present value of an investment discounted at 12 percent per year, which has a $2,000 return only at the end of years 4, 5, and 6, can be determined as follows:

Year	Amount		Present Value at 12 Percent		Present Value Amount
1	$ —	×	0.893	=	$ —
2	—	×	0.797	=	—
3	—	×	0.712	=	—
4	2,000	×	0.636	=	1,272
5	2,000	×	0.567	=	1,134
6	2,000	×	0.507	=	1,014
Total					$3,420

Computation of the present value of the deferred annuity can also be performed using the annuity tables if the cash flow amounts are equal for each period. The present value of an annuity for six years, minus the present value of an annuity for three years, yields the present value of an annuity for years 4 through 6:

Present value of an annuity for six years at 12 percent:	$2,000 × 4.111 =	$8,222
Present value of an annuity for three years at 12 percent:	$2,000 × 2.402 =	−4,804
Present value of the deferred annuity		$3,418*

*The difference between the $3,420 above and the $3,418 is caused by rounding error.

TABLE 1   Present Value of $1.00

Present value of $1.00 $= \dfrac{1}{(1 + r)^n}$.

Periods	6%	8%	10%	12%	14%	16%	18%	20%	22%	24%	26%	28%	30%
1	0.943	0.926	0.909	0.893	0.877	0.862	0.847	0.833	0.820	0.806	0.794	0.781	0.769
2	0.890	0.857	0.826	0.797	0.769	0.743	0.718	0.694	0.672	0.650	0.630	0.610	0.592
3	0.840	0.794	0.751	0.712	0.675	0.641	0.609	0.579	0.551	0.524	0.500	0.477	0.455
4	0.792	0.735	0.683	0.636	0.592	0.552	0.516	0.482	0.451	0.423	0.397	0.373	0.350
5	0.747	0.681	0.621	0.567	0.519	0.476	0.437	0.402	0.370	0.341	0.315	0.291	0.269
6	0.705	0.630	0.564	0.507	0.456	0.410	0.370	0.335	0.303	0.275	0.250	0.227	0.207
7	0.665	0.583	0.513	0.452	0.400	0.354	0.314	0.279	0.249	0.222	0.198	0.178	0.159
8	0.627	0.540	0.467	0.404	0.351	0.305	0.266	0.233	0.204	0.179	0.157	0.139	0.123
9	0.592	0.500	0.424	0.361	0.308	0.263	0.225	0.194	0.167	0.144	0.125	0.108	0.094
10	0.558	0.463	0.386	0.322	0.270	0.227	0.191	0.162	0.137	0.116	0.099	0.085	0.073
11	0.527	0.429	0.350	0.287	0.237	0.195	0.162	0.135	0.112	0.094	0.079	0.066	0.056
12	0.497	0.397	0.319	0.257	0.208	0.168	0.137	0.112	0.092	0.076	0.062	0.052	0.043
13	0.469	0.368	0.290	0.229	0.182	0.145	0.116	0.093	0.075	0.061	0.050	0.040	0.033
14	0.442	0.340	0.263	0.205	0.160	0.125	0.099	0.078	0.062	0.049	0.039	0.032	0.025
15	0.417	0.315	0.239	0.183	0.140	0.108	0.084	0.065	0.051	0.040	0.031	0.025	0.020
16	0.394	0.292	0.218	0.163	0.123	0.093	0.071	0.054	0.042	0.032	0.025	0.019	0.015
17	0.371	0.270	0.198	0.146	0.108	0.080	0.060	0.045	0.034	0.026	0.020	0.015	0.012
18	0.350	0.250	0.180	0.130	0.095	0.069	0.051	0.038	0.028	0.021	0.016	0.012	0.009
19	0.331	0.232	0.164	0.116	0.083	0.060	0.043	0.031	0.023	0.017	0.012	0.009	0.007
20	0.312	0.215	0.149	0.104	0.073	0.051	0.037	0.026	0.019	0.014	0.010	0.007	0.005

TABLE 2   Present Value of an Annuity of $1.00

Present value of an annuity of $1.00 = \dfrac{1}{r}\left(1 - \dfrac{1}{(1 + r)^n}\right)$.

Periods	6%	8%	10%	12%	14%	16%	18%	20%	22%	24%	25%	26%	28%	30%
1	0.943	0.926	0.909	0.893	0.877	0.862	0.847	0.833	0.820	0.806	0.800	0.794	0.781	0.769
2	1.833	1.783	1.736	1.690	1.647	1.605	1.566	1.528	1.492	1.457	1.440	1.424	1.392	1.361
3	2.673	2.577	2.487	2.402	2.322	2.246	2.174	2.106	2.042	1.981	1.952	1.923	1.868	1.816
4	3.465	3.312	3.170	3.037	2.914	2.798	2.690	2.589	2.494	2.404	2.362	2.320	2.241	2.166
5	4.212	3.993	3.791	3.605	3.433	3.274	3.127	2.991	2.864	2.745	2.689	2.635	2.532	2.436
6	4.917	4.623	4.355	4.111	3.889	3.685	3.498	3.326	3.167	3.020	2.951	2.885	2.759	2.643
7	5.582	5.206	4.868	4.564	4.288	4.039	3.812	3.605	3.416	3.242	3.161	3.083	2.937	2.802
8	6.210	5.747	5.335	4.968	4.639	4.344	4.078	3.837	3.619	3.421	3.329	3.241	3.076	2.925
9	6.802	6.247	5.759	5.328	4.946	4.607	4.303	4.031	3.786	3.566	3.463	3.366	3.184	3.019
10	7.360	6.710	6.145	5.650	5.216	4.833	4.494	4.192	3.923	3.682	3.571	3.465	3.269	3.092
11	7.887	7.139	6.495	5.938	5.453	5.029	4.656	4.327	4.035	3.776	3.656	3.544	3.335	3.147
12	8.384	7.536	6.814	6.194	5.660	5.197	4.793	4.439	4.127	3.851	3.725	3.606	3.387	3.190
13	8.853	7.904	7.103	6.424	5.842	5.342	4.910	4.533	4.203	3.912	3.780	3.656	3.427	3.223
14	9.295	8.244	7.367	6.628	6.002	5.468	5.008	4.611	4.265	3.962	3.824	3.695	3.459	3.249
15	9.712	8.559	7.606	6.811	6.142	5.575	5.092	4.675	4.315	4.001	3.859	3.726	3.483	3.268
16	10.106	8.851	7.824	6.974	6.265	5.669	5.162	4.730	4.357	4.033	3.887	3.751	3.503	3.283
17	10.477	9.122	8.022	7.120	6.373	5.749	5.222	4.775	4.391	4.059	3.910	3.771	3.518	3.295
18	10.828	9.372	8.201	7.250	6.467	5.818	5.273	4.812	4.419	4.080	3.928	3.786	3.529	3.304
19	11.158	9.604	8.365	7.366	6.550	5.877	5.361	4.844	4.442	4.097	3.942	3.799	3.539	3.311
20	11.470	9.818	8.514	7.469	6.623	5.929	5.353	4.870	4.460	4.110	3.954	3.808	3.546	3.316

Glossary

The number enclosed in parentheses after each term refers to the chapter where the term is first defined.

Absorption Cost Basis of External Reporting   (2) A method of external reporting under which all manufacturing costs are product costs and all selling and administrative costs are period costs.

Absorption Costing   (10) A product costing procedure where all manufacturing costs (fixed and variable) are assigned to products and inventoried (also called **Full Costing**).

Accelerated Cost Recovery System (ACRS)   (15) An asset depreciation method created by the Economic Recovery Tax Act of 1981 that allows personal property to be depreciated for tax purposes over a period much shorter than an asset's estimated useful life.

Accounting Rate of Return   (14) A method used to evaluate capital expenditures that ignores the time value of money. It is computed as the average annual net income associated with an investment divided by the average investment amount.

Acid Test Ratio   (16) A measure of the availability of cash and other current monetary assets to pay current liabilities. It is computed as the sum of cash, current receivables, and marketable securities divided by current liabilities.

Allocation Base   (12) The factor or characteristic common to cost objectives that is used to determine how much of a cost (or cost pool) is assigned to each objective.

Annuity   (Appendix) A series of equal cash flows received or paid over equal intervals of time.

Appropriation Budgets   (6) Budgets used in not-for-profit organizations to provide the authorization for expenditures during a specified period.

Asset Depreciation Range (ADR)   (15) Guidelines for determining the appropriate useful life for depreciable assets as set by the 1969 Tax Act.

Asset Turnover   (16) A ratio that measures the ability of an organization to use its assets to generate sales. It is computed as sales divided by average total assets.

Bail-Out Period   (14) The time required to recover the initial investment in a capital project from any source of funds.

Bottom-Up Approach to Budgeting   (6) See **Participation Budget.**

Break-Even Point   (4) The unit or dollar sales volume where total revenues equal total costs.

Budget   (1) A formal plan of action expressed in monetary terms.

Budget Committee   (6) A group responsible for supervising budget preparation that also serves as a review board for evaluating requests for discretionary funds and new projects.

Budgetary Slack   (6) Occurs when managers intentionally request more funds in the budgets for their departments than they need to support the anticipated level of operations.

By-Product   (12) A product with relatively insignificant value produced jointly with one or more other products.

Capacity Costs   (3) Fixed costs that are related to capacity.

Capital Asset   (15) Generally defined for tax purposes as an asset held for investment gain.

Capital Budgeting   (14) A process that involves the identification of potentially desirable projects for capital expenditure, the subsequent evaluation of capital expenditure proposals, and the selection of proposals that meet certain criteria.

Capital Expenditures   (14) Investments of significant financial resources in projects to develop or introduce new products or services, to expand current operations, or to change current production or service facilities.

Capital Gain   (15) A gain on the sale of a capital asset.

Capital Loss   (15) A loss on the sale of a capital asset.

Cash Budget   (6) A summary of all cash receipts and disbursements expected to occur during the budget period.

Centralization   (9) The retention of decision-making authority by top management.

Certainty   (13) A condition that exists when the probability of an event's occurrence is 100 percent.

Certified Management Accountant (CMA)   (1) A designation intended to recognize professional competence and educational attainment in the field of management accounting.

Certified Public Accountant (CPA)   (1) A designation intended to recognize professional competence and education attainment in the field of public accounting.

Chartered Accountant (CA)   (1) A designation similar to the CPA. It is used in Canada and several other countries for people who perform independent evaluations of public organizations and the other activities normally associated with being a CPA in the United States.

Chief Financial Executive   (1) A position that often combines the duties of the controller and the treasurer.

Coefficient of Determination   (3) A measure of the percent of variation in the independent variable that is explained by the cost estimating equation; it indicates how good the equation fits the historical data.

Committed Fixed Costs   (3) Costs required to maintain the current service or production capacity.

Common Costs   (12) Costs incurred at a given level for the benefit of two or more cost objectives.

Common Segment Costs   (10) Costs related to more than one segment of an organization and not directly traceable to any particular segment (also called **Indirect Segment Costs**).

Constant Dollar Accounting   (17) A method of restating the nominal dollar amounts presented in financial statements into dollars of uniform purchasing power.

Constant Dollars   (17) Dollars of uniform purchasing power.

Consumer Price Index (CPI)   (17) A widely used measure of the cost of living for the typical consumer household prepared by the U.S. Department of Commerce, Bureau of Labor Statistics.

Continuous Budgeting   (6) A budget based on a moving fixed time frame that constantly extends over the same fixed period.

Contribution Income Statement   (4) A type of income statement in which costs are classified according to behavior. All variable expenses are grouped together and subtracted from revenues to produce contribution margin. All fixed costs are subtracted from contribution margin to produce net income.

Contribution Margin   (4) The difference between revenues and variable costs.

Contribution Margin Ratio   (4) The ratio of contribution margin to sales revenue. It indicates the portion of each sales dollar available for fixed costs and profits.

Controller   (1) The chief accountant of an organization.

Controlling   (1) The process of ensuring that results agree with plans.

Conversion Costs   (2) Direct labor and factory overhead costs incurred to convert raw materials into finished goods.

Corporation   (15) A legal entity recognized by an act of the state and empowered to conduct business activities.

Correlation Coefficient   (3) A standardized measure of the degree to which two variables move together.

Cost   (2) A monetary measure of the economic sacrifice made to obtain some product or service.

Cost Behavior Analysis   (3) The study of how costs respond to changes in the volume of an activity.

Cost Center   (7) A responsibility center held accountable only for the incurrence of costs. It does not have a revenue responsibility.

Cost Elements   (2) The detailed categories of costs assignable to a cost objective.

Cost Estimation   (3) The determination of previous or current relationships between cost and activity.

Costing Purpose   (2) The basic reason a cost concept is used and a cost measurement is made.

Costing Techniques   (2) The procedures used to assign cost elements to cost objectives.

Cost Objectives   (2) Objects or activities to which costs are assigned.

Cost of Capital   (14) The average cost, expressed as a percentage, of obtaining the resources necessary to make investments.

Cost of Goods Manufactured   (2) Total costs assigned to products completed during a period of time.

Cost of Production Report   (11) A summary of the unit and cost data of each department in a process cost system. It includes the summary of units in process, equivalent units, the computation of unit costs, the total costs to be accounted for, and the total costs accounted for.

Cost Pool   (2, 12) A group of related costs, such as factory overhead and service department costs, that are allocated together to other cost objectives.

Cost Prediction   (3) The process of forecasting the future relationships between cost and activity.

Cost Prediction Error   (5) The difference between a predicted future cost and the actual amount of the cost when, and if, it is incurred.

Cost Reduction Proposal   (5) A proposed action or investment intended to reduce the cost of an activity that the organization is committed to keeping.

Cost-Volume-Profit Analysis   (4) A technique used to examine the relationships between volume, total costs, total revenues, and profit.

Cost-Volume-Profit Graph   (4) Illustrates the relationship between volume, total revenues, total costs, and profit.

Current Cost Accounting   (17) The updating of balance sheet items to their current value and then adjusting the income statement to reflect the changes.

Current Manufacturing Costs   (2) Total additions to Work-in-Process inventory during a given period.

Current Ratio   (16) A measure of short-term solvency. It is computed as current assets divided by current liabilities.

Cycle Budgeting   (6) A budget method based on the life cycle of a project.

Days Receivables Outstanding   (16) The number of days, on the average, required to generate the sales uncollected at year end.

Debt-to-Equity Ratio   (16) A measure of long-term solvency. It is computed as total liabilities divided by total stockholders' equity.

Decentralization   (9) The delegation of decision-making authority to successively lower management levels in an organization.

Decision Package   (6) Identifies activities, departments, or agencies in budget planning. They may be related to goods, services, geographic areas, capital projects, or any other activity as related to an organization's goals and objectives.

Deflation   (17) The purchasing power of money increases as prices fall.

Denominator Variance   (8) See **Fixed Overhead Volume Variance.**

Depreciation Tax Shield   (15) The reduction in taxes due to the deductibility of depreciation from taxable revenues.

Descriptive Model   (13) A type of quantitative model that specifies the relationships between a series of independent and dependent variables.

Differential (Cost) Analysis   (5, 14) The determination of the difference between the cash flows of competing alternative actions that management is considering.

Direct Allocation Method   (12) A procedure whereby all service department costs are allocated directly to the producing departments without any recognition of interdepartmental activities.

Direct Costing   (10) See **Variable Costing.**

Direct Department Costs   (12) The department to which costs are assigned at the time of their incurrence.

Direct Labor   (2) Wages earned by production employees for the time they actually spend working on a product or process.

Direct Labor Ticket   (11) A document used in product costing systems to record direct labor hours and cost.

Direct Materials   (2) The cost of primary raw materials that are converted into finished goods.

Direct Product Costs   (2) Direct materials costs plus direct labor costs.

Direct Segment Costs   (10) Costs that are directly identifiable with a segment and avoidable if the segment is discontinued.

Discount Rate   (14) The minimum rate of return required for a project to be acceptable.

Discretionary Cost Center   (7) A cost center that does not have clearly defined relationships between effort and accomplishment.

Discretionary Fixed Costs   (3) Costs that are set at a fixed amount each year at the discretion of management (also called **Managed Fixed Costs**).

Divisional Segment Margin   (10) The difference between a division's contribution margin and all direct fixed expenses identifiable with the division.

Earnings per Share (EPS)   (16) A measure of profitability. It is computed as net income divided by the average number of shares of stock outstanding during a given period.

Economic Order Quantity (EOQ)   (13) The order quantity that results in the minimum annual costs of ordering and carrying inventory.

Electronic Data Processing (EDP)   (1) The storage, manipulation, retrieval, and communication of data by electronic means.

Employee Fringe Benefits   (2) The additional labor costs paid by the employer on behalf of employees.

Equivalent Completed Units   (11) The number of completed units that is equal (in terms of manufacturing effort) to a given number of partially completed units.

Excise Tax   (15) A tax on an activity performed by, or a privilege granted to, a taxed party.

Expected Value   (13) The weighted average of the possible cash flows associated with a decision alternative.

Expired Costs   (2) Expenses that are deducted from revenues on the income statement.

Factory Overhead   (2) Manufacturing costs other than direct materials and direct labor (also called **Indirect Product Costs**).

Favorable Variance   (1) The resulting difference when actual costs are less than allowed costs.

Feasible Region   (13) In a linear programming problem, the area that represents all possible production volumes and mixes. It is depicted by the area between the vertical axis and horizontal axis, and the first set of enclosing lines in a graphic analysis of product mix.

FIFO (First-in, First-out) Inventory Method   (11) An approach to process costing in which beginning inventory units each period are costed as a separate group consisting of the portion processed during the previous period plus the additional processing required to complete them during the current period.

Financial Accounting   (1) A segment of accounting concerned with providing financial information to persons outside the firm, especially investors, labor unions, creditors, and the general public.

Financial Leverage   (16) The use of capital funds from debt or equity that have a fixed interest or dividend rate.

Financial Statement Analysis   (16) The process of interpreting and evaluating financial statements by using data contained in them to produce additional ratios and statistics.

Finished Goods Inventory   (2) The manufactured products held for sale outside the organization.

Finished Goods Inventory Record   (11) A document maintained for each completed product indicating the number of units produced, sold, and on hand, as well as the related product costs.

Fixed Cost   (3) A cost that does not respond to changes in the volume of activity within a given period.

Fixed Overhead Budget Variance   (8) The difference between budgeted and actual fixed overhead cost.

Fixed Overhead Volume Variance   (8) The difference between total budgeted fixed overhead and total standard fixed overhead assigned to production.

Flexible Budgets   (7) Based on cost-volume-profit or cost-volume relationships, they are used to determine what costs should be at the actual level of production.

Flexible Budget Variance   (7, 8) The difference between the actual cost and the flexible budget cost of producing a given quantity of product or service.

For-Profit Organizations   (1) Organizations that have profit as a primary goal.

Full Costing   (10) See **Absorption Costing.**

Full Costs   (5) Costs that include all fixed and variable product costs and all period costs.

Functional Income Statement   (4) A type of income statement in which costs are classified according to function, such as manufacturing, selling, and administrative.

Future Value   (Appendix) The amount a current sum of money earning a stated rate of interest will accumulate to at a future period.

General and Administrative Expense Budget   (6) A schedule that presents the expected costs and disbursements for the overall administration of the organization.

Gross National Product Implicit Price Deflator   (17) A broad-based price index published by the U.S. Department of Commerce encompassing the entire U.S. economy.

High-Low Method of Cost Estimation   (3) An approach that uses two observations to estimate the variable and fixed elements of a mixed cost.

Home Office Expenses   (12) Central corporate expenses, including the salaries of the president and other executive employees, public relation expenses, legal and tax department expenses, and corporate planning and development costs.

Idle Time   (2) The time employees are not working on the product or performing other production-related tasks.

Imposed Budget   (6) An approach to budgeting whereby top management decides on the goals and objectives of the organization and communicates these to lower management levels (also called **Top-Down Approach**).

Income Tax   (15) A tax based on the income of individuals, corporations, estates, or trusts.

Incremental Approach to Budgeting   (6) A method that budgets cost for a coming period as a dollar or percentage change from the amount budgeted for (or spent during) a prior period.

Indirect Department Cost   (12) A cost reassigned to a department from another cost objective to which it was directly assigned.

Indirect Labor   (2) The salaries and wages earned by production employees for the time they spend performing tasks not directly related to production.

Indirect Materials   (2) Low-cost materials that are difficult to associate with specific units of a final product.

Indirect Product Costs   (2) See **Factory Overhead.**

Indirect Segment Costs   (10) See **Common Segment Costs.**

Inflation   (17) Purchasing power of money declines as prices rise.

Input-Output Approach to Budgeting   (6) A method of budgeting physical inputs and costs based on a planned activity level.

Interdepartmental Services   (12) Support activities that one service department provides to another service department within the same organization.

Internal Auditing   (1) An accounting function intended to ensure that the records are adequate and accurate, that management's operating policies are being followed and that the organization's assets are properly safeguarded from fraud or theft.

Internal Rate of Return (IRR)   (14) The discount rate that equates the net present value of a project's cash inflows with the initial investment in the project (also called the **Time-Adjusted Rate of Return**).

Inventory Turnover   (16) A measure of the number of times the average stock of inventory was sold and replenished during the period. It is computed as cost of goods sold divided by average inventory amount.

Investment Center   (7) A responsibility center held accountable for the relationship between its profits and total assets.

Job Cost Sheets   (11) A record used to accumulate the costs for specific jobs in a job cost system.

Joint Costs   (5, 12) The costs of producing joint products that are incurred prior to the split-off point for joint products.

Joint Products   (5, 12) Two or more products simultaneously produced from common inputs by a single process or common manufacturing activity.

Labor Efficiency Variance   (8) The difference between the standard cost of actual labor inputs and the flexible budget cost for labor.

Labor Rate Variance   (8) The difference between the actual labor cost and the standard cost of actual labor inputs.

Lead Time   (13) The amount of time between the placement and the receipt of an order.

Least-Squares Method of Cost Estimation   (3) An approach that uses the mathematical criteria of least-squares to estimate the variable and fixed elements of a mixed cost.

Linear Algebra Allocation Method   (12) A procedure whereby all service department costs are allocated simultaneously both interdepartmentally and to producing departments.

Linear Programming   (13) An optimizing model used to assist managers in making decisions under constrained conditions when linear relationships can be assumed.

Line-Item Budget   (6) A type of budget in which revenues and expenditures are assigned to specific categories and items of responsibility, often used in not-for-profit organizations.

Lump-Sum Budget   (6) A type of budget that is very popular with not-for-profit organizations in which only general areas are allocated revenue and expenditures.

Managed Fixed Costs   (3) See **Discretionary Fixed Costs.**

Management Accounting   (1) A segment of accounting concerned with providing financial information to managers and other persons inside specific organizations.

Management by Exception   (1) A concept where managers focus their attention on those aspects of operations that are not operating as planned, rather than constantly monitoring all activities.

Management by Objectives   (1) A concept where the head of an agency or department and the immediate superior agree to a set of short-run nonmonetary objectives, which are subsequently used as a basis of performance evaluation for the agency or department head.

Managers   (1) The employees who direct the affairs of the organization.

Manufacturing Cost Markup   (5) Used for pricing, it is computed as the total predicted selling and administrative costs plus the desired profit divided by the predicted manufacturing costs.

Manufacturing Disbursements Budget   (6) A budget used to plan materials, labor and factory overhead requirements, and costs for a future period.

Manufacturing Margin   (10) Segment sales minus direct manufacturing costs.

Manufacturing Organizations   (2) Organizations that process raw materials into finished products for sale to others.

Marginal Cost   (3, 5) The varying increment in total costs required to produce and sell an additional unit.

Marginal Revenue   (5) The varying increment in total revenue derived from the sale of an additional unit.

Margin of Safety   (4) The excess of actual or budgeted sales over break-even sales. It indicates the amount that sales could decline before the organization would show a loss.

Materials Price Variance   (8) The difference between the actual materials cost and the standard cost of actual materials inputs (also see **Materials Purchased Price Variance**).

Materials Purchased Price Variance   (8) The actual cost of materials purchased minus the standard cost of materials purchased (also see **Materials Price Variance**).

Materials Quantity Variance   (8) The difference between the standard cost of actual materials inputs and the flexible budget cost for materials.

Materials Requisition Form   (11) A record used to record transfers of direct materials from raw materials to work-in-process.

Merchandising Organizations   (2) Organizations that buy and sell goods; included in this category are most retail organizations.

Minimum Level Approach to Budgeting   (6) An approach to budgeting in which a base amount for all budget items is established and an explanation or justification is required for all amounts in excess of the base.

Mixed Costs   (3) Costs that contain both a fixed and a variable cost element (also called **Semivariable Costs**).

Model   (1, 13) A simplified representation of some real-world phenomenon.

Monetary Items   (17) Assets and liabilities whose values are fixed in terms of nominal dollars.

Mutually Exclusive Investments   (14) Where acceptance of an investment causes the automatic rejection of all other alternative investments under consideration.

Net Present Value Method   (14) A method used to evaluate capital expenditures that compares the initial investment to the present value of all future cash flows using a predetermined discount rate.

Net Sales Volume Variance   (7) Indicates the impact of a change in sales volume on the contribution margin, given the budgeted selling price and the budgeted variable costs.

Nominal Dollars   (17) Amounts actually recorded in historical cost accounting records and presented in traditional financial statements.

Nonmonetary Items   (17) Assets and liabilities whose values are not fixed in terms of nominal dollars.

Normal Equations   (3) Equations used to compute the constant term and the slope that best meets the least-squares criteria.

Normal Factory Overhead Accounting   (11) A method of accounting for factory overhead that uses a multiyear overhead and eliminates the need to close the balance in Factory Overhead at the end of each year.

Not-for-Profit Organizations (1) Organizations that do not have profit as a goal.

Objective Function (13) In linear programming, this is the goal to be maximized or minimized.

Operating Activities (6) Normal profit-related activities performed in conducting the daily affairs of an organization. They include such things as purchasing, production, and sales.

Operating Budget (6) A formal financial document that indicates planned revenues and expenses and other activities for a future period.

Operating Leverage (4) A measure of the responsiveness of income to changes in sales.

Operating Loss (15) For tax purposes, the excess of operating expenses over operating revenues that ordinarily may be carried back three years and carried forward fifteen years.

Opportunity Cost (2) The net cash inflow that could be obtained if the resources committed to one action were used in the most desirable other alternative action.

Optimal Solution (13) In linear programming, this is the feasible solution that maximizes or minimizes the value of the objective function.

Optimizing Models (13) A type of quantitative model that suggests a specific choice between decision alternatives.

Order Filling Costs (7) Costs incurred to place finished goods in the hands of the purchasers.

Order Getting Costs (7) Costs incurred to obtain a customer's order.

Order Quantity (13) The amount of inventory ordered at a particular time.

Organization (1) A group of people united to achieve a common goal.

Organization Chart (1) An illustration of the formal relationships that exist among the elements of an organization.

Organizing (1) The process of making the organization into a well-ordered whole.

Outlay Costs (5) Future costs that require future expenditures of cash or other resources.

Overtime Premiums (2) Bonus wages in excess of the regular hourly rate paid to production employees who are working more than the regular number of hours.

Participation Budget (6) An approach to budgeting in which managers at all levels, and in some cases even nonmanagers, become involved in budget preparation. Because this budget approach often starts at the lowest levels of management, it is sometimes called **Bottom-Up Budgeting.**

Partnership (15) An unincorporated business ordinarily owned by two or more individuals.

Payback Period (14) The length of time necessary for the cumulative operating cash inflows from a project to equal the initial cash investment for the project.

Payoff Table   (13) A table used to enumerate the alternative actions management may take and the possible monetary outcomes of each.

Performance Reports   (1) Reports provided to management during and after the budget period that compare actual results with plans.

Period Costs   (2) Expired nonproduct costs; they are always an expense.

Physical Models   (13) Scaled-down versions or replicas of physical reality.

Physical Quantity Method   (12) A method of allocating joint costs on the basis of relative quantities of specific common physical characteristics possessed by the various joint products.

Planning   (1) The formulation of a scheme or program for the accomplishment of a specific purpose or goal.

Planning, Programming, and Budgeting Systems (PPBS)   (6) A concept that emphasizes outputs, rather than inputs, of an organization in programmed areas.

Predetermined Factory Overhead Rate   (2) An overhead rate determined at the start of the year by dividing the predicted overhead costs for the year by the predicted activity level.

Present Value   (Appendix) The current worth of a specified amount of money to be received at some future date at some discount rate.

Present Value Index   (14) The number of present value dollars generated per dollar of initial investment (also called the **Profitability Index**).

Price Earnings Ratio   (16) The current market price of a firm's stock divided by its earnings per share of stock.

Price Index   (17) A standardized measure of the amount of money needed to purchase a standardized package or basket of goods and services.

Price Variance   (8) The actual costs of actual inputs minus the standard cost of actual inputs.

Prime Product Costs   (2) Direct materials costs plus direct labor costs.

Product Costing   (2) The process of assigning costs to inventories as they are converted from raw materials to finished goods.

Product Costing System   (11) A system used to assign manufacturing costs to products consisting of the records of manufacturing inventories, activities, and costs.

Product Costs   (2) Costs assigned to products as they are produced that are expensed when the products are sold.

Production Budget   (6) A budget indicating the number of units of product an organization plans to produce in a coming period. It is based on predicted sales, adjusted for beginning inventory and desired ending inventory.

Product Margin   (10) Product sales revenue less direct product costs.

Product Reporting   (10) A type of reporting in which revenues and expenses are presented for product lines of an organization.

Profitability Index (PI)   (14) See **Present Value Index.**

Profit Center   (7) A responsibility center held accountable for both revenues and costs and evaluated on their differences.

Profit-Volume-Graph   (4) A graph used to illustrate the relationship between volume and profits.

Pro Forma Financial Statements   (6) Hypothetical financial statements that reflect the "as if" effects of budgeted activity on the financial position of a firm.

Property Tax   (15) A tax based on the ownership of property. It is usually determined by multiplying a statutory tax rate (referred to as a tax millage) times the assessed value of the property.

Purchases Budget   (6) A schedule of raw materials and supplies that must be acquired to meet production needs and inventory requirements.

Purchasing Power Gains and Losses   (17) Gains and losses that result from changes in the purchasing power of money during a given period.

Quantitative Models   (13) A series of algebraic relationships intended to represent some real-world relationships.

Quantity Variance   (8) The standard cost of actual inputs minus the standard cost of inputs allowed for the outputs produced.

Quick Ratio   (16) See **Acid Test Ratio.**

Raw Materials Inventories   (2) The physically existing items that are to be converted into a finished product.

Raw Materials Inventory Record   (11) A record used to record increases and decreases in the available balance for each type of raw material.

Relevant Costs   (2) Future costs that differ among competing alternatives.

Relevant Range   (3) The area of operation, within which a linear cost function is a good approximation of the economists' curvilinear cost function.

Reorder Point   (13) The inventory level at which an order for additional units is placed.

Replacement Cost   (17) The current cost to purchase or reproduce an asset or its productive capacity.

Residual Income   (9) The excess of investment center income over the minimum return set by the company.

Responsibility Accounting   (7) The structuring of performance reports addressed to individual or group members of an organization in a manner that emphasizes factors controllable by them.

Responsibility Center   (7) A person or organizational unit that has been assigned certain responsibilities. Examples are investment centers, profit centers, revenue centers, and cost centers.

Return on Assets   (16) A measure of the ability of the firm to profitably use its assets. It is computed as net income plus net-of-tax interest expense divided by average total assets.

Return on Equity   (16) A measure of the profits attributable to the shareholders as a percentage of their equity in the firm. It is computed as net income divided by average stockholder's equity.

Return on Investment   (9) A measure of the earnings per dollar of investment. It is computed by dividing the income of the investment center by its asset base.

Return on Sales   (16) A measure of the ability of the firm to generate profits from sales. It is computed as net income plus net-of-tax interest expense divided by sales.

Revenue Budgets   (6) Budgets that establish the amount expected to be collected from each revenue source during the upcoming period.

Revenue Center   (7) A responsibility center held accountable for generating sales revenue.

Robinson–Patman Act   (5) A law of the United States that prohibits firms from charging purchasers different prices when the purchasers compete with each other in the sale of their products.

Safety Stocks   (13) The actual units of inventory carried to prevent stockouts due to variations in the demand for units during the lead time.

Sales Budget   (6) A forecast of unit and dollar sales volume. It may also contain a forecast of sales collections.

Sales Mix   (4) The relative portion of unit or dollar sales that is derived from each product or service.

Sales Price Variance   (7) The total difference in revenues for the actual sales volume resulting from a change in the selling price from the budgeted price.

Sales Value Allocation Method   (12) A method of allocating joint costs based on the relative sales values of the joint products.

Sales Volume Variance   (7) The impact on revenues of a change in sales volume, assuming no change in selling price.

Scatter Diagram   (3) A graph of volume and cost data.

Segment Margin   (10) The amount that a segment contributes toward the common (indirect) costs of an organization and toward profit of the organization.

Segment Reports   (10) Income statements that show operating results for some portion or segment of a business.

Selling Expense Budget   (6) A schedule of the costs and disbursements the organization plans to incur in connection with budgeted sales and distribution.

Semivariable Costs   (3) See **Mixed Costs.**

Sensitivity Analysis   (4) The study of the responsiveness of a model's dependent variable(s) to changes in one or more of the model's independent variables.

Service Costing   (2) The process of assigning costs to services.

Service Department   (12) A department that provides support functions for one or more production departments.

Service Organizations (2) Nonmanufacturing firms that perform work for others. Included in this category are banks, hospitals, and real estate agencies.

Simple Rate of Return (14) See **Accounting Rate of Return.**

Simplex Method (13) A mathematical technique used to solve linear programming problems.

Sole Proprietorship (15) An unincorporated business owned by one individual.

Solvency (16) The ability of a firm to pay its debts as they come due.

Split-Off Point (5, 12) The point in a process where the joint products emerge as separately identifiable products or units.

Standard Cost (7) A budget for one unit of product. It indicates what it should cost to produce one unit of product under efficient operating conditions.

Standard Cost Center (7) A cost center that has clearly defined relationships between effort and accomplishment and uses a standard cost system.

Standard Cost Variance Analysis (8) The process of analyzing flexible budget variances.

Standard Error of the Estimate (3) A measure of the variability of actual costs around the cost estimating equation. It is used to construct probability intervals for cost estimates.

Statement of Cash Flows (16) A summary of resource inflows and outflows stated in terms of cash.

Statement of Cost of Goods Manufactured (2) A financial summary of the activity in the Work-in-Process inventory accounts. It may also summarize activity in the Raw Materials inventory account.

Statement of Cost of Goods Manufactured and Sold (2) A financial summary of the activity in all major inventory accounts.

Statement of Resource Flows (16) An overall summary of all major transactions that cause changes in the balance sheet (statement of financial position) between two statement dates.

Statement of Working Capital Flows (16) A statement of resource inflows and outflows that generated and used working capital during the period.

Static Budget (7) A budget based on a prior prediction of expected sales and production.

Step Allocation Method (12) A procedure whereby service department costs are allocated in a manner that gives partial recognition to interdepartmental services among the service departments.

Step Costs (3) Costs that are constant within a range of activity, but different between ranges of activity.

Subchapter S Corporation (15) A business legally organized as a corporation, that has opted under a special provision of the tax law to be taxed as a partnership with income flowing directly to the individuals holding the shares of stock.

Sunk Costs (2) Historical costs that result from past decisions that management no longer has control over.

Tax Avoidance   (15) The reduction of taxes by legitimate means.

Tax Base   (15) A monetary measurement of the conditions or activities subject to taxes, such as taxable income and assessed value.

Tax Deferral   (15) The planning and timing of transactions to cause legal delays in the payment of taxes.

Tax Rate   (15) A percentage that is multiplied times the tax base to determine total taxes.

Time-Adjusted Rate of Return   (14) See **Internal Rate of Return.**

Times Interest Earned   (16) A measure of interest paying ability, computed as the earnings available to pay interest divided by the total interest expense.

Top-Down Approach to Budgeting   (6) See **Imposed Budget.**

Total Cost Approach (to capital budgeting)   (14) The calculation of the present value of the cost associated with each alternative, with the low-cost alternative being preferred.

Transfer Price   (9) The internal value assigned a product or service that one division provides to another.

Treasurer   (1) The officer responsible for money management in an organization.

Uncertainty   (13) A condition that exists when the probability of an event's occurring is less than 100 percent.

Unexpired Costs   (2) Incurred costs recorded as assets on the statement of financial position.

Unfavorable Variances   (1) Variances that result when actual costs exceed allowed costs.

Unit Contribution Margin   (4) The difference between unit selling price and unit variable costs.

Value Added Tax   (15) A tax based on the value added to the goods produced during a period.

Value of Perfect Information   (13) The maximum amount a manager would be willing to pay for additional information.

Variable Cost   (3) The uniform incremental cost of each additional unit.

Variable Costing   (10) A product costing procedure whereby only variable manufacturing costs are assigned to products (also called **Direct Costing**).

Variable Cost Markup   (5) Used for product pricing, it is computed as the total of the predicted fixed costs plus targeted profit divided by the predicted variable costs.

Variable Cost Ratio   (4) The ratio of variable costs to sales revenue. It indicates the portion of each sales dollar that is used to cover variable costs.

Variable Overhead Efficiency Variance   (8) The difference between the standard variable overhead cost for the actual activity base inputs and the flexible budget variable overhead costs for the actual outputs.

Variable Overhead Spending Variance   (8) The difference between the actual variable overhead cost incurred and the standard variable overhead cost for the actual activity base inputs.

Variance   (1) The difference between actual and allowed costs.

Variance Analysis   (8) The process of analyzing the difference between the actual cost and the standard cost allowed by the flexible budget for manufacturing a product or providing a service.

Volume Variance   (8) See **Fixed Overhead Volume Variance.**

Weighted Average Method   (11) In process costing, an inventory valuation procedure where all equivalent units in process are assigned the same average cost.

Working Capital   (16) The difference between current assets and current liabilities.

Work-in-Process Inventories   (2) The raw materials that are in the process of being converted into a finished product.

Zero-Base Budgeting   (6) An approach to budgeting based on the premise that every dollar of a budget expenditure must be justified.

Checklist of Key Figures

CHAPTER 3

3–5 Fixed costs $40,000

3–6 Fixed costs $12,000

3–7 Fixed costs $5,200

3–8 $2.75 per direct labor hour

3–9 $13.46 per direct labor hour

3–10 **b)** Fixed costs $10,000

3–11 **b)** Fixed costs $500

3–12 **b)** 50,000 servings

3–13 **c)** 120 participants

3–14 Fixed costs $5,000

3–15 **b)** $6.875

3–16 **b)** For 10,000 tickets, overestimated by $4

3–17 **b)** For 500 inspections, overestimated by $300

3–18 **b)** 30,000 rolls

3–19 **b)** 1,060,000 copies

3–20 Fixed costs $3,000

3–21 Fixed costs $94.50

3–22 **c)** $20,410

3–23 **c)** $55,090

3–27 **c)** $3,750

3–28 **b)** $586.80

3–29 Fixed costs $7,285

3–30 **b)** Fixed costs $600

3–31 **c)** $4 per direct labor hour

CHAPTER 4

4–1 **d)** $2,400 increase

4–2 **d)** $3,000 increase

4–3 **d)** 5,200 units

4–4 **d)** $5,000

4–5 **b)** $400,000

4–9 **b)** $475,000

4–10 **c)** 23,200 units

4–11 **b)** 54,000 units

4–16 **b)** 7,500 units

4–17 **b)** $700,000

4–20 Fixed costs $21.67 million

4–21 **4.** Increase $160,000

4–22 **a)** 16,900 patient days

4–23 **c)** 6,600 pairs

4–24 **b)** 311,111 units

4–25 **c)** 175 percent

4–26 **c)** 32 percent

4–27 36,000 units

4–28 **b)** Margin of safety $137,500

4–29 **b)** Break-even point 3,750 units

4–30 **a) 3.** Profit $33,240

CHAPTER 5

5–8 **b)** Disadvantage of accepting $630,000

5–9 **b)** Advantage of buying $5,500

5–10 Advantage of subscribing $6,700

5–11 **c)** Opportunity cost $1,000

5–12 Monthly commissions $4,900

5–13 Disadvantage of further processing $700

5–14 Advantage of further processing $6

5–15 **c)** 17,520 units

5–16 $0.80

5–18 **e)** Increase $33,000

5–19 **f)** Decrease $100

5–20 **e)** $36

5–21 **c)** Manufacturing cost markup price $313.20

5–22 **b)** Advantage of replacement $30,000

5–23 **c) 2.** Decrease in profits $20,000

5–24 **d)** Profit $240

5–25 **e)** Advantage of making $10,100

5–26 **f)** Advantage of full service $7,800

5–27 **a)** 37,500 boxes

5–28 **f)** Sales dollars $1,350,000

5–29 **a)** Cost to make $335,000

5–30 **b)** Minimum price $66,727

5–31 **a)** Incremental profit $5,695

CHAPTER 6

6–1   April ending balance $64,500

6–2   December ending balance $77,000

6–3   Total receipts $192,365

6–4   June ending accounts receivable $106,200

6–5   June cash disbursements $219,000

6–6   May purchases $612,000

6–7   **b)** February purchases $301,000

6–8   Net income $154,385

6–9   Net income $3,000

6–10 **b)** Fall quarter sales $3,850

6–11 Fourth quarter sales $822,000

6–12 **a)** Balance from general fund $5,000

6–13 **a)** Balance to general fund $105,000

6–14 Balance to general fund $19,000

6–15 June ending cash balance $105,600

6–16 **b)** Total cost of raw materials $2,241.60

6–17 July purchases of pecans 61,200 pounds

6–18 **c)** September ending balance $5,037

6–19 **d)** Excess of disbursements over receipts $2,563

6–20 **b)** May budgeted purchases 67,800 pounds

6–21 **b)** Total assets $504,400

6–22 **f)** Total assets $123,500

6–25 **f)** Net income $100,000

6–26 **e)** Cash balance end of second quarter $148,000

6–28 **b)** Excess revenues over appropriations $3,000 F

6–29 Total administration $375,000

6–30 **b)** Cost per vocational pupil $412

CHAPTER 7

7–1   Total for 20,000 units $736,000

7–2   Total for 40,000 units $74,850

7–3   **b)** Total flexible budget variance $18,100 U

7–4   **b)** Total flexible budget variance $13,000 F

7–5   Sales volume variance $80,000 U

7–6   Sales volume variance $90,000 F

7–7   Sales volume variance $50,000 F

7–8   **c)** $125 F

7–9   **c)** $750 U

7–10   **b)** Net sales volume variance $30,000 U

7–11   **b)** Net sales volume variance $24,000 U

7–12   Net sales volume variance $700 F

7–13   Net sales volume variance $2,250 F

7–16   **b)** Total flexible budget variance $842 F

7–18   Total flexible budget variance $173,300 U

7–19   Total flexible budget variance $7,000 U

7–20   Total flexible budget variance $3,300 U

7–21   Net sales volume variance $62,500 F

7–22   **d)** Net sales department variances $12,000 U

7–23   Cost variances $51,500 U

7–24   **d)** Net sales department variances $40,000 F

7–25   Cost variances $9,900 U

7–29   **b)** Production department variances $13,500 F

7–30   Net sales department variances $36,000 F

CHAPTER 8

8–1   Quantity variance $1,000 U

8–3   **d)** Materials quantity variance $1,200 F

8–4   **b)** $500 U

8–5   **c)** $1,350 F

8–6   **b)** $500 U

8–7   **a)** $400 U

8–8   **a)** $375 U

8–11   **b)** $10

8–12   **a)** Total materials quantity variance $315 U

8–13   **a)** Materials quantity variance $560 U

8–14   **d)** Total flexible budget variances $8,600 U

8–15   **b)** Materials quantity variance $60 U

8–16   **c)** Materials price variance $183 F

8–17   **c)** Total flexible budget variance $1,360 U

8–18   Total variable overhead variances $100 U

8–20   **1.** Effect on labor rate variance $262.50 U

8–22   **a)** Materials quantity variance $30 U

8–23 **a) 5.** Total flexible budget variances $1,565 U

8–24 **2.** 25,000 pounds

8–25 **c)** Total flexible budget variances $1,190 U

8–26 **d)** $10,000 F

8–27 **8.** $360,000 U

8–28 **c)** Flexible budget variance $4,615 U

CHAPTER 9

9–1 **a)** Central 0.169

9–2 **a)** Tex 0.28

9–3 **b)** C $700

9–4 **b)** $26,000

9–5 **b)** $32,400

9–6 ROI with investment 0.20

9–7 K operating assets $625,000

9–8 Sun ROI 0.40

9–9 **b)** Division 200, current value residual income $400

9–10 **b)** Trinket replacement value residual income $(25,000)

9–11 **a)** Tax Consultants gross profit $240,000

9–12 **a)** Pulp gross profit $0

9–13 **a)** Yes. Contribution is $16 per wheel.

9–14 **a)** $3,720,000

9–16 Beta net income $310,000

9–17 Jeff gross profit $2,000,000

9–18 Contribution of proposed sale $45,000

9–19 **a)** No. Contribution margin is negative.

9–20 **a)** 19x6 net income $276,000

9–21 **a)** ROI with new investment 0.176

9–23 **b)** Profit increase for company $210,000

9–25 **c)** Disadvantage of accepting offer $750

9–27 **a)** Division 11 19x1 ROI 0.11

CHAPTER 10

10–1 **b)** Cost of goods sold:
　　　Absorption $1,912,500
　　　Variable $1,312,500

10–2 May cost of goods sold:
　　　Absorption $180,000
　　　Variable $160,000

10–3   **a)** Net income $36,000   **b)** Net income $30,000

10–4   **a)** 19x1 net income $(10,000)   **b)** 19x1 net income $(30,000)

10–5   **a)** 19x1 net income $350,000   **b)** 19x1 net income $150,000

10–6   **b)** Absorption and variable net income $50,000

10–7   **b)** Net income:
          Absorption $30,400
          Variable $26,000

10–8   19x8 net income:
          Absorption $1,600,000
          Variable $(2,150,000)

10–9   Net income $185,000

10–10 Net income $484,000

10–11 Net income $54,000

10–12 Net income $92,000

10–13 **a)** 19x2 net income $3,328,571   **b)** 19x2 net income $2,900,000

10–14 **a)** 19x6 net income $2,900,000   **b)** 19x6 net income $2,900,000

10–15 **a)** Alaska territory margin $10,600

10–16 Service 14 product margin $55,000

10–17 **a)** First quarter income $426,000   **b)** First quarter income $446,010

10–18 **a)** 19x1 net income $70,700   **b)** 19x1 net income $45,700

10–19 **a)** First quarter net income $(15,000)

10–20 19x5 net income:
          Absorption $5,625
          Variable $(10,000)

10–21 19x2 Left Division $541,000

10–22 **c)** January net income $26,000

10–23 **a)** Net income $(124,800)   **b)** Net income $(140,800)

10–24 **a)** Net income $10,000

10–25 **b)** Southeast umbrellas product margin $20,000

10–26 **b)** Retail customer margin $1,500

10–27 **b)** Europe territory margin $52,000

10–28 **b)** Donuts product margin $260

10–29 **b)** Auditors market margin $(12,800)

10–30 **c)** Product A product margin $185,000

CHAPTER 11

11–1   **b)** Debit Finished Goods Inventory $3,950

11–3   Transferred out $276,000

11–4   **a)** 12,750 equivalent units

11–6 **a)** $36,800

11–7 **c)** Underapplied $1,000,000

11–8 **a)** 27,825 equivalent units   **b)** 26,325 equivalent units

11–9 **a)** $74,800.00

11–10 **b)** Debit Work-in-Process $1,600

11–12 **a)** Debit Finished Goods Inventory $96,900

11–13 **e)** Underapplied $5,000

11–14 **a)** Debit Finished Goods Inventory $136,872

11–15 **b)** Overapplied $20,000

11–16 **b)** Overapplied $14,600

11–17 **c)** Credit Work-in-Process $3,520

11–19 **c) 1.** $75,000

11–20 **b)** Debit Finished Goods Inventory $393,000

11–21 **c)** Conversion $4.125

11–22 **b)** Debit Work-in-Process: Finishing Department $237,750

11–23 **b)** Debit Finished Goods Inventory $1,434,800

11–24 Transferred out $473,520

11–25 **b)** $80,000

11–27 **a)** Ending Work-in-Process $136,000

11–29 Transferred out of Finishing Department $516,850

11–30 **b) 3.** Total transferred to Finishing $366,176

CHAPTER 12

12–2 **1.** Allocation to Molding $30,000

12–3 **1.** Allocation to P1 $45,000

12–4 **b)** Accounting/Finance $110/student credit hour

12–5 **c)** Total Housewares $15,217

12–6 Total P1 $77,103

12–7 Total P1 $72,324

12–8 Melting overhead rate $16

12–9 **b)** Total Cutting $745,750

12–10 **c)** Total Cutting $539,400   **d)** Total Cutting $538,189 (rounding)

12–11 **b)** Stamping $46/machine hour

12–12 **b)** Total P1 $3,760

12–13 **a) 2.** Cafeteria to Mixing $99,000

12–14 **c)** $970

12–15 **c)** West Division income $400

12–16 **c)** $947.50

12–17 **b)** Total P1 $220,178

12–18 **a)** **1.** Allocation to Spinning $53,100

12–19 **b)** Medical $17/patient visit

12–20 **b)** Total operating costs of Education $149,000

12–21 **b)** $6.14

12–22 **b)** Allocation to A based on sales $1 million

12–23 **c)** Micro Division net income $18,500

12–24 **c)** Bugoff gross profit percent 56.25

12–25 **a)** Grade A gross profit percent 60   **b)** Grade A gross profit percent 51.2
      c) Grade A gross profit percent 45.6

12–26 Total Fabrication with direct allocation $7,071,760

12–28 **a)** Joint costs to X $60,000   **b)** Joint costs to X $50,640

12–29 **d)** Gross profit of Slices $22,321.40

12–30 **b)** Branch net income $26,000

CHAPTER 13

13–1 **a)** EOQ 200 units

13–2 **a)** EOQ 400 units

13–5 **b)** Annual cost savings $800

13–6 **b)** Annual cost savings $2,250

13–7 Value of objective function $28,000

13–8 Value of objective function $56

13–9 **b)** Value of objective function $680

13–10 **b)** Value of objective function $24,000

13–11 **a)** Expected value of I $4,000

13–12 **a)** Expected value of I $10,000

13–13 **b)** Expected value of perfect information $36,800

13–14 **b)** Expected value of perfect information $18.75

13–15 Expected cost of do not inspect $1,000

13–16 Expected cost of do not inspect $350

13–17 Expected cost of do not inspect $120

13–18 EOQ 40 units

13–19 EOQ 50 units

13–20 **a)** **4.** 10 days

13–21 Case 1 total cost $1,000
Case 2 total cost $3,000
Case 3 total cost $200
Case 4 total cost $2,000

13–22 **2.** 0.45/dollar

13–23 c) $3,700

13–24 c) $1,150

13–25 b) $200,000

13–26 Coefficient of B1 $1.61

13–27 Coefficient of A $16.5

13–30 Expected value of perfect information $2,800

CHAPTER 14

14–1 6. $3,570

14–2 6. $5,568

14–3 a) $4,282   **b)** 24 percent

14–4 a) $1,702.50   **b)** 18 percent

14–5 18.99 percent

14–6 14.5 percent

14–7 a) $7,659   **b)** 22 percent

14–8 a) $6,500   **b)** 24 percent

14–9 a) Proposal A 2.5 years   **b) 2.** Proposal A 0.30

14–10 a) Proposal X 2.4 years   **b) 2.** Proposal X 0.333

14–11 1. $(1,052)   **2.** 12 percent   **3.** 4.0586 years
4. On average investment 14.34 percent

14–12 1. $2,807.76   **2.** 14 percent   **3.** 4.7059 years
4. On average investment 16.59 percent

14–13 a) 1.6 years   **b)** 2.4 years   **c)** 24 percent   **d)** $44,610

14–14 a) 1.7 years   **b)** 2.7 years   **c)** 18 percent   **d)** $92,656

14–15 a) Rankings of A:
Payback 1
Accounting rate of return 3
Net present value 3

14–16 a) Rankings of X:
Payback 2–3
Accounting rate of return 1–2
Net present value 1

14–17 a) Present value index of plastic containers 1.6406

14–18 a) Present value index of plastic 1.2793

14–19 b) 5.65 years

14–20 b) 0.25

14–21 Net present value $3,779

14–22 Net present value $14,210

14–23 Advantage of old processor $1,650

14–24 Advantage of new system $27,880

14–25 Advantage of new equipment $58,208

14–27 **b)** $37,983

14–28 **a)** Proposal A is selected

14–29 **c)** Net present value $64,320

14–30 **d)** Present value of restaurant $513,213

CHAPTER 15

15–1 **a)** $20,880

15–2 $33,000

15–3 **b)** Present value of tax shield, ACRS depreciation $5,019

15–4 **c)** Present value of tax shield, ACRS depreciation $57,882

15–5 **a)** After-tax cost of machine $8,892

15–7 **c)** $792

15–8 **d)** $7,515

15–10 **a)** $990,000

15–11 **a)** Acme common stock $9,490

15–13 **b)** $27,120

15–15 **a)** Income taxes $51,595

15–16 **b)** $4,760

15–18 **b)** Payback period 4.29 years

15–19 Net present value $(6,885)

15–20 **a)** Net present value $19,993

15–21 **a)** Net present value $(496)

15–22 **b)** $169,783

15–23 **b)** Total taxes $19,000

15–24 **a)** 19x1 income taxes $44,370

15–25 **b)** Total taxes $25,500

15–26 **b)** $0

15–27 19x4 net income $69,300

15–28 **b)** $(164,711)

15–29 **c)** 21.79 percent

15–30 Net tax liability $27,350

CHAPTER 16

16–8 Decrease in working capital $5,300

16–11 **b)** Net change $0

16–13 **d)** $85,000

16–14 **b)** $86,100

16–16 **c)** Return on sales 0.103

16–17 **a) 3.** Return on sales 0.080

16–18 **b)** $503,000

16–19 **b)** Net cash provided by operations $66,475

16–20 **a)** Net working capital provided by operations $22,725

16–21 Net cash provided by operations $23,125

16–22 **a)** Net working capital provided by operations $236,000

16–23 Net cash provided by operations $284,000

16–24 **b)** Net cash provided by operations $18,900

16–25 **b) 4.** 0.109

16–27 **a)** Net cash provided by operations $2,130,000

16–28 **b)** Net cash provided by operations $240,000

16–29 **c)** Net working capital provided by operations $(5,500)

16–30 Net cash provided by operations $10,000

CHAPTER 17

17–8   Total assets in constant dollars $1,326,500

17–9   Total assets in constant dollars $374,250

17–10   Net income in constant dollars $42,400

17–11   Net income in constant dollars $(116,083)

17–12 **a)** Loss on accounts receivable $16,000

17–13 **a)** Gain on cash $4,800

17–16 **b)** Gain on sale $2,720

17–17 **b)** Loss on sale of A $250

17–18 **a)** 19x8 constant dollar income after taxes $67,200

17–19 **b)** 19x5 $342,720

17–20 **b)** Total flexible budget variance $23,250 F

17–21 **b)** Total flexible budget variance $500 F

17–22 **c)** Cost prediction error $137,700

17–23 **d)** $63,550

17–24 **a)** 19x1 constant dollar net income $5,775

17–25 **c)** Net present value discounting nominal dollars $236,896

17–26 **b)** $4,869

17–27 **b)** $7,819

17–28 **b)** $1,943

17–29 **b)** $(10,656)

17–30 **b)** $26,469

Index